The Economist

YEAR BOOK

The following companies
are advertising in this edition of
The Economist Yearbook:

The Economist

YEAR BOOK

1993 EDITION

1992 IN REVIEW

The Economist's main editorial office is at:

25 St James's Street, London SW1A 1HG

For inquiries about subscribing to The Economist please contact:

The Economist, Subscription Services Department
PO Box 14, Harold Hill
Romford, Essex RM3 8EQ
United Kingdom
Tel (44) (0) 708 381555 Fax (44) (0) 708 381211

The Economist, Subscription Department
North America, tel 1-800-456-6086
Colorado & Mexico, tel 1-303-447-9330

The Economist Newspaper Ltd
2 Jurong Port Road, Singapore 2261
Republic of Singapore
Tel (65) 264 4891 Fax (65) 264 1545

THIS YEARBOOK is *The Economist*'s second retrospective album. It has three aims. First, it is a book to browse through for a portrait of an unsettling year, presented in a style and format that readers of *The Economist* will find familiar. There are essays that evoke 1992 and its lessons, subject by subject, accompanied by articles whose worth (or misguidedness) seems to us to have outlived the week in which they were written.

Second, it is a work of reference. When, precisely, did that civil war start? At what level was this or that statistic on such and such a date? Who was the foreign minister of Utopia before it broke apart last spring? (Or was it summer?) The yearbook's chronologies plot 1992's history, area by area, theme by theme, day by day. *The Economist*'s particular way of presenting the world's statistics is adapted to cover the whole year. And there is an up-to-date list of who was in power at the year's end, where and since when.

Last, this yearbook will form part of a history of *The Economist*'s view of the world. Together with its predecessor, it offers a compact solution to people who have neither the space nor the desire to collect back-numbers of *The Economist*, but who cannot bring themselves to discard the yellowing pile until it starts to topple.

The people, events, numbers, attitudes and arguments of 1992 are distilled in this book for years to come.

CONTENTS

CONTENTS

Contents

LEADERS

Back to earth

AFTER the party, the hangover. The excitements of the late 1980s, most of them stemming from the collapse of communism, could not last for ever, and in 1992 they stopped. Almost everywhere, euphoria slipped into sullenness, and even to despair. The queen of England talked of an *annus horribilis* for her and her family. The same phrase could have applied to the world. It was only right at the end of the year that the mood showed any sign of turning from *horribilis* to hope.

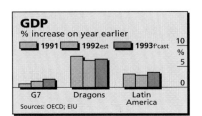

GDP
% increase on year earlier
1991　1992est　1993f'cast
G7　Dragons　Latin America
Sources: OECD; EIU

The sourness of 1992 sprang from two sources. One, as so often before, was economic. This was supposed to be the year when economic growth picked up; the OECD's forecasters were expecting the combined GDP of their 24 rich member countries to grow by 2¼% in 1992. In the event, it managed a rise of only 1½%. The difference between those figures is equivalent to losing the entire GDP of Austria, or of Thailand and the Philippines combined. More prosaically, the continuing sluggishness meant jobs lost, incomes squeezed and investments shelved. Capitalism, having won the war of ideas with communism, seemed to perform about as badly as any Marxist critic would have predicted.

The year's other source of disappointment was, in the broadest sense, political. The dream had seemed so simple: after the cold war, a new world order would emerge. It would be free of the superpower rivalry that had threatened to obliterate mankind. It would be based on a new consensus about pluralism and decent behaviour. The world, in short, would be safer and nicer. What 1992 provided was far harsher: a new world disorder, created by the poisonous rivalries of race and culture. They had always been there, but they had been largely suppressed by the internal disciplines of communism and contained by the cold-war framework. Places that many people would not previously have been able to mark on a map—Bosnia, Somalia, Ayodhya—came bloodily on to the television screens. It was not a safer world.

In both economics and politics, then, the euphoria faded. It would be nice to report that it was replaced by a gritty realism, and there was a bit of that. But something more fatalistic was also in the air. Both economically and politically, there was a casting back to times past, dreadful times.

Economic ghosts

As the recession dragged on through 1992, it prompted a new brand of unease. Perhaps, mused many, this was not a typical cycle, with downturn leading to recovery just as night turns to day. There was much talk of economic "long waves", of the 1990s being a re-run of the 1930s. After all, even Japan was in a fearful mess. Its stockmarket fell by more than a quarter in 1992; and if its companies were struggling, their performance was not half as dismal as that of its politicians. Large, impersonal forces were gripping the world, and would not let go for years to come.

As with so much in economics, even the wildest talk may start from a germ of truth. It was indeed true that conditions in the early 1990s were different from, say, ten years earlier, when the world came out of a painful recession to enjoy one of the longest booms on record. In particular, companies and individuals in 1992 were weighed down with more debt than ever, relative to their assets and incomes. And governments were not well placed to inject a familiar Keynesian stimulus of their own. Among the OECD countries, which account for four-fifths of world output, budget deficits were already large. In 1992 they reached almost 4% of GDP, their highest for ten years. The budgetary boost was there already, and still the wheels turned slowly.

Nor, the Depression worriers pointed out, was cheap money doing much good. The Federal Reserve brought American interest rates down to 2½%, their lowest in 30 years. But this did not push American consumers and companies into a spending spree. Instead, the size and persistence of the budget deficit cast a shadow over the bond market. Long-term interest rates hardly budged, and at 7½% were a powerful deterrent to borrowing—unless, that is, you were the government. For much of the year, events seemed to support the gloomy view that something odd was going on, something that would not yield to the usual treatment.

While many national economies seemed mired, internationally there was another inviting parallel with the 1930s. The world's trading system was frequently in the balance, its fate dependent on an arcane dispute between the United States and the European Community over agricultural subsidies and quotas. The Uruguay round of talks, launched by the GATT in 1986, should have been finalised in 1991. The round almost broke down at the end of that year, but was rescued. This set a pattern for 1992: alternating bouts of near-collapse and revival, and always confusion. Everybody seemed to lose sight of the fact that governments had made some remarkable mutual concessions, in areas—services, intellectual know-how, procurement policies—which had never been subject to GATT rules and procedures before.

The Uruguay round was ready, at almost any time, to

Milosevic, Super-Serb

Downbeat for Delors

make a triumphant entry into 1992, bringing with it a boost to economic growth that was variously calculated at up to ¹₂% of gross world product every year for ten years. In the event, the round's fate was still undecided by the year end. And, no doubt, in the American Congress there were dozens of politicians waiting to play the roles of Messrs Smoot and Hawley, the two men who in the 1930s had sponsored the bill that took an economic downturn and made it into a trade war.

The political year also produced its historical echoes, but from further back. The Balkans, microcosm of Europe's ancient hatreds, were the most intractable and distressing of the world's trouble spots. In one sense, the details of each gory week mattered less than what they revealed about Europe as a whole. There are other potential Bosnias in Eastern Europe and the ex-Soviet Union: not as ruinous, perhaps, but involving the same deadly brew of ethnic tension and disputed geography. If 1992 is any guide, such tensions are dauntingly hard to contain, let alone to solve.

And, as history has shown, they can spread. Hence the outside world's concern, and involvement. During 1992 the European Community and the United Nations were engaged in the old Yugoslavia, applying a mixture of diplomacy, relief work and threats. They were acting the parts written into the script of the new world order, but their efforts served mainly to prove the depth of disorder. Each new initiative and each new rebuff raised the stakes; what had started out as unthinkable—active military intervention against the Serbs—was by end year coming to constitute the new consensus.

The awkwardness of the Balkans could serve as a metaphor for the whole European Community. This was, after all, supposed to be the year of triumph: 1992 and the completion of the single market, 1992 and the ratification of the Maastricht treaty. In fact, much good work was done to develop the single market, but its significance was overshadowed by recession and by political doubt. The Danes said No to Maastricht, and the whole equation changed. The apparently clear path to economic and monetary union was suddenly strewn with uncertainties. The exchange-rate mechanism that had bound currencies together for five relatively calm years was stretched and all but broken.

Nor was this the only way in which Europe's political leaders were reminded of the limits to their creative powers. Across Europe, but particularly in Germany, nastier voices were raised—against unemployment, against immigrants, against foreigners in general. The notion of a strong, united, European Europe took a fearful knock in 1992. It was largely a product of the image-makers anyway, but images can please and persuade. This one, it appears, did not.

A tail of hope

For all its disappointments, 1992 had a hopeful side, and a more cheerful finish. The hope lay in the developing world where market-based economic policies showed their worth. China's annual growth spurted to 11%. The Asian "dragons" continued to grow at 7% a year. The moral was not lost on India and Latin America, as once dirigiste governments turned bravely to economic reform.

The end-year cheer in the rich world was created in one country: America. Public opinion at last recognised what the statisticians had been reporting for almost two years: that the American economy was growing. When word came out that GDP in the third quarter increased at an annual rate of almost 4%, the effect was startling. And not just in America: people everywhere began to forget all that talk of another Depression. If the mighty United States was on the move, so, surely, was everybody else.

The 4% magic came just too late for the man who had been trying to conjure it up. George Bush went down with the economy, but then decided to leave office with a flourish. He sent American troops into Somalia, which proved (however temporarily) that poor people do not have to starve because local thugs steal food given by well-meaning outsiders. Mr Bush went to Mogadishu to applaud the change; then, as the year turned, on to Moscow to sign a treaty that could rid the world of most of the most dangerous nuclear weapons.

For all that rush of international activity, it was not Mr Bush who was America's beacon in the closing weeks of the year. The man who beat him for the presidency, Bill Clinton, came suddenly to represent all that is best and most hopeful about America. Young, vigorous, can-do: these are qualities as engaging as they can be dangerous. As 1992 drew to its close, it was all too easy to be left with one pessimistic thought: that the world is placing a disconcerting amount of faith in the leadership of a man whose CV says that he has governed Arkansas.

Upbeat for Clinton

As we reported then

Sam, Sam, the paranoid man

JANUARY 18TH **Economic self-disgust set the tone in America's election year.
It threatened to become self-flagellation**

WHEN Americans look at their economy these days, they are horrified by what they see—or think they see. A "double-dip" recession, with the second dip possibly worse than the first; crumbling international competitiveness in industries crucial for long-term growth; an economy hobbled by a naive commitment to "free trade", while competitors play by rules of their own. Sapped of strength at home and conspired against abroad, America is failing. This amounts to a national emergency, no less. Something must be done.

To outsiders the image looks hopelessly distorted. But, you might ask, what else is new? Economic paranoia has become an American habit. For the past 20 years America has watched other economies, notably Japan, narrow its lead in living standards, and most of the time has complained. That has not stopped it from growing richer, at a rate that is disappointing only by the standards of the comparative handful of countries that are close to catching up. America worries as it prospers. So be it.

The trouble is that in recent months these fears have become so intense that they threaten to do real, not imaginary, harm. This time, for once, the demands for something to be done may actually result in something being done—and in all likelihood that will be a setback. An emergency budget package to revive the economy; a tougher line on trade, especially with Japan; new policies to rebuild the industries that have been unfairly disadvantaged in the past. These and other false remedies are not merely, as always, being pressed by Washington lobbies that exist for no other purpose. At the beginning of 1992, they stand an ominously good chance of being tried. That is why it is urgent for America to look carefully at its true economic strengths and weaknesses, and to think hard about the proper goals of economic policy.

The fear of fear itself

Confusion is helping to feed the present mood of despair—a confusion caused because two sorts of economic worry have been run together. The first concerns the short term: how far might the economy fall in the current recession? The second looks further ahead: what price will America have to pay for its failure to compete in international markets? Taken separately, these fears are based on false premises and are greatly overdone. Lumped together—as when cyclical changes are offered as proof that America is in chronic decline, or when the recession is blamed on foreigners' trade policies—they have caused a spurious and potentially destructive panic.

Start with the recession. From the tone of most recent commentary, you would conclude that it has been ferocious. In fact, measured by the decline in output since its peak in 1990,

or by the rise to date in unemployment, it has been unusually mild. True, you would also conclude from your reading that the recession has hardly started, and that much worse is on its way. In fact, the recovery may already have begun.

There are good reasons to think that the coming expansion may be weaker than most of its predecessors; the mildness of the recession that preceded it is the main one. And the danger of a worsening slump cannot be ruled out, least of all in an economy which so delights in talking itself into trouble. Yet signs of recovery are there for those who would see—in recent months' figures for construction, durable goods' orders, share prices, the money supply, bank reserves and indices of leading indicators. The recent rally in the dollar is itself a sign that the financial markets have scented the upturn.

Yet Congress and the White House are preparing to abandon their hard-won budget accord in order to stimulate the economy with tax cuts and increases in public spending—changes in policy that will, in any case, take months to work through to output and employment. That budget accord was agreed to during an earlier panic over the size of the government's deficit. For George Bush, its price was steep: the humiliation of having to break his promise not to raise taxes. Despite its political cost, the accord proved inadequate to the task. In the current fiscal year, the deficit is expected to be roughly $350 billion, compared with the pact's (non-binding) target of $317 billion. Most of the rise in the deficit since 1990 is due to the recession, but there has been a rise in the underlying deficit too.

Now, it seems, Congress and the White House may agree to cast aside their flimsy instrument for curbing the deficit. In negotiating a fiscal package to reflate the economy, they may also decide to unravel the Tax Reform Act of 1986. If so, another flawed but worthwhile piece of economic legislation will be torn up for no good purpose. Some argue, despite this, that a properly designed fiscal initiative need do no long-term harm. What matters, they say, is to make sure that its effects are temporary and that nothing happens to increase the underlying deficit. In other words, it will be all right as long as the package is designed by a right-minded economist rather than by a Republican president squabbling with a Democrat-controlled Congress in an election year. This year's bold fiscal initiative is all too likely, by 1993, to have turned into that year's intractable economic problem; and fiscal policy will itself have rejoined the queue for emergency remedies.

The irony is that America's inability to restrain public borrowing is one of the country's main economic handicaps. By rushing in with needless short-term measures, politicians and lobbyists will make America's longer-term economic problems worse. Here too, however, it is important to see these difficulties as they really are. The present despair over America's ability to compete in the world economy is utterly misconceived.

America the strong

Over the past five years the volume of America's manufactured exports has nearly doubled; over the same period the volume of exports from other industrial countries went up, on average, by a quarter. As a result, America's share of the OECD's manufactured exports increased from 14% in 1987 to an estimated 18% in 1991. The fall of the dollar since the mid-1980s helped, but so too did a fact that is less well-known: the American economy is much the most efficient user of manpower. Measured across the whole economy, it is about twice as productive as Japan. Even measured across manufacturing, where Americans fear they are being thrashed, it is roughly as productive as Japan overall, and retains a clear lead in many industries. American firms continue to dominate most of the businesses that embody leading-edge technologies, such as pharmaceuticals, biotechnology, aerospace, computers and new materials.

Committed pessimists and those lobbying for government hand-outs will at once reply that all this is changing. Japan is catching up and before long will overtake; South Korea and a following army of Asian unfair traders are close behind. But consider this: in itself, catch-up is not merely natural but desirable—even to the country whose lead is diminishing. Japan's ability to make cars and videos that are good and cheap has made America and the other importers of those goods better off. Fierce competition from abroad not only means better, cheaper products to consume; it is also a spur to production, because it promotes innovation and efficiency, and shifts resources to better uses. If that looks like sophistry, cast an eye over Eastern Europe and the Soviet Union, whose producers long enjoyed protection from unfair competition, all the zero-cost capital for investment they could use, and governments bold enough to engage in carefully co-ordinated industrial strategies. My, how they thrived.

The narrowing of America's industrial lead is not in itself a cause for alarm—but it is worth paying attention to, if it indicates that the American economy is doing less well than it might be. Undoubtedly, successful as it is, it could do much better. American businesses are investing far too little in their future. At only 9% of national income, they spend less than half as much as Japan each year on new capital, and roughly one-third less than Germany. And America has to struggle with several burdens that would crush a weaker economy: an outlandishly wasteful and expensive health-care industry; a legal system that acts as a heavy tax on American business; and an education system that leaves too many children unequipped for work.

These are the issues that policy-makers need to tackle. The two best ways to boost investment would be to bring the budget deficit under control (because that would raise the national saving rate and lower the cost of long-term capital) and make a firm commitment to low inflation.

Both ways will demand economic leadership, which raises questions about the timbre of the man in the White House. America needs a president who can respond to misguided gloom with calm proposals to promote long-term growth. Instead it has Mr Bush, who has surrendered to panic and is making things worse.

Upbeat China

MARCH 21ST **The old guard in Beijing is conceding that its old ideas are no match against new wealth**

REFORM is winning in China, and the fortune-makers of Hong Kong are winning with it. That old Communist turned capitalist roader, Deng Xiaoping, now 87, has long been pressing his country to return to the path of reform. Now it looks as though he has succeeded. China is still far from free, but the omens for it are good.

Mr Deng is a practical man, who, like Old Possum, likes practical cats. "It doesn't matter whether a cat is black or white," he says, "so long as it catches mice." Earlier this month the Communist Party Politburo officially came round to the same heresy: if an economic reform, however non-communist, delivers the goods, argued the Politburo (in stuffier language than Mr Deng's, of course), it is acceptable. Almost three years after the bloodshed of Tiananmen Square, and four years after the previous burst of economic reform was smothered, China's 1.2 billion people are entering a new stage in their long march out of poverty and communism.

The real point, however, is not that another stage in this march has opened; it is that the march has become irreversible. This does not mean continuous. Chinese politics is un-

stable, shot through with nepotism and corruption. China specialises in stop-go cycles, of both the political and the economic sorts. Likelier than not, the latest renewal will be followed some day by more repression. That will be sad, but probably not fatal to a happy outcome. The lesson of the failed clampdown of 1988-91 is that the economic reforms begun by Mr Deng 14 years ago have unleashed a new China that only full-scale civil war could now stop from becoming capitalist.

The world's businessmen and investors have come to realise this. China is still no market for the faint-hearted, but it has become a market whose opportunities are hard to ignore. Its foreign trade last year was $135 billion. That equalled a third of GDP, a high proportion for a continent-sized country. The stock of foreign direct investment in China is now around $40 billion, which must be the envy of other would-be reformers like Russia and India.

Most of the foreign investment in China consists of low-wage factories that have moved there from Hong Kong and Taiwan. Some of it, however, is the work of big multinational companies. Procter & Gamble and Avon are both doing booming business across the border from Hong Kong in Guangdong province, whose 65m people now have incomes high enough to allow them to buy cosmetics. Motorola is planning a state-of-the-art electronics factory in the northern city of Tianjin.

Hong Kong is the place most touched by the lifting of the post-Tiananmen gloom about China. With good reason: under the terms of a deal that Britain signed with China in 1984, Hong Kong and its 6m people will be returned to Chinese sovereignty on June 30th 1997. As that date inches closer, the views of outsiders about Hong Kong—and Hong Kong's own view of itself—must increasingly reflect hunches about China's future. In the despair after Tiananmen, Hong Kong's link with China cost it much shine. Today it adds lustre.

Few people are naive enough to believe that, after 1997, Hong Kong will be a place whose citizens can choose their rulers or freely speak their minds. But more and more people already believe that Hong Kong will still be a place where money can be made: maybe, as China itself booms, even more than they make there now.

The economic motor of change

The border between Hong Kong and Guangdong is, despite formalities that irritate the 15,000 lorry-drivers and several thousand other people who cross it each day, an increasingly insubstantial affair. Hong Kong firms already employ 2m-3m workers in their factories in Guangdong; a large share of the colony's manufactured exports are now made there. Hong Kong is thriving on the back of China. Its economy is expected to grow by 6% this year and next. Capital is coming in, not fleeing. Unemployment is below 2%, and it seems that last year there was a brain gain rather than a brain drain; certainly more people came to the colony than left it. Foreign institutional investors have helped make Hong Kong's stockmarket one of the world's perkiest over the past 18 months. These investors, frustrated by the thinness and obscurity of China's own infant stockmarkets, say that one big reason they are in the Hong Kong bourse is to capture reflections of China.

All this has happened because the reforms Mr Deng brought in during the years 1978-87 spread their benefits far and wide—the 80% of Chinese who still live on the land prospered most—and because foreign trade and investment were welcomed instead of spurned. The crackdown of 1988-91 proved pretty ineffective. Too much wealth and authority had already seeped away from Beijing for hardliners to do much but stop further reforms from being proposed. Mr Deng has now grabbed even that stopping-power from them.

As China's leaders prepare the next stage of reform, they are acting in an atmosphere of what one former political prisoner calls "political devolution". He means that the conclusion most Chinese drew from Tiananmen Square was that politics had become meaningless and should be avoided. The rulers should be left to enjoy their dynastic games in Beijing, so long as they let everybody else get on with making money. Keep politics quarantined, in other words.

If that is really what is happening, it will amount to a revolution in a country whose official dogma just 20 years ago was that politics should be everywhere, not nowhere. The best test of the hypothesis will be found in the behaviour of the leadership towards state industry in the next few months. All the gains China has enjoyed have come from the exuberant growth of non-state industries since the early 1980s: their share of industrial output has zoomed from under 15% to a little over half. If China is at last ready to break the backbone of communism, it will start turning the state industries from welfare agencies and political clubs into competitive businesses. There are hints it could do this in the most imaginative way, by bringing foreign investors into the good state factories and letting these then absorb the bad ones.

The China thus created would still make western democrats uneasy. It would be an authoritarian anti-democracy that paid little attention to human rights. But it would also be a China where civilising influences could begin to emerge, as they are already doing in the parts of the country that are growing richer fastest. This has, in general, been the way of Asia's most successful countries, from Taiwan and South Korea to Singapore and Malaysia. It will, over the next 20 years, become China's way too.

May the worst lot lose

APRIL 4TH   As Britain's election campaign neared its end the Conservatives seemed to us to be less unconvincing than Labour

THE Britain that goes to the polls on April 9th is in fractious mood, a strange mixture of impatience and indifference. The recession has gone on too long. The election campaign has gone on too long. Almost all the opinion polls have pointed to an inconclusive result, with no single party getting an overall majority. The voters are right to be bored. Although this election ought to be of great moment, the politicians have not risen to the occasion.

Their failure does not go back just to last month, when John Major named the date. Party inadequacies have been all too plain throughout the past five years. The Conservatives have been confused and divided over the poll tax, the exchange rate, Europe. The Labour Party under Neil Kinnock has behaved as though politics could be reduced to a dark suit, a white shirt and a programmed chorus of "the government is wrong". The voters are not impressed: after 13 years of Tory rule and now a long recession, Labour ought to be far more popular. Only the third party has shown real vitality, going from the collapse of the Alliance to the birth of the Liberal Democrats and now, under Paddy Ashdown, to almost 20% in the polls. But none of the parties has paid sustained attention to the challenge facing Britain. All talk about recession, though that is probably already over, which means they ignore the lessons of the past and the demands of the future. The result is that too few Britons grasp what they have to do to create a land of hope, let alone of glory. The task of creation centres on the economy; and the choice of creator starts with a choice between Tory and Labour.

Just the beginning

No Briton under the age of 35 has voted in an election that did not involve Margaret Thatcher as Tory leader. Those who are

18, and voting for the first time, can hardly remember Britain before Mrs Thatcher. The result is that 12m voters have no reason to think about the origins of what came to be called Thatcherism, no yardstick to judge it by. To them, it was the norm. They may have loved her or loathed her, but they were not particularly curious about her. The same has increasingly been true of people over the age of 35.

Mrs Thatcher herself is irrelevant to this election. But what she did and why she did it still count enormously, and will go on counting no matter who is in government after next week. In economic terms, her significance stems from the fact that the election in 1979 came when Britain was slipping from the second rank of countries and heading for the third. It was losing touch with France. The next stop was going to be alongside somewhere like Spain, and even that only briefly.

Britain's economic sluggishness was not just a statistic. It was visible, palpable, in every part of British life. While other OECD economies were satisfying the spending hopes of both private individuals and the state, Britons were squabbling over money that was not there. Increasingly, visitors saw the place as a joke, shabby and strike-ridden. Even Anglophiles were shaking their heads and starting to mutter behind their hands.

The Thatcher years stopped the slide: in 1979-90 Britain's productivity growth was faster than Germany's and France's. Given the momentum of history, given that economics tends to reward success with more success and to pile failure on to failure, this was a huge achievement. If people have lost sight of its scale, it is because Mrs Thatcher was around for so long. Yet the economic imperatives of 1979-90 are not history. In terms of both ends and means, they are as powerful today as ever.

On ends, the British economy needs another 20 years or so of above-average productivity growth to raise real incomes to German and French levels. To achieve that will require macroeconomic stability as a background to microeconomic sharpening, and both those means are far more elusive than politicians like to pretend. Witness Mrs Thatcher's own difficulties.

Her years in government were notable for their lack of macro stability. Financial deregulation led to an excessive credit boom, and sterling became a full member of the European monetary system at least five years later than it should have done. Both these factors have now lost their force: the credit boom was one-off, the EMS is reality. A credible macro framework is in place in Britain, for the first time in more than 20 years. But there is nothing inevitable about its future. The next government could strengthen macro stability, or destroy it.

The microeconomic sharpening has also made progress, but it too could be blunted. On tax particularly, the achievements of the Thatcher years were fragile. The proportion of people's incomes going to the taxman has been cut since 1979, but not for those on average earnings and below. The cuts were made possible only by shifting the tax burden from income on to spending, and even more because of the revenues from North Sea oil and the privatisation programme. The fundamental cause of Britain's growing tax burden in 1950-80—the rise in public expenditure—was slowed down, but it was not turned back.

Macro stability, micro sharpening: these are the yardsticks for judging the promises of Messrs Major and Kinnock. The judgment begins with three figures: £1.6 billion, £36 billion and £1 billion. The first is how much the Tory government felt able to afford in net tax cuts in its budget last month. That modest sum was part of the huge second figure, the projected size of public borrowing (excluding receipts from privatisation) in the fiscal year that starts next week. And the trivial £1 billion is how much the Treasury estimates will be available for future tax cuts or extra spending—but only in three years' time. Britain, in short, is boxed in: virtually no room for lower taxes or higher spending, yet massive borrowing.

Nothing better illustrates the tightness of the box than Mr Kinnock's about-turn this week, when he said he would retain some of the Tories' privatisation plans. For years he has railed against them. Now he sees he would need the money. Yet privatisation is a dwindling pot; so is North Sea oil. The need to control public spending is therefore greater than ever.

But no senior political figure has the stomach to control public spending, or even to explain why it is necessary. Instead, Mr Major and his ministers have spent the past 15 months showering money on the voters, while Labour has chanted "mean, mean". That has been the central failing of this protracted campaign, and it is why Britain is again threatened with a slide into the third league.

A cruder test

If neither Labour nor the Tories would do the economy any good, voters should use a different test: which party would do the least harm? Even by that low standard, the Tories are flawed. On the plus side, they have learnt the harsh lesson of the 1986-90 boom and bust. Their commitment to sterling's parity in the EMS seems real, which greatly reduces the chances of resurgent inflation. But Mr Major is far too relaxed about public spending and borrowing, and he has been wildly optimistic about the scope for cutting income tax. The best hope for the Tories is that this insouciance is just a charade that would be replaced, after April 9th, by a serious effort to curb spending and borrowing. Lies born of cynicism are bad, but they are not as harmful as lies born of delusion.

Cue for Labour, which claims to have changed its economic thinking since the 1970s. Could it now avoid doing harm? Some of its policies—on education and training, for example—are designed to be supply-side improvements, and might well act as such. But Labour seems to think that these are an alternative to radical policies on competition and incentives. They cannot be regarded as an alternative; they are a useful supplement.

This confusion runs through much of the rest of Labour's economic programme. It promises to reduce unemployment; but it would also introduce a minimum wage, which would destroy jobs. It says it will concentrate on investment; but its two strongest public-spending commitments are to raise pensions and child benefit, which are both pure consumption. It says it wants markets to work; but its policy papers in the past five years have been littered with new committees that would interfere with market outcomes. It says it has abandoned nationalisation as a doctrine; but its plans to regulate and guide industry would be just as damaging. It sounds firm about not devaluing within the EMS; but a stable currency comes about because an economy is competitive and can hold its own with

Germany. Labour would make Britain less competitive.

That list is completed by the biggest flaw in Labour's programme: income tax. When Labour was last in office, most Britons—including, privately, senior Labour ministers—and every foreigner agreed that British taxes were too high. Thirteen years later, while almost every government in the world has been cutting taxes, the new-look Labour Party plans much higher taxes than it had before.

Look at this table of average rates—the amount that the taxman takes in income tax and national insurance from people on three illustrative levels of earnings, using some stereotypical assumptions:

	Person on average earnings	Twice average earnings	Four times average earnings
1978-79 (actual Labour budget)	14.5%	20.7%	29.5%
1992-93 (proposed Labour budget)	16.9%	24.3%	37.5%

* Married man, two children; mortgage equal to twce his salary up to tax-relief limit; pension contribution equal to 8% of gross salary

These figures give the lie to Labour's claim that its tax plans would affect only the "rich". In Britain average earnings for men with full-time jobs are now £17,500 a year, the princely sum of $30,000. For those plutocrats, Labour plans to boost the tax-take by 2½ percentage points—ie, more than a sixth—compared with when it was last in office. For the person on £70,000 ($120,000), the tax take would be up by eight points—more than a quarter higher than when the last Labour government was triumphantly claiming to be taxing the rich "until

the pips squeak". Rich? With Labour in power, nobody who works for a salary and pays his taxes honestly would ever get rich.

That leaves till last the Liberal Democrats. Some of the party's favourite policies—proportional representation, an independent central bank—are close to this newspaper's heart. And, with Mrs Thatcher's departure, Mr Ashdown has often shown a keener awareness of the task facing Britain than any other politician. Yet his party's election manifesto was disappointing. In several crucial areas—health, most of all—the Liberal Democrats sound as unimaginative as Labour. On taxes, too, the possibilities for reforming the whole system are ignored in the party's rush to raise income tax.

The positive case for supporting the Liberal Democrats is therefore smaller than once seemed likely. It is overshadowed by the cruel arithmetic of the voting system; on the latest opinion polls, the party will be lucky to hold on to the 22 seats it had in the last Parliament. Nor is voting reform likely to come directly from a hung Parliament, because the Liberal Democrats would almost certainly be ignored by whichever party had the largest number of seats. Mr Ashdown's best long-term hope for a Liberal revival lies in overturning the history of the past 92 years, so that the Labour Party and the Liberals rejoin each other. For that to happen, Labour must lose this election, and the bigger its loss the better.

And that, given the depressing state of British politics, is the best reason for wanting the Conservatives to win next week.

The Danes say No

**JUNE 6TH   Their referendum on the ratification of the Maastricht treaty
burst the bubble of Europhoria**

THE gamble of the Treaty on European Union has failed, bringing the European Community's high-rolling phase of the past three years to an abrupt end. It failed by only a Viking's whisker in a referendum in Denmark, the third-smallest state in the Community and, like Britain, a habitual Eurosceptic. No matter: the rule was always clear. Amendments to the Treaty of Rome, such as this treaty contained, must be ratified by the Community's entire membership. Now the other 11 members will seek ways around this rule to keep the treaty afloat. The quest will be wearying, and they risk repeating the mistake that has landed them where they are.

The Maastricht treaty is, or was, far more than a constitutional amendment: it was a redesign. Not content with giving the Community one currency, a central bank and lots of macro-economic authority, Maastricht would have given it a citizenship, a fledgling foreign policy and an embryonic defence policy. It would have extended the rule of Community law into just about every area of government that a modern nation-state could concern itself with. All this, and more, was appreciated by the Danes, for their government had honourably showered them with copies of the Maastricht text.

The fact that a uniquely informed people snubbed its own parliament points up the error of Maastricht, and tells why a lost vote in a little nation may yet wreck something which, with the backing of just 24,000 more Danes, would still today be imperturbably on course. Maastricht was a rushed job, bounced upon the Community by the governments of France

and Germany in an urge to fulfil their dream of European union before its basis in cold-war Europe vanished.

A conference of governments then hurried great changes past their voters, like the White Rabbit muttering "train to catch" and "this or nothing" before plunging down a dark hole. Even in France and Germany it soon became clear that government had moved ahead of many of the governed. Thus the Danes' refusal to be mass-tricked is not an irritant to be brushed aside by 11 other confident members. It will rightly work upon embarrassed governments and uncertain peoples and steer the pell-mell development of Europe on to a new and more gradual course. Already the French government has conceded that its people must have a referendum on Maastricht. The British government will come under justifiable pressure to do the same. Though Maastricht was the stuff of lively politics in Westminster, Britons still have only a vague grasp of what it promises to do to their system of government.

The Danish veto will also disrupt and delay another hectic change in the EC: its enlargement. The Nordic countries have been toppling towards the Community like dominoes: first Sweden, nudged by its forcefully Europhile prime minister, Carl Bildt; then Finland, not to be left out; leaving only Norway wobbling in lonely indecision. Now that the Community's resident Norseman has said No, imagine the impact. The Austrians and Swiss—two more peoples whose governments have probably run ahead of them in their Euro-enthusiasm—will take note too. The would-be members in central Europe

16

will not. For them the EC remains a Golconda.

It is hard to say what in the Maastricht treaty the Danes found unpalatable. Probably it was a combination of the treaty and much wrangling over enlargement. The European Commission, curiously disappointed by Maastricht, was worried that the inrush of new members would further dilute its vision of the union. So its president, Jacques Delors, counter-attacked, musing about the need for a strengthened commission, a trimming of the power of smaller members and another conference of governments to decide such things. Another Maastricht? Already? No wonder many Danes felt they were falling down a black hole.

The whiff of the thing

There will be those who, detesting the whole idea of a confederation of states with a degree of supranational authority, will be gleeful that the EC has brought turmoil upon itself. For *The Economist* the mistake was never the goal, always the immoderate manner of its pursuit. Europe's single market is not even up and running yet. The detailed plan for monetary union offered more than enough to be getting on with. The Community was marching into areas of centralised lawmaking—particularly on social policy—which scoffed at its own principle of "subsidiarity". Above all there was the whiff of coercion in the air, of governments frog-marching public opinion along or of "saving the Germans from themselves". Coercion was Comecon's most damaging ingredient.

Europe's governments now face a constitutional mess. Maastricht is not a separate treaty from which 11 members can simply exclude Denmark. It is a mass of changes to the rules of

a club of which Denmark is already a full member: the EC will go on existing without those changes. Nor can selected bits of Maastricht be easily abstracted to make the treaty more acceptable. Such treaties are always confections of something-for-everyone, devilish hard to unmix.

The commission and member-states are toying with two solutions, to be explored after the 11 have ratified Maastricht. Invite Denmark to opt out of the Community's joint efforts in foreign, immigration and defence policy, and then to hold another referendum on what remains. Or dump the Treaty of Rome, incorporate Maastricht into a completely new treaty between 11 members, and relegate Denmark to membership of the European Economic Area, in which the other Nordic countries currently repose. The former is the flexible way of the EC's future. The latter sounds like more frog-marching.

The rest of the 1990s was bound to be troubling for the EC. It had stored up too many promises in a deeply changed Europe. With the Danish vote the storm has broken early. Whatever emerges from the storm will confirm two truths. The driving force of European union remains the fact that modern European nation-states cannot run their economies independently of each other. The single market will forge on, embracing ever more of Europe. The second is that the Community will have to be built more flexibly from now on, with more scope for members to opt, or be kept, out of its different realms of joint government. It is even conceivable that the original six members will re-emerge from this crisis bent on forming a new core within the EC's growing diversity—safe from disgruntled Vikings.

GATT will build the world

JUNE 27TH   America, the country that gave the world the GATT, appears to have forgotten why it was worth giving

THE Uruguay round of trade talks is now delicately balanced between success and failure. Success is there for the taking. If the round fails, it will be because governments around the world—but, above all, the government of the United States—prefer no deal at all to one they regard as an unsatisfactory compromise. Their purist approach might be right if it were defending a fine principle; actually, if the round fails, a fine principle will have been trampled down. If the talks collapse, it will be because governments judge it politically expedient to let that happen, despite what they know to be a massive cost to their own electorates. That would be a failure of leadership on a historic scale.

In trade policy, no government is blameless. For reasons that political economists have understood for centuries, almost every government succumbs to pressure from special interests demanding protection from foreign competition: losses may outweigh gains, but those who stand to gain are usually vocal and well-organised, whereas those who stand to lose are not. This protectionist logic works everywhere. America has resisted it better than most. For years it championed the cause of freer trade through the General Agreement on

Tariffs and Trade (GATT). Decades of American leadership after 1945 opened markets worldwide. In miserable contrast, the European Community has written the book on new methods of protection. Why then, if the round fails, should America's government be singled out for criticism?

For two reasons. First, precisely because the former champion of liberal trade now seems willing to betray that cause. And second because, surprising as it may seem, the American economy would itself be much the biggest gainer if a compromise to conclude the round could be agreed upon. Look at it this way: for the sake of surrendering his free-trade principles, George Bush is willing to make most Americans worse off.

Know your ally

The GATT, regrettably, is not an institution that wins the hearts and minds of popular opinion. Its discussions drag on, as though negotiators need a month merely to clear their throats; arcane rules and regulations, which no right-thinking person could ever take an unpaid interest in, are its meat and drink. Yet the fact is that GATT has been a great success. Witness the American economy. Thanks to the lowering of trade barriers after the second world war, American firms became exporters to the world. Despite its self-doubt, in many of the industries likely to grow fastest in the years ahead, America remains the strongest and most competitive producer in the world—precisely because its companies are obliged to test themselves in the global marketplace. In this sense, GATT built America.

It also built the prosperity that much of the world now takes for granted. This remarkable history of success can continue. Thanks to the pro-trade policies that so many third-world governments have lately adopted—unilaterally, mind, without seeking "concessions" from trading partners—it can spread its blessings to countries hitherto left out.

Consider the trade deal that is now within reach, defects and all. For the first time, it would bring farm trade within the GATT's rules. Into the bargain, the European Community has proposed a substantial liberalisation of its insanely protectionist common agricultural policy. Admittedly, that reform is not as radical as it should be—in the dispute that is the main obstacle to an overall agreement in the Uruguay round, America is insisting on further changes—but it is real reform nonetheless. The round is ready to liberalise trade in textiles; to bring services into the GATT and start liberalising trade there, too; to establish clearer rules for the protection of intellectual property; to lower tariffs and strengthen disciplines over non-tariff barriers to trade; and more.

This is not free trade at a stroke—supposing that that is what America wants. But each of the previous rounds of trade talks failed to deliver that, too; even so, they were deservedly judged a success. If anybody had predicted at the start of the present round that such a compromise would be achieved, they would have been told not to set their sights so recklessly high.

The gains within reach are not a theoretical fantasy; they are a matter of cold, hard cash. In sum, the flawed package that the Uruguay round is poised to deliver would immediately raise global income, according to one careful (and conservative) study, by $120 billion a year—roughly ½% of today's gross world product. America's share of that pot would be $35 billion a year. Japan's share would be $28 billion, about the same as the EC's. These gains are roughly half as big as those that would flow from a comprehensive trade-liberalisation package. But, belying the claim that only a much more radical deal could provide gains big enough to draw in developing countries and producer-alliances (such as farm-goods export-

ers), it turns out that even a half-loaf would be shared widely across the world.

There is, of course, no such thing as a free half-loaf. Freer trade would reduce employment in some industries and increase it in others. The truth is that freer trade works by forcing economies to change. Disruption is the source of its benefits. The forces that would reduce farm employment would increase jobs not just in services (the biggest part of the economy) and construction, but also in capital goods, high technology and other leading-edge manufacturing.

The challenge for governments is to defeat resistance to these changes, partly by compensating losers in ways that do not retard growth (eg, by helping with retraining and relocation) and partly by mobilising support among the large majority of firms and workers who stand to gain directly from freer trade. Too often, America's government, like others, does exactly the opposite. Its farm policy is a case in point. It encourages people to stay where they are not best employed.

The same is true of America's approach to industrial trade. When Mr Bush went to Asia in January he took with him not a strategy for America's future, but representatives of its past: the bosses of failing, protection-seeking industries. Mr Bush and his trade negotiators, always claiming to be outsmarting the protectionists, have often merely pandered to them. Lately, with Ross Perot angling to form the most protectionist administration since the Great Depression, Mr Bush has seemed less willing than ever to set trade policy on its proper course.

For years American politicians have railed against the GATT. They have made vigorous use of section-301 and other weapons to retaliate against countries they deem to be trade offenders. They have promoted the mercantilist fallacy that trade must be "fair" (whatever that means) rather than free. And they have pursued the regional alternative to multilateral negotiations on trade—an alternative intended to foster trade on America's terms. The free-trade agreements with Canada and Mexico have the potential to do great economic good, but it is a trap to think of them, as the administration appears to, as an alternative to multilateralism. Without a strong GATT (ie, without a GATT made strong by the support of its member governments), regional trade blocks are likely to become regional trade fortresses. That would be a disaster for America and the world economy.

Mr Bush's critics are right. It is time the president put America first. He must not allow the GATT to fail.

Out of Bosnia

AUGUST 1ST   **Ex-Yugoslavia's miseries presented Western Europe with a test it had neither the will nor the joint-means to face up to**

THE clothes say prosperous, the faces say destitute. It is the refugees' faces that are the more eloquent in describing the misery of the war in what was once Yugoslavia, but the prosperous clothes bear a message, too, and it is an uncomfortable one for Europe. The message is that wars are not confined to history books and poor countries. They happen in places

where people are well dressed: they happen in Europe, and Europe is being found wanting.

It has taken an exodus of refugees to bring this message home. The fighting, after all, has been going on for more than a year, but Europe has wanted to believe that this squabble need not affect anybody other than the wretched belligerents.

In their affluence West Europeans have forgotten their own past, the centuries of going at each other, the two world wars. They have forgotten how recently they turned their attention to making markets not wars. They have taken comfort in their institutions, in the European Community and NATO and the other bodies that have brought nearly half a century of peace and prosperity for their members. These have helped West Europeans bury their old antagonisms, but their writ does not run in ex-Yugoslavia. No outsider is prepared to quell the fighting, so it goes on. And as it goes on, the refugees multiply, and have now reached numbers that cannot be ignored.

So much for European progress. This war cannot even be confined behind a *cordon sanitaire*, let alone stopped. That is one shock for West Europeans. The other nasty truth has yet to sink in. It is that some of the rules that they, with their allies, have tried to set over the past 45 years in faraway places like the Middle East are about to be broken on their doorstep. The West teaches that aggression will not be rewarded, that land will not be acquired by conquest or even frontiers adjusted by force. Iraq tried it, and was bombed and beaten back. Israel is scolded day after day for not returning the land it occupies. But Serbia, and perhaps Croatia, may be allowed to get away with it.

Serbs and Croats may succeed where others have failed chiefly because no outsider cares enough to risk more lives to hold the antagonists apart. But that is not the only reason. The other is that the old patterns of territorial division in ex-Yugoslavia are plainly incompatible with lasting peace. Even had the Yugoslavs tried to settle their differences by negotiation rather than fighting, some redrawing of boundaries and movements of population would have been sensible. Now that hatreds have been inflamed, not just by the usual horrors of war but by atrocities, it is unimaginable that a settlement involving the return of every displaced family to its former home could be achieved. And now that Serbs (and Bosnia's Croats) have grabbed so much territory, it is hard to see them being made to hand it all back.

The peace-makers' task will therefore be to win agreement for the least inequitable redrawing of boundaries that is compatible with resettling the maximum number of refugees. It seems a distant objective to be discussing when no peace is in sight and in a week when the United Nations has been trying to concentrate minds on the immediate problems of the refugees still flooding out of Bosnia. Yet there should be a political connection between (a) those displaced by the war and (b) a settlement, no matter how distant. And in the meantime the refugees will be given a much warmer welcome by their reluctant hosts if their eventual return to somewhere near home is at all likely. At present it isn't.

Western Europe, with some exceptions, has not responded well to the refugees. Although the vast majority of the 2m-plus have not yet tried to leave the territory of ex-Yugoslavia, borders have been closed with alacrity. Before this week's conference in Geneva, ex-communist Hungary had taken more (50,000) than any other country except Germany (275,000); Britain and France had taken barely 1,100 each. No country has matched the welcome routinely extended by nations far poorer than Western Europe's. Malawi, for instance, a country of 9½m with an income per person of barely $180 a

year, is host to 950,000 refugees; Pakistan has given shelter to 3.6m Afghans.

The one excuse for such inhospitable behaviour lies in the aggressors' aims. The war in the Balkans is not just about winning territory; it is also about moving whole populations, ethnically defined, in the interests of tribal purity. Indeed, "ethnic cleansing", the Serbs' contribution to the euphemisms of war, is a policy of driving non-Serbs out of their homes never to return. Those who help the refugees thus cleansed are therefore both performing an act of basic human decency and acquiescing in a practice of which Stalin and Verwoerd would have approved. The easier it is for refugees to find a haven abroad, the greater the number of those who will elect to flee, and the better pleased their persecutors.

True as this is, it is not an excuse for rejecting refugees; nor is the fear of setting precedents when future bust-ups occur in Eastern Europe or parts of the former Soviet Union. Instead, the countries of Western Europe should treat the refugees generously, bearing in mind the following. First, most refugees will want to stay as close to home as possible. That means that countries farther away should compensate neighbouring ones for some of the burdens they will disproportionately bear. Second, refugees need not be wholly dependent on charity. Although many of those allowed to leave ex-Yugoslavia will be very old or very young, and although Western Europe's economies are weak, refugees who want to work should be allowed to. They need not be given EC citizenship but, if some eventually settle down and become citizens, the European Community will be the winner. It is also important to recognise now that some refugees are unlikely ever to go home; nothing is to be gained by keeping them, like Palestinians, indefinitely in camps.

The Palestinian example is instructive in other ways. Most refugees will want to go home, and the world should not forget them. Serbia may be aiming for an all-Serb state, but it will not achieve it, any more than the architects of apartheid achieved racial tidiness in South Africa: this is the age of migration and miscegenation. If Serbia is ever to regain international respectability, its readiness to accept the return of refugees, with suitable guarantees of their rights, will have to be part of the bargain. A glance at Palestine shows why. Four decades after the 1948 war, the 2.5m Palestinian refugees are still a huge obstacle to a settlement.

For good reasons the outside world has avoided direct military intervention in the Balkans, though some kind of action—air strikes, for instance—may yet be justified if Serb atrocities do not end. Serbia has expanded its territory; Croatia has made gains as well as suffered losses; the main victims are the Muslims of Bosnia—45% of the population, left with barely 5% of the land. Western Europe cannot impose peace in an area where so many people are determined to have war. It will have to acknowledge that Serbia, and maybe Croatia, will end up bigger than they started; indeed the sooner that is recognised, the sooner the war will end. But meanwhile Europe can do more to help the innocents who want to get out. That means welcoming refugees. It also means explaining to Serbia that it will remain a pariah state until it hands back most of the territory it has grabbed and puts an end to ethnic cleansing.

Open the club

AUGUST 29TH **If the United Nations is to be the world's voice, its Security Council must be seen to be more than a western clique**

WHAT a bad business it would be if the United Nations Security Council, freed from the east-west confrontation, were to be trapped in a north-south one. It could happen. The council, exult northerners, has been reborn to keep the peace in a manner that fits with modern times. No, grumble southerners, the council is becoming a flag of convenience for old-time neo-imperialists. The argument matters. If the UN loses its credibility, the Security Council would still be able to order governments about, but its orders would have lost their international sheen and look more like big-power bullying.

The council is an anachronism. Its five permanent veto-wielding members are the victors of the second world war (the ten other members are chosen on a rotating basis for two years). America, Britain and France dominate decision-making; Russia is out of things and China intent on its own affairs. This is an absurdity that cannot last. Japan, for one, has made it plain that it expects to be welcomed to the top table when the UN celebrates its 50th anniversary in 1995. Germany, less pushy, has let it be known that it is on Japan's heels. The developing world, uncomfortable at having to accept China as its representative, presses its own claims.

If the system ain't broke, don't fix it, argue advocates of the status quo. They have a point. Peacekeeping, in the broadest sense of the term, has blossomed since the end of the cold war: the UN's efforts to set the world to rights stretch from El Salvador's legal system to the reconstruction of Cambodia. Yet the peacekeepers are coming in for a lot of flak. They are, it is said, doing the wrong things in the wrong way.

Doing things the wrong way is more a matter of the UN's lack of co-ordination and of governments not paying their dues than of the council's composition. But getting priorities wrong reflects on council membership. Look, say critics, how long it took the council to respond to the tragedy unfolding in Somalia, a country now remote from western interests. Compare this with the energy that goes into issues that the West is excited about: ex-Yugoslavia, Iraq and Libya. The contrast feeds the suspicion that the top three are using the council as an instrument to promote their own foreign policy.

The vetoers would veto a veto veto

Any change to the Security Council requires the General Assembly to revise the UN charter. But the veto-wielders have the power to prevent revision. Thus there is a world of difference between what should be done and what can be done.

The Permanent Five's own preferred solution would be to sneak in Japan, whose money is needed, on its own. Japan already pays handsomely for peacekeeping ventures, second only to America. But if Japan is let in, Germany will not accept being kept out. The awkwardness is that three permanent seats for Western Europe are two too many (and maybe Russia, which inherited the Soviet seat, does not deserve, by the criteria of wealth, military clout or bossiness, to keep an East European seat).

One neat solution would be to keep the overall numbers as they are but to replace France and Britain with Japan and the European Community. Germany, the outsider, would accept this if the EC could get its act together. France may be prepared to think about it. Britain is adamantly against the idea, though long an enthusiast for the EC showing solidarity at the UN. The quest for a common EC foreign policy does not depend only upon the Maastricht treaty, and a single West European seat on the Security Council would nicely concentrate attention on that quest. Perhaps Germany, France and Britain could agree to fill the single seat on a rotating basis in the absence of a European union to take over.

Sorting out the European complication, and bringing in Japan, would still leave the developing world feeling hard done by, scowling at the Security Council as a rich man's club. By their size and/or geography, India, Nigeria (or possibly Egypt) and Brazil are high in the queue for permanent seats. They are likely to be kept waiting for a time. Some argue that their addition would make the club unwieldy (there was a bit of fuss when council numbers were raised from 11 to 15 in the 1960s). But the true stumbling-block is the veto.

The veto has not been formally exercised for several years. But it was always a lamentable affair, used by the Soviet Union to spike capitalist plans and by the United States to protect Israel. Now that the cold war is over, and Israel is protecting itself with peace talks, these uses are redundant. The veto would be better done away with, and decisions made in a straightforward way on the basis of a two-thirds majority. But this is a fantasy: those that have the veto would veto its removal. By common consent the veto is not now used. Yet its possession guards self-important governments from the prospect of being obliged by lesser folk to do something they do not want to do.

A third tier of permanent but veto-less seats is often suggested as a way of broadening the Security Council. It might work. But it would not heal the resentment that lies at the heart of the Security Council's problems: if a country merits a permanent seat, why should it not merit a veto too? The reason is that it might use it—and the council find itself stuck in the impasse of its bad old days.

Moreover, there has been a profound change since those days: the council is now prepared to reconsider the traditional UN view that governments have a sovereign right to be as beastly as they like to their own citizens. Many countries, but particularly third-world ones, are uncomfortable about this new interventionism. A third-world representative might see itself duty-bound to act as blocking agent.

A risk, to be sure. But so is the UN's loss of credibility. Cosy though it is for those inside, the rest of the world cannot for ever be kept out of the world's top peace-making body. Better to welcome newcomers in, and garland them with responsibility, than to leave distrust to fester.

Mayhem

SEPTEMBER 19TH   The near-death of the European Community's quasi-fixed exchange rate system showed up the need for a fully fixed one

EUROPE'S monetary system now faces a test that puts its very survival in doubt, yet which challenges the old logic of a Europe of independent national currencies as never before. On September 16th overwhelming currency-market speculation forced Britain to suspend sterling's membership of the exchange-rate mechanism (ERM) that links the currencies of the European Community. What had, only weeks earlier, seemed a measured march towards a monetary union in Europe became a rout.

In mid-recession, Britain was asked to endure its steepest-ever one-day jump in interest rates—a rise of five percentage points. Yet the pound still fell, until the government abandoned its pledge to defend it, and reversed the interest-rate increase announced just hours before. Italy, having devalued the lira only days earlier, was pushed out too. Spain kept the peseta inside the ERM but devalued it by 5%. Sweden, also in recession, had to raise its overnight interest rate to 500% merely to shadow the ERM. The system's critics were left triumphant. If such currency mayhem is not a *reductio ad absurdum*, they could ask, what is?

At this cruelly testing moment for Europe's economic policy-makers, two points need to be clearly understood. First, the British government, though brought in the end to a clumsy and humiliating defeat, was right to try to defend sterling with high interest rates. Its mistake was in failing to do so earlier. More important, the near-breakdown of the ERM makes a strong case not for abandoning the system, still less for making it more flexible, but for striving all the more urgently to create a single European currency.

Don't ditch the monnet

Britain's ERM commitment was worth a fight. The system never offered an economic panacea, though two years ago many commentators in the press and the markets promised exactly that. It merely offered valuable advantages—as it still does. Recent shocks to Europe's economy would have challenged any currency regime—fixed, floating and everything in-between. If the ERM had never happened, Europe's governments would now be facing not the happy prospect of quiet markets, high employment and non-inflationary growth but, now or in due course, economic troubles at least as bad as today's, if in a different form.

Europe has lately been caught between two formidable forces: German unification and cheap dollars. The demands of unification have widened Germany's budget deficit, so the Bundesbank, determined to contain the inflationary consequences, has been raising its interest rates. In America, however, the Fed has for years been cutting rates to revive demand in its own economy. This divergence caused the D-mark to rise and the dollar to plunge. That, in turn, put the weaker currencies in the ERM under strain.

Without the ERM, those currencies would still have been under strain. Consider sterling—and assume that British interest rates had been held below German rates, as the ERM's critics say they should have been. Sterling would have fallen steeply. It is anybody's guess how far, but it is likely that this other sort of sterling crisis would have destroyed any hope of containing, let alone defeating, inflation in Britain. And, since trade with Europe matters to Britain so much, wild swings in exchange rates are harmful to it in another way: they make nonsense of the price signals that guide firms on where to do business. Any British government without an exchange-rate policy would soon decide it needed one. Which is where the whole business began.

Then why not a different sort of ERM? Instead of a rigid system, in which parities are defended until the grid is torn apart, why not be more flexible? This suggestion looks sensible, but it begs a crucial question: why do the markets call for realignments? The answer, in Europe in 1992, is certainly not "because of economic fundamentals". According to the test of purchasing power, the pound was, by and large, "correctly" valued at DM2.95, its central rate in the ERM since 1990; and at its ERM floor of DM2.78 it was somewhat undervalued.

Mountaineers climb mountains because they are there; markets seek currency-realignments because they might happen. In recent days, the mere possibility of a currency realignment has been the ERM's most destabilising feature. To make the system less rigid—ie, to increase the probability of a realignment within any given time—is not merely to settle for a permanently higher rate of inflation, but also to ask for greater instability in both interest rates and exchange rates. That is why the commitment to defend a parity within the ERM, once made, is worth keeping—even at the heavy short-term cost of lower output and higher unemployment.

As the markets have made clear, however, even a rigid ERM—one in which realignments happen only rarely, and under duress—is vulnerable to crippling instability. With time this vulnerability can only increase, because of the growth in international capital flows. These are now so huge that governments are helpless before them. Doubts over Europe's plans for full monetary union greatly increased the pressure on the ERM in recent weeks. So, to its shame, did the Bundesbank.

In the past several days, statements from Bundesbank officials played a decisive role in the system's unravelling. Germany's central bank has long made it clear that it wanted the D-mark to be revalued against the system's weaker currencies—as ever, because that suited its domestic purposes. Its hints have been especially unsubtle of late. On Sunday September 13th its promise of lower interest rates was so timed as to be good news for the weaker currencies when markets were closed; then, when the markets opened on Monday, the Bundesbank redoubled the strain on those same currencies by announcing an interest-rate cut that was much smaller than expected. Whether deliberately or not, the ERM's anchor helped deliver the system to the currency traders, and the traders chose to sink it.

Europe's small, open economies cannot work well, let alone as a truly single market, with floating exchange rates. But their efforts to create a semi-fixed system have received a bruising setback, and may yet receive more. One way to make either of these approaches work better—as some governments may soon start to argue—is to rebuild the barriers to international capital flows that have been taken down over the past ten years. With extensive controls on capital, floating exchange rates float more gently, and semi-fixed exchange rates face a manageable opponent. But that is the wrong answer. Rebuilding capital controls is beyond the wit of governments, and even if it could be done, the cost in international misallocation of resources would be huge.

Much the best answer for Europe—ambitious though it now seems—is to create a single currency. With one European money, Germany's demand for capital after unification could have been supplied at lower interest rates; and the inflationary consequences of its western boom would have been dissipated across Europe as a whole, by means of a larger, but much more readily financeable, trade deficit. Currency instability within Europe would be abolished by definition. And an inflexible and narrow-minded central bank—explicitly charged to look at Europe as a whole—could safely aim for price stability, on average, across the EC.

As governments try to repair the damage of recent days, many are likely to conclude that the goal of a single European currency should disappear altogether from view, whatever the French say in this weekend's referendum on the Maastricht treaty, whose centrepiece is a programme for monetary union. That conclusion would be a terrible mistake. And, in a way, an odd one. For events like those of September 16th are exactly what a single currency—and no other workable European monetary arrangement—can promise to avoid.

Break up General Motors

OCTOBER 31ST   **The world's biggest manufacturer is too inefficient
to survive as it is**

ROSS PEROT was right. "Get rid of the 14th floor," he used to say of the plush executive offices at the top of General Motors' Detroit headquarters. This was not just a soundbite. Mr Perot wanted GM's managers to learn their business by working alongside the people who actually make cars—which is what the top managers of Japan's car firms do. Unwilling to listen, GM's directors squandered $700m in 1986. Ostensibly they were buying Mr Perot's GM shares; in fact they were buying his silence and his departure from the board. Instead of running for president of the United States, the Texan billionaire would have done better to turn that deal down, stay on the board and keep trying to fix the world's biggest company.

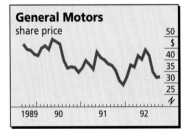

General Motors
share price

What followed Mr Perot's departure was a corporate disaster of Titanic proportions. Roger Smith, the company's chairman, blew $80 billion on a clumsy effort to automate GM's factories, only to see the firm's share of the American market tumble towards 30%. By the time his successor, Robert Stempel, realised that GM would never again sell every other car in America—as it did a decade ago—it was too late. After failing to slim down GM fast enough and facing a third successive year of enormous losses, Mr Stempel lost the confidence of the board. On October 26th he resigned. His replacement now faces a task so immense that it will be impossible to save GM in anything like its present form.

The road to oblivion

The most urgent task facing the board is to end months of uncertainty among GM's bewildered employees about who is actually running the company. A boardroom coup in April was led by John Smale, an outside director of GM and a former chairman of Procter & Gamble. He gave Jack Smith, once boss of GM's successful European operations, day-to-day control. As this newspaper went to press, Mr Smale was tipped to take over the top post until a permanent chairman could be found.

Whoever ends up running GM will face not only a dispirited American workforce, but a company with no obvious strategy to stop what looks like a slide towards bankruptcy. Many of GM's employees believe there is nothing to look forward to but more job cuts, more plant closures and an ugly battle with the United Auto Workers union which could destroy the company's chances of survival. Confidence has to be restored because in the car business a bright image is precious: people like to buy cars from winners, not losers.

Nevertheless, deep cuts are inevitable. GM's production costs in America are $795 a car more than those of its two Detroit rivals, Ford and Chrysler. Those firms already have much leaner operations after brushes with bankruptcy several years ago. Time and again, GM promised to change, but never really did. If it could keep its costs in check, it might be a strong company once again. It does, after all, still sell about 7m vehicles a year worldwide, which is 2m more than Toyota.

What is needed is the emergency treatment that a break-up would bring. Unfortunately, GM is so vast and complex that people who have considered doing just that have always shied away. Lee Iacocca, Chrysler's boss, explored the possibility of a GM takeover on behalf of a corporate raider in 1987, but dropped the idea after deciding "it might be easier to buy Greece". Lacking an outsider determined and able to break it up, the job will have to be done by GM's own managers instead.

They should start by disposing of two costly acquisitions: Hughes, an aerospace company, and EDS, the computer firm which Mr Perot founded. These were supposed to pump lots of high technology into GM's cars and manufacturing processes. It has not happened. If the companies still have anything to offer a car maker, their services can be hired, probably at far less cost. Next to go would be most of GM's in-house components companies. Compared with other car firms, GM is much too vertically integrated. It produces about 70% of the components that go into its vehicles, twice the level of many of its rivals. Mr Smith has made a start by declaring that GM's assembly plants will buy parts only from the most efficient supplier, whether that supplier is inside or outside GM.

Breaking up the car business will be trickier. Mr Smith has begun to streamline GM's product development, but he needs to do much more. Parts of GM are successful, such as its new

small-car subsidiary, Saturn; its European operations, Opel and Vauxhall; and its Cadillac and Buick divisions. But the mainstream car businesses of Chevrolet, Pontiac and Olds-mobile are in terrible trouble. These brand names might be worth retaining, but their product lines are going to have to be heavily pruned. Saving GM is likely to be the toughest job in American corporate history, a challenge ideally suited to a ruthless, self-confident outsider. Once America's voters have chosen their next president, perhaps Mr Perot might care to return to Detroit.

Time to choose

**OCTOBER 31ST   We liked George Bush, but were weary of him. We were wary
of Bill Clinton, but endorsed him**

THE race has been memorable, and America's voters have made it that way. The campaign razzmatazz has not dazzled them; glib arguments have not impressed them; they have not been sidetracked by bimbos, bigotry or draft-dodging. As No-vember 3rd approaches, voters are registering in record num-bers to make a choice grounded in frustration. They want jobs. They want visible signs of economic growth. They long for a leader who is patently in command. And, though this theme is more subdued, they want to recover their confidence in the world. The themes run together. America should have basked in triumph after the fall of communism, but instead found its nose rubbed in inadequacies at home. Falling real incomes, growing debt, raw social divisions, moral drift: these, rather than glory, seemed to be the fruit of the new decade. Unless these failings could be set right, the next century would belong to Europe or Asia.

These feelings, strong as they are, have been brought to life largely because of one man: Ross Perot, who was rewarded for it with a late and short-lived surge in the polls. This newspa-per believes neither that Mr Perot knows how to govern Amer-ica, nor that he should get the chance to try. Particularly in the past two weeks, he has preached the worst kind of xenophobic populism. Yet his effect on the campaign has been extraordi-nary. He has concentrated minds on the country's real imper-ative, to tackle the budget deficit; and, in doing so, he has re-minded Americans that both the Republican and the Democrat lack the nerve to do what is necessary.

In George Bush and Bill Clinton, America has two politi-cians who have built their careers, with care, within the sys-tem. Neither will break moulds. Both are good at the game, ambitious, solicitous of their friends. But they have few sparks of political courage, and no clear vein of principle. Both have shown themselves masters of the flexible posture, the dis-ingenuous slide and the convenient mem-ory lapse. Mr Bush has weaselled on abor-tion, taxes and civil rights; Mr Clinton on the Vietnam draft, free trade and sodomy laws in Arkansas. If the issues of the election are seen as "trust" and "character", Mr Bush wins by the slimmest margin.

But the issue of this election is not "trust"; it is "change". Whether under a Re-publican or a Democrat, Americans do not want government-as-usual. That, above all,

is the lesson of Mr Perot's campaign. And although "change" is a theme Mr Clinton has easily claimed as his own, change must be more than mere difference of party. In America, the ideological gap between the parties is slight. A keener distinc-tion between Mr Clinton and Mr Bush is that one man has exhausted the possibilities of office, while the other pants to put into practice the ideas he has been developing for 12 years.

The known quantity

America has had four years of George Bush, of which the last two have coincided with what is commonly seen as a reces-sion. In fact, output and spending have been rising. The rate of growth has certainly been sluggish: overall, in the Bush presidency, it has averaged 0.9% a year. Mr Bush and his ad-visers have held to the reasonable belief that the slowdown, being worldwide and cyclical, is not their fault; that recovery will come in due course, will be stronger (and less inflation-ary) for coming slowly, and that stimulus is unnecessary. But because they have never bothered to sell this policy to the pub-lic, economic sense has led to deep political unpopularity.

Fiscal policy, meanwhile, has been all at sea. The federal debt has been growing at almost three times the rate of GDP, and now stands at about $4 trillion. Not all the blame can be laid at Mr Bush's door. It was Ronald Reagan who ran up the debt as if it were Old Glory. But Mr Bush has not tried to haul it down. He raised taxes once, and was vilified so much that he now talks only of cutting them. His sensible deal with Con-gress in 1990 set limits on spending, and he has promised more; but no programme that carries any political risk (mean-ing no programme to which Americans believe they are enti-tled) will ever be more than snipped at.

Mr Bush blames Congress, and it is true that he has been only the second president to face two houses controlled by the oppo-site party. He has had to fall back on veto-power, a destabilising tactic which also sug-gests that government is incapable of moving forwards. But many of his chances in domestic policy—in education, training, urban reform—have been missed for sim-ple lack of interest. The president's pro-fessed belief in smaller and less intrusive government is a sham; during his term, the burden of federal regulation has increased. "Less government", in the Bush lexicon, seems to mean a distant and distracted leadership whose defining vision is to cling to power.

Mr Bush must be given credit for successes abroad. In a world turned upside down, America has become, almost to its surprise, a steadying and collegial force. His management of the Gulf war deserves applause; the Middle East peace process still looks a triumph of patience; the free-trade agreement with Mexico has been doggedly driven through. Yet on the larger issue of preserving and enhancing the GATT trading system, Mr Bush's lack of vision has been painfully clear. The Uruguay round has produced changes which, though not perfect, would be good for America. But Mr Bush has allowed the round to drift on, playing a dangerous game of bluff with the European Community at a time when the world economy has needed decisiveness. At this stage in his term, Mr Bush appears to lack the will even to pursue those things that he, and we, believe in. This being so, we cannot support him.

Although Mr Bush would be the wrong president for America's next four years, that does not make Mr Clinton into a paragon. Anybody who wants the governor of Arkansas to be the president of the United States has to hope hard and take much on trust. On two points in particular, Mr Clinton has to prove himself: that he is not a protectionist, and not an isolationist. A successful president will be one who enables America to be a high-skill, export-minded economy, trading freely with the world and, secure in its economic health, able to take on the security burdens the new world may require.

Risking the unknown

Mr Clinton often endorses that philosophy. But he also talks brusquely of making Europe and Japan shoulder their own defence burdens, and of cutting more defence spending and bringing home more troops than Mr Bush would. Diplomatic bumps are bound to occur when this eager but untrained man is seized by conflicting advice; and Mr Clinton's well-known caution about American adventuring abroad may translate, in office, into paralysis. The voter mood he has been so carefully matching contains a mean streak of indifference to the world outside America. In reality, that world will demand of him his most outward-going and forward-looking self.

At home, Mr Clinton presents himself as the standard-bearer of a new Democratic Party: fiscally responsible, socially hard-headed, business-minded. That is a welcome change, but how deep does it go? Mr Clinton's record in Arkansas shows an encouraging emphasis on education, training and investment, without which America will never create enough high-paying jobs. It shows, too, that Mr Clinton is serious about getting people off welfare, and can promote his ideas in ways that are attractive to both blacks and whites.

The Arkansas record also has a darker side. Earlier this year, when medical services had to be cut to balance the state budget, Mr Clinton left the job to his deputy, and bowed out. The governor's relations with business, too, sometimes go beyond a helpful partnership; he seems to be over-ready with the tax breaks to keep firms sweet, and sometimes to be in their pocket. This is a man who, on a local level, often plays the legislature like a violin. When it comes to Congress—a Congress that has waited 12 long years to have its way with a Democratic president—Mr Clinton may be played in turn, and find himself handing out favours on a national scale.

It is on the economy that he most needs to prove himself. Mr Clinton has said, more than once, that "tax-and-spend doesn't work". Yet his plan to spend $80 billion on infrastructure over four years, added to his plans to raise the tax rate on annual incomes over $200,000, has more than a hint of tax-and-spend; and his advisers are known to be split between Keynesian pump-primers and deficit-cutters. A hardscrabble background in a poor state has convinced Mr Clinton that government should sometimes intervene. Hence his proposals for mandatory health care and worker-training, and his devotion to mandatory entitlement programmes. When it comes to cutting the budget deficit, he has no more clue than Mr Bush.

The choice

What choice between these two? On past occasions *The Economist* has sometimes joined in with American elections and stated its preference; and it has sometimes opted out. In 1988, when George Bush faced Michael Dukakis, we felt we could recommend neither. Four years on, Mr Bush has done nothing to prove himself. The man is spent, and his party with him. The Republicans, tired to distraction, out of ideas, have become prey to a far right whose economic nostrums run to demonising taxes, and many of whose social ideas would rub salt in the country's wounds.

The issue of ideas is central. The Democratic Party, to be sure, has not yet proved that its new look goes beyond Mr Clinton and his circle. But it has been working for 12 years on how to become a plausible modern party of government, and should be given a chance to try. During the campaign, Mr Clinton has proved himself to be far more than a token candidate. He is intelligent; he is diligent; he is energetic; he has grasped most of the issues, and found persuasive solutions to some. He could mark an end to divided government and could, if he used the presidency well, begin to bring Americans, black and white, rich and poor, closer together. Despite the risks, the possibilities are worth pursuing. Our choice falls on him.

Japan's chance for change

NOVEMBER 21ST   **Shocked by scandals and depressed by recession, the Japanese are starting to lose patience with their odd form of politics**

ALOOF, tradition-bound and impenetrable though it might seem to outsiders, Japan has passed through more changes than any other industrial country in the past half century. Yet while its economy and its companies have made flexibility a Japanese byword, in one respect at least the country has made glaciers look nimble: its politics. Corrupt and uninspiring,

the Liberal Democratic Party (LDP) which has ruled Japan for the past 37 years becomes more embarrassing by the day. But it shows no sign of losing power. Or does it? For the first time in many years, Japan has a chance for political change. It arises from the economy that has forced and accepted so many changes in the past. This change is not inevitable and cannot yet even be called probable. But the remarkable thing is that it does, at last, look possible.

To western eyes, reports on Japanese politics tend to display a certain sameness. They open with a sentence or two describing an incomprehensible tussle between various factions of the LDP, or a scandal involving bribes and gangsters, or a complicated election result, or the possibility that someone about whom you know little, and care less, might become prime minister. Then come the disclaimers: all policies will stay the same; the Liberal Democrats will stay in power; nothing will really change. Japanese politics has become a page-turner—not as a thriller but a bore.

This is not supposed to happen in democracies, which is why it is common to assume that Japan is not one. It certainly is a democracy in the sense that every few years the public has the chance to kick the rascals out. But the voters never take their chance. Since the Liberal and Democratic parties merged in 1955, Japan has been, in effect, a one-party state. That might not matter if it could be said that the LDP was really a coalition of parties which share a name but alternate in power. In a way this is true, for the party consists of several factions that compete with one another as fiercely as they do with opposition parties. Yet theirs is not a battle of ideas, ideologies or even policies: to display any of these would impress nobody. The tussle is over flows of money and prestige, nothing more.

The result is a foul cocktail of scandal, policy stagnation, a disregard for foreign affairs (no money there) and public disillusion. All attempts at reform are either blocked or phoney, or both. Yet the LDP still wins elections. One reason is that the public has long been disillusioned but not discontented: strong economic growth has delivered rising incomes and secure jobs for most of the past 30 years. Another is that the alternatives are lousy: the biggest opposition party, the Socialists, still mouths Marxist slogans and talks of the dangers of fascism. But the third, and biggest, reason is money: the Liberal Democrats have been by far the best channel for bribes and donations from business pressure groups. This gives the party a huge advantage in elections, as well as powerful friends in all parts of the economy. And those friends have been careful always to pass a little of their money to the opposition, so that it will not oppose too enthusiastically. Scandals invariably involve politicians from several parties—even one that calls itself the "clean government" party.

Unpopular but entrenched: that is the governing party of Japan. On grounds of morality, decency, democracy, international relations and even the national interest, this state of affairs should change. But little in Japan changes in response to the word "should", and the LDP has no intention of making itself an exception. Things in Japan do change, however, when they have to, when the change is forced by self-interest. It is that test which must be applied to the perennial question: when will one-party rule collapse?

When the money dries up

Japan is experiencing something it has not had at all since 1975, and before then not since the 1950s: a recession. By western standards, certainly, it remains mild, but to the Japanese even sluggish economic growth is disconcerting. The signs are everywhere: collapsing corporate profits, a frail stockmarket,

empty restaurants and abundant taxis. Officials are optimistic that next year will be better. They are probably wrong, because Japan is suffering the same sort of recession as America and Britain, and will be slow to shake off its burdens of consumer debt and tumbling property prices. And something fundamental has changed: nobody believes officials any more.

The biggest casualty of the financial troubles Japan has faced since 1990, and the recession it has entered this year, is faith in officialdom. The abuses of the LDP did not matter as long as bureaucrats could be trusted to run things properly and, more to the point, prosperously. In many eyes, they have lost that trust. The effects of recession are spreading from boardrooms into households. Even unemployment is on the rise. Next year, corporate Japan may be forced to shake out its surplus labour rather than keeping and coddling it as it has done in the past. The dole queue could double or treble in length.

Disillusion meets discontent: the first protection for the LDP, economic growth, is fading. The party has some ways to ease this, but it is failing even at that. A huge fiscal package, worth ¥10.7 trillion ($86 billion), was announced in August but is now stranded in parliament, held up by the party's scandals and factional disarray. It looks unlikely to pass before this year's parliamentary session ends on December 8th, delaying any boost it might bring to the economy. It will be an extraordinary failure. If there is one thing you might expect Japanese politicians to do briskly, it is to pass big public-spending measures through which they can line their own pockets and please their constituents and lobbyists.

If it happens, such a failure will cast doubt on the LDP's greatest skill: its ability to attract finance. That ability is already weakened by the economy, for the party's traditional backers—construction firms, stockbrokers and even manufacturers—have less cash to throw around. But the money-raising magic is in danger of being destroyed if the party proves unable to deliver what the cash-providers want: favourable laws for some, public spending for others, economic growth for all.

There lies Japan's chance for change. Those backing the LDP are losing patience. Voters are switching from apathy to anger. But one thing is still missing: an alternative. Nothing can change in Japanese politics until someone seizes the chance to exploit the disarray in the ruling party. That someone will have to lure away a large chunk of the LDP's financial backing; it is thus more likely to be right-wing and pro-business than left-wing and populist.

Will the alternative arrive? All that can be said, so far, is that it is possible. There is more talk in Japan of creating new parties and splitting old ones than there has been for years. The lower and middle ranks of the Liberal Democrats feel their future power and prestige are being imperilled by their octogenarian leaders. The chance that some will break away gets higher with every piece of bad economic news, and will get higher still as unemployment climbs. Somewhere in Japan, someone is wondering whether he might now have a chance to make history, to bring one-party rule to an end and to bring a new generation to the top. The chance is there to be taken.

Contents

AMERICA

Frustration begets hope

THE old order changed in America in 1992, and the Democrats returned to the White House for the first time in more than a decade. Although the election was close-run and the campaign volatile, the result was not greatly in doubt for most of the year. The Republicans, it was felt, had run out of ideas; their long lock on the presidency had turned into sleeping at the wheel. Against that, the Democrats seemed to offer something new. Their ideas, to be sure, might turn out to be a skin-deep cover for the old ways of special interests and big government: but voters decided to give them the benefit of the doubt. America voted less out of enthusiasm than out of a paroxysm of frustration.

Time for a change

That frustration had its roots in economic gloom. America was not in recession in 1992; the economy continued to grow, but at so slow a reported rate that Americans could not see it. Although unemployment, at around 8% for much of the year, was not unnaturally high, the voting middle classes felt particularly threatened by it. All the main-party candidates began their campaigns by pledging to help the "forgotten" middle class, usually by offering a tax cut that could not be paid for. Half-way through the campaign, however, the economic emphasis shifted to the loss of manufacturing jobs abroad and the part that might be played in that by the NAFTA and GATT treaties which were then in negotiation; and America felt a shudder of xenophobia, which had not completely passed as the year ended.

The depth of popular anxiety about a dragging economy was made clear to candidates in the New Hampshire primary in February; and that primary, as so often, set the tone for what followed. In May, the acquittal of five white policemen for beating a black in Los Angeles caused the worst race riots since the second world war, with 42 people killed and $1 billion-worth of property destroyed. The riots, the looting that went with them and the apathy that followed them, showed to what extent America had become socially divided and morally indifferent. In August, the Republican Party at its convention de-

Los Angeles burns

clared that its answer to the nation's social ills was godliness, self-righteousness and intolerance. This set the seal on the Republicans' defeat; although that defeat was already predicted in economic figures that ticked up too late.

Time and again, voters said they wanted "change". Their dissatisfaction took the extraordinary form of lighting on a Texan businessman, Ross Perot, who promised little more than to "clean out the barn". Mr Perot played with voters for much of the year, tantalising them from television talk-shows, and even dropping out of the race in July only to re-emerge in October. Because at one point he had led George Bush and Bill Clinton in the polls, they treated him with almost exaggerated respect, and allowed his priority of cutting the budget deficit, then running at around $400 billion, to dominate the campaign for a while. Neither, however, dared to endorse his deficit-cutting ideas. Mr Perot's final result, 19% of the poll, was the best showing by a third-party candidate since Theodore Roosevelt's in 1912; and was the more remarkable because his last weeks of campaigning had showed him in full flood of xenophobia, neurosis and bad temper.

Mr Bush had a wretched campaign. Even the poaching of James Baker from the State Department, which he left with manifest reluctance, could not give it focus. Dirty tricks were attempted, including the searching of Mr Clinton's passport files for evidence of youthful pro-Soviet sympathies; but they predictably backfired. The president seemed bemused that his foreign-policy triumphs of the years before had been so quickly forgotten, and puzzled that the signs of recovery he could detect in the economy were not obvious to everyone. By November the economic figures, especially for GDP and retail sales, proved he had been right all along. By then, their only effect was to render academic and inconclusive the economic summit on fiscal stimulus called by the Democratic president-elect.

Mr Clinton's year, though it ended jubilantly, had notable ups and downs. His campaign was nearly derailed, before New Hampshire, by allegations of adultery and revelations about his attempts to dodge the Vietnam draft. Mr Clinton met the adultery charges head-on, and they evaporated; on Vietnam he waffled and trimmed, ensuring that his draft-dodging haunted him right up to election day. He succeeded, however, in convincing most of his audiences that he was a new sort of Democrat, outward-looking, business-minded, non-protectionist and not a tax-and-spender; and Americans voted for him with a measure of hope, as well as an awareness of the risk they were taking.

The campaign as a whole produced many departures from old ways, some of them striking. Although the print-press was often accused of favouring Mr Clinton (and the accusation had some truth to it), the newspapers no longer shaped opinions as they have done in the past. Instead, the public watched (and quizzed) candidates on talk-shows and took them on in live debates. At times, even the presenters and moderators would fade into the background, leaving an almost unimaginable experiment in democracy: the candidate, even the president, in direct and sometimes acrimonious conversation with the voter. Far from disliking this, the candidates—especially Mr Clinton—appeared to relish it, and it is likely to form the main structure of future presidential campaigns.

In general, the election showed a higher level of interest and commitment among voters than had been seen for years. Registration and voting rates shot up; the proportion of the over-18 population voting, at 55%, was the best for 20 years. The campaign was not without its moments of trivia: in particular, a storm over criticisms made by Dan Quayle, the vice-president, of the decision of a TV sit-com character, Murphy Brown, to bear a child without a father. Even this, however, was made to seem representative of serious issues. For some months, the Republicans, spurred on by religious hardliners in their party, tried to shift the campaign to the theme of "family values": a code-word for attacks on homosexual rights, working women, abortion, divorce rates and spreading secularism.

Most Americans responded to this with dignified good sense. Although many of them were worried about a decaying social fabric, they did not imagine that government could do much about it. Issues such as divorce, homosexuality and abortion, far from being party-political, were matters of private moral choice. The public was helped to this conclusion, on June 29th, by a particularly finely-tuned judgment on abortion from the Supreme Court. The case in question, *Planned Parenthood of Southeastern Pennsylvania v Casey*, had been expected to show the court in its conservative colours, and to result perhaps in the overturning of *Roe v Wade*, the 1973 ruling legalising abortion. In fact, the court ruled 5-4 to let *Roe* stand, although allowing states to

Moral issues to the fore

hedge it about with certain limitations. The ruling contained the eminently sensible statement that although abortion was not a "fundamental" right, it was "a rule of law and a component of liberty we cannot renounce".

The court's ruling did much to remove abortion from the hustings. The Republicans, recognising that their own party was divided on the issue, eventually left the subject to the religious right, which regrouped at the end of the year in happy anticipation of wars to come with the Clinton administration.

In the end, the nation's moral indignation found a different, but familiar, target: the condition of Congress. The chief cause of frustration among voters, after the economy, was the sense that divided government no longer worked. The legislative record of the Bush years—a record string of sustained vetoes, and almost no new laws on the books—convinced many Americans that as long as a Republican sat in the White House and Democrats controlled Congress, nothing

Time's up

could get done. To this was added a lively disgust with Congress inspired, in March, by the news that dozens of members had floated cheques at the House bank. Desperate to "throw the bums out", 14 states approved measures in November to limit the terms of their congressmen. Oddly enough, however, the same disgust did not appear when it came to voting for representatives already in place. Only 24 House incumbents failed to win re-election, and all the acknowledged masters of pork-barrel survived comfortably.

America ended the year both revived and apprehensive. The president-elect was slowly gathering his team and formulating his policies. Congress was making soothing noises of co-operation. The economy was looking better. But all these pleasant scenes, bathed in sunlight, were backed up by towering clouds. For a year, obsessed not only with its election but with its own racial wounds, America had virtually ignored the world. In November, however, the ambassador to Russia scurried back to Washington, saying there was no more he could do. In early December, the first of many troops—a force of 1,800 Marines—set sail for Somalia. The war in Yugoslavia became daily more urgent; Europe seemed daily more volatile. Old enemies in the Gulf began to flex their muscles. With a neophyte in the White House, it was time for America to try to cope with a world in turmoil.

Louis Vuitton. The spirit of travel

Louis Vuitton luggage and accessories are sold only in exclusive Louis Vuitton shops :
Australia, Austria, Belgium, Brazil, Canada, Chili, China, Denmark, France, Germany,
Great Britain, Greece, Guam, Hawaii, Hong Kong, Indonesia, Italy, Japan, Korea,
Kuwait, Malaysia, Mexico, New Zealand, Philippines, Portugal, Saipan, Singapore, Spain,
Switzerland, Taiwan, Thailand, United States.

V Some travellers are particularly adventurous. In far flung places, whilst challenging the elements, they rediscover the spirit of travel. For such individuals, Louis Vuitton creates travel instruments; luggage and accessories that are both elegant and functional.

Since 1854, the Louis Vuitton craftsman has preserved and maintained the traditions of the Company which pioneered the art of travel. Louis Vuitton products are sold only in their exclusive shops in Paris, London and the major cities of the world.

LOUIS VUITTON
MALLETIER A PARIS

MAISON FONDÉE EN 1854

Wednesday 1st
President Bush spent new year's day in Australia, as part of a visit to **Asia and the Pacific**. Mr Bush, troubled by the American recession, had promised to promote trade—but he had to fend off complaints by Australian farmers, who felt they were the victims of American protectionism.

Saturday 4th
In Singapore **George Bush** sought to reassure his hosts that the closure of American bases in the Phillipines would not spell the end of American engagement in the Asia-Pacific region. Gok Chok Tong, the prime minister of Singapore, said that a big American security and economic presence was needed to balance growing Japanese power in the region.

Wednesday 8th
President Bush fell ill and collapsed at a state banquet in Tokyo. Before falling to the floor, he **vomited** on the Japanese prime minister, Kiichi Miyazawa. The White House later announced that the president was suffering from intestinal flu, and his visit to Japan continued. But the incident was seized upon by commentators in America and Japan, who saw it as symbolic of American weakness.

Douglas Wilder, the governor of Virginia, became the first candidate to bow out of the presidential election. He said that his duties as governor were too onerous to allow him to campaign. Translation: his campaign was going nowhere.

Monday 13th
Returning to the attack on issues of **trade**, George Bush accused the European Community of hiding behind an "iron curtain of protectionism". His speech to American farmers was timed to coincide with the reopening of the GATT trade talks in Geneva.

Tuesday 14th
The New York **stockmarket** jumped 60 points to a new high of 3,246, despite the continuing recession. Dealers expressed confidence that the economy would recover in the second half of 1992.

Thursday 16th
The **New York Times** announced that its publisher, Arthur Ochs Sulzberger, was retiring and would be replaced by his son, Arthur Ochs Sulzberger Jr. The senior Sulzberger had been in charge of the paper since May 1963.

Friday 17th
Bill Clinton, the governor of Arkansas and a leading contender for the Democratic Party's presidential nomination in 1992, was accused of adultery by the *Star*, a tabloid magazine sold in supermarkets. The governor dismissed the allegations as "trash". But they were quickly picked up by the mainstream media and began to erode his position as the frontrunner in the New Hampshire primary.

Monday 20th
A new storm about **relations with Japan** was provoked when American newspapers reported the remarks of Yoshio Sakurauchi, the speaker of Japan's lower house of parliament. Mr Sakurauchi had said that the American economy was suffering because so many American workers were lazy and illiterate.

Tuesday 21st
The possibility that the Supreme Court would reopen the vexed debate on **abortion** before the November presidential election was increased when the court announced that it would soon consider a recent Pennsylvania law, restricting abortion rights. But some observers pointed out that the court could uphold the Pennsylvania law without specifically overturning *Roe v Wade*, the 1973 ruling which had established constitutional protection for abortion rights.

President Bush announced that he would propose an extra $600m for **Head Start**—a pre-school programme for poor children and one of the few anti-poverty programmes in America to enjoy widespread support.

Wednesday 22nd
Testifying before Congress, the director of the CIA, Robert Gates, said that the **threat of attack** by the forces of the former Soviet Union had "all but disappeared". On the same day, President Bush announced that he would ask Congress for a further $645m in aid to the former Soviet republics.

Thursday 23rd
Evidence of a populist **backlash against Japan** mounted, with the announcement that Los Angeles County was to cancel a contract to buy $122m-worth of rail cars from a Japanese company, Sumitomo Corporation. The contract was instead awarded to an American company, despite the fact that the cars would have been manufactured by an American-based subsidiary of Sumitomo.

Sunday 26th
In an effort to salvage his **presidential election** campaign, Governor Bill Clinton and his wife, Hillary, gave a live television interview after the Super Bowl—a time guaranteed to maximise their audience. Mr Clinton denied having an affair with Gennifer Flowers, a former television reporter, but refused to issue a blanket denial of adultery.

Monday 27th
Gennifer Flowers, the "smoking bimbo" dogging the Bill Clinton campaign, gave a press conference in New York at which she played tapes of telephone conversations between herself and the governor. Against a background of laughter from a raucous press corps, she declared that she had been in love with Mr Clinton.

An opinion poll found that President Bush's **"approval rating"** had dropped to an all-time low of 43%. In the immediate aftermath of the Gulf war, 88% of Americans had expressed approval of the president's handling of his job.

Tuesday 28th
George Bush tried to use his **"state of the union"** address to Congress to rebuild his popularity. In a deliberate echo of the Gulf war, Mr Bush declared that the recession "will not stand"—the same words he had used about the Iraqi invasion of Kuwait. But the president's economic proposals were fairly mild: a further $50 billion-worth of defence cuts over five years, some tinkering with tax codes, the familiar call for a cut in the capital-gains tax, and a promise of reform of the health-care system.

February

Saturday 1st
Boris Yeltsin paid a lightning visit to Camp David for talks with George Bush. Dispensing with the pomp and ceremony of old-style Soviet-American summits, the two leaders discussed arms control and economic aid to Russia.

Wednesday 5th
The House of Representatives voted to set up a congressional task force to investigate the **October Surprise**: the allegations that in 1980 Ronald Reagan's campaign struck a deal with Iran to delay the release of American hostages until after the presidential election.

Thursday 6th
George Bush unveiled his administration's **health-care** plan in a speech in Cleveland. The centrepiece of the plan was tax-credits to help those without insurance to pay for it. The White House scheme was immediately attacked by Democrats who pointed out that Mr Bush had yet to explain how it would be paid for.

The presidential election campaign of **Bill Clinton** suffered a further blow when the *Wall Street Journal* reported allegations that he had evaded the draft during the Vietnam war.

Monday 10th
Mike Tyson, the former world heavyweight boxing champion, was found guilty of rape after a trial in Indianapolis. Mr Tyson's conviction was hailed as a victory by those

seeking to prove that convictions could be secured in cases of "date rape", where the victim and the attacker were known to each other.

The first vote in the presidential election campaign, the **Iowa caucuses**, took place. Senator Tom Harkin, the Democratic victor, was a local man and so the results were widely dismissed. George Bush faced no opposition among the Republicans. Meanwhile polls in New Hampshire showed that Bill Clinton's lead among the Democrats had disappeared under an avalanche of allegations about his personal life. The new front-runner was Paul Tsongas, a former senator from Massachusetts.

Thursday 13th
Richard Truly, the administrator of NASA, the **space agency**, was dismissed after pressure from the vice-president and head of the National Space Council, Dan Quayle. Mr Truly had presided over a series of public-relations mishaps at NASA—including the discovery of flaws in the Hubble space telescope and a number of delayed space launches.

Friday 14th
James Baker, the secretary of state, toured one of the former Soviet Union's two major **nuclear weapons** plants, amid concerns that poverty-stricken nuclear scientists might soon sell their expertise to the highest bidder. Mr Baker proposed the creation of an international institute to employ the scientists.

Saturday 15th
A jury in Milwaukee decided that Jeffrey Dahmer, a **serial killer** who had murdered, dismembered and possibly partly eaten 15 men and young boys, was sane. Mr Dahmer had admitted the killings but

pleaded not guilty on grounds of insanity.

Tuesday 18th
The **New Hampshire primary**, the first major event of the 1992 presidential election campaign, delivered a severe jolt to George Bush. His right-wing challenger, television pundit Patrick Buchanan, received 37% of the vote in the Republican primary. Mr Bush's advisers rued their earlier decision to ignore the Buchanan campaign.

In **the Democratic race** Paul Tsongas prevailed, proving the virtues of dogged persistence after a campaign which had been widely dismissed by the media. But Bill Clinton finished a respectable second, encouraging his supporters to hope that his campaign could bounce back in their candidate's native south.

Thursday 20th
H. Ross Perot, a self-made billionaire from Texas, appeared on "Larry King Live", a television programme. He told the audience that he would consider running for president if volunteers could raise enough signatures to get him on the ballot in every state.

Monday 24th
James Baker made it clear for the first time that America would not grant Israel $10 billion in **loan guarantees** for the resettlement of Soviet Jews until the Israelis agreed to stop construction of new settlements on the occupied West Bank.

General Motors announced the largest loss in its history. In 1991 GM lost $4.5 billion and went "down like a rock", according to its chairman Robert Stempel.

Tuesday 25th
Bob Kerrey, a Democratic senator from Nebraska, recorded his first victory of the primary season in neighbouring South Dakota. There was more bad news for George Bush: even though Patrick Buchanan was not on the ballot, 31% of Republican voters voted for an uncommitted slate of delegates.

A monthly survey showed American **consumer confidence** in January at a 17-year low. Alan Greenspan, the chairman of the Federal Reserve, called the survey "quite disturbing", but repeated his prediction that the economy would pick up in the second quarter.

George Bush travelled to Los Angeles to announce an "**integrated border plan**", aimed at cleaning up America's polluted 1,600-mile frontier with Mexico.

Wednesday 26th
Ronald Reagan issued a statement of support for George Bush. The three-paragraph statement had been solicited by the Bush campaign after Mr Reagan had failed to appear at a fundraising lunch for Mr Bush in Los Angeles, prompting speculation that the former president was unhappy with his one-time deputy.

Thursday 27th
The House of Representatives passed a measure giving 90m voters a one-year **tax-cut**, to be financed by permanently raising taxes for the richest 1% of Americans. The president called the House's action "a sorry performance".

March

Tuesday 3rd
George Bush beat Patrick Buchanan in three **primaries in Georgia, Maryland and Colorado**. But Mr Buchanan's strong showing, particularly in Georgia, where he won nearly 36% of the vote, troubled the White House. In the Democratic race, Bill Clinton won Georgia by a convincing margin—his first victory. But Paul Tsongas won in Maryland and Jerry Brown, the former governor of California, won a surprise victory in Colorado. The contest remained wide open.

The trial of **John Gotti**, the reputed head of New York's biggest Mafia family, took a dramatic turn. Salvatore Gravano, once Mr Gotti's right-hand man, testified for the prosecution and gave a chilling account of Mr Gotti's role in the 1985 murder of Paul Castellano, the boss of the Gambino crime family.

Tuesday 10th
Bill Clinton swept the states of his native South in the primaries of **Super Tuesday**. His victories—particularly in Florida, where his chief rival, Paul Tsongas, had been expected to do well—established him as the firm front-runner for the Democratic Party's nomination. In the Republican primaries, George Bush regained the initiative after Patrick Buchanan did worse than expected.

Friday 13th
The House of Representatives voted unanimously to make public the names of 355 current and former members who had overdrawn their accounts at the House bank. The **check-kiting** affair swiftly became another occasion to bash Congress for enjoying privileges unavailable to ordinary Americans.

Monday 16th
President Bush rejected a Senate compromise over **loan guarantees to Israel**. Mr Bush had opposed granting $10 billion in guarantees, to help the settlement of Soviet Jews, because of the Israeli policy of building settlements in the occupied West Bank. The rejection of the compromise, which would have freed some of the money and fudged the settlements issue, came during a visit to Washington by Israel's defence minister, Moshe Arens.

Tuesday 17th
The **Illinois and Michigan primaries** ended in sweeping victories for Bill Clinton. In the Republican race, Pat Buchanan's challenge continued to fade. The most surprising single result was the defeat of Alan Dixon, a Democratic senator from Illinois, in his party's primary for the Senate election in November. The victor was Carol Moseley Braun, a black woman.

Thursday 19th
Paul Tsongas dropped out of the race for the presidency. He said that his campaign for the Democratic nomination had run out of money. His departure seemed to leave the field clear for Bill Clinton.

The United States warned all Americans living in **Libya** to leave the country before the United Nations imposed an air embargo. The UN, spurred on by Britain and America, was trying to secure the surrender of two Libyans suspected of taking part in the 1988 bombing of a Pan-Am jet over Lockerbie in Scotland.

Friday 20th
Bill Clinton apologised for having played golf at an **all-white country club** in his home state of Arkansas.

Sunday 22nd
George Bush **vetoed** a bill which proposed a small tax-cut for the middle-classes and higher taxes for wealthy Americans. The bill was part of the Democratic campaign for greater "fairness" for middle-income Americans.

Mr Bush and **Helmut Kohl**, the chancellor of Germany, ended two days of informal talks at Camp David by reiterating their determination to achieve a breakthrough in the GATT trade talks in Geneva. They gave no hint about how this long-revered goal might be achieved.

Monday 23rd
The City College of New York decided to fire Leonard Jeffries, who had been head of its Black Studies department for 19 years. Mr Jeffries had preached a **racist philosophy**, based on the claim that blacks were humanitarian "sun people" and whites ruthless "ice people". He had a particular animus against the Jews, whom he accused of plotting to denigrate blacks in Hollywood films.

Tuesday 24th
Jerry Brown narrowly defeated Bill Clinton in the Connecticut primary. His victory undermined the assumption that Mr Clinton was assured of the Democratic Party's nomination. Attention now turned to the New York primary on April 7th.

Senator **Warren Rudman**, famous as the architect of the ill-fated Gramm-Rudman Act of 1985 which had attempted to control the budget deficit, announced that he was leaving the Senate. He issued a parting warning of congressional paralysis in the face of mounting government debt.

Thursday 26th
Mike Tyson, the former world heavyweight boxing champion, was sentenced to ten years in prison for raping a contestant in the "Miss Black America" beauty contest. In a statement before sentencing, Mr Tyson denied his guilt and he launched an appeal immediately.

Sunday 29th
Bill Clinton admitted that he had smoked **marijuana** as a student in England in the 1960s. "I didn't inhale and I didn't try it again," he said.

Monday 30th
"Silence of the Lambs", a thriller about a serial killer with a penchant for eating his victims, swept the board at the **Oscars** ceremony. The film won awards for Jonathan Demme as best director, Anthony Hopkins as best actor and Jodie Foster as best actress, as well as the overall award for best film.

Tuesday 31st
Talk of a possible run for the presidency by **H. Ross Perot**, a self-made billionaire from Texas, was given a boost by a poll in the *Los Angeles Times*. This suggested that Mr Perot would receive 21% of the votes in a race against Bill Clinton and George Bush.

April

Wednesday 1st
Bill Clinton delivered a much anticipated speech on **foreign policy** in New York. He lambasted the Bush administration for its slowness in providing aid to Russia and the other republics of the Commonwealth of Independent States. But, as Mr Clinton spoke, George Bush staged a press conference at the White House—interrupting television coverage of his likely Democratic challenger to announce a package of $24 billion in western aid to those very countries, 20% of which was to come from America.

Thursday 2nd
John Gotti, the fashionably-dressed head of New York's biggest Mafia family, was found guilty of murder and racketeering. Three previous attempts to convict him had ended in acquittal.

Monday 6th
The Supreme Court ruled that a Nebraska farmer convicted of buying child pornography had been entrapped by the FBI and was, therefore, not guilty. The ruling cast into doubt the future of "**sting operations**" by the police.

Tuesday 7th
Bill Clinton won the **New York primary** after a bruising campaign, marked by relentless attacks on his integrity by the local tabloid press. Mr Clinton received 41% of the vote and also won primaries in Wisconsin, Kansas and Minnesota. Exit polls in New York, as elsewhere, showed a marked lack of enthusiasm for Mr Clinton among Democratic voters, but the primary seemed to mark the end of real opposition to his nomination. Despite a big effort in New York, Jerry Brown, Mr Clinton's chief rival, finished third—behind Paul Tsongas, who had already abandoned his campaign.

Wednesday 8th
Arthur Ashe, the first black tennis player to win Wimbledon and the US Open, announced that he had AIDS. Mr Ashe made his announcement reluctantly after it became clear that a newspaper would soon reveal the fact. He had contracted the HIV virus from a blood transfusion in 1983.

Tim Wirth, a Democrat from Colorado, became the seventh Senator to announce that he would not seek re-election. His announcement was greeted as a further sign of demoralisation in Congress.

Thursday 9th
General Manuel Noriega, the former dictator of Panama, was found guilty of drug and racketeering crimes, ending a marathon trial in Miami.

Wednesday 15th
On the day that Americans had to submit their annual tax returns, **Leona Helmsley**, the New York hotel owner dubbed the "queen of mean", started a prison sentence for tax evasion.

Thursday 16th
The **trade deficit** fell to its lowest level for nine years. The February deficit was $3.4 billion, down from $5.95 billion the previous year. Officials at the Commerce Department attributed the improvement to a surge in American exports.

Friday 17th
Alan Greenspan, the chairman of the Federal Reserve, reassured Congress that the **collapse in the Japanese stock market** would have only a limited impact on the American economy.

Tuesday 21st
California carried out its first **execution** for 25 years. Robert Alton Harris was put to death after the failure of a last-minute appeal to the Supreme Court. Harris, who had been on Death Row for over a decade, received four last-ditch stays of execution—the final one as he was strapped into a chair in the state gas chamber—before eventually being put to death. Opponents of capital punishment feared that California would now proceed with several long-delayed executions.

Wednesday 22nd
The Supreme Court started hearings on a Pennsylvania law restricting **abortion** rights. Many observers believed the court's decision might determine whether American women had a constitutional right to an abortion, as the court had ruled in the case of *Roe v Wade* in 1973.

David Duke, a former Ku Klux Klan leader, abandoned his effort to win the Republican nomination for the presidency and announced that he would not run as a third-party candidate.

Monday 27th
Dan Quayle, the vice-president, told reporters that he thought that the Texan billionaire, **Ross Perot**, might offer a more serious electoral challenge to George Bush than Bill Clinton. Mr Perot had spent much of April giving a series of television interviews and taking soundings over whether to run as a third-party candidate in the presidential election. Some opinion polls had already put him ahead of Mr Clinton.

Tuesday 28th
First-quarter GDP figures showed that **economic recovery** was finally under way. The Commerce Department estimated that in the first three months of the year, the economy grew at an annual rate of about 2%.

Bill Clinton easily won the Democratic **primary in Pennsylvania**. His supporters took heart from the fact that the numbers of voters expressing doubts about his integrity had declined sharply. His detractors noted that the turn-out in the primary had been, once again, discouragingly small.

Wednesday 29th
Riots broke out in Los Angeles after four police officers, filmed in the act of savagely beating a black motorist, were acquitted of assault. The trial of the police officers had been moved out of Los Angeles to Ventura county, a largely white suburban area.

Thursday 30th
Rioting and looting in Los Angeles spread from the black ghetto of south-central Los Angeles to more affluent areas. The National Guard was deployed. Over 2,000 buildings had been set on fire by the end of the day. Unrest spread to other cities: San Francisco was placed under a state of emergency; rioting broke out in Las Vegas and young blacks attacked white businessmen in central Atlanta.

May

Friday 1st
As rioting continued in Los Angeles, **George Bush spoke to the country** on television. The president tried to strike a balance between condemning the riots and pledging to remedy their underlying causes. In an attempt to show that justice could still be done in the Rodney King case, the Justice Department started to investigate whether federal civil-rights charges could be brought against the police officers who had beaten Mr King.

Saturday 2nd
George Bush declared Los Angeles a "**disaster area**", opening the way for the federal government to provide the kind of assistance given after natural disasters like earthquakes and hurricanes. In Los Angeles itself, Peter Ueberroth, who had organised the triumphantly successful Olympic Games in 1984, agreed to organise the city's response to the riots.

Mr Bush clinched the **Republican nomination** for the presidential election after winning primaries in Maine and Wyoming.

Sunday 3rd
After two days of relative calm in Los Angeles, the city's mayor, Tom Bradley, announced that the dusk-to-dawn curfew could be lifted the following day. The **final death toll** in the riots was put at 58—more deaths than in any of the riots of the 1960s; 4,000 people were injured, 12,000 people were arrested and the cost of the damage was put at over $1 billion.

Monday 4th
The president's press spokesman, Marlin Fitzwater, said much of the blame for the riots could be laid at the door of the **social programmes of the 1960s and 1970s**. Mr Fitzwater said that they had emphasised government hand-outs and eroded pride in local communities.

A national opinion poll in the *Los Angeles Times*, the first since the riots, showed a virtual **three-way tie** between Bill Clinton, George Bush and Ross Perot, the Texan billionaire threatening to run as an independent candidate for the presidency.

Tuesday 5th
Mr Fitzwater's attack on the Great Society programmes of the 1960s provoked a **sharp reaction from the Democrats**. Bill Clinton, the likely Democratic nominee for the presidential election, said that it was the erosion of the programmes, not their creation, which had created despair in the cities. It was noticeable, however, that Mr Clinton's policy prescriptions for the cities—emphasising private-sector initiative, home ownership and discipline in schools—were similar in many respects to those pushed by conservative Republicans, like Jack Kemp, the secretary for urban development.

Thursday 7th
George Bush toured Los Angeles. The president expressed his "horror and dismay" at the devastation in the South-Central area, but pervasive security prevented him from spending much time talking to local residents, some of whom booed him.

Monday 11th
The Census Bureau released a report showing that the number of **low-paid workers** had risen sharply during the 1980s. The report claimed that in 1979 12.1% of full-time workers earned $12,195 or less, but by 1990 that figure (adjusted for inflation) had risen to 18%.

Tuesday 12th
The CIA announced that it was releasing a hitherto secret 110-page file on the activities of **Lee Harvey Oswald** before the assassination of John F.Kennedy in 1963. The agency's decision came in response to mounting public pressure for the release of secret documents relating to the killing—pressure which had been largely created by "JFK", a recently-released film.

Saturday 16th
For the first time, a national opinion poll showed **Ross Perot** leading both George Bush and Bill Clinton in the race for the presidency.

Tuesday 19th
Dan Quayle, the vice-president, attacked **Murphy Brown**, the eponymous hero of a television series, for having a child out of wedlock. Miss Brown, played by Candice Bergen, had become a mother in an episode watched by 38m Americans. Mr Quayle said the breakdown of the American family was a leading cause of poverty and lamented the fact that a role-model like Miss Brown should "mock the importance of fatherhood by bearing a child alone."

Friday 22nd
America announced that it would expel the **Yugoslav military attache** from Washington and close two Yugoslav consulates, as part of its effort to help force the Serb-dominated Yugoslavian army out of Bosnia. James Baker, the secretary of state, warned that punitive sanctions against Yugoslavia could follow.

After almost 30 years in the job, **Johnny Carson** retired as host of the "Tonight" show on NBC.

Sunday 24th
President Bush, holidaying in Maine, instructed the Coast Guard to intercept all **Haitian refugees** heading for Florida and to return them to Haiti without giving them an opportunity to apply for asylum. The president feared that previous, more tolerant, policies had merely encouraged the flow of refugees.

Tuesday 26th
Benno Schmidt resigned as president of Yale University to become chief executive officer of the **Edison Project**, which aimed to build 1,000 new technologically advanced (and profit-making) schools.

Friday 29th
The Census Bureau released the most detailed statistics yet to emerge from the latest census. They showed that in 1990 America had the largest foreign-born population in its history. Over 19m Americans, just under 8% of the population, were foreign-born. Foreigners were concentrated in big cities like New York, Los Angeles and Miami where 75% of residents spoke a language other than English at home.

Ross Perot gave an interview in which he pledged not to appoint homosexuals or adulterers to his cabinet, if elected president.

Monday 1st
George Bush, attempting to polish up his his **environmental record** ahead of the Rio Earth Summit, announced an extra $150m in aid to help save the world's forests.

Tuesday 2nd
The **primary season ended** with elections in several states including California. Bill Clinton and George Bush both recorded easy victories, but exit polls in California suggested that Ross Perot would have beaten both men.

Wednesday 3rd
The **Perot campaign** announced that Edward Rollins, Ronald Reagan's campaign manager in 1984, and Hamilton Jordan, once Jimmy Carter's chief of staff, would be co-managers of the Texan billionaire's still undeclared bid for the presidency.

Thursday 4th
The Postal Service announced the results of a special vote to decide the design of a stamp commemorating **Elvis Presley**. Over a million Americans cast ballots in a contest between a stamp showing the young Elvis and one showing a fatter, older version. Youth won by three-to-one.

The State Department published 53 documents concerning **American-Iraqi relations** before the Gulf war. The documents had been requested by a congressional committee investigating allegations that America had ignored, or even connived in, Iraq's arms build-up.

Friday 5th
The Labour Department reported that **unemployment** had risen from 7.2% of the work force to 7.5%—reaching its highest level since 1984.

Thursday 11th
President Bush's plans to address a rally in **Panama City** were disrupted when riot police attacked demonstrators with tear gas. The president, his wife and entourage were forced to beat a hasty retreat from the platform.

Saturday 13th
Bill Clinton spoke to the Rainbow Coalition, a pressure group headed by Jesse Jackson, and startled his audience by criticising **Sister Souljah**, a rap singer who had addressed it the previous day. Mr Clinton said that her recent comments suggesting that blacks stop killing each other and kill some whites instead were "filled with hatred". His speech was interpreted as an attempt to distance himself from the Jackson wing of the Democratic Party.

Sunday 14th
The **Earth Summit** ended in Rio with America cast in the role of villain. The United States refused to join 152 other countries in signing a legally binding convention on biodiversity. President Bush said that the proposals would hurt American businesses. America did sign a treaty on climate control.

Monday 15th
The Supreme Court ruled that the American government could **abduct suspects** from foreign countries and bring them to trial, even if the United States had an extradition treaty with the country in question. The ruling cleared the way for the trial of a Mexican doctor accused of partici-

pating in the murder of a Drug Enforcement Administration (DEA) agent, and subsequently kidnapped in Mexico by the DEA.

Tuesday 16th
President Bush and Boris Yeltsin, the Russian leader, announced a sweeping new **agreement to cut nuclear weapons**. The deal, reached at a summit in Washington, committed Russia to eliminating its land-based multi-warhead heavy missiles and America to halving the number of its submarine-based missiles. The two countries agreed that by 2003 neither would have more than 3,500 warheads.

Caspar Weinberger, once defence secretary for Ronald Reagan, was indicted on charges that he had committed perjury about his knowledge of the Iran-contra affair.

Wednesday 17th
Boris Yeltsin addressed Congress and reassured his audience that Communism was dead and that he would press ahead with economic reforms. His audience seemed more inclined to pass a large package of economic aid to Russia.

Sunday 21st
Bill Clinton released an economic programme which called for **higher taxes** on the rich, a phased reduction in the budget deficit and more money for education.

Wednesday 24th
Sighs of pleasure and relief could be heard from the State Department at the news that

the Labour party had won the Israeli elections. James Baker called for an early resumption of **peace talks in the Middle East**.

Ross Perot and the Bush campaign engaged in a bitter feud. The Bush team had made much of Mr Perot's penchant for employing private investigators to look into the doings of his foes. Mr Perot responded by using his favourite forum, the "Larry King" show on CNN, to accuse the president's aides of "dirty tricks".

Friday 26th
The navy secretary, Lawrence Garrett, resigned in the aftermath of the "Tailhook" affair, which had involved the sexual harassment of 26 women attending a convention for naval aviators in Las Vegas.

Sunday 28th
The strongest **earthquake** in America for 40 years hit California. Fortunately, its epicentre was in the desert 100 miles east of Los Angeles.

Monday 29th
The Supreme Court issued a long-awaited ruling on **abortion**. The court upheld restrictions on access to abortions imposed by a Pennsylvania law, but made it clear that an outright ban on abortion would be unconstitutional. Anti-abortion forces seemed more disappointed than the pro-choice lobby, but the latter fretted about the narrow 5-4 majority.

America announced that it would provide air cover for relief convoys in **Bosnia**. The decision, prompted by the ruthless Serbian bombardment of Sarajevo, was America's first attempt to intervene directly in the war occasioned by the disintegration of Yugoslavia.

July

Wednesday 1st
President Bush expressed strong reluctance to deepen **American intervention in Bosnia.**

The Senate voted to shelve the **balanced-budget amendment**, which had been supported by Mr Bush.

Thursday 2nd
The Federal Reserve cut its discount rate to 3%, pushing **interest rates to their lowest level for 29 years.** The decision came on the same day that the unemployment rate reached 7.8%, its highest level for eight years.

Sunday 5th
President Bush spoke in Warsaw and assured Poles they were on the right path, despite the pain of economic adjustment following the collapse of communism.

Wednesday 8th
The leaders of the Group of Seven rich countries wound up their summit in Munich by reaffirming a promise of $24 billion in **aid to Russia**, the first $1 billion of which would arrive in about a month. An enlightened gesture, but the Americans were less pleased by the summit's failure to advance the stalled GATT trade talks.

Thursday 9th
Bill Clinton selected **Al Gore**, a senator from Tennessee and a fellow-southerner, as his running mate. The selection of Mr Gore bucked the convention that a vice-presidential nominee should balance the presidential candidate by coming from a different region of the country or wing of the party. Mr Gore, like Mr Clinton, had long been regarded as a moderate. The Clinton camp hoped that the relative youth of the two Democrats, both in their 40s, would contrast favourably

with a 67-year-old president.

Mr Bush promised to bring **humanitarian relief** to Bosnia "no matter what it takes", but rebuffed an appeal from the president of Bosnia for international military intervention. Behind the scenes, the Defence Department was arguing firmly against risking American troops.

Sunday 12th
Three national opinion polls released on the eve of the Democratic convention showed Ross Perot, Bill Clinton and George Bush heading for a **dead-heat**.

Monday 13th
The Democratic convention opened in New York. Its first night attracted the smallest television audience ever recorded for a convention.

Wednesday 15th
Bill Clinton was nominated as the Democratic candidate for the presidency. A rousing nominating speech by Mario Cuomo, the governor of New York, was followed by an easy first-ballot victory for Mr Clinton. To end the night the candidate, his wife, Hillary, and daughter, Chelsea, walked over to the convention hall to be cheered by delegates. As Mr Clinton pointed out, the last Democratic candidate to do this had been John F. Kennedy in 1960.

Thursday 16th
The last day of the Democratic convention was thrown into turmoil by **Ross Perot's statement that he would not run** for the presidency. Mr Perot, who had been feuding with

his advisers, said that the "revitalisation" of the Democratic Party had convinced him that he could not win the presidency outright. Others speculated that he had been dismayed by the political difficulties involved in advancing a plan to eliminate the federal deficit.

In the evening, Bill Clinton gave a long and warmly received speech accepting the Democratic nomination. He outlined his idea of a **"New Convenant"** between the government and the people, in which the government would provide better education and health care, but would also impose more obligations on recipients of public benefits.

Sunday 19th
Three separate opinion polls showed Bill Clinton jumping into a **lead of 20 points** or more over George Bush.

Monday 20th
James Baker visited Israel at the start of a five-day tour of the Middle East. Mr Baker's talks with Yitzhak Rabin, the new Israeli prime minister, and leaders of the Palestinian delegation to the Middle East peace talks, were overshadowed by rumours that he would soon quit his job at the State Department to take over the management of President Bush's re-election campaign.

Wednesday 22nd
The White House gave a warning that **new military action against Iraq** was possible, if the government of Saddam Hussein continued to defy UN inspectors, charged with investigating Iraq's nuclear-weapons programme.

George Bush denied "crazy rumours" that **Dan Quayle** would step down from the Republican ticket. But Mr Quayle did his cause no good by suggesting on a television

programme that he would allow his daughter to have an abortion—a contradiction of his staunchly "pro-life" stance. Mr Quayle was swiftly corrected by his wife, Marilyn.

Thursday 23rd
James Baker made a **surprise visit to Lebanon,** to demonstrate America's support for the Lebanese president's efforts to re-establish his country's independence and to encourage a withdrawal of Syrian troops.

Monday 27th
America sent **Patriot missiles and a third aircraft carrier** to the Gulf to underline its determination that Saddam Hussein should comply with all UN resolutions. Meanwhile, the White House called Bill Clinton "reckless" for proposing the use of American air power in Bosnia.

Wednesday 29th
The Field poll in **California**, a state with one-fifth of the electoral votes needed to win the presidency, showed Bill Clinton 34 points ahead of George Bush.

Clark Clifford, a close adviser to every Democratic president from Harry Truman to Jimmy Carter, was indicted for allegedly taking bribes from the owners of the Bank of Credit and Commerce International, in return for hiding BCCI's ownership of American banks. Mr Clifford, now aged 85, staunchly protested his innocence.

August

Sunday 2nd
The Bush campaign issued a press release accusing Bill Clinton of being a "snivelling hypocrite". The statement aroused particular interest, both because of its juvenile tone and because its author Mary Matalin, a senior aide in the Bush campaign, had been romantically involved with James Carville, Mr Clinton's campaign manager. President Bush quickly disavowed Ms Matalin's broadside and vowed to stay out of the "sleaze business".

Wednesday 5th
Four white police officers who had been videotaped beating a black motorist were charged with **federal civil-rights offences**, three months after their acquittal on state charges set off the Los Angeles riots.

Thursday 6th
President Bush announced that **America would recognise Bosnia & Hercegovina**, Slovenia and Croatia, following similar steps by the European Community. Mr Bush also endorsed a UN resolution authorising the use of force to deliver humanitarian aid in Bosnia.

Tuesday 11th
President Bush concluded his talks with the new Israeli prime minister, Yitzhak Rabin, by announcing that he could now recommend the approval of $10 billion in **loan guarantees** to Israel. Mr Bush's decision symbolised the improvement in American-Israeli relations, following the fall of the Shamir government.

The *New York Post* published allegations that Mr Bush had had an affair with **Jennifer Fitzgerald**, an official at the State Department. Mr Bush was asked about the allegations at his press conference with Mr Rabin. Visibly an-gered he called the charges "a lie" and blamed the "screwy atmosphere" of the election.

Wednesday 12th
America, Canada and Mexico announced a draft agreement on the formation of a **North American Free Trade Area**. If ratified, NAFTA would create a single free-trade zone of 360m people—as large as the proposed European Economic Area. But the plan faced difficulties in Congress where many feared the loss of manufacturing jobs to Mexico.

Thursday 13th
James Baker took charge of the Bush re-election campaign, assuming the post of White House chief of staff. In a statement explaining this long-awaited development, the White House said that Mr Baker would develop a co-ordinated approach to domestic and foreign problems. Mr Baker himself, making a fare-well speech to the State De-partment, laid out a conservative agenda, stressing the virtues of smaller government, freer trade and individual initiative.

Sunday 16th
The *New York Times* published a report claiming that America was planning to provoke a confrontation with **Iraq** over UN inspections of Iraqi ministries, and that this could lead to renewed bombing of Baghdad. President Bush, embarrassed by the implication that this action was being planned to coincide with the Republican conven-tion, denied that he would ever take military decisions for political reasons and inveighed against a "clear breach of security".

Monday 17th
The **Republican convention** opened in Houston. Patrick Buchanan, the conservative television commentator who had challenged George Bush for the Republican nomination, endorsed Mr Bush in a long speech. Mr Buchanan told his audience that there was a "religious war" going on in America between God-fearing conservatives and per-missive liberals. He was followed by Ronald Reagan who cheered the party's delegates with a rousing invocation of the old conservative values. But some moderate Republi-cans expressed fears that the party had conceded too much to the evangelical right. In particular they worried that the Republicans' commitment to outlawing all forms of abor-tion might alienate women voters.

Tuesday 18th
Woody Allen called a press conference in New York to deny allegations that he had sexually abused his adopted daughter, Dylan. The charges came after the acrimonious break-up of Mr Allen's 12-year-long relationship with an actress, Mia Farrow, which in turn followed Mr Allen's ad-mission that he was having an affair with Miss Farrow's 21-year-old adopted daughter, Soon-Yi.

Wednesday 19th
The Republican convention's stress on **family values** culmi-nated with a long speech by Barbara Bush. She praised her husband and said that he had always put his family first.

Thursday 20th
George Bush accepted the Re-publican nomination for the presidency. He apologised to the party for having agreed to raise taxes as part of the 1990 budget agreement, and prom-ised fresh tax-cuts (balanced by spending cuts), in a second term as president. Mr Bush's speech was peppered with at-tacks on Bill Clinton for his inexperience and alleged evasiveness.

Friday 21st
Polls taken in the aftermath of the Republican convention showed that Bill Clinton's lead over the president had narrowed substantially. Most surveys showed the Democrat leading by 6-8 points.

Monday 24th
Hurricane Andrew smashed through southern Florida kill-ing 15 people and causing an estimated $30 billion-worth of damage. Buildings in central Miami were badly hit, but this was nothing compared to the devastation further south in small towns like Homestead and Florida City. President Bush declared Florida a disas-ter area, making it eligible for federal disaster relief. But crit-ics were swift to condemn the ineffectiveness of Washing-ton's response.

The **dollar** fell to record lows against the D-mark. The Bush administration appeared un-concerned. Nobody expected it to raise interest rates in the middle of an election campaign.

Mr Bush announced that his administration would spend an extra $2 billion a year to expand American **job-train-ing** programmes.

September

Tuesday 1st
Hurricane Andrew's **damage in Florida and Louisiana** was put at $7.3 billion. President Bush and his wife, countering criticism of federal government inefficiency, flew to see the relief operations "to be sure that nothing is falling through the cracks."

Wednesday 2nd
George Bush decided to **sell 150 F-16 fighters to Taiwan** before electioneering in Fort Worth, Texas, where the planes are built. China, in reply, threatened to leave UN arms-control talks.

California's Republican governor, Pete Wilson, signed a **compromise budget** after the state authorities had existed for 65 days on $3.4 billion of IOUs they had issued. Wilson's Democratic opponents agreed to big cuts in school spending, welfare and other state costs to cover a $10.7 billion shortfall.

Prince, the diminutive rock star, signed a **$108m recording deal** with Warner Brothers, making him the highest-paid artist in history.

Thursday 3rd
President Bush announced he was **tripling** the amount of American wheat eligible for export subsidies.

A CNN/USA *Today* poll showed Bill Clinton's **lead rising** to 15 percentage points, 5 points above the level it climbed to after the Republican convention.

Friday 4th
The Federal Reserve Board **cut its interest rate** from 3.25% to 3%, the lowest since June 1963.

Americans in **poverty** were reported to have risen by 2m to 35.7m in 1991, the highest since 1964. (Definition: those below the official poverty lines of income of $6,932 a year for individuals and $13,924 for families of four.)

Monday 7th
Bill Clinton urged the media to investigate a memorandum of a talk between George Schultz (then secretary of state) and Caspar Weinberger (then defence secretary), raising the possibility of George Bush's "illegal conduct" in the **Iran-Contra operation**. They both opposed it. Mr Bush did not.

Fay Vincent **resigned** as baseball commissioner after major team owners passed a no-confidence motion.

Wednesday 9th
George Bush said he was wrong to have agreed with the Democrats to **raise taxes** in 1990 if they would accept a deficit-reducing budget: "I'm not going to do it again. Ever, ever."

Thursday 10th
White House spokesman Marlin Fitzwater said President Bush **had not pledged** himself never to raise taxes again.

Friday 11th
President Bush said he would **sell 72 F-15 fighters to Saudi Arabia**, despite Israeli protests. He was talking at the McDonnell Douglas plant in St Louis, Missouri.

Sunday 13th
Dan Quayle insisted on television that President Bush would **never raise taxes** again.

Wednesday 16th
Geraldine Ferraro, former Democratic vice-presidential candidate, was **beaten** in a primary to contest a New York Senate seat.

Thursday 17th
Barbra Streisand sang to Bill Clinton and his wife in Hollywood about George Bush and Dan Quayle: "One doesn't look well, the other can't spell, those fellas won't do, it has to be you."

Friday 18th
Arizona became the fiftieth and final state to place Ross Perot's **name on the ballot** for November.

Sunday 20th
Space shuttle Endeavour returned to Cape Canaveral after eight days' flight. The crew included the first black woman and the first married couple in space.

Tuesday 22nd
George Bush's campaign manager, James Baker, had a **secret meeting** with Ross Perot.

Legislation allowing mandatory but unpaid leave from work for pregnancy, adoption or family illness was **vetoed** by President Bush for a second time.

Candice Bergen, an actress in the television series "Murphy Brown", which was criticised by Dan Quayle because it glamorised single motherhood, had a lorryload of **potatoes** (a word Mr Quayle found difficult to spell) dumped in the driveway of the vice-president's home. He had sent her a stuffed Republican **elephant toy**.

Wednesday 23rd
President Bush proposed $20 billion-worth of **tax breaks** and deregulatory measures over five years to help small businesses.

Thursday 24th
Richard Secord, a former American air force major-general convicted for his part in the Iran-Contra affair, declared that George Bush had not only **known about the operation** but had persuaded Ronald Reagan to persevere with it when it was "dead in the water".

Friday 25th
The Senate and House both approved stopping all **underground nuclear testing** in the United States by late 1996.

Tom Bradley, Los Angeles mayor for 20 years, **said he'd stand down** in June 1993. He said the riots in the spring "tore at my heart".

Monday 28th
Gregory Kingsley, a twelve-year-old, had his request to be "**divorced**" from his Florida parents upheld in court. He had hired his own lawyer. He wished to be adopted by a Mormon couple who had been his foster parents since October 1991.

Tuesday 29th
"**Magic**" **Johnson**, the retired HIV-positive basketball star, said he would return to play between 50 and 60 games a year for the Los Angeles Lakers. (It's an 82-game season.) He endorsed Bill Clinton and resigned from the National Aids Commission, saying the administration had "utterly ignored" its work.

Wednesday 30th
President Bush, having previously rejected the idea of debating with Governor Clinton, sent out a challenge for each of the four Sunday evenings immediately before the election. 'It's a crime we're not having **debates**,' he said. Bill Clinton hesitated, saying the dates clashed with baseball's World Series games.

October

Thursday 1st
Ross Perot re-entered the presidential race, criticising George Bush and Bill Clinton for failing to address the economic issues, particularly the budget deficit. He was accused of being a distraction, motivated by ego.

Friday 2nd
The **unemployment rate** in September was 7.5%, down from 7.6%, marginally better than expected. Wall Street concluded it meant no prospect of a further interest-rate cut.

The Senate Judiciary Committee reported that more than 21,000 American women were **assaulted, raped or murdered** weekly in 1991.

Sunday 4th
The three candidates for the presidency agreed to compress **three 90-minute debates** into nine days. The first would have questions from three journalists; the second, questions from the audience; the third, questions by a moderator and then by a journalists' panel. It was also agreed there would be one vice-presidential debate.

The *Washington Times* said Bill Clinton visited Moscow in 1969 and could have been a **recruitment target** for Soviet intelligence.

Monday 5th
Congress overrode **President Bush's veto** on legislation to regulate cable television companies, its first such success in 36 attempts over four years.

Tuesday 6th
The **Bush campaign denied** tampering with Bill Clinton's passport file. Mr Clinton said of a claim that he had thought of renouncing American citizenship: "They are stirring everything they can, but this old dog won't hunt."

Wednesday 7th
President Bush flew to Texas to initial the **North American Free Trade Agreement** with Mexico's President Salinas de Gortari and Canada's prime minister, Brian Mulroney.

Saturday 10th
Iraqi security police seized an American contractor working on mine-clearing close to the Kuwait-Iraq border; he was quickly released.

Sunday 11th
In the **first presidential debate**, George Bush was cautious and low-key; Bill Clinton had a hoarse voice; Ross Perot admitted: "I don't have any experience–in running up a $4 trillion debt." Mr Bush let it be known he wanted James Baker to run domestic policy after the election, and would dismiss the treasury secretary, Nicholas Brady, and his economics team.

Tuesday 13th
In the **vice-presidential debate**, Dan Quayle was aggressive, insisting that Bill Clinton "has trouble telling the truth". Al Gore condemned "trickle-down" economics. Ross Perot's Admiral James Stockdale asked "Who am I? Why am I here?" and had trouble with his hearing aid.

Wednesday 14th
White House spokesman Marlin Fitzwater said the State Department did instruct the embassy in London to **search for files on Bill Clinton**, including documents on his draft status and citizenship. Al Gore called it "an abuse of power" smacking of a police state.

Thursday 15th
Second debate. The audience demanded the candidates kept to policy issues and stopped "trashing each other". Bill Clinton had a superior command of facts and figures. George Bush was caught looking at his watch.

Attorney-general William Barr **appointed a special counsel,** but not an independent prosecutor, to investigate the administration's possible connivance in, and concealment of, $4 billion in illicit pre-Gulf war loans to Iraq by the Atlanta branch of the Italian Banca Nazionale del Lavor.

Friday 16th
The **trade deficit** rose to $9 billion in August, with exports showing their biggest decline in five years.

Monday 19th
Third debate. George Bush, no longer lethargic, told Americans to "watch your wallet". Bill Clinton said Mr Bush was the "biggest practitioner" of what he had once called "voodoo economics". Ross Perot said he was sick of Republicans blackening his name. Some 18.6m households watched.

Wednesday 21st
Madonna's **much-hyped** book "Sex" reached the stores, priced $49.95.

Thursday 22nd
American negotiators flew home from the **stalled GATT talks**, threatening immediate sanctions on up to $1 billion of EC exports, especially white wine. America wanted the EC to shrink its subsidised food exports by 24%; the EC refused to go beyond 18%.

Friday 23rd
President Bush announced thatHanoi would turn over its entire archives on **Americans still missing** from the Vietnam war.

America gave the EC until November 4th, the day after the election, to come to terms or face **sanctions**.

Saturday 24th
The Toronto Blue Jays beat the Atlanta Braves 4-3 in 11 innings, to win baseball's **World Series** 4 games to 2, the first time the series had gone to a team from outside the United States. The winning hit was a two-run double by Dave Winfield (aged 41).

Sunday 25th
A CBS-*New York Times* poll gave Bill Clinton a **lead of just 5 points**; *Time*'s poll one of 7 points. Ross Perot's performance was said to be responsible.

Ross Perot said he had dropped out of the presidential race for 11 weeks because the Bush campaign had been planning to disrupt the wedding of his daughter, Carolyn, in August. Most of the media said Mr Perot was "obsessed with conspiracy theory".

Monday 26th
Robert Stempel **resigned** as chairman and chief executive of General Motors. The corporation's North American operations had lost $5 billion in 1991; Ford and Chrysler continued to gain in the lorry and car market.

Tuesday 27th
The American economy grew at an annual rate of 2.7% in the third quarter, almost doubling the spring rate of 1.5%. Inflation fell to 2.1%.

Monday 2nd
Four **surveys** put George Bush an average of 7.5 points behind Governor Clinton. Mr Bush said: "When Bill Clinton is playing that 'taxophone' middle-class Americans will be singing the blues". Mr Clinton said: "Tomorrow we will drown out the negative voices that we have heard for too long." Ross Perot said: "We'll landslide this thing if the people vote their conscience."

Tuesday 3rd
Mr **Clinton won** the presidency (370 electoral college votes to George Bush's 168) but not by a landslide. The popular vote divided: Clinton 43%, Bush 38%, Perot 19%. The Perot vote was the second-best ever by a third candidate, but was not enough to carry a single state. The Democrats kept their majorities in the Senate and in the House of Representatives, although with some losses in the House. Carol Moseley Braun (of Illinois) became the first black woman senator. The Democrats also won eight of the 12 elections for governor, with three gains and one loss.

Thursday 5th
Carla A. Hills, the American trade representative, said **tariffs** would be put on $300m of EC goods in 30 days' time unless Brussels changed its tune in the GATT negotiations.

Sunday 8th
Detroit police said a black motorist had been **beaten to death** by two white officers while five others looked on, in a case resembling the attack in Los Angeles on Rodney King in 1991. Police chief Stanley Knox called it a disgrace.

Monday 9th
President-elect Clinton said he would **call a conference** of business leaders and economists, "some of the brightest people in the country", on urgent problems to "get as many good ideas as I can."

Tuesday 10th
George Bush **fired** Elizabeth Tamposi, assistant secretary of state for consular affairs (and a former Republican fund raiser), the official who handled the pre-election search of Bill Clinton's passport and citizenship files.

Judge Sol Wachtler, the chief judge in New York state, **resigned** after a federal court put him under house arrest amid charges that he had blackmailed a woman with whom he had had an affair. He was ordered to wear an electronic monitoring bracelet.

Thursday 12th
In his **first press conference** since the vote, Bill Clinton said: "We need increased investment and gradual, disciplined reduction of the deficit." He wanted tax credits for business investment and money for roads, water and other public works projects that were ready to go.

In California a federal district judge, Terry Hatter, ordered the navy to reinstate immediately Keith Meinhold (aged 30) to his former position as a sonar instructor. Meinhold had been discharged for **homosexuality** in 1991.

Monday 16th
Bill Clinton met Democratic congressional leaders at Little Rock to **end the "gridlock"** between the executive and legislature. He pledged to create jobs, raise middle-class incomes, provide comprehensive health insurance cover for all, and devise a disciplined plan to trim the deficit.

Senator Sam Nunn, chairman of the Armed Services Committee, said he **opposed Mr Clinton's plan** to end the ban on homosexuality in the military. So did Senator Robert Dole, the Republican minority leader.

Tuesday 17th
In issue 75 of **Superman** Comics, the patriot from Krypton expired at the hands of Doomsday, a supervillain. The question of a recovery, like Sherlock Holmes's, was not, however, ruled out.

Wednesday 18th
Bill Clinton had a 90-minute talk with George Bush in the **Oval Office** on the transfer of power. He then took a walk in a poor district. He stayed at the Hay-Adams Hotel, not at Blair House, as Mr Bush had offered.

Senator Robert Byrd, chairman of the Appropriations Committee, opposed the idea of allowing Mr Clinton **line-item veto power on spending.** He refused to "transfer additional authority to the executive branch."

Thursday 19th
Barbara Bush, back from house-hunting in Houston, showed **Hillary Clinton** round the second-floor private residential quarters in the White House.

Friday 20th
President Bush approved a **trade compromise** with the EC, dropping the demand that the EC accept firm output limits on rapeseed, sunflowers and soya. The EC agreed (France dissenting) to restrict farm acreage devoted to oilseed. Both sides agreed to reduce internal supports for agriculture by 20%.

Monday 23rd
The Coast Guard forecast massive **attempts by Haitians to flee to America** in hastily-built boats. Bill Clinton had already retracted an election promise, denying he would promote a refugee exodus from the island.

Tuesday 24th
Georgia's junior Democratic senator, Wyche Fowler, was **defeated** in a run-off contest by Republican Paul Coverdell, despite support from Bill Clinton and Al Gore. The Democrats expected to end with a Senate majority of 57-43.

The last American servicemen left the **Subic Bay** naval base in the Philippines, held since 1898. Filipino President Ramos said his country was free from foreign troops for the first time since the Spaniards arrived in 1571.

Wednesday 25th
Revised Commerce Department figures showed **third-quarter growth** at an unexpected annual rate of 3.9%. President-elect Clinton said: "It won't change my long-term plans at all."

Thursday 26th
UN relief agencies in Somalia **rejected an American offer** of up to 30,000 troops to protect aid supplies from looting by armed bands.

Wednesday 2nd
American economists declared that **Bill Clinton's economic programme** would add just 0.2 percentage points more to growth than expected from a second Bush term.

Friday 4th
President Bush ordered up to 28,000 American **troops to Somalia**, under United Nations instructions, to prevent mass starvation in the country. He said on television that Operation Restore Hope was "God's work."

Saturday 5th
Ben Nighthorse Campbell, the **first Indian** to be elected to the Senate since 1929, said he planned to wear warpaint and ride his horse War Bonnet at the Clinton inauguration.

Sunday 6th
Bill Clinton put off a meeting with the British prime minister, John Major, but denied it was a **snub**. He said he would meet no foreign leaders until after he was inaugurated.

Tuesday 8th
The first American troops went ashore in Somalia (with orchestrated television coverage) in **Operation Restore Hope** to guarantee the distribution of food to the starving and keep the local warring factions apart. No shots were fired. The warlords ordered their gunmen to avoid the advance marine force.

Thursday 10th
Mr Clinton appointed Lloyd Bentsen **treasury secretary**, with Roger Altman, a Wall Street investment banker, his deputy. He also named Leon Panetta **budget director** and Alice Rivlin, a vocal critic of budget deficits, Mr Panetta's deputy.

A Los Angeles judge ruled that the **will** of William Kane, a millionaire who committed suicide, was **invalid**. Mr Kane had left his sperm to his girlfriend, Deborah Hecht, who said she wanted his child. The judge ordered the sperm to be destroyed.

Friday 11th
Bill Clinton named his Oxford friend Robert Reich as his **labour secretary**, and Donna Shalala **secretary of health and human services**. Critics said both were radicals.

New York city was declared a **disaster area** after being hit by 90mph winds. The storm caused flooding in the subway, and forced the closure of La Guardia airport and the evacuation of seaside homes.

Saturday 12th
Ron Brown, the black Democratic Party chairman, was picked as **secretary of commerce** in the new cabinet and Thomas "Mack" McLarty, a childhood friend of Bill Clinton and a newcomer to national politics, **White House chief of staff**.

Monday 14th
Bill Clinton and Al Gore heard industrialists, economists and union officials setting out **ideas for the economy** at a summit in Little Rock, Arkansas. Mr Clinton called the national debt "an economic ball and chain dragging us down."

Tuesday 15th
The secretary of state, Lawrence Eagleburger, called for a partial lifting of the UN **arms embargo** to help the Bosnians defend themselves.

Wednesday 16th
Mr Eagleburger listed seven Serbs who, he said, were suspected of being **involved in genocide**, particularly in the siege of Sarajevo. He said Serb leaders might eventually be charged with war crimes.

Thursday 17th
President Bush signed the **North American Free Trade Agreement** with Canada and Mexico, predicting an "explosion of growth" across the continent.

President-elect Clinton appointed Henry Cisneros, a Hispanic and former mayor of San Antonio, Texas, his **secretary of housing and urban affairs**.

Friday 18th
Attorney-general William Barr appointed a **special investigator** to see if James Baker, the former secretary of state and Bush campaign manager, broke the law in the examination of Bill Clinton's passport files during the election.

Saturday 19th
President Bush and British prime minister John Major were reported to have agreed on a 15-day deadline for the enforcement of a **"no-fly zone"** over Bosnia.

Sunday 20th
Defence secretary Dick Cheney confirmed the no-fly plan, but John Major **denied** it, saying: "That was nothing we discussed over the weekend."

Tuesday 22nd
Bill Clinton chose Warren Christopher, who served in three previous Democratic administrations, as **secretary of state**. Les Aspin was appointed to the Pentagon and Anthony Lake as **national security adviser**. The choices were said to be conservative.

Thursday 24th
President Bush **pardoned** former defence secretary Caspar Weinberger and five other officials in the Reagan administration who had been named in the Iran-contra affair. Lawrence Walsh, the independent prosecutor, said Mr Bush himself was now the subject of investigation.

Sunday 27th
An American F16 fighter **shot down** an Iraqi MiG after what the Bush administration called a grave challenge to the air exclusion zone over southern Iraq.

Monday 28th
President Bush warned the Serbs that the United States would **use force** if they provoked a military conflict in Kosovo province, bordering on Albania.

The American aircraft carrier *Kitty Hawk* was ordered from Somali waters to **confront Iraq** in the Gulf.

Tuesday 29th
America and Russia agreed to **cut their nuclear arsenals** by two-thirds; both countries would lose their deadliest intercontinental weapons—land-based ones armed with multiple warheads. Presidents Bush and Yeltsin agreed to sign at a summit in January.

Thursday 31st
George Bush landed at Mogadishu and told American troops in Somalia they were showing "that same expertise, that same kind of devotion" as in the Gulf war. He visited the United States embassy, a hospital, a school and a relief centre for mothers and children. Somali factions exchanged artillery and machinegun fire.

Louis Vuitton. The spirit of travel

LAppointment in Jaipur, arriving by car or by elephant... Imbued with all the magic of a golden age of travel, creations by Louis Vuitton in Epi leather belong to the realm of the exceptional. Crafted to exacting standards in the finest leatherworking tradition, they perpetuate the proud heritage of a House which, since 1854, has endowed travel with its symbol of nobility.

LOUIS VUITTON
MALLETIER A PARIS

MAISON FONDÉE EN 1854

*Louis Vuitton luggage and accessories are sold only
in the 167 exclusive Louis Vuitton shops, among which :
Paris, 78 bis avenue Marceau · London, 7 Royal Exchange, Cornhill ·
Frankfurt, Goethestrasse 7 · Tokyo, 7-6-1 Ginza, Chuo-Ku. ·
Hong Kong, Peninsula Hotel.*

As we reported then

A triumph of expediency

JANUARY 4TH, WASHINGTON, DC *George Bush's trip to Japan, accompanied by America's leading car manufacturers, became a symbol of his less-than-wholehearted commitment to free trade*

POLITICALLY, it is a neat solution. Needing to seem less preoccupied with foreign affairs, but having no domestic initiative to offer, George Bush has redefined the recession as a trade issue and set off on a two-week tour of Asia to complain about barriers to American exports. The consultants who dreamed this up must be congratulating themselves. Never mind that it stems from some mercantilist nonsense borrowed from the Democratic Party.

The presidential trip—to Australia, Singapore and South Korea and culminating on January 7th with a visit to Japan—was planned long ago and was to be brimming with goodwill towards Pacific nations. These, Mr Bush has long rightly recognised, are quickly becoming America's most vital trading partners. Yet first the Gulf war and then an autumn panic about the American economy delayed the tour. Now its purpose has been hijacked by that domestic panic. Out has gone the goodwill; in comes a jingoistic brand of economic crusading. And look who the infidel is: that trusty villain Japan, now being blamed for the American recession by Americans who ought to know better.

In case Mr Bush should forget these flawed lines, a chorus of American businessmen has been brought along to echo them. On January 7th they will all complain loudly about Japan's closed markets and the harm they are causing valiant American exporters. Closed markets there are aplenty in Japan. But the 21 hand-picked executives could hardly be a less comely bunch to deliver this hissogram. For they represent much that is wrong with American business.

Many are yesterday's men, such as Lee Iacocca of Chrysler, from yesterday's companies (the other two heads of Detroit's Big Three are also present). Most pay themselves munificently—on average, six times more than their Japanese equivalents and 100-plus times more than their own employees—come good times or bad. Mr Iacocca himself (1991 salary: $4.65m, excluding stock options) never misses an opportunity to insist that Japan has a God-given duty to dig Detroit out of its giant hole (1991 losses: $6 billion) by buying more American cars. He is calling for fresh restrictions to prevent Americans from buying the Japanese cars they want.

The irony is not lost on the Japanese. They shun American cars for much the same reason as many Americans do: the cars are not the best for the buck. Certainly, unnecessarily stringent certification procedures help to keep imported cars from Japan, but Japanese consumers still buy plenty of European cars. Last Sunday on an NBC talk show Japan's deputy foreign minister, Koji Watanabe, was asked what the Japanese could learn from American car makers. He was completely stumped for an answer.

Fair play it isn't

All this palaver matters because it is suddenly fashionable again in Washington to be a protectionist. Of course, you will call yourself a "fair trader". But discrimination is America's only implied problem, and retaliation its only implied response, whatever that might cost the American consumer. A trade deficit is taken as conclusive proof of "unfairness".

This stand is to be expected from old protectionists like Richard Gephardt, the House majority leader and a gofer for the American car industry. Before Christmas Mr Gephardt introduced in Congress a bill that would restrict imports of Japanese cars if America's $40 billion merchandise-trade deficit with Japan did not shrink to under $5 billion by 1997.

It is quite another thing to hear the outgoing commerce secretary, Robert Mosbacher, join in. He was on the same NBC talk show as the Japanese minister, along with John Dingell, a Democratic congressman from Detroit who has done much to hinder American business and would love to do the same to Japan. Mr Dingell said flatly that Japan, by blocking American exports, had caused America's current recession. Mr Mosbacher, pressed on the same point, seemed to agree, though not "totally". Mr Mosbacher also mentioned the possibility of restricting Japanese car imports. The Japanese embassy pronounced itself outraged at the recession slur.

Mr Mosbacher will now head Mr Bush's re-election campaign, so more criticism of Japan will flow from him if that is what opinion polls seem to dictate. At least his tenure at the Commerce Department had the advantage of being relatively low-key. It is uncertain whether his successor, Barbara Franklin, a management consultant, will follow a more activist course. But

Mr Bush, if he is pushed in an election year to start bashing the Japanese, could smother his better instincts.

If the result were simply lower import barriers in Japan, fine. But the rumours already spilling from the Japanese government suggest otherwise. Various possible appeasement measures include fresh voluntary export restraints for America-bound cars, and tax subsidies for those at home who buy foreign ones. Such a return to more managed trade would benefit only those bureaucrats from whose regulatory grip so much Japanese business has escaped in the past 10-15 years.

Intellectual deficit

This current bout of American protectionism is different from previous recent ones in that the current-account deficit has been shrinking for four years. In nominal terms the current-account deficit peaked at $162 billion, or 3.6% of GNP in 1987. Since then it has fallen sharply, due mostly to an improvement in the merchandise trade balance (see chart). In 1990 the current-account deficit was $97 billion, or 1.8% of GNP. The deficit in 1991 will be only about $4 billion, thanks in part to foreign contributions towards the cost of the Gulf war;

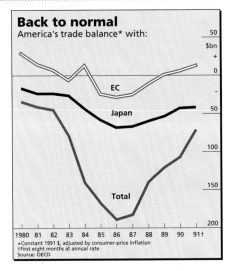

Back to normal
America's trade balance* with:

```
                                          50
                                          $bn
                                          +
                        EC                0
                                          -
              Japan                       50

                                          100

                                          150
         Total
                                          200
1980 81 82 83 84 85 86 87 88 89 90 91†
```

*Constant 1991 $, adjusted by consumer-price inflation
†First eight months at annual rate
Source: OECD

but thanks also to record volumes of exports, despite a slowing world economy.

Although this means that America now runs a trade surplus with Europe, its deficit with Japan remains above $40 billion a year and will probably rise soon. True, nearly two-thirds of that deficit is accounted for by car imports into America. But that does not mean that Japan's car industry should be singled out for special

"blame". Americans buy two-fifths more cars than they produce, whereas the Japanese buy cars equivalent to half their production. Why? Because Japan has a comparative advantage in making cars.

Not every Washington economist preaches managed trade. This week Fred Bergsten of the Institute for International Economics argued that Mr Bush should be seeking from the Japanese a promise of domestic fiscal expansion and a revaluation of the yen, which Mr Bergsten reckons is presently 15-20% undervalued. Such a plan presupposes that unpegged currencies are controllable, through international co-operation—which may be a little wishful.

Rather than worry about Japan's problems, Mr Bush would do better to dwell upon his own country's. The current-account deficit is unlikely to shrink further. The Gulf war dividend will not be repeated. And as America's petrified economy comes back to life, so it will suck in imports. Once again, an untackled budget deficit will weigh heavily upon America's external accounts, with or without a deficit with Japan. Mr Bush could usefully remind himself of one thing while he roams abroad. The economy really does begin at home.

King George humbled

FEBRUARY 22ND, MANCHESTER, NEW HAMPSHIRE *The New Hampshire Republican primary dealt a rude shock to George Bush: disgruntled voters plumped for his conservative rival, Pat Buchanan. It was an omen of humiliations to come*

NOT since Gene McCarthy knocked Lyndon Johnson from his perch in 1968 has New Hampshire dealt such an unkind blow to an elected president. In the primary on February 18th, Patrick Buchanan and his bash-'em conservatism took 37% of the Republican vote, against George Bush's 53%. Mr Bush, as Mr Buchanan himself pointed out on the eve of the election, is no Johnson: "When he says he'll do anything to get re-elected, I take him at his word." Even so, the harrying that Mr Bush received from Mr Buchanan in New Hampshire is the most humbling moment of his presidency.

What went wrong? Six weeks ago Mr Bush had seemed to have put together a formidable and pugnacious re-election team. Robert Mosbacher, the campaign chairman and a former commerce secretary, had some of the richest business friends in the country. Robert Teeter, Fred Malek and Charles Black were all veterans of earlier campaigns. Jim Pinkerton, a White House staffer, won his spurs for the negative campaigning that demolished Michael Duka-

kis in 1988. He was set to work on Mr Buchanan's particularly indefensible past utterings, of which there are many.

Only three weeks ago the Bush team looked set to be nasty to Mr Buchanan, while ignoring the Democrats. Mr Buchanan's challenge, after all, was Republican treason, akin to attempted regicide. Inside the Republican court, the Bushmen argued, you had to get nasty with traitors. So they bought space on New Hampshire's radio and television stations and prepared to put on some anti-Buchanan commercials.

Then the Bush campaign fell oddly mute. Right-wing Republicans loyal to Mr Bush, including Bill Bennett (a former education secretary with a conservative, Irish-Catholic upbringing similar to Mr Buchanan's), had urged a change of course. They warned Mr Bush that, by attacking the Buchanan campaign, he risked splitting the Republican Party into its right and moderate wings. Mr Bush's place in the history books, they argued, would not be embellished if he won the soubriquet of a "Rockefeller" Republican. Mr Bush there-

fore could not bring himself to mention by name "the other guy", a habit he also used to employ against Mr Dukakis in 1988.

The result was drift. The president was warned by his handlers to steer clear of foreign policy, on which he is deemed to spend too much time. So, on the three occasions when Mr Bush visited New Hampshire, he was reduced to mouthing banalities, some of them incoherent, about the economy (such as "Message: I care"). Occasional sightings of the presidential cavalcade incongruously crossing the snowy valleys of New Hampshire heightened the other-worldliness of it all. Right-wing Republicans from Washington, dispatched to press the president's conservative credentials, neither impressed the fierce right-wingers of the state nor comforted the moderates.

If Mr Bush was forbidden to campaign on the confident territory of his foreign policy, Mr Buchanan was happy to fight him on just that patch. True, Mr Buchanan's commercials were all about tax increases and Mr Bush's promises, past and present, of tax cuts and tax credits. But his speeches were as much about America's role in the world.

Mr Buchanan inveighs against Israel, China, the IMF—indeed, against any foreign state "mainlining out of the Treasury". He paints Mr Bush as the enemy of freedom—by refusing to recognise early enough the independence of the Baltic states and of Slovenia and Croatia, and by backing a corrupt regime in China.

Mr Buchanan's campaign is truly an insurgent one. His bid for the presidency is just ten weeks old. His campaign team, which consists of little more than himself, his "baby sister", Bay Buchanan, and a young lawyer and film-maker, Paul Erikson, was held together in New Hampshire with string and sealing wax. The question now is how much further it can surge.

The campaign's funding has a lot to do with it. Mr Buchanan has been able to draw upon unparalleled mailing lists. Direct-mail shots have provided him with much of his money, federal matching funds with most of the rest. In New Hampshire, Mr Buchanan spent more than the president—and $1.7m on media alone. His campaign now expects $2m more in the next couple of weeks. Mr Buchanan will spend as

Vanquished victor, with sister

much of that as allowed in the Georgia primary on March 3rd.

Georgia will make or break Mr Buchanan. Georgians strongly backed the Gulf war, which Mr Buchanan did not. Even peace-loving Jimmy Carter would make

sure he was seen in quail-hunting gear. Mr Buchanan, for all the tales of his youthful street fights, has the look of one who has never lifted a water-pistol.

Newt Gingrich, a congressman from Georgia, described Mr Buchanan's success in New Hampshire as a "primal scream". Surveys of voters there confirm that most were voting against Mr Bush rather than for Mr Buchanan. But the Georgia economy is far more robust.

That leaves Mr Buchanan with one card with which he might try to trump Mr Bush—race. He has already denounced Mr Bush for signing a civil-rights act that he feels gives blacks quotas of jobs. In Georgia there will be many Republicans who respond to talk like that. Mr Buchanan is no crude racist. But then, before he came to New Hampshire, he had little sympathy for those who complained about their economic plight.

Pat Buchanan won no primaries, but took his revenge with a hate-filled speech at the Republican convention that was widely thought to have contributed to Mr Bush's defeat.

Jesse Jackson's long shadow

MARCH 7TH **The Democratic Party felt so assured of the black vote that it made no particular effort to court either blacks or their nominal spokesman, Jesse Jackson**

THE scene is a New York courtroom. John Gotti, the head of the Gambino Mafia family, is on trial. Salvatore Gravano, once his consigliere, now a stool-pigeon, is testifying against him. Mr Gotti cracks—"It's an outrage, it's a dirty double-crossing back-stabbing thing to do. For him to do this to me is an act of dishonour," he yells.

Right quote, wrong person. The man with the Mafiosi mouth was not the Dapper Don at all, but Slick Willie: Bill Clinton, the governor of Arkansas and candidate for the Democratic presidential nomination. And why did he come so close to saying that the object of his rage would soon sleep with the fishes? Because he thought he was in danger of losing the black vote in the Democratic primaries, that's why.

Mr Clinton's outburst came before an open microphone in a television studio, after an interviewer had erroneously given him the impression that Tom Harkin, a rival of his for the nomination, had been endorsed by Jesse Jackson. In 1984 and (especially) 1988, when he won nearly 7m votes in Democratic primaries, Mr Jackson had shown himself able to mobilise blacks for a

presidential campaign like no one else. Mr Clinton's outburst was twice revealing: first, in showing how important black support is to him; and second, in showing how long a shadow Mr Jackson still casts.

The unspoken assumption behind Mr Clinton's anger was that, although Mr Jackson is not running this year, the black vote was his to dispose of—or, at the least, that an endorsement by Mr Jackson of someone else would be so powerful that it would do Mr Clinton harm. This assumption of Mr Jackson's importance was not Mr Clinton's alone. No sooner had he stuck his foot in his mouth than St. Paul Tsongas, his main rival for the nomination, was airing commercials on black radio stations saying, among much else, "Paul Tsongas doesn't go around attacking respected national leaders like Jesse Jackson." As for Mr Harkin himself, he has tried to rescue his flagging campaign by padding through South Carolina in Mr Jackson's footsteps. And Jerry Brown has said that, if nominated, he would ask Mr Jackson to be his running mate ("Jerry and Jesse"—it has a ring to it).

In the event, the impact of Mr Clinton's

gaffe was far smaller than many pundits had predicted. Mr Clinton was endorsed by Kurt Schmoke, the black mayor of Baltimore, and by the whole of the black political establishment in Atlanta. In both Maryland and Georgia he won the black vote easily. Offending Mr Jackson (which

Mr Clinton has done many times before) does not seem to have done the governor much obvious harm.

Working out why that might be is a fascinating exercise. In the absence of Mr Jackson, the message sent to black voters by the Democratic campaign is very different from that sent when he led his poor people's crusades in 1984 and 1988. Both Mr Clinton and Mr Tsongas believe that economic growth must precede the elimination of inequality; both rail against a Washington party establishment which they see as pledged to liberal special-interest groups (which is code, in some parts of the country, for a party that is too kind to blacks). Both have had associations with groups that are less than popular among Mr Jackson's supporters. Mr Clinton used to be chairman of the Democratic Leadership Council, a self-styled "moderate" pressure group. Mr Tsongas is a boardroom lawyer.

At the same time, both Mr Tsongas (with his message that all Americans are part of "the same team") and Mr Clinton (with his stress on the American "community") use language that is designed to convince blacks that they have not been forgotten.

Both men have made vehement and undoubtedly sincere condemnations of the racism that they believe is at the heart of the candidacy of Pat Buchanan: racism which they suspect will be a part of George Bush's own campaign in the autumn. In essence, both men are saying to blacks: "Economically, we are more conservative than the Democratic candidates, white or black, whom you have supported in the past. We are not promising anything special for you; we think that what is good for the American economy as a whole is also good for blacks. But we are no less committed to civil rights or opposed to racism than your heroes of years past."

How this line sells among blacks is going to be one of the most intriguing questions of 1992. It is hard to see how it is going to bring in many more black votes for the Democrats than in 1988, when Michael Dukakis won about 90% of the black vote. It may woo a few conservative blacks who voted for Mr Bush or abstained in 1988, but those numbers are not significant.

Of course, this year's strategy may appeal (indeed, may be designed to appeal) to white voters who did not much like Mr Bush but did not support Mr Dukakis either, because he was the candidate of Mr Jackson's party. But this boost from white voters could come at a price: its reverse may be that blacks simply do not go to the polls in the numbers that Democrats need to win the presidential election. Without Mr Jackson in the field, the turnout in Georgia on March 3rd was significantly lower than in 1988. If that is an omen for November—if large numbers of black voters just withdraw from politics entirely this year—it would be bad for the Democratic Party. It would be worse for America.

....

Blacks did not withdraw. Their turnout was higher than usual, and almost all voted Democratic.

Scandal of the year

MARCH 21ST, WASHINGTON, DC *The House banking scandal provided ammunition against congressmen that wounded them right until November, and could still be live*

THE baying pack has Congress between its teeth and it will not let go. In the coming weeks a reluctant House of Representatives will publish the list of nearly 300 current House members, and 59 former ones, who "floated" 8,000 cheques a year for the past three years at the House bank, now defunct. Next week, before the full list is published, the 19 current and five former members who are the most egregious culprits will be offered up to the hounds as a propitious first bundle of bones for scrunching.

That may not be enough. Most congressmen behave as if they believe Mencken's dictum that "the only way to success in American public life lies in flattering and kowtowing to the mob." Fully 100 members have played contrite, but angry Americans may want more. One ten-term Texan congressman, Charles Wilson, who floated 75-85 bad cheques, dared a small joke: "I called in the posse and gave myself up." His re-election in November now looks shaky.

Many think he will not be the only one to fall. The House of Representatives, for many years almost as comfortable for incumbents as Britain's House of Lords (where only death can dislodge a member), may be, from now on, a less secure resting place. Bob Beckel, a television commentator, bets that 100 representatives will be sent packing in the November elections, which would mark the biggest congressional clean-out since the Credit Mobilier scandal of 1872-73. But some caution is called for.

First, the saga does not involve cheque-kiting, which therefore lessens its claim to be called a scandal. A kited cheque, according to Webster's dictionary, is one "written for an amount greater than that on deposit and covered with another bogus cheque drawn on a different bank." Bogus cheques were not involved here; the House bank simply allowed members' cheques to "float" until cash was deposited to cover them. Nor is this a cheque-bouncing scandal. The scandal, if there is one, is that cheques were not bounced often enough. Even the House bank's lax staff, however, drew the line at one congressman who wrote 31 bounced cheques over the 39-month period to last October for a value of $180,937.87.

Second, no taxpayers were bilked, as

'NEXT OUT OF THE CHUTE, FOLKS, IS BIG TOM FOLEY ON RUBBER CHECK!'

they were in the savings-and-loan mess, nor were losses incurred. The House bank, which was closed at the end of 1991, was just a depository for members' pay cheques. The dupes were those congressmen who allowed their balances to cover the interest-free overdrafts of others. One former California congressman, a Democrat, used his overdraft to pay for his campaign.

Third, this is a scandal that American journalists have chosen to inflate, probably because they had little better to do. The hullaballoo began last October, when the General Accounting Office (GAO) criticised the bank's management. Yet this was far from the first GAO report. And congressmen had been floating cheques for the previous 161 years. This may be why even the most dogged publications have found it hard to keep up the impression of a full-blown scandal.

Other factors have helped to fuel the "perception" of scandal. Wishing to distance itself from the House, the Senate passed, in a 95-2 vote, what must be its most vacuous resolution ever: to wit, that the upper chamber had no equivalent bank. And on the House side Republicans are playing the partisan card for all it is worth, on the assumption that the law of averages will ensnare more Democrats than Republicans. Newt Gingrich, minority whip and gangleader of the righteous, has pointed to the procrastination of the House Speaker, Tom Foley, called it a cover-up, and demanded Mr Foley's head. Democrats, though tempted for a moment, declined to provide it.

Mr Gingrich himself has written 20 bad cheques, up from an original admission of one. He remains sanctimonious. Nor has his zeal diminished with the news on March 17th that three members of George Bush's cabinet, Dick Cheney, Lynn Martin and Edward Madigan, former congressmen all, had written a few bad cheques, too.

Despite this slight embarrassment, the whole furore fits the White House script for the November election, in which President Bush will blame all America's ills on a corrupt, recalcitrant and Democrat-controlled Congress. One Republican, Guy Vander Jagt, has ludicrously suggested that the scandal is "as serious as Watergate". Another, Jim Nussle, a first-term congressman, appeared on the House floor with a paper bag over his head in shame.

All this might seem farcical. Yet it has the effect of strengthening partisan lines in Congress, and of reinforcing what Norman Ornstein, at the American Enterprise Institute, calls its "psychological gridlock". This gridlock needs to be broken if the real scandal is to be put right: the refusal of American voters to give either Congress or the President the mandate to plug a budget deficit of outrageous proportions, which will lead to the giant bilking of future generations.

Charles Wilson kept his seat. In general, the scandal had less electoral impact than people had predicted. The budget deficit remained untouched.

H. Ross Peron

APRIL 4TH   *The campaign was remarkable for the emergence, withdrawal and re-emergence of Ross Perot. Our initial summing-up, though rude, proved accurate enough*

THE cartoons say it. In *USA Today*, he walks on the water; in the *Washington Post* he appears as Uncle Sam, a large mallet ready to crush the little Bush and Clinton bugs who cower at his feet. This saviour figure, H. Ross Perot, is in fact a short little man, with a yapping Texas drawl, sticking-out ears and a head like a bottle brush. But his myth makes a giant of him. Even the whisper of an independent Perot candidacy—and it is not yet much more than that—has the press at his heels and the Republicans, in a lather, shoring up their Texas defences.

Businessmen know Mr Perot as the man who founded Electronic Data Systems in 1962 with $1,000 and sold it to General Motors in 1984 for $2.6 billion. Ordinary Americans know him as the man who thumbed his nose at Hanoi by trying to run supplies to POWs, and at Iran by organising a commando raid to spring two employees out of jail. Equally impressive, he tried to take on the board of GM and make the company shrink, a policy that now looks prescient; and he struggled, with some success, to shake up the public schools in Texas.

Party labels have never stuck to Mr Perot. He is both the snappish little man fed up with government, and the brutish chief executive determined to run the country like a corporation. Sensible on the deficit (cutting it is his first priority) and on entitlements, he would also emasculate Congress by turning its tax-raising power over to the people. In a Perotist America the Leader would address the people; and the people, using computers linked to their television screens, would signal their desires directly to the man at the top.

Diffidently, Mr Perot says he will not announce his candidacy until the people call him. Providently, he has opened 100 telephone lines to the Draft Perot office in Dallas.

Twelve blind jurors

MAY 2ND, LOS ANGELES   *The worst race riots in America since the second world war caused few ripples elsewhere, least of all in the urban policies of the Bush administration*

APRIL 29th may well be remembered as the day that Southern California finally lost its reputation for tolerance and justice. For several weeks the city had been steeling itself for an expected string of guilty verdicts in the trial of four policemen who were filmed savagely beating a black motorist, Rodney King, last March. In the event, the jury's verdict—not guilty on ten of the 11 counts against the four men—proved still more devastating. By the end of the day, the scores of burning buildings throughout southern Los Angeles resembled oilfields ablaze in the Gulf war.

As *The Economist* went to press, five people had died and over 100 were injured. Thousands of homes were without power as fire engines, escorted by police cars (to protect the firemen), thundered around the city. Downtown Los Angeles looked like a battlefield. The first place to erupt was South Central Los Angeles, a depressed black area, famous for the machine-gun-toting gangs of "Boyz N' The Hood". Other riots and fires broke out around the city. Many of the rioters were barely in their teens and only half of them were black. Robbery appears to have been as much a motive as racial grievance.

In 1965, riots in Watts, a relatively small black district of the city, led to more than 30 deaths. This time damage was spread out over a far greater area, but with less lethal concentration. Whatever the final tally, the pictures of rioting thugs pulling motorists out of cars and beating them may haunt Los Angeles as long as those of Mr King being kicked and beaten.

California's governor, Pete Wilson, made the National Guard available, pointing out as he did so that the rioting will not help Mr King. But it is not difficult to understand the widespread fury among blacks at the verdict. From the start, the trial of the four officers took an unorthodox course. It was moved out of Los Angeles to Ventura county, a prosperous conservative suburb. After a lengthy search for a jury, the seven men and five women selected included no blacks.

The prosecution relied heavily on an amateur film which shows the officers beating, kicking and firing a 50,000-volt stun-gun into Mr King. Defence lawyers tried to limit its impact by slowing it down into a frame-by-frame analysis; but one of the policemen, Theodore Briseno, in effective testified against the others, calling the beating "a holocaust of batons, boots and blood", which he tried to stop.

By the end of the trial, experts predicted that Mr Briseno might well be acquitted. He was—but, to most observers' surprise, the jury also completely acquitted two other officers, Stacey Koon and Timothy Wind. For reasons best known to itself, the jury was unable to decide whether Laurence Powell, who was seen hitting Mr King 43 times and sent a computer message saying that he "hadn't beaten anybody that bad in a long time", had used excessive

Los Angeles goes up

force. Mr Powell may face a retrial on that charge. Mr King's civil case against the Los Angeles Police Department (LAPD), from which he is seeking over $80m in damages, will also continue. Governor Wilson, who admitted he was surprised by the verdict, said that federal lawyers were also looking at the case on a civil-rights basis.

At the centre of the city's longer-term future is its police department and two men: its controversial chief, Daryl Gates, who has agreed to step down in June, and his recently chosen successor, Willie Williams, formerly police commissioner in Philadelphia. Mr Gates, who has run the police department as if it was a private army, retains the support of his men, but he has long

since lost the confidence of minority groups, making him an anachronism in such a diverse city. Mr Williams, who is black, has promised to set things straight.

The beating of Mr King led to a long-overdue investigation into the Los Angeles Police Department by an independent commission chaired by Warren Christopher, Jimmy Carter's deputy secretary of state. It concluded that the department was unnecessarily racist and brutal—and urged a variety of reforms, including making the police more accountable to the city's politicians. In June many of those reforms will be put before Los Angeles voters in an initiative called Charter Initiative F. Characteristically, Mr Gates has delayed his resignation to June in order to fight the initiative which Mr Williams supports. Mr Gates has also made much of the fact that Mr Williams has not, like himself, got a university degree.

Mr Williams is rightly determined to introduce community policing. That looks a fearsome job—and not just because of the events of the past year. The biggest challenge in a city as sprawling as Los Angeles may well be economic. Pundits guess that putting more policemen on the streets could increase the police department's budget by as much as 50%. The city of Los Angeles faces a budget deficit of close to $200m: it is keeping the police force at its current level only by raiding its community redevelopment agency, and raising taxes will anger voters. But if the citizens of Los Angeles want a decent police department, they will have to pay for it.

By the end of the year, large parts of South Central remained in ruins. Only a fraction of the promised federal aid had appeared, and no extra police on the beat.

California failing

AUGUST 8TH, LOS ANGELES *America's largest state, buffeted by the economic slowdown, limped through the year with the help of drastic budget cuts*

BY ANY reasonable standard—be it efficiency, popularity or even electoral interest—the government of the most advanced state of the most powerful country in the world is failing. For over a month California has been unable to pass a budget. Like a gambler fallen on hard times, the state has been reduced to handing out IOUs to its creditors. Since July 1st it has issued $1.6 billion-worth of these demeaning scraps of paper.

Sad to say, many Californians greeted this week's refusal by some banks to honour the state's IOUs (warrants, as they are properly known) with an ironic cheer. State employees left holding the warrants may not see the grisly logic, but in theory the banks' decision should at last force a deal to remedy the state's $11 billion budget deficit. The state's unpopular Republican governor, Pete Wilson, and his even less-loved opponents in the Democrat-run leg-

islature, will have to compromise.

Mr Wilson has a simple explanation for the budget crisis humbling his state's government: the poor. "Welfare", he says, "is the prime engine driving California's perennial over-spending." The number of welfare recipients, he says, is growing four times faster than the state's population.

Despite $7 billion in budget cuts last year, further enormous cuts in state services are inevitable. On education, the Democrats and Republicans are simply arguing over how much to cut: the governor wants a reduction of $2.3 billion, but the legislature is holding out for cuts of less than half that amount. The argument over health and welfare is more complicated: the Democrats object both to the extent of Mr Wilson's reductions (such as cutting off money for dental and mental-health programmes for the poor) and to his plan to shift more of the responsibility for such services to local government, which they believe will lead to services disappearing altogether.

In the short term, Mr Wilson may have the stronger nerve. Only a few of the more liberal Democrats are talking about tax increases. Many of those worst hit by the banks' refusal to cash the IOUs will be Democrats rather than Republicans—increasing the pressure on the Democrats to compromise. Some of the governor's supporters talk of toughing it out until the legislative elections in November, when voters will also consider an initiative, sponsored by Mr Wilson, which calls for even greater cuts in welfare and gives the governor more power over the budget.

Mr Wilson, who was treated like a leper by his own party when he agreed to $7 billion-worth of tax increases last year, has come up with a new system of trickle-down taxation. Just as the federal government has been shifting burdens on to the states, so California is devolving power—and costs—to the cities and counties.

The problem dates back to a 1978 initiative, Proposition 13, which halved local property taxes and hobbled local government in the process. In its wake the state government rushed in to salvage services like welfare programmes and county hospitals, which might otherwise have collapsed. Easy then. Today, with more welfare cases and less prosperous times, Mr Wilson is intent on moving some social-security programmes back to local government.

He started the process last year. Now he plans to go further, handing back many more programmes and also granting local governments the right to raise money through sales taxes (a strategy which means that they rather than he will have to carry the accompanying stigma). Cities may be able to persuade voters to pay for the "popular" programmes they administer, like the police and fire departments; but counties, which are responsible for most of the big welfare programmes, have a harder task. All of which points to the need for radical reform of the state's governmental structure. The po-litical map of California is a mess: there are 58 counties, 468 cities, 1,012 school districts and some 6,000 other special districts to deal with anything from treating sewage to air quality. Many of these organisations were born of a healthy belief in strong local government; now they tend to be merely confusing. Various voter initiatives have made that map still messier. Thanks to a 1988 initiative, 40% of the state's general fund has to go to education. Nearly as much again is mandated to various health and welfare programmes.

Dismal politicos

But radical reform is unlikely. Californians are not in the mood to trust any of their politicians. Mr Wilson's approval rating is now a dismal 20%—a figure that still leaves him twice as popular as the state legislature. Thanks to new limits on terms in the legislature, Willie Brown, the Democratic speaker and for many years arguably the most powerful black administrator in America, is no longer a permanent fixture.

Look more closely and the alienation of voters from traditional politics runs deeper and wider. In the six poorest council districts of Los Angeles, an area with 1.4m inhabitants, a mere 37,000 people voted in recent council elections. Only 125,000 out of the state's 5m registered Republicans give money to their party. By contrast, 1m Californians signed a petition for Ross Perot and 500,000 of them stump up $30 to belong to Greenpeace.

It is fashionable in Sacramento, the state capital, to blame such apathy (like the problems of the budget) on the state's crumbling economy, which, by some measures, is stuck in its worst recession since the war. Unemployment stands at 9.5%—higher than in any other industrialised state. California has lost 600,000 jobs in the past two years—roughly a third of all the jobs lost in America.

This makes a nice excuse, but not a particularly convincing one. California's recession may be bad, but it is not so much worse than those in other states. Moreover, in past recessions, Californians turned to politicians to get them out of trouble. As Kevin Starr, the author of a forthcoming book on California in the 1930s points out, the state's voters approved a host of huge publicly financed projects, including the Golden Gate Bridge and the Shasta Dam water system.

Mr Starr argues that the state has since lost its "positive progressive mindset". That change has little to do with the budget or the recession. Instead it stems from Californians' growing contempt for, and steady disengagement from, politics and politicians.

Which raises the most important question of all: do Californians really want better government? So far the only reaction to the budget debacle has come from a few well-organised lobby groups—even though the cuts envisaged by Mr Wilson will affect millions of people. Bill Bradley, a Sacramento commentator, argues that in California, politics has become "another consumer market—and a luxury one at that". Many Californians prefer to buy their politics outside government from groups like Greenpeace or even their local housing association. Millions of others do not bother to shop at all.

In this sense at least, this year's budget crisis may represent a nadir rather than just another chapter in an increasingly unread book. For many Californians it will come as a rude shock when their salary or income-tax refund cannot be cashed. If the inefficiency of Mr Wilson and the legislature can teach the state one small lesson—that people who do not vote should not complain when their government's cheques bounce—then it may have a brighter side.

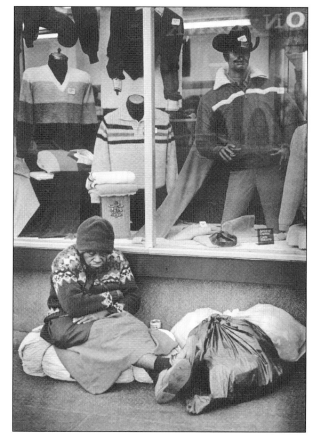

Budget-buster

Country style

AUGUST 22ND *Country-and-western music enjoyed an unexpected vogue as the white answer to rap. Even politicians joined in*

GEORGE BUSH claims to be a devotee of the Nitty Ditty Nitty Gritty Great Bird, Bush-speak for the Nitty Gritty Dirt Band, a country-and-western outfit. James Baker, his friend and lieutenant, turns up to formal dinners in cowboy boots and stetson. Not to be outdone, Bill Clinton and Al Gore take every opportunity to prance around in western wear, prattling about their love of fiddle and steel guitar.

Predictably, the politicians are simply two-stepping where the public has two-stepped before. All of a sudden, country-and-western is the hippest thing in America, as popular with city sophisticates as with rural rednecks.

The music charts are full of people with first names like Vince (Gill), Randy (Travis), Clint (Black) and Billy Ray (Cyrus). Garth Brooks, a sort of stetson-wearing Elton John, is outselling Michael Jackson and Guns N' Roses. Investment bankers try to outperform each other at the achy breaky dance. To accommodate them, discos throughout the country are being converted into dance halls.

Country-and-western entrepreneurs are busy making hay, flogging cowboy gear, coaching novices in the two-step, and generally glamorising the country lifestyle. *Country America*, a magazine, has doubled its circulation to 1m in two years. The Nashville Network, a cable-television channel devoted to all things country, has 50m subscribers.

The popularity of country music came as something of a surprise to the music moguls of Hollywood and Manhattan. The introduction in 1991 of an electronic method that could accurately measure record sales—the charts had hitherto been based largely on oral reports—immediately boosted the number of country records in the top 200. It seems that 30-40-year-olds (who account for about 30% of record buyers) had been turning to country in their millions, deafened by heavy metal and revolted by rap.

Businessmen quickly set to work turning a boomlet into boom, refashioning country-and-western to appeal to a more cosmopolitan crowd. The rising stars in the country firmament now include a Canadian feminist (k.d. lang) and a black cardiologist (Cleve Frankland). Country has increased its share of record sales from

Pity about the gritty ditty

8.8% in 1990 to 12.5% today and Coca-Cola and McDonald's are hiring country singers to sell their products.

The unacknowledged strategists of the United States are now more likely to be country crooners than poets. "If I want a little free advice about Saddam Hussein", George Bush once said, "I listen to country music." Cheering thought.

God and man

AUGUST 22ND, HOUSTON *The Republican convention attacked the Democrats as despisers of family life, scorners of American values and rejecters of God. The theme went down so badly in the country that it was soon abandoned*

"IF MY people, who are called by my name, shall humble themselves and pray, and turn from their wicked ways," said the platform speaker, and 3,000 voices then joined him, "then shall I hear from heaven, and will forgive their sin, and will heal their land." And with that passage from the scriptures (II Chronicles, 7:14), the God and Country rally on the first day of the Republicans' convention in Houston broke into a thunderous chorus of Amen! and Halleluia!

The rally, organised by Pat Robertson, a televangelist turned businessman who was a Republican candidate in 1988, featured 1950s crooner Pat Boone and vice-president Dan Quayle. It was, without any doubt, the most fervent and triumphant meeting of the convention. Children by the score were hoisted aloft; pregnant women beamed with heartland fecundity; home video-cameras whirred away. And through it all came the message that the evangelical movement, once thought to have been sidelined by the failure of Mr Robertson's candidacy four years ago, was well and truly back.

The evidence for that, and the source of the triumphalism at the rally, was in the Republicans' platform. In the week before the convention, evangelicals had won battle after battle to get language to their liking in the platform. They won not just on abortion (against) and school prayer (for), but on references to "the Judeo-Christian heritage that informs our culture" and to the party's belief in the American people as "free men and women with faith in God". The platform committee spent much time debating whether it was appropriate to say that America was the "last best hope for man on earth", since the evangelicals argued that Christ was (on that battle between America and God, America won).

From the podium, speaker after speaker pointed out that the word God did not appear in the Democrats' platform.

Four years ago few would have predicted that a Republican Party led by George Bush, an Episcopalian, would fall so heavily under the influence of the religious right. Although, by Mr Robertson's estimate, 83% of evangelicals supported Mr Bush in 1988, they have had scant encouragement from him since. Mr Robertson says that the White House personnel office has blocked the appointment of evangelicals to important administration positions. But the Republicans know where their base is, and the president's electoral weakness makes it all the more urgent to mobilise their keener supporters. Mr Quayle's campaign this year for "family values" and against the "cultural elite" was aimed squarely at evangelicals. He told the God and Country rally that it "wasn't me" his opponents were laughing at; "it was you". They went wild.

Bill Clinton will be a harder candidate to demonise than the genuinely secular

Michael Dukakis was as the Democratic candidate in 1988. A southerner who can use all the cadences of the Baptist preachers whose sermons he lapped up as a child, Mr Clinton mentioned God six times in his acceptance speech at his party's convention and quoted from the scriptures too. Mr Robertson, needless to say, does not think much of Mr Clinton's appeal to evangelicals. He said this week that Mr Clinton's use of the term "New Covenant" was implying that he was "like a new messiah". "The only person in our history who has used that term before", said Mr Robertson, "is Jesus Christ."

In November, though, will all these claims and counter-claims of godliness and blasphemy mean much? Many people in Houston thought they would not. Some see the evangelicals' success in drafting the platform as a moment of hubris rather than triumph. Gary Wills, a historian, argues that the evangelicals have overreached themselves; where once they spoke for more people than themselves in articulating a sense of outrage at the moral relativism of the 1960s, now they are trying to force a reluctant nation into their own narrow moral confines.

If that is so, the reaction will not be long

delayed. At the Republican convention itself, those in favour of abortion rights were remarkably upbeat about the future. They believe the party will never again tie itself to such an absolutist position. Bill Weld, the governor of Massachusetts, spoke from the podium in favour of abortion rights—and he is undoubtedly one of the party's coming men.

Even though the evangelicals may find

it harder to corral the Republican Party in future, they are not going to disappear either. The religious commitment of its people is still one of the things that sets America apart from other modern democracies; the number of spick-and-span churches in any small American town astounds visitors from abroad. America is still the only modern democracy where random twiddling of the radio dial so often brings the voice of preachers into one's car. The very fact that such modern men as Mr Clinton and Al Gore, his running mate, feel duty-bound to stress their religious credentials suggests that the nation is not yet ready for openly secular leaders.

The question at issue is the one that has dogged America since the Pilgrims arrived. It is whether a privately godly people is duty-bound to establish institutions and principles of public government that reflect its godliness. The argument between those who argue that God must be in the government and those who argue he must not goes back and forth, with first one side and then the other triumphant. But given the fervour at the God and Country rally, it is difficult to believe that the secularists will have things all their own way as the century draws to its close.

Ears 2: The Return

SEPTEMBER 19TH, WASHINGTON, DC *The first stirrings of Ross Perot's return began to be heard in the land*

HE MAY have left the race, sniping and licking his wounds, but Ross Perot has a way of lingering on. His supporters have continued to file petitions on his behalf, and he is now on the ballot in every state. Mr Perot still keeps 64 campaign offices round the country, and spends about $500,000 a month maintaining them. The latest ABC News/*Washington Post* poll reveals that 16% of voters still plan to vote for him. And Mr Perot himself, infuriated by the tag of "quitter", has been making appearances again. On September 15th he told the *Los Angeles Times* that if neither candidate did anything serious about the deficit, he would have to re-enter the race. That is a condition more than likely to be met.

Failing a re-entry by their hero, Mr Perot's legions have been hoping that someone else can carry the banner for them. They have set up a centrist third party, the Independence Party, which will

be launched formally in Washington in October. By 1994, they hope to be fielding candidates. So far, there is one plank: fiscal responsibility. If Mr Perot runs after all, he will be their man; if he does not, they hope to inherit his organisation. In any event, they need his endorsement.

The party approached Lowell Weicker, the independent governor of Connecticut, to be its chairman. Mr Weicker said No, but remains its most prominent supporter. Another leading light is Theodore Lowi, a professor of political science at Cornell. Mr Lowi believes that the middle class is still enraged, still feels ignored, and needs only a political vehicle to express itself. Polls taken by Gordon Black, another founder-member, suggest that as many as 50% of voters would seriously consider switching to a third party.

Meanwhile, Mr Perot's deficit-cutting plans have been taken up in other quarters. Paul Tsongas, a rival of Bill Clinton for the Democratic nomination, is joining a Re-

publican senator, Warren Rudman (of Gramm-Rudman fame, now retiring), and Peter Petersen, a banker who served as Richard Nixon's commerce secretary, to launch a campaign to bring the deficit down. They started on Monday, September 14th. The goal, says Mr Tsongas, is "to provide a political constituency for the hard choices".

That constituency used to belong to a small, tough Texan. Mention that to Mr Tsongas and his aides, and they smile in an awkward way. They acknowledge, however, that many of the proposals put forward by the Concord Coalition are very similar to those proposed in Mr Perot's plan to cut the deficit, which (in its paperback version) is now at the top of the bestseller lists. A 50-cent rise in the petrol tax over five years; a capital-gains-tax cut for long-term stock holdings; higher taxes on tobacco, social security, Medicare and health-insurance benefits; a 15% cut in federal discretionary spending. All proposed by people who, as luck would have it, are no longer running for office.

The Concord Coalition has also linked

up with a grassroots effort called "Lead . . . or Leave", which aims to energise the young and restore fiscal responsibility to government. It is waging a campaign to get all House and Senate candidates, challengers and incumbents alike, to sign a pledge promising that they will not run for re-election if the federal deficit is not reduced by half in the next four years. So far, 61 main-party candidates have signed.

Will voters follow after them, and register their fury too? Mr Tsongas thinks they will. Many, presumably, will be the same people who signed petitions urging Mr Perot to run for president. They now have a choice of champions.

Mr Perot won 19% of the popular vote. After the election, nothing more was heard either from him or from the other "independent" parties; but they may re-emerge with time. The deficit continued to grow.

A sip of something good

OCTOBER 10TH, NEWARK, NEW JERSEY *After a depressing year on the race-relations front, we found a development to celebrate—in Newark*

WHERE CAN you find your groceries in the centre of a city? Over the past two decades, supermarkets have fled to huge suburban malls. Inner-city residents, particularly those without cars, have come to rely on "mom and pop" convenience stores, generally defined as shops of less than 6,000 square feet, for their everyday purchases of food. But these stores rarely sell healthy foods, offer little variety, and can be both dirty and over-priced.

Studies by the Department of Labour have found that the poorest 20% of Americans spend 34% of their after-tax income on food; the richest 20% spend 8%. A 1991 study by New York city's Department of Consumer Affairs found shoppers in poor neighbourhoods paying 8.8% more for the same groceries than those in middle-income and upper-income areas. And most of what they buy is not particularly good for them. A study by Nielsen Marketing Research in 1990 found that the four items most frequently purchased by low-income households were frozen pizza, pork rinds, beef patties and corn dogs. What the poor buy reflects what they are offered.

Supermarkets began fleeing to the suburbs in the early 1960s, following their customers. Between 1970 and 1988 40% of America's central cities lost people. In the same period Los Angeles, Chicago, Brooklyn and Manhattan lost almost half their supermarkets. A study of 28 large cities by the Conference of Mayors in 1991 found eight (including Boston, Miami, San Antonio and Minneapolis) reporting a decline in the number of supermarkets in poor neighbourhoods over the previous year.

High labour costs push them out, as well as high insurance premiums, low sales volume, high levels of stock loss (from pilfering, pricing and checkout errors, and damage), high rents and low profits. And new supermarkets, if anybody is thinking of putting one up, need site approval, which often takes twice as long in cities as it does in the suburbs.

Newark, New Jersey, presents both the worst face of inner-city decline and a ray of hope. About a third of the city's 275,000 people are on welfare. The supermarket exodus from the inner city was made complete by five days of riots in 1967. Every one of the city's supermarkets was looted and ultimately destroyed. Not one was rebuilt.

Three-quarters of the people in the city's central ward do not have cars, and there are no direct bus links to markets in outlying areas; so residents fell back on Newark's convenience stores. These rarely sold fresh fruit, vegetables or meat, and lack of competition and high labour costs led to prices 38% higher than at suburban supermarkets. At the beginning of each month, when the welfare cheques were sent out, prices would be put up another notch.

After some years of this, the city's New Community Corporation began to float the idea of a suburban-style supermarket. In 1982, New Community began working with Supermarkets General, a supermarket chain based in Woodbridge, New Jersey, to open a store in central Newark. After eight years of litigation and money-scrounging, the result was a 48,000 square-foot Pathmark supermarket with a doughnut shop, print shop and food emporium. New Community owns two-thirds of the store, and has put up all the money. Supermarkets General owns a third, and provides the management and other expertise.

To the surprise of many executives in the supermarket industry, the Newark store is one of the most profitable in its division. It is expected to make a profit of $1.2m this financial year. Some of its success is unsurprising. It has, after all, no competitors, and no fewer than 93,000 people live within a mile of the store. Because it is in an enterprise zone, taxes on non-food items are 3.5% instead of the usual 7%. But the managers have also responded to demand. When surveys showed that 93% of the store's customers were black, the managers brought in collard greens, liver pudding and tongue, items that seldom appear in suburban stores. They also offered clean and well-lit fresh-fish and vegetable departments.

The store also strives to maintain strong ties with the community. It sponsors on-site tests for diabetes, hypertension and high blood pressure (all of which afflict blacks more than others), and holds an annual festival in the car park. The store is on a local bus route and, for $5, offers customers a shuttle service. Behind its barbed-wire fence, with a single entrance manned by security guards, this—as shoppers say—is probably the safest place in Newark.

Other cities may follow. Fiesta supermarkets in Houston and Vons in Los Angeles have announced plans to open stores in inner cities. First National Supermarkets of Ohio has spent $28m over the past five years to open or refurbish stores in central Cleveland, and Dominick's opened an inner-city supermarket in Chicago's South Shore two years ago as part of a redevelopment plan. The Food Marketing Institute has set up a taskforce to identify potential inner-city supermarket sites and to help communities with education and training. Profits are there for the taking.

Feeding the masses

No margin for error

NOVEMBER 7TH, LITTLE ROCK *The Democrats won back the White House, after 12 years, less on their own merits than because of huge frustration with George Bush and the status quo*

IN THE end it was very close. Despite crushing George Bush in the electoral college, where he won 370 votes to the president's 168, Bill Clinton has won the White House by a far smaller margin than most had expected. His edge in the popular vote over Mr Bush was just five points–the closest result since 1976. Had Mr Bush won all the states in which he trailed Mr Clinton by just four points, he would have had a bare majority (274 votes) in the electoral college.

No more than five days before the election, a narrow Bush victory seemed quite possible. The Clinton camp was in a tizzy as internal polls showed the race tightening; the challenger was convinced that something was going wrong with his campaign but, unhelpfully, could not decide what. On October 29th both candidates travelled round Michigan, perhaps the fiercest contest of all. At lunchtime Mr Clinton was at a heavily black rally in downtown Detroit. At the same time Mr Bush was just a few miles away, in suburban Macomb county, home of the famous (and white) "Reagan Democrats" who have fled the city. There he held one of the most spirited rallies of his campaign. By the time his entourage had reached Grand Rapids, in the west of the state, that evening, those with him were starting to think that he might pull off an amazing upset.

It was not to be. Mr Bush's team, with some bitterness, think their momentum was halted by the revelation on October 30th of details in the indictment of Caspar Weinberger, Ronald Reagan's defence secretary, on charges related to the Iran-contra scandal. Contemporaneous notes made by Mr Weinberger, newly released, made it plain that Mr Bush had known all along of the plan to swap arms for hostages. The Bush team, in their own eyes, wasted a vital day replying to the charge.

But even if the Weinberger memo had not been made public, the polls might once more have turned against Mr Bush. In one of the many bizarre moments of the campaign, he wasted Halloween by spending the whole day on a train trip through one state—Wisconsin—with just 11 electoral college votes. In the last two days he

picked up the pace again, but his speed was nothing like Mr Clinton's, who, starting at dawn in Philadelphia on the eve of the election, campaigned for 29 hours across eight states. The trip took him from within a few miles of the Canadian border in shivering Michigan, where a grunge-rock band played in an airport hangar, to the edge of Mexico in McAllen, Texas, where 12,000 Latinos came out on a balmy night to shout "Adelante con Clinton" while the press corps gulped frozen margaritas. The Dem-

Got it

ocrat lost just one state—Texas, and that by only three points—of the eight that he visited. Who says campaigning makes no difference?

Although much conventional wisdom will now be abandoned, one bit should not be. Despite having two southerners on the ticket for the first time since the Civil War, the Democrats came nowhere near to capturing the "new" Republican stronghold in the south. Mr Bush won seven of the 11 states of the Confederacy. Outside the home bases of Mr Clinton and Al Gore, his running-mate, the Democrats won just two southern states—Georgia, by one

point, and Louisiana, by four.

By contrast, the Democrats swept New England, the first time they had done so since 1964, and built on the strength that Michael Dukakis had demonstrated four years ago in the Rocky Mountains and the Pacific Coast. In addition to Hawaii, Washington state and Oregon, all won by Mr Dukakis, Mr Clinton took Colorado, New Mexico, Montana, Nevada and—the biggest prize of all—California. Mr Clinton's brand of modern Democratic politics, suspicious of government and in favour of entrepreneurship, has always seemed to have its natural base not in the south but in the west. On the day that mattered, the westerners obliged.

There were two bits of conventional wisdom that now deserve to be dumped. At the beginning of the year, as the 1990 census results were analysed, it was fashionable to say that America had become a "nation of suburbs"; and to conclude that, since suburban voters disliked both taxes and cities (for which, read places where poor blacks live), the Republicans would be the political beneficiary of a demographic shift.

Not so. Mr Clinton won classically "suburban" states like New Jersey, Connecticut, Michigan, Ohio, Illinois and Missouri, and all but Ohio by comfortable margins. In the north-east and along the Great Lakes, his message that the economy was in a mess was far more powerful than Mr Bush's attack on him as a tax-and-spend liberal. As far as the exit polls could reveal, "social" issues—like abortion and fear of crime—played virtually no part in the campaign, except possibly in California, where women candidates picked up 70% of voters favouring choice on abortion. Yet it was these issues that were supposed to keep the Reagan Democrats for ever in the Republican camp.

The second bit of dumped conventional wisdom concerns the youth vote. For reasons that it would take a psychologist to explain, Ronald Reagan was wildly popular with young voters. Mr Bush initially benefited from that, winning 52% of the votes of 18-29-year-olds in 1988. This year he got just 33%, whereas Mr Clinton had 44%. Some people may wonder how Mr Clinton and Mr Gore, two rather stiff, unhip, middle-aged men, came to be heroes of the young, but there surely is no mystery about that: many young people

The swing to the Democrats

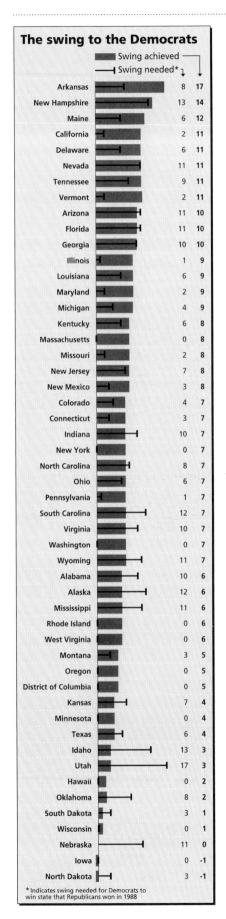

Swing achieved
Swing needed*

State	Achieved	Needed*
Arkansas	8	17
New Hampshire	13	14
Maine	6	12
California	2	11
Delaware	6	11
Nevada	11	11
Tennessee	9	11
Vermont	2	11
Arizona	11	10
Florida	11	10
Georgia	10	10
Illinois	1	9
Louisiana	6	9
Maryland	2	9
Michigan	4	9
Kentucky	6	8
Massachusetts	0	8
Missouri	2	8
New Jersey	7	8
New Mexico	3	8
Colorado	4	7
Connecticut	3	7
Indiana	10	7
New York	0	7
North Carolina	8	7
Ohio	6	7
Pennsylvania	1	7
South Carolina	12	7
Virginia	10	7
Washington	0	7
Wyoming	11	7
Alabama	10	6
Alaska	12	6
Mississippi	11	6
Rhode Island	0	6
West Virginia	0	6
Montana	3	5
Oregon	0	5
District of Columbia	0	5
Kansas	7	4
Minnesota	0	4
Texas	6	4
Idaho	13	3
Utah	17	3
Hawaii	0	2
Oklahoma	8	2
South Dakota	3	1
Wisconsin	0	1
Nebraska	11	0
Iowa	0	-1
North Dakota	3	-1

*Indicates swing needed for Democrats to win state that Republicans won in 1988

Short of a sweep

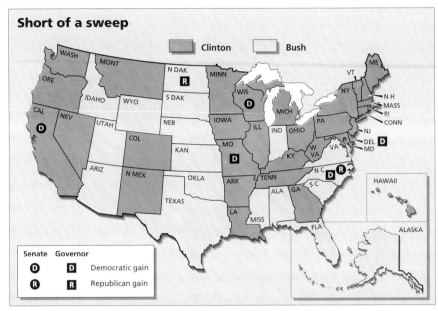

Clinton / Bush

Senate Governor
D D Democratic gain
R R Republican gain

like to pretend they are hip, but they would like a job even more. Young Americans may mildly have approved of Mr Clinton's appearances on MTV and (with shades and saxophone) on the Arsenio Hall show, but the bigger truth is that they lack the sunny optimism that used to be their birthright. Mr Bush, at bottom, is a man with an unquenchable faith in the continuing greatness of America. This year that message did not sell.

Even more than Mr Clinton, the candidate who told the electors that America was in decline was Ross Perot, the independent billionaire candidate from Texas. He did phenomenally well, winning 19% of the popular vote, the best third-party result since Teddy Roosevelt's Bull Moose run in 1912. Mr Perot won 20% of the vote or more in 31 states, and pushed Mr Clinton into third place in Utah.

His vote was distributed in a fascinating way. The policy with which he is most closely associated is his effort in support of Vietnam veterans and prisoners of war. Yet he did poorly in the militaristic south, and best in Maine (which had shown its independent spirit in February by backing Jerry Brown for the Democratic candidacy). In no fewer than 20 states he improved on the 22% he won in Texas. He did remarkably well not just in the mountain west, where he has always shown strength, but across the whole of the "northern tier" from Massachusetts (23%) to Washington state (24%). A decent rule of thumb is that wherever Mr Dukakis did well, so did Mr Perot. Of all the oddities of the election campaign, the oddest is the idea that Mr Perot would be able to mine the seam of Scandinavian/Anglo-Saxon concern for "good government", extending westwards from New England along the Canadian

border, that Mr Dukakis unearthed.

At his victory speech in Little Rock, delivered in bitter cold before a crowd of 50,000 who had waited for hours, Mr Clinton made a special appeal to Perot supporters. They, like those who supported Mr Clinton, presumably feel that the country now desires "change". This being America, much that is essential will not change; the country is going to remain God-fearing, patriotic and capitalist. But there will be some shifts in economic and social policy, and the principal task of Mr Clinton now is to prepare for them.

The Progressive Policy Institute (PPI), Mr Clinton's in-house think-tank, is preparing a briefing book for him called "Mandate for Change". That title touches the nub of the problem, for a president with just 43% of the vote does not have a mandate for much. Mr Clinton's job now is to pull off the same sleight of hand that Margaret Thatcher managed in Britain in 1979: to transform the support of 43% (or, in her case, 44%) of the voters into a ringing endorsement of his programme. This will not be easy; traditional Democratic interest groups and congressional Democrats do not have at all the same agenda as the bright young things in the PPI. Ominously for what Mr Clinton calls "new" Democrats, exit polls show that his shilly-shallying on the North American Free Trade Agreement was popular in the vital Great Lakes states.

Still, at least the Democrats can work out their differences in the warmth of government. No such luck for the Republicans, who now seem doomed to engage in public blood-letting. The religious right, vaguely represented by the vice-president, Dan Quayle (who carefully kept his nose clean during the campaign), will say that the party is not conservative enough. The "progressive" conservatives, led by Jack Kemp, Mr Bush's housing secretary, will try to appeal to black and Latino voters. The libertarians, led perhaps by Bill Weld, the governor of Massachusetts, will try to argue–as Mr Weld did to some effect at the Houston convention–that government should keep its hand out of Americans' wallets and its nose out of their bedrooms.

Few Republicans, if any, will argue for the woolly, business-minded, internationalist conservatism which, if he believed in anything, was at the core of Mr Bush. He will now be cast as the party's pariah. It is a cruel fate for a man who, whatever his other failings, handled the momentous diplomatic challenges of the end of the cold war with tact and finesse. But such is the lot of losers: even those who lost as close an election as that of 1992.

Ignore touch paper and retire

NOVEMBER 28TH, WASHINGTON, DC *Once George Bush was defeated, the economy began to show the signs of life he had always maintained were there*

IT WAS first billed as an economic summit to rival Gerald Ford's, the one that promised to Whip Inflation Now. Then Bill Clinton's people saw that summits which fed unrealisable expectations served no one. Robert Reich, the co-ordinator of Mr Clinton's economics team, pulling cowl over head, now speaks of the summit as a "retreat".

Whatever eventually takes place in Little Rock on December 14th and 15th, it was predicated upon Mr Clinton inheriting a moribund economy. His first days as president were going to kick the economy into life with a $20 billion public-works programme and an investment-tax credit (ITC). Fortunately, it is now hard for Mr Clinton to claim that the economy is any longer in the dismal state he once described: so hard, that on November 25th he said he might have to think again about his stimulus package. Signs of recovery are coming, if not thick and fast, at least quite steadily. In October orders for durable goods rose by 3.9%. This month the Conference Board's index of consumer confidence has leapt, suggesting that the growth in retail sales since the summer (see chart) can be extended.

Hopes of recovery have come before, only to be dashed. Companies and consumers have had to bear a heavy load of debt. They have also faced bankers unwilling to lend much money. This is why present bank-lending figures are so encouraging. Banks provided $11 billion in new loans in September, the highest monthly figure for over 20 months. The broad money supply, measured by M2, has risen strongly for more than two months, almost back into its target range (see chart).

Final confirmation of a recovery came on November 25th, when the figure for GDP growth in the third quarter was revised up to an annual 3.9% compared with the second quarter. Plenty of economists expected the initial estimate of 2.7% to be revised downwards. But the economy showed strong and broad growth—in exports, stocks (inventories), consumer spending and business investment. The economy had not grown that much in any quarter since the last months of Ronald Reagan's presidency. George Bush must feel sick.

The debate about fiscal stimulus should now fade. The bond markets, for one, would not tolerate a large package if growth continues. Moreover, after cutting interest rates for nearly three years, the next move of the Federal Reserve may well be to tighten monetary policy. Having cut inflation to 3%, it does not want to ruin that record with a widening budget deficit.

The deficit is the most pressing problem, as the OECD's new report on the American economy highlights so well. The 1992 fiscal year is set to produce a deficit of 5.5% of GDP. Stripping out cyclical factors and such transitory factors as the cost of deposit insurance still leaves a structural deficit of 3% of GDP. The deficit soaks up three-fifths of net private saving, which, at 4.6%, is already chronically low. The OECD suggests a six-point list for wiping out the structural deficit, including capping health spending, taxing social security and raising the petrol tax by 25 cents a gallon. This list does not even include the contentious issues of introducing a value-added tax or raising income taxes.

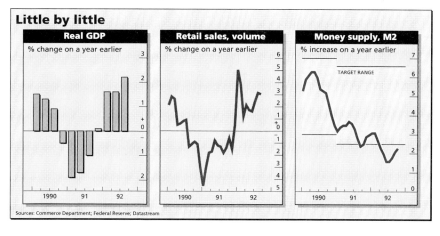

Little by little

Real GDP — % change on a year earlier

Retail sales, volume — % change on a year earlier

Money supply, M2 — % increase on a year earlier — TARGET RANGE

Sources: Commerce Department; Federal Reserve; Datastream

American values

The ideas that once held America together seem to be forcing it apart. Can the centre hold?

AS EXPERIMENTS go, the United States is a risky one: a nation of individuals held together not by blood, but by language, aspiration and an idea. That idea, expressed in the declaration of independence, is "that all men are created equal, and endowed by their Creator with certain inalienable rights, among them life, liberty and the pursuit of happiness." Fine words, better philosophy; and a hell of a creed to live up to. Lincoln himself asked whether "any nation so conceived and so dedicated, can long endure"; and Americans go on wondering.

In this election year, the symptoms of doubt are everywhere. Many are caused by a new nervousness about the strength of American democracy itself. The Soviet Union provided both an enemy and a system with which Americans could make proud and unquestioning comparisons. That evil empire gone, America is starting to recognise the flaws in its own system: among them endemic violence, racial inequality and political indifference. As new democracies look to America, cheerfully parroting its values, Americans no longer feel sure they project them with the confidence they once did.

Values cannot often be credibly attributed to nations, nor peoples imagined to act in reliable concert with them. But they can come to obsess nations; and this is what has happened in the United States. Out of the original founding idea, Americans periodically pluck one value, ignoring others, to cement the nation in a new age. Lincoln plucked equality; the progressives of the late 19th century plucked opportunity; the Supreme Court in the 1960s plucked individual rights. These are taken, in their time, as the building-blocks of civil society. They are not immediately achieved, but the promise of them keeps America's dangerous volatility in check.

"Family values", the unlikely war-cry of the present Republican campaign, would seem to be in a different category. This is surely sentiment, and not particularly American sentiment at that: it is not just Americans, nor yet all Americans, who believe in motherhood and apple pie. Most voters these days, the polls show, are more worried about the economy, and hence about whether America is still the

land of equality, liberty, opportunity and "the dream". Yet the traditional version of the dream includes the stable family, the hard-working, fortune-making father and the fecund mother. Even abstract ideals come to rest, as George Bush puts it, round the kitchen table.

From melting pot to salad bowl

Worries about values are not new. In the 1890s a wave of nervousness seemed to descend on the country, so that all looked

gloomy, progress seemed doubtful, and the centre surely could not hold. Those feelings, however, were largely caused by fears that the crowds of new immigrants pushing into the cities would never be assimilated as Americans. For, throughout its history, America's sense of itself as an idea-based nation has coexisted with a much more humdrum view: that America is basically a white, "Anglo-Saxon" nation wherein, as elsewhere, the ruling tribe sets the tone. Worries about "values" begin, typically, when the ruling majority finds itself in decline and on the defensive.

It is on the defensive now. Immigration is at the highest levels since the 1890s. Between 1965 and 1990, 14m newcomers arrived legally, of whom 85% were non-European, mostly Hispanics and Asians. Each year 2m-3m illegal immigrants arrive from Mexico. By 2000 barely half of the people entering the workforce will be native-born and of European stock. The new immigrants are not only more visible than ever

before, because of the colour of their skins; they are also encouraged, as never before, to cling on to what they have, to keep their language and customs, to be different.

The favoured phrase now is not "melting pot" (the invention of Israel Zangwill, a Jewish Briton), but "salad bowl", a tag with a longer ancestry. The motto on the president's seal, "E pluribus unum", comes from a recipe for salad in an early poem by Virgil: "Garlic, parsley, rue and onions, seasoned with cheese, salt, coriander and vinegar, and finally sprinkled with oil." In a salad, the ingredients do not merge; the union is simply the sum of its parts.

Unamalgamated parts are bothering to Americans. The nation did not amalgamate its black citizens, keeping them at a distance both socially and legally until 1965. As a result, it is now faced with two kinds of black separatism. The first, academic and rarefied, is a distaste for "Euro-centrism" in schools and universities. At the latest count, the nation's universities offered 400 courses, many faculties even, in black studies; each faculty comprising, as one conservative black writer has put it, a little sovereign state in which different values obtain from those of the white world.

The second kind of separatism, horrible and visible to all, is the drug-ridden and crime-infested black counter-culture of the inner cities. Although blacks are only 12% of the population, they account for almost half the inmates of America's prisons. The "values" that obtain in the ghetto—dominance, violence and each-man-for-himself—have a way of coming back to haunt America. When they are set beside the crass and violent video images that make up much of America's cultural exports, from westerns to rap, it is no wonder that foreigners are surprised at the liberty-and-equality talk.

Ethno-consciousness has this to be said for it: not before time, it has corrected the idea that there is only one, white, experience of America. It has fed through into a kind of general sensitivity (so that people do not say "nigger" on television, and so that school textbooks now give as much weight to black experiences of history as to white). But it has also underlined a strong disruptive tendency in America: the elevation of group and race "rights" over the interests of either the individual or the whole. What is presumed to be equality has turned into balkanisation, one camp

An odd place, America

Which is more important: equality or freedom?		
% choosing	Equality	Freedom
United States	20	72
Britain	23	69
France	32	54
Italy	45	43
West Germany	39	37
Japan	32	37
Spain	39	36

Source: Gallup International Research Institute, 1987-88

Is it government's responsibility to reduce income differences?	
%	Yes
Italy	81
Hungary	77
Holland	64
Britain	63
West Germany	56
Australia	42
United States	28

Are you affiliated with a church or religious organisation?	
%	Yes
United States	57
Holland	35
Britain	22
Spain	15
West Germany	13
Italy	7
France	4

Are you very/quite proud of your country?	
%	Yes
United States	96
Britain	86
Spain	83
Italy	80
France	76
Japan	62
West Germany	59

Source: GIRI, 1981

against another; what is presumed to be an expression of the best American values, such as individual liberty, may get in the way of trying to impose other values, like responsibility, in the inner-city streets.

To the splits created by ethnicity (which have always been present, to some degree, in American society) have been added other, more foreign, sensibilities. Americans are now much readier to talk of class, to know which class they are in (though 80% would opt for the all-embracing "middle"), and to notice, and remark on, class differences. In some cases, as in "underclass", the word is virtually a synonym for race. In others, such as "the merit class", it is used to explain the dominance of new elites that are supposed to have taken over from the old Protestant establishment, vaunting their computer skills rather than their money.

The seeds of this new class-consciousness seem to have been sown partly by a sluggish economy, which has been growing at a rate of 2% or less since 1989, and partly by a startling discrepancy in the 1980s between the real hourly wages of the college-educated, which rose by 2% over the decade, and those of people who went no further than high school, which fell by almost 10%. These discrepancies, together with an unemployment rate of nearly 8%, reflect a once-in-a-century adjustment, the departure of low-skilled jobs to third-world countries; and although the numbers of those defined as poor are actually falling (by 14% between 1984 and 1989), there is a growing sense of inequity and of opportunities closed off.

America's most evident value, to many of its citizens, is the freedom specifically to make money. Effort is individual, and it is according to their efforts, by and large, that individuals are rewarded. The sense of group rights has undermined even this most basic belief; for the political favour that such groups demand is also economic, from job quotas to

higher pensions to industrial protection. If in the future hard work in the anterooms of Capitol Hill is to carry more weight than hard work on the factory floor, one of America's most vital values will have perished.

The political enthusiasm evident in group lobbying is, however, untypical. In general, citizen democracy, in which the founding fathers placed their hopes, has lost much of its attraction. Instead, Americans believe group entitlements to this or that are more likely to be gained through the courts. About half the electorate declines to vote even in presidential elections, and party membership is falling. As incumbents stay put in the legislature, kept in place by sheer inertia, the citizenry is out on the streets, where the clamour for rights grows ever louder, less tolerant and more particular.

America has common symbols that are meant to foster unity: the flag, the constitution, the bill of rights, the statue of Liberty, the pledge of allegiance. All are invoked in the "rights" arguments, usually on both sides, since liberals and conservatives alike see themselves as more truly American than the other lot. Even the Almighty gets

dragged in. Around 90% of all Americans profess to believe in God, and a sunny confidence in divine favour fires people and even politicians. Yet to invoke God in public places is still deemed to threaten an "establishment" of religion (or, more likely, to promote the interest of one group, usually Christians, over the rest). Such invocations, harmless as they seem to most Americans, keep many a lawyer in work.

Liberty or anarchy?

What values then are shared? Listen to the politicians and you could think all decent Americans still believe in marriage, family, hard work, community, parental authority, filial piety and unlocked doors. In fact, many believe that a "stable relationship" is as good as (and more free and equal than) a marriage. According to the Census Bureau, barely a quarter of America's households now contain that Rockwellian (and Republican) ideal, a married couple with a child or children under the age of 18.

Moreover, Americans increasingly feel that the word "family" should include the 60% of black households headed by women struggling to raise their children on their own. They believe too that the fact that 60% of women with children under six are in the workforce is less a threat to "family values" than a natural expression of another founding American principle, "I'll do as I please."

"I'll do as I please" is not quite the same as the pursuit of happiness. It is a practical value, not an abstract ideal. It goes with two others cited recently by a journalist in the *Washington Post*: "I'm as good as you are," and "You can't do that to me." Sentiments like these are as likely to end in gunfire as in civil-rights laws. Lewis Lapham, a political columnist, wrestling with the question of "Who, or what, is American?", concluded that the nation's chief unifying idea was the chance for each individual to reinvent himself.

These ideas are prosaically

borne out in the movement of households. Americans are always ready to up sticks and seek progress, or a fortune, preferably both, in another place. In search of the dream, each man looks out for himself.

This restlessness lies behind both the plight of some blacks and the success of others. Those who cannot move, in city or country, are stranded; they become the intractable poor. Those who leave the ghettos in search of the dream (the house in the suburbs, the car, the VCR, college for the children) tend to prosper: two-thirds of blacks now qualify as middle-class, a quarter of black adults have attended college, 80% have completed high school. Yet even their share of the once-white dream does not lead them to amalgamate with the nation as a whole. Their preferred college may be black; their suburb is black; and what they are looking for, in the words of Henry Louis Gates, a pioneer of Afro-American studies, is "the company of other African-Americans . . . who care about the race". In other words, the dream is the ghetto, no matter how green.

Anyone can play at that game. Increasingly, the rich and white are fleeing not merely to the suburbs but to enclaves within the suburbs, where there may be security guards at the gate, rules against dogs, rules against children, and unearthly quiet. At the latest count, one-eighth of the population lived this way, and 150,000 home-owners' associations were protecting their right to do so. In such places, self-interest is paramount, to the extent that people pay private taxes to avoid crime and maintain their comforts, and resent paying anything for the needs of the wider area in which they are set. Yet why should anyone condemn them? The freedom to live as one likes is quintessentially American; helping one's neighbour needs more inculcation. In any case, he ought first to try to help himself.

America shows, in many ways, a surface homogenisation. Far-flung regions now increasingly look, sound, shop and vote alike; the suburban sprawl and freeways outside Madison, Wisconsin, look just the same as those outside Little Rock, Arkansas. Yet for all that, separatism seems to move faster. Modern communications, which might be supposed to blend the country together, actually strengthen divisions. Televised politics, with its nine-second sound bites, turns each issue into a galvanising slogan. Soap operas bring fantasies of material wealth into every living room, but remind the poor how far they are from sharing it. Black rap music becomes the favourite listening of middle-class white teenagers, because it lets them enjoy

vicariously a world they will never enter.

America still possesses that set of abstract values, as opposed to practical ones, which are meant to allow its diversity to take coherent shape as a nation. But do they still hold? Certainly liberty, equality and democracy are still invoked *ad nauseam* by politicians seeking moral stature. These values are what Americans have in mind, however vaguely, when, by huge majorities, they tell pollsters that they are proud of their country. But they are not well understood.

The glue of tolerance

The essential underlying principle, although the word is nowhere in the founding documents, is tolerance. Tolerance of race; of religion; of neighbour; and of the other man's point of view. Modern Amer-

ica shows all too acutely the dangers that arise when a nation of many peoples, beliefs, races and traditions keeps to the rallying cries of liberty, equality and happiness, but neglects the glue of mutual regard, attention and respect.

Some in America, now as in the 1890s, fear that increasing immigration will make matters worse. It need not. Ben Wattenberg, a senior fellow at the American Enterprise Institute, has called the United States "the first universal nation". From the offspring of many nations, it shaped—in the 19th century rather than in 1776—a national identity. Today's Americans need to learn afresh the tolerance that helped to achieve that.

How are they to be taught? America has a great longing for statesmen who can persuasively invoke the old ideals; but even Ronald Reagan, whose power of invocation was next to none, was content to preside over a nation in the grip of violent crime, racial distrust and fiscal extrava-

gance. The political career of Ross Perot suggested, however, that America's bipolar political system might eventually be shaken up into the sort of constructive consensus that the founders hoped for. Likewise, the latest ruling by the Supreme Court on the contentious issue of abortion suggests that the court may be struggling, not towards an imposed tolerance, but to a careful recognition and amalgamation of the merits of both sides' arguments.

Tolerance is hard to teach; but a start could be made in the schools. A core curriculum for elementary schools, developed by E. J. Hirsch and his disciples in Charlottesville, Virginia, requires teachers to devote half their time to the basics of American history, world history, geography and literature. It has been tried in inner-city schools and in all-white suburbs; and although this is not a civics lesson in the old style, a pledge of allegiance to the flag, the result is a set of children, differing in colour, creed and class, who understand why their country was founded, where it stands in the world and the chief influences that shaped it.

With a better understanding of the place of each in the whole, and of mutual civility and obligation, the present emphasis on "rights" might begin to fade away. There is evidence already that Americans are beginning to object to the hijacking of the media and political debate by those who are loudest and most bigoted; that the great, quiet middle, those people who would rather compromise and get along and try unobtrusively to improve themselves, would like to be heard. They could be heard if they voted. They might vote more readily if registration were easier, and suburban shopping malls became centres of civic as well as commercial life. And by making a habit of voting they might lose a little of their excessive regard for litigation, which has done much to divide the nation into intolerant camps.

There remains an economic element. Nothing will persuade Americans, moving ever on to fresh fields, to go back and pick up the pieces of projects that have failed. But those who are left behind may be helped in other ways. While America's public finances sink into ever deeper debt, it can hardly claim to embody the values of progress and self-reliance. Public solvency, and the soundly based economic growth that springs from it, would be powerful answers to the nagging sense of inequality and the disturbing measure of intolerance in American life. Much of the present anxiety about values may sink to rest as the economy rises.

Louis Vuitton. The spirit of travel

LV Ready to cross the Irish sea... the whisky set in Epi leather, lined with Alcantara. Imbued with all the magic of a golden age of travel, creations by Louis Vuitton belong to the realm of the exceptional. Crafted to exacting standards in the finest trunkmaking tradition, they perpetuate the proud heritage of a House which, since 1854, has endowed travel with its symbol of nobility.

LOUIS VUITTON
MALLETIER A PARIS

MAISON FONDÉE EN 1854

*Louis Vuitton luggage and accessories are sold only
in the 167 exclusive Louis Vuitton shops, among which :
New York, 49 East 57th Street · Zurich, 11 St. Peterstrasse ·
Milan, Via Monte Napoleone 14 · Taipei, Fu Shing North Road ·
Sao Paulo, Rua Haddock Lobo, 1545.*

Contents

BRITAIN

Annus horribilis

THE queen summed it up in just two words: *annus horribilis*. For her family, 1992 was a dreadful year. Her two married sons separated from their wives, amid speculation about the succession to the throne and even about the future of the monarchy itself. Bowing to public pressure, the queen promised to start paying taxes. The fire at Windsor Castle in November seemed to symbolise the state of royal affairs, and prompted the queen to produce her famous bit of Latin.

Annus horribilis happens to be an apt description of 1992 for many Britons besides the royals. A few did manage to prosper. Irish terrorists, for example. They shrugged off setbacks—such as the loss by Sinn Fein, the IRA's political wing, of its seat at Westminster and, for loyalists, the outlawing of the Ulster Defence Association—and got on with the killing. The number of deaths from terrorism since Northern Ireland's Troubles began climbed above 3,000; the IRA intensified its bombing blitz in England; talks aimed at a political settlement ended with barely any visible progress. The tabloid newspapers had a fine year too, as they competed for sordid scoops about the royal family and cabinet ministers. But most people, like the queen, will remember 1992 as a lousy year.

The recession dragged on, with almost daily distress stories about troubled businesses, collapsing consumer confidence and, above all, disappearing jobs. The jobless total rose inexorably towards 3m, with nearly 500,000 more people out of work at the end of the year than at the start. Despite the recession, interest rates remained punishingly high for much of the year, as the government tried (but eventually failed) to stick with the anti-inflationary discipline of Europe's exchange-rate mechanism (ERM). Homeowners saw the value of their properties plunge: the Bank of England estimated in August that about 10% of mortgage-payers were trapped with homes worth less than the value of their loans.

These were ideal circumstances for an opposition party to fight a general election. Yet 1992 turned out to be *annus horribilis* for Labour too

Labour changes leader

(as well as for the opinion pollsters who predicted Tory defeat). On April 9th, John Major's Conservatives were returned to a fourth term in office with a clear overall majority, albeit one reduced from 101 to 21.

What went wrong for Labour? The party was quick to blame the power of the Tory press. But Labour made mistakes of its own. Some voters were deterred by the triumphalist tone of a pre-election rally in Sheffield. Many more disliked the tax policies set out in Labour's "shadow budget", which fuelled fears that even the new-look Labour Party was still out to soak the rich. Personality counted too. Labour's leader, Neil Kinnock, lacked gravitas; Mr Major, using an old-fashioned soap-box for his campaign prop, seemed likeable and dependable. In the end, it came down to a question of trust: Labour failed to win enough of it.

The result had disturbing implications not only for Labour, but for the health of British democracy as well. By the next general election, the economic cycle would almost certainly be more favourable to the government and changes in constituency boundaries would in effect give the Tories another handful of seats. Did the 1992 result mean that Britain had become, like Japan, a country stuck under one-party rule?

As its new leader, Labour chose John Smith, a Scottish lawyer with the gravitas Mr Kinnock lacked—but also the person responsible for the party's disastrous tax policies. He quickly rejected the most radical strategy for defeating the Tories: an alliance with the Liberal Democrats. Mr Smith preferred cautious reform, starting with the establishment of a Commission for Social Justice to look afresh at the entire system of taxes and benefits. Conservatives looked forward to a fifth term in office, if only they could avoid future blunders.

Major trouble

After the government's performance in 1992, however, few would underestimate its capacity to blunder. With his triumph at the polls, this should have been Mr Major's *annus mirabilis*. He had emerged from the shadow of Lady Thatcher (as she became with her elevation to the Lords) to win power in his own right. He could promote more of his own chums to the cabinet (though one of them, Chris Patten, lost his seat and left to be governor of Hong Kong). He could sit back and take the credit for the expected economic recovery. There was even heady talk—given France's lame-duck presidency and Germany's post-unity woes—of Britain under the re-elected Mr Major becoming the strong man of Europe.

But it turned out that Lady Thatcher's shadow was still a

Lamont keeps smiling

force to be reckoned with and that a majority of 21 seats in the Commons left Mr Major vulnerable to bolshy back-benchers. One of his closest cabinet chums—David Mellor, the national-heritage secretary—was hounded from office for being too friendly with a Spanish actress and too ready to accept free family holidays. Worse, the economy stubbornly refused to recover and the government's economic policy was left in ruins on "Black Wednesday", September 16th. As for Europe, far from showing leadership, Britain was criticised for its failure to ratify the Maastricht treaty on schedule and ridiculed for the way it ran its EC presidency during the second half of the year: "like a Rolls-Royce without a steering wheel" was one of the kinder continental comments.

Three traumatic episodes encapsulated the government's troubles. First, sterling's ejection from the ERM. ERM membership was a painful policy, especially with the cost of German unity keeping interest rates high across Europe, but pain was in fact the point: the idea was to use Germanic discipline to defeat inflation and provide the basis for stable economic growth. Mr Major and his chancellor, Norman Lamont, dismissed growing calls for interest-rate cuts to breathe life into the economy and vowed to defend the currency come what may. But on September 16th, four days before France's Maastricht referendum, the defence collapsed. The assault on sterling had become irresistible, as currency speculators rightly reckoned that the government would not maintain interest rates at the heights needed to keep the pound within its ERM limits. The pound was allowed to float free—ie, devalue. The government lost its main economic policy, a lot of money (one estimate put the bill for the failed defence of sterling at £1.3 billion) and much of its credibility.

It had also helped prepare a second trauma: the prospect of defeat in the "paving motion" for the Maastricht treaty on November 4th. The ERM fiasco swelled the ranks of Tory Euro-rebels. Sensing the chance to unseat the government, Labour decided to ignore its pro-European policy and vote against the motion. On the day insiders said that, just seven months after his election triumph, the prime minister was prepared to resign if the vote went against him, as looked quite possible. In the end, he squeaked through by three votes, but only by abandoning his own timetable for the ratification of the treaty. Europe, a surprising non-issue in the election campaign, was plaguing the government again.

No outside help was needed for the government's next mishap. The drama over its plans to close 31 pits was entirely of its own making. It seemed unaware of the furore that would follow its decisions on the coal mines (taken without a full cabinet discussion and, the High Court later ruled, without proper consultation with the miners). Within days the minister responsible for energy policy, Michael Heseltine, was forced into an ignominious retreat.

The cumulative effect of Mr Major's triple trauma was to create the impression of a weak, incompetent government, prone to U-turns and without any clear sense of direction. Even staunchly pro-Tory newspapers turned savagely critical, with a sense of nostalgia for the good old days of firm Thatcherite leadership.

Reassessing Thatcherism

Yet the woes of 1992 prompted a look back at the Thatcher years for another reason. How much did Thatcherism really change Britain? Sterling was ejected from the ERM on Black Wednesday because of the underlying weakness of the British economy. Inflation and high public spending, ills supposedly cured by Thatcherism, still threatened Britain's economic health (true, inflation came down to 3% by the end of 1992, but it looked likely to rise again under the post-ERM "growth" policy of interest-rate cuts and devaluation). The Thatcherite homeowners' dream turned for many in 1992 into a debtors' nightmare. Was the lesson of the year that Britain was still on a path of long-term decline?

Maybe not. Perhaps the troubles afflicting the pillars of the state, such as the monarchy and the church of England (which in 1992 was threatened by a schism over its decision to allow the ordination of women priests), were merely all part of a healthy process of modernisation. At the end of the year there were signs of spluttering economic recovery. Even amid the gloomy talk of British manufacturing decline, a brighter future could be glimpsed as Japanese-built car plants revved up for mass production. The Edinburgh summit in December brought success for Britain's much-criticised EC presidency and a sense that the Tory Euro-rebellion might have peaked. Continuing radicalism in education policy, with encouragement for schools to opt out of local-authority control, showed that the government had not entirely abandoned its reforming mission.

It is possible to tell an optimistic tale about Britain in 1992 and keep a straight face. But in that *annus horribilis*, few were prepared to take optimists seriously.

Divided royalty

January

Wednesday 1st
A prosperous new year was the last thing most people seemed to be expecting. A survey by the Institute of Directors registered **less optimism** in company boardrooms than had been evident three months earlier. A MORI poll suggested ordinary voters, on balance, had also grown gloomier. Tory MPs were not immune to the general mood: the chancellor, Norman Lamont, had to stamp on talk of a sterling devaluation among his own backbenchers.

The **new year's honours** included the CBE for the four returned Beirut hostages. Several sportsmen and artists on the list were less expected—except to those familiar with the new status of cricket and opera in Downing Street.

Among the **cabinet papers** for 1961 released under the 30-year rule was a string of letters recording one of Harold Macmillan's lesser known battles during his premiership: a campaign to press for bounty payments on grey squirrels. SuperMac nagged the agriculture ministry about it for 17 months. But grey men from the ministry sided against the idea and finally saw him off.

Sunday 5th
Squabbles over **tax rates** kicked off a frenetic start to the unofficial election campaign, as the two main parties rubbished each other's sums. The chancellor, Norman Lamont, said Labour was planning to drop a "tax bombshell" of 10p on the standard rate of income tax to pay for £35 billion ($66 billion) of extra spending. John Smith, his shadow rival, dismissed this as "a big lie".

Monday 6th
Belfast businessmen criticised lax security after two massive IRA **bombs** blasted shops and offices in the city centre.

Tuesday 7th
British Steel confirmed that its **Ravenscraig** steelworks in Strathclyde would close in the autumn. The prime minister, John Major, said the closure, axing 1,220 jobs, was "a matter of deep regret"; the local region was earmarked to become an enterprise zone.

Monday 13th
The collapse of the late Robert Maxwell's business empire returned to the headlines. Kevin and Ian Maxwell, two of the disgraced tycoon's sons, risked **imprisonment for contempt** of the House of Commons social-security select committee, whose questions about the Mirror Group's pension funds they refused to answer. The brothers' lawyers told MPs that the couple did not want to ruin their chances of a fair trial if they had to face criminal charges.

A 49-year-old Australian **statistician**, Bill McLennan, was made the new boss of the Central Statistical Office. Widely credited as the man who modernised the Australian government's handling of economic data, his appointment offered the hope he might do the same one day for Whitehall.

Tuesday 14th
Heavy hints from John Major fuelled speculation that the government planned a **tax-cutting budget**. Meanwhile the polls suggested that a Tory onslaught on Labour's own tax plans had payed off handsomely: Labour's steady lead of recent months was reversed to leave the Tories with a one point lead.

A brain-storming session in Downing Street failed to sort out a gathering row over how to proceed with the planned privatisation of **British Rail**. (After further meetings failed to break the impasse over the next few weeks, plans for a privatisation white paper were shelved until after the election.)

Monday 20th
A remorseful Peter Brooke, the Northern Ireland secretary, offered his **resignation** after an insensitive appearance on Irish television—singing "Clementine" on a late-night chat show—only hours after an IRA bomb on January 17th had killed eight Protestant workmen. They were returning home from a day's building work at a British army base. John Major refused Mr Brooke's offer; and Mr Brooke went back to trying to restart all-party talks about talks on the future of the province.

Wednesday 22nd
A former British army **intelligence agent** and senior figure in the Ulster Defence Association pleaded guilty to five charges of conspiracy to murder. But the crown dropped two charges of murder against the man, Brian Nelson, averting a trial that had threatened to disclose links between the army and loyalist gunmen. Nationalist politicians alleged a cover-up—but the accused emerged from the trial with a ten-year sentence.

The 1992 edition appeared of Crawford's Directory, a leading digest of business information. It listed 4,000 **boardroom directors**; remarkably, only 20 of them were women. The Tories said this showed John Major's good sense in pushing for the promotion of more women to top jobs. The working-women's lobby said few would take them, without some tax relief against child-care costs.

Sunday 26th
George Gershwin, Diana Ross, Elgar and a 1948 cricket commentary—just some of the sounds that John Major told **Desert Island Discs**, a radio programme, he would like to serenade him in his solitude. And his final choice? Frank Sinatra singing "The Best Is Yet To Come."

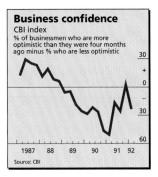

Business confidence
CBI index
% of businessmen who are more optimistic than they were four months ago minus % who are less optimistic

Source: CBI

Tuesday 28th
News of record exports in the final quarter of 1991, up 0.5% on the previous quarter, provided a brief glimpse of economic sunshine. The clouds soon drifted back: the Confederation of British Industry reported a sharp fall in **business confidence**.

Wednesday 29th
For the first time ever, an opinion poll among Scots suggested half of them wanted an **independent Scotland**. Support for devolution and a Scottish parliament as a halfway house came from only 27% of those polled—a sharp drop. Scottish nationalists were cock-a-hoop; the government tried to deflect charges of neglect by scheduling a Westminster debate on the issue for Scottish MPs—but could not dampen it.

February

Sunday 2nd
Pre-election nerves were set jangling in Westminster by a story in the *Sunday Times* newspaper about meetings between the leader of the Labour Party, Neil Kinnock, and the Soviet ambassador in 1984. Labour said Mr Kinnock had been "smeared" and accused Downing Street of giving the go-ahead for a **dirty election campaign** by sanctioning the story's publication. The row prompted a bizarre week of conspiracy theories about what covert operators on both sides of the main party divide might be up to.

Monday 3rd
A boardroom quarrel prompted the resignation of David Plowright as chairman of Granada, the **independent television** network's most successful company. Cue industry *Angst*: worried TV executives said it was a blow against the high-quality programming that Mr Plowright had always championed—and that opponents of the government's shake-up of the industry had always warned would be imperilled by the Tories.

Tuesday 4th
A 24-year-old RUC officer bluffed his way into Sinn Fein's Belfast press office and **shot dead** three men. He later killed himself. His superiors said the constable was suffering from stress caused by a colleague's death. The next day loyalist gunmen burst into a Belfast bookmaker, **shooting bystanders** at random. Five people were killed, nine others injured. "It looked like a butcher's shop," said a survivor.

Wednesday 5th
Paddy Ashdown, the Liberal Democrat leader, admitted having a "**brief relationship**" in 1987 with his former parliamentary secretary. Mr Ashdown's announcement came after he had tried in vain to stop the press from publishing details of the affair, extracted from papers stolen from his solicitor's office. His fellow Liberal Democrat MPs rallied to his support; the other party leaders said the affair should not become an election issue. A few days later, Mr Ashdown's party advanced four percentage points in the opinion polls.

Thursday 6th
Barbara Mills, the head of the Serious Fraud Office, was appointed **director of public prosecutions**. Widely credited with establishing the SFO's reputation as an investigator of complex fraud cases, her appointment seemed likely to strengthen the growing demand for a reform of the courts' approach to fraud.

Monday 10th
The prime minister, John Major, revived his government's bid to settle **Ulster's future** by talking at a Downing Street meeting to leaders of the four main Northern Ireland parties. As they were making their way to Downing Street, an IRA bomb was defused in a Whitehall telephone booth. The government later announced it was sending 500 more troops to strengthen security in Ulster.

The government approved **pay rises** well above inflation for more than 1.3m public servants, at a cost of £1.8 billion ($3.2 billion). Teachers were told they would get an average rise of 7.5%, nurses 6%, doctors 5.5% and the armed forces 6%. The most controversial decision—how much to give top people like judges and civil-service mandarins—was put off until later in the year.

The **Channel tunnel** opening was rescheduled for autumn 1993, a delay of several months. Eurotunnel, the tunnel's operator, blamed contractors for the setback, which will lose it the peak season summer traffic.

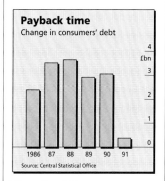

Payback time
Change in consumers' debt

Source: Central Statistical Office

Thursday 13th
A spate of gloomy statistics on the economy had political pundits talking of a "**Black Thursday**" for the Tories, and their chances of re-election. The seasonally adjusted unemployment figure jumped to its highest for four years, and a record number of house repossessions (more than 75,000) was reported for 1991. The bad news underlined the Bank of England's confirmation on the 11th that the recession was the longest since 1945; the Bank also drew attention to the continuing slide in consumer confidence—consumers in December had made their biggest monthly debt repayment since 1976.

Sunday 16th
An **ambush** by SAS soldiers left four IRA gunmen dead and two others injured after they had attacked a police station in Coalisland, Northern Ireland; one of the dead turned out to be a 21-year-old acquitted of arms offences at the Old Bailey in 1991 in the week that the Birmingham Six were released.

Wednesday 19th
A historic judgment in the appeal court ruled that government bodies could not use **English libel law** against hostile comment in the press. Reversing a lower court judgment, in which Derbyshire county council had won the right to sue the *Sunday Times* newspaper for attacking it over various pension transactions, the judges cited a European Court of Human Rights decision as grounds for overruling the common law.

Thursday 20th
Richard Ingrams, a founder and for many years the editor of *Private Eye*, a satirical magazine, launched **a new title** on the magazine shelves: the *Oldie*, aimed at the country's more senior citizens. Might it soon be the *Mouldie*? No, said Mr Ingrams, he had "good vibes" (to coin a relatively new-fangled phrase).

Tuesday 25th
Hopes of making the judiciary more responsive to change and reform were bolstered by the appointment of Sir Peter Taylor as **Lord Chief Justice**. He replaced Lord Lane, who retired early to a less than flattering send-off from the press.

Would Baden-Powell have approved? To jazz up their camp-fire ditties and put a gloss on their image among inner-city youngsters, the **boy scouts** announced that they had hired a black rap singer, named T-Love, to record a boy-scout rap.

Friday 28th
An IRA **bomb** exploded at British Rail's London Bridge terminal in the middle of the morning rush hour, injuring 28 commuters.

March

Monday 2nd
Oftel, the regulatory watchdog for the telecoms industry, told **chatline-services** companies their days were numbered; plans were disclosed to cut off their access to the public networks. The companies allowed callers to dial up and get connected to others ringing the same number—but at a premium rate that had hit some unsuspecting subscribers (or their parents) hard.

Tuesday 3rd
The strongest evidence yet that an election was on its way: the Liberal Democrats published a **pets' charter**. They claimed to be the first party with a policy on pets. Under their proposals, dog- and cat-owners would have to get the equivalent of an MOT certificate of road-worthiness. An animal-protection commission would enforce the law.

Tuesday 10th
The chancellor, Norman Lamont, fired off what many at Westminster fully expected to be the opening volley of the general election campaign: his **budget.** He introduced a new 20p rate for the first £2,000 of taxable income and predicted that public borrowing would double to £28 billion ($48 billion) in 1992-93. He also unveiled plans to merge the Treasury's autumn statement (on spending) and the spring budget (on taxes). The markets gave Mr Lamont's handiwork a generally cool reception; most City pundits reproved him for doing far too little to help spark economic recovery—or even to boost the Tories' chances of re-election.

Wednesday 11th
At last. John Major **called the election** for April 9th. The media celebrated with gleeful predictions of the toughest (and dirtiest) campaign in recent memory. The City gave Mr Major an uncomfortable start: sterling came under heavy pressure and equities had their worst day since the attempted Soviet coup of the previous August. Suddenly it was the consensus wisdom that the Tories were going to lose the election.

Monday 16th
After a breathless race through outstanding government business, Parliament was dissolved and the Commons raised a **farewell cheer** for the most famous of many departing MPs: Margaret Thatcher.

John Smith, Labour's shadow chancellor, unveiled an unashamedly redistributive **shadow budget**, confirming his party's role as the champion of the lower-paid. Earners of more than £22,000 ($37,800) were to be worse off under his proposals, which included a new 50% tax-band for income over £36,375—about twice average male earnings. Most of the media applauded a polished performance by Mr Smith. Those who focused on the arithmetic of his tax proposals, though, were sharply critical of their potential impact on the recovery—especially since Mr Smith said nothing about phasing in his changes.

Wednesday 18th
The two main parties published their election **manifestos**, neither of which contained any significant surprises—most of their ideas had been well trailed in advance. The Tories ran their first party-political broadcast, entitled "John Major. The Journey." Earlier in the day, the first clear lead for either party had emerged, with two polls giving Labour a five-point edge on the Tories. But other polls the same evening confirmed a general impression that an unusually large number of voters were still far from decided about which way they intended to vote.

Thursday 19th
Bad unemployment figures, showing the total at its highest level for 4½ years, gave the Tories an uncomfortable end to the first full week of election campaigning.

Buckingham Palace announced that the **Duke and Duchess of York** were to separate after five-and-a-half years of marriage. The Palace said the queen had decided to issue a statement in view of intense press coverage of the story, which was undesirable during a general election campaign.

Sunday 22nd
Margaret Thatcher made one of her few starring appearances in the Tory campaign, before flying off to meet prior engagements in America. She joined John Major at a rally in London, and warned that a hung parliament would "hang the future of our country". Her target was revealing: more and more pundits were beginning to believe that a hung parliament was the election's most likely outcome.

Tuesday 24th
An opinion poll from the Harris organisation gave the Tories a five-point lead; but it was way out of line with the other polls, and generally disregarded as a rogue result.

A highly emotive party-political broadcast by Labour focused on the Tories' handling of the **national health service**: a little girl was shown in distress, waiting months for an operation that had to be delayed for lack of funds. When her name and fuller details emerged soon after, a furore broke out over the ethics of the broadcast. No one seemed clear whether the episode had helped Labour or hurt it.

The publishers of *Punch*, United Newspapers, said the 150-year-old **funny magazine** would have to close unless a buyer could be found within a couple of weeks. (No buyer came forward; it closed on April 8th.)

Wednesday 25th
Cricket fans stumbled into work bleary-eyed after rising early to catch the whole of the radio commentary on England's performance in the **cricket world cup**, live from Australia. England lost.

Tuesday 31st
Three opinion polls were released, pointing to a Labour lead over the Tories of between four and seven percentage points. They seemed to confirm a growing consensus among the media that **Neil Kinnock** was turning rapidly into the prime-minister-in-waiting; and criticisms of John Major as a wooden and rather uninspiring campaigner—now reduced to standing on a soapbox and addressing market-square crowds through a megaphone—grew more strident even among Tory supporters.

April

Wednesday 1st
The stockmarket plunged, gilt prices dropped sharply and short-term interest rates began pointing to a rise in base rates, as the consensus forecast among City pundits shifted decisively towards expecting a Labour victory at the polls. Neil Kinnock and his shadow-cabinet colleagues were certainly anticipating one: at a triumphalist **party rally** in Sheffield, the biggest of its kind ever held in Britain, the Labour leader told 10,000 supporters that a Labour government was nine days away.

Thursday 2nd
The two main parties in the general election moved in opposite directions over **electoral reform**. Labour said it would welcome other parties joining its own inquiry into future reforms, opening up the possibility of some kind of deal with the Liberal Democrats. John Major flatly rejected the idea: there were "no circumstances", said Mr Major, in which he would go for proportional representation.

Saturday 4th
Even sport failed to keep off the subject of the election: a horse named Party Politics won the **Grand National** at Aintree. On the same day, Oxford beat Cambridge for the 16th time in 17 years in the annual university boat race.

Wednesday 8th
Three last minute polls indicated a sudden break with the general pattern of poll results over the campaign: Labour's small but consistent lead had evaporated. John Major told the press he was "**stone cold certain**" that he was going to win an overall majority.

Thursday 9th
Fine weather over most of the country helped ensure an unusually high turnout (77%) for the **general election**. It proved a cliff-hanger until the last possible moment. Exit polls by the BBC and ITN predicted at 10pm that the Tories would emerge the largest party, but well short of an overall majority. For the next three hours, individual constituency results showed no clear national pattern; but the Tories steadily inched ahead, with a tiny overall majority predictable by 2am. Its size grew hourly after that—and the Tories ended the election with 336 seats, a majority of 21 over Labour (271), the Liberal Democrats (20) and all other parties (24).

Friday 10th
The IRA exploded a car bomb—the biggest bomb to go off on the mainland of Britain since the second world war— in the heart of the City of London. It killed three passers-by, injured dozens more and caused widespread devastation that first estimates reckoned might cost over £1 billion ($1.8 billion). A second IRA bomb later the same evening damaged a north London fly-over, and was expected to cause months of traffic chaos.

Saturday/Sunday 11th-12th
John Major reshuffled his cabinet to reflect his own meritocratic-but-compassionate Conservatism. He appointed **women and wets** to some big spending departments (with Virginia Bottomley to health and John Patten to education) but ensured that Thatcherites kept their hands on some important purse-strings (with Peter Lilley to social security and Michael Portillo to the Treasury as chief secretary). Michael Heseltine moved to trade and industry, Kenneth Clarke to the Home Office and Michael Howard to the environment department.

Monday 13th
Neil Kinnock announced that he was **resigning as the Labour leader**. Ditto Roy Hattersley as deputy leader. Blaming Labour's defeat on the Tory tabloid press, Mr Kinnock said he was quitting immediately to let a new leader emerge before the autumn party conference. John Smith and Bryan Gould stepped forward as the two candidates to replace him.

Thursday 16th
John Patten made a surprising debut as education secretary: writing in the *Spectator* magazine, he argued that growing crime among young people was partly due to a dwindling belief in hell and the "**fear of eternal damnation**". Criminologists suggested that unemployment and too few bobbies on the street might be additional causal factors.

Monday 20th
More than 72,000 rock fans spent Easter Monday packed into Wembley stadium for a concert in memory of **Freddie Mercury**, a flamboyant rock star who died in 1991 from AIDS, aged 45. A Hollywood celebrity better known for getting married than for giving sex-counselling, Elizabeth Taylor, joined the cast of veteran singers with a plea to the fans: "use a condom, whoever you are."

By an unhappy coincidence, two of the most successful of popular comedians, Frankie Howerd and Benny Hill, died over the same weekend. Benny Hill, a well-known TV face in 100 countries, lived just long enough to see himself reinstated on the ITV television schedules, which dropped his humour as "sexist" in 1989.

Monday 27th
Traditions fell like nine-pins when the **new parliament** assembled at Westminster. The Commons had a contest for the speaker's job for the first time since 1951. Unusually, it elected an MP from the opposition benches—and Betty Boothroyd became the first woman in the job. She then dispensed with the past by discarding the speaker's wig.

Tuesday 28th
In an upbeat speech to the Institute of Directors, John Major claimed that **recovery** was on its way: "As spring advances, so will confidence." He defended his chancellor, Norman Lamont, who had "done an outstanding job." The currency markets seemed to agree: continuing a post-election trend, sterling strengthened further against the dollar and the D-mark.

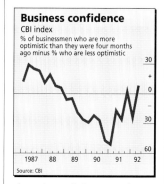

The prime minister's optimism got some support, too, from the latest quarterly-trends survey by the Confederation of British Industry. It showed **business confidence** at its highest level for four years.

May

Tuesday 5th
The chancellor, Norman Lamont, shaved half a point off **base rates**, bringing them to a four-year low of 10%. Shares soared.

Wednesday 6th
With the usual pomp and pageantry the **queen opened Parliament**. Among the forthcoming bills announced in her speech were ones to privatise British Coal, encourage private services on the railways, curb union powers further, crack down on bogus asylum-seekers, set up a national lottery and promote the Welsh language.

Ofgas, the gas-industry watchdog, told **British Gas** to cut domestic prices by 2p a therm—promising average annual savings of £15 ($27) per household—or face the courts.

Thursday 7th
The Tories consolidated their general election triumph with the best **local-election** results in England and Wales for 13 years, winning control of 126 councils. But those who had earlier thirsted for a hung parliament could take some comfort: the results produced 137 hung councils.

Saturday 9th
Liverpool won the FA Cup for the third time in six years, beating Sunderland 2-0.

Sunday 10th
At a service in Derby cathedral to give thanks for the achievements of British business, the Archbishop of Canterbury, George Carey, criticised the much-publicised high pay awards granted to captains of industry during the recession and said that the **purpose of business** was to benefit humanity, not to "make profits for shareholders."

Labour dismissed a call by the Liberal Democrat leader,

Paddy Ashdown, for a **non-socialist regrouping** on the centre-left to oppose the Conservative Party. Labour said it remained open to dialogue on ideas, but was not convinced that Mr Ashdown's party represented more than a "wishy-washy centre that will do a deal with anyone."

Monday 11th
Yet another in a long series of embarrassments for the judicial system: Judith Ward, jailed in 1974 for an IRA bombing, was **freed by the Court of Appeal** after it ruled that her conviction, based largely on her own confession, was unsafe and unsatisfactory. The defence was later alleged to have withheld evidence in 1974 that would have greatly reduced the chances of a guilty verdict.

Tuesday 12th
The **queen** stepped into a Euro-row. A misleading Whitehall press briefing, released just ahead of her first ever address to the European Parliament in Strasbourg, had indicated that she would say the differences in parliamentary traditions were "insignificant" within the Community. Incensed anti-federalist MPS howled in protest—only to discover on the day that her speech referred merely to insignificant differences in debating styles.

Monday 18th
Nine **British servicemen** had been "unlawfully killed" by American "friendly fire" during the Gulf War, a jury decided at an inquest in Oxford. The verdict caused consternation among lawyers, but followed several days in which the jury had heard evidence of "massive discrepancies" between accounts of the deaths given by the American pilots involved and those provided by air-traffic controllers; the American government had re-

fused to allow the pilots to testify in person. John Major ruled out any official moves to press charges against them.

A leading private school, Malvern Girls' College, disclosed that it had had to employ a **debt-collecting agency** to pursue parents in arrears with their fees.

Police sealed off Coalisland, in **Northern Ireland**, to search for a machinegun stolen from soldiers during clashes with civilians. A paratrooper had shot three civilians while being attacked by a mob. Locals alleged that several townspeople had earlier been beaten up by members of the 3rd battalion of the Parachute Regiment, stationed there.

BSkyB, a **satellite television** channel, announced that it had won an auction held by the soon-to-kick-off Premier League, for the exclusive right to broadcast its football matches live. Bitter recriminations followed over the conduct of the auction, which ITV claimed had dealt with its own bid unfairly.

Tuesday 19th
Bringing a touch of *glasnost* to **Whitehall**, William Waldegrave, the minister for the Citizen's Charter, revealed details of key ministerial committees and published "Questions of Procedure for Ministers", the collection of handy tips traditionally given to cabinet newcomers.

Barbara Mills, the recently appointed director of public prosecutions, ruled out **criminal proceedings** against more than 200 police officers of the discredited West Midlands serious crime squad, disbanded in 1989. Mrs Mills ruled that a (hugely expensive) two-year inquiry into the activities of the squad had not produced sufficient evidence for charges to be pressed successfully.

Wednesday 20th
Kenneth Clarke, the home secretary, attended his first annual conference of the Police Federation, at Scarborough. Announcing a government review of pay and career structures, he promised that a big shake-up of the **police force** was on its way. (Three weeks later, he duly extended the terms of the review to cover the structure of the force and the procedures for funding it.)

Monday 25th
As the country baked in an unusually warm May, the environment department announced it was reviewing **water policy** and ways to cope with a four-year drought.

Meanwhile, 25,000 new-age people, ravers and assorted lay-abouts turned up for an **illegal festival** in the Malvern hills, some threatening to stay for weeks. Locals said the music was driving them mad and the police were not doing enough to protect them.

June

Tuesday 2nd
Labour's front bench lost another of its dwindling band of former ministers. **Gerald Kaufman**, the party's foreign-affairs spokesman, said it was time at the age of 61 for him to "make way for another political generation". But Mr Kaufman said he would stay on in Parliament and was confident that Labour would win the next election.

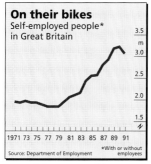

On their bikes
Self-employed people* in Great Britain

1971 73 75 77 79 81 83 85 87 89 91

*With or without employees

Source: Department of Employment

One of the most striking trends of the labour market in the 1980s, the rapid growth in the number of **self-employed** people, had run into problems since the end of that decade, a new survey revealed.

Wednesday 3rd
Cheered by Denmark's surprising rejection of the Maastricht treaty, over 100 Tory MPs signed a Commons motion urging the government to help build a **Common Market** trading-block, not a European superstate. John Major announced he was postponing further debate in the House on a bill to ratify the treaty, but insisted it could not be renegotiated. In private, other cabinet ministers were less sure.

Friday 5th
The Other Place picked up strong reinforcements for its role in the political fray, as 21 new peers were created in the **Dissolution Honours List**. They included all the former cabinet ministers who had retired from the Commons at the April election, with the

exception of the former Labour leader, Michael Foot. Margaret Thatcher headed a list of nine of her former ministers; former opponents who moved with them to the Lords included Denis Healey and David Owen.

Sunday 7th
The press revelled in speculation about the **private lives** of the Prince and Princess of Wales, inspired by a serialisation in the *Sunday Times* of a former tabloid journalist's book about their marriage. The Press Complaints Commission quickly condemned the coverage as "odious", and several MPs spoke of the need for tighter laws on privacy. But newspaper sales soared, as did sales of the book when published later in the month.

Monday 8th
Peter Lilley, the social security secretary, said the government was setting aside an immediate £2.5m ($4.6m) to keep the **Maxwell pension funds** afloat. But as the Department of Trade and Industry announced that it was appointing a formal inquiry into the affairs of Mirror Group Newspapers, MPs from all parties vowed to keep pressing for compensation for the pensioners from the banks that unwittingly accepted the pension funds' assets as collateral for loans to Maxwell.

Tuesday 9th
The ex-factory **prices** of manufactured goods, a good pointer to core inflation, rose by 3.5% in the year to May. Stripping out food, drink and tobacco, it was the index's smallest annual increase since the 1960s. Other economic news, though, was less encouraging: the Treasury was reported to have cut its projection of economic growth for 1992 to under 1%, and new figures showed consumer borrowing still falling.

Wednesday 10th
One of the better conspiracy theories of the second world war began to wear terminally thin, when secret government papers were released on the **Rudolf Hess affair**. Some historians of the whodunnit school had worked for years on the idea that the German who landed in Scotland with a peace plan in 1941 was an impostor. But the papers left little doubt that he was indeed the deputy-führer—apparently more than a little deranged, and acting entirely on his own initiative. Another triumph for the cock-up school.

Monday 15th
More military cuts. Malcolm Rifkind, the defence secretary, announced that the navy was to scrap its stockpile of **sea-borne nuclear weapons**—leaving nuclear deterrence increasingly in the hands of the Trident-submarine programme. George Bush and Boris Yeltsin unveiled dramatic arms cuts the next day. A coincidence, said Mr Rifkind.

Tuesday 16th
The bell tolled for **Neddy**, the National Economic Development Council set up in 1962 to promote co-ordination between government, business and the trade unions on economic planning. Businessmen cheered, Labour jeered and trade unionists wailed. Tory MPs were less sure of how to read the news: as another

coup for anti-corporatism, or a harbinger of a fresh start by Michael Heseltine at trade and industry?

Monday 22nd
A lock of **Lord Byron's hair** was sold for £4,620 ($8,590) at Bonhams, a London auctioneer. "An incredibly romantic gift" for one of his children, said an incredibly romantic buyer.

After a woman died from AIDS, and three others with the HIV virus said that the same man had infected them on purpose, MPs called for **deliberate infection** to be made a criminal offence. Health officials insisted the man was guilty of "regrettable irresponsibility" and needed psychiatric help.

Tuesday 23rd
Adding to concern on the Tory benches at Westminster over yet another **delay to the economic recovery**, output figures for the first quarter of 1992 showed that GDP had shrunk by 0.5%. But the chancellor, Norman Lamont, rejected calls for fresh measures to lift the housing market.

A report by the King's Fund, an independent think-tank, said that at least 15 big **London hospitals** should be closed, allowing more money to be channelled into community health care.

Thursday 25th
The Royal Navy's fishery protection squadron had to intervene after Cornish and Breton fishermen clashed in an area just north of the Scilly Isles. A long-standing dispute over fishing techniques flared into a violent confrontation when four **French trawlers** cut the Cornishmen's nets. Stiff protests went off to Paris, and the French government warned the culprits they would be harshly dealt with.

July

Wednesday 1st
Britain took over from Portugal the **European Community's presidency.** EC countries take turns to do the job for a six-month stint.

A breakthrough in negotiations over **Northern Ireland** came with the announcement that Ulster Unionist MPs had agreed to formal talks with Irish ministers for the first time in nearly 20 years. The first session opened in London on July 6th, as part of the three-tiered discussions on the province's future.

Thursday 2nd
Baroness Thatcher of Kesteven used her maiden speech in the House of Lords to attack the Maastricht treaty.

Monday 6th
The two **dentists' unions**, outraged by the government's 7% cut in their fees, voted to deny treatment to new NHS patients. Virginia Bottomley, the health secretary, claimed the cut was to avoid overpayment: dentists, on new contracts which pay per patient, registered more people than the government had expected.

With an opening scene involving ladies' knickers being thrown out of a window, the BBC launched "Eldorado", a thrice-a-week **soap opera** about expats in Spain, dubbed "Costa del Bonk" by the tabloids.

Tuesday 7th
Malcolm Rifkind, the defence secretary, set out Britain's post-cold-war defence strategy in a white paper. It promised a "peace dividend" but confirmed the order of a fourth Trident nuclear submarine. Plans for the four-country European Fighter Aircraft were thrown into confusion by Germany's withdrawal from the project.

Channel Five Holdings, a group led by Thames Television, emerged as the only bidder for the franchise for **Channel 5**, a new TV channel due to start in 1993. Others were put off by an obligation to retune some 7m video recorders to avoid technical interference, and by the prospect of competition from satellite and cable TV.

Wednesday 8th
The British smoke, drink and weigh too much, said a white paper on **"The Health of the Nation"**. It set targets for reducing obesity, smoking, sexually transmitted diseases, suicides and teenage pregnancies.

Thursday 9th
John Major rejected a review body's recommendation for a rise of up to 24% in **top people's pay** in the public sector, offering 4% instead. But this failed to impose similar stringency on MPs, who voted themselves a rise of 38% in their expense allowance.

Tuesday 14th
Ministers shunted out their plans for **privatising British Rail**. It would be split in two: one part running the tracks and remaining in state hands, the other handling train services and being offered to bidders in 30 to 40 franchises. Only freight services would be sold outright.

Musical chairs began among **newspaper editors**. *The Times's* Simon Jenkins announced his departure. His job had been offered to Paul Dacre of London's *Evening Standard*, who turned it down in favour of the *Daily Mail. The Times* job eventually went to Peter Stothard, a deputy editor.

Saturday 18th
By a thumping majority, John Smith, formerly shadow chancellor, was elected **Labour Party leader,** to replace Neil Kinnock. His unofficial running mate, Margaret Beckett, won the deputy leadership.

Sunday 19th
The *People*, a tabloid newspaper, revealed that **David Mellor**, the national-heritage secretary who had been dubbed "minister for fun", was having extramarital fun with an actress. John Major rejected his offer to resign.

Monday 20th
The Treasury was forced to cut the interest rate on a new **National Savings** bond, launched to help finance the public-sector deficit, after it proved too successful. The Cheltenham & Gloucester building society had had to raise its rates because it was losing investors.

Wednesday 22nd
The Treasury announced a new "top-down" system for **setting public spending**. The cabinet would decide on a supposedly unchangeable control total for all spending. Ministers would then have to fight for their share of the pie.

Police in riot gear moved into a housing estate in Bristol, afer several **nights of rioting**. The violence began after two local men riding a stolen motorbike died in a collision with a police car. Other outbursts of rioting followed in Burnley and Blackburn.

Thursday 23rd
Labour elected five newcomers to its **shadow cabinet**. The cabinet had a record number of women (five), but men held the top jobs of shadow chancellor, foreign secretary and home secretary.

Friday 24th
Hundreds of British holidaymakers had their **holidays cancelled** and others were stranded abroad after Land Travel, a coach-tour firm, collapsed.

Monday 27th
Five years' of fierce debate ended when Britain conceded the principle that for the sake of the single market the European Community needed a minimum standard rate of **value-added tax.**

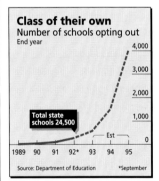

Class of their own
Number of schools opting out
End year

Total state schools 24,500

Source: Department of Education   *September

Tuesday 28th
John Patten, the education secretary, unveiled his **white paper on schools**. Schools would be encouraged to opt out of local-authority control; a national agency would be set up to finance them. Hit-squads would take over management of bad schools. Mr Patten said he was giving more power to parents; critics said he was centralising it in his own hands.

Friday 31st
The battle over the **pricing of gas** moved into a new phase. British Gas, the privatised supplier, was unable to reach agreement with the industry's regulator, Ofgas, and asked for a review by the Monopolies and Mergers Commission.

August

Monday 3rd
Pressure mounted on the government to give a boost to the **housing market**. Abbey National, Britain's second-largest mortgage lender, suggested tax relief of up to £10,000 ($19,000) on any loss when people sold their home and bought another. Several other mortgage lenders—their profits hit—came up with similarly desperate schemes.

Tuesday 4th
An inquiry into Ashforth hospital, one of England's three "special" hospitals for dangerous mentally-ill patients, criticised **staff brutality**. The government ordered a review of top-security mental care.

The rail passengers' watchdog reported that **complaints about British Rail** had reached record levels in the year to March. The Central Transport Consultative Committee blamed the government for not investing enough in the railways.

Thursday 6th
Television gained access to the courts—though only in Scotland. Scotland's senior judge announced the decision to allow limited **televising of courts**: cameras could be permitted in cases where this was "without risk to the administration of justice".

Sunday 9th
Travellers camping at a site near Winchester vandalised and set light to a rubbish incinerator, causing up to £1m ($1.9m) of damage.

Monday 10th
Millions of **credit-card customers** were advised to check their statements after a mess by a card-processing company which had installed new computer software. High-street banks warned customers they may be charged the wrong amounts, have their credit cards rejected or have them gobbled up at cashpoints.

The government outlawed the **Ulster Defence Association**, the biggest loyalist paramilitary group operating in Northern Ireland, because it was "actively engaged" in terrorism. In London, police appeared to have foiled an IRA bombing plan when they discovered a van packed with explosives.

Tuesday 11th
BT agreed with its regulator, Oftel, to restrict price increases for **telephone calls** to 7.5 percentage points below inflation for its 19m residential and 6.5m business customers. Connection charges would also fall.

Wednesday 12th
Lord Justice Bingham was appointed the new **Master of the Rolls**, the top civil judge in England and Wales.

Thursday 13th
It was announced that **unemployment** had risen to a five-year peak, with 2.75m out of work at the end of July.

Tuesday 18th
About one in every ten **mortgage-payers** was trapped with homes worth less than the value of their loans, reported the Bank of England.

John Major interrupted his holiday in Spain to get cabinet agreement that the RAF should join an international force to stop Saddam Hussein killing Iraq's Shias. At a six-hour meeting of the defence and overseas policy committee, ministers also agreed to send up to 1,800 **British troops** to protect United Nations aid convoys in Bosnia.

Wednesday 19th
End-of-school **exam results** showed the number of people taking A-levels up by 4.5% on the previous year, with a record pass rate of 79.6%. Officials denied that better grades were due to less exacting standards.

The two biggest car makers in Britain, **Ford and Rover**, both announced plans to put plants on short-time work. This was in response to weaker-than-expected demand at home and in export markets.

Thursday 20th
John Bryan, a Texan, failed to prevent the *Daily Mirror* from publishing intimate poolside pictures of himself and the **Duchess of York** on holiday in France. The paper sold out in hours.

Monday 24th
As the disgraced Duchess of York went into hiding, the *Sun* stirred up more **royal scandal**. It printed a transcript of a telephone conversation allegedly between the Princess of Wales (on the tape, called "Squidgy") and a male admirer. The *Sun* claimed to have refrained from using the tape for two years.

Wednesday 26th
The Institute of Directors reported a plunge in **economic confidence**. Only 13% of directors claimed to be optimistic about the economy, compared with 50% two months earlier.

The Bank of England's biggest intervention in six years helped to steady **the pound** against the D-mark and avoid an interest-rate rise. But sterling remained perilously close to its floor in Europe's exchange-rate mechanism.

Thursday 27th
Foreign ministers gathered in London for a two-day **conference on ex-Yugoslavia**, chaired by John Major (on behalf of the European Community) and Boutros Boutros-Ghali (for the United Nations). The conference adopted a package of tough-sounding proposals. The fighting in Bosnia went on.

After a year of thankless toil, **Lord Carrington**, a former foreign secretary, resigned as head of the European Community's peacemaking effort for ex-Yugoslavia. Another former foreign secretary, **Lord Owen**, replaced him.

Controversy over **exam standards** flared up after the announcement of the best-ever results in GCSEs (the exam for 16-year-olds).

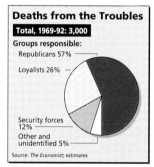

Deaths from the Troubles

Total, 1969-92: 3,000

Groups responsible:
Republicans 57%
Loyalists 26%
Security forces 12%
Other and unidentified 5%

Source: *The Economist*; estimates

The death toll in the 23 years since **Northern Ireland**'s Troubles began reached 3,000 with the murder of a young Catholic by a republican splinter group.

Monday 31st
Torrential bank-holiday rain kept both people and criminals away from the **Notting Hill carnival**. According to the organisers, the attendance still topped 1m. Scotland Yard's more sober estimate was 300,000.

September

Thursday 3rd
In an **effort to support sterling**, the government borrowed £7.3 billion-worth of D-marks and other currencies. The scheme was widely described as "innovative", but the euphoria proved short-lived.

Kevin Maxwell became Britain's **biggest-ever bankrupt**, with debts of over £400m ($800m). "Bankruptcy is a very public humbling," admitted Mr Maxwell.

Monday 7th
Threatened with closure at the end of the month, **London Zoo** won an indefinite reprieve. The head of the zoo's parent body said extra revenue had guaranteed the zoo's survival until April 1994, by which time a long-term rescue package should be in place.

Tuesday 8th
For the first time in its 124-year history, the **Trades Union Congress** was addressed by the head of the bosses' club, the Confederation of British Industry. Howard Davies of the CBI called for wage restraint in the public sector, with increases linked to productivity. Arthur Scargill, the miners' leader, staged a walk-out.

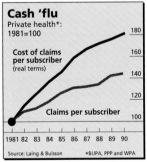

Cash 'flu
Private health*:
1981=100

Cost of claims per subscriber (real terms)

Claims per subscriber

1981 82 83 84 85 86 87 88 89 90

Source: Laing & Buisson   *BUPA, PPP and WPA

Sir Bryan Carsberg, the director-general of fair trading, triggered a Monopolies and Mergers Commission investigation into **private medical fees**. Rising bills had prompted much higher premiums for private medical insurance.

Wednesday 9th
John Patten, the education secretary, announced a review of the **teaching of English** in schools. The inquiry would concentrate on the teaching of standard English, basic writing and great literature.

Women in full-time work earned 23% less than men, said a report by the Equal Opportunities Commission. It urged the government to encourage employers to upgrade **women's pay**.

Sunday 13th
Several Labour MPs turned up to speak to fringe meetings at the start of the **Liberal Democrats' conference** in Harrogate. During the conference, the Lib-Dems ruled out any formal pact with Labour, but decided to "develop and debate ideas by working with people of all parties".

Sara Parkin resigned as leader of the **Green Party**. She told its conference in Wolverhampton that the party must "reform or fold".

Monday 14th
David Mellor, the national-heritage secretary, already in the news because of an extra-marital affair, made headlines again during a libel hearing brought by a friend whose father was a PLO member. He had paid for a holiday by Mr Mellor's family during the Gulf crisis.

Two brands of vaccine used for immunisation against measles, mumps and rubella were withdrawn by the **Department of Health** because they had caused meningitis in some children.

Wednesday 16th
"Black Wednesday". Desperate efforts to shore up sterling, through interest-rate rises of first two points and then a further three, came to grief. The government "suspended" sterling's membership of Europe's **exchange-rate mechanism**. That meant devaluation—something John Major's administration had sworn it would avoid.

Thursday 17th
In an atmosphere of recrimination, the government sought to **blame Germany**, and the Bundesbank in particular, for sterling's exit from the ERM. John Major's cherished special relationship with Helmut Kohl began to look as damaged as his anti-inflationary strategy.

Saturday 19th
A hospital consultant was convicted of **attempting to murder** a patient who had asked hospital staff for a drug to "finish her off". The terminally ill patient was in agonising pain from acute rheumatoid arthritis.

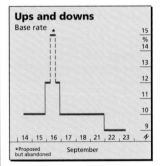

Ups and downs
Base rate

15
%
14
13
12
11
10
9

14 15 16 17 18 21 22 23

*Proposed but abandoned   September

Tuesday 22nd
The government cut **base rates** by one percentage point, to 9%, bringing them below German short-term rates for the first time in 11 years. The pound continued its slide against the D-mark.

Wednesday 23rd
More **job losses** hit the headlines. British Aerospace said it was to shed 3,000 jobs and close its Hatfield factory. The following day, Ford and Rolls-Royce blamed the recession for their plans to axe 2,500 jobs.

Thursday 24th
The pressure on the national-heritage secretary, **David Mellor**, to resign eventually proved irresistible. He had been accused of loose morals with an actress and of unwisely accepting free holidays. His replacement was Peter Brooke, a former Northern Ireland secretary.

Tuesday 29th
In his speech to the **Labour Party conference** in Blackpool, John Smith described John Major and Norman Lamont as the "Laurel and Hardy of British politics". On the eve of the conference, Bryan Gould caused a stir by resigning from the shadow cabinet in protest over the leadership's pro-Maastricht stance.

In a dawn raid, police **arrested a television researcher**, Bill Hamilton, who had worked on a Channel 4 programme that alleged collusion between the Royal Ulster Constabulary and loyalist death squads. He was charged with perjury.

Wednesday 30th
The **row with Germany** over the devaluation of sterling flared up again when a "confidential" paper delivered by the German Embassy to the Foreign Office was made public by the embassy. The paper set out the Bundesbank's rebuttal of British criticisms of its behaviour in the run-up to "Black Wednesday".

The Department of Trade and Industry ordered the troubled Municipal Mutual Insurance, the leading provider of **insurance for local authorities**, to stop paying claims or taking on new business. Councils panicked that they might soon be without insurance cover.

October

Thursday 1st
The new **Criminal Justice Act** came into force. One of its aims was to deal with more non-violent offenders by community penalties rather than custody.

Sunday 4th
Akio Morita, the head of the Sony Corporation, was awarded an honorary knighthood by the queen in recognition of his contribution to Anglo-Japanese relations. Sir Akio invented the **Sony Walkman**.

Tuesday 6th
The **Conservative Party conference** in Brighton argued with unaccustomed fury over Europe. Calls by Lord Tebbit for policies that put "Britain first" brought roars of approval. Douglas Hurd, the foreign secretary, described the risk of splitting the party over Europe as "madness".

Thursday 8th
At his speech in Brighton, Norman Lamont, the chancellor of the exchequer, gave a first glimpse of the government's **new economic policy** following sterling's exit from Europe's exchange-rate mechanism. Low inflation remained the goal, he said, but there would be no early return to the ERM.

Friday 9th
John Major wrapped himself in the flag in a bid to unite his party in his speech to its Brighton conference. He warned Euro-sceptics that failure to ratify the Maastricht treaty would leave Britain "scowling in the wings". But he pandered to their nationalism by using the words "Britain" and "British" 52 times in a 58-minute speech.

Monday 12th
The IRA intensified a **bombing campaign** in London. One of eight bombs in a week exploded in a crowded pub in Covent Garden.

The first **surveys of business confidence** since sterling's withdrawal from the ERM were grim. Dun & Bradstreet reported a sharp decline in businesses' expectations of sales, and a CBI survey revealed deepening pessimism in financial services.

The pits
Miners employed in Britain

1966-93, years ending March 31st
Source: Brtish Coal   *Estimate

Tuesday 13th
British Coal announced the closure of 31 pits and the loss of 30,000 jobs. The announcement caused an outcry, and threats of rebellion by Tory backbenchers.

The **Booker Prize** judges shared out the prize between the two favourites—Michael Ondaatje for "The English Patient" and Barry Unsworth for "Sacred Hunger".

Thursday 15th
More dismal news about **jobs**. The number out of work had risen to 2.84m, 10.1% of the workforce. In September the jobless total rose by 32,200.

British Rail announced average fare increases of 7.5% from January for season-ticket holders on InterCity and Network SouthEast. It blamed the higher-than-inflation rise on the recession.

Friday 16th
The one-day EC **Birmingham summit**, called by John Major in response to last month's currency-market saga, resulted in a pledge by leaders to make the Community more open and to respect national traditions. The declaration was overshadowed by the domestic political drama.

Monday 19th
"We British *are* Europeans," proclaimed **the queen** on a wound-healing state visit to Germany. But "like all close friends", she admitted, the British and Germans "do not always see eye to eye".

Tuesday 20th
The prime minister appeared to promise a **new economic strategy** for "growth and jobs". The government cut interest rates by one percentage point and hinted at plans for further investment in infrastructure. The share market perked up, but sterling remained depressed.

Sir Michael Checkland, the BBC director-general, accused his chairman, Marmaduke Hussey, of being too old to **lead the Beeb** into the next century. Mr Hussey, 69, has been given a second five-year extension to his contract. Sir Michael, 56, was given only a one-year extension.

John Major dashed **Neil Kinnock**'s hopes of becoming a European commissioner. Bruce Millan would keep his post for a further two years.

Wednesday 21st
The government narrowly escaped defeat in the Commons over British Coal's proposed pit closures—but only after conceding almost every concession demanded by Tory rebels. There would be more aid for the mining areas, consultation galore, a white paper, and 21 pits got a temporary reprieve to allow for a "full review" of the decision.

Thousands of miners arrived in London for a **protest march** against the pit closures. An opinion poll, by MORI, suggested only 16% of the country had any confidence in John Major.

Friday 23rd
The 1991 census showed that there are almost as many Catholics as Protestants in **Northern Ireland**. Protestants had been thought to outnumber Catholics by two to one. But many Catholics had boycotted the previous census, carried out in 1981 at the time of IRA hunger strikes.

Wednesday 28th
Scenting a chance to unseat John Major, the **Labour Party** decided to override its pro-European policy and vote against a "paving" motion for Maastricht. It hoped that its own votes, plus those of Tory rebels, would be enough to defeat the government.

The government accepted the conclusion of an independent inquiry, headed by Sir Bernard Tomlinson, that at least **ten London hospitals** should be closed or merged. The hospitals included St Bartholomew's, established in 1123. The report said that money should be shifted to GPs and provincial hospitals.

Friday 30th
A **car bomb in Whitehall** exploded only yards from Downing Street. The method of delivery was one well known in Northern Ireland: a minicab driver was forced to take the bomb to the target.

Wednesday 4th

The government narrowly avoided defeat in a crucial Commons **vote on Maastricht**: it won with a majority of just three. Bitter feuding promptly broke out within the Tory party, as rebels who returned to the fold at the last moment accused the government of intolerable "arm-twisting, thumb-screws, persuasion and inducements".

Thursday 5th

John Major created fresh doubts about the future of the **Maastricht treaty** by saying that final ratification by Britain would wait until mid-1993, after the second Danish referendum.

A dispute between BAA, the company that runs most of Britain's airports, and British Rail threatened to sink plans for a £300m ($450m) **express link from Heathrow** airport to Paddington station. BAA argued that the issue of track fees must be resolved before it could seek financing.

Monday 9th

Allegations that ministers broke government guidelines prohibiting **arms sales to Iraq** weeks before the invasion of Kuwait caused a furore. The allegations arose after the collapse of the trial of three company directors accused of making illegal sales to Iraq. John Major ordered a judicial inquiry.

President Boris Yeltsin visited John Major in London, signed the first bilateral treaty between Russia and Britain since 1766, pledging peace and friendship, and went to lunch with the queen.

Tuesday 10th

Six months of talks on the future of **Northern Ireland** broke up without agreement. The talks had produced only microscopic progress.

Wednesday 11th

The Archbishop of Canterbury made a plea for peace following a vote by the synod—the Church of England's governing body—to allow the ordination of **women priests**. The reform, which broke with four centuries of tradition, provoked stirrings of rebellion. More than 1,000 priests threatened to resign.

Thursday 12th

In his autumn statement, the chancellor, Norman Lamont, unveiled his **public-spending plans** for 1993-94. There would be tight controls on public-sector pay, to make way for capital spending—especially on housing—as part of the government's new growth strategy. The chancellor also cut interest rates by a further one percentage point.

Saturday 14th

The first **rugby match** between England and South Africa since 1969 was overshadowed by accusations of foul play. F.W. de Klerk, who attended the match, hailed it as a symbol of the restoration of normal relations between the two countries. John Major cancelled his plans to attend at the last minute.

Sunday 15th

A huge IRA **bomb at Canary Wharf** in London's Docklands was found by security men and defused.

The editor of the *Daily Mirror*, the only **pro-Labour tab-**loid, was replaced by someone "without any of the Maxwell experience", as the paper's owners explained. The Labour leader, John Smith, expressed concern.

Tuesday 17th

The government provoked an outcry by refusing entry visas to 180 **Bosnian refugees** on the Austria-Slovenia border. Kenneth Clarke, the home secretary, made concessions to six with family ties in Britain. Since Yugoslavia's break-up, Britain had accepted 4,500 refugees. Germany had taken in 235,000.

Wednesday 18th

The government's first set of **exam league tables** for schools was greeted by an education minister as a "catalogue of achievement". Parents' groups and teachers claimed the tables were misleading. Scilly Isles and suburban London schools came top, inner-city schools dominated the bottom ranks.

Thursday 19th

The government announced Britain's withdrawal from the European Fast Reactor **nuclear-research programme**, on which it had been collaborating with France and Germany since the 1950s at a cost of £2 billion ($3 billion). The decision ended Britain's development of "fast-breeder" nuclear reactors.

Friday 20th

A **fire at Windsor Castle** gutted a big part of the building, which the queen uses but which belongs to the state. The government quickly announced that it (that is, the taxpayer) would pay for repairs. This led to renewed controversy over the cost of the monarchy.

Tuesday 24th

In the wake of the Windsor fire and other royal disasters, **the queen** dubbed 1992 an *annus horribilis* and called for "a touch of gentleness, good humour and understanding" in royal reporting. Two days later the prime minister announced her offer to start paying taxes and to finance most members of her family herself.

Peter Brooke, the national-heritage secretary, issued the government's "green" (tentative) paper on the **future of the BBC**. The corporation then released its own long-awaited treatise on the subject. Both considered radical ideas, but it was not clear whether many of them would be put into practice.

Thursday 26th

The environment secretary, Michael Howard, announced details of the new **council tax**, due to replace the hated poll tax in April 1993. He eased Tory fears of another local-taxation fiasco by revealing plans for a transitional relief scheme to help those hardest hit by the new tax. No household would face an increase of more than £3.50 a week.

Sunday 29th

The chancellor, **Norman Lamont**, refused to resign in the wake of a spate of embarrassing newspaper stories. Tabloid newspapers had leaked details (partly accurate, partly not) of his credit-card bills. It was also revealed that Mr Lamont had accepted public money to help pay his legal fees involved in evicting a "sex therapist" tenant.

Tuesday 1st
After a tip-off, police evacuated Christmas shoppers from a large area of London's West End and made safe a van packed with explosives. People in Belfast were not so lucky: an **IRA bomb** in Ann Street injured 25.

John Gummer, the agriculture minister, announced his resignation from the Church of England's General Synod over its vote to allow **women priests**. He also signalled his intention to leave the Church once the legislation on the ordination of women was enacted.

Wednesday 2nd
Parts of the West of Britain suffered their **worst flooding in ten years**. Among the damage: part of an 18th-century toll bridge over the river Wye, washed away.

Thursday 3rd
The IRA's **bombing blitz** intensified. Two bombs exploded in the centre of Manchester, injuring 64 people.

Saturday 5th
Police put on a show of strength in their effort to counter IRA terrorism in England. They mounted random **road blocks** of the sort long used in Ulster, promising that the measures would be temporary.

Tuesday 8th
Following the destruction by Hindu fundamentalists of the mosque at Ayodhya, a wave of **ethnic violence** rolled from India into Britain: six Hindu temples were firebombed. Community leaders appealed—successfully—for calm.

Wednesday 9th
Buckingham Palace announced the separation of the **Prince and Princess of Wales**, after 11 years of marriage. John Major said their decision had "no constitutional consequences" and that there was "no reason why the Princess of Wales should not be crowned queen in due course". Not everyone was convinced.

Saturday 12th
The two-day **European summit** in Edinburgh ended with agreement on the two biggest issues: the Community's future finances and how to solve the "Danish problem". After months of growing criticism for the way he was handling Britain's six-month EC presidency, John Major had managed to succeed when it mattered most.

In a private ceremony in Scotland, the **Princess Royal** remarried. Her second husband, Commander Timothy Lawrence, was a former equerry to the queen.

Wednesday 16th
Sir Patrick Mayhew, the **Northern Ireland** secretary, said that the army would "return to its garrison role" only if the IRA renounced violence. Otherwise, he said, to withdraw would be to abandon Ulster to Yugoslav-style ethnic cleansing.

Thursday 17th
The government announced its plans for a **national lottery**, starting in 1994. Tickets would cost £1 and there would be a top prize of at least £1m ($1.6m) a week. Operators of the football pools, in whose market the lottery would compete, said the plans could cost 3,000 jobs.

The Labour Party launched its long-awaited **Commission on Social Justice**, with the job of re-thinking the tax and benefits system. Under the chairmanship of Sir Gordon Borrie, a former director-general of fair trading, the 16-member, quasi-independent commission was expected to take about 18 months to produce its conclusions.

Friday 18th
The Independent Television Commission rejected the only bid for a fifth terrestrial **television channel**. The ITC said the bid—by Channel Five Holdings, a consortium led by Thames Television—lacked sufficient "investor commitment".

Sunday 20th
The chairman of British Rail, Sir Bob Reid, criticised the government's plans for **railway privatisation**, saying there would be a lot of upheaval for no quick improvement in service and some worry about safety.

Newspapers revelled in the story of an ex-millionaire, Trevor Deaves, who received £1,830 ($2,940) a week from the state in income support to help pay mortgage interest on his 66-acre farm and mansion. It was believed to be Britain's **biggest-ever benefit payout**.

Monday 21st
The High Court ruled that the way the government had attempted to close 31 **coal pits** in October was illegal. It said the miners' right to proper consultation had been ignored.

The government bowed to pressure from the insurance industry and agreed to act as a **re-insurer of last resort** for cover against damage from terrorism in mainland Britain. In the wake of the IRA's attacks on property in England, insurers had frightened businesses by threatening to withdraw such cover.

Tuesday 22nd
Tristan Garel-Jones, the minister for Europe, announced his intention to resign once the Maastricht bill was passed. He explained he wanted to see more of his family.

Friday 25th
The queen, in her **Christmas message**, emphasised the value of "continuity", after her year of troubles. Her troubles with the media continued: the *Sun* had leaked her message in advance.

Monday 28th
The start of the **winter sales** was one of the busiest in years. Traffic in several city centres was clogged up as shoppers flocked to hunt for bargains. Optimists saw the rush as a sign that the economic mood was changing.

Thursday 31st
The new year **honours list**, the last of its kind before planned modernisation of the system, produced just one life peer: Shirley Williams, one of the "gang of four" Labour defectors who founded the now-defunct Social Democratic Party. Knighthoods went to, among others, David Frost, a political interviewer, and Anthony Hopkins, an actor.

As we reported then

Embattled bobbies

FEBRUARY 8TH *With a general election looming, the Tories looked short of fresh ideas for a new mandate. But one item on their agenda promised a rude break with Tory traditions: reforming the police*

ASK a policeman about the impending general election and you could be in for a surprise. He will tell you that he is an apolitical sort of bloke. But then he will reveal a detailed knowledge of voting trends and secret manifestos. He will say that this is the most important election for more than a decade. He will mutter about broken promises and hidden agendas. Then he will pull his biggest surprise: the promise-breakers and agenda-hiders in question are the Tories.

The word among the police is that the Tories are out to get them. The Conservative Party was happy to give the police what they needed to defeat striking miners and printers. But now the dirty work is done, the police can be treated like everyone else in the public sector. A fourth Conservative government will do for the police force what the last government did for the national health service and the education system—reorganise it along market lines.

The Tories will privatise what they can, selling off specialised services to private contractors and, more sinister still, restricting money so much that ever more companies and individuals will have to start hiring private security firms. The rest of the service will be reorganised on quasi-commercial—and highly parsimonious—lines. The Police Federation argues that the sell-off has begun. In January the government sold the docks police, the oldest police force in the country, to a private firm.

How much truth is there to these rumours? None, if the official Tory line is to be believed. Listen to Kenneth Baker, the home secretary, and you learn that the police are doing a wonderful job. Read Tory statements and you find endless guff about putting more bobbies on the beat. But talk to Conservatives in private and you hear a different story. The police need an officer class to stiffen their fibre. The police are the last of the old-style trade unions: over-manned, overpaid and riddled with restrictive practices. Clearly, police bashing is no longer a monopoly of the loony left.

The reason for the spat between the Tories and the police is that the Thatcherite approach to law and order proved to be an expensive disaster. The Tories gave the police the men and resources they asked for to fight crime—real spending on the police rose by almost 70% in the 1980s—but crime continued to soar and public confidence in the police slumped. A poll in 1959 revealed that 83% of those surveyed had great respect for the police; that figure had fallen to 43% by 1989.

A fresh approach is on its way. In 1988 a Home Office circular made it clear that police forces would in future be given more resources only if they were making the best use of the ones they already had. At the

same time, the Audit Commission revealed problems with police management stretching from the Home Office downwards. The Home Office, for example, ties the financing of local police forces to the number of uniformed officers they recruit—a perverse arrangement which discourages chief constables from employing (much cheaper) civilians or installing fancy computers. Police work is hampered by top-heavy and inefficient management structures.

So much for the assumption that the best way to prevent crime is to employ policemen. Suddenly, the Home Office is keen on voluntary initiatives, such as neighbourhood watches, and rehabilitation schemes, such as a £17.5m ($31.5m) initiative for drug counselling. John Patten, a minister at the Home Office, wants to shift attention away from crime prevention to criminal prevention—a neat ruse for playing the law-and-order card while spending less on the police.

This new thinking is being embedded in policy. The Home Office is looking a little less like an arm of the Police Federation and more like an organ of government. It has beefed up the Inspectorate of Constabulary, recruiting high-flying officers and requiring it to publish annual reports on the efficiency of each police force. It has also asked local forces to produce reports on the performance of every police officer, a precondition for weeding out the lazy and incompetent. The citizen's charter will add still further to the impetus to create a powerful and independent inspectorate.

A rejuvenated Home Office is producing initiatives on the police force by the dozen. It plans to recruit 10,000 more part-time, unpaid special constables. It is extending its fast-track graduate-recruitment scheme to include people in their 40s, possibly as a way of creating an officer class. It is even taking a critical look at itself. A newly appointed committee is examining the Home Office formula for police funding. The betting is that it will eventually decree fixed budgets for local police forces—just as the Audit Commission has recommended.

A new generation of well-educated and efficiency-conscious chief constables is enthusiastic about these reforms. (Indeed, some of them suggested the changes.) They welcome the idea of a Home Office which acts as a monitor of standards rather than a hands-on manager. They are anxious to get rid of sloppy management and over-manning. Go-ahead police authorities such as Kent's and Derbyshire's are doing away with layers of middle management and devolving more authority to local levels. But the unreconstructed elements in the ranks are determined to resist any change. Their chosen vehicle for resistance is the Labour Party.

Since the late 1980s the Police Federation and the Labour Party have been conducting a secret courtship. The Police Federation calculates that a Labour government would be too nervous of being accused of going soft on law and order to risk taking on the police. For its part, Labour is anxious to win friends in respectable places. Neil Kinnock, the Labour leader, once delighted the police by telling them that his childhood ambition was to be a policeman (an ambition which some of Labour's left-wingers think he has achieved). Roy Hattersley, the shadow home secretary, has delighted them even more by repeatedly promising that a future Labour government will put more bobbies on the beat.

A nervous Labour government or an impotent hung parliament may delay reform. It will not put it off indefinitely: the police are well aware that the 1990s will not be a repeat of the bountiful 1980s. Reforms are on their way—and the question is not whether it will happen, but when.

Red in tooth and claw

MARCH 21ST *Labour's shadow chancellor, John Smith, unveiled a plan for higher taxes that soon became a serious electoral liability—deservedly so*

JOHN SMITH should be congratulated for his candour in publishing Labour's "shadow budget". It is a bold move. Beyond boldness and candour, however, there is little to praise. If you ask whether the numbers in Mr Smith's budget add up to a plausibly costed programme of Labour government, the answer is no. If you ask whether, taken at his word, Mr Smith has offered a budget as calm, competent and moderate as his popular reputation, the answer again is no. The shadow budget is reckless, and its underlying economic philosophy—so far as one can be discerned—is not just flawed, it is dangerous.

Start with macroeconomic policy. Mr Smith has tried hard to appear "credible". He has promised not to devalue sterling within the European exchange-rate mechanism (ERM). And, rather than adding to public borrowing, he has adopted the Tories' projected public-sector borrowing requirement (PSBR) of £28 billion ($48 billion) for 1992-93. A week before he had called that deficit excessive and promised never to pay for tax cuts with borrowing. In his budget, he could have indexed personal allowances, instead of raising them (ie, cutting taxes) in real terms, and thereby cut public borrowing by £1 billion. Instead he chose to match the Tory budget's tax-bribe with one of his own.

That's politics. But why is Mr Smith's macroeconomic policy less credible than the government's? Certainly, the would-be chancellor cannot be accused of planning to over-stimulate the economy. Compared with the Tories' recent budget, Mr Smith's budget delivers no aggregate boost to the economy; within the new total for public spending, the "recovery programme" of £1.1 billion is vanishingly small. On the face of it, therefore, Mr Smith's budget is correctly austere. But there are two difficulties.

First, Mr Smith's promise to maintain sterling's value within the ERM is hard to believe. The shadow chancellor betrays no understanding of what that undertaking implies. Since October 1990, when sterling entered the ERM, interest rates have gradually come down. Mr Smith has greeted every change as too little and too late—as though a chancellor can choose to accelerate interest-rate reductions within the ERM. The commitment to the ERM implies a willingness to keep interest rates high if need be, however inconvenient for the domestic economy. In that inflexibility lies the ERM's anti-inflationary power. The shadow budget argues, in contrast, that the only way to defeat inflation is to "build efficient and competitive industry". That hardly implies a willingness to raise interest rates during the first post-election run on sterling.

Second, Mr Smith's numbers must in any case be regarded with suspicion. His shadow budget's increases in public spending are tiny when set against the promises that Labour's various departmental spokesmen have made. True, these promises have all been carefully qualified: "when circumstances allow", and so forth. But expectations have been created that will be hard to disappoint. Moreover, Mr Smith has not said how he intends to make good the shortfall of income that would presumably be caused by the curtailment of the government's privatisation plans. This might deprive a Labour government of £2 billion in 1992-93 and larger sums thereafter. Something would have to give: either Mr Smith's "prudence" on borrowing, or his pledge not to raise taxes for most taxpayers.

It is in the plans for personal taxation that the shadow budget is most radical. Elements of Mr Smith's reforms undoubtedly make sense. Higher income-tax

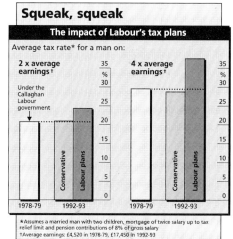

Squeak, squeak

The impact of Labour's tax plans

Average tax rate* for a man on: 2 x average earnings†, 4 x average earnings†. Under the Callaghan Labour government. Conservative, Labour plans. 1978-79, 1992-93.

*Assumes a married man with two children, mortgage of twice salary up to tax relief limit and pension contributions of 8% of gross salary
†Average earnings: £4,520 in 1978-79, £17,450 in 1992-93

thresholds are a better way to help the low-paid than the lower-rate band proposed by the government (though neither measure helps the really poor, who pay little or no tax in any case). It is also sensible to remove the dip in marginal tax rates between £21,060, the ceiling for national insurance contributions (NICS), and £23,700, the threshold for the present 40% rate of income tax (to be retained). But Mr Smith does these things as part of a reform that causes a sudden and massive increase in the tax burden for those with incomes of £21,000 a year and more.

At 49% and 59%, Labour's higher rates of income tax plus NICS are not outlandish by international standards. But the incomes at which such rates start to bite are outlandish. In Britain a married person starts paying the current 40% top tax-rate on roughly 1½ times average male earnings; the top-rate (31%) threshold in America is four times average earnings and in France (57%) and Germany (53%) more than six times. Already, British executives pay more of their income in tax than their foreign counterparts.

Labour's policy would do far more than reverse the higher-rate cuts introduced since 1979. Mr Smith would impose a much heavier burden of tax on technical and professional staff, on middle and senior managers, and on owners and directors of small and medium-sized companies than that of the previous Labour government, whose chancellor boasted of taxing the rich "until the pips squeaked". Almost everywhere in the world, top tax rates fell sharply during the 1980s. For those on higher-than-average earnings, the shadow budget would therefore make Britain's tax regime one of the most severe in the world—and conspicuously so.

The reform would take a big risk with the economy. In London and the southeast, the recession has hurt many prosperous but over-borrowed families; the links between indebtedness, collapsing house prices and the slow recovery in consumer spending are all too clear. A budget that imposes—all at once—the heaviest tax increase for decades on this part of the economy is an extraordinary gamble.

If this budget is any guide, the reformed Labour Party, the moderation and competence of John Smith, the fine talk of "an active policy to create the supply-side environment within which enterprise can thrive" all come down to this: soak the "rich". That is the message that will go out to foreign investors, to footloose capital and footloose managerial talent. Mr Smith's budget would blunt incentives to seek promotion, to take the risk of starting a business and to acquire skills, not just for the rich but across a large part of the economy. A Labour Party that rightly emphasises education and investment remains as contemptuous as it ever was of those hoping to reap the returns on education and investment.

Many of Britain's political and economic commentators have taken the view that there is little to choose between the Tories' recent budget and Mr Smith's effort. The *Financial Times* described it merely as a choice between "monetary rectitude and fiscal profligacy in the blue corner and fiscal profligacy and monetary rectitude in the red one". Such a curious misjudgment suggests that Britain, as well as the Labour Party, may have changed much less over the past 13 years than had been supposed.

Give 'im the kippers

MARCH 21ST *Once the general election got under way, many were bemused by the anti-hero figure leading the Tories*

DURING the heyday of Margaret Thatcher, fastidious Conservatives would bemoan the "cult of the Blessed Margaret" that developed around her. Never again, they promised. And now what has happened? In much the same way, the Tories' campaign is shaped around the personage of John Major.

The Conservative manifesto cover is a giant blow-up of the John Major grin. The first party broadcast is an autobiographical film called "John Major. The Journey". Mr Major's whistle-stop tours around the country feature "meet-the-people" events in which the prime minister sits on a bar-stool taking questions from an invited audience.

To an extent, this was inevitable. Mr Major charms almost everyone he meets and his rise from a relatively poor family background and an early stint on the dole queue is a Conservative morality tale that the party finds irresistible.

Even so, the dangers are apparent. The party broadcast, on March 18th, was in many ways impressive; but it showed that building up a leader-cult risks bathos—particularly with Mr Major, who positively trades on his ordinariness. The film script carries the following exchange, for example, in London's Brixton market:

PM: "Can I have a pound of those tomatoes, nice to see you." Greengrocer: "Nice seeing you." PM: "We used to come in and buy kippers." Fishmonger: "Well we still sell kippers." PM: "I'll have some kippers, I'll have some kippers."

Mr Major already suffers from being lampooned as a Mr Pooter who has wandered into Downing Street almost by accident. Such exchanges do not necessarily help him. Similarly, Mr Major's bar-stool chats with carefully selected audiences have produced unflattering comparisons with a bland Irish singer, Val Doonican. They are not the absorbing television the Tories had hoped for.

So are the Tories in danger of wasting their best asset? Transmitting Mr Major's decency and niceness to a wide audience is clearly proving a problem. Perhaps they have been protecting him too much. Unscripted moments of humour and confrontation are just what nervous handlers try to avoid; yet they have an electric quality that Mr Major's campaign currently lacks—and badly needs.

The insider–out

MARCH 28TH *With less than two weeks of campaigning to go, the Tories looked like losing the election. Here's why*

THE Conservatives' campaign oozes uneasiness, and a surprising insecurity of tone. At the centre of the problem is John Major himself, or rather the selling of him. Curious, that, since he has always been so popular. But Neil Kinnock's cheery derision when told that Mr Major was promising "no more Mr Nice Guy" is one of the more memorable images of the campaign so far.

The Tories set out to sell Mr Major as John Commoner, the ordinary man who got to the top as an outsider. But the image was carried too far and now seems phoney, not only to observers but probably to the prime minister himself.

For the reality is starkly different: Mr Major is the ultimate insider. True, as a teenager he suffered periods of relative poverty, took labouring jobs and was unemployed for eight months. But a year later Mr Major was in a white-collar job. Since then he has had 28 years of adult employment. For 14 of them he was a banker. For much of that time he was a Tory councillor or Westminster candidate, networking his way up the party. For nine of those 28 adult years he has been in government, occupying four of the most powerful jobs in Whitehall.

And this man is supposed to be an outsider? Only, perhaps, at the top of the Conservative Party could Mr Major's lack of a university education and the bumps in his early career be seen as something worthy of wonder. Of the other 21 members of Mr Major's cabinet, 19 went to Oxbridge or to ancient Scottish universities; the odd two out are David Hunt, who attended Bristol and Montpellier, and John Wakeham, one of the wealthiest of them all. Among those advising the Major campaign are a clutch of multi-millionaires.

Perhaps, for them, having a once-unemployed Brixton man chairing their meetings did seem like the arrival of a Kalahari bushman for tea at the Ritz. They then made the basic mistake of thinking that the rest of the country would agree. Like pasty-faced courtiers confronting a surly mob (known in the pollsters' jargon as "the C2s"), they made too much of their leader's humble origins. Go on, they urged him, you used to speak fluent oik. You talk to them. No wonder they burble on endlessly about his ordinariness. No wonder either, that he is sensitive to their condescension.

Political history suggests that British voters are patriotic and hard-headed, susceptible neither to soft-soap nor to flattery. If they decide to back Mr Major, it will be because they trust him as a sophisticated and experienced insider, not because he has persuaded them that he is the boy next door. It would have been more sensible, then, to emphasise Mr Major's un-ordinary qualities—the drive, political antennae, retentive memory and capacity for hard work that got him the job in the first place. This week the foreign secretary,

Whitehall man made flesh

Douglas Hurd, started to do just that, telling a press conference that he had watched Mr Major in private meetings with other world leaders "build his own authority . . . quickly and impressively."

But Mr Hurd's line is rarely heard. Suppose the other politicians around Mr Major were less obsessed by his early life, and tried to sell him as he is. What would their message be then? Perhaps: "Here is a capable mandarin with strong, conventional views about economic management, who has proved his resilience and common sense. As you can see from his citizen's charter, he is not a visionary, but an administrator.

"He has risen through the salariat. Unlike Cecil Parkinson and Michael Heseltine, he has never been a businessman, doing it for himself. Unlike Margaret and Norman Tebbit, he is a stranger to the ferocity and heartache of parliamentary opposition. He is accustomed to power. Under him, life will be duller but safer. We British are unimpressed by politics, and rightly so. We would prefer to be left alone to get on with our lives under a lowish-tax but compassionate and anonymous government. After the Thatcher whirlwind,

that is what John offers."

Would such bold blandness win votes? According to the polls, more than a quarter of the electorate is still undecided about how (or whether) to vote. No doubt some of these people are poring over manifestos, annotating newspaper reports, and carefully compiling lists of pledges before deciding. But for every uncommitted voter like that, surely nine more, or 99, are dazed by the hyperbole and sickened by the abuse.

These are the people being wooed by Paddy Ashdown's rehearsed high-mindedness. But they are also the voters Mr Major could be winning over—and is failing to. It is hard to believe they are moved by the nonsensical chatter from Tory briefers about "unleashing the dogs of war" on Labour. Ministers keep talking about "just letting John be himself". If they really meant it, they would let him be as reasonable and uncombative as usual. That would be more effective than pretending he is the man from the mean streets, streets he has not walked since about 1964.

There are few other options. Mr Major's friends often say that if only he were able to meet every voter face to face, he would win by a landslide. Impossible? Well, as it happens, psephologists reckon that this election will be decided by only 80,000 or so people—the swing voters in the most marginal seats. Assuming Mr Major could have managed 300 two-minute chats per day, and that Central Office could have tracked these awkward souls down, he could in theory have met every one of them between July 22nd last year, when he launched his citizen's charter, and polling day.

Short of that (it has some small logistical drawbacks), the idea of a mildly apolitical prime minister might have gone down rather well in this mildly apolitical country. Mr Major has a story to tell, but it is a real one about administrative efficiency and tax rates, not a fairy-tale about evil socialists and good boys from Brixton market. As it is, he could yet become the first prime minister in British history to be defeated at an election because he was overpackaged.

A plea for bloodshed

APRIL 18TH *Labour reacted to its general-election defeat with a stoicism that many non-Tories deplored*

HAVING lost the 1992 election, Labour is now wondering how best to lose the next one. Can there be any other explanation for the tranquil reaction by some of its senior politicians to their defeat, or their enthusiasm for a smooth change of leadership, with the minimum of fuss or bloodshed? Do they still not realise what has happened?

As the results were being declared, Michael Portillo, one of the newcomers in John Major's refashioned cabinet, insisted: "The important thing to remember is that we can be defeated. There is no reason at all for Labour to give up." Much the same thing was being said by some of Labour's leaders. Roy Hattersley said in an interview: "We are far nearer to winning than the gloomy predictions over the weekend have suggested . . . We're down in round three but the fight goes on for many more generations . . . "

Many more generations? That is the kind of Labour Party Mr Portillo and his mates like fighting. Plucky old thing—bonk—keeps being knocked over—split lip, wonky nose, water on the brain—staggers to its feet every time—bonk—knocked over again. Never wins. Never gives up.

How British. And how useless. The nearness of the win this time is now a matter of history, not politics. The Boundary Commission changes (giving the Tories perhaps another 20 seats, a possible net switch of 40) and the continuing political and demographic shifts mean that the 1996-97 election will be harder still for Labour. And it is not just the electoral boundaries that are being changed: another five years of Conservatism will further weaken the trade unions and make it harder for them to finance Labour.

Only the most ruthless scrutiny of Labour's structure, policies, philosophy and even its name, followed (perhaps) by an electoral pact with the Liberal Democrats, might (just might) get it back into power five years hence. Then the immediate introduction of voting reform could scupper the idea of majority rule by any single party, making John Major the last leader of an all-Tory government. All alert Tories know this. Mr Major's big task now is to keep the anti-Tories apart.

He will be helped, lucky fellow, by Labour politicians who explain away their defeat with the minimum of soul-searching. Some, including Mr Hattersley, blame the recession (it made people more easily frightened). After 1987 they were saying the boom was to blame (it had made people more selfish). These are excuses, not explanations. Ditto the argument, made by Neil Kinnock, that the Tory tabloids were responsible: "I express no bitterness when I say that the Conservative-supporting press has enabled the Tory party to win yet again when the Conservative Party could not have secured victory for itself."

Mr Kinnock, who has been on the receiving end of more abuse than most mortals could take, has a perfect right to hit back. But the press was not to blame for Labour's defeat. Most people get their news from national television, which bent over backwards to be fair, and relayed a campaign in which the most vivid images were Labour ones. Much was made of the fact that in marginals like Basildon (which stayed Tory) half the households take the *Sun*. But Basildon does not—thus far—employ sinister civic thought-police to ram the *Sun* through letter-boxes. Maybe people choose it because they happen to agree with it.

Labour's inquest needs to be about more than the press. It is hard to see quite how it can be divorced from the business of choosing the new leader. Or why it should be. Labour now needs a leader as single-minded and brave as Mr Kinnock—but one less sentimental about Labour as an institution. Perhaps this individual cannot be found; but the party owes it to its supporters to look long and hard at the two contenders, John Smith and Bryan Gould. Mr Kinnock's attempt to force the pace with a vote in June was rightly overturned by the party's national executive in favour of a mid-July election.

Cheerful Mr Smith has the thing virtu-

Gould, the outsider

ally sewn up already—the union and MPs' pledges are neatly tucked behind his immaculate breast-pocket hanky. It all seems a touch premature. He may be the right person to lead Labour—but how can anybody really know until both men have gone through months of open debate about Labour's future, explaining and defending their visions and strategies? Mr Smith is as discreet as an Easter Island statue, so he would dislike that. But the thinking should precede the voting, not the other way about. If Labour switches bosses like some decaying *quattrocento* court on a Tuscan hilltop, then it will rob its new leader of authority in the party and of credibility beyond it.

Bryan Gould, the party's environment spokesman, has drawbacks too. He is rocky on the currency, a less effective debater than Mr Smith, and sceptical about voting reform. But he scores by not being a gut "Labour man". He wants a cross-party constitutional convention, along Scottish lines, to build up a consensus on reform. And, unlike most Labour leaders, he is a southerner (very southern, being once a New Zealander). Whereas Mr Smith, a Scot, underestimated the impact of his tax proposals in the south, Mr Gould knows all too well about the people Labour needs to attract.

But his main claim is that, as the outsider, he wants the maximum debate. One asset, at least, the party has in abundance: the time to think. It does not matter, frankly, if a bit of blood is spilled now; better that than rushing into the wrong long-term strategy. There will be no pact with the Liberal Democrats (whose disastrous election result has passed almost without comment) for years. But the direction of anti-Tory politics may be decided within weeks.

Labour's inquest and its choice of leader are not matters for Labour alone, or even mainly. They are not enclosed territory, surrounded by barbed-wire and roses, marked "trespassers beware". They belong in the public domain, where the electorate can at least wander and question. Why? Because they are questions about the very future of a healthy multi-party democracy.

The Whitehall jester

MAY 9TH *The most intriguing move in the new Tory government was to set up a "minister for fun"*

IT WOULD be too unBritish to call it the Ministry of Culture: the word smells French, and takes itself seriously. The Department of National Heritage, as the new ministry run by David Mellor is called,

sounds safer: old, stuffed, and probably kept in a glass case. Even that, though, is a bit too grandiose for ministers, including Mr Mellor, who swiftly dubbed it the ministry of fun. But a ministry of culture it is,

with bits and bobs like sport and press regulation thrown in. The big arguments will be over the BBC's future, but the big bucks will go into persuading the British that they are a cultured people after all.

The Tories did not advertise such a ministry in their manifesto. Labour did. For a prime minister who wants to gather support among groups who do not have much time for his party, there is a lot of sense in stealing the idea. Arty types are held to be pinkos, and rather influential. Young people, who are well-known for lounging about in galleries all day long, also vote Labour more than their parents. Jack Lang, France's socialist minister of culture for the past 11 years, has scattered money around the artists and built himself a following among the young.

Can Mr Mellor become a Tory Jack Lang? Mr Lang has certain advantages. He looks like a film star. His ministry got FFr22.4 billion ($4 billion) last year. The British government's arts budget was £600m ($1.1 billion). The aesthetics are immutable, but the financial constraints are shifting. Thanks to Mr Mellor, first as arts minister and then as chief secretary to the Treasury, finance for the arts has been rising sharply. And now the arts have been promised the proceeds of the new national lottery, predicted to be somewhere between £500m and £1 billion.

Mr Mellor certainly has the tastes and character to turn himself into a cultural tsar. Whereas most of those in public life limit themselves to a fondness for the jollier bits of opera, Mr Mellor is not just vaguely enthusiastic; he is a passionate lover of serious music and a trustee of the London Philharmonic Orchestra. He

knows what he likes—even in those arts that he does not know well—and he interferes.

The art world, which has long been begging for a ministry and lots more cash, is getting a little nervous. The trouble about having powerful, well-financed, ministers in charge is that they may start taking control. Suddenly the old British way of doing things, with worthies on the Arts Council distributing money at arm's length from the politicians, and volunteers around the country promoting ballet in North Wales or pottery in Lincolnshire, does not look so shabby.

Nor is Jack Lang-ism an unqualified good thing. People have started pointing to "L'Etat Culturel", a new book that has pricked France's cultural self-confidence. The author, Marc Fumaroli, argues that France's *grandes oeuvres* programme succeeded in building plenty of palaces to culture—the Pyramide du Louvre, the Grande Arche, the Très Grande Bibliothèque—and in stifling the individual creativity that should have produced the works of art to fill them. Mr Mellor, in an interview with the *Financial Times*,

started talking about "memorials" or "permanent examples of the nature of our culture that future generations will have pride in". Oh. Maybe somebody should lend him the book.

Mr Mellor was forced to resign the ministry of fun on September 24th after a series of scandal-mongering disclosures about his private life.

Small bang

MAY 9TH *Winning his own electoral mandate as prime minister gave John Major the chance to signal a deeper break with the past. One result, little fanfared, was a new start for government policy on science*

FOR the first time in more than 30 years Britain has a cabinet minister with direct responsibility for science. The last such minister, in the early 1960s, was regarded as an eccentric spokesman for the other culture. Lord Hailsham was an Old Etonian who read classics at Oxford before winning a prize fellowship at All Souls.

But the Conservative Party moves with the times. To prove it, John Major has given the science portfolio to William Waldegrave—an Old Etonian who read classics at Oxford before (you guessed it) winning a prize fellowship at All Souls. Mr Waldegrave is adding stinks-and-bangs to his ragbag portfolio of responsibilities as the quaintly named Chancellor of the Duchy of Lancaster. (Others include the Citizen's Charter and the civil service.) As a non-departmental minister, he will be based in the Cabinet Office.

But it would be unfair to dismiss Mr Waldegrave as Lord Hailsham without the wig. Lord H is the eldest son of a peer; Mr

W is a younger son. Lord H went to aristocratic Christ Church; Mr W attended the relatively classless Corpus Christi (and then the even more classless Harvard). Lord H started his career as a barrister; Mr W spent some time working for Lord Weinstock at GEC. Lord H once had to summon help to work an electric toaster; Mr W probably knows how.

Certainly, scientists are delighted by his appointment. It raises the profile of science in higher government circles. The science portfolio used to be fobbed off to a junior minister at the Department of Education and Science (DES). But a junior minister lacks cabinet clout, and the DES inevitably devotes much more thought to schoolchildren than to scientists. Now science will have a cabinet member to champion its cause in the annual battle for money. A more co-ordinated science policy may also emerge; before, half-a-dozen departments had a finger in the science pie. Now one minister will at least scruti-

nise what they are up to.

But the biggest reason for the cheering from the science lobby is that Mr Waldegrave will be supported by a revamped bureaucracy. The Office of Science and Technology, based in the Cabinet Office and led by the government's chief scientist, Professor William Stewart, will become bigger and more powerful, taking in the former science branch of the DES. It will be responsible for the science budget and for a range of scientific quangos including the five science-research councils. (All, alas, is not as simple as it seems: the DES will go on financing university research.)

Many of these changes were foreshadowed in the Labour rather than the Conservative manifesto. Why has the government suddenly decided to outbid the left on science policy? The obvious answer is Europe. Lack of a science minister has long been an embarrassment at Euro-bashes. Most European Community countries send a science minister (with an expert adviser in tow) to represent them at the EC research council or the OECD. Britain has had to make do with a junior minister from the Department of Trade and Industry.

In July Britain takes over the presidency of the EC, a job that includes a good deal of co-ordinating of science policy. Now Mr Major will be represented by a cabinet minister (albeit one with a quirky title) and his chief scientific officer.

The new move also signals an attempt to build bridges between the Tory party and scientists. One of the first things John Major did when he arrived in Downing Street was to invite the bigwigs of the scientific world to meet him for tea and a chat. He has decided to let the science budget increase in real terms every year for the next three years. And he has strengthened Mr Waldegrave's hand with a junior minister who has long been interested in science. Robert Jackson (yet another fellow of All Souls) has a cluster of scientific laboratories in his constituency, held the science portfolio when he was a minister for science at the DES from 1987 to 1990, and helped to launch a pressure group, Save British Science.

Margaret Thatcher failed to get her honorary doctorate from Oxford largely because the scientists hated her. Can Dr Major (Oxon) be far away?

Forging his future

JULY 18TH,   *John Smith took over from Neil Kinnock as Labour Party leader. Bagehot delved beyond the Scottish lawyer's telegenic exterior*

IN 1994 a senior, anonymous Labour MP is widely quoted thus: "I never thought I'd say it—but come back, Neil, all is forgiven." John Smith is a disaster: stiff and reproving on television, a weak and old-looking Labour leader who is too timid to reform the party thoroughly and too unimaginative to build the anti-Tory coalition Britain desperately needs.

For Mr Smith, gravitas has turned out to be merely the Latin for boring. His enthusiasm for high taxes has proved, as in the 1992 election, a turn-off for the southern voters. At the Commons there are continual and demoralising rumours about the health of this heart-attack survivor. "Everyone knows" he is lazy. The Westminster in-crowd mutter about the superior sex appeal of Tony Blair.

These are some of the things that will be said about Mr Smith over the next couple of years. He had better get used to them. After he becomes Labour leader on July 18th, he will enjoy a brief honeymoon. Then the pro-Tory papers, the Conservative Party and even some Labour dissidents will try to destroy him. Every angle will be used, every line of attack attempted. If Mr Smith thinks he can continue to receive the flattering press he enjoyed when he was a useful stick with which to beat Mr Kinnock, he had better think again.

Of course, Mr Smith does not think this. He told friends that if Mr Kinnock won the election and he became chancellor, he expected to be the most unpopular man in the Labour Party. He had steeled himself to be booed down at party conferences as he kept the lid on spending and kept the pound in the European exchange-rate mechanism. (If he is to prove a successful leader, he may face the booing yet.) For someone who is routinely described as being straightforward and simple, Mr Smith is rather a complicated man—as smooth and glossy as a Russian doll, but as multi-layered too.

On the outside is the Smith of the television studio. This fellow is decorated with every English cliché about the lowland Scots—bankerly, cautious-but-dull, trustworthy. Packed inside that Mr Smith is the conviction socialist who is in politics to help the poor and who never forgets it. This less public Smith is the man who is (in contrast to Mr Kinnock) on genial personal terms with hard-leftists like Tony Benn

The outer layer

and Dennis Skinner and who is regarded by the Labour left as being that rare commodity, a "good right-winger".

Inside that man is the genial, social Smith recognised by scores of friends as the mirthful, whisky-drinking companion, whose language can be surprisingly crude. And finally, deep inside social-Smith, is a quiet but self-reliant man. If cockiness can run deep, it runs deep here. This self-assuredness means that he will be harder to hurt than Mr Kinnock. One shrewd minister says: "We regard him as an *homme sérieux*"—and he means Mr Smith's private toughness.

He is a man with the capacity and will to make his party as serious as he is. His admirers say he will be more radical than most outsiders have realised. He will allow previously unsayable things to be said about taxation and the poor; and will vigorously push for electoral reform for the Commons after a Labour committee reports on it next spring. The 1993 Labour conference will be the culmination of an energetic burst of reform and change that will start this weekend.

But then comes the question of Mr Smith and the much-touted realignment of the left. He may be sceptical about the practicality of a pact with the Liberal Democrats, but he cannot rule it out. Most observers still see it as one possible key to unlocking the next election. But there are already signs that Mr Smith and Paddy Ashdown, the Liberal Democrats' leader, will find it hard to deal at all. Granted, Mr Smith was the main conduit between the government and the Liberals during the Lib-Lab pact of the late 1970s. But his self-certainty and instinctive Labour loyalism mean he will not be a natural power-sharer. He is quite partisan. He is not humble. On the floor of the Commons these are necessary virtues. Behind closed doors, they may turn out to be vices.

He is near-contemptuous of many Liberal Democratic policies (sometimes with justice) and speaks often of the weakness of that party. Mr Ashdown signals his unease about Mr Smith thus: "Many people have rightly asked this question: are Labour able to take part in the building of the new politics, or will they continue to act as a barrier to its progress? The answer we have received in the past few months has been in the negative. I regret that Labour has been moving away from the future, not towards it."

The two parties are not rebounding from one another quite as smartly as Mr Ashdown's comments suggest. Mr Smith seems to have encouraged colleagues such as Robin Cook and a young Highland MP, Calum Macdonald, to engage in a little verbal flirtation with the Liberal Democrats. He wants to make sure his proposed commission on social justice will not be a wholly owned Labour outfit. But the longer-range forecast must be for squalls. Both Mr Smith and Mr Ashdown are inclined to be high-minded: were one of them to be a cheerily cynical fixer, their relationship would probably be easier.

The expected size of Mr Smith's majority as leader will reflect a warmth throughout the party about a man who seems both modern and genuine. He is wary enough to expect the attacks which started this column, and probably tough enough to withstand them (though the deepest recesses of anyone's character are mysterious and unpredictable). He is sharp enough to find ways of raising taxes that might even sell in the south. He has only one chance to get to Downing Street: Bagehot guesses he will be ruthlessly radical in reforming his party.

And none of that will be quite enough. Pride, as any good presbyterian knows, is a sin. It is a sin to which the Scots are peculiarly prone, just as the Scots can be too loyal to their own kind. But Mr Smith has to reach out and bring new people into the Labour fold—ex-Tory voters, wishy-washy English Liberals, all manner of dubious characters. To do this, he will need to suppress some of his deepest prejudices and instincts, and reach out. He will need to do so at the very moment when the attacks on him will make him want to recoil, and stick with his own people, his Labour clan. It is an unfairly difficult thing to ask of anyone. But if he cannot manage it, Mr Smith will fail.

Britannia rules the waverers

AUGUST 15TH **Pictures of Bosnia's agony shocked the world. Yet this was a drama in which Britain failed to live up to its Thatcherite reputation for forthrightness**

A POLITICIAN, it was once said, thinks of the next election; a statesman, of the next generation. No other country is as well-placed as Britain to be statesmanlike over Bosnia. Not only does it currently have the job, as the European Community's president until the end of the year, of setting the EC's agenda and co-ordinating its policies. It also faces none of the inhibitions distracting the other big western players—the presidential campaign in the United States, the imminent referendum on the Maastricht treaty in France, Germany's constitutional qualms about sending any forces abroad. John Major's government, which showed its capacity for leadership with its safe-haven plan for the Kurds last year, is fresh from its election victory. The British might reasonably be expected to be making the running in the Bosnian imbroglio.

Indeed they are. But not the official British. The most influential intervention of the past week came from a British news team: Independent Television News's pictures from Omarska camp in Bosnia shocked the world. Second-most-influential, arguably, was a former British prime minister: Margaret Thatcher's call for a vigorous western response did much to sway opinion in America. In Britain itself, the most visible politician in reports from the Balkans has not been any government minister, but Paddy Ashdown, the leader of the Liberal Democrats, who has been airlifting himself to Bosnia and arguing for intervention. Where, meanwhile, are the officials who are supposed to be in charge of British policy?

On holiday, mostly. Mr Major is in Spain. His foreign secretary, Douglas Hurd, is in Tuscany. Two of the top three Foreign Office officials handling policy towards ex-Yugoslavia are away. In London it has been left to Lynda Chalker, the overseas-aid minister, to field questions about Bosnia.

Few would begrudge busy ministers a well-earned rest. Yet even before the ministerial holiday season, Britain's policy towards ex-Yugoslavia was earning a reputation for its absence of urgency and imagination. Now, while the *New York Times* approvingly compares Lady Thatcher to Winston Churchill, the British government is increasingly criticised for neo-Chamberlainism: treating Bosnia as a faraway country about which it can do little.

In Sarajevo, Bosnia's Muslim leaders express their frustration with British statements about non-intervention. In Bonn, Germany's foreign minister, Klaus Kinkel, complains about Britain's failure to share the refugee burden. Germany has well over 200,000 refugees from ex-Yugoslavia; Britain has little more than 1,000, and has even been expelling some of those.

In Brussels, a top official at the European Commission criticises Britain for calling a multinational conference with too much advance notice—an invitation, he complains, for Serbs to press on for maximum military gains until the London conference begins on August 26th. On August 10th, while the commission's president, Jacques Delors, was urging armed intervention at an emergency meeting of the European Parliament, Douglas Hogg, a junior Foreign Office minister who was in town for the day en route for the Balkans, was upsetting Euro-MPs by failing to turn up (a representative of the presidency always attends normal sessions of the parliament). A feeling is spreading that Britain is making a hash of its EC presidency.

Minds versus hearts

Does Britain really deserve such criticism? No more than other countries, its defenders can fairly claim. The blame for the disasters in ex-Yugoslavia is widely shared. Critics tend to confuse incompetence with impotence: sometimes, there is not a lot outsiders can realistically do.

The British have specialised in realism. They know from their own experience in Northern Ireland—and from earlier lessons in India and Palestine—about the dangers of getting caught in the middle of ethnic feuds. They have been cool-headed in calculating the costs and benefits of possible policies. At strategy sessions, diplomats and generals have pored over ethnic maps and military options. British policy has been meticulously thought through. Nor have British diplomats been idle behind the scenes.

The trouble is that cool-headedness can easily be mistaken for heartlessness. And if the basic policy is to "do nothing", there is always the danger of losing the initiative to others who "do something". That is exactly what has happened at several key moments of the Yugoslav crisis.

Against the Foreign Office's better judgment, Britain was dragged into recognising Slovenia and Croatia by a Germany threatening to break ranks with its more cautious EC partners. In June, hours after Mr Major had carefully explained at a press briefing how over 100,000 troops would be needed to intervene effectively in Bosnia, President Mitterrand showed how to take Sarajevo airport single-handed. Now Britain has found itself having to respond to American (election-driven) pressure for a UN resolution authorising "all necessary means" to back the delivery of humanitarian help.

So much for British leadership. Boldness is not to be expected from the prudent diplomats at the Foreign Office, whose boss, Mr Hurd, is himself by training and temperament more of a prudent diplomat than a politician. Any bold initiatives—from welcoming thousands of refugees to agreeing to send troops—would almost certainly have to come from the prime minister, as was the case over the Kurds. But before proposing anything remotely risky, Mr Major would want to be sure that there was a strong demand for such risk-taking from the British public. In other words, if Britain is ever to take a lead over ex-Yugoslavia, it will come above all from the force of its public opinion, not from any statesmanship of its ruling politicians.

House of Windsor

AUGUST 29TH **As the royal family was rocked by scandals, we irreverently analysed its troubles from a business perspective**

THE problems of "the firm", as it is affectionately called, are not immediately financial. Although the value of some of the assets in its large property portfolio have undoubtedly slumped, cash-flow is healthy (see table). Its problem lies in increasing worries about the reliability of some of its offshoots. There has been a perceptible fall in customer goodwill, and some analysts are beginning to wonder whether this may not eventually result in this once-unassailable operator losing its state franchise. Or, in the jargon of the business, how many devaluations of the crown does it take to create a constitutional crisis?

The firm has seen, and survived, much turbulence. The Welsh takeover which created House of Tudor in the 15th century was followed by a handover to a Scottish subsidiary in the 17th century. As House of Stuart, it lost touch with the market and briefly went out of business. After it was acquired by German interests in the 18th century, it went through a long period of stability. In the early 20th century, when the German connection became an embarrassment, the firm had a successful relaunch under a new, British, name.

The current management has diversified into younger brands and raised the firm's profile through a new emphasis on public relations. The strategy was designed to increase consumer awareness and stave off the distant possibility that customers might consider switching to a cheaper, presidential, product. But, as happened with Perrier's troubles during the benzene scandal in 1990, high brand awareness can cause problems when quality is in doubt.

The oldest product in the royal range, the queen mother, remains an impressive design, its antique sparkle ever-popular; but it may be coming to the end of its life cycle. The queen provides solid reliability for less adventurous tastes. The Princess of Wales, developed in the early 1980s, quickly became the star brand and transformed the firm's fortunes. The Duchess of York, a more downmarket version of a similar concept, had some initial success; but there have been problems recently with both. The Princess Royal and Princess Margaret, both of which had image difficulties in the past, have been successfully repackaged as plucky single mums.

The men have been harder to sell than the women. Prince Philip, a spin-off from the queen, proved decorative but dated. Prince Charles was well received at first, but in recent years customers have been complaining that there may be a bug in his software. The Duke of York's laddish, militaristic flavour was originally reckoned to be an inspired bid for

Royal favours

Annual salary from the state	£'000
Queen*	7,900
Queen Mother	643
Duke of Edinburgh	359
Duke of York	249
Princess Royal	228
Princess Margaret	219
Prince Edward	96
Princess Alice	87
Prince of Wales†	2,177

Source: Report of the Royal Trustees-1990
* The queen pays £636,000 to be shared between the Dukes of Gloucester and Kent and Princess Alexandra
† Income received tax-free from 75% of revenue from Duchy of Cornwall

The monarchy matrix

the macho market, but the brand does not age well. Prince Edward flopped.

The firm's principal dilemma is that it aims to cater to two separate types of demand. On the one hand there is its core business: constitutional functions like dissolving governments and opening parliament, along with the associated activities of visiting foreign countries and cancer patients. On the other hand, as it has raised market profile it has expanded its role as mass entertainment. Our matrix shows how Windsor's various brands perform in the two areas.

No match for Grimaldi

Similar firms abroad have been more cautious, specialising in one area or the other. The Monaco-based House of Grimaldi has concentrated on entertainment and done well with Princesses Caroline and Stephanie. North European firms in Holland, Denmark and Sweden have stuck to the core business.

Unlike House of Grimaldi, which took

the entertainment business seriously enough to buy in a model from Hollywood in the 1950s, House of Windsor's approach has been amateurish. Its problems stem from a piece of good luck. The Princess of Wales was a runaway success, and her instinctive ability to serve both markets simultaneously encouraged the firm to expand the entertainment side.

Result: the Duchess of York fiasco. Customers for the constitutional business are sensitive to, and incensed by, any hint of tackiness on the entertainment side (just as there is little room in the fiercely competitive celebrity market for frumpy, dowdy royals plying their traditional constitutional trade). That makes the two businesses dangerous to mix. The higher the product's profile, the more likely its flaws are to be exposed in the glare of publicity. Serious questions arose first about the

Duchess of York's usefulness, then about her reliability when she was pictured in close financial negotiations with a supposedly independent adviser.

Current difficulties with the Princess of Wales illustrate a different problem created by the dash into the entertainment business. The princess was promoted so heavily that many customers transferred their loyalty to this one product, at the expense of the rest of the range. Like Vidal Sassoon, the Princess of Wales manages her own brand; and a recording of what may be a private conversation between her and a confidant suggests dissatisfaction with the way the firm is run. If she were to leave, there would be trouble for Windsor: she has outperformed the rest of the range so dramatically that she could carry the customers with her.

There is as yet no real competition to

threaten House of Windsor, so it looks likely to survive its current woes. But it should learn from them. It has diversified too fast, with too little attention to quality, and thus devalued its better products. And it has moved too far away from its core business.

A leveraged buy-out?

The troubles have highlighted what customers require from royal brands. They must be functional and may, within limits, be entertaining as well. There is no demand for those brands that are bad at the dreary bits. Scrapping the brands that fall below the horizontal axis on our matrix might help to restore the Windsor range, and phasing out the glitz would limit future damage. Otherwise, analysts speculate, it should watch out for the possibility of a bid from House of Thatcher.

Harold Major

SEPTEMBER 19TH *Amid a currency crisis, sterling was withdrawn from Europe's exchange-rate mechanism and allowed to devalue. This brought back disturbing memories*

ALL political dramas are about character as well as about policy. John Major briefly displayed it, putting up interest rates and putting on a display of determination—only to give in to the humiliation of devaluation. Within months of a personal triumph at the hustings, Mr Major risks finding himself routinely compared to Harold Wilson, the least-admired of all Britain's post-war leaders.

Even those who always advocated devaluation for economic reasons accept that the very word reeks of political menace. Devaluations tend to happen only after politicians have been firmly, repeatedly and unequivocally promising that they will not succumb: which makes politicians seem liars. And since the currency is a symbol of national potency, cutting its value is a singularly public admission of national failure.

Of the two post-war devaluations within the Bretton Woods system—the only reasonable parallel to the exchange-rate mechanism today—both were carried out by Labour governments. But whereas the Attlee administration kept its reputation, and is fondly remembered by historians, the Wilson government found its devaluation an ominous turning-point. Some believe the Labour Party itself has never been quite the same since.

It is instructive now to distinguish the longer-term political impact of the 1949 devaluation from the 1967 one. Attlee's government had a hugely ambitious domestic

and foreign-policy programme. It was busily nationalising and building the welfare state at home, and decolonising and helping create the post-war

Nightmare in Downing Street

world abroad. Like it or hate it, no one could possibly ask what the Attlee government was for.

Harold Wilson, though, was a different kettle of fudge. Well before 1967 his colleagues and parliamentary opponents had started to express unease about a perceived lack of direction and strategy—indeed purpose—beneath the surface glitter of verbal cleverness and tactical brilliance. Like Mr Major, Lord Wilson prided himself on his

extraordinary appetite for absorbing details, for hard work and for the hypnotic complexities of party management. But, unlike Attlee, Lord Wilson attracted the dangerous question: what was his government for?

The 1967 devaluation crystallised those doubts about Lord Wilson. He had firmly, repeatedly and unequivocally ruled out the thing he now authorised. It demonstrated, therefore, either the prime minister's comparative impotence (the correct conclusion) or his deviousness (a general one). Either way, it humiliated and undermined him. It was a moment of truth when the Great Fixer was illuminated, stark naked.

Mr Major is not Lord Wilson. He is widely perceived as straighter, nicer and more principled. But there is a connection: except for his determination to eradicate inflation by keeping the pound in its ERM band, and to put Britain firmly at the core of Europe, his administration seems to lack the sense of purpose that drove Margaret Thatcher. Unfair? Perhaps, but that is how it seems. A devaluation cripples his anti-inflationary strategy and severely damages his European policy too. In addition, as with Lord Wilson, it demonstrates his weakness, or damages his reputation for plain dealing, or (some will say) both. Devaluation could, in short, hurt Mr Major's administration as severely as it did the 1966-70 Wilson one.

The chancellor, Norman Lamont, faces calls for his resignation. But although that is the precedent, ministers resign with far less alacrity these days. This is not primarily a Lamont issue, just as 1967 was not primarily a James Callaghan (the then chancellor) issue. The big question is whether Mr Major's post-devaluation administration, having lost its only important policy anchors, merely drifts helplessly. The Citizen's Charter and the Patten education reforms are not a sufficient answer to the question: what is the Major government really for? John Smith, the Labour leader, is in a position of potential strength unheard-of for the chief of a beaten party just

months after an election. Whether he is the Edward Heath of the 1990s, reshaping his party and ready to pounce, remains to be seen.

Devaluation was resisted by Mr Major for so long because he believed—and where that belief has now hidden itself remains a mystery—that it was likely to be fatal to his economic ambitions. He may still be the calm administrator and expert negotiator he has already proved himself to be. But as Lord Wilson found, short-term manoeuvring is no substitute for loss of authority

and loss of direction.

The morality-tale from 25 years ago is a chilling one. But history never repeats itself—quite. The success or failure of this administration may be settled within the next week—as may Mr Major's place in history. There is one other clue from 1967, though whether it is a good or a grim omen it is too early to say. Then, the crisis was aggravated by the French (through General de Gaulle, on the issue of British membership of the European Community) saying a simple word: *Non*.

Three sides of an argument

OCTOBER 24TH *The government suddenly announced it was "going for growth". We looked at the background to its economic acrobatics*

ANOTHER week, another economic policy. The political vocabulary needs to be enriched: what you have seen in the past few days is not so much a U-turn as a pirouette. Or perhaps—as Norman Lamont may try to explain in his Mansion House speech next week—no change in substance at all, merely a presentational adjustment.

Whatever Mr Major and his chancellor mean, or think they mean, by their recent pronouncements, a vigorous debate about British economic policy is going on in newspapers, in the City and in economics faculties around the country. The table below offers a guide for the bemused. Simplifying outrageously, it says that there are three broad schools of thought, identifiable by responses to seven questions. The three schools are:

•**Growth merchants.** They think Britain is in danger of economic collapse. To fret about inflation at such a time, they believe, is a mistake—either because (some would say) a bit of inflation would help the economy, or else because (as others would say) no amount of stimu-

lus will cause inflation to rise in such a depressed economy. They want to see much lower interest rates yesterday; care little for intermediate targets of the sort that Mr Lamont spelt out with such care on October 15th; regard a devalued currency as a good thing; favour fiscal ease; are not much interested in talk about an independent central bank; and tend to be at least mildly doubtful about Europe.

They are an ill-matched bunch. In or near this category fall Winston Churchill ("Inflation is yesterday's battle") and quite a few other Tory MPs, virtually all of the Labour Party, Christopher Dow (formerly the economics director at the Bank of England), Wynne Godley (head of the neo-Keynesian Cambridge Economic Policy Group, long a thorn in the Treasury's flesh) and most newspaper editors.

•**Monetarists.** Until September 16th they were almost indistinguishable from the growth merchants. Both agreed that the exchange-rate mechanism was bad for Britain. Getting sterling out of the ERM was their priority—because floating

exchange rates are better than fixed, and because it was essential to cut interest rates. Now the differences are easier to see.

Monetarists do care about inflation. They are against steering policy by targets for real economic growth; they prefer a target for the money supply (most would choose M4). In the main, they are fiscal conservatives: many would wish to see tighter fiscal policy (even at the cost of some tax increases) alongside a further loosening of monetary policy. Many regard an independent Bank of England as indispensable. Nearly all are Eurosceptics.

Their spiritual leader is Lady Thatcher. In or near this camp are many Tories; a good few City economists, especially Tim Congdon of Gerrard & National; academics such as Sir Alan Walters and Patrick Minford; and Martin Wolf, the economics leader-writer of the *Financial Times*.

•**Gradualists** (for want of a better term). Like monetarists, this third school is already worried about the next inflation. Unlike them, it urges caution on further interest-rate cuts; its fear is a collapse in sterling, which would be bad for inflation eventually. Like monetarists, gradualists forswear targets for output, but prefer nominal GDP and the exchange rate (supplemented by other "nominal" indicators) to particular measures of the money supply. Compared with monetarists, many are

The battlelines

	Is it right to worry about medium-term inflation now?	What should the government do to interest rates?	Intermediate targets?	What about sterling?	What should the government do to fiscal policy?	New economic constitution?	EMU and all that?
Growth merchants	No	Cut them sharply (to 5% or less).	None. Go for growth.	Forget it.	Increase spending. Perhaps cut taxes; on no account raise them.	Talk about it later.	Views differ. Talk about it later.
Monetarists	Yes	Cut them (to 6%).	Money supply (some say broad, others narrow).	Moderate devaluation is fine. If lower rates cause a rout, raise interest rates.	Curb spending and public borrowing; raise taxes if need be.	Yes, crucial. Make Bank of England independent.	A curse on Maastricht and all its works.
Gradualists	Yes	Nothing for now, unless the pound stabilises and German interest rates fall.	Money GDP, exchange rate, other nominal indicators.	Avoid a collapse, because of effects on inflation and, above all, confidence.	Let automatic stabilisers work (ie, tolerate modest overshoot of public-spending targets); squeeze public-sector pay.	Yes, important. Make Bank of England independent.	Further integration desirable, with caveats.

soft on public borrowing. They too favour an independent central bank. They are pro-Europe, with reservations.

In or near the gradualist camp—the loosest of the three coalitions—are assorted former chancellors and officials in the Treasury and Bank of England; academics such as David Currie at the London Business School; Samuel Brittan, chief economic commentator of the *Financial Times*; and this newspaper.

This week John Major, with one foot in gradualism and the other in monetarism, was attempting a backwards somersault to join the growth merchants.

Admitting the obvious

DECEMBER 12TH   *The separation of the Prince and Princess of Wales raised questions not only about the succession to the throne but also about the future of the monarchy*

IN THE days when every British schoolchild rote-learnt the kings and queens of England, one ditty helped them through the paramours of Henry VIII:

Divorced, beheaded, died,
Divorced, beheaded, survived.

One day, the offspring of Elizabeth II may be similarly remembered. This week the first line—"Divorced, separated, re-wed"—took shape.

On Wednesday Buckingham Palace announced that the Prince and Princess of Wales are to separate after 11 years of marriage. Three days later the Prince's divorced younger sister, Anne, was due to wed a naval officer in a private ceremony in Scotland. The queen's second son, Andrew, is separated from his wife, the Duchess of York, who wants a divorce and has comforted herself in the company of her financial adviser. She at least had a good week, extracting the equivalent of $132,000 in damages from French newspapers which published pictures of them discussing her affairs in the south of France. The queen's youngest son, Edward, is unmarried.

The queen had already called 1992 her *annus horribilis*; in fact, the 20th century looks like the House of Windsor's *saeculum horribile*. After Henry VIII,

there were only two proper royal sex scandals in four centuries, admittedly before tabloid newspapers had been invented. George I divorced before coming to the throne, then when king flaunted two German mistresses. Worse, George IV ducked out of his forced marriage to a cousin, Caroline of Brunswick (she fled to Italy, but returned in 1820 to claim her rights as queen, a claim resolved only by her death). But since 1900, one disaster has followed another: Edward VII cavorting with Lillie Langtry before the first world war, Edward VIII abdicating for love of a twice-divorced American in 1936, and now Prince Charles. Where will it all end?

Not, according to the prime minister, in constitutional change. "The decision to separate has no constitutional implications," John Major told the House of Commons on December 9th. MPs, on their best behaviour, just about swallowed that. But when he went on to say that there was "no reason why the Princess of Wales should not be crowned queen in due course", there was a murmur of disbelief.

Formally, the prime minister is right. If princess stays married to prince, and if he becomes king, she becomes queen. But although the couple say they have "no plans

to divorce", it is not flatly ruled out. No one even bothered to speculate about a possible reconciliation between the pair, such is the feeling between them. Though they will carry out some joint engagements, the thought of them kneeling together before the Archbishop of Canterbury at the sacred moment of coronation now seems wildly implausible. A penny to the Crown Jewels would be a fair price against.

Without the widely popular princess, can the Prince of Wales be sure of his crown? He often seems to want it, if only more effectively to propagate his mildly eccentric anti-materialist views. But he sometimes seems not to, preferring to commune with nature in his garden. The queen is a woman of duty, unlikely to abdicate before the present turmoil subsides. By the time her job becomes vacant, her eldest son may refuse it, or be manifestly unsuitable.

There is loose talk of regents: another royal could fill a regent's role until Charles's elder son, ten-year-old William, achieves his maturity. This strategy makes sense only if Prince William turns out to be the missing paragon of regal virtues.

Hence the larger question: will the queen have a successor at all? Even to ask may seem ridiculous. Here is an institution beloved of tourists, toffs and *hoi polloi*; here reside important constitutional reserve-powers. Yes, but the mood towards royalty is changing.

The change showed in complaints about the queen's exemption from tax, forcing her to abandon that privilege in November. It is reflected in opinion polls: though 55% of those questioned by MORI in May thought Britain would be worse off without the monarchy, that compares with 77% in 1984. Even in the Commons, Mr Major's expressions of support for the royal pair failed to evince full-throated "hear-hears". Labour republicans like Dennis Skinner were not shouted down.

When institutions have to change, it is quintessentially British to pretend that everything remains as it was. But the royal family would delude itself if it mistook such rhetorical cover for reality. After this week, things can never be the same again for Britain's royalty. The more wholeheartedly they adapt to that fact, the better their chances of a 21st *saeculum mirabile*.

Contents

EUROPE

A year of living dangerously

EUROPE in 1992 earned itself the unhappy reputation of being the world's most unstable continent. Here of all places, the end of the cold war had raised hopes of a new continental togetherness. Instead, the after-shocks from the collapse of communist power in the East, combined with recession and resentment at swelling numbers of refugees in the West, seemed to blow the place apart.

In Europe's newly ex-communist parts, from former Yugoslavia to Ingushetia, ethnic and religious hatreds brought forth a barbarity that most Europeans

Ex-Yugoslavia at war

thought had been exorcised half a century earlier. From these war-torn places to Czecho-Slovakia, new splinter-states were in the making. In Russia, a year of ruling courageously ended in near-rout for Boris Yeltsin's band of brave reformers. Even in the continent's richer, more stable parts, from Germany in the north to Spain in the south, anti-foreigner resentment bred violence and claimed lives. The dream of a "Europe whole and free" fell victim to a series of jarring shifts in what the continent's Marxists used to call the "forces of history".

History had looked like shaping up forcefully for the better. From the ruins of the old Soviet Union stepped Mr Yeltsin's Russia, dedicated to the pursuit of peace, democracy and a market economy. The Maastricht treaty, freshly initialled by the 12 members of the European Community, laid out ambitious steps to a political, economic and monetary union in the West that would encompass an ever-widening group of countries, including the three fastest reformers of Central and Eastern Europe: Poland, Hungary and Czechoslovakia. Russia, too brash and bulky ever to be properly clubbable, would be drawn by its own marketising reforms closer to Western Europe's expanding hub of prosperity.

This vision of spreading pan-European stability was not so very far-fetched. Certainly, there were worries: about the fate of ex-Soviet nuclear weapons, about the employment of ex-Soviet nuclear scientists, and about the testy relations between Russia and Ukraine. But these seemed manageable, given enough western diplomatic attention, and dollops of technical help and cash. The war between Serbs and Croats in ex-Yugoslavia—Europe's first real shooting war in recent memory—pounded mercilessly on, but the shrapnel did not fly very far.

Not for the first time this century the complacent calculations of Europe's statesmen were blown away by forces they could not—or had not thought to—control. In the Balkans it was the relentless mortars, in Western Europe it was disgruntled voters, and in Russia it was unrepentant Russia-firsters who knocked history off its expected course.

The determination to forge a greater Serbia out of disintegrating Yugoslavia had already led to war with Croatia. Western recognition of Slovenia and Croatia prompted Bosnia & Hercegovina to seek independence, too. Swiftly the Serb siege of the Croatian port of Dubrovnik was matched, and then surpassed in medieval ferocity, by the siege of Sarajevo. The "cleansing" of the Muslim population from Serb-won parts of Bosnia created Europe's greatest flood of refugees since the second world war.

By year's end, 3.5m people—mostly Muslims—had been displaced by ex-Yugoslavia's war. Over 600,000 had fled to Western Europe. According to the International Red Cross, 128,000 had died in Bosnia alone. In all of ex-Yugoslavia, at least 17,000 more had been killed directly in the fighting; more than 100,000 had disappeared. The methods employed by the Serbs—the systematic torture, rape and execution of civilians, the deliberate pulverising of villages and towns—led to calls for a war crimes tribunal. But the perpetrators would be caught, if at all, only when the war ended.

Repeated attempts by western mediators failed to reconcile Serb demands to run their own show with Muslim demands (backed by the West) that Bosnia should not be broken up along ethnic or religious lines. Serb promises at the London conference in August—a ceasefire, the inspection or closure of internment camps, the surrender of heavy weapons, unhindered access for relief agencies—were made to be broken. A UN-decreed no-fly zone over Bosnia was routinely flouted.

Western consciences had been pricked, but western interest was not fully engaged until the war threatened to spread to Serbia's Albanian-populated province of

Maastricht up in the air

Kosovo, possibly sucking in Albania, Greece and Turkey. Of the four courses of western military action being canvassed—destroying Serb gun positions, creating military safe havens for refugees, letting Bosnian Muslims and Croats buy arms, and enforcing the no-fly zone over Bosnia—enforcing the no-fly zone garnered most support. But it would not end the war.

The EC, to which America and others looked for a lead in this crisis, was less ready for joint action than even its own diffident diplomats might have guessed. In June Denmark's voters narrowly rejected the Maastricht treaty. In September what looked like being at best a barely audible Yes from French voters plunged the currency markets into turmoil, forced the lira and sterling out of the exchange-rate mechanism and threatened to destroy Maastricht's goals of economic, monetary and political union.

What was to have been the start of a confident new era of constitution-building and problem-solving became instead a scramble to reassure voters distrustful of governments that had attempted to foist Maastricht on them unawares. Germany's high interest rates, sharing out involuntarily the burden of German unity, the cost of making economies converge to meet the agreed criteria for economic and monetary union (EMU), the rigours of a single market, worries about the free flow of refugees, dislike of rule-making from Brussels—all contributed to disenchantment with Project Europe. With Denmark and Britain still to ratify Maastricht, continued talk by German bankers and politicians of a D-mark zone to replace EMU, and muttering in France about a multi-speed Europe, the Maastricht plan seemed destined for a re-think.

Worse to come?

The EC's doubts about its own future distracted attention from other tasks. Luckily, dire predictions of falling living standards and mounting unrest in Eastern Europe proved wrong. Indeed, 1992 saw Poland, Hungary and Czechoslovakia turn the corner to a sustainable market economy. Bulgaria and Romania slowed their fall. The collapse of the Soviet Union reduced the biggest potential military threat in the region. However, the fate of Russia still mattered. All year it hung perilously on the skill, determination and survival of one man, Boris Yeltsin. But as the year wore on, not even Boris the Brave could hold back the forces of reaction to his attempts to transform Russia.

The effort to hold together a post-Soviet

Czechoslovakia splits

Mockery versus regret in Russia

Commonwealth of Independent States foundered, leaving 26m or so Russians stranded as foreigners in other people's countries. From the Baltic states and Moldova to Central Asia, they became pawns in a struggle for influence in Moscow between the westernisers, like the Russian foreign minister, Andrei Kozyrev, who thought their interests best defended by diplomatic means, and the Russia-firsters, determined to flex military muscle.

Leaning to the nationalists seemed a price Mr Yeltsin was prepared to pay for a free hand on the home front. In January many prices were set free; later the rouble was allowed to float; the government of Yegor Gaidar started the biggest sell-off of state-owned services, farms and factories ever attempted. Inevitably, the costs of this bravery showed up before the benefits. Although goods reappeared in the shops, industrial production dropped by 20%; inflation by year's end was zooming towards 2,000%. The government's weak grip on the money supply (the central bank owed its allegiance to parliament, not president) threatened to overwhelm the reform effort. In December Mr Yeltsin bungled a confrontation with parliament and was forced to drop Mr Gaidar as prime minister. The battle for reform was not yet lost, but Mr Yeltsin was in retreat.

At the start of 1992, the chances seemed good that the inevitable turmoil in the East would eventually be quelled by a combination of western diplomatic and economic assistance and Russian determination to re-attach itself to the rest of Europe. By year's end Western Europe was only just recovering its political footing; Russia was in danger of slipping back into isolation, or worse. Without Russian co-operation, the war in Bosnia would be harder to contain, and the problems of Eastern Europe that much harder to resolve. Was 1992 just an unhappy interlude, or a foretaste of even harder times to come?

January

Thursday 2nd
Real economic reform began in Russia. Boris Yeltsin's government took the **big-bang** approach, freeing most prices overnight and announcing ambitious plans to sell off state businesses. It was in effect the end of central planning and the painful beginning of market economics.

Cyrus Vance, the United Nations' special envoy, negotiated a **ceasefire in Yugoslavia**. This looked more durable than all previous attempts, despite opposition from local warlords in Serb enclaves of Croatia. Serbs in Belgrade, increasingly tired of war and worried about international isolation, seemed ready to sue for peace.

Monday 6th
After months of tension and two weeks of fighting, Georgia's elected president, **Zviad Gamsakhurdia**, fled a shell-shattered parliament building in Tbilisi to take refuge in Armenia. Rebel leaders took power. Yet demonstrations by Gamsakhurdia supporters soon made it clear that Georgia's troubles were far from over.

Tuesday 7th
A Yugoslav air-force jet shot down a helicopter carrying a European Community observation team, killing all five people on board and causing outrage. If the aim was to scupper **peace-keeping plans for Yugoslavia**, it failed. The next day the UN Security Council voted to send 50 observers to prepare for an even-tual deployment of blue-helmet peacekeepers.

Thursday 9th
A power struggle within France's ruling Socialist Party was won by **Laurent Fabius**, a former prime minister. He became party leader, replacing another ex-prime minister, Pierre Mauroy. His immediate aim was to halt the decline in the party's electoral support. His longer-term objective was to use his new power-base for a future bid for the presidency.

Friday 10th
President Mitterrand for the first time raised the possibility that France's nuclear **force de frappe** might one day have a part to play in a European nuclear doctrine. The reference was tantalisingly vague, but it was a sign of the reappraisal under way of French defence policy.

Tuesday 14th
A German Christian Democrat, **Egon Klepsch**, was elected president of the European Parliament—an increasingly important job, in view of the new powers planned for the parliament at Maastricht a month before. Eurosceptics were confident that the mediocre Mr Klepsch would do more to boost their cause than the parliament's.

Spain's health minister, Julian Garcia Valverde, resigned over a scandal involving land deals made by Renfe, the state railway company, at the time when Mr Valverde was its president. The number of scandals coming to light in Spain was causing alarm. The welcome novelty in this case was the prompt resignation of a senior figure prepared to accept responsibility.

Wednesday 15th
The European Community recognised the independence of **Croatia and Slovenia**. Germany had insisted on the deadline, and a ceasefire in the civil war seemed to be holding. Two other ex-Yugoslav republics, Bosnia & Hercegovina and Macedonia, were told they would have to wait for recognition.

Thursday 16th
A Greek drama at last came to an end: a special court acquitted **Andreas Papandreou**, ex-prime minister and leader of the Socialist Party, on corruption charges. Two former members of his cabinet were found guilty and given short sentences. The drama had gone on for too long, distracting attention at a time when the problems of the Greek economy should have been centre-stage.

Joe Bossano's Socialist Labour Party was returned to office with an increased majority in **Gibraltar's election**. Spanish officials despaired: they saw little prospect of progress in the dispute over the British colony so long as the uncompromising Mr Bossano was in charge.

Sunday 19th
A former dissident, Zhelyu Zhelev, became **Bulgaria**'s first directly elected president. Mr Zhelev, a philosopher who had been appointed president by parliament in 1990, defeated a candidate backed by the Socialist (ex-Communist) Party.

Monday 20th
Two former **East German border guards** were convicted for shooting a man as he tried to escape to West Berlin in February 1989. Germans continued to wonder whether it was right to punish those who carried out orders while the people who issued the orders remained largely unpunished. And the opening to public scrutiny of 120 miles of Stasi (East German secret police) files gave plenty more scope for agonising over the painful past.

Wednesday 22nd
A two-day conference opened in Washington on co-ordinating rich countries' **aid to the ex-Soviet Union**. Some European governments were angry at what they saw as America trying to steal the limelight in the hitherto mostly European aid effort. Meanwhile the Russian government lobbied for a package of at least $15 billion in various types of aid to support its economic reforms.

Tuesday 28th
Boris Yeltsin paid a sudden visit to the naval base at Novorossisk, missing the opening in Moscow of the Middle East peace conference. The reason: the mounting conflict with Ukraine over control of the **Black Sea fleet**. At stake was how the fleet, based at the Ukrainian port of Sevastopol in the Crimea, was to be divided between the two countries.

Thursday 30th
Ireland's Fianna Fail prime minister, **Charles Haughey**, announced he would resign. New allegations about his part in a ten-year-old telephone-tapping scandal made it impossible for him to stay on any longer. He had dominated the political scene in Ireland since he first became prime minister in 1979. Without him, Irish politics was expected to be simpler but duller.

February

Tuesday 4th
President Mitterrand declared that the **George Habash affair** was closed. There had been uproar over the decision—officially said to have been taken without consulting the president—to allow the leader of the Popular Front for the Liberation of Palestine into France, supposedly for urgent medical treatment. Unfairly or otherwise, the affair was widely seen as the latest evidence that France's president was losing his grip.

The run-up to **Italy's election** on April 5th grew ever more colourful. An actress granddaughter of Mussolini announced that she would be standing as a neo-fascist—yet more entertainment for voters already being wooed by a Party of Love, led by a former porn star.

Saturday 8th
A spectacular ceremony marked the opening of the **Winter Olympics** in Albertville in the French Alps. The rendering of the *Marseillaise* prompted some people in France to call for a change to less bloodthirsty lyrics.

Sunday 9th
Romania's ruling National Salvation Front, led by ex-communists and dominant in the first free elections in 1990, suffered a setback in local elections. In the first round of voting it won under a third of contests for mayor, while the opposition Democratic Convention won nearly a quarter—including big cities such as Bucharest and Brasov.

Russia's first big **anti-government demonstration** since January's price liberalisation was held in the centre of Moscow. A smaller, pro-Yeltsin demonstration was held in front of the Russian parliament. The real surprise was that popular reaction to the economic shock-therapy remained relatively restrained.

Tuesday 11th
Albert Reynolds, sacked just three months before as finance minister, was confirmed as Ireland's new prime minister. He quickly showed his determination to be his own man: in his new cabinet he replaced nearly two-thirds of the ministers from the government of his predecessor, Charles Haughey. Mr Reynolds's top priority was to reduce Ireland's 20% unemployment rate.

Wednesday 12th
Jacques Delors unveiled the European Commission's spending proposals for the five years beginning in 1993, the so-called **Delors package**. He wanted to raise the EC's spending limits from 1.2% of GDP to 1.37%, to pay for (among other things) a doubling of aid to the poorer members. Mr Delors argued that the extra money was needed to pay for commitments made in the Maastricht treaty. But Germany and Britain, which would have to foot most of the bill, were not happy with the scale of Mr Delors's spending ambitions.

Thursday 13th
Boris Yeltsin dealt with a political trouble-maker in the traditional way: giving him the poisoned chalice of responsibility for agriculture. His populist vice-president, **Alexander Rutskoi**, had been openly critical of the Yeltsin government's economic reforms. Mr Yeltsin hoped the farm portfolio

would keep him quieter.

Monday 17th
Controversy flared up over Ireland's constitutional **ban on abortion**. The High Court in Dublin prevented a 14-year-old girl, pregnant by an alleged rape, from travelling to London to have an abortion. Protesters said the case showed the absurdity of the law. On appeal to the Supreme Court, the High Court's decision was later softened, and the abortion went ahead.

Karol Lutkowski resigned as **Poland**'s finance minister. He feared that the new government under Jan Olszewski intended to relax the country's unpopular economic reforms.

Wednesday 19th
Basque terrorists of ETA continued their campaign to disrupt **Spain's year of festivities**, which included the Universal Exposition in Seville and the Barcelona Olympics. Three people died when a car bomb exploded in the northern city of Santander. The Expo had just suffered a more direct setback: a fire destroyed one of its five theme pavillions.

Saturday 22nd
The conservative Nationalist Party held on to power in **Malta's general election**, but only just. The Nationalists won 51.8% of the vote to Labour's 46.5%, and a majority in Parliament of just three seats. Among the Nationalist government's priorities was Malta's bid to join the European Community.

Tuesday 25th
The savagery of the **conflict in Nagorno-Karabakh** became clearer. Armenian fighters took Khojali, an Azeri stronghold that had been shelling the local capital, Stepanakert. Reports of a massacre of Azeri men, women and children

from Kholaji soon emerged. The withdrawal of the last ex-Soviet troops from the region fuelled fears that the fighting would get worse unless outsiders moved fast to mediate.

Thursday 27th
Chancellor Kohl and President Havel signed a **Czechoslovak-German friendship treaty** in Prague. The treaty did not settle the controversial issue of the claims of Sudeten Germans expelled after the second world war. But it marked another step in the reconciliation between the two countries.

The International Expositions Office in Paris awarded **Budapest** the right to hold a World Fair in 1996. The city had rejected the idea in 1991 as too expensive, but the Hungarian parliament decided to proceed with scaled-down plans, as a way of putting post-communist Hungary on the map.

Saturday 29th
Two days of voting began in **Bosnia & Hercegovina's referendum** on independence. More than 99% of those who voted said Yes to independence. But most of them were local Croats and Muslims. Bosnia's Serbs (about a third of the population) boycotted the vote. Some briefly erected barricades in the capital, Sarajevo, raising fears that Yugoslavia's war would break out again in Bosnia.

March

Friday 6th
After months of post-election negotiations, **Belgium** finally got a new government. Jean-Luc Dehaene took over from his long-serving fellow Christian Democrat, Wilfried Martens. He led a coalition of the same four parties—the French-speaking Socialists and Christian Democrats and their sister parties in Flanders—that had formed the previous querulous government.

Tuesday 10th
Edward Shevardnadze, ex-Soviet foreign minister, was named head of Georgia's ruling state council. A former Communist boss of Georgia, Mr Shevardnadze had a mixed reputation in his native land. But his reputation in the West was excellent and was expected to win the international recognition for Georgia that its civil war had so far prevented it from being given.

Thursday 12th
Just as Italy's general-election campaign was gathering momentum, a **Mafia murder** stunned the country. Salvo Lima, the power-broker in Sicily of Italy's Christian Democratic prime minister, Giulio Andreotti, was shot near his home. Italians were shocked not only by the brutality of the Mafia's campaign tactics, but also by what many saw as a reminder of the unsavoury links between the main political parties and gangsters.

Sunday 15th
Jordi Pujol won a fourth term as leader of **Catalonia**. His co-

alition of nationalists won 70 of the regional parliament's 135 seats. Mr Pujol's success lay in pressing for maximum autonomy, but within Spain. By keeping his absolute majority, he also put himself in a strong bargaining position should the Socialist government in Madrid need a coalition partner after the general election due in 1993.

Wednesday 18th
Finland's parliament voted in favour of membership of the European Community. The same day, Finland formally applied to join the EC, in time to be in the group of countries—including Austria and Sweden—hoping to gain entry by the mid-1990s.

Ukraine was said to have reversed its decision earlier in the month to stop transferring **tactical nuclear weapons** to Russia for destruction. The Ukrainians had claimed that the weapons were not being destroyed as agreed. Outsiders suspected that the Ukrainian move had been meant to strengthen its bargaining position with Russia. But it had swiftly brought expressions of alarm from the West.

Friday 20th
A summit in Kiev of the 11-member **Commonwealth of Independent States** ended in public disagreement. Ukraine's president, Leonid Kravchuk, was unrestrained in his criticism of the proceedings. There was speculation that before long Ukraine would withdraw from the Commonwealth and bring about the collapse of the grouping.

Saturday 21st
Violence surrounded the Kurdish new year (Nevruz) in south-east **Turkey**. More than 50 people were killed, mainly when the security forces used live bullets to disperse demon-

strators supporting the Kurdistan Workers' Party (PKK). Within days Germany responded by suspending arms sales to Turkey.

The oil-rich republic of **Tatarstan**, home to the biggest minority in Russia, held a vaguely worded referendum on sovereignty. Just over 60% of those who voted said Yes to the idea—though it was unclear whether the real aim was a looser relationship within a federal Russia, or outright independence.

Sunday 22nd
France's ruling Socialists suffered a big blow in regional elections, winning a mere 18% of the vote, their worst score ever. The mainstream conservatives did poorly too, managing only 33%. Voters migrated to the fringes—to the extreme-right National Front and to green parties. Pressure mounted on **President Mitterrand** to change his unpopular government.

Communism was defeated in **Albania**. The communists (renamed as Socialists) lost the general election to the Democratic Party, led by Sali Berisha. The Democrats won nearly two-thirds of the vote. They faced the unenviable job of grappling with the appalling economic and social legacy of the communist years.

Tuesday 24th
A smallish accident at a **nu-**

clear-power plant near St Petersburg created fresh alarm about the safety of the civilian nuclear industry in the former Soviet Union. The accident was at a reactor of the same type as the one at Chernobyl.

Wednesday 25th
Voters in **Amsterdam** narrowly supported a proposal to ban cars from the city centre. But the turnout in the referendum was so low (just 27%) that the idea seemed likely to be wartered down.

Sunday 29th
French police arrested the three most-wanted leaders of the **Basque terrorist organisation**, ETA. Spain hoped this would help its efforts to prevent ETA from upsetting its big year of festivities.

Moldova declared a state of emergency after weeks of mounting violence over the breakaway Dniestr region, where Russian-speakers form a majority. The dispute threatened to widen to involve Romania, Ukraine and Russia.

Tuesday 31st
In Moscow, 18 of Russia's 20 republics signed a **federal treaty** dividing powers between the centre and the regions. President Yeltsin hoped this would keep Russia together. The two dissidents were Tatarstan and the Chechen republic, which had proclaimed its independence. In the Chechen capital, Grozny, a state of emergency was announced in response to what local officials described as an attempted coup.

King Juan Carlos of Spain and President Chaim Herzog of Israel marked a new stage of reconciliation between **Spain and Jews**. On the 500th anniversary of the edict expelling Jews from Spain, they joined together in a ceremony in Madrid's synagogue.

April

Wednesday 1st
A $24 billion package of **aid for Russia** was announced by the United States and other rich western countries. The reason for the announcement's timing was clear: it was meant to support Boris Yeltsin's reforms before a tough session of Russia's parliament. Less clear was exactly where the money would come from, and how much of it consisted of new pledges.

Thursday 2nd
In the wake of the ruling Socialist Party's disastrous showing in local elections in March, Edith Cresson was replaced as France's prime minister by **Pierre Bérégovoy**. This was taken to be more a change of style than of substance: the main cabinet posts were not reshuffled in the new government, and France's economic policy (masterminded by Mr Bérégovoy as finance minister) was thought unlikely to change.

Sunday 5th
A political earthquake was registered in **Italy's general election**. The long-ruling Christian Democrats sank to their lowest score since the war (29.7% of the votes), and their main partners in government, the Socialists, dropped from 14.3% to 13.6%. The renamed communists in the Democratic Party of the Left fell from 26.6% of the votes to 16.1% (while a hardline splinter party won 5.6%). The big gainer was Umberto Bossi's protest movement, the Northern League, which soared from 0.5% of the votes to 8.7%.

Complex negotiations on forming a government began.

Far-right parties did alarmingly well in two **German regional elections**. The Republicans won nearly 11% of the votes in Baden-Württemberg (where the Christian Democrats lost outright power for the first time in 20 years), and the German People's Union won 6.3% in Schleswig-Holstein (where the Social Democrats under Björn Engholm clung to their majority in parliament by just one seat). Worry over the growing numbers of asylum-seekers in Germany was the main explanation for the far-right surge.

Monday 6th
EC foreign ministers decided to **recognise Bosnia & Hercegovina** as an independent state (another republic of the old Yugoslavia, Macedonia, was told it would have to wait until the dispute with Greece over its name was sorted out). But any hopes that international recognition would bring calm to Bosnia were quickly dashed. Fighting between ethnic groups intensified, with Serb attacks in the east creating tens of thousands of Muslim refugees.

Wednesday 8th
The most striking initiative announced in the programme of the new French government was a **freeze on nuclear testing** at least until the end of the year. Sceptics saw the move as a cynical attempt to woo green votes rather than any fundamental change in French nuclear policy.

Thursday 9th
Sali Berisha, the heart surgeon who had led the Democrats to victory in the general election in March, became **president of Albania**. He replaced Ramiz Alia, the former communist boss, who had resigned in the wake of the re-

named communists' electoral defeat. Albania's communist era thus came to its end.

Sunday 12th
Euro Disneyland, just outside Paris, opened to the public. Its organisers hoped that Mickey Mouse and the other familiar attractions would draw 11m visitors a year.

Monday 13th
It emerged that **Germany's terrorists** of the Red Army Faction had sent a letter suggesting they were prepared to give up violence. The authorities took the letter seriously, but were wary of false optimism: the RAF was responsible for the deaths of many businessmen and officials over the years.

Constantine Mitsotakis, Greece's prime minister, sacked his foreign minister, Antonis Samaras. The reason: a dispute over **Greek policy towards Macedonia**. Mr Samaras had insisted that Macedonia would have to change its name (to distinguish it from the Greek province of Macedonia) if it wanted recognition as an independent state. Mr Mitsotakis, who took over the foreign ministry himself, seemed ready to take a less strident approach.

Wednesday 15th
After days of doubt and threats of resignation, **Boris Yeltsin's reformist government** survived a fight in parliament, emerging bruised but intact. Its survival made it likely that a large western aid effort would go ahead.

Monday 20th
King Juan Carlos opened the **Universal Exposition in Seville**. The organisers were expecting 18m visitors during the six months of the Expo—an occasion, 500 years after Columbus's discovery of the new world, for the world's re-

discovery of the new Spain.

Sunday 26th
Political confusion deepened in **Italy** with the resignation of President Francesco Cossiga ten weeks before his mandate ended. He said he lacked the power and authority necessary to steer the country through the uncertainty following the inconclusive general election earlier in the month.

Monday 27th
Double turmoil hit **Germany**. A wave of public-sector strikes began, the first for nearly 20 years, over pay. And Hans-Dietrich Genscher, Germany's Free Democratic (liberal) foreign minister for 18 years, announced he would resign within a month. The sense of disarray deepened with a fiasco over the appointment of Mr Genscher's successor. Liberal deputies rebelled against their leaders' initial choice and nominated Klaus Kinkel, the justice minister and a former Genscher aide, instead.

The creation of a **new Yugoslavia** was proclaimed in Belgrade, a shrivelled version of the former federation. The "new" state would consist only of Serbia and Montenegro, though other areas were welcome to join if they wanted. Western countries did not rush to recognise the new Yugoslavia as the legal successor to the old one. Meanwhile, fighting in neighbouring Bosnia continued, despite a negotiated ceasefire.

May

Monday 4th
Italy's Socialists appointed their deputy secretary, Giuliano Amato, to investigate the party's involvement in a growing corruption **scandal in Milan**, the power base of the Socialist leader, Bettino Craxi. The affair undermined Mr Craxi's hopes of heading the next Italian government.

Tuesday 5th
Tragedy struck in **Bastia** on the French island of Corsica when a temporary stand collapsed during a soccer match. More than a dozen people were killed and hundreds injured.

Relations between the two post-Soviet giants, Russia and Ukraine, took a turn for the worse when the parliament of **the Crimea** declared a vaguely defined independence, subject to a referendum. The Crimea has a Russian-speaking majority but was transferred to Ukraine in 1954. Ukraine's President Kravchuk, fearing that Crimean "independence" might be a first step towards reunification with Russia, called the decision illegal.

Wednesday 6th
Already shaky, **Poland**'s government wobbled close to collapse with the resignation of the finance minister, Andrzej Olechowski. The reason: decisions in parliament undermining his pledge to the IMF to limit the budget deficit to 5% of GDP. The consequence: a further loss of credibility for Poland's macroeconomic management.

A church scandal rocked **Ireland**. Eamann Casey, the popular Catholic bishop of Galway, resigned when details became public of his affair with an American divorcée. Mr Casey had borrowed from church funds to pay his ex-mistress, who had had a child from the affair. The revelations threatened to damage the church's authority in advance of referendums on abortion due in the autumn.

Thursday 7th
Leaders of **Germany**'s public-sector workers recommended acceptance of the government's improved pay offer. This ended the chaos caused by public-sector strikes. But it added to the disorders in public-sector finance: the pay offer was over 5%, higher than inflation at 4.5%.

Thursday 14th
A botched semi-coup briefly restored **Azerbaijan**'s former communist boss, Ayaz Mutalibov, to power, but a popular uprising quickly removed him and his fellow apparatchiks. The nationalist Popular Front took control in Baku. Its immediate priority was to cope with the crisis with Armenia over the disputed territory of Nagorno-Karabakh. Armenian forces had been making big gains in a conflict threatening to escalate into all-out war.

Sunday 17th
Switzerland's long tradition of splendid isolation was eroded when in a referendum voters decided narrowly in favour of joining the IMF and the World Bank. The vote was a prelude to the bigger decision about whether to join the European Community. The following day, the government announced that it would join the queue of would-be EC members.

Thursday 21st
European Community farm ministers agreed on a **reform of the common agricultural policy** (CAP). The emphasis would shift from price support (farm prices were expected to be cut by up to 29%) to income support for farmers. Though brave by EC standards, the reform was not expected to remove Europe's food mountains or to reduce the amount the Community spends on the CAP.

Friday 22nd
At a summit in La Rochelle, France's President Mitterrand and Germany's Helmut Kohl, announced the birth of a Franco-German defence force. The French saw the new "**Eurocorps**" as the embryo of a future European defence force distinct from NATO; the Germans claimed it would help draw the French closer to NATO. The Americans and British watched and worried.

Saturday 23rd
Gangsters took their gruesome revenge on Italy's leading Mafia-fighter. **Giovanni Falcone** was blown up with his wife and three bodyguards on a motorway in Sicily. Mr Falcone's work as an investigating magistrate had led to the convictions of many *mafiosi*. His murder shocked politicians out of their dithering over a new president: within two days they had elected Oscar Luigi Scalfaro, a Christian Democrat.

With allegations of corruption swirling around him, **Bernard**

Tapie resigned as France's minister for urban affairs. A flamboyant businessman, Mr Tapie had been brought into the new government two months earlier to lend a bit of colour. Too much colour, it turned out.

Sunday 24th
The unhappy Waldheim era came to a close when Thomas Klestil was elected as **Austria's new president**. The conservative Mr Klestil comfortably beat his Social Democratic rival in the run-off for the largely ceremonial job.

The president of the ex-Soviet republic of **Moldova** appealed to the United Nations for help in its dispute with Russian-speaking separatists in the Moldovan region of Trans-Dniestria. Fighting over the region was escalating.

Wednesday 27th
International **outrage over Serbia**'s aggression in Bosnia led to the imposition of western sanctions. On the day a mortar attack killed a score of people in a bread queue in Sarajevo, the European Community agreed on sanctions (including a trade embargo) against Serbia and Montenegro, the two republics left in the rump of Yugoslavia. Three days later the United Nations Security Council voted unanimously to impose economic sanctions.

Thursday 28th
A half-day **general strike in Spain**, called by the two main unions in protest against government austerity measures (notably cuts in unemployment pay), was something of a flop. The unions failed to mobilise the sort of mass support they managed in the previous general strike, in 1988. For the moment, anyway, the pressure on the government to compromise on its austerity plans was off.

June

Tuesday 2nd
In a referendum, **Danish voters** rejected the European Community's Maastricht treaty on political and economic union. The result was close—50.7% of the vote to 49.3%—but it was enough to throw the whole of the EC into disarray. The treaty has to be ratified by all 12 EC members to become law. The other 11 decided to press ahead with their own ratification processes in the hope that the Danes would somehow eventually change their minds. But the Danish vote suggested that politicians had moved too fast for their electorates.

Wednesday 3rd
President Mitterrand responded to the Danish vote by announcing that **France** too would hold a referendum on Maastricht, in the autumn. It was a calculated gamble. He hoped both to rally France behind the treaty and to divide the right (which was split between Euro-federalists and doubters) in the run up to France's general election. He risked losing the vote and all credibility.

Thursday 4th
After tottering for months, Jan Olszewski's government in **Poland** finally fell. Mr Olszewski had constantly feuded with President Lech Walesa, and had desperately tried to cling to power by releasing to parliament a list of top people (including even Mr Walesa) who had allegedly informed for the secret police under communist rule. The move backfired. A 32-year-old, Waldemar Pawlak, a lightweight leader far more to Mr Walesa's liking, was asked to try to form a new government.

Saturday 6th
Two days of voting in **Czechoslovakia**'s general election produced a divided parliament that looked likely to propel the country towards a split. In the Czech federation, the winners were the free-marketeers led by the finance minister, Vaclav Klaus; in Slovakia, the nationalist-socialists under Vladimir Meciar triumphed. Either side could block legislation in the federal parliament. So both had an incentive to go their own way: the Czechs to speed ahead uninhibited with market reforms, the Slovaks to gain statehood and protect their heavy industries.

Sunday 7th
Abulfaz Elchibey, the leader of the nationalist Popular Front, won the presidential election in **Azerbaijan**. Azeris reckoned he was the man most likely to wrest back control of Nagorno-Karabakh from Armenians.

Thursday 11th
With sceptics around the European Community feeling freer to express their **doubts about the Maastricht treaty** in the wake of the Danish referendum, 60 German economists issued a joint criticism of the plan for economic and monetary union. Opinion polls showed Germans to be worried about the prospect of giving up their beloved D-mark.

Sunday 14th
With external pressure on Serbia mounting, there were signs too of growing internal pressure on its strongman, **Slobodan Milosevic**. A peace demonstration in Belgrade was led by Patriarch Pavle of the Serbian Orthodox church. The next day several thousand students marched throught the city demanding Mr Milosevic's resignation.

Wednesday 17th
After weeks of wrangling, **Italy** at last got a new prime minister-designate: Giuliano Amato, the deputy leader of the Socialist Party. Mr Amato faced a tough task: keeping together a coalition government with only a fragile majority in parliament while pushing through tough policies to control Italy's chaotic public finances.

Friday 19th
Czech and Slovak negotiators paved the way for a likely divorce between their two republics. They agreed that the federal government stripped of real power should remain while the parliaments of the two republics sorted out the future status (if any) of the federation by September 30th.

Tuesday 23rd
At a summit meeting, Presidents Boris Yeltsin and Leonid Kravchuk signalled a change for the better in the strained relationship between **Russia and Ukraine**. They did not discuss the most vexed issue (the Crimea), but they made progress in other areas: the ownership of the Black Sea fleet, the price of Russian energy exports, the prospect of a separate Ukrainian currency, the effort to keep open borders.

Thursday 25th
A new club of **Black Sea co-operation** was ushered into existence at a summit meeting in Turkey. Though the summiteers were ostensibly gathering to discuss economic co-operation, they also had other urgent business to talk about: such as avoiding wars. The 11 members included Armenia and Azerbaijan, as well as Moldova, Georgia and Russia, plus Greece and Turkey.

In **Ireland's referendum on Maastricht**, two-thirds of voters said Yes to the treaty. This did not cancel out the Danish No earlier in the month, but it gave hope to supporters of Maastricht that the treaty could be saved.

Friday 26th
Germany's Bundestag voted for a more liberal law on **abortion**, allowing it on demand (after compulsory counselling) during the first three months of pregnancy. The country had struggled to produce a new law ever since the two Germanies, with different rules on abortion, came together in 1990.

European Community leaders gathered for their two-day **Lisbon summit**. They agreed to postpone most tricky decisions—on the EC budget, on the site of the future European central bank, and on how to tackle the problem of Denmark's rejection of the Maastricht treaty. They did, however, agree to re-appoint Jacques Delors for another two years as president of the European Commission. The newly humble Mr Delors had (post-Denmark) been stressing "subsidiarity", the idea that Brussels should intervene only when strictly necessary.

Sunday 28th
France's President Mitterrand boldly showed the way for the relief of beleaguered **Sarajevo** by braving the bullets and making a six-hour visit to the Bosnian capital (he set out straight after the European Community's Lisbon summit, without telling his EC colleagues of his plans). The following day a first contingent of United Nations troops took shaky control of Sarajevo airport, soon to be joined by more UN forces. Humanitarian aid began to arrive.

July

Wednesday 1st
French troops flew into Sarajevo, capital of Bosnia & Hercegovina, to improve security before the start of an **international relief operation**. There were repeated breaches of a ceasefire in the city.

Friday 3rd
Lord Carrington, chairman of the EC's peace conference on Yugoslavia, said he had made no headway in trying to bring peace to Bosnia & Hercegovina. Meanwhile the Serbs continued their programme of "**ethnic cleansing**" in areas under their control in Croatia and Bosnia.

Saturday 4th
Socialist Giuliano Amato took office as prime minister of Italy at the head of a **four-party coalition**, ending a protracted government crisis after the resignation of Giulio Andreotti. Mr Amato promptly proposed revenue-earning and cost-cutting measures to reduce the huge budget deficit.

French truckers protested against new rules for driving licences by blocking many of the country's *autoroutes* and delaying holidaymakers.

Monday 6th
The Group of Seven (G7) industrialised countries **opened their summit in Munich** with the International Monetary Fund ready to give Russia a credit of $1 billion for a short-term economic stabilisation programme. The British prime minister, John Major, pressed G7 members for an early agreement on the Uruguay round of the General Agreement on Tariffs and Trade (GATT). Fruitlessly.

Tuesday 7th
G7 leaders warned the warring parties in Bosnia & Hercegovina that **they would use force if necessary** to ensure that relief supplies reached Sarajevo. Fears were voiced that Croatia and Serbia were carving up Bosnia & Hercegovina. President Yeltsin said more economic aid was essential for the survival of Russian democracy.

Wednesday 8th
The G7 summit ended with leaders promising to consider **letting Russia suspend the servicing of its foreign debt** and with no agreement on GATT.

Thursday 9th
The 51-nation Conference on Security and Co-operation in Europe (CSCE) opened in Helsinki with a promise from President Bush to make sure relief reached Sarajevo "**no matter what it takes**". Bosnia's president, Alija Izetbegovic, said up to 60,000 people had been killed by Serb forces and 1.4m people had been driven from their homes. The three Baltic republics, Latvia, Lithuania and Estonia, appealed to the CSCE for help in pressing Russia to withdraw its remaining troops from their territory.

Friday 10th
Poland's five-week government crisis ended as parliament gave a vote of confidence to a **seven-party coalition** headed by Hanna Suchocka, Poland's first woman prime minister.

The CSCE ended its summit by criticising governments which left their **troops** in other countries—but without naming names. It adopted a security framework giving it an enhanced peace-keeping role. The Western European Union and NATO decided to launch separate air and sea operations in the Adriatic to observe if UN sanctions against Serbia were being respected.

Sunday 12th
Serbian authorities in Kosovo pressed forward with their "colonisation" programme of putting Serbs into official jobs held by ethnic Albanians ranging from university professors to factory workers.

Friday 17th
The lower house of Belgium's parliament voted to ratify the EC's **Maastricht treaty** by 146 votes to 33. The Senate would vote on it in the autumn.

Vaclav Havel stepped down as president of Czechoslovakia after Slovaks in parliament opposed his bid for re-election, saying the split in the country was "a major failure for all of us".

Sunday 19th
The **Mafia** intensified its campaign of intimidation against Italy's judiciary by killing the magistrate most directly concerned with fighting organised crime, Paolo Borsellino.

The recently appointed prime minister of Yugoslavia (consisting of Serbia and Montenegro), **Milan Panic**, paid a surprise visit to Sarajevo offering to hold peace talks with Bosnia & Hercegovina. There was no let-up in Serbian shelling of the city and of counter-attacks.

Monday 20th
The decision was taken to wind up an Italian state holding company, Efim, which could not service its debts of 8.5 trillion lire ($7.3 billion). This was seen as another sign of the country's **economic crisis**.

Facing a higher-than-expected budget deficit, **Spain** increased value-added tax and income tax by 2%.

Tuesday 21st
A new peace plan for Bosnia & Hercegovina by Lord Carrington, in which artillery would be placed under UN supervision, collapsed when the UN secretary-general, Boutros Boutros-Ghali, said the plan was "not realistic". He broke tradition by publicly criticising the Security Council for trying to force his hand.

General **Lewis MacKenzie** of Canada, the senior UN soldier in Sarajevo, said that for a UN peace force to be effective in the city alone he would need 40,000 troops.

Monday 27th
EC finance ministers agreed to a Community-wide **minimum level of value-added tax** at 15% until the end of 1996. Critics in Britain of a closer European economic union objected.

Wednesday 29th
At a 60-nation Geneva conference on the refugee crisis in **ex-Yugoslavia**, delegates pledged more than $170m in aid. The UN High Commissioner for Refugees, **Sadako Ogata**, said 500,000 people were likely to need shelter. Aid officials said more than 2m people had been displaced.

August

Monday 3rd
The United States confirmed the existence of Serbian-run detention camps in Bosnia & Hercegovina where **torture and killings** had taken place.

Franjo Tudjman, a communist turned nationalist, won a second term as **president of Croatia** by defeating a moderate candidate and a more extreme nationalist. Tudjman's reported desire to grab Croatian-occupied parts of Bosnia did him no harm.

Tuesday 4th
The weekly Serb magazine *Epocha* said of northern Bosnia that "our army surrounds Muslim villages. If the Muslims do not raise the white flag on the minarets, **we raze the villages to the ground.** Serb villages will be built there." Serbian bombardments of the city centre and airport of Sarajevo, the Bosnian capital, continued. Muslim forces fired back.

Sunday 9th
The British foreign secretary, Douglas Hurd, underlined the reluctance of the United States, Britain and Germany to commit ground troops to help bring peace to Bosnia & Hercegovina. At the United Nations it was revealed that a report dated July 8th on Serbian-run detention camps and **"persecution, deportation and intimidation"** of the republic's Muslims had been received at the New York headquarters but not published. At Omarska detention camp, the Serb police chief said some detainees were emaciated because they had been fasting.

Monday 10th
The president of the European Commission, Jacques Delors, condemned the EC for inaction in ex-Yugoslavia and called for **"realistic military intervention"** to prevent the "cunning and murderous strategy of the Serb leaders" from spreading. The German foreign minister, Klaus Kinkel, said Germany would "unfortunately" be unable to send troops to guard convoys bringing food and medical aid to Sarajevo and elsewhere in Bosnia.

Tuesday 11th
UN officials said the Serbs were **trying to force 28,000 people** living in north-west Bosnia to move to neighbouring Croatia.

Militant supporters of the ousted president of Georgia, Zviad Gamsakhurdia, **kidnapped the interior minister**, Roman Gventsadze.

Wednesday 12th
Croatia's President Tudjman, backed by the leader of Bosnia's Serbs, Radovan Karadzic, called for Bosnia & Hercegovina to be made a UN protectorate, thus challenging the republic's right to exist. The proposal **suggested that Serbia and Croatia might be working together** on the issue and that it was their aim to get a further opportunity to carve up the republic while it was technically in UN hands. At Sarajevo, in an action that protected lives while speeding the process of Serbian "ethnic cleansing", the UN escorted a convoy taking 300 Muslim women and children out of the city. Bosnia's second city, Banja Luka, was described as "a city of daytime arrests, midnight beatings and round-the-clock terror".

Thursday 13th
The UN Security Council **authorised the use of force** as a last resort to ensure that relief supplies got through to the beleaguered population of Bosnia & Hercegovina but stopped short of any further military involvement. France's President Mitterrand said: "Adding war to war would not solve anything". Holland proposed that the EC countries should close their embassies in Belgrade.

Sunday 16th
At least **22 people** were killed in fighting in the breakaway Abkhazia region of western Georgia.

Tuesday 18th
After an emergency cabinet meeting the British prime minister, John Major, announced that **1,800 troops would be sent to Bosnia** under the UN flag to escort convoys operating with the consent of the warring parties— but not to fight their way through to besieged towns. Turkey called for a graduated military response with air strikes on the Serb operations in Bosnia.

In Georgia, government troops using tanks and helicopters **recaptured Sukhumi**, capital of the breakaway Abkhazia region.

Thursday 20th
Finland's economic crisis, caused partly by a slump in trade with Russia, deepened. The government announced **spending cuts of FM6 billion ($4 billion)** because of a soaring budget deficit fuelled by the cost of growing unemployment, reckoned at about 13% of the workforce.

Wednesday 26th
Mr Major opened an **international conference on the Yugoslav crisis** in London by serving notice on the Serbs that the world would quarantine them unless they agreed to co-operate with the western powers and bring the conflict to an end. The acting American secretary of state, Lawrence Eagleburger, called for inspectors to monitor arms movements and human-rights violations in Serbia and Bosnia.

Sweden's economic crisis of confidence worsened. The central bank **increased lending rates** by three percentage points to 16% to stop a massive outflow of funds caused by the government's unwillingness to cut the budget deficit.

Thursday 27th
The London conference on ex-Yugoslavia **ended with an agreement on paper** under which detention camps would be closed, borders would be recognised, violence and sieges would end, humanitarian aid would be delivered more speedily, sanctions on Serbia would be tightened and negotiations would continue in a committee in Geneva. Radovan Karadzic said, however, that the Bosnian Serbs, who control more than half of the republic, were prepared to give up only 20% of it. Lord Carrington stepped down as EC mediator and was replaced a few days later by Lord Owen, a former Labour foreign secretary who had advocated the threat of force and air strikes to bring the fighting to an end. Earlier in the day five people were killed and 20 injured in Sarajevo by a mortar while queuing for bread.

September

Tuesday 1st

Continued neo-Nazi violence against **asylum-seekers in eastern Germany** provoked fears of a foreign boycott of German products and criticism of the government and police for reacting too slowly.

A **struggle for power** in what remained of Yugoslavia (Serbia and Montenegro) began between the moderate federal prime minister, Milan Panic, and the ultra-nationalist Serbian president, Slobodan Milosevic. The respected federal president, Dobrica Cosic, backed Mr Panic.

Wednesday 2nd

Workers in Ukraine **went on strike** for more industrial subsidies as the country joined the International Monetary Fund (which intended to demand, in return for a loan, that subsidies be reduced).

Thursday 3rd

President François Mitterrand took part in a televised debate on the EC's Maastricht treaty as the campaign for a **national referendum** on the treaty gained momentum. Fears grew that if France voted No, the European exchange-rate mechanism could unravel, leading to numerous devaluations.

An Italian aircraft bringing humanitarian aid to Sarajevo was **shot down**, apparently by a missile, near the airport. Aid flights were temporarily suspended.

Sunday 6th

EC economy ministers discussed their **currency worries** and the head of the German Bundesbank said Germany "did not plan to increase interest rates in the current circumstances".

Bosnian Serbs were given a week to **keep their promise** to place their heavy weapons around four Bosnian cities under UN control.

Tuesday 8th

The Nordic countries had a bout of financial jitters and took some **drastic actions**. The Bank of Sweden, worried about the state of the currency, raised its lending rate by 8% to 24%. Finland, in contrast, allowed its currency to float (it was devalued by 13%). Earlier, Norway increased its rate from 13% to 17%.

Two French soldiers in an aid convoy to Sarajevo were **killed in a machine-gun attack**, apparently by Bosnian Muslims.

Police in Athens clashed with striking workers protesting against the government's plans to tighten rules for the loss-making and inefficient **state pensions system**.

Wednesday 9th

Italy's prime minister, Giuliano Amato, worried about the deteriorating economy and its political impact, sought **emergency powers** from parliament enabling him to rule by decree in an emergency.

Russia's President Boris Yeltsin postponed his much-awaited **visit to Japan**, citing domestic problems. The main reason was stalemate over the future of the Russian-held Kurile islands off the northern tip of Japan, which Japan claims.

Sunday 13th

Italy **devalued the lira** by 7% while remaining in the ex-

change-rate mechanism amid growing tension among European political leaders and currency dealers about the outcome of the French referendum.

Germany asked other European countries for more help in dealing with the **flow of refugees**, saying its political stability was at risk because of violence against foreigners. Britain declined.

Monday 14th

The UN Security Council voted to send **5,000 more troops** to try to keep the peace in Bosnia & Hercegovina.

Responding to political pressure, the German Bundesbank **cut its key lending rate by 0.25%**. Britain welcomed the move but would have liked a bigger cut.

Serb artillery **shelled Sarajevo**, damaging the prospects for negotiations due to be held in Geneva.

Wednesday 16th

In a day of chaos on the money markets, Britain raised its interest rate from 10% to 15% and intervened massively to fend off pressure to devalue sterling. In the end the government admitted failure, suspended sterling's membership in the ERM and **let the pound float**. It promptly lost more than 10% in value. The move was a serious political reverse for the prime minister, John Major. Italy's lira, under similar selling pressure, also left the ERM. Sweden raised the central bank's overnight rate to 500% to discourage speculation against the krona.

Thursday 17th

Spain **devalued the peseta** by 5% but stayed within the ERM.

Sunday 20th

In its referendum on the Maastricht treaty, **France**

voted in favour, but by a margin of less than 1%. The result was greeted with widespread relief by governments in Europe but concern at the closeness of the result.

Russia's acting prime minister, Yegor Gaidar, promised that the government would tighten monetary policy after conceding that the **budget deficit was now "very bad"**.

Thursday 24th

Thousands took to the streets in Hungary to protest against the **rise of the far right**, led by Istvan Csurka, vice-president of the ruling Democratic Forum, who published a booklet attacking Jews as enemies of the Hungarian people.

Germany indicated to the UN it would like a **permanent seat** on the Security Council and promised to revise its constitution so that its troops could take part in UN operations.

Sunday 27th

Romania's ex-Communist president, Ion Iliescu, unexpectedly won 48% of the vote in a **presidential election** against 30% for the opposition candidate, Emil Constantinescu. A run-off was to be held on October 11th.

Tuesday 29th

The UN High Commissioner for Refugees said 400,000 people in ex-Yugoslavia could **die from cold and hunger** in the winter without emergency assistance and a renewed airlift.

October

Thursday 1st
The Czechoslovak federal parliament voted down a government proposal for a constitutional break-up of the country into two republics, **delaying plans for a quick divorce** between the Czechs and the Slovaks.

Sunday 4th
An El Al Boeing 747 cargo jet **crashed** into a block of flats in Amsterdam after take-off when it lost its two right engines. Initially some 250 people were feared to have died but the toll was eventually put at about 70. The exact number was unknown because many illegal aliens lived in the building. After the authorities offered an amnesty to those affected, more than 1,000 illegal aliens claimed they lived there.

Monday 5th
Russia's President Boris Yeltsin admitted that his cabinet had made mistakes in its **economic reforms**. He said corrections were needed, implying that he accepted some of the criticism aimed at him by conservative ex-Communist industrialists.

Wednesday 7th
The **Gorbachev Foundation** was ordered to vacate its Moscow building hours after a newspaper published an interview in which Mikhail Gorbachev said President Yeltsin was "clearly not coping with his duties".

Sunday 11th
In one of several racist incidents in Germany, police in the eastern city of Magdeburg **arrested 60 neo-Nazi youths** who were hurling stones and shouting insults at an immigrants' hostel.

Edward Shevardnadze, former Soviet foreign minister, won a presidential election in Georgia amid fighting by Muslim minorities against the Christian-dominated government. Shevardnadze said the "chances for a political solution **have significantly deteriorated**".

Serbian forces captured Bozanski Brod, in Bosnia & Hercegovina, after Croatian forces pulled out, leaving the town defended only by Bosnians. This led to more speculation about **secret deals** between the Serbs and Croats to carve up Bosnia & Hercegovina. At the same time Serbian aircraft, defying a UN Security Council ban on flights over Bosnia, bombarded two Bosnian strongholds.

Monday 12th
Romania's ex-communist President Ion Iliescu easily won the run-off in his country's **presidential election**, defeating anti-communist Emil Constantinescu. There were numerous complaints about voting irregularities.

Tuesday 13th
Ukraine's parliament voted overwhelmingly for the appointment of the manager of the world's largest missile factory, Leonid Kuchma, as prime minister. A political unknown, his appointment on the recommendation of President Leonid Kravchuk appeared to represent a victory for big industrial groups which are hostile to economic reform and seek continued state subsidies.

Thursday 15th
As fighting continued in Bosnia & Hercegovina, the UN negotiator, Cyrus Vance, said the deployment of UN units to protect relief convoys was "extraordinarily slow" and the UN High Commissioner for Refugees, Sadako Ogata, said: "**We are poised on the edge of a humanitarian nightmare.**" Almost 3m people—refugees, displaced persons and people trapped in besieged cities and regions—were affected.

Friday 16th
The 12 EC heads of government, meeting in Birmingham, issued a statement designed to still the fears of EC citizens that the Maastricht treaty was leading towards a tighter union directed by the European Commission. The summit leaders reaffirmed the support for the treaty but also recommended more openness in EC decision-making and that decisions be taken "**as closely as possible to the citizen**". The language was also designed to take account of Danish demands prior to Denmark's second referendum on Maastricht next year.

Sunday 18th
Serbian shelling knocked out Sarajevo's **last remaining flour mill**, delivering a severe blow to the 400,000 people surviving in the city partly on bread and pasta.

Thursday 22nd
Arguments between Russia's President Yeltsin and conservatives led by his vice-president, Alexander Rutskoy, grew more heated as Mr Yeltsin warned against "**skidding to the right**". Mr Rutskoy demanded the sacking of five cabinet ministers and said the sweeping privatisation plan was designed "to rob the country".

Saturday 24th
Rebels in the ex-Soviet republic of Tajikistan **seized the presidential palace** and government buildings in the capital, Dushanbe. The next day, they withdrew. The republic was split between forces loyal to the acting president, Akbarcho Iskandarov, an Islamist, and the ousted president, Rakhmon Nabiyev, an ex-communist.

Slovakia began **damming the Danube** to divert its waters through the controversial Gabcikovo hydro-electric barrage despite furious protests from neighbouring Hungary and criticism from Germany. Hungary said it was taking its complaint to the World Court and the Conference on Security and Co-operation in Europe.

Thursday 29th
Russia's President Yeltsin **suspended the withdrawal** of troops from Lithuania, Latvia and Estonia on the grounds that the civil rights of ethnic Russians in the three ex-Soviet states were being violated. The troops would be withdrawn, he said, after agreements protecting their rights had been signed. Earlier, the defence ministry had said the withdrawal of some forces was suspended—but for a different reason: a shortage of housing for servicemen in Russia. Mr Yeltsin's move appeared to be designed to placate his nationalist critics and to maintain Russian influence over the Baltic republics. Estonia's Russians, who make up 40% of the population, were excluded from presidential and parliamentary elections in September because they have no automatic right to Estonian citizenship.

Tuesday 3rd
Russia's President Boris Yeltsin imposed a **state of emergency** in North Ossetia to stop fighting between Ossetians and Ingush.

Wednesday 4th
Hundreds of Bosnian Muslims, forced out of their homes in Jajce by Serb forces, trekked to safety in Croatia but were **turned back at the border**. The Croats said they could absorb no more refugees. Serb gunners fired thousands of shells on Gradacac and besieged Tuzla. In Belgrade, the Serbian capital, supplies of petrol were ample despite UN and EC sanctions.

Russia's parliament voted overwhelmingly to ratify the treaty with the United States on **reducing nuclear arms**, against the opposition of hardline conservatives. But Ukraine's new prime minister, Leonid Kuchma, said he would find it difficult to sell the treaty to his parliament without "inducements" from the West.

Thursday 5th
A German official in Rostock apologised for the statement of the chairman of the city's committee on internal affairs to a German Jew that his "homeland is Israel". The chairman resigned. The incident came after several outbreaks of violence against im-

migrants and refugees by neo-fascist thugs.

Saturday 7th
A Japanese freighter accompanied by a guard-ship left the French port of Cherbourg for Japan with a controversial cargo of **1.5 tons of plutonium** reprocessed from spent Japanese power-station fuel, to be used as fuel in fast-breeder reactors.

Sunday 8th
More than 250,000 Germans led by President Richard von Weizsäcker and Chancellor Helmut Kohl demonstrated in Berlin against **outbreaks of racism** including attacks on foreigners. A small group of anarchists and leftists pelted the two men with paint bombs, eggs and tomatoes, chanting "hypocrites".

Relief flights into Sarajevo were delayed as **heavy fighting** raged around the airport. British troops in Bosnia in a convoy checking a road used for relief supplies came under fire from Serb gunmen.

Monday 9th
President Yeltsin **signed a friendship treaty** with Britain during a visit to London where he conferred with the prime minister, John Major, lunched with Queen Elizabeth and addressed parliament.

Tuesday 10th
Another ceasefire was agreed in Bosnia & Hercegovina, this time signed by middle-ranking Serb, Croat and Muslim military men at a meeting in Sarajevo, the capital, under the auspices of the UN Protection Force.

Wednesday 11th
France's President François Mitterrand criticised Britain's prime minister, John Major, for **delaying ratification of the Maastricht treaty** until some time next year. The Ger-

man chancellor, Helmut Kohl, said he understood Mr Major's political difficulties.

Sunday 15th
President Yeltsin agreed with conservative ex-communist industrialists, led by Arkady Volsky, to **slow down his economic reforms** without (he claimed) diluting them.

The ex-communist Lithuanian Labour Party won a clear majority of seats in parliament in the second round of a general election, humiliating President Vytautas Landsbergis. The Labour leader, **Algirdas Brazauskas**, said he favoured closer ties with Russia and slower economic reforms.

Monday 16th
The UN Security Council voted to allow warships in the Adriatic to **stop and search** freighters suspected of breaking the ineffectual UN trade embargo on Serbia and approved other measures to end violations of the embargo on the Danube and elsewhere.

Tuesday 17th
Germany's opposition Social Democratic Party approved at a special congress a possible amendment to the constitution that would end a ban on **sending German soldiers on UN peace-keeping missions** outside the NATO area. But it would not allow them to take part in combat operations such as the Gulf war. The party also made a tentative agreement with the government to tighten up rules on admission of asylum-seekers

and to take quicker action to deport those who had been refused admission. But there was more haggling to come.

Wednesday 18th
In a U-turn on economic policy, Ukraine's prime minister, Leonid Kuchma, told parliament that there was **no alternative to a thorough-going reform**.

Sunday 22nd
Serb forces **shelled Sarajevo** (as usual) and pushed forward towards two Muslim towns, Travnik and Gradacac.

Police in Sicily ordered the seizure of **nearly $750m in assets** of an alleged Mafia family, the Madonias.

Monday 23rd
A **neo-Nazi firebombing** in the German town of Mölln killed three Turkish-Germans including a ten-year-old girl.

UN officials said there had been **more than 100 Serb violations** of the "no-fly" zone over Bosnia & Hercegovina that was imposed by the Security Council on October 9th.

Wednesday 25th
Ireland held a **general election** and the small Labour Party led by Dick Spring made most gains. But the result was inconclusive and several recounts were ordered.

Sunday 29th
A UN aid convoy in Bosnia was allowed past Serb roadblocks and reached the Muslim town of Srebrenica, which had been **cut off since April**.

Monday 30th
Russia's Constitutional Court ruled that President Boris Yeltsin was **right to ban the Communist Party** after its attempted coup in August 1991 but should not have closed down local party organisations.

December

Tuesday 1st
President Boris Yeltsin opened a session of the Congress of People's Deputies with a call for greater presidential powers and a declaration that he would not be deflected from the goals of his reform programme. He had previously called for the founding of a **new political party** to defend reform, and offered to join it.

Thursday 3rd
A Greek-registered oil tanker **caught fire** off the Spanish port of La Coruna, spewing thousands of tons of North Sea crude into the Atlantic.

Sunday 6th
Switzerland **rejected closer European integration** in a referendum, with 16 out of 23 cantons voting No to joining the European Economic Area. The popular vote was closer: 50.3% said Yes and 49.7% said No. The EEA was to have linked the European Community with all members of the European Free Trade Association (including Switzerland) in an enlarged common market.

Germany's ruling coalition and the opposition Social Democrats worked out the precise terms to amend the constitution to **tighten the rules on the admission of foreigners** as alleged refugees. It confirmed the right to asylum but allowed border guards to turn back "manifestly unfounded cases". The measure, which would go to the Bundestag (lower house) after Christmas, was also designed to reduce the influence of neo-Nazis opposed to immigration. About 250,000 Germans demonstrated against racism in Munich.

Voters in the ex-Yugoslav republic of Slovenia **preferred moderates** in their elections for a president and parliament. They re-elected the cautious President Milan Kucan and gave most votes to the centrist Liberal Democrats and Christian Democrats in parliament.

Monday 7th
Opponents of President Yeltsin in Russia's Congress of People's Deputies failed twice in an attempt to change the constitution to give the legislature the power to **appoint all members of the cabinet except the prime minister**. Although the second vote favoured the move the majority fell short of the necessary two-thirds.

Sunday 13th
Leaders of the 12 EC countries, meeting at a summit in Edinburgh, agreed on the EC's future finances, a formula for **ratifying the Maastricht treaty** that Danish voters might approve in a referendum in 1993 and the start of negotiations with Austria, Sweden and Finland on membership. The agreement was an unexpected success for Britain's six-month EC presidency.

Italian voters, fed up with years of corruption, misgovernment and the unimpeded rise of the Mafia, **turned away from their traditional parties**, the Christian Democrats, the ex-Communist Party of the Democratic Left and the Socialists, in local elections. All three parties lost votes, which went instead mostly to the anti-Rome Northern League, the anti-Mafia "Network" and the neo-fascist Italian Social Movement.

Ignoring mighty Switzerland, voters in neighbouring Liechtenstein (population 29,000) **voted heavily** in favour of joining the European Economic Area. The week before Switzerland had voted against joining the zone.

Monday 14th
In a sudden reversal, Russia's embattled President Yeltsin **replaced his reformist acting prime minister**, Yegor Gaidar, with Viktor Chernomyrdin, a conservative deputy prime minister and former industrial manager. Mr Chernomyrdin said hesitantly that he favoured reform, "but not through the impoverishment of the people", and the market economy, "but not a bazaar".

Tuesday 15th
Moves were under way for the UN Security Council to **authorise the use of force** to prevent any Serbian flights over Bosnia. NATO was making contingency plans for limited uses of force in ex-Yugoslavia. But some western governments were still wary of actions which might put the poorly defended Bosnian Muslims, outside aid workers and foreign soldiers helping them more at risk from Serbian guns than they are already.

Sunday 20th
Serbia's hardline President Slobodan Milosevic emerged as the clear winner in a **presidential election** over the conciliatory Milan Panic, prime minister of the remnant of Yugoslavia (Serbia and Montenegro). Mr Panic claimed the result was null and void because of "fraud, theft and cheating" during vote-counting.

Monday 21st
Fifty-four passengers and crew were killed when a chartered DC-10 airliner of the Dutch airline Martinair **crashed on landing** at Faro airport, in southern Portugal. There was speculation that cross-winds were to blame.

Tuesday 22nd
Jacques Delors, president of the European Commission, carried out **a shake-up** of old and new commissioners. Britain's Sir Leon Brittan took the important trade portfolio and Holland's Hans van den Broek was put in charge of negotiations over new members and common foreign policies. Turf battles seemed inevitable.

Wednesday 23rd
President Yeltsin re-appointed most of his **reform-minded cabinet ministers** including the minister for privatisation, Anatoly Chubais.

Friday 25th
Pope John Paul marked Christmas by lamenting that the world seemed at times ''**deaf and impenetrable**'' to a message of healing and hope. He denounced the "planned and inhuman" ethnic war in Bosnia & Hercegovina.

Tuesday 29th
The United States and Russia agreed on the text of a SALT-2 treaty that would cut their **nuclear arsenals** by two-thirds during a meeting in Geneva between the secretary of state, Lawrence Eagleburger, and the Russian foreign minister, Andrei Kozyrev.

As we reported then

Vorsprung durch Panik

FEBRUARY 15TH, BONN *Angst abounds in Germany over the state of the economy. The growing sense of unease is only partly explained by the rising costs of unity. Can Germany continue to compete?*

ROUGHLY once a decade the Germans get the urge to question their economic prowess. At the start of the 1980s they moaned that foreign rivals were streaking ahead with newer technology and fresher ideas—and then resolved to catch up. Ten years and a run of record trade surpluses later, they are in a blacker mood than ever.

Unity is partly to blame. While many foreigners fret about a too-mighty Germany, the Germans themselves reel under new economic blows and bills. Record public borrowing, highish inflation, more than 3m out of work: this was not what the Germans expected unity to bring (on the rare occasions when they considered the topic at all).

Even apart from the unity strains, firms in Germany are being crippled, according to the hand-wringers, by high taxes, expensive labour and big environmental and power costs. As a result, foreign investors are shunning Germany and German bosses are moving production (and hence tens of thousands of jobs) abroad. Edzard Reuter, head of Daimler-Benz and one of the loudest groaners, gives warning that his group may be forced to start building even luxury Mercedes cars outside Germany. Heinrich Weiss, president of the Federation of German Industry, sadly reflects that Germans nowadays prefer to "reap instead of sow".

As the charts show, cost-cutting is one reason for German firms' foreign invest-

ment. But it is usually not the main one. Allianz, the country's biggest insurer, expanded abroad because cartel rules stopped it growing much more at home; Deutsche Bank swept into Italy and Spain the better to position itself for the single European market; Siemens (electricals) and the German chemical giants bought heavily in America to be inside markets they could not feed with exports alone. But why haven't foreigners been ploughing more money into Germany?

Not, in many cases, for lack of trying, as Pirelli's recent abortive bid for Continental, a German tyre company, showed. For all their claims to the contrary, the Germans can be as hostile to foreign buyers as the Japanese. (Like the Germans, the Japanese are huge net investors abroad, but unlike the Germans they rarely suffer from economic self-doubt.) True, plenty of foreign firms have made it to Germany and thrived, such as General Motors with its Opel subsidiary. The government is also keen to get more foreigners to put cash into the still ramshackle east. But, that apart, Germany's market is hard to penetrate and tough to stay in—though not quite as tough as the groaners say. Three issues are illustrative.

First, corporate tax rates look unbearably high, profits often piffling. But Germany's gloriously flexible accounting rules let firms bury earnings in reserves for accelerated depreciation and the like, which re-

Hand-wringer Reuter

sults in less revealed profit and a lower tax bill (a technique of which Daimler's Mr Reuter in particular is a master). That still leaves the tax burden a bit heavier than in most competitor countries, so the centre-right government of Helmut Kohl has pledged to lighten it. The bosses' squeals now are meant in part to ensure that the promise is kept.

Second, the bill industrial firms face to keep the place clean—DM21 billion ($13 billion) in 1990 alone—looks a lot higher in Germany than in most competitor countries. Hence the corporate squawks against still tougher environmental rules being mooted by the government. This is understandable. But the German car industry at first complained about government prodding to install catalytic converters, and then went on to make a packet out of them, while also picking up the biggest world market share in fuel-injection systems. Now lots of other German firms are forging into environmental technology, partly because the government is setting a hot pace but also because big market chances beckon, especially in the heavily polluted east.

Third, German workers, who already take the world's longest holidays and are, apart from Norway's, the most expensive to employ, are treating themselves to pay rises this year probably averaging around 6%. Too high, most pundits say, even al-

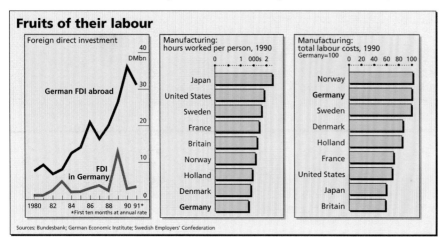

Fruits of their labour

Foreign direct investment (DMbn)	Manufacturing: hours worked per person, 1990 (000s)	Manufacturing: total labour costs, 1990 Germany=100
German FDI abroad; FDI in Germany	Japan	Norway
	United States	Germany
	Sweden	Sweden
	France	Denmark
	Britain	Holland
	Norway	France
	Holland	United States
	Denmark	Japan
	Germany	Britain

1980 82 84 86 88 90 91*
*First ten months at annual rate

Sources: Bundesbank; German Economic Institute; Swedish Employers' Confederation

lowing for German labour's discipline, high productivity and a widely admired on-the-job training system. More rationalisation is inevitable; jobs will go. Similar chants have been heard in most years and have often proved true. But over the past decade around 1.5m more new jobs have been created than have been lost. Unrelenting pressure for more goodies from strong trade unions is one big reason why German firms have had to strive so hard to make themselves more efficient, pushing into new fields and higher-value products.

A nice trick if you can keep it up. Plenty of employers doubt it—citing, for one

thing, the soaring costs of unity, which are pushing up prices and interest rates, and aggravating union demands. This is true for the moment, although unity means huge business chances too. Otherwise western German industry would not be investing DM36 billion ($23 billion) in the east this year alone. By the end of the 1990s, according to a recent poll of businessmen and politicians, the east will have emerged as the showcase of Germany, with more modern plant and infrastructure than the west. This view is strongly at odds with the present gloom.

Germany's competitors have grown steadily stronger in part thanks to German-

type virtues: the British by cutting strikes, the French by reducing inflation, the Japanese by (among other things) better organisation. That means the Germans need to do more: for instance, by cutting state subsidies; by encouraging more privatisation (both the federal railways and the postal service are now on the government's list); by simplifying chronically complex regulation; and by using more efficient production methods. What are the prospects? Not bad, thanks to that corrective ten-year itch. The Germans have a habit of spurring themselves into action just when it seems they might be falling into a self-satisfied doze.

Italy's earthquake

APRIL 11TH, ROME   *The voters stunned the politicians by sending them an unusually powerful message in Italy's general election. Italians, tired of misgovernment, were in a mood for change*

IT IS many years since a general election in Italy registered more than a quiver on the Richter scale. But after the vote on April 6th and 7th, the earth shook, and cracks appeared in the structure of power. Horrified Christian Democrats saw their share of the vote drop to its lowest since the war—29.7% in the lower house of parliament. Though still the biggest party, their long dominance of Italian politics is under threat. Italians are fed up with the shabby politics of the ruling parties in Rome, and they are no longer afraid to vote for alternatives.

The Christian Democrats had expected to lose ground in northern Italy, where a mass protest vote rallied to the regionalist Lombard League and its allies in neighbouring regions. But they were not prepared for big losses across the country.

The election was a personal triumph for Umberto Bossi, the leader of the Northern League, an alliance of regionalists that swept to second place in the north. The League won 8.7% of the national vote (and over 20% in Lombardy). The raucous Mr Bossi, who has given voice to dissatisfaction with misgovernment by Rome, is by far the most popular politician in Milan—something of a humiliation for Milan-born Bettino Craxi, the Socialist leader.

Mr Craxi has acknowledged a "slight erosion" in Socialist support, which dipped from 14.3% to 13.6% of the vote—the party's first general-election setback since Mr Craxi took over the leadership in 1976. The Socialists suffered conspicuous losses in Milan, where the recent arrest of a party

official on corruption charges took its toll. Losses throughout northern Italy were not quite outweighed by gains in the south, where the Socialists are now the second-largest party, having overtaken the Democratic Party of the Left (PDS), Italy's renamed communists. Forty of the Socialists' 92 deputies were elected in southern constituencies—a substantial geographical shift for a party whose roots lay in the industrial north.

The vote has left Italian politics deadlocked. The outgoing four-party coalition under Giulio Andreotti (which includes the tiny Liberal and Social Democratic parties as well as the Socialists and Christian Democrats) has kept a slender majority in parliament. But no one seems to think this is enough to form a new government.

Mr Craxi has already withdrawn his candidacy for the prime ministership. Christian Democratic leaders instructed their party secretary, Arnaldo Forlani, to open talks with all parties in parliament except the League and the neo-fascist MSI. After talking to his party's old allies, he has been told to approach the ex-communist PDS, the Republicans and the Greens.

The response has been cool. The Republican leader, Giorgio La Malfa, whose move into opposition last year fatally weakened the ruling coalition, says he will support only a government of "experts", with ministers chosen for technical competence rather than political allegiance. The PDS leader, Achille Occhetto, warned his party this week not to heed the Christian Democratic "siren-song". Christian Democratic emissaries are not the only ones wooing Mr Occhetto. Mr Craxi is too.

So much attention must be of some comfort to Mr Occhetto. He had set his sights low, hoping to poll 17%—nearly ten points below the Communist score in the last general election. But his party won just 16% of the vote. Mr Occhetto expected some damage from hardline Communists who left last year to found their own party. But the hardliners did better than expected, winning 5.6% of the vote.

Still, Mr Occhetto won strong personal support and his party remains the second-largest nationwide. His leadership is therefore not at stake. The same cannot be said of Mr Forlani. The Christian Democrats' faction chiefs are notoriously merciless in their treatment of party leaders who have outlived their usefulness. But the time is probably not yet ripe for a coup within the party. The grand old men of the Christian Democrats, like Mr Andreotti, are determined to survive through the manoeuvres to patch together a government.

Enter the joker in the pack: Italy's un-

predictable president, Francesco Cossiga. It will be up to Mr Cossiga to pick Mr Andreotti's successor after parliament meets on April 23rd. And Mr Cossiga has already made it clear that unless he is presented with a clear-cut parliamentary majority by the end of the month, he will pick a new prime minister at his discretion. Who this could be is now the subject of endless Roman debate. Mr Cossiga's mandate expires on July 3rd, and voting for his successor is due to begin on June 4th. So if he intends to spring a surprise, he will have to do so soon.

Mr Cossiga has swung wildly in his recent political hates and sympathies. He has quarrelled with the Christian Democratic Party from which he rose to the presidency, and crossed swords with Mr Andreotti, only to stage public and affectionate recon-

ciliations a few weeks later. He attacked Mr Occhetto, then announced his suitability to join a future government.

Italians might be hoping for a reforming prime minister, such as Mario Segni, the Christian Democrat who successfully championed a referendum on electoral reform last year. He saw that vote as a vindication of his own demand for new voting rules designed to produce clear-cut majorities. Mr Segni is demanding an extraordinary party conference to elect a new Christian Democratic leadership. He wants a broad-based government with support from all th____rties for a programme of elector___omic reform. Anyone trying to___ether the old four-party govern____ce, says Mr Segni, "has not ___d what happened in this electio."

Street capitalism

APRIL 25TH, MOSCOW
Economic reform began in earnest in Russia under Boris Yeltsin's radical government. The capitalist revolution quickly turned the streets of Moscow into a giant bazaar

THE centre of Moscow is now home to one of the most extraordinary sights in the world. Knotted around a children's department store opposite the former KGB headquarters, thousands of people stand all day long holding up for sale a shirt, glassware or shoes. There are few stalls: people simply stand around.

Something similar happened in Poland after economic reform. Moscow's giant bazaar stretches for almost two kilometres, its tentacles reaching into new alleys almost daily. On weekdays 7,000 to 10,000 people are out selling; at weekends the figure doubles. In December 1991 the market did not exist.

Here, it seems at first sight, is an explosion of entrepreneurial spirits. How can anyone have thought that Russians could

not be capitalists? The size and vitality of the market surely show that a presidential decree, signed in January, allowing unrestricted street trading to challenge the state retail system has worked triumphantly.

Then doubts creep in. People stand all day to sell a plastic toy for 160 roubles ($1.50). How can this be worthwhile? Sooner or later trading must move back to where it is economically rational—in shops (as has happened in Poland). A pensioner stands clutching half a dozen packets of tea from her kitchen. She is selling them, she says, because she cannot make ends meet.

In an attempt to find out how this strange bazaar fits into the wider economy, *The Economist* asked a sample of 100 traders about their activities. Nearly 20 were students on tiny stipends; 26 were skilled blue-collar workers, including a machine-tool operator and an oil-field driller; 22 were white-collar workers, including an aircraft designer. All but four who had been in regular jobs had left them, mostly voluntarily.

Few of the goods on sale came from home. Three-quarters of the traders claimed they had bought their stock at state shops. This is odd. You might expect customers to be prepared to pay a modest premium to avoid queuing. But in the Moscow

bazaar the average mark-up was 100%.

If goods are in the shops for half the price, why don't consumers buy from there? Because of continuing shortages. Consumers simply do not know what is available where. The traders are mostly Muscovites with local knowledge. The customers often come from outside Moscow. Russia's capital is unusual in attracting so many out-of-towners, which is why other cities, even St Petersburg, lack such huge bazaars.

Why don't shopkeepers put up prices? Because state shops are not allowed by law a mark-up of more than 25%. This keeps prices down but makes supplies erratic. The market reflects rigidities in Russian pricing.

The profits are huge. Out of the 100 in our sample, the least successful group are the pensioners. They earn on average 26 roubles an hour and work eight hours a week (excluding the time spent shopping for supplies). The most successful, four students selling Turkish leather jackets, make 135 roubles an hour and work over 50 hours a week. Most of the sample make 80-100 roubles an hour, working 20 hours a week. Compare that with an industrial worker on a mere 17 roubles an hour. One student said she earns four times as much in one day at the market as both her parents earn in a week.

This makes the market one of Moscow's biggest enterprises. Some 10,000 people earn on average about 100 roubles an hour. The market runs ten hours a day—providing a profit of 10m roubles. In the name of public order Moscow's deputy mayor wants to close it down. He must be mad.

Eager to consume

Genscher's last act

MAY 2ND **Out of the blue, Hans-Dietrich Genscher resigned after 18 years as Germany's foreign minister. "Genscherism", as it came to be called, defined a whole era of German foreign policy**

REMINDED by a former American secretary of state of the old joke that "two aircraft collided over the Atlantic and Genscher was in both of them," Germany's peripatetic and seemingly perpetual foreign minister shot back: "And in both cases he was the only survivor." But survival is also about knowing when to eject. After 23 years in cabinet, 18 of them as his country's foreign minister, Hans-Dietrich Genscher is still the Germans' favourite politician. But even his fans admit that, since Germany became whole again, Europe's master diplomat seems to have lost his touch.

German unity was unexpectedly a crowning achievement for a man whose name has entered Europe's political lexicon. Genscherism did for East-West relations what Thatcherism did for economics: defined an era, but also a personal style that generated awe and respect among some, anger among others. Genscherism was above all—some say at any cost—about compromise.

To detractors, the search for accommodation in divided Europe smacked of appeasement. His former boss, Helmut Schmidt, who doubted Mr Genscher's loyalty to him but not to the West, described him as a "tactician without a strategy". Which is perhaps why to many Germans he personified the Germany they long for: one that could remain secure and well-loved, while avoiding hard choices.

Genscher loyalists, who dominate the foreign office, reject the charge that he lacked principle. He made European integration, and most recently the cause of monetary union, the cornerstone of his small Free Democratic Party—and that of German foreign policy. His mastery of the political platitude and his determination to keep a dialogue going with the communist world may at times have infuriated the White House, but it made his the acceptable face of Germany in the Kremlin. As the collapse of the Soviet empire accelerated, that may have helped Mikhail Gorbachev to let the former East Germany go.

In the run-up to German unity, Mr Genscher pressed Chancellor Helmut Kohl

for a clear recognition of Poland's frontiers, and has steadily argued for political as well as economic generosity to Eastern Europe. But the policies that were his strengths have also shown up his weaknesses.

He deserves credit for suggesting early that Mr Gorbachev should be taken at his word. He then nurtured his Gorbachev connection with the Soviet Union to the virtual exclusion of all others, and was caught flat-footed when Mr Gorbachev was swept aside. Others made the same mistake. But none seemed so determined to overdo concessions in advance: from Mr Genscher's early opposition (to the fury of the German defence ministry) to continued deployment of short-range nuclear weapons in Germany, to his insistence that eastern Germany would not become a full part of NATO—a presumed sticking-point with the Kremlin over German unity that in the end not even Mr Gorbachev stuck at.

Mr Genscher's final success may be recognising the right time to go. He has found it hard to adapt to the world he helped to change. He was slow to endorse the Gulf war. Partly for domestic reasons, he rammed through recognition of Croatia and Slovenia, despite the hesitation of his EC allies, thus undermining the common approach to foreign policy of which he was himself a prime champion. He has done little to prepare Germany for a new role in a different world. After 18 years on the stage, Mr Genscher's will be a hard act to follow. With luck, his successor will not try.

Why the Danes wouldn't

JUNE 6TH, COPENHAGEN **By rejecting the Maastricht treaty on European union, Danish voters threw the European Community into confusion**

DENMARK'S libraries and post offices had been offering, free, 500,000 copies of the full text of the Maastricht treaty, one for every tenth man, woman and child in the country. It may have been a mistake. Many Danes took one look at the near-incomprehensible legalese and said, "If they think I'm voting for this, they are in for a surprise." "They"—the political establishment, both sides of industry, and almost the entire press—duly got their surprise on June 2nd, when Denmark's voters, in a referendum that parliament has to obey, narrowly but resoundingly rejected the treaty, 50.7% against to 49.3% in favour.

Those who voted against may not have spent much time on the details of Maastricht, or of their own motives in saying No, but they knew what they chiefly disliked. They felt that this treaty, even if it did not go all the way, pointed towards Superpower Europe, a European army, yet more power to Brussels. Opinion surveys and conversations in the street alike suggest

that, for many Danes, such a Europe would destroy national independence, perhaps even national character. Now was the moment to prevent it.

Such fears existed, more hesitantly, when the Danes voted by comfortable majorities to join the European Community in 1972 and then, in 1986, to endorse the Single European Act. But on both those occasions the politicians presented the issue as chiefly one of economics. In 1972, especially, it was a question of being able to sell Danish-grown food (now 24% of Denmark's total exports) to the rest of Western Europe. Even in 1986, little was heard

And Nay they said

about political Europe. This time, however, there was no way for the pro-Maastricht parties—ranging from the Conservatives and the Liberals, both members of the coalition government, to the opposition Social Democrats—to deny that the issue was Europe's political future. Most politicians' views on that have changed since 1972, and even since 1986. They have convinced themselves that German unification has made it even more desirable to bind Germany into a European Union. But they could not sell the argument. The machinery of the union frightened people.

Even men as amiably persuasive as

Poul Schlüter, the prime minister, and Uffe Ellemann-Jensen, the foreign minister, failed to persuade a majority that "European Union" was not a phrase to send a shiver down the spine. The anti-Maastricht forces—a curious assortment of peace and environment enthusiasts, the ex-Marxists of the Socialist People's Party and the right-wing populists of the Progress Party—could not put much money into their campaign. But they won the day.

The defeat for Maastricht is especially serious for the leaders of the Social Democrats, by far Denmark's largest party, which got 37% of the vote in the 1990 election. Its

supporters appear to have gone two to one against the treaty. This adds an extra item to the explanation of why the Danes voted as they did on June 2nd.

The Social Democrats long ago ceased to be a party of the industrial working class; they are now chiefly the party of old-age pensioners and of the third of the labour force that works in government services. Danish women, who apparently voted 57% against the treaty, thus deciding the issue, are employed in large numbers in the schools, the health service and the welfare services. Denmark's government wants to reduce the country's taxes, now the highest in the EC, to something nearer the European average, partly by cutting government spending on such things. These women saw Europe as an economic threat as well as a political one.

But if Denmark leaves the Community as a result of Tuesday's vote, or even slides down into the sort of relationship the countries of the European Free Trade Association used to have, the economic consequences will look very different. Denmark now has the highest GDP per head in the Community. If investment drifted away from Denmark, and if the Danes could no longer be part of the common agricultural policy, the pain would be severe. And why, as one furious, pro-Maastricht woman voter said, should the other 11 countries be nice to a Denmark that "only wants the benefits and won't share the responsibilities of creating a wider Europe"?

The nightmare continent

JUNE 13TH *The optimism that followed the collapse of the Soviet empire gave way to a sombre mood during 1992. Troubles in both East and West crowded in on a worried Europe*

A SPECTRE is haunting Europe. It is the ghost of chaos past, in a continent that has produced two world wars this century. The European Community was meant to be a beacon of stability in the aftermath of communism's collapse. But the Community is in disarray, thanks to Danish voters' rejection of its Maastricht reforms. Europe is threatening to become the world's problem continent once again.

With the crumbling of the Soviet empire, a degree of turmoil was inevitable. The question was: would instability in the East spread westwards, or would the West's stability expand eastwards? At first things seemed to be going the right way. Now the reasons for alarm are multiplying.

The worst worries are still in the East, afflicted not only by economic slump but by local wars (from Bosnia to Nagorno-Karabakh) and a growing refugee problem.

Two new items must now be added to the list. First, the disintegration habit is spreading from ex-Yugoslavia and the ex-Soviet Union into Central Europe. After Czechoslovakia's election, the country looks likely to split in two. There is talk of a "velvet divorce" to follow the country's "velvet revolution" of 1989. But once squabbling begins over the division of assets—not to mention the explosive matter of the Hungarian minority in Slovakia—a separation may become far from smooth.

The second, less-noticed and more dangerous novelty is the gathering conservative backlash across much of Eastern Europe. In Russia, Boris Yeltsin has diluted his government of radical young reformers with some cautious older faces (notably from the military and energy industries, the mainstays of the old regime); the freeing of energy prices, a litmus test of the will

to reform, has been postponed and even reformers are proposing to bring back centralised controls on foreign trade. The ex-communist mafia is tightening its grip on Ukraine. Slovakia has voted for nationalist socialism. In Poland, which had such westernising zeal before it sank into ungovernability, the latest governing team has a distinctly eastern look.

Indeed, a new division of Europe may be in the making, with the two halves separated not by an iron curtain but by differences in attitude to reform. The divide bisects Czechoslovakia and old Yugoslavia. Hungary is on the western side, Poland is in danger of joining the east. West of the divide lies wholehearted capitalism; to the east lies half-hearted capitalism which relies on old elites to run broken economies (perhaps it should be called *kaputtalism*).

With such a commotion next door, the EC ought to be devoting more energy to helping its eastern neighbours. But the Community has been distracted. First there was the effort of putting together the

Bayern.
The Quality Edge in
the New Europe

Strength at the center

Over the last two decades, Germany's
economy, generally regarded as one of
the strongest in Europe, has grown
by 60%. Consistently the growth leader
among the country's states, Bavaria has
surpassed that figure by 50%. Today,
the state's more than DM 479 billion in
annual output and around DM 100 billion
in annual exports would make it (were
it an independent nation) the OECD's
12th largest economic power. Over half
of the airplanes, electronics, production
systems and other high-tech goods
Germany ships to the outside world
originate in the state. With 20.8 million
arrivals, Bavaria is the country's foremost
tourist area; Munich alone ranks among
Europe's top 5 destinations.

These facts detail a remarkable transformation, which began after World War II.
Bavaria, large (its 70,554 square kilo-
meters now comprise 19% of the
Federal Republic of Germany's surface)
and rural, had areas of secondary
industrial importance in Nuremberg,
Munich, Würzburg and Augsburg. Seen
from the geopolitical perspective of the
time, Bavaria was not centrally located.
Its neighbors were either members of
the East Bloc (Czechoslovakia), under
joint Soviet administration (Austria) or,
looking beyond the Alps, themselves
reconstructing (Italy).

Stability from the start

One asset Bavaria did have: political
stability, expressed in an unswerving
commitment to creating the preconditions for business growth and thus
improving standards of living. Coming to
this haven in southern Germany were
such major German companies as
Siemens and such American pioneers as
NCR and Texas Instruments.

In the mid '50's, the Bavarian government launched an unprecedented
program of investment in its human
capital and in transport infrastructure. At
the 19 universities and polytechnics the
state either founded or expanded, young
scientists and entrepreneurs developed
their products and ideas. Through an
extensive technology transfer program,
"seedling companies" concentrating on
electronics and information technology
were planted (initially) in the greater
Munich and Nuremberg/Erlangen area.
In the late '70's, the flourishing of these

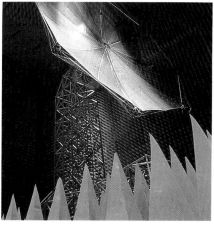

young companies helped catapult
Bavaria to the top of Europe's high-tech
regions. Today, the nearly 280,000 persons employed in Bavaria's electronics
sector represent a quarter of the
country's total.
Other factors were the emergence of a
domestic European aerospace industry,
centered in Germany around Munich's
Deutsche Aerospace AG and the
German Space Operations Center in a
western suburb, and the remergence of
two famous automobile manufacturers:
BMW and Audi.

Development is the whole state's business

Over the last three decades, a key policy focus has been to spread this rapid economic growth throughout the entire state – with commendable success. An integrated system of business promotion incentives and advisory services was set up. It took in all levels of government and all sectors of industry. The Bavarian Ministry for Economic Affairs and Transport coordinates this system's outreach, providing "one stop service" to potential investors.

The result: the state's long-time "corporate citizens" have increasingly located their new facilities in such places as Regensburg (Siemens, BMW), Augsburg (MAN), Dingolfing (BMW), where they have been joined by such non-German high-tech leaders as Murata (Nuremberg), Hitachi (Landshut, Landsberg), Toshiba (Regensburg) and Microsoft (Unterschleißheim).

Products from Bavaria's farms – and television studios

Some things, of course, didn't change. Re-organized and reequipped, Bavaria's agricultural sector has remained Germany's largest, with its hops, dairy products, wine and grain earning DM 16 billion a year for the state's farmers.

Media, surprisingly enough, has always been a traditional state specialty. Ever since the Second World War, Munich has been the world's second largest book publisher. Attracted by the city's glamour and favorable business conditions, much of the nation's film and television production industry set up shop in the city. Bavaria Film studios, currently Europe's second largest, heads the list of Munich's 320 companies in the field.

The achieving of this "critical mass" of technological and economic power had important ramifications, especially for the state's financial sector. Today, the Bayerische Vereinsbank and the Hypo Bank (Bayerische Hypotheken- und Wechselbank) are ranked among Germany's top five universal banks. To serve the needs of the state's companies and private investors, 24 of the EC's 80 private banks are located in the state.

But it is in the insurance sector where Bavaria stakes its claim to being "Europe's investment center". With DM 158 billion in assets, Allianz is Europe's largest insurer. Its associate, Münchener Rückversicherungs-Gesellschaft, is the world's leading re-insurer. Other prominent names include Frankona and Bayerische Rück.

Fast tracks
to European unity

In 1989 and 1990, the political barriers fell in eastern and western Europe, creating whole new avenues of political and economic interaction. Showing considerable foresight, Bavaria had been constructing several major infrastructure projects. With the coming on line of Munich's state of the art airport, the Rhine Main Danube canal (which connects the North and the Black Seas) and the reopening of some 8 rail and road connections to eastern Germany and eastern Europe, the state has thus been in a position of facilitate pan-European development by giving the two halves of Europe access to each other's markets. Beneficiaries of the boom in Bavaria's north and east: such towns as Hof, Bayerisch Eisenstein and Waidhaus, once on the margins, today sporting the state's highest tourism and investment growth rates.

Two major challenges of the '90's are continuing the integration of both Germany and the EC. In the planning and study stages are high-speed ICE train lines between Bavaria and Thuringia and Berlin, and between the state and Paris via Mannheim, as well as a rail-road tunnel under the Alps. Another development enhancing the state's ties to the world will be Munich's new trade fair centre, to be located in the eastern suburb of Riem. This new facility will have 200,000 square meters of covered floor space. It will provide badly needed room to grow to Systems, Electronica, ISPO and other events making Munich one of the world's five largest trade fair venues. Both trade fair exhibitors and organizers in Munich as well as in Nuremberg and in Augsburg can avail themselves of the state's 150,000 self-employed professionals, whose skills range from translation to graphic arts.

Some things don't change, they just get better

In the midst of this galloping progress, it is reassuring to note that many items in Bavarian life have remained the same over the decades, generations, even centuries. Such industries as glass and porcelain manufacturing have been pursued in the cities of Selb and Weiden for three quarters of a millenium. Half of Bavaria's workforce is employed by small and medium-sized companies. While many of their products, including Rosenthal china, Loden-Frey clothing and Nachtmann crystal are world-known, a great portion of these companies are still managed by their founding families. And preserving the vitality of these companies is another of the policy focuses of the Ministry for Economic Affairs and Transport, which works closely with them to develop their products, marketing strategies and personnel.

In one very important way, the state hasn't changed at all. Despite being a favourite with both employees and employers – creating a net intra-German migration of some 25,000 persons a year – Bavaria is still relatively underpopulated, with an average of 162 persons per square kilometre. Whole stretches of the state, including the southern rim of Alps and lakes and its eastern reaches of pristine forests, are reserved exclusively for nature and sports lovers.

Nor is the past forgotten in Bavaria. It manifests itself in the state's historical and cultural sights, which range from the spectacular (King Ludwig II's three castles) to the intimate (the Frauenchiemsee island in Lake Chiemsee). Its festivities include the raucous Oktoberfest, the dignified Richard Wagner festival in Bayreuth, the avant-garde Biennale in Munich and the Mozart festival in Würzburg.

Four and a half decades of stable economic growth, a millenium of culture and history and a few aeons of unspoiled natural beauty are proving an irresistible mix for an increasing number of investors. But it is other units of time which these investors are now noticing upon arrival in the state: the hours and minutes saved by the direct flights to and from the new airport. Bavaria is a lot closer than it used to be.

For further information, please contact

Bavarian Ministry
for Economic Affairs
and Transport
Prinzregentenstraße 28
8000 München 22
Germany
Tel.: (89) 21 62-26 42
Dr. Georg Orlitsch

Maastricht treaty (and, for Germany, of coping with unification). Now there is the mess of Maastricht ratification.

The sudden sense of uncertainty in the wake of the Danish No to Maastricht does not mean that Western Europe is about to experience the sort of traumas now afflicting the ex-communist half of the continent. Local wars are not waiting to break out in the Community, nor are EC countries in danger of collapsing into poverty. Nevertheless, even in prosperous Western Europe there is a palpable new unease.

The Danish referendum was the latest in a series of electoral blows to the political establishment—in France, Germany and above all Italy, where politicians are still dazed from the power of the protest vote at the general election in April. In France and Germany, far-right parties have been doing distressingly well. All this, plus the struggle against recession, has kept EC governments busy with difficulties at home. The ramifications of the Danish referendum herald another period of European introspection.

That is unfortunate. It means that the Community's ability to radiate stability eastwards will remain weak. A club consumed with anxieties about its own future hardly provides the example that the boldly uniting Community seemed to have in the early days of the new European order.

Distracted by the Maastricht morass, EC governments will not give priority to policies—notably the lowering of trade barriers, especially for farm products—that would help East Europeans pull out of their economic morass. Worse, there will be a delay in the EC's efforts to work out a framework of enlargement that could give East Europeans something specific to aim for. Neglect by the West Europeans may even be partly responsible for the emergence of Europe's new east-west divide. With the EC beacon shining too feebly, some East Europeans are being drawn to more familiar lights.

The Community's introversion also risks causing damage beyond Europe. EC governments are liable to find it harder to take big decisions together. That could damage efforts to reach agreement in the GATT trade-liberalisation talks. As they grapple with the consequences of the Danish referendum, EC leaders should try to keep an eye open to what is happening in the world around them. Otherwise, old European nightmares could all too easily return.

An inch deeper into a quagmire

*JULY 18TH   **Everyone wanted the spreading war in ex-Yugoslavia to end. But outside powers could agree on little else, reluctant to be sucked in to Europe's first full-scale war in more than 40 years***

AFTER a fortnight of declarations about the war in Bosnia, the outside world is clearer at least about what it should not be doing there. At the Helsinki meeting of the Conference on Security and Co-operation in Europe (CSCE) on July 9th and 10th, George Bush made it plain that America was not thinking of using military force to halt the conflict. The Europeans agree. No foreign power wants its soldiers dragged into a Balkan quagmire. Beyond that differences surface. Though bent on joint diplomacy towards what was Yugoslavia, the Americans and various Europeans have their own aims to pursue.

International pressure is growing on Serbia to halt its aggression. At the Helsinki meeting Serbia was at least temporarily denied Yugoslavia's seat in the CSCE, to which it lays claim with Montenegro. Support from Russia prevented harsher action against Serbia & Montenegro (such as im-

mediate expulsion from the CSCE). This bodes ill for an attempt to suspend or expel the Yugoslav rump state from the United Nations, where Russia has another veto.

The Europeans and the Americans have sent naval vessels and reconnaissance aircraft to the Adriatic as a possible first step towards monitoring the UN's trade embargo of Serbia. This is largely for show. Without a new UN resolution, this tiny flotilla has no right to stop or search merchant ships. There is scant evidence that goods are reaching landlocked Serbia from the Adriatic coast in quantity.

More serious outside efforts are diplomatic mediation and humanitarian relief for Sarajevo. Lord Carrington, the European Community's negotiator, invited the leaders of Bosnia's rival groups to London at mid-week to talk to him, even if they would not talk to each other. The Bosnian Serbs and Bosnian Croats would break

Bosnia up into ethnic cantons and might settle for a lasting ceasefire. Each group has won land from Bosnia's Muslims. Yet Muslims make up around 45% of the Bosnian population and account for a large share of the 1.6m Bosnians made homeless by the war. No peace leaving out Bosnia's Muslims could endure.

At the Munich summit of the G7 rich nations, the French had floated the idea of placing the diplomatic work in the hands of the UN, with the ultimate aim of calling an international conference for Yugoslavia. The Serbs, rightly, feel they would have more friends in the UN than in the EC, which sponsors Lord Carrington's work.

The British, who this month took over the six-month presidency of the EC, and the Americans are against France's idea. The UN, they argue, has its hands full with peacekeeping in Croatia and relief in Sarajevo. Changing negotiators would bring a settlement no nearer.

The British are irritated with the French on other counts. President Mitterrand's bold visit to Sarajevo last month caught them short. As if in imitation, Douglas Hurd, Britain's foreign secretary, this week began a visit to five ex-Yugoslav republics. More seriously, the British complain that the French are using the war to encourage the strictly European defence organisation, the Western European Union (WEU), at the expense of NATO. This is theology to suffering Bosnians, say the French, who are the most engaged there of all the Europeans. A lot of the troops under UN command at Sarajevo are to be French.

The Germans are confused. They pressed hard last autumn for international recognition of Croatia and Slovenia, despite British and French warnings that an un-negotiated break-up of Yugoslavia would leave Bosnia exposed. Spokesmen justify Germany's low profile now in two ways: given its history, German peacekeepers would be unwelcome in the Balkans; and, by its calculations, Germany has spent more money than any other outsider on humanitarian relief in Yugoslavia.

The German government this week decided to do more. It sent a destroyer, the *Bayern*, to join the naval cordon in the Adriatic and dispatched reconnaissance aircraft to the area as well. The opposition Social Democrats say this may be unconstitutional. Germany may send military forces abroad only under international agreement (here NATO). The government wants Germany to take on more peacekeeping and defence responsibilities and is glad to have a test case it thinks clear cut.

The British take a Hippocratic view of Bosnia: the priorities are not to make things worse and to prevent the war spilling over into neighbouring countries. If they have a peace plan, they are keeping quiet about it. One aim may be to open up "safe areas" in Bosnia, including Sarajevo, with the help of UN peacekeepers. Cost, which delayed the sending of peacekeepers to Croatia, is not currently a problem. The Security Council this week voted for an extra 500 UN troops to go to Sarajevo.

Even if Europe cannot bring peace to Yugoslavia, it cannot ignore its refugees. According to the United Nations High Commissioner for Refugees (UNHCR) in Belgrade, there are 1.8m "displaced people" in ex-Yugoslavia (almost all of them in private homes) and up to 500,000 Yugoslav refugees outside. Around 580,000 are in Croatia alone. This week the government of Croatia said it would take no more. Most European countries, frightened by the rise of anti-foreign far-right parties, are also closing the door. The UNHCR wants countries to create a new legal category of "temporary asylum" and to agree to burden-sharing under which governments not letting in temporary refugees would pay into a fund for those who did.

The mess in ex-Yugoslavia, it is being said, shows the limits of collective diplomacy in post-communist Europe. The international bodies—the EC, the UN, the WEU, NATO and the CSCE—have been weak or slow. Resisting local bullies needs single-minded leadership. Only individual governments can give that. The new Balkan statelets thrown up by the collapse of communism are like those that emerged at the end of the Habsburg and Ottoman empires: they expect big powers to boss them about, and, as the Serbs under Mr Milosevic have shown, are quick to misbehave when nurse looks the other way.

Yet part of the Yugoslav tragedy is that there are no easy steps outsiders, together or alone, can take to stop the war. By going it alone, an outside power could well make things worse. Europe's governments have not prevented war in Yugoslavia. They have so far stopped it from driving a serious wedge between them. This was not always true of Balkan disputes in the past.

The cracks in Russia widen

SEPTEMBER 5TH, MOSCOW **The sudden end of the Soviet Union stunned the world. But the unravelling has not stopped. Russia itself is fraying at the seams**

LAST year it was the Soviet Union that was under threat; now it is Russia. The Soviet Union exploded. If Russia goes too, erosion will have done it, the erosion of ethnic differences and economic rivalries.

On the face of it, the danger was eased by the signing in April of a "federation treaty", which distributes power between the federal and the local governments. True, two of Russia's 21 "republics" (regions populated by minorities with substantial self-governing powers) refused to sign. One, called Chechnya, in effect seceded last year, but nobody noticed. The other, Tatarstan, which contains Russia's largest minority, held a referendum in April in which 61% of those who voted backed "independence". But Tatarstan says it does not want to break with Russia; its president claims that a special treaty between the two will be ready this month.

But the signing of the federation treaty has not settled the matter. First, the Russian government has insisted that all regions sign the treaty before it will make any bilateral deals with them. Tatarstan is likely to sign only a bilateral treaty, and this may cause the others to demand the same privilege. Another republic, Bashkiria, has agreed to sign the treaty only on condition that it gets special concessions, including the right to exclusive control of property (which would exempt it from privatisation).

Trouble outside Russia, in Georgia's rebellious district of Abkhazia, could also help to unravel the treaty. People in the part of Russia adjoining Georgia have banded together into an organisation called "the Confederation of Mountain Peoples" to help the rebellion in Abkhazia. This could pull them away from Russia.

Anyway, the treaty is caught up in a wrangle over a new constitution, of which it forms part. Russia's President Boris Yeltsin, having threatened to impose a new constitution on a reluctant parliament in May, then seemed to drop the idea. Recently, however, he has revived it.

At this delicate point, enter economics. In the country's general economic confusion, many local authorities have been quietly expanding their powers in this field. In Tyumen, Russia's largest oil-exporting region, oil producers need an export licence from the local commodity market, in which the local government has a large stake. Despite January's price liberalisation, nearly a third of Russia's cities still control the local prices of many basic foods. Tatarstan issues special coupons for local food purchases.

It may be getting worse. Sergei Alexashenko (one of the few good economists not working for the government) says local governments are using their economic clout—as owners of land and providers of water and electricity—to intervene more in local economics. They make factories and farms in their area sell them 10-15% of their output at low prices, and then barter the goods with other local authorities that are doing the same thing.

Russia's deputy prime minister for regional affairs, Valery Makharadze, claims that this is not all bad: the regions are taking an active interest in economic issues. But this will not help if they undermine the central government in the process.

The decision of the Tyumen authorities to insist on local export licences makes the oil-exporting business more bureaucratic. Local-authority barter trade distorts the nationwide market and sometimes leads to local protectionism. Farmers have been refusing to sell grain to the central government on the ground that, until recently, the price was too low. This has caused food shortages in some cities and encouraged Krasnodar, the region that includes some of Russia's richest farmland, to suspend grain "exports" to other parts of Russia.

Worst of all, local authorities are beginning to undermine one of the most basic functions of government—raising and spending taxes. Russia's regions have usually run budget surpluses that help to offset the centre's deficit. But the accumulated regional budget surplus fell from 95 billion roubles in May to less than 85 billion in June, thus increasing the net federal deficit.

This decline is caused partly by a rise in local-government spending, but it is also partly the Russian government's fault. In January the central government exempted coal-mining regions from part of the taxes they should have paid, to prevent a threatened coal strike. That was one of several deals granting regions preferential tax arrangements at the centre's expense.

Local governments are also spending money they have no right to. They are withholding tax revenues that should be handed over to the centre. In an attempt to stop this, the Russian parliament in July threatened sanctions on areas not fulfilling their tax obligations. This made things worse. The three biggest "republics" (Tatarstan, Yakutia and Bashkiria) have threatened unspecified retaliation in the event of sanctions being imposed.

Because local taxes account for only a third of Russia's tax take, this poses a smaller danger to Russia than Russia did to the Soviet Union when it withheld taxes in 1991 (Russia had contributed half of Soviet tax revenues). Moreover, Russia's regions have few tax-raising powers of their own, getting most of their money from fixed shares of federal taxes. So the centre in theory has more control over tax policy than its American and German counterparts.

In practice, Russia's centre lacks their established authority. Mr Yeltsin's attempt to stop the regions ignoring his decisions by appointing local governors does not seem to have worked. Under communist rule, Russia was over-centralised. Some loosening-up was needed, and is happening. The danger is that it is getting out of hand, and that the federation treaty will fail to prevent a sensible loosening from becoming disintegration.

Population, m	
All Russia	**149.4**
Adygei	0.43
Bashkiria	3.95
Buryatia	1.04
Chechnya & Ingushia	1.27
Chuvashia	1.34
Dagestan	1.79
Gorno-Altai	0.19
Jewish region	0.22
Kabardino-Balkaria	0.76
Kalmykia	0.32
Karachevo-Cherkess	0.42
Karelia	0.79
Khakasia	0.57
Komi	1.26
Mari	0.75
Mordovia	0.96
North Ossetia	0.63
Tatarstan	3.64
Tuva	0.30
Udmurtia	1.60
Yakutia	1.08
Source: 1989 census	

Map legend:
1 ADYGEI
2 KARACHEVO-CHERKESS
3 KABARDINO-BALKARIA
4 NORTH OSSETIA
5 CHECHNYA & INGUSHIA

An idea that is sinking fast

SEPTEMBER 26TH, BRUSSELS **A French No to the Maastricht treaty would have sunk it without further ado. It was reprieved but only to face blow after blow**

BOTH the exchange-rate mechanism (ERM), a European Community success story of the 1980s, and the Maastricht treaty, its blueprint for the future, are on the brink of oblivion. France's narrow vote in favour of the treaty on September 20th failed to convince other Europeans or the money markets that the European venture was still sufficiently seaworthy for the voyage ahead to European union.

In a flurry of diplomacy reminiscent of previous panicky moments in Community politics, President François Mitterrand met Chancellor Helmut Kohl on September 22nd to reaffirm Franco-German support for the treaty. Yet a day later, despite massive intervention by the Bundesbank and others, currency speculators almost added the French franc to the list of those—the lira, the pound and the peseta—which had either dropped completely out of the ERM or devalued within it the previous week. Like the narrowness of France's vote, the renewed pressure on the franc appears to strengthen the hand of those Britons who want to see the Maastricht treaty abandoned. They argue that the treaty's core—the plan for economic and monetary union (EMU)—cannot proceed now that the mechanism for powering it, the ERM, is breaking apart.

The rest of the Community worries that Britain may not be willing, or indeed able, to ratify the treaty. John Major's government—shaken by sterling's departure from the ERM, plus what it construes as Germany's high-handedness and its own divisions on Europe—has said little to give reassurance.

Britain is the current president of the EC. It has called a special meeting of heads of government in London on October 16th. That summit will discuss reform of the ERM—or perhaps, by then, its postmortem; what to do about Denmark, which voted down the treaty in June; and how to respond to popular concerns reflected in the worryingly large No vote in France, but also increasingly in other EC countries, that Community institutions are remote and unaccountable. Mr Major says that Britain will not ratify the treaty until the EC has decided how to tackle these problems.

Many countries now suspect Britain's intentions and good faith. Countries are not supposed to exploit the presidency to pursue national interests. But many governments fear that Mr Major will now do just that to slow the pace of integration. German diplomats are afraid that he may encourage the Danes to ask for a special deal that could undermine the Maastricht treaty. France's foreign minister, Roland Dumas, worries about the summit. "It should not open the door to ambiguities or allow the thought to spread that we could take another look at the treaty," he said this week, after a meeting of foreign ministers in New York.

That meeting revealed the extent of Britain's isolation. Douglas Hurd, the foreign secretary, proposed a statement on the ratification of the Maastricht treaty which set no dates and left open the possibility of amending it. The other ministers forced him to accept references to the original timetable for ratification and to the impossibility of "reopening" the text.

Whatever its shortcomings, most governments want to avoid renegotiation. Since the treaty was the outcome of a finely balanced compromise between the 12 partners, they fear that changing some parts could mean unravelling the whole.

Yet the treaty cannot come into force until its 12 signatories ratify it. Luxembourg, Greece, Ireland and France have done so. Belgium's lower house has approved the treaty. The Spanish, Italian, Portuguese and Dutch parliaments are on target to ratify it before Christmas.

The German parliament will start ratification next month. The *Länder* (regional states) want more influence over German policy in the Council of Ministers. The opposition Social Democrats also want a parliamentary vote in 1996 on whether the final phase of EMU should proceed. The government will probably give in to the *Länder*, but will try to stop any vote on EMU from being binding.

All the major parties want the treaty ratified this year. The only party to oppose Maastricht is the far-right Republican Party. Yet many Germans are sceptical about the timetable for EMU, and public opinion is firmly opposed to giving up the D-mark. If the current chaos in the EC sets off a new wave of anti-Brussels sentiment, ratification may not look so certain.

Still, the chances are that by the end of this year only Britain and Denmark will not have ratified the treaty. Denmark's partners now believe that a way round its problem is in sight. On October 12th the Danish government will publish a white paper setting out a list of options covering policy towards the EC. In November parliament will decide on the line the government should take when it starts talking to the EC about a special deal for Denmark.

It will probably ask for additions to the Maastricht treaty that would leave the original text unchanged. The opposition Social Democrats have suggested provisions stating, among other things, that the single currency and common defence would not apply to Denmark, and that its system of social security would be safe. Poul Schlüter, the Danish prime minister, has

floated the idea of opening the Council of Ministers and the European Commission to the public. He predicts a second Danish referendum by early autumn next year.

The British problem appears much harder to solve. Mr Major is unlikely to try to push the Maastricht bill through the House of Commons before January. If and when he does, members of Parliament may not approve it.

The furious debate on Maastricht within the Conservative Party has pushed Mr Major and his foreign secretary towards caution and ambiguity. Mr Hurd says that the Community cannot carry on with Maastricht as if nothing had happened. "There have got to be changes," he said this week. "Whether they are changes to the treaty, or alongside the treaty, clarification, clearing things up that are obscure or messy, that is something which the October summit will have to talk about."

Since some changes must be made to suit Denmark, British diplomats hope that they can, at the same time, push through others to suit Britain. Britain will avoid any "renegotiation" (the R-word is taboo) of the original treaty. "Saying that we won't 'reopen' the text doesn't stop us add-

ing new things," says a British diplomat.

Such a ploy would not necessarily upset the rest of the Community. If Britain and Denmark could think up changes that boosted openness and accountability—and included some ritual bashing of that universal scapegoat, the commission—they might be on to a winner. Nearly every government now has a problem convincing its public that Maastricht is a worthwhile venture. Even Mr Kohl said this week, after meeting Mr Mitterrand, that it was time to cut back the powers of the commission.

So a kinder, gentler Maastricht treaty may yet emerge this winter—the old text plus some extra pieces of paper. But what if Britain still failed to ratify it? Some of the countries that had already done so would threaten to carry on regardless, searching for some legal jiggery-pokery that would allow them to leave Britain behind.

It is more likely that a British No would kill the treaty. That would result in a two-speed Europe, in which some countries went ahead with monetary or military cooperation, beyond what is left of the framework of the Community. Britain would be once more cut off from Europe.

At the gates

DECEMBER 5TH *If European countries had been quicker to take a tough line on asylum-seekers, they might have been kinder to the people fleeing what was once Yugoslavia*

THERE was a curious unreality about the meeting of immigration ministers from European Community countries in London this week. Most of the meeting was taken up with the EC's faltering plans to remove all internal border-controls at the beginning of 1993. Much less time was devoted to pleas from Germany, speaking on behalf of the countries that border on ex-Yugoslavia, for a concerted policy to share the refugee burden. Yet refugees and their plight could well become, in the course of the winter, a problem of terrifying proportions.

The ministers' discussions were shaped mainly by what has been happening back in their home countries: a sharp increase in immigration, a nasty upsurge of racism, a general move to make it more difficult for non-EC citizens to enter the Community. The precise level of immigration is hard to measure. The best guess is probably that of the secretariat of the Inter-governmental Consultations on Asylum, Refugee and Migration Policies in Europe, North America and Australia, based in Geneva. This speech-stoppingly named organisation thinks that, between 1985 and 1992, about 15m people have poured into the countries of Western Europe. Of course, some have since left. But in several European countries, as the chart shows, a rising proportion of the total have been asylum-seekers. Indeed, in Sweden the influx of asylum-seekers far outstrips the arrival of all other immigrants.

Predictably, ex-Yugoslavs now dominate Europe's asylum-seekers. So far this year, the secretariat reckons, 210,000 Yugoslavs have sought asylum in Western Europe. That is more than double last year's inflow and more than six times the influx in the calmer days of 1990. But by no means all ex-Yugoslavs are asylum-seekers, and not all asylum-seekers are ex-Yugoslavs. Of the 607,300 ex-Yugoslavs who have come into Western Europe since the start of the Balkan conflict (more than a third of them to Germany), only half have applied for asylum. At the same time, others also hope for shelter in Western Europe. Romanians are now seeking asylum in the same sort of numbers (98,000 so far this year) as Yugoslavs did last year. Turks and Sri Lankans also apply for asylum in Western Europe in large (though not increasing) numbers.

In several countries rising immigration has brought with it rising racial tension. In Germany recorded attacks on foreigners rose nearly tenfold last year. This year's violence culminated last month in the murder of a Turkish woman and two young girls. In Sweden on Monday, black-garbed right-wingers had to be protected by the police from a rival demonstration against racism. But prejudice and violence have been on the march even in countries that have accepted few Yugoslavs.

In England attacks on foreigners last year were up by nearly a fifth. Spain has just suffered its first racially motivated murder in recent times. Only in France, where last year one centre-right politician complained about the "noise and smells" of immigrants and another likened their presence in France to the German occupation, do racist passions seem to have cooled this year.

For European idealists, anxious to create a barrier-free Europe, this is sinister news. The EC has been making painfully slow progress towards the commission's

ideal of a Europe without passport controls. The nine members of the Schengen group, which had hoped to lead the way, have been thwarted mainly by practical difficulties. Some hope to scrap controls in May or June next year, although they may have second thoughts: the northern European members also feel increasingly uneasy about opening their borders to the southern Europeans, with their porous frontiers. In London the 12 agreed to differ: the British, Irish and Danes will keep their passport officers.

As Europe's internal borders open, doors to the outside world shut. Legislation is being toughened across Europe. Sometimes, the call has come from liberals. In Italy the Catholic church, long an advocate of relatively liberal immigration rules, has begun to call for quotas, arguing that too many migrants are now homeless and destitute. Germany's Christian Democrats have pressed the Social Democratic opposition to amend the constitutional right to asylum.

Elsewhere, governments have simply become more brutal. France has been weeding out and repatriating "economic" refugees, and has thereby cut the number of asylum-seekers to half the 1989 level. Spain plans a sharp restriction in the definition of asylum-seekers, and a system of quotas for immigrant workers. Most European countries are now introducing "fast-track" procedures to speed up decisions on which asylum-seekers should be admitted and which turned away. Once in, they become hard to throw out.

These national changes have been aimed mainly at all immigrants, rather than specifically at refugees or at fleeing Yugoslavs. But the effect has been to make escape from ex-Yugoslavia ever more difficult. A growing number of countries (Britain is the latest) now require visas from ex-Yugoslav visitors. And on November 30th the EC ministers decided that refugees who enter the EC from a third country that is

deemed safe can be sent back there. As no EC country actually borders Bosnia, it will be possible for EC countries to return refugees to those that do, including Austria, Hungary, Slovenia or Croatia.

Britain's home secretary, Kenneth Clarke, insists that the provision is not intended to immure Bosnians in the countries of their desperate neighbours, but to catch those who stay for several months in one country before moving on to another. The neighbours, however, will note the reluctance of EC ministers to accept proposals from Austria, Switzerland and Germany for formal arrangements to share the burden. Germany's EC partners were unanimously hostile to the idea; their only concession was to ask Denmark, when it takes up the EC presidency in January, to start negotiations on burden-sharing.

Balkan tremors

In the nick of time, a cynic might say. The outpouring of refugees from ex-Yugoslavia is likely to grow much worse in the coming months, for two reasons. First, the states inside the dismembered country, which have received the bulk of displaced humanity, can no longer cope. And second, fighting may well break out again on a scale that will make the recent past look mild.

By far the largest number of ex-Yugoslav refugees are in ex-Yugoslavia itself. Some 1.7m homeless people are still in Bosnia & Hercegovina. Croatia, a country of 4.7m people, has taken in about 750,000 refugees. Its hotels are crammed, and it is running out of electricity (which it imports) and food. Inflation and the far right are both on the march.

To try to stem the flood, Croatia has shut its borders with Bosnia. As a result, many of the 6,500 wretches released by the United Nations from Bosnia's detention camps have nowhere to go. European countries have offered a total of 4,300 places.

Croatia's problems would ease if it re-

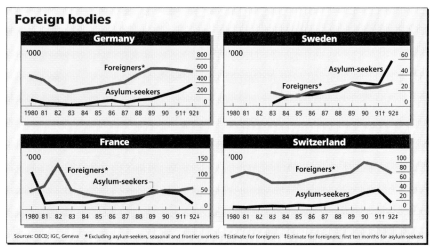

Foreign bodies

Germany — '000: Foreigners*, Asylum-seekers (0–800) 1980 81 82 83 84 85 86 87 88 89 90 91† 92‡

Sweden — '000: Asylum-seekers, Foreigners* (0–60) 1980 81 82 83 84 85 86 87 88 89 90 91† 92‡

France — '000: Foreigners*, Asylum-seekers (0–150) 1980 81 82 83 84 85 86 87 88 89 90 91† 92‡

Switzerland — '000: Foreigners*, Asylum-seekers (0–100) 1980 81 82 83 84 85 86 87 88 89 90 91† 92‡

Sources: OECD; IGC, Geneva   *Excluding asylum-seekers, seasonal and frontier workers   †Estimate for foreigners   ‡Estimate for foreigners; first ten months for asylum-seekers

ceived more cash from the outside world to offset the bill of $100m a month; or if it could send home the 260,000 or so refugees who have fled from the territory protected by UN troops. But this is not the moment for the UN to start allowing displaced Croats back into territory that Serbs have captured. On December 20th Serbia goes to the polls; the build-up of Serbian troops in Kosovo suggests that Slobodan Milosevic, the Serb president, may be planning an attack—before or after the election—on Kosovo's ethnic Albanians. That could suck in Albania, Bulgaria, Greece and Turkey. The number of asylum-seekers who would beg Western Europe for shelter could run, not into hundreds of thousands, but into millions.

Hope fades

DECEMBER 19TH, MOSCOW **After a year-long push for reform, Russia's hardliners pushed back hard. The year ended with Boris Yeltsin on the run**

THE best that can be said of the turn of events at the Congress of People's Deputies is that Russia's president, Boris Yeltsin, is more important to the succesful defence of economic reform in Russia than its acting (and now ousted) prime minister, Yegor Gaidar, was. If a choice had to be made between them, it was better that Mr Yeltsin should survive at Mr Gaidar's expense, than that both should be turned out of power.

But did that choice have to be made? President and parliament had been at loggerheads for days. When Congress came to vote on who it thought should be Russia's prime minister, it was no great surprise that only 400 deputies supported Mr Gaidar in the first round, compared with the 621 who supported the man Mr Yeltsin eventually put forward, Viktor Chernomyrdin, and the 637 who voted for the hardline secretary of Russia's security council, Yuri Skokov. Under the peculiar rules governing the choice of prime minister, Mr Yeltsin could still have insisted on appointing Mr Gaidar.

By doing so, Mr Yeltsin would undoubtedly have provoked a challenge to his own power when parliament next convenes, in April. Faced with that possibility, Mr Gaidar offered to resign (remarking, reportedly, that though Mr Skokov would cause disaster tomorrow, Mr Chernomyrdin might postpone it for a few weeks).

Mr Yeltsin had proved to be his own worst enemy. On December 10th he strode into the chamber, denounced Congress for "re-establishing the old communist system rejected by the people" and demanded a referendum to decide who ruled Russia: president or parliament. He then called on his supporters to leave the chamber. Had more of them done so, the outcome of the dispute—and perhaps the future path of Russia—might have been different. Congress would have ended its session in confusion.

But Mr Yeltsin had failed to prepare his supporters for the walk-out and only 150 left. Congress still had enough deputies present to continue work. Buoyed by support from the vice-president, Alexander Rutskoi, it retaliated by passing an amendment to the constitution which would have stripped the president of his powers had he attempted to dissolve Congress. The next day it went on to ban all referendums aimed at abolishing or curtailing the powers of the parliament, the president or the Constitutional Court.

The ministers of defence, internal affairs and security all promised to stay out of the dispute, thereby showing Mr Yeltsin's implied threat to impose emergency rule to be an empty one. The chairman of the Constitutional Court said that, if the legislature and executive did not compromise, the court would begin impeachment proceedings against "responsible officials".

The compromise that emerged was not wholly bad for the president. Mr Yeltsin persuaded Congress to sign its own death warrant by agreeing to a referendum on April 11th on the "principles of a new constitution". Once a new constitution is passed, a new parliament will have to be elected. The question now is: how powerful should this parliament be?

Mr Yeltsin would no doubt prefer Russia to be a "presidential republic", in which he would have powers similar to those of the French or American president—and at parliament's expense. A president subservient to parliament would be a recipe for chaos, especially in a country which still lacks proper political parties.

Under the compromise, Mr Yeltsin also persuaded parliament to sign a self-denying ordinance not to upset the balance of power between executive and legislature before the referendum. The result is a truce in the constitutional wrangle, until the issue can be settled by popular vote.

Yeltsin stands alone

But parliament and president may be unable to reach agreement either on the wording of a referendum question, or on a constitution. In return for an agreement that may backfire, Mr Yeltsin has made sacrifices that undermine his authority. He had promised to protect Mr Gaidar and failed to do so. He conceded to parliament the right to approve four ministers—those of defence, security and internal and foreign affairs. The liberal foreign minister, Andrei Kozyrev, now seems certain to go.

If he does, Russia may start bullying its immediate neighbours and veer away from co-operation with the West. Mr Kozyrev dramatised this possibility at a meeting this week of the Conference on Security and Co-operation in Europe, by giving a startling mock-cold-war speech in which he pretended that Russia would defend its interests in the ex-Soviet Union by force if need be. Those who gunned for Mr Gaidar accuse Mr Kozyrev of demeaning Russia. They are only too ready to pursue the policies Mr Kozyrev spoke of.

Most worryingly, as he set off this week on an official visit to China, Mr Yeltsin left behind a prime minister who does not fully support him and whose record does not augur well for the continuation of reform. Mr Chernomyrdin's main achievement as energy minister was to exempt the oil industry from privatisation. His first remarks as prime minister—that reform must not result in "mass pauperisation", and his emphasis on reversing the decline in industrial output rather than curbing inflation—echo the complaints of those most hostile to reform.

There are only two glimmers of hope. First, the minister in charge of privatisation, Anatoly Chubais, seems likely to stay on long enough to see through the critical early stages of privatisation-by-voucher early next year. Removing a critical mass of large companies from state control would make it hard to reverse this reform.

The other reason for hope is that the government's room for manoeuvre is small. With food prices rising by over 30% a month, Russia is on the verge of hyperinflation. Mr Chernomyrdin has promised to stick to Mr Gaidar's proposed budget for 1993 and not to reimpose price and wage controls. Yet those promises will be hard, if not impossible, to keep. Disdain for money, or sheer ignorance of its importance, may yet lead Mr Chernomyrdin to plunge the country into hyperinflation by mistake, thereby destroying all hope of reform.

Westward no?

JULY 4TH **Boris Yeltsin had overturned communism in Russia and seen the break-up of the Soviet Union. He wanted the new Russia to turn westwards. Others did not. What place in the world should a reborn Russia seek?**

IN THE 19th century, two schools of thought dominated political and intellectual life in Russia. The westernisers wanted to use European ideas and technology to modernise a feudal autocracy. The Slavophiles also wanted to modernise, but looked inwards for Russian ideas to do it with. Westernisers saw Russia as a European great power. Slavophiles saw it as the centre of a group of Slavic nations embracing Poland, Ukraine and Bulgaria. Turgenev was a westerniser, Dostoevsky a Slavophile. The battle is alive today.

On the face of things, westernisers have swept the board, in Russia's government at least. Last month Boris Yeltsin signed the Washington charter, which aims to set up a "Euro-Atlantic peacekeeping capability", in which Russia would like to play a leading role. His prime minister, Yegor Gaidar, looks to western capitalism for the means of reviving Russia's economy: $24 billion of aid, for a start.

Aid explains only part of the westernising policy. The galloping Americanisation of Russian culture, evident in the Russian language, in shops and on television, testifies that the turn to the West is more than government-deep. Mr Yeltsin and his foreign minister, Andrei Kozyrev, argue that the new Russia shares the West's basic values of democracy, market economics and respect for individual human rights. That is why they are working within western-dominated institutions such as the International Monetary Fund, the

Conference on Security and Co-operation in Europe (CSCE) and even the North Atlantic Co-operation Council, a talking shop admittedly, but still a NATO spin-off.

There has been no such drive to win membership of, say the Asian Development Bank or the economic co-operation organisation that in theory embraces Turkey, Pakistan, Iran and the Central Asian states of the former Soviet Union. Yet more of Russia lies east of the Urals than west, and that territory contains most of the natural resources—oil especially—on which it pins its economic hopes. And not only has Russia a substantial non-European minority—10m Muslims, for a start—but its majority population is influenced by non-western ideas, as the long Slavophile tradition shows.

In fact, after a spasm of activity in which policy has been wholly western, other ideas are being quietly but unmistakably reasserted. Some come from groups which, to varying degrees, oppose Mr Yeltsin (some of whose members, in Russia's peculiar politics, hold high government office). First are the communists who want Russia to turn its back on the West. They hated Mr Yeltsin's agreement to cut Russia's stockpile of strategic nuclear weapons by two-thirds, branding it "criminal" and "insane". The Soviet Union used to support the third world, they argue, and Russia should do the same.

Then there are former reforming communists, like Vice-President Alexander

Rutskoi, who are nostalgic about the Soviet past and hesitate to jump into capitalist democracy. Russia's ministers of internal and external security have both in recent weeks referred to the West as Russia's "adversary". Some critics are isolationists, who want a Russia-first policy untrammelled by conditions that the West puts on its aid. Others argue more thoughtfully that Russia either should not or cannot meet these economic conditions. The recent drift of economic policy away from radical reform suggests that their influence is growing.

The third source of criticism is the armed forces. Though the defence minister, Pavel Grachev, has gone along with the arms-reduction agreements signed in mid-June, he and the army are emerging as powers in a way that will not endear them to the West. Some of his recent remarks on the army, for instance, suggest that, to him, it represents all that is best in Russia and—a sinister idea—that the army should protect Russians living outside Russia.

To see the implications for foreign policy, read a recent article on the Yugoslav conflict in the army newspaper, *Red Star*. This argued against sanctions on Serbia, casting its analysis largely in terms of familiar spheres-of-influence considerations. Serbia, it said, is part of Russia's sphere. Its diplomatic isolation showed the danger if other Slavic states were to be isolated. Russia should resist sanctions on fellow Slavs.

A stronger case

In all these cases, criticism of the westward drive of foreign policy reflects criticism of Mr Yeltsin's domestic, and especially economic, policies. His opponents have not shifted him on these, so their dislike of his foreign policy may not weigh much. But there is a stronger case to be made against Russia's current foreign policy. This emphasises the country's unique geographical position and argues that shifts in the balance of power in the world should dictate a foreign policy less closely aligned with that of the West. This criticism is being made by Russians who cannot be counted among the opponents of Mr Yeltsin's reforms and who cannot be dismissed so easily.

The argument runs as follows. First, Russia cannot wholly trust the West, because it is not certain that western interests really are served by having a rich and powerful Russia. At the moment, the considerable western aid programme stands in contrast to that assertion. But the balance of western interests may change. An unstable Russia which possesses nuclear weapons and is on the brink of bread riots is undesirable for the West. But as those weapons are destroyed, under Russian-American arms-control agreements, and as Russia's economy begins to recover, the West may well begin to wonder whether it really does want such a powerful neighbour.

Nor should Russia trust the West to produce the sort of investment it needs. The $24 billion in aid over five years is just a start. Estimates of the total required to upgrade Russia's industry run into hundreds of billions of dollars. David Roche, of Morgan Stanley International, has calculated that the country needs every year $15 billion-50 billion for infrastructure, $30 billion-60 billion for energy, and $5 billion-10 billion each for agriculture and unemployment benefit, in addition to $21 billion-38 billion in balance-of-payments support. In sum, between $76 billion and $167 billion each year, excluding money to clean up the environment or stabilise the rouble.

Such calculations can only be illustrative. But what they illustrate to some Russians is that, if this is the sum really needed, and if western governments cannot be counted on to give anything like that amount, then it may not be worth tying Russia closely to the West.

Look south, not west

More seriously, even if Russia could trust the West to deliver the goods, the question remains whether it should. Over the past four decades, this part of the argument runs, the world has been divided between communist East and capitalist West. As that division disappears, it will replaced by a division between rich north and poor south. In that division, Russia's interests do not lie in membership of the north. Russia is not rich now, and, even if economic reform goes well, it will take 30 years before it can join a rich-country club.

Even when Russia is rich, its interests will still differ from those of other northern states. In particular, it has long borders with the poor south, as they do not (America's border with Mexico excepted). That means that, in the case of a north-south confrontation, Russia will be on the front line.

To take one example of how it could be threatened, two of its richest agricultural regions are the Kuban and the area around Stavropol. Both are in the south, on the borders of the turbulent Transcaucasus, one of whose leaders has several times threatened to wage holy war on Russia. For its own security, Russia cannot afford to ignore its neighbours to the south and east. It needs to pursue a more active policy towards its neighbours in the Common-

wealth of Independent States (CIS)—and, in particular, it cannot be too pro-western, if that means alienating Islamic countries.

Shifts of power

Three other strategic changes reinforce these arguments. First, the growth of Japan and the Asian dragons is tipping the balance of economic power eastwards to the Pacific rim. Russia should therefore be seeking to develop its closest ties there. This is especially true because the Asian dragons are the countries nearest to Russia's own far east and its raw materials, and their technology is still relatively unsophisticated, like much of Russia's. They also have experience of effective state intervention (and of lessening it) in a market economy.

Second, Russia's "westward ho" policy is, to be precise, an Atlantic policy. It is dominated by relations with the United States and the countries of Western Europe. But just as the increasing power of the Pacific rim provides a reason why Russia should not hitch its wagon too closely to America, so the likely recovery of the countries of Eastern Europe provides reasons for caution in Russia's approach to the European Community.

United Germany, on this argument, not the EC, will in practice be the linchpin of Russia's future relations with Europe. The last time there was free trade in Europe from the Atlantic to the Urals—as long ago as 1913—45% of Russian trade was with Germany. Germany is Russia's largest western trading partner even now. If Russia's economy recovers, Russian-German trade will rise sharply. Even if it does not attain its pre-1914 significance, closer economic links between Europe's two largest nations imply closer political ties. This

would alarm other EC countries (and, in fact, the Germans, for all their aid, are not showing any enthusiasm for it). But so be it. For Russia, what matters in Europe will be its relations with Germany and Eastern Europe, not the EC and the Atlantic.

The third reason has to do with the break-up of the former Soviet Union. The emergence of Ukraine and Belorussia as independent states means that Russia is now geographically farther from the centre of Europe than at any time since the 18th century. Moreover, the long-term foreign-policy aim of both Ukraine and Belorussia is to join the EC. Though its sheer size and muscle will always command the respect of European governments, Russia can never hope to become an EC member. It is simply too big and too complex a state to swallow. In so far as it is in competition with Ukraine for the EC's attention, it will fail. Ergo, it should not let Europe dominate its foreign policy.

There are alternatives

How should these arguments be weighed against those of the westernisers? It is tempting to dismiss them by saying that few influential Russians support them and that Russia's foreign policy is securely anchored in the western camp by its overriding need for aid. Tempting, but wrong. It is true that few influential Russians have openly espoused these arguments (the notable exception is Sergei Stankevich, Mr Yeltsin's adviser on relations with Russia's various political parties). But Russia's westernising policy is not secure, because its foreign-policy-making institutions and domestic politics alike are themselves in confusion.

Russia at the moment has no real foreign policy. Its relations with the rest of the

Not all Russians live in St Petersburg

world are governed by domestic necessity. One result is that foreign-policy decisions are often improvised, not thought through. Another is that the foreign ministry has lost much of its influence. The foreign minister, Mr Kozyrev, who is one of the leading westernisers, has little access to the president. He has come under attack in parliament and is isolated in his own ministry (which is hardly surprising, given that he has publicly accused some of his staff of betraying him).

Russia's westernising policy relies largely on Mr Yeltsin himself. Though he shows few signs of wanting to change course, he has proved in economic policy that he is capable of trimming. It should not be taken for granted that the current "western" consensus will remain for long.

Looking all round

What might replace it? Some people suggest a vigorous Asian policy, to re-establish Russia in its "historic role" as a bridge between West and East. This will not fly. Except in Muslim Central Asia, the East in fact took most of its western influences direct from the West. But even if that had been Russia's role, what need is there of it now? Japan—whose navy thrashed Russia's in 1905, and which was again briefly at war with it 40 years later—is a member of the Group of Seven. South Korea and the other dragons get on perfectly well dealing directly with the West. If Russia ever had an opportunity to act as go-between, it has missed it.

Further, in the short run, two particular obstacles stand in the way of a vigorous Asian policy. The first is the Kurile Islands. Japan's claim to these islands is preventing closer relations, and the dispute shows few signs of resolution. In addition to conservatives who oppose giving any territory away, Mr Yeltsin faces opposition from the governor of Russia's far-eastern region, which administers the Kuriles. Given the secessionist tendencies already evident in that region, Mr Yeltsin cannot afford to confront him over the issue.

The second obstacle is the ideological conflict between today's Russia and China. The Chinese are wary of Mr Yeltsin, not only as the man who brought down communism in Russia but as an arch-"splittist" of the Soviet Union (a nasty thought in a country that fears splits of its own). After Mikhail Gorbachev's visit to Beijing in 1989, Russia's relations with China improved. The two countries have settled most of their border disputes and have withdrawn many of their border troops. In the short term, though, there seems little scope for improving relations further.

Another alternative is a policy neither Asian nor exclusively western, but "Eur-

A bridge to Asia? The Russian fleet at Tsushima, 1905

asian". Just as, in the 19th century, the Slavophiles too wanted modernisation, those who argue for a Eurasian foreign policy want co-operation with the West, recognising the importance of its economic aid. But, they say, Russia should not put all its eggs in one basket.

It should not neglect its southern frontiers, as it has been doing (in Afghanistan, for example, its policy has been merely to get the United Nations involved). It must pay more attention to its relations with other members of the CIS. Here a strong case can be made that Russia's westernising policy has costs, as well as benefits. In pursuit of it, Russia has tried to keep Ukraine from leaving the commonwealth. To that end, it accepted a much greater weakening of CIS institutions than the Central Asian members wanted. For instance, the Russians overruled the most powerful of them, Kazakhstan, which said that the Soviet army should not be broken up into national units. But this policy is doomed to failure. Ukraine says it will leave the CIS anyway when all its strategic nuclear weapons have been dismantled, by 1994, if it has not left already.

Russia, say the "Eurasians", will then be left with the worst of both worlds. It will have failed to keep Ukraine inside the CIS. And it will have offended the Central Asian states, losing time at forging links with them that it could have had for the asking—time during which Turkey and Iran have been vying with each other to supplant Russian influence on its own southern border.

Some straws in the wind

A mutual-defence treaty signed in May by Russia, Kazakhstan, Uzbekistan, Tajikistan and Armenia may be an early sign that Russia is already trying to correct the neglect of its southern border. And an agreement signed in mid-June by Mr Yeltsin

and the Ukrainian president to settle their differences outside the CIS framework suggests the corollary. While Russia forges closer links with Central Asia within a multilateral institution, the CIS, it is moving its relations with Ukraine to a bilateral, state-to-state basis.

Elsewhere, too, there are signs of change. Those who argue that Russia cannot trust America, because the Americans will work against Russian national interests if their own are threatened, seem to have been justified by events in India. The United States imposed sanctions on Russia's space agency after it offered to sell India a rocket engine that would enable the Indians to launch heavy, long-range rockets. This was the first case in Mr Yeltsin's time when Russia's and America's interests plainly clashed. The Russians decided to go ahead with the sale anyway.

Arguably, the case of Serbia also shows Russia's unwillingness to sacrifice other interests for the sake of its alliance with the West. Though the Russians voted at the United Nations for sanctions, defying protests at home, they have backed a proposal to let Serbia simply inherit Yugoslavia's seat in the CSCE.

Should the West worry if Russia waters down its current pro-western foreign policy? The answer is surely no. Russia's geography ensures that it will always have one foot in the south. That fact cannot be ignored, however much Russia depends on western aid. And from a western point of view, a Russia pursuing an autonomous foreign policy has its advantages. An economically successful Russia could provide an alternative to the rival pulls of Turkey and Iran in Central Asia. And still less than in the days when Dulles saw communists under Nehru's bed, would the friendship of a now free-market Russia with India do either country, or the West, any harm.

Contents

ASIA

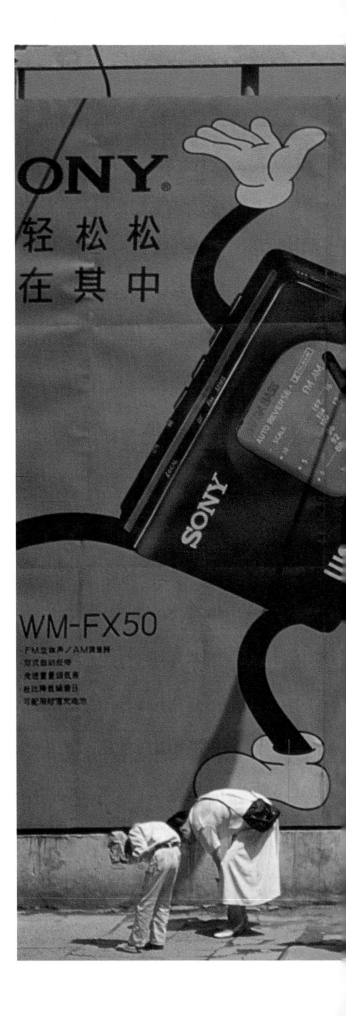

Present still imperfect

I F MIGHT is right, three countries in Asia must surely determine their continent's destiny: China and India, by the power of their populations; Japan by the influence of its economy. Yet the hypothesis is not necessarily self-fulfilling: as 1992 drew to an end, India had just bathed itself in the bloodshed of sectarian violence, while Japan's politicians were still immersed in the Sagawa Kyubin affair, a bribery scandal every bit as bad as the Recruit company "shares-for-favours" scam three years earlier. Only the People's Republic of China, with the world's most dynamic economy, was confidently playing to the full its role on the world stage.

Deng, still driving China along

For that performance, thank Deng Xiaoping, who remained China's paramount leader for all his lack of official titles. It was Mr Deng who in 1978 broke the deadlock of Maoism: his liberal economic reforms brought prosperity first to the countryside, home for four-fifths of China's 1.2 billion people, and then to the cities. Add the burgeoning underground economy to the official statistics and the People's Republic is probably as productive and prosperous per person as the Philippines or Indonesia. In October, the 14th national congress of the Chinese Communist Party enthusiastically backed Mr Deng's liberalism, and called for more; hardline traditionalists found themselves pushed to the political periphery. When President Boris Yeltsin visited Beijing in December, the contrast between shambolic Russia and self-assured China was proof to Beijing's gerontocrats that they had found the right formula of economic liberalism and political authoritarianism—while Mikhail Gorbachev had betrayed communism and reduced his nation to virtual penury.

But could the formula last, or would China's people demand greater political freedoms to go with their rising standard of living? The question was one China's leaders would doubtless prefer to avoid.

On October 7th, however, it became too loud to ignore: Chris Patten, installed in July as Hong Kong's 28th (and, he presumed, last) governor, announced modest proposals to extend democracy in the British colony before it reverted to China's sovereignty in 1997. China saw them as a perfidious attempt to subvert the spirit, if not quite the letter, of

Patten takes on Beijing

its agreements with Britain over Hong Kong and also of the "Basic Law", the constitution devised by China for Hong Kong after 1997. China was determined not to lose "face"; it feared too that Hong Kong's political liberalism would infect Guangdong, the province that has become China's richest because it is next door to capitalist Hong Kong. Accordingly, China promised to reverse reforms implemented by Mr Patten. Hong Kong's self-confidence, always fragile and febrile, began to falter badly.

For how long remains to be seen. The conflict of ideas between West and East is never likely to disappear: Mr Patten, a friend of Britain's prime minister, John Major, and former chairman of its Conservative Party, represents an individualism and openness that are alien in much of East Asia, with its Confucian values of consensus and obedience. Lee Kuan Yew, Singapore's former prime minister, visited the Philippines in November and told his hosts (who included President Fidel Ramos) that they had made a mistake in embracing American-style democracy: "What a country needs to develop is discipline rather than democracy. The exuberance of democracy leads to undisciplined and and disorderly conditions which are inimical to development."

Such an argument finds ready agreement in China, which is, after all, the world's largest developing country. Indeed, it finds agreement among many Filipinos: in May they had had a festival of representative democracy, electing a president, a Senate, a House of Representatives and thousands of local officials—and still the Philippine economy looked likely to remain mired in corruption and inefficiency.

But the argument has rather less relevance for those countries whose economies are maturing. In May, it was Bangkok's growing middle class that took to the streets and, after a bloody interlude, forced Thailand's generals to step down from government. On December 18th South Koreans chose Kim Young Sam as their new president, the first for 32 years not to have a military background. The next day Taiwan elected a legislature which for the first time did not include "old thieves" (as their critics called them) elected on the Chinese mainland before 1949, when Chiang Kai Shek's regime fled the victorious communist army of Mao Zedong. Such elections should give heart to those, such as Mr Patten in modern, dynamic Hong Kong, who believe representative democracy is an inevitable consequence of material, middle-class prosperity—not an obstacle in its way.

The difficult question is what kind of democracy. Mr Kim Young Sam was once an opposition leader, until in 1990 he merged his party with the ruling Democratic Justice Party. The result was the Democratic Liberal Party, consciously created to emulate Japan's Liberal Democratic Party (LDP). In Singapore the People's Action Party was also an admirer of the LDP, and so was Taiwan's Kuomintang (Nationalist Party). What they saw in the LDP, which has governed Japan continuously since 1955, was the answer to the problems of reconciling democracy with Confucianism: a benign party which governed by consensus, having resolved any differences of opinion through a system of factions.

Would that politics could be so simple. In 1992, however, the LDP looked sadly tarnished. Because candidates must spend lavishly both to get elected and to fulfill their constituency duties, the real power in the LDP rests with those who can

Kanemaru in trouble

provide money: the faction-leaders. Their power of patronage, and the loyalty it inspires, depend not on their ideas or policies but on their ability to raise money. The inevitable consequence is their need to accept, indeed solicit, illegal donations—hence the Lockheed bribery scandal that toppled Kakuei Tanaka in the mid-1970s and the Recruit scandal that befell Noboru Takeshita in the late 1980s. In 1992, the victim was Shin Kanemaru, who, having assumed control of the Takeshita faction, had long been the party's "godfather", choosing which men to make prime minister—and when to remove them. But not even Mr Kanemaru could remain unscathed by the Sagawa Kyubin affair, in which a parcel-delivery company used *yakuza* (gangster) organisations to bribe politicians. Such was Mr Kanemaru's prestige that he was fined a mere ¥200,000 in September for accepting a bribe of ¥500m ($4.2m); such was the public outrage that in October he was forced to resign from the Diet (parliament).

Those shenanigans were hardly signs of a mature democracy, of the kind to be emulated by the rest of Asia. What seemed to make them worse was the onset of economic recession, and so the realisation that Japan's bureaucrats did not have some magic formula for the economy that made politics irrelevant. The irony is that the shenanigans occurred in a year when Japan seemed ready to assume a political responsibility in the world more commensurate with its economic clout. One sign of this was the Diet's approval in June—after 20 months of squabbling—of a bill to allow Japanese troops to take part in UN peacekeeping operations overseas, with Cambodia their destination later in the year. Another sign was the

visit to China in October of Emperor Akihito, followed in November by the resumption of aid to Vietnam. Clearly Japan was becoming willing to make its own foreign policy, rather than simply follow America's lead.

For all the bitter memories of the second world war, that willingness should be welcomed. One reason is that America, which at the end of September closed its last base in the Philippines, will become less ready to be Asia's policeman. A second reason is that North-East Asia remains potentially a dangerous region: China and Russia are nuclear powers; North Korea may be close to joining them (and its talks with the South failed to build on the rapprochement reached at the end of 1991). Suspicious of its own militarist traditions, Japan is inclined to achieve regional stability through economic investment. Whether it will succeed is another matter: the problem of the region is its lack of multilateral security organisations, equivalent to NATO or the Western European Union.

Thankfully, such worries concern the possibility, not the actuality, of conflict. If only that were true of the Indian subcontinent. Sadly, the civil war in Sri Lanka, begun in 1983, continued, while secular India edged closer to sectarian schism. The ostensible cause was the dispute over a four-centuries old mosque at Ayodhya, in Uttar Pradesh, built on the supposed birthplace of the Hindu god, Ram. In December Hindu zealots demolished the mosque, setting off nationwide violence that left around 1,600 dead and put in question the government of Narasimha Rao, with its brave (and sensible) programme of economic reform. Add to that the simmering unrest among the Sikhs of Punjab and the atrocities between the Indian army and the Muslim majority in Kashmir, and "the world's largest democracy"—a familiar Indian boast—looked again to have more problems than solutions.

Should India therefore be written off, as Asia's giant weakling? On balance, not. Great nations have the resilience to recover from even the worst disasters. The sceptics need only remember how far Japan has come from its devastation in 1945, or China from its chaotic Cultural Revolution.

India's fragile democracy

To appreciate the *bigger* picture, consider the *smaller* detail

One global city has the vision to make you more **COMPETITIVE**. Cohesive and dynamic. Integrated **BUSINESS ARCHITECTURE** combining highly skilled manpower networked with superb physical and technological infrastructures. Planned for efficiency. Geared for **EXCELLENCE**. Designed to respond to the **GLOBAL** needs of world-class corporations. A total commitment to a total business environment. Not surprisingly, this is **SINGAPORE UNLIMITED**.

January

Wednesday 1st
Just as **Hong Kong's governor**, Sir David Wilson, was made a lord in the queen's list of new year's honours, so it was announced that he would retire sometime during the year. The naming of the next (and last) governor was to await the British general election, leaving Sir David politically a lame duck.

More than 70 Indian revellers **died after drinking** at a government-licensed bar in Bombay. The bar's liquor had been contaminated with methyl alcohol.

Beginning his postponed Pacific tour in Australia, America's President Bush promised to guard the region's security. **Australia's farmers** ignored the pledge and attacked America's agricultural subsidies.

Friday 3rd
Singapore banned the import and manufacture of **chewing gum**. The government said it was a "perennial nuisance" and sometimes delayed subway trains by stopping their doors from closing.

The founder of the giant Hyundai group, **Chung Ju Yong**, said he would leave business and start a political party to contest South Korea's National Assembly elections due in the spring. Speculation was strong that Mr Chung, recently given a $180m tax bill by the government, would also try for the presidency.

Sunday 5th
President Bush warned his South Korean hosts to beware their rapprochement with **North Korea**. The president, alarmed by the North's nuclear progress, was unconvinced by a joint declaration by the North and South in late December in favour of a nuclear-free Korean peninsula.

Tuesday 7th
North Korea said it would sign, in the last week of January, the **nuclear safeguards** agreement of the International Atomic Energy Agency, allowing foreign inspection of its nuclear facilities. On January 30th it kept its promise.

Imelda Marcos announced she would contest May's Philippine presidential election. The announcement came as Mrs Marcos pleaded not guilty in a Manila court to charges of corruption during the rule of her late husband, Ferdinand.

China expelled a Canadian **human rights** delegation, three of whose four members were MPs, for "engaging in activities incompatible with their status".

Wednesday 8th
President Bush **collapsed** and vomited at a state banquet in Tokyo. His doctor blamed "a touch of the flu". The incident cast further embarrassment on Mr Bush's three-day visit to Japan. The president was likened to a car salesman after demanding that Japan should import American cars and parts to reduce the American trade deficit.

Monday 13th
Fumio Abe, the secretary-general of the party faction led by Japan's prime minister, Kiichi Miyazawa, was **arrested** on charges of taking a ¥80m ($630,000) bribe. He was the first member of parliament to be arrested since the Lockheed bribery case of 1976.

Tuesday 14th
Prime minister Kiichi Miyazawa, two days before an official visit to Seoul, apologised for Japan's conscription of around 100,000 South Korean women to act as "**comfort girls**" for Japanese troops during the second world war.

Cambodia said it would open its **prisons** to foreign inspection, free political prisoners and allow the formation of political parties. Political prisoners and POWs from the civil war that officially ended in October were thought to number 2,000.

Friday 17th
Most of Punjab's Sikh groups said they would **boycott** elections called for February 19th to end direct rule from Delhi. Sikh militants, seeking Punjab's secession from India, had threatened to murder all candidates.

Monday 20th
Japanese newspapers reported Yoshio Sakurauchi, speaker of the lower house of parliament, as saying that American workers were lazy and 30% of them were **illiterate**. He appeared not to know that during the previous decade America's productivity had grown faster than Japan's.

Tuesday 21st
The **Khmers Rouges** said they had repulsed Phnom Penh government troops and recaptured villages in Cambodia's Kompong Thom province. The fighting, begun on January 5th, ended the ceasefire agreed the previous autumn.

Thursday 23rd
Six Hindus were killed when Sikh gunmen disguised as police attacked a convoy of buses belonging to the **Hindu-** nationalist Bharatiya Janata Party (BJP). The convoy was passing through Punjab on its way to Kashmir on a "unity pilgrimage" for India.

Friday 24th
China and Israel established full **diplomatic relations** at the end of a visit to Beijing by Israel's foreign minister, David Levy. China, a strong supporter of the Palestine Liberation Organisation, said it would seek to narrow the gap between Israel and the Arabs at peace talks due in Moscow the following week.

Saturday 25th
Corazon Aquino chose **Fidel Ramos**, her former defence secretary, as the candidate to succeed her in the Philippine presidential election due on May 11th. General Ramos had helped put down at least six coup attempts against Mrs Aquino.

Sunday 26th
Murli Manohar Joshi, leader of the Hindu-nationalist BJP, flew to Srinagar and, surrounded by 1,000 security men, planted the Indian flag in the heart of **Kashmir**. The BJP had halted its march because of threats by Kashmir's Muslim separatists.

Tuesday 28th
Ending a two-day **summit**— only their fourth in 25 years— the six heads of government of the Association of South-East Asian Nations (ASEAN) agreed to cut tariffs on 15 groups of manufactured goods to a maximum of 5% over the next 15 years. They expected Vietnam would be an ASEAN member within five years.

Sunday 2nd
China's prime minister, Li Peng, arrived in Lisbon to talk about the return of Portugal's colony, **Macao**, to Chinese sovereignty in 1999. Portuguese officials said they would also discuss China's poor human rights record.

Monday 3rd
A fight in Hong Kong's Shek Kong camp for Vietnamese **boat people** left 23 dead, burned alive in their hut. The fight, between inmates from the north and the south of Vietnam, apparently started over the distribution of water.

A court in Bangladesh sentenced the former president, **Hossein Ershad**, to three years' jail for corruption and confiscated money equal to $500,000 found in his house. He had earlier been sentenced to ten years' jail for the illegal possession of firearms.

Japan's prime minister, **Kiichi Miyazawa**, annoyed Americans by saying that their "work ethic is lacking." The Japanese embassy in Washington quickly sent President Bush a message saying that no criticism of America's workers was intended.

Wednesday 5th
America's secretary of state, James Baker, said China had agreed to comply with international restrictions on exporting **ballistic missiles** and their technology. However, written confirmation would be needed before America would lift sanctions imposed after China's missile sales to Pakistan.

Friday 7th
By the deadline for the May 11th **Philippine elections**, there were 78 candidates for the presidency, 18 for the vice-presidency and 265 for the 24-seat Senate. An independent commission promptly

disqualifed all but 8 of the presidential candidates. The survivors ranged from Imelda Marcos to Joseph Estrada, a film star.

Sunday 9th
Japan's ruling Liberal Democratic Party, already tainted by scandal, was further undermined by **defeat** in an upper-house by-election for the Nara constituency. In protest at alleged corruption, the opposition parties were meanwhile delaying the budget by boycotting parliamentary hearings.

Monday 10th
Tiny **Singapore** announced that from September 1st it would ban the import of cars more than three years old. To combat pollution and traffic congestion, a mix of auction and lottery was already in use to determine car ownership in Singapore.

Tuesday 11th
A march by **Kashmiri militants** to cross the ceasefire line from Pakistan-controlled Kashmir to the part under Indian control was thwarted by Pakistani troops worried lest it provoke war with India. A few militants were killed and their leader, Amanullah Khan, gained valuable publicity for the cause of an independent Kashmir.

Wednesday 12th
Japan said that it was worried about instability in Russia. But Kiichi Miyazawa rebuffed a German request for aid to Russia. He said such aid

would depend on Russia ceding to Japan four islands in the Kuriles chain occupied by the Soviet Union at the end of the second world war.

Hong Kong forced 36 boat people back to Vietnam. Their deportation went smoothly, in contrast to the first mandatory **repatriation** almost two years before and a second in November 1991. Meanwhile, some 3,000 boat people were waiting to leave under a voluntary repatriation scheme.

Thursday 13th
It was announced in **Hong Kong** that China had chosen 40 prominent, but conservative, Hongkongers to advise it on the British colony's affairs. Pro-democracy activists said China was trying to strip Hong Kong of any autonomy before its transfer to Chinese sovereignty in 1997.

Saturday 15th
New Zealand's National Party government received an unexpected boost with a by-election victory in the seat vacated by Sir Robert Muldoon, a former party leader and prime minister. The current prime minister, **Jim Bolger**, whose popularity had reached a record low, claimed that the win vindicated his policies of deregulation.

Wednesday 19th
Because of death threats (several of which were carried out) to voters and candidates by

militant Sikh secessionists, the turnout for **Punjab**'s federal and state election, postponed from June 1991 because of violence, was under 25%. Congress Party candidates won most of the federal seats, boosting the minority government of Narasimha Rao.

The prime ministers of South and North Korea began a two-day meeting in the North's capital, Pyongyang, to confirm agreements of peace and a **non-nuclear** Korean peninsula. American sceptics, however, believed the North was still building a nuclear bomb.

Thursday 20th
Secretary-general Boutros Boutros-Ghali said 15,900 soldiers would go to **Cambodia**, part of a 22,000-strong UN peacekeeping operation costing over $2 billion. Money squabbles were certain.

Sunday 23rd
China's official *People's Daily* praised **capitalism** in a front-page essay. Clearly senior leader Deng Xiaoping, 87, was pushing for more economic reform ahead of the 14th Chinese Communist Party Congress, due later in the year.

Wednesday 26th
Australia's prime minister, Paul Keating, announced a reflationary economic package. He also gained popularity by saying Britain had left Australia undefended in the second world war—and had then **hurt Australia** by joining the European Community. Earlier he had angered monarchists by putting an arm around Queen Elizabeth.

Thursday 27th
The Indonesian army said it had punished six senior officers for the November 12th massacre of civilians in **East Timor**. Aid donors had threatened to cut off assistance because of the killings.

March

Sunday 1st

Major-General Asad Durrani was sacked as boss of Pakistan's powerful **Inter-Services Intelligence** agency. Two days later Lieutenant-General Javed Nasir was appointed in his place. Durrani was a supporter of the Afghan mujahideen and, it seemed, had been too feeble in backing the UN peace plan for neighbouring Afghanistan.

Police in Osaka raided more than 100 offices of the Yamaguchi-gumi, Japan's biggest **yakuza** organisation. The raid coincided with the implementation of a new law requiring the yakuza gangs—amazing as it may seem—to register themselves.

Thursday 5th

America promised **aid to Vietnam**. In return, Vietnam agreed to search for Americans missing-in-action during the Vietnam war. America refused, however, to lift its 17-year-old trade embargo. It said full diplomatic relations with Vietnam must await free elections in Cambodia, where Vietnam had backed the Phnom Penh government.

Philippine officials said America was "hard-hearted" in deciding to tow away three dry-docks from its **Subic Bay** base rather than leave them for civilian use. In September 1991 the Philippine Senate had rejected a new lease for the base, prompting President Aquino to order the Americans to leave by the end of 1992.

An American lawyers' group said "at least hundreds, perhaps thousands" of Vietnamese **boat people** were being denied refugee status by flaws in Hong Kong's screening process. Of the 29,939 people who had been screened up to January 1st, 86% were classified as economic migrants, to be repatriated to Vietnam.

Sunday 8th

Japan's ruling Liberal Democratic Party lost a by-election. With the party already mired in corruption scandals, the defeat increased doubts that **Kiichi Miyazawa** would complete his two-year term as prime minister.

President Aquino said a referendum might be needed after a settlement under which America's Westinghouse would operate a $2.1 billion **nuclear plant** in the Philippines. The company was to pay the Philippines $10m in cash and $90m in credits and discounts to settle a bribery suit over the plant, which was built in 1985 but never run.

Monday 9th

China signed the **Nuclear Nonproliferation Treaty** during a visit to London by its foreign minister, Qian Qichen. China, often accused of irresponsible arms sales, was the last official nuclear power to sign the treaty.

Malaysia broke the silence of the Association of South-East Asian Nations when it protested to Myanmar over its treatment of its **Rohingya Muslim** minority. Over the past year some 140,000 Rohingyas had fled to neighbouring Bangladesh, alleging a Buddhist Burman campaign of rape, forced labour, and the confiscation of their land.

Wednesday 11th

India's most senior foreign ministry official said in Washington that India had the capability to build a **nuclear bomb**, but that its programme was less advanced than Pakistan's. He said India wanted direct security talks with America before joining any multilateral talks on nuclear weapons in South Asia.

Thursday 12th

China's newspapers proclaimed that the Communist Party Politburo had endorsed the call by senior leader **Deng Xiaoping** for more economic reform. Doctrinaire Marxists were clearly losing strength.

Saturday 14th

Sikh militants on motor scooters shot and killed 20 people in Ludhiana, in Punjab state. The Sikhs wanted an independent homeland, to be called Khalistan.

Sunday 15th

Myanmar troops crossed into Thailand in their pursuit of **Karen insurgents**. A day earlier the troops had overrun Sleeping Dog Mountain, near the Karen stronghold of Manerplaw. Myanmar has often accused the Thais of allowing the Karen minority refuge in Thailand.

Monday 16th

India announced that its navy would hold joint training exercises with the **American navy**. Farewell India's policy of non-alignment?

Wednesday 18th

Afghanistan's **President Najibullah** offered to hand power to an interim government which the UN was hoping to set up as part of its plan to end 13 years of civil war. Some doubted the president's sincerity.

Saturday 21st

During the annual National People's Congress, China's finance minister announced a 13.8% budget increase for the **People's Liberation Army**.

Sunday 22nd

Thailand held its first general election since a military coup 13 months earlier. Three days later **Narong Wongwan** was chosen as prime minister of a pro-military coalition. In 1991 Narong had been denied an American visa for suspected links with the drugs trade.

Tuesday 24th

South Korean **voters deprived** the Democratic Liberal Party of President Roh Tae Woo of its parliamentary majority. Miffed by economic woes, they gave Chung Ju Yong's new Unification National Party a tenth of the seats.

Sunday 29th

At last some good news for Japan's prime minister, **Kiichi Miyazawa**: his Liberal Democratic Party won two by-elections, including a seat previously held by the opposition.

Monday 30th

Some 527 **Cambodian refugees** went home by bus, so starting the repatriation of 375,000 Cambodians from camps in Thailand.

Tuesday 31st

India's foreign minister, Madhavsinh Solanki, charged with delaying inquiries into the five-year-old **Bofors scandal**, resigned. The Swedish company allegedly bribed the Congress government of Rajiv Gandhi. Congress came back to power in 1991.

Wednesday 1st
A setback for China's hard-line prime minister, **Li Peng**: the National People's Congress, normally a rubber-stamp, reportedly told him to amend a speech he had made to the NPC on March 20th. He was told to insert some criticism of hard-line leftism. Li's humiliation was a boost for China's reformist senior leader, Deng Xiaoping.

Malaysia's cabinet met to discuss the role of the country's nine **hereditary sultans**. The prime minister was furious because the Sultan Ismail Petra, of Kelantan state, had driven away from customs officers in his new Lamborghini Diablo car without paying duties of $810,000. The sultan said he was above the law.

Thursday 2nd
America's globe-trotting evangelist, **Billy Graham**, delivered a verbal message from President Bush to North Korea's President Kim Il Sung. The preacher's visit was another sign of Kim's desire to end his country's isolation.

Monday 6th
Police killed at least seven demonstrators killed and wounded some 50 others in a protest strike in **Katmandu** against inflation and corruption. The strike, called by Nepal's far left opposition, was the most serious challenge so far to the Nepali Congress Party, which came to power in 1991 in the first multiparty elections for 30 years.

A report in *China Daily* alarmed South-East Asia: the deputy commander of the navy said China would develop weaponry to protect its claims in the South China Sea. The obvious reference was to the **Spratly Islands**, claimed also by Taiwan, the Philippines, Malaysia, Brunei and Vietnam.

China's Communist Party boss, Jiang Zemin, arrived in Tokyo for a five-day visit and said Emperor Akihito should visit China. Japan's prime minister, Kiichi Miyazawa, politely said no. Japan, it seemed, was not yet ready to normalise relations. That would involve apologising for **Japanese war crimes**.

Tuesday 7th
General **Suchinda Kraprayoon**, the power behind the military coup of February 1991, became Thailand's new prime minister. The first choice as prime minister after the general election of March 22nd had been Narong Wongwan—until America confirmed it had refused him a visa for alleged connections with drug trafficking.

Thursday 9th
North Korea's parliament formally approved an accord allowing the International Atomic Energy Agency to inspect the country's **nuclear facilities**. South Korea said it hoped the inspection would take place "without delay".

Saturday 11th
Australia's ruling Labor Party lost a by-election for the seat vacated by its former leader, Bob Hawke. But the opposition Liberal candidate lost, too. Disgruntled voters chose Phil Cleary, coach of a local Australian-rules football team. Mr Cleary thus became only the second independent MP in the past 25 years.

Tuesday 14th
Afghan mujahideen captured the Bagram air base and the town of Charikar, north of Kabul. The fall of the capital looked only a matter of time.

America said it would restore direct telecommunications **links with Vietnam**, broken with the fall of Saigon in 1975. The decision came because Vietnam had taken "positive steps" on Americans missing-in-action and was supporting the peace settlement in neighbouring Cambodia.

Wednesday 15th
North Korea's President **Kim Il Sung** celebrated his 80th birthday. The "Great Leader" marked the occasion with an interview with the *Washington Times* predicting better relations with America.

Vietnam's National Assembly adopted a new constitution guaranteeing **economic freedoms**. But it was also made clear that the Communist Party would still provide the nation's "leadership".

Thursday 16th
Afghanistan's President **Najibullah resigned**, leaving his ex-Communist government to negotiate the surrender of Kabul after 14 years of war to the mujahideen guerrillas. The ousted president sought sanctuary in the Kabul office of the UN, while his foreign minister denounced him as "a hated dictator who had been an obstacle to peace".

Sunday 19th
China said its **population** reached 1.158 billion at the end of 1991, with 1.25m fewer babies born in 1991 than in 1990. But despite strict birth control, there could still be a "baby boom": some 123m women in 1992 would be in the prime child-bearing age of 23-29, up by 16% on the 1985-90 period.

Monday 20th
The head of Japan's nuclear power programme said Japan might delay plans to use a **fast-breeder reactor**. Critics of the programme hoped this was a sign that Japan was reconsidering its intention to produce and import plutonium. The next day the government said it was not.

Some 50,000 Thais demonstrated in Bangkok against the prime minister, General **Suchinda Kraprayoon**, because he had been appointed without being elected.

Thursday 23rd
General Saw Maung, said to have become both ill and mad, was replaced as head of the military junta in **Myanmar** by General Than Shwe. The junta later freed many political prisoners, and said the detained opposition leader, Aung San Suu Kyi, could be visited by her British husband.

Friday 24th
Britain named Chris Patten, the Conservative Party chairman, to be **Hong Kong's governor**. He had just lost his seat in the British election, but was thought to have the political skills to prepare Hong Kong for its return to China in 1997.

Tuesday 28th
Sibghatullah Mujaddidi arrived in Kabul at the head of a coalition of resistance groups to receive the surrender of the Afghan capital. Afghanistan, once Communist, was renamed an **Islamic republic**.

May

Sunday 3rd
Cardinal Jaime Sin, the archbishop of Manila, attacked as "godless" **Fidel Ramos**, the man favoured by President Corazon Aquino to succeed her in the May 11th election. Ex-General Ramos, a Protestant, helped administer martial law in the Marcos era.

Monday 4th
Gulbuddin Hikmatyar, leader of the fundamentalist Hizb-i-Islami, began a two-day barrage of Kabul, hoping to oust rival mujahideen guerrillas from the Afghan capital. Mr Hikmatyar's men had been expelled from Kabul the previous week.

About 70,000 protesters demonstrated in Bangkok to denounce the appointment in April of General Suchinda Kraprayoon as Thailand's **unelected** prime minister. Chamlong Srimuang, ascetic leader of Bangkok's main political party, began a fast "until I die or Suchinda resigns."

A government delegation left Seoul for Los Angeles to seek reparations for the South Korean shopowners who had suffered damages—estimates went as high as $300m—during the previous week's **riots**. Up to 400,000 South Koreans live in Los Angeles.

Tuesday 5th
President Rakhmon Nabiyev declared a **state of emergency** in Dushanbe, capital of Tajikistan, after demonstrators took over the radio station and demanded his resignation.

Wednesday 6th
Officials of the International Atomic Energy Agency expressed surprise at the details North Korea had given of its **nuclear programme**. A 100-page submission to the agency went further than required and also disclosed previously unknown facilities.

Saturday 9th
Hong Kong announced that the **Chinese police** would set up a liaison office in the British colony. The move, requested by Hong Kong's police chief, Li Kwan-ha, followed an increase in violent crime, much of it involving guns and criminals brought in from China.

Sunday 10th
Yasushi Akashi, the UN's special representative in Cambodia, set a deadline of early June to start disarming the armies of the **Khmers Rouges** and other Cambodian factions. The task was reckoned to be the most difficult facing the UN peacekeeping force.

In the largest rally so far, over 120,000 **demonstrated in Bangkok** to demand the resignation of General Suchinda Kraprayoon, the unelected prime minister. At the same time the opposition leader, Chamlong Srimuang, agreed to end his hunger fast.

Monday 11th
The Philippine electorate voted for a **new president** to succeed Corazon Aquino—and also for senators, congressmen and local government officials. The result was not expected for several weeks, but pollsters predicted the next president would be Fidel Ramos. His rival, Miriam Defensor Santiago, was already calling foul.

America **imposed sanctions** on the space enterprises of Russia and India because of a deal in which Russia agreed to sell India booster motors for long-range rockets. India said it wanted to launch commercial satellites. America said it wanted to curb the spread of military technology.

Tuesday 12th
Britain and Vietnam agreed that most of the 55,700 **boat people** in Hong Kong would be returned to Vietnam whether they liked it or not. An earlier agreement had applied only to recent arrivals. News of repatriation programmes had so far in 1992 reduced to a handful the number of boat people seeking refuge in Hong Kong.

Thursday 14th
India outlawed the Liberation Tigers of Tamil Eelam, who seek a separate Tamil state in Sri Lanka and who were accused of assassinating a year earlier the former Indian prime minister, Rajiv Gandhi. The move allowed India to crack down on **Tamil Tiger** sanctuaries in the southern Indian state of Tamil Nadu.

Monday 18th
Thailand's prime minister, General Suchinda Kraprayoon, declared a **state of emergency** and sent troops to clear the streets of Bangkok after a weekend of huge demonstrations there calling for his resignation. Scores of civilians were reported killed or wounded.

America formally protested to China after security officials, a day earlier, **ransacked** the office of the Beijing correspondent of the *Washington Post*.

Wednesday 20th
King Bhumibol Adulyadej summoned Thailand's prime minister, Suchinda Kraprayoon, and opposition leader, Chamlong Srimuang. They approached him on their knees. Four days later General Suchinda agreed to step down and to let the constitution be amended so that only an elected MP could become prime minister.

Japan's parliament ended the requirement that all foreign residents be **fingerprinted**. The requirement was viewed as discrimination by over 600,000 Koreans and Taiwanese, many of whose families had been brought by force to Japan during the Japanese colonial era.

Thursday 21st
America accused China of conducting, in Xinjiang province, its biggest ever underground **nuclear explosion**.

Friday 22nd
Three **North Korean infiltrators** were killed and two South Korean guards wounded in the demilitarised zone. It was the first clash since 1986.

Monday 25th
Afghanistan's **rival mujahideen** leaders, Ahmad Shah Masoud and Gulbuddin Hikmatyar, agreed to end hostilities, withdraw forces from Kabul and hold elections within six months. However, mujahideen kidnappings continued, and President Sibghatullah said it might take two years to hold an election.

Friday 29th
India test-fired its Agni intermediate-range ballistic missile, defying America's concern over missiles in the region.

June

Tuesday 2nd

A presidential spokesman said America would renew China's **most-favoured-nation** trading status, despite concerns over human rights in China. Meanwhile, weeping was officially banned in Beijing's Tiananmen Square, where pro-democracy demonstrations had been bloodily suppressed on June 4th 1989.

Fiji's President Ratu Penaia Ganilau appointed ex-General **Sitiveni Rabuka** as prime minister. His government was the first to be elected since 1987, when Mr Rabuka (then a colonel) led a military coup to topple a government dominated by Indian Fijians.

Wednesday 3rd

Rival Sunni and Shiite Muslim **mujahideen kidnapped** hundreds of civilians on the streets of the Afghan capital, Kabul.

Thursday 4th

The International Atomic Energy Agency said a video made by its experts of a North Korean **nuclear installation** showed it to be "extremely primitive". In February the head of America's CIA had said North Korea was a few months away from producing a nuclear weapon.

Monday 8th

After 20 months of political squabbling and four days of opposition filibustering, an exhausted upper house of Japan's parliament passed a bill allowing up to 2,000 troops, subject to strict conditions, to join UN **peacekeeping operations**. Japan's constitution forbids overseas military activity. Approval by the lower house was a formality.

The Taiwan High Court sentenced George Chang, a Taiwanese-American, to ten years in jail for plotting to overthrow the Nationalist government, which claims to represent mainland China as well as Taiwan. Mr Chang, a supporter of **Taiwan's independence**, had returned to Taiwan in December after 30 years in America.

Chung Ju Yung, a tycoon turned presidential hopeful, said South Korea should allow a **legal Communist Party**. The South is on permanent guard against the communist North, but Mr Chung said legal communism had not harmed Japan and its economy.

Tuesday 9th

The ruling Golkar party won some two-thirds of the 107m votes cast in the **Indonesian election**, compared with 73% in the 1987 election. Some saw the vote as an endorsement of President Suharto's 27 years in power; others saw it as a sign of waning confidence in Mr Suharto ahead of the 1993 presidential election.

Wednesday 10th

King Bhumibol turned down Somboon Rahong, a retired air chief marshal, and appointed **Anand Panyarachun** as Thailand's prime minister. Mr Anand, a civilian and unelected, promised elections within four months. By a constitutional amendment his successor would have to be an elected MP.

Monday 15th

The lower house of Japan's parliament, brushing aside the threat of resignation by the opposition socialists, approved the bill to allow troops to join UN **peacekeeping** operations.

Troops of the Phnom Penh government were reported to be launching a counter-attack on the **Khmers Rouges** guerrillas, further imperilling the Cambodian peace accord. The Khmers Rouges said they would not let the UN disarm their fighters in the phase of the accord due to start on June 13th.

America's State Department said it was cutting its request to Congress for **aid to the Philippines** by almost two-thirds to $219.1m. A big reason for the fall was the Philippines' rejection in 1991 of a new lease for the American base at Subic Bay.

Wednesday 17th

America warned India to help stop **nuclear proliferation** or risk losing American aid. India, which is capable of making nuclear weapons, had argued that the non-proliferation treaty was discriminatory.

Thursday 18th

China said members of Hong Kong's United Democrats should not be included in the Executive Council of **Chris Patten**, who was to take over as governor on July 9th. The United Democrats in 1991 almost swept the board in the first direct elections to the British colony's legislature.

Malaysia's foreign minister expressed concern that Japan's decision to take part in UN peacekeeping operations might revive **Japanese militarism**. Other Asian countries had expressed similar worries.

Sunday 21st

Li Xiannian, formerly China's president, died at the age of 83. He was the youngest of the "Eight Immortals", men of influence from the days of the Communist revolution. His death meant one fewer conservative opponent for the immortal Deng Xiaoping.

Monday 22nd

A meeting of 33 governments, the EC and 12 international organisations pledged $880m to **rehabilitate Cambodia**—far exceeding the $600m estimated by the UN to be needed for the coming 18 months.

Wednesday 24th

Japan said it would send a mission to Cambodia to prepare for Japanese participation in UN **peacekeeping** there. A poll showed most Japanese to be against the recent peacekeeping bill.

Thursday 25th

Hong Kong's Legislative Council, 18 of whose 60 members are **directly elected**, narrowly rejected a motion that half their number should be directly elected.

Sunday 28th

The ruling Mongolian People's Revolutionary Party won handsomely in **Mongolia's general election**. The result was a rebuff to the Democratic Alliance, which favoured faster economic reform than the ex-communist MPRP.

Sibghatullah Mujaddidi ended his two-month term and handed **Afghanistan's presidency** to Burhannudin Rahbani—the first peaceful accession since 1901.

Thursday 2nd
The **Khmers Rouges** refused a UN appeal to allow their guerrillas to be disarmed as part of the Cambodian peace plan. They insisted that the withdrawal of Vietnamese troops first be verified and the powers of the Vietnam-backed government in Phnom Penh be lessened in favour of Cambodia's Supreme National Council.

China said it would hold negotiations with Vietnam over the **Spratly Islands**, where the two countries came to blows in 1988. China added that the rival claims to the islands "will not affect the normal development of relations".

Sunday 5th
Rocket **attacks on Kabul** by the fundamentalist Hizb-i-Islami killed at least 100 and left the Afghan capital without power and water.

Monday 6th
Three days of talks between Britain and China over **Hong Kong's new airport** ended without agreement. China objected to the cost of the project, estimated overall at $21.2 billion; Britain thought the objections were politically motivated by China's opposition to the democratisation of Hong Kong.

Tuesday 7th
Taiwan's National Assembly voted to lift a decades-old ban on the return of exiled **Taiwanese activists**. More than 270 had been barred for advocating that Taiwan abandon its official goal of reunification with China.

Japan thanked its G7 colleagues at their summit in Munich for agreeing that the issue of the Russian-occupied **Kurile islands** to the north of Japan was more than a bilateral problem for Japan and Russia. Japan said its aid to

Russia would be in part conditional on the return of its "Northern Territories".

Thursday 9th
Chris Patten, former chairman of Britain's Conservative Party, was sworn in as Hong Kong's **last governor**. He warned China, which takes over the British colony in 1997, that "trust is a two-way street".

Thailand's prime minister, **Anand Panyarachun**, curbed the military by revoking power of its supreme commander to tackle civil unrest. Army action in May had killed scores of civilian demonstrators in Bangkok.

Japan's foreign minister, **Michio Watanabe**, was operated on in a Tokyo hospital, reportedly for the removal of gallstones. His ill health seemed likely to scuttle his chance of replacing Kiichi Miyazawa as prime minister.

Saturday 11th
South Korean diplomats arrived in Hanoi to prepare their country's first **liaison office** in Vietnam since 1975. The visit marked another step in South Korea's improved relations with the traditional allies of North Korea.

Tuesday 14th
Li Ximing, leader of the Beijing Communist Party and hitherto a Maoist ideologue, supported economic reform in a front-page article of the *Beijing Daily*. The article was another sign that China's senior leader, Deng Xiaoping, had won a battle for liberal-

ism ahead of the 14th Chinese Communist Party congress.

Cambodia's **Khmers Rouges**, in one of the worst violations of the UN-monitored truce, launched an artillery barrage and then overran two villages in the north of the country. Meanwhile they promised to send their guerrillas to UN-run barracks within a month if the Vietnam-backed government in Phnom Penh was first disbanded.

Wednesday 15th
China warned France not to jeopardise bilateral economic relations by selling **Mirage** fighter aircraft to Taiwan.

Thursday 16th
After almost two years of debate the **Taiwan** National Assembly authorised the government to lift bans on direct links between capitalist Taiwan and the communist mainland of China. This might mean permission for Chinese communists to visit Taiwan or for the hiring of workers from the mainland.

Friday 17th
By a single vote the parliament of **Papua New Guinea** chose Paias Wingti as the new prime minister following a general election at the end of June.

Sunday 19th
Hindu extremists defied a court order to halt the construction of a temple on the site of a mosque in Ayodhya, in Uttar Pradesh state. Hindus believe the site is the birthplace of the god Ram. Riots over the issue had caused 2,000 deaths in the previous three years.

Tuesday 21st
Bao Tong was sentenced to nine years' jail for counter-revolutionary incitement and leaking state secrets during the events of Tiananmen Square

in 1989. Mr Bao was the aide of the ousted Communist Party boss, Zhao Ziyang. His sentence was reduced to seven years, of which three had been served awaiting trial.

Wednesday 22nd
Vietnam and Laos signed treaties of "**amity and co-operation**" with the Association of South-East Asian Nations, so moving towards eventual membership of ASEAN. Russia's foreign minister told an ASEAN meeting in Manila that it might agree renewed access to Vietnam's naval base of Cam Ranh Bay.

Sunday 26th
Japan's ruling Liberal Democratic Party won 69 of the 127 seats being contested for the upper house of the Diet (parliament). The result, achieved from a record low turnout, brought the party within striking distance of the majority it lost in the **upper-house election** three years earlier. It was thus a triumph for the prime minister, Kiichi Miyazawa.

Wednesday 29th
Myanmar announced that its universities would re-open on August 24th. The military junta had closed them in December after demonstrations for democracy.

Thursday 30th
The official *China Daily* said China was negotiating to sell **nuclear-power plants** to Egypt, Iran and Bangladesh.

August

Sunday 2nd
Mujahideen of the fundamentalist Hizb-i-Islami, led by Gulbuddin Hikmatyar, shelled rival **mujahideen** groups in the Afghan capital of Kabul. Pakistan's prime minister, Nawaz Sharif, called off a visit to Kabul because of the violence.

Monday 3rd
Malaysia's prime minister, **Mahathir Mohamad**, declared that the Non-Aligned Movement was still needed to counter powerful western nations, despite the end of the cold war. Dr Mahathir was scheduled to attend a summit meeting of the movement the following month in Indonesia.

Tuesday 4th
Reports from Tokyo said that Russia was planning to involve America in talks to resolve its territorial dispute with Japan. Russia occupied four islands in the **Kurile chain** at the end of the second world war. Japan maintained their return was a pre-condition for any substantial economic aid to Russia.

Wednesday 5th
A Beijing court sentenced Gao Shan to **four years' imprisonment** for leaking state secrets. Mr Gao, detained after the crushing of the Tiananmen democracy movement in June 1989, was a subordinate of Bao Tong, sentenced in July for his role in the Tiananmen events.

Ruslan Khasbulatov, the chairman of the Russian parliament, said Russia would go ahead with a $250m deal to supply India with **rocket technology**. His assertion came despite opposition to the deal by America, which had imposed sanctions on both countries.

Singapore and Indonesia announced joint measures to combat **piracy** in the Malacca Strait. In 1991 203 cases of piracy were reported; the toll reported so far in 1992 was 50 incidents.

Saturday 8th
Tamil Tiger separatists exploded a land mine to kill Major-General Denzil Kobbekaduwa, the leader of the government troops in Sri Lanka's civil war. Eight of the general's aides were also killed. The war had claimed over 22,000 lives since it began in 1983.

Monday 10th
Ignoring criticism, Japan's prime minister, Kiichi Miyazawa, officially decided that **Emperor Akihito** should visit China in October to mark 20 years of normal diplomatic relations. It seemed the emperor would express regret, but not an outright apology, for the 13m or more Chinese said to have perished after Japanese troops invaded China in 1937.

A spokesman said Japan would send troops, as early as October, to rebuild roads in Cambodia. Their dispatch would be the first deployment of **Japanese soldiers** overseas since the second world war.

About 3,500 police stormed two university campuses in Seoul in an attempt to thwart rallies in favour of **Korean reunification**. Among those arrested were a German and a Turk.

Tuesday 11th
Taiwan's foreign ministry refused to comment on reports that Russia was offering to sell Taiwan 50 jet fighters. **Taiwan's airforce** was said to prefer American F-16s, but the government was also considering the French Mirage 2000. China threatened sanctions against any country supplying aircraft to Taiwan.

Chinese authorities temporarily closed the stock exchange in **Shenzhen** after three days of riots by up to 1m would-be share-buyers from all over China. Many accused the police of keeping application forms for themselves.

Wednesday 12th
New Zealand's defence minister, Warren Cooper, said his country needed to re-establish strong **security ties** with America. These had been virtually broken in 1985, when New Zealand's then Labour government banned visits from nuclear-armed or powered ships.

Thursday 13th
Internal security officials in **Singapore** raided the offices of the local *Business Times* newspaper. Apparently, it had used secret official documents in accurately reporting the island republic's economic growth rate.

Islam Karimov, president of **Uzbekistan**, arrived in Islamabad to sign three agreements with Pakistan on investment and economic co-operation. Pakistan had been competing with China, Turkey and Iran for influence in former Soviet Central Asia.

Sunday 16th
The United Nations **evacuated** all but seven of its personnel from Kabul because of renewed rocket-fire. Afghanistan's coalition government said it had expelled Gulbuddin Hikmatyar, the fundamentalist Muslim leader responsible for the bombardment.

Wednesday 19th
India and Pakistan signed an agreement prohibiting the use of **chemical weapons**. They also agreed a code of conduct on the treatment of diplomats. Predictably, negotiations in Delhi failed to resolve the dispute over Kashmir.

Monday 24th
South Korea and China formally established **diplomatic relations**. The move meant the end of South Korea's diplomatic ties with Taiwan, which claims to represent all of China. Taiwan, now diplomatically isolated in Asia, was not happy; nor was China's traditional ally, North Korea.

Universities and colleges in **Myanmar** reopened after being closed for nine months because of pro-democracy activism.

Thursday 27th
The **Khmers Rouges** said they would rejoin a UN-supervised body monitoring violations of the ceasefire in Cambodia, ending a boycott of more than two months. The UN was hoping for elections in the spring.

Sunday 30th
Hong Kong's liberal United Democrats were defeated in a **by-election** for the Legislative Council. The election of a pro-China candidate was praised by Hong Kong's conservatives.

September

Tuesday 1st
Communist insurgent **Saturnino Ocampo** was freed from detention in the Philippines. President Fidel Ramos had ordered his release to show good faith before peace talks with the banned communists. Also to be released was Romulo Kintanar, head of the insurgents' New People's Army.

Kiyoshi Kaneko, governor of Japan's Niigata prefecture, resigned. He said there was a "high" probability that an aide had received illegal payments from Sagawa Kyubin, a delivery company linked to organised crime. It seemed certain that the scandal would soon claim other political victims.

Wednesday 2nd
President Bush ordered the sale of 150 F-16 **jet fighters** to Taiwan. The decision flouted a 1982 agreement with China in which America undertook to reduce both the quantity and quality of its arms sales to Taiwan. China, which claims Taiwan as its own, accused Mr Bush of electioneering, and said it would boycott big-power arms-limitation talks.

A four-day meeting of the **Non-Aligned Movement** opened in Jakarta. Cuba's Fidel Castro and Libya's Muammar Qaddafi stayed away. Indonesia's President Suharto emphasised the need for free-market economic development.

Thursday 3rd
Vietnam sent a protest note to China demanding the removal of an oil-drilling ship in the Gulf of Tonkin. Vietnam believed China was expanding its claims of sovereignty in the South China Sea. In the past, **conflicting claims** to the Spratly Islands had led to naval clashes.

Sunday 6th
The island's government-owned radio said Taiwan would soon buy 60 Mirage 2000 **jet fighters** from France for $2.6 billion. If so, it would be another blow to mainland China, which had been trying for months to block the sale.

The Indian state of **Punjab**, racked for years by separatist violence, held municipal elections. Unlike February's state and federal elections, these were not boycotted by the Sikh Akali Dal party. Independents won most of the seats—and both the Akali Dal and the Congress Party claimed them as supporters.

Monday 7th
Rakhman Nabiyev stepped down as president of Tajikistan after weeks of clashes between his supporters and the opposition Islamic Renaissance Party and the Democratic Party. Mr Nabiyev, formerly boss of the Communist Party, had been elected in November 1991.

Tuesday 8th
Taiwan and Russia agreed to exchange permanent missions in another example of Taiwan's "**pragmatic diplomacy**". Anti-communist Taiwan had previously been loth to make contact with the old Soviet block. All changed with the collapse of European communism.

Wednesday 9th
Russia's President **Boris Yeltsin** abruptly cancelled a

visit to Japan scheduled for September 13th-18th. The unstated reason was Japan's pressure for the return of four islands in the Kurile chain seized by the Soviet Union at the end of the second world war. Japan had connected the return of the islands with its willingness to give aid.

Thursday 10th
China, the biggest customer for American wheat, said it might stop its purchases immediately if America went ahead with the sale of **jet fighters** to Taiwan.

Sunday 13th
A coalition of four anti-military parties won **Thailand's election**. It seemed, however, that they would need a fifth party to consolidate their position. Meanwhile, the armed forces promised not to interfere.

Monday 14th
Pakistan's cabinet was briefed on the damage caused by a week of **floods** that began in Kashmir and swept south along the country's five main rivers. It seemed that at least 2,000 were killed and hundreds of villages destroyed. Critics said the authorities had ignored flood warnings.

Thursday 17th
The **Khmers Rouges** attended a UN-supervised military committee of the rival Cambodian factions, ending a boycott of three months.

North and South Korea agreed to install a **military hot-line**. This was one of the first steps to implement the non-aggression accord signed the previous December.

Saturday 19th
New Zealanders voted in two **referendums**. In the first they agreed to hold a referendum to choose a new voting system. In the second they agreed that

the proposed alternative to the existing first-past-the-post system should be Germany's "mixed member proportional" system.

The Labor government of Premier Wayne Goss was **re-elected** in Queensland's state election. Given the parlous condition of the economy, Australia's ruling Labor Party did not expect to repeat such success in other forthcoming elections.

Sunday 20th
Japanese troops arrived in Cambodia to assist the UN peacekeeping operation. They were the first Japanese soldiers to be deployed overseas since the second world war.

Saturday 26th
Myanmar's military junta revoked two **martial law** decrees that had allowed regional commanders to try civilians in military courts.

Sunday 27th
Roh Tae Woo arrived in Beijing for the first state visit to China by a South Korean president. His hosts warned him that too much pressure on North Korea to stop its nuclear programme might be counterproductive.

Monday 28th
The "godfather" of Japan's ruling Liberal Democratic Party, **Shin Kanemaru**, agreed to pay a trivial fine of ¥200,000 for accepting a bribe of ¥500m ($4.2m). Many were outraged that Mr Kanemaru had not even had to go to the prosecutor's office.

October

Thursday 1st
The Afghan government appointed 33 **mujahideen** commanders as generals in the nation's armed forces. It seemed unlikely, however, that the appointments would end fighting between the various mujahideen groups who had toppled the government of President Najibullah the previous April.

A welfare office in the Japanese city of Osaka ran out of cash, sparking three days of rioting in the slum district of Airin.

Monday 5th
The **Sultan of Brunei**, allegedly the world's richest man, celebrated 25 years as an absolute monarch. A royal banquet for 5,000 diners was supplied with meat from the sultan's Australian ranch—which is bigger than all of Brunei.

Cambodians began registering for **free elections** after two decades of civil war and totalitarian rule. Seven parties monitored the registration process; they did not, however, include the radical Khmers Rouges. Voting, according to a UN peace plan, was scheduled for May 1993.

The Labor government of Paul Keating announced that Australians would no longer accept **knighthoods** and other decorations from the British monarchy. The decision was more evidence of a republican trend in Australia, whose head of state is the Queen.

Tuesday 6th
Hong Kong's governor, **Chris Patten**, announced political reforms for the British colony designed to spread democracy. China, which takes over Britain's colony in 1997, accused Mr Patten of being "extremely irresponsible" and said the reforms, if implemented, would be reversed.

Wednesday 7th
Thailand's parliament unanimously voted to **repeal** the **amnesty** granted to those generals who in May had ordered soldiers to fire on unarmed pro-democracy demonstrators.

Saturday 10th
China backed away from a **trade war** with America by agreeing to phase out import quotas and other controls on American-made goods. America, fearing a trade deficit with China that might reach $17 billion by the end of the year, had threatened to impose tariffs on Chinese exports worth $3.9 billion.

Monday 12th
Opening the 14th national congress of the **Chinese Communist Party**, Jiang Zemin, the party chairman, promised that China would hasten capitalist-style reforms to its economy. However, he insisted there was no alternative to the party's monopoly of political power.

President **Fidel Ramos** said he was willing for American troops to be stationed in the Philippines, despite the contrary decision a year earlier by the Philippine senate. Mr Ramos's remarks came less than two weeks after the American flag was lowered on the giant Subic naval base. The Clark air base, damaged by the Pinatubo volcano, had already been abandoned.

Wednesday 14th
Shin Kanemaru, the "kingmaker" of Japan's ruling Liberal Democratic Party, resigned from the Diet (parliament), taking responsibility for a scandal in which he and other politicians took bribes from Sagawa Kyubin, a delivery company. The resignation threw into turmoil the party's Takeshita faction, which Mr Kanemaru had led.

Thursday 15th
Tamil Tiger separatists massacred at least 160 people in attacks on four villages. It was the worst carnage in Sri Lanka for two years, adding to a death toll since the civil war began in 1983 of around 25,000.

Taiwan's ministry of health, hoping to encourage **breast-feeding**, announced that advertising powdered milk for babies would be banned from the following April.

Monday 19th
America's presidential envoy, General John Vessey, ended a three-day visit to Hanoi. He said Vietnam had agreed to search its archives for information on Americans **missing in action** during the Vietnam war. The issue of some 2,000 MIAs remained an obstacle to the normalising of America's relations with Vietnam.

Tuesday 20th
Hong Kong's governor, Chris Patten, began a three-visit to Beijing to explain his proposals for political reform. China's prime minister, Li Peng, refused to meet him, a **snub** that reflected continuing attacks on the governor by Chinese officials.

Wednesday 21st
The head of the UN mission in Cambodia said the **disarmament** of Cambodia's factions might have to stop because the Khmers Rouges were refusing to comply with the country's UN-brokered peace accord. The disarmament was a key step on the way to elections due in May 1993.

Friday 23rd
Japan's **Emperor Akihito** began a six-day visit to China, celebrating the 20th anniversary of the normalisation of relations between the two countries. The visit showed that China, three years after the Tiananmen bloodshed, was again internationally respectable. In return, China did not press the emperor for a proper apology for Japan's brutality in China in the 1930s and '40s.

Sunday 25th
China **deported** Shen Tong, a 24-year-old student, to America. He had been arrested the previous month after returning from exile in America and touring China to promote democracy.

Wednesday 28th
Japan told America that after the American election it would resume its **aid to Vietnam**, suspended for 14 years. The decision was another breach in the American-led ostracism of Vietnam.

Thursday 29th
Kim Woo Choong, chairman of the Daewoo group, announced he **would not run** for the South Korean presidency in December's election. His decision was a relief for the government's candidate, Kim Young Sam.

November

Sunday 1st
China **expelled** a Hong Kong journalist after she admitted offering bribes for state secrets. Expulsion rather than jail was seen as a Chinese move to ease tensions with Hong Kong.

Monday 2nd
Hong Kong's governor, **Chris Patten**, promised he would make no secret deals with China over the colony's future. China had been claiming, against British denials, that the governor's plans for increasing democracy conflicted with earlier, secret agreements between Britain and China.

Tuesday 3rd
The Thai cabinet decided to end the 1976 Internal Peacekeeping Act, which had given the army free rein to curb civil unrest. The move was another **curb** on the armed forces following their bloody crackdown on pro-democracy demonstrators in May.

The Phnom Penh government, one of Cambodia's four factions, called on the United Nations to abandon the disarmament phase of its **peace plan**. It said it wanted to combat the Khmers Rouges, who had refused to disarm.

Wednesday 4th
Lawyers for **Imelda Marcos**, widow of President Marcos, agreed to ask Swiss banks to transfer to the Philippines Marcos family deposits worth $356m. The Philippine government, which said the money was illegally gained, would drop some of its legal cases against Mrs Marcos.

Thursday 5th
Japanese prosecutors said seven top officials of the ruling Liberal Democratic Party had offered a rightist group $25m to stop attacking the prime ministerial campaign of Noboru Takeshita in 1987.

Ultimately, the prosecutors said, **gangsters** had intervened to silence the rightists' loudspeaker trucks.

Friday 6th
Japan signed a ¥45.5 billion ($380m) loan to Vietnam, so breaking away from the **embargo** imposed on Vietnam by America in the late 1970s.

Saturday 7th
A Japanese ship, the *Akatsuki Maru*, left the French port of Cherbourg with a cargo of **plutonium** for use in Japan's fast-breeder reactor programme. Environmentalists were outraged. Several countries warned the ship to stay out of their territorial waters.

Monday 9th
A special constitutional panel ruled that the Thai government had no right to put on trial generals who had ordered the bloody suppression of demonstrations in May. The House of Representatives had in October rejected an **amnesty** for the generals.

Wednesday 11th
Hong Kong's Legislative Council by a vote of 32 to 21 backed the proposals by Chris Patten, the governor, to **increase democracy**. China, which will take over the British colony in 1997, was vehemently against the proposals.

America eased its embargo on Vietnam by allowing direct **telephone links**, with American telephone companies permitted to make payments direct to Vietnam.

Sunday 15th
Singapore relaxed a 26-year-old restriction order on Chia Thye Poh, a **political prisoner** accused of communist activity. Instead of being confined to Sentosa island after nightfall, he was now allowed to live at his father's home on the main island of Singapore.

Monday 16th
India's Supreme Court upheld the decision of the former V.P. Singh government to reserve 27% of government jobs for "**backward castes**". The allocation was in addition to the 22% of jobs reserved for the "untouchables" and tribal groups. The court rejected the current government's bid to reserve 10% of jobs for poor members of the upper castes.

A **suicide-bomber** killed Sri Lanka's navy chief, Vice-Admiral Clancey Fernando, and three aides in the heart of Colombo. Police said the assassin, who rammed his motorcycle into the admiral's car, was a Tamil Tiger separatist.

A Chinese deputy prime minister, Zhu Rongji, said that China might abandon its agreement with Britain over Hong Kong if **democracy proposals** were not withdrawn. China later said Mr Zhu had been mistranslated.

Singapore announced that both its deputy prime ministers, Lee Hsien Loong and Ong Teng Cheong, were suffering from **cancer**. It had been assumed that Mr Lee, the son of Lee Kuan Yew, would take over as prime minister from Goh Chok Tong.

Wednesday 18th
Lee Kuan Yew, Singapore's former prime minister, said in Manila that the Philippines needed discipline more than western-style democracy. His hosts disagreed, at least in public.

Opposition leader **Benazir Bhutto** led hundreds of thousands of demonstrators in a march on Pakistan's capital, Islamabad. The prime minister, Nawaz Sharif, barricaded the city against the march and arrested Miss Bhutto.

Thursday 19th
Imoli Rakhmonov was elected acting president of **Tajikistan**, becoming the third head of state in two months. Fighting seemed certain to continue between Islamic groups, who held the capital, Dushanbe, and pro-communist groups.

Friday 20th
Indonesian troops captured **Xanana Gusmao**, leader of the Fretilin guerrilla movement fighting for the independence of East Timor. Portugal, East Timor's former coloniser, offered asylum and warned Indonesia not to mistreat him.

Monday 23rd
Australia's government, overriding military protests, decided **homosexuals** could serve in the armed forces.

Monday 30th
The UN Security Council threatened sanctions against the Khmers Rouges and said **Cambodian elections** would go ahead in May with or without them.

The row over Hong Kong worsened: China said all contracts signed without its approval by Hong Kong's government would be **invalid** when the British colony passes to China in 1997.

December

Tuesday 1st
The day after the UN Security Council announced economic sanctions on Cambodia's **Khmer Rouge** guerrillas, the government in Phnom Penh criticised the measures as inadequate and gave warning of a Khmer Rouge offensive.

Wednesday 2nd
Six UN peacekeepers in Cambodia were **kidnapped** by the Khmers Rouges and another seven were wounded by mines or gunfire. The hostages were soon released, but other kidnappings followed.

Thursday 3rd
A Chinese spokesman said Hong Kong's governor, Chris Patten, must **abandon democratic reforms**; otherwise he would jeopardise agreements already reached between Britain and China for the transfer of Britain's colony to China in 1997. The statement was the strongest diplomatic threat so far by China in its campaign against Mr Patten.

Sunday 6th
A mob of **Hindu zealots** demolished a 16th-century Muslim mosque in Ayodhya, in India's Uttar Pradesh state, claiming it defiled the birthplace of the Hindu god Ram. The storming of the mosque sparked sectarian violence across the country, killing over 1,500 people.

Tuesday 8th
Bill Clinton, America's president-elect, signalled his sympathy for Hong Kong's governor, Chris Patten, by saying he

was "very concerned" at Hong Kong's dispute over democratic reform. China, Mr Clinton said, must understand that Hong Kong's economic success requires "personal freedom, liberty and human rights".

The Khmers Rouges stayed away from a meeting of Cambodia's Supreme National Council. It was the first time the hardline faction had **boycotted** a meeting of the body that advises the UN authorities in Cambodia.

Wednesday 9th
Two fighter jets, belonging to the militia of General Abdul Rashid Dostam, strafed the presidential palace in Kabul as **mujahideen factions** in Afghanistan's coalition government fought for power.

The editor of Singapore's *Business Times*, two stockbrokers and an official of the country's central bank were charged under Singapore's **Official Secrets Act**. Their alleged offence was to publish GDP data ahead of schedule. They faced a fine of S$2,000 ($1,220), or two years' jail, or both.

Friday 11th
The official news agency announced that North Korea's President **Kim Il Sung** had dismissed his prime minister, Yon Hyong Muk. The apparent reason was that Mr Yon had failed to push through economic reforms.

Saturday 12th
The Indonesian island of Flores was **devastated** by a combination of earthquake and tidal waves. The death toll was estimated at around 2,200.

Monday 14th
Singapore's former prime minister, **Lee Kuan Yew**, told an audience at Hong Kong University that the pro-de-

mocracy proposals of Chris Patten were unrealistic. The Hong Kong governor, who was sitting beside Mr Lee, wryly asked for a right of reply after 1997, "perhaps in Singapore".

Tuesday 15th
India's prime minister, **Narasimha Rao**, dismissed the governments of Madhya Pradesh, Rajasthan and Himachal Pradesh, having earlier sacked the government of Uttar Pradesh. All four states had been run by the Hindu-nationalist Bharatiya Janata Party. Mr Rao argued he was calming sectarianism; the BJP said he was undemocratic.

Thursday 17th
Khmer Rouge guerrillas released 21 UN **hostages** in Cambodia—and then took captive 46 more.

Friday 18th
Electors in South Korea chose **Kim Young Sam**, candidate of the ruling Democratic Liberal Party, as their new president. He won 42% of the vote, compared with 34% for the opposition leader, Kim Dae Jung, and 16% for Chung Ju Yung, a recently-retired tycoon.

Saturday 19th
Taiwan's ruling **Kuomintang** was abashed when it won just 53% of the vote in the island's first fully democratic election for the legislature. With 31% of the vote, the Democratic Progressive Party—which favours abandoning Taiwan's dream of political reunification with the Chinese mainland—surpassed expectations.

Singapore's prime minister, **Goh Chok Tong**, won a by-election he had called for his own constituency. The slate of the ruling People's Action Party took 73% of the vote. Although this was down from the 77% of the 1991 general

election, Mr Goh could still claim it as a vote of confidence in his leadership.

Monday 21st
America's commerce secretary, Barbara Franklin, on a visit to Beijing, **warned China** not to invalidate contracts in Hong Kong. She was the first cabinet member to intervene in the dispute between China and Hong Kong. China, which takes over in 1997, had threatened to ignore contracts unless plans for democracy in Hong Kong were withdrawn.

Wednesday 23rd
Emerging from four years in hiding, Colonel **Gregorio (Gringo) Honasan** agreed to hold peace talks with the Philippines' government. He had been linked to three coup attempts against the former president, Corazon Aquino.

Tuesday 29th
China announced that **North Korea** must henceforth pay for imports with cash, not barter. The move seemed certain to intensify the economic plight of the North. Recent reports had spoken of severe food shortages in North Korea.

Wednesday 30th
Malaysia's prime minister, Mahathir Mohamad, announced plans to allow citizens to lodge complaints against the nation's **hereditary sultans** and to end the sultans' power to pardon themselves. He had earlier promised to end the sultans' immunity from the law.

THE FORCES OF COMPETITION.

The **POWER** behind the forces. Down to the smallest detail, one **GLOBAL CITY** boosts your competitive edge with an unequalled **CONFIGURATION** of business infrastructure. With IT and telecommunications more sophisticated than most. Skilled manpower **NETWORKED** at every level. A multi-faceted support base for high value-added manufacturing and world-class services. And creating **STRATEGIC** alliances that generate opportunities in Asia-Pacific and beyond. Without a doubt, this **TOTAL** business environment is **SINGAPORE UNLIMITED.**

As we reported then

Greeting America's salesman

JANUARY 4TH, TOKYO **President Bush's trip to Japan turned into a public-relations disaster when he fell ill at a state banquet. His mission had already messily mixed trade with politics.**

HOW times have changed. Charles de Gaulle once dismissed a visiting Japanese prime minister as a transistor salesman—a gibe the Japanese have neither forgotten nor forgiven. Because of good manners, and self-interest, they will not call George Bush a mere car salesman when he arrives in Tokyo on January 7th, after stops in Australia, Singapore and South Korea, for three days of talks on security, trade and world affairs. But since he will be accompanied by the bosses of General Motors, Ford and Chrysler, a car salesman is what the American president will pretend to be.

"Pretend" because no one on either side of the Pacific seriously expects the Japanese to forsake their own well-made and affordable motor cars for dubious products from Detroit. But with America's presidential election just 11 months away, the Japanese understand Mr Bush's need to be seen as the booster of American exports and protector of American jobs. These same Japanese also understand that Kiichi Miyazawa, Japan's prime minister, is destined to become the hapless fall guy—even though, after only two months in office, his popularity has already started to plummet.

Deservedly so. Mr Miyazawa has mishandled every big policy initiative presented during the extraordinary session of the Diet (parliament) which started with his appointment and ended just before Christmas. First, the bills to allow Japanese soldiers to participate in United Nations peace-keeping and disaster operations had to be dropped. Then he failed to include a special tax in the new budget so Japan would not be caught dithering, in Gulf war fashion, in the next international crisis. Now he has had to abandon plans to revise Japan's money-grubbing electoral system. The electorate senses that the undoubtedly clever Mr Miyazawa is short of gumption.

His lack comes at a bad time. Like Mr Bush, Mr Miyazawa also faces a crucial test at the polls in 1992. The ruling Liberal Democratic Party (LDP) is desperate to regain the upper-house majority that it lost after the Recruit shares-for-favours scandal two years ago. Ever since, the government has been stymied when it has tried to push controversial legislation through the Diet. Mr Miyazawa knows that he must deliver that majority in July's election or his party bosses will boot him out.

His best ploy will be to play the international statesman. Using just such a ploy,

his predecessor, Toshiki Kaifu, who bungled even more disastrously at home than Mr Miyazawa, became Japan's most popular prime minister since the war. The Japanese enjoy seeing their leaders on television hobnobbing with the great and the good around the globe.

Mr Miyazawa's difficulty is that he has only two brief opportunities to capture public attention before the Diet becomes embroiled in the annual budget debate. One is Mr Bush's visit to Japan. The other is the compromise on agricultural protection that America, the European Community and Japan will have to achieve to save the GATT's Uruguay round from acrimonious failure. In both cases, Japan will see itself giving more than it gains—so Mr Miyazawa's place in the spotlight could end up being more dangerous than valuable.

What he wants from the Americans is a "Tokyo Declaration"—a high-minded proclamation outlining the next 50 years of co-operation between the United States and Japan to help solve the world's problems. Mr Miyazawa will propose an international conference in Tokyo to consider the economic issues confronting the Middle East; and he will join Mr Bush in stressing the need to prevent the proliferation around the world of both nuclear and conventional weapons. All this will be drafted with fine phrases about peace and mutual understanding. Innocuous documents that promise no risk or expense go down especially well in Japan.

In return, the Japanese will let Mr Bush have his "Action Plan". This will be explicitly concerned with bilateral trade issues—and will give the president a few economic souvenirs to take home.

One, gift-wrapped on the eve of Mr Bush's departure from Washington, was a cut in Japan's discount rate from 5% to 4.5%—the second half-point reduction in less than two months and one which, in unlikely theory, could expand Japan's demand for American goods. Another is the squeeze that the Ministry of International Trade and Industry (MITI) has already put on Japan's car makers to limit their exports to America for at least another year. Japan's "voluntary" agreement to export no more than 2.3m cars a year to America was due to expire in March. In practice, the new deal will cost Japanese car companies nothing. They export only 1.8m cars a year to the United States now that their big American factories are up and running. A similar export restraint on Japanese machine-tool makers is to be extended for a further two years.

MITI's other token is to get Japan's car dealers to sell American models alongside Japanese ones. The transport ministry has meanwhile agreed to relax some import requirements on American cars. Even the budget has been skewed to reap American praise after complaints that Japan has been diverting public investment into industry at the expense of ordinary Japanese people—who are then forced to put up

with third-world standards of roads, airports, sanitation, housing and recreation facilities.

As a gesture to the Americans, money for the government's construction projects is to be increased by 5.3%, compared with an overall rise of 2.7% agreed on December 28th for the next fiscal year's ¥72.2 trillion ($580 billion) budget. In addition, local governments are expected to spend 11% more on public works and there will be a 10.9% rise in the "fiscal investment and loans programme" to allow more money to find its way into public works.

All this, Mr Miyazawa can argue, is evidence that Japan is delivering on its prom-

ise to spend ¥430 trillion over ten years modernising its infrastructure. True, none of Japan's promises is likely to put more than a handful of Americans back to work—but they will sound good when Mr Bush hits the campaign trail.

The question is what Mr Miyazawa will get in return. Will Mr Bush be as accommodating in the final haggling over the Uruguay round—and the necessity for Japan to open its sacred rice market to foreign growers? Probably not, in which case Mr Miyazawa's reward for playing the obliging host could be to see his support from the party and the public disappear altogether.

Tycoons of crime

FEBRUARY 29TH, TOKYO **Japan's social peculiarities are often exaggerated, not least to explain its economic success. But one social oddity needs no exaggeration**

THE one activity the bureaucrats have failed to regulate into nice orderly behaviour in post-war Japan has been crime. Now even gangsters are to be brought under ministerial fiat. New legislation which comes into force on March 1st will, among other things, allow district governments to designate shady characters who hang out together as official *boryoku-dan* (violence groups).

To qualify, gangs will have to demonstrate threatening behaviour, have members with criminal records, and belong to an organisation made up of various ranks. That, amazingly, is what the preamble to the legislation says. Once thus designated, the gangsters can go about their business unmolested provided they do not break the law.

Being a *yakuza* (gangster) is a legitimate profession in Japan. The gangs have headquarters with their names on polished brass plates. Like other enterprises, they advertise for recruits and go about their business openly. Between them, the gangs now boast some 90,000 members—with the three biggest syndicates (Yamaguchi-gumi, Inagawa-kai and Sumiyoshi-rengo-kai) accounting for half the membership. Their main source of revenue is from trafficking in stimulants, especially crystal methamphetamine (known as ice). American narcotics agents reckon that 90% of the ice on the streets of Hawaii is smuggled in by Japanese gangsters. As a business, organised crime in Japan is thought to make around ¥1.5 trillion ($11 billion) a year. And that excludes the gangs' new interests in property development and golf clubs.

The gangs became interested in prop-

erty in the 1980s when land prices were going through the roof. Anyone who happened to own some land next to a vacant plot risked becoming the victim of strongarm tactics by a gang. Its aim was to help a property agent put together a plot big enough for a developer to build a large office block on. It did not take the gangs long to decide to become property developers themselves.

The Japanese police have been unable to prevent gangs from laundering illicit earnings by investing in property and other legitimate businesses. Nor have they been able to stop them from collecting protection money or forcing businesses to deal with the gangs' affiliated suppliers. A profitable new sideline is collecting damages

on behalf of motorists involved in traffic accidents. Often the motorists are the gangsters themselves, and the incidents are not so accidental. The gangsters stop just short of breaking the law on blackmail or coercion by using insinuation rather than violence to get results. However, under provisions of the new legislation coming into force next week, insinuation will be illegal, too.

What does the ordinary Japanese say about the gangsters' licence to misbehave? The *yakuza*, with their tattooed bodies and strict rituals, used to have a romantic reputation. They were once given credit for defending the interests of local neighbourhoods. But now they tend to be associated with violence and drugs.

Open warfare between the bigger gangs is threatened. The Yamaguchi-gumi gang, with its 30,000 members, has outgrown its provincial base in Kobe and the surround-

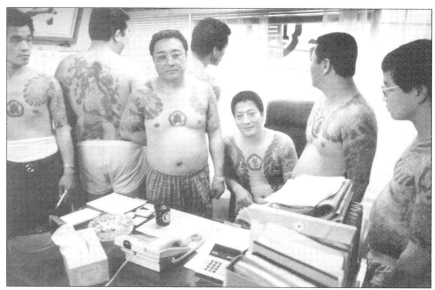

Dressed for the office party

ing region of Osaka. It has recently been trying to muscle into Sumiyoshi-rengo-kai's territory in the Tokyo area.

One night two years ago Yamaguchi-gumi's top boss, along with an army of bodyguards, brazenly had a night out in a Ginza bar that was Sumiyoshi-rengo-kai's home turf. A mêlée ensued as some 150 young thugs bloodied one another, startling the police in what was previously a peaceful patch. Since then Yamaguchi-gumi has been setting up property and financial-services companies in and around Tokyo.

The new laws, which also cover drugs and restrict the use of firearms and swords, will unquestionably make life tougher for organised crime in Japan. But they are not going to drive the gangs out of business. Many people suspect Japan's crime syndicates could move even deeper into commercial business. Yamaguchi-gumi has ordered its 117 affiliated gangs to register as boards. Local bosses were told to make themselves chairmen or presidents of their companies and elect their most talented lieutenants as directors. Each company is to be capitalised at ¥10m.

Gangs all over Japan have been tearing down their old headquarters signs and turning themselves into businesses. One enterprising gang in Kyushu tried to become a co-operative. Just in time, the police managed to get the application thrown out. Had the gang succeeded, it would have been eligible for ¥2 billion worth of business loans from the district and national governments. Other gangs are turning themselves into political organisations. Using rightist groups with loudspeaker vans blaring accusations at petty wrongdoers has long been a *yakuza* way of practising extortion.

But the prize for audacity goes to a gang in the Osaka area that plans to evade the new legislation by registering itself as a religious order. "My religion will be Ninkyodo, the way of the chivalrous spirit," a straight-faced boss told reporters, "and I will be the spiritual leader." Judging from the wealth pouring into many Japanese temples, organised religion could well be more profitable than even organised crime.

Buddhists against Muslims

MARCH 21ST, COX'S BAZAR Relations between Bangladesh and neighbouring Myanmar have often been strained. They became more so when Myanmar's Muslim minority was put to flight

THEY tell of forced labour, the confiscation of their fields, the rape of their women. When Bangladesh's prime minister, Begum Khaleda Zia, visited the Rohingya Muslims on March 13th, she found them crowded in squalid shelters—most of them simply brushwood torn from the forest—in the poorest part of one of the world's poorest nations. The 140,000 refugees from Myanmar's Arakan state have been intimidated by Buddhist Burman nationalism. They are a burden on Bangladesh that increases by around 4,000 refugees a day. When will the load be lightened?

Only when foreign pressure prompts a change of heart by Myanmar's military rulers. Hence Begum Zia's eagerness to discuss the Rohingyas with George Bush in Washington on March 19th. Meanwhile, it was reported that the United Nations plans to send an envoy to Bangladesh and, if possible, to Myanmar, in an effort to halt the abuses against the Rohingyas.

Begum Zia's government has been late to recognise the need for foreign help. The flight of the Rohingyas began almost a year ago, but Bangladesh decided that quiet diplomacy with Myanmar would work better than a call for international assistance.

This approach had, it is true, worked in 1979, when Burma, as it then was, took back 200,000 of the 300,000 Rohingyas it had expelled a year earlier. This time, however, Myanmar appears unmoved. Mostafizur Rahman, Bangladesh's foreign minister, says the intransigence on the part of Myanmar's junta is "a plan to destabilise Bangladesh's democracy lest it inspire democracy in Myanmar."

More likely, the junta is pandering to Burman nationalism by campaigning against Myanmar's minorities. The Rohingyas are an easy target. Descended from Arab and Indian traders, they claim to have lived in Arakan since the 7th century. But they were not represented in the Burmese union that negotiated independence from Britain in 1948. The junta says they are illegal immigrants, to be driven out so that their land can be given to Buddhists.

Bangladesh has no economic leverage over Myanmar and would be foolish to press an argument of force against Myanmar's battle-hardened troops. However, Begum Zia's government is not completely helpless, nor is Mr Bush its only friend to turn to. The Muslim world is providing much of the relief assistance for the south of Bangladesh; Muslim Malaysia is urging its regional colleagues to condemn the junta.

The fear, though, is that bad will simply get worse. Bangladesh, people nervously expect, will grow tired of giving forced hospitality; the Rohingya camps will turn into quagmires when the rains come in June; and desperate people will seek desperate solutions.

The Rohingya guerrilla organisations in Arakan are small, but they could get bigger. An angry 23-year-old Rohingya refugee said outside his hovel of plaited twigs, "When the mujahideen call, I'll go back and fight." Poor Bangladesh: such action would give Myanmar an excuse to hit back at the Rohingyas and all who give them sanctuary.

And the rains are to come

Begum Zia's burden

APRIL 4TH, DHAKA **Bangladesh, beset with more problems than most developing countries, is belatedly trying democracy to help cure its ills. The initial treatment, however, promises no quick miracles**

IS THERE nothing good to say about Bangladesh? Its 116m people are among the poorest in the world; the economy is a wreck, kept floating only by injections of foreign aid; the low-lying countryside is regularly devastated by cyclone and flood. In the days when it was East Pakistan, before a vicious "war of liberation" in 1971, Bangladesh—the Bengal Nation—was already an economic basketcase, cut off by the partition of British India from Bengal's entrepot of Calcutta. Today the population is 70% bigger—and so Bangladesh is an even bigger basketcase. The typical Bangladeshi has no access to a doctor or a telephone, cannot read and will survive barely beyond 50.

The untypical, who can read, will see dismal headlines: Dhaka varsity student killed in gun battle; Garbage hurled at Mayor's residence; Baby killed in city sweepers-police clash; Substandard drugs flood markets; Bombs exploded in bid to rob women; and so on, newspaper after newspaper, day after day. Whether in Dhaka, the drab beggar-infested capital, or in the lush paddy-fields of the south, it is easy to despair.

A little hope is more constructive. On February 27th last year, two months after "people power" demonstrations in the streets of Dhaka toppled President Hussain Mohammad Ershad (he is now serving prison terms for corruption and firearms offences), Bangladesh had the first free and reasonably fair election in its history.

The victor was Begum Khaleda Zia, leader of the Bangladesh Nationalist Party and widow of General Zia ur Rahman, an unusually uncorrupt president who was assassinated in 1981. Leading the vanquished was Sheikh Hasina Wajed, the head of the Awami League and the daughter of Sheikh Mujib ur Rahman, who led Bangladesh to independence in 1971 and became its first president, only to be assassinated in 1975. Perhaps to its own surprise, Bangladesh has now become one of the Muslim world's rare democracies and, since a referendum last September, a parliamentary one.

But will democracy last, and will it help the country? Mrs Zia has an impressive manner, but spends hardly any time in parliament; the more educated Sheikh Hasina relishes parliamentary debate, but concentrates on the obsessive pursuit of her father's killers (they are protected by an "indemnity ordinance" that the Awami League is determined to overturn). Meanwhile, the momentum that overthrew President Ershad is being lost. As one Dhaka businessman puts it: "The Bangladesh Nationalist Party came to power with the strongest mandate possible, and is behaving as though it was the weakest."

He is right. In June 1991 the government announced a budget to cut its deficit—and two months later gave government workers pay rises averaging 50%. More capitulations followed, to the jute workers and to the road and rail workers. There was even an agreement to waive all agricultural loans of 5,000 taka ($130) or less—a vote-buying pledge from the election campaign that will hardly change the "default culture" of a country where some banks recover only 30% of their loans. In a country of poor farmers and share-croppers, the government is strangely reluctant to resist the fraction of the industrial workforce that is unionised.

But the reluctance has its apologists. Mrs Zia's advisers know that it was the Dhaka students and the Dhaka mob that ended the Ershad era—which is why the prime minister respects the Awami League's threat to resort to street politics. She knows, too, that General Ershad's Jatiya Party is still a force in parts of the country. Equally to the point, the parties all have student wings ready to use guns (often supplied by venal policemen) in support of political slogans and ready, also, to defy the restraints of their political parents. As Abdus Salam Talukdar, the minister of local government and secretary-general of the Bangladesh Nationalist Party, wryly explains: "I don't anticipate anything peaceful in this country."

His pessimism could be self-fulfilling. One parallel for Bangladesh today is the Philippines of six years ago. For the competent but corrupt President Ershad, read Ferdinand Marcos; for Mrs Zia, Mrs Aquino—also a housewife turned politician by the assassination of her husband. But will the parallel become still more complete? Will Mrs Zia, like Mrs Aquino, squander international sympathy for her country's new democracy? Will foreign aid be wasted in corruption and bureaucracy? Will natural catastrophes emphasise government incompetence?

The answers could all be yes. Saifur

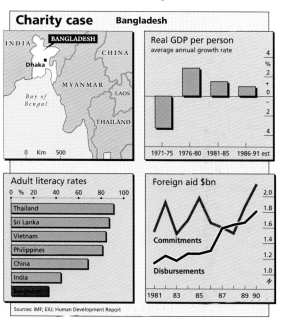

Charity case — Bangladesh

Real GDP per person
average annual growth rate

1971-75 1976-80 1981-85 1986-91 est

Adult literacy rates
0 % 20 40 60 80 100

Thailand
Sri Lanka
Vietnam
Philippines
China
India
Bangladesh

Foreign aid $bn

Commitments

Disbursements

1981 83 85 87 89 90

Sources: IMF; EIU; Human Development Report

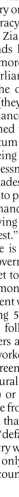

Rahman, the minister of finance, is doing or saying many of the right things: a value-added tax has been introduced; import tariffs are to be reduced (albeit slowly); and state enterprises are up for sale. For all the backsliding over wage rises and labour relations, Mr Rahman says Bangladesh is "absolutely on track" with every macroeconomic demand by the International Monetary Fund. But in the same breath he admits that his cabinet colleagues do not understand free markets: "The prime minister is my only supporter."

No wonder, then, that the privatisation programme, begun a decade ago under General Ershad, is virtually stalled; the state sector is hugely overmanned; and the country's development projects are delayed (not least because many potential bidders, having been publicly named on Mr Rahman's list of loan-defaulters, have decided to lie low). As the aid pipeline silts up through lack of efficiency and local matching funds, there is an obvious danger that foreign donors will become less generous to a country in which aid counts for about 7% of GDP.

But that danger is not critical. The pipeline is stuffed with over $5 billion in committed aid; any fresh disaster such as the cyclone a year ago (which killed 139,000 and revealed the new government's administrative inadequacies) would doubtless bring more.

The bigger danger is complacency. Today's assumption is that the army will stay in its barracks. Maybe. But democracy would be a lot more secure with a healthier economy. That means recognising Bangladesh's problems: one is that its labour costs are higher than Sri Lanka's (where GDP per person is 2.5 times higher); another is that it will soon face competition for investment and for markets from Vietnam. It then means accepting the medicine of free markets and economic reform. Unhappily, neither Mrs Zia nor Sheikh Hasina inspires confidence as a doctor.

The Afghans' nervous end-game

APRIL 25TH   *Afghanistan was once the battleground for a proxy war of the superpowers. When that war ended, with the collapse of the Soviet Union, it was up to the Afghans to make their own peace*

PUT on your rose-tinted spectacles and Afghanistan looks tantalisingly close to peace. Take them off and the country is teetering on the brink of a new war.

The regime of Muhammad Najibullah, installed by the Soviet Union six years ago, has collapsed three years later than expected, but more suddenly and less bloodily than most people had foreseen. Cities have fallen to the mujahideen guerrillas, who have formed a loose alliance with armed tribesmen and disaffected government troops. In Kabul a group of generals and ministers is ready to hand power to a mujahideen government.

However, a peaceful transfer of power is far from certain. Jealousies among the mujahideen and rivalry between the Pathans, the largest ethnic group, and the country's half-dozen minorities could still erupt into fighting.

Thanks to the support of Russia and to his own grip on the army, the tribal militias and the Khad secret police, Mr Najibullah was able to survive the withdrawal of Soviet troops in February 1989. But on December 31st last year Russia stopped supplying arms to the Kabul government. Although America also stopped its supplies to the mujahideen, they could still count on aid from Pakistan and Saudi Arabia. In January Mr Najibullah failed to crush an army mutiny in Hairatan. His generals began to doubt his durability, and prepared to switch horses.

The switching began in Afghanistan's second city, Mazar-i-Sharif, in March when Uzbek and Ismaili tribal militias (one of them led by Mr Najibullah's closest ally, General Abdul Rashid Dostam) joined forces with local mujahideen. Mr Najibullah's promise to step down at the end of April in favour of a stopgap government of 15 neutral Afghans assembled by the United Nations merely hastened his downfall. Government garrisons sought to protect themselves by making alliances with local mujahideen, with whom they often shared tribal or family ties.

They did so in Charikar on April 14th; at the Bagram air base north of Kabul on the 15th; in Herat and Kunduz on the 18th; in Kandahar, Samangan and several other places on the 19th. By the 23rd only Jalalabad and Kabul, the capital, remained in "government" hands, and both were negotiating terms of surrender.

Powerless to stop the defections, Mr Najibullah tried to flee during the night of April 15th. He was turned back at the airport by General Dostam's militia, and sought refuge in the UN office in Kabul. Benon Sevan, the UN special envoy to Afghanistan, tried to arrange for Mr Najibullah to join his family in Delhi, but by April 23rd had not succeeded. His departure was opposed both by the mujahideen and by some erstwhile supporters: the foreign minister, Abdul Wakil, said he should stand trial "as a traitor".

Ahmad Shah Masoud, the most successful of the mujahideen commanders, has emerged as the most powerful figure in the country. A Tajik, he belongs to the Jamiat-i-Islami guerrillas, who call for a mild sort of Islamic government in Afghanistan. The supposedly broadminded Mr Masoud leads the Islamic Jihad Council, a loose coalition of mujahideen and tribal groups that controls most of the (non-Pathan) north and west of the country. He also enjoys a fair amount of support among Pathans in the south and east, though that might turn to enmity if Mr Masoud tried to rule Afghanistan, a job that Pathans think is by tradition theirs. Mr Masoud is already opposed by Gulbuddin Hikmatyar, the leader of the Hizb-i-Islami and a fanatic who wants to run a radical Islamic government in Kabul.

Mr Hikmatyar's forces are deployed to the south of Kabul; he has threatened to attack the city unless it surrenders unconditionally by April 26th. His forces may not, however, be strong enough to carry out this threat (and his commanders may not obey any order to try). But, just in case, Mr Masoud, whose fighters are gathered to the north of Kabul, has sent men to guard Kabul's southern approaches against Mr Hikmatyar, a safeguard that will not still all the fears of the 2m Kabulis that their city is about to become a battleground.

In Kabul authority has been assumed by a group of generals and ministers under the nominal command of Abdul Rahim Hatif, who was Mr Najibullah's vice-president but not a member of Mr Najibullah's Homeland (ex-Communist) Party. The strongman of the group is the former deputy defence minister and Kabul garrison commander, General Nabi Azimi. On

April 19th Mr Hatif sent the foreign minister to negotiate with Mr Masoud in Charikar; on April 21st he offered to surrender the city to a mujahideen government in return for an amnesty, or guarantees of safe conduct, for members of the hated Khad and for senior figures in the Homeland Party. The implicit threat is that otherwise these well-armed people will turn a mujahideen entry into Kabul into a bloody fight to the finish.

Mr Masoud is apparently prepared to accept these terms, although some other mujahideen leaders (including Mr Hikmatyar) are said to be less merciful. For the moment, however, the issue is academic: Mr Hatif is offering to transfer power to an interim mujahideen government that is not yet formed.

Representatives of the mu-

jahideen groups have spent the best part of a week in Peshawar, in neighbouring Pakistan, trying to agree who should take part in the government and who should lead it. So far their efforts have been in vain, despite the encouragement of the Pakistani prime minister, Nawaz Sharif. Mr Masoud is an obvious choice for leader, but would probably not be acceptable to the Pathans. Mr Hikmatyar is demanding the lion's share of power in a mujahideen administration, prompting one of Mr Masoud's spokesmen to say that Mr Hikmatyar is "in danger of dealing himself out of the game".

And if the mujahideen do agree on a transitional government, what next? Mr Sevan, who had been trying for months to set up a broad-based interim government including representatives of all Afghan parties (mujahideen, the Kabul government, tribal chiefs and supporters of the exiled former king, Zahir Shah), now hopes that a stop-gap government of the mujahideen alone will hold a democratic election. But although Mr Masoud talks about "elections under UN supervision", he speaks in the same breath of "mujahideen government". Does that mean that nonmujahideen—be they nationalists, monarchists or leftists—would be barred as candidates? If so, Mr Masoud could be sowing the seeds of further conflict.

The ensuing months proved pessimists right as the victorious mujahideen turned to internecine warfare.

With him, chaos

MAY 9TH *The collapse of the Soviet Union was always likely to cause problems in Central Asia. Solutions were less obvious*

FOR a month the political conflict in Dushanbe, the capital of Tajikistan, was peaceful. The worst calamity was the smell as many thousands of opponents of the government squatted in the city centre, while nearby an equal number of government supporters were similarly encamped. This week the conflict turned violent. On May 5th, in a night of gun battles, the opposition took control of parts of the city and captured the television station and airport.

For a while the government held on to the radio station and the parliament building, but on May 7th jubilant eyewitnesses said President Rakhmon Nabiev had fled the capital.

Might this be a warning of what is to come in Central Asia now that the Soviet Union has broken up? Optimists say no. Tajikistan, they say, is unlike its neighbours. It is Persian-speaking. Other states speak Turkic languages. It is the place where the Islamic Renaissance Party (IRP) has made its biggest mark. Opponents of the Nabiev government are said to be a mix of Muslims and liberals. The president of neighbouring Uzbekistan says dismissively that "all sorts of strange things happen in Tajikistan". Yet the strange things may spread.

Islam in the region is represented by the Islamic Renaissance Party, which has never had contact with the secular authorities, and the larger "official" form of Islam,

The call for change

represented by Muslims once tolerated or supported by the government. The more serious challenge to the Tajikistan government probably came from the "official" lot. There is a similar challenge by moderate Muslims to the rulers in Uzbekistan. Both groups, IRP and "official", seek to avoid extremism; neither wants a Khomeini-style revolution. But both want changes in the government.

Despite the demise of communism elsewhere in the ex-Soviet Union, all Central Asian republics except Kirgizstan are ruled by former Communist bosses. Tajiki-stan's Mr Nabiev was appointed by Brezhnev and kicked out by Mikhail Gorbachev. He regained power in September and was confirmed in office in November, winning 58% of the vote on a platform of "without me, chaos". He then lost support by filling his government with cronies and favouring the north—not the south and west, where Islam is strong.

During this week's violence a desperate Mr Nabiev appealed for unity. "The homeland is in danger," he said. In the past the Communist regimes of Central Asia have been able to call on Soviet soldiers to put down riots, usually caused by ethnic differences and unemployment. Mr Nabiev and other rulers now know the dangers of being on their own.

Revolt of the rich

MAY 16TH, BANGKOK *The military has long dominated Thai politics. But the growing middle class is determined to send soldiers back to their barracks*

ONE thing Thais take seriously is *sanuk*, which means having fun. Good food, shopping and gossiping in the office are *sanuk*; politics usually is not. Hence the apathy that greeted the last military coup in February 1991. What then stirred 100,000 Thais to take to the streets of Bangkok for almost a week this month? The explanation lies in one of the biggest problems facing Thailand: the gulf between Bangkok and the rest of the country.

Bangkok and its surroundings account for almost three-quarters of Thailand's industrial production. Bangkok's GDP per person is ten times higher than that of Esarn, the poor north-east of the country, where a third of Thailand's 56m people live. While Bangkok is getting rich, rural Thailand remains poor, and has politics to match. Every Sunday morning in hundreds of provincial hotels the local fat cats, who may be members of parliament, or are in charge of a string of MPs, hand out brown paper envelopes to policemen and civil servants. At election time individual votes are bought. For millions of poor farmers, selling their vote makes sense.

At the other end of the spectrum are the people who demonstrated in Bangkok. Dressed in polo shirts and trainers, and often carrying video cameras, these represen-tatives of Bangkok's middle class demonstrated, and browsed among the food stalls, in an orderly fashion. They are fed up with being governed by corrupt politicians elected by peasants, or by generals.

The man who has convinced the middle class he offers an alternative is Chamlong Srimuang. A former major-general and former governor of Bangkok, Mr Chamlong led the Palang Dharma Party in the March general election and helped it win 32 of Bangkok's 35 seats.

In a city of conspicuous consumption, Mr Chamlong is an ascetic. He and his wife are vegetarians and celibates. Their wooden house has no television, air-conditioning or mattresses. While he was governor, Mr Chamlong lived on his army pension and gave his governor's salary to charity. After a government had been formed, led by General Suchinda Kraprayoon, the leader of last year's coup, Mr Chamlong announced that his MPs would not attend parliament. On May 4th he went on hunger strike.

The size of the demonstrations in support of Mr Chamlong clearly rattled the army, which tried to block television and radio broadcasts of them, thus drawing more crowds keen to see what was happening. On May 9th, with the momentum be-hind Mr Chamlong's protest apparently irresistible, the government coalition and the opposition parties agreed to amend the constitution so that prime ministers must henceforth be elected. Mr Chamlong ended his hunger strike, and two days later told the demonstrators to go home. He may have feared that otherwise the army would use guns to clear the streets. Or he may have felt that the protests would obstruct Buddhist celebrations being held this week. Mr Chamlong is a member of the radical Santi Asoke sect, which General Suchinda claims wants to establish a new national religion in Thailand.

Mr Chamlong may just have decided that his movement needed a breathing-space. He says street protests will start again on May 17th and will continue if the governing coalition reneges on its commitment to amend the constitution.

Will it? General Suchinda is stubborn. However, his first month in office has not been a happy experience. He may even have been telling the truth when he told reporters on May 12th, "On learning that there is an initiative to amend the constitution I am delighted, although I may have to lose my position as a result." If he lives up to his words, Bangkok's middle classes will have scored a significant victory.

....

General Suchinda resigned on May 24th after his troops had shot scores of unarmed demonstrators.

Salt of the earth

JUNE 27TH *Three-fifths of the world's 5 billion people live in Asia, which has only a fifth of the world's arable land. Will irrigation help grow enough food?*

ASIA faces a dilemma. Farms in India, Pakistan, north-western China and Soviet Central Asia are rapidly becoming barren as the salt dissolved in irrigation water is dumped on the land. With the population soaring over the next few decades, these countries cannot simply abandon their farms. But neither can they afford the reclamation that is needed.

Unlike rainwater, which is usually pure, all water from irrigation contains dissolved salt. As it evaporates, this water leaves its salt behind on the surface, where it gradually accumulates. If there is enough irrigation water to wash salt out of the top-soil, it will flow into rivers or, if there are none, into the water table instead. Because there is no natural drainage on Asia's plains, where many farms are, this irrigation water becomes trapped in the water table, which rises. Eventually the top of the water table is close enough to the soil surface for evaporation to draw water up, depositing the salt it contains among the roots of growing crops. That spells tragedy.

Not immediately. Salination is slow to show, especially if salt-tolerant crops such as cotton are planted. But after a few decades during which a yearly dose of several tonnes of salt has been dumped on each

Poor soil, poor Pakistan

hectare, the land will have become desert—much as it was before irrigation first made it fertile as part of Asia's Green Revolution. Not so long ago research suggested that the world was losing 100,000 hectares (250,000 acres) of farmland a year to salt; more recent research puts the loss at more like 1.5m hectares a year.

The process of salination has long been understood. The first large irrigation schemes in the Indian subcontinent, carried out by the British in the 19th century, showed signs of salination as early as the 1930s. Even as irrigation projects went ahead in the 1960s, it was recognised that further investment in drainage would eventually be needed, so that groundwater could carry away the salt. But the investment has been too little, and too late.

At the end of the 1950s Pakistan began to sink wells to pump water out of the salt-laden water table in areas where it had risen to the surface. Nevertheless, in Sindh province almost half the area surveyed at the end of the 1970s was saline. Pakistani academics say that more than 260,000 wells have been sunk, but as fast as one field is reclaimed, another is lost.

Moreover, the effort is expensive. Between 1971 and 1985 the cost of managing Pakistan's wells and canals increased tenfold. It now costs five times as much to construct adequate drainage as it does to irrigate in the first place. Already, Pakistan spends far more on reclaiming land than on irrigating it. Other investment, in roads and bridges and education, for example,

A pinch too much		
Mid-1980s	Saline land, hectares m	As % of irrigated land
India	20.0	36
China	7.0	15
United States	5.2	20
Pakistan	3.2	27
Soviet Union	2.5	12
World	**60.2**	**24**

Source: FAO

has a stronger call on government money than invisible drainage that may not produce a benefit for several years.

The World Bank, the United Nations Development Programme and the International Commission on Irrigation and Drainage between them last year created an organisation with the catchy name of the International Programme for Technology Research in Irrigation and Drainage. This month it set up a help-line, on which scientists and engineers can consult each other. It is none too soon. While parts of Asia turn into desert, its farmers will have an extra 1.8 billion mouths to feed by 2025.

Where Hong Kong has the edge

AUGUST 22ND, HONG KONG *The cities of Hong Kong and Singapore are perennial rivals—in economic activity and social style. Will their competition eventually show one to be a winner, and the other a loser?*

ONE of the most momentous and least understood events of this half-century is East Asia's rise from poverty. The high rates of economic growth consistently achieved over decades by the Asian tigers—Hong Kong, Singapore, Taiwan and South Korea—have almost no equal anywhere at any time. Growth theory has trouble explaining this. The difficulty is compounded by the wide divergence in circumstances and economic policies of the four countries. Alwyn Young, a business professor at the Massachusetts Institute of Technology, has written a paper* looking at how Hong Kong and Singapore did it. If his analysis is right, it augurs ill for Singapore in the next decade or two.

Hong Kong and Singapore started on a similar footing in 1945. Both were city-states, British colonies (with a British legal and administrative system) making their living as trading ports. Neither manufactured much. Both were populated mainly with immigrants from southern China.

In 1960 the two territories had roughly the same GDP per head, which over the following quarter-century grew at an astonishing and virtually identical 6% a year in

real terms. Both were free traders, allowing foreign goods and money to flow where they would. Both climbed the same industrial ladder, moving up from textiles to plastics to consumer electronics to financial services.

There were two crucial differences. First, Hong Kong, its population luckily swollen by sophisticated Shanghainese refugees from Communist China, had a

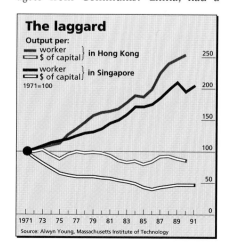

The laggard
Output per:
▬ worker ⎱ in Hong Kong
▭ $ of capital⎰ in Hong Kong
▬ worker ⎱ in Singapore
▭ $ of capital⎰ in Singapore
1971=100

1971 73 75 77 79 81 83 85 87 89 91
Source: Alwyn Young, Massachusetts Institute of Technology

vastly better educated population than Singapore's until well into the 1980s. Second, Hong Kong had a laisser-faire government (to the point of not investing even in needed infrastructure until street riots forced it to); Singapore had an extremely interventionist one.

The government decided which industries Singapore should go into and when. Through its Central Provident Fund levies on companies and workers, it compelled private savings of around 40% of GDP. Through state-owned companies and boards the government channelled much of these savings, as well as its large excess of current tax revenues over current spending, into investment it favoured. It welcomed, indeed heavily subsidised, direct investment by foreign multinationals.

The sources of growth in the two territories turned out to be startlingly different. Between 1960 and 1985 Hong Kong saved and invested a more or less consistent 20% of GDP. Singapore, which in 1960 invested half as much as Hong Kong, surpassed it in 1967 and has invested a larger share ever since: by the late 1980s Singapore's investment as a share of GDP was more than 40%, more than twice Hong Kong's rate.

In the two decades after 1970, Hong Kong's output per worker went up more than 2½ times, Singapore's a little more than twofold. Not much difference there. However, Hong Kong's output per unit of capital stayed roughly constant over the 20 years; Singapore's was more than halved (see chart on previous page).

The alarm bells about Singapore's use (or misuse) of capital keep ringing louder. By the mid-1980s Singapore's incremental capital-output ratio—meaning how much extra capital was needed to produce an additional unit of output—was twice Hong Kong's. As you would expect from an ever-increasing use of capital, Singapore's return on capital, which in the early 1960s had been 40%, by the late 1980s had fallen to 11-12%, one of the lowest rates in the world.

Most damning of all, Mr Young finds that over the two decades after 1970, 56% of Hong Kong's increase in output per worker came from a rise in "total factor productivity" (how much can be produced by combining given units of land, labour and capital). Singapore's total factor productivity fell by 6% over those years: in other words, 106% of Singapore's growth in output came from adding capital. To put it crudely, Hong Kong got richer by becoming a lot more efficient in the way it used people, capital and technology. Singapore became richer by thrusting its hands ever deeper into its citizens' pockets—through taxes, forced savings and subsidies to multinationals—and throwing the money at the

problem.

Economic-growth buffs will find it interesting that Hong Kong seemed to benefit so much from the better education of its people. For Singapore, however, Mr Young's analysis has a gruesome and more or less immediate practical implication. If he is right, Singapore has very few years of growth left along the old lines: it simply cannot extract much more savings from its people—already the biggest savers in the world—to support its growing craving for capital. Mr Young's cruel comparison is with the Soviet Union, which turned in respectable growth rates from the 1930s to the 1960s by pouring on the capital. Everyone knows what happened after that.

Changing partners

AUGUST 29TH, BEIJING, SEOUL AND TAIPEI

Alliances in Asia were once a product of the cold war—so with the cold war over it was not surprising that they should change

RATTING on old friends is part of innovative policy-making, as China and South Korea demonstrated this week. These two countries established diplomatic relations on August 24th. In doing so China turned its back on North Korea, a fellow authoritarian state with which "in blood-cemented friendship" it fought shoulder to shoulder in the Korean war. South Korea cut its links with Taiwan, for decades its capitalist friend and trading partner.

That said, the event did not come as a total surprise. The two countries set up trade offices in each other's capitals last

year. Two-way trade amounted to nearly $6 billion last year and is expected to rise to around $10 billion this year. China now tends to regard North Korea as it would a rather potty and embarrassing relative who is always asking for money. The South's high technology and wealth is a far more attractive prospect. China is now the third most popular place for South Korean investment after Thailand and Indonesia.

Even ratting, when applied internationally, requires some concession to diplomacy. China is believed to have spent a lot of time trying to persuade North Korea that, in a changing world, recognition of the South was necessary. It may have argued that the reunification of Korea, which both countries constantly demand, could be hastened with the help of a China friendly to both sides. A Chinese foreign ministry spokesman said this week that it would continue to have "good-neighbourly, friendly and cooperative relations" with the North.

Still, it was a hard blow for the North to take, already abandoned by the countries of the former Soviet Union. Until now it has been comforted by the fact that on Chinese maps South Korea was not even marked as a country. When the North's leader, Kim Il Sung, visited Beijing last year the entire Chinese leadership lined up on the railway platform to greet him. After all, Mao's son had died fighting for the North in the Korean war. Now that is all nostalgia. There is not much comfort in the hard-up Stalinist

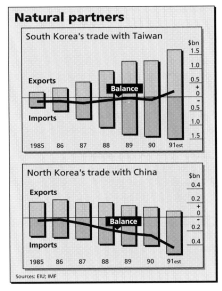

Natural partners

South Korea's trade with Taiwan

North Korea's trade with China

Sources: EIU; IMF

North at the moment.

At least North Korea was given advance warning of the blow to come. That politeness does not seem to have been extended by South Korea to Taiwan. Last week Taiwan got wind of the deal and made it public. Even at that stage South Korea dismissed the report as an old rumour. When the truth came out Taiwan was vitriolic in its condemnation of the deal, which, it said, "violated our trust and trampled on international justice". In Taipei protesters threw eggs at the South Korean embassy and trampled on the Korean flag. Cannily, Taiwan put in hand plans to sell its embassy building in Seoul, just in case China took it over.

South Korea was Taiwan's last formal diplomatic ally in Asia. In sealing its deal with China, South Korea has had to accept the official Chinese line that Taiwan is not a country, let alone the "real China", but is

Bad eggs, says Taiwan

merely a Chinese province in rebellion.

Taiwan will survive the setback, albeit its worst for many years. "Fortunately, we still have some money in our pocket," President Lee Teng-hui said in the understatement of the week.

Taiwan is rich. Its foreign currency reserves of more than $86 billion are the largest in the world. Rich people usually find friends. Taiwan can still claim diplomatic relations with 29 countries, although many are small ones. Its most recent catch was Niger, acquired in June, and it accorded its prime minister a 19-gun salute on his arrival in Taipei last week. More important, Taiwan has trade ties with almost every

country. President Lee said Taiwan was setting up "an international aid fund" to help the country's "flexible foreign policy". No doubt there will be plenty of applicants.

China can only gain from the deal. Apart from tapping South Korean resources it will continue to get investment from Taiwan. The Taiwanese government has declined to criticise China over the deal. In South Korea, President Roh Tae Woo was chided for his "unethical" act against an old friend. But Koreans feel a bit safer now that their huge neighbour, once an enemy, is officially a friend.

The main question that the deal has

thrown up is what its effect will be on North Korea. A possible danger is that its increased sense of isolation may make it do something silly. It is believed to be close to making a nuclear weapon. On the other hand, it has opened its nuclear plants to international inspection. Diplomatic ties with the United States and Japan, which it wants, and which would lead to economic aid, depend on acceptable behaviour. Some hint of the North's thinking following the China deal was awaited with interest by its neighbours. But amid the flow of comment from the rest of the area, there was not a sound, not even a moan, from the North.

The fire this time

OCTOBER 10TH, OSAKA *Few people associate Japan with social unrest—but not even successful Japan could avoid the effects of a slowing economy*

IT MAY not be south-central Los Angeles, but the Airin district of Osaka—home for vagrants, alcoholics and ex-convicts—is the nearest thing in Japan to a smouldering ghetto. This month it caught fire for three days when a welfare office closed on October 1st after running out of cash for handouts. Some 700 angry locals ran wild, burning cars and smashing bicycles when baton-wielding police moved in to disperse a demonstration. By the weekend 1,500 riot police had been drafted into the area.

With its 35,000 residents, Airin is the largest slum in Japan (followed by the Sanya district in Tokyo). Since mid-September, Osaka's municipal government

had been doling out ¥2,000 ($17) a day to the neighbourhood's needy—enough, just, for a meal and a night in a local flophouse. Nine out of ten of Airin's male population are casual workers, hired by the day by local gangsters for work on building sites. With bankruptcies spreading throughout the building trade, the number of Airin's residents applying for help had swollen from a few dozen a day a month ago to almost 1,000 a day by last week. By October 1st the centre's meagre ¥7m ($58,000) fund had been exhausted—and the hungry took to the streets.

People hanging around Airin's littered streets fear the cops—with their 24-hour surveillance cameras on street corners—

even more than they do the local gangsters. Two years ago the spark for a week of rioting was corruption among the local police. A police sergeant had been sacked for taking bribes from gangland bosses for tipping them off whenever raids were planned. When word got out, a mob of some 1,600 people attacked the police station, set fire to the local railway station and looted shops. They were quelled only when 2,500 police, equipped with water cannon, were rushed to the area.

This year's rumpus was a stroll in the park by comparison. But the recession in the building industry has barely begun—and Osaka, Japan's third biggest city, has more vulnerable construction projects under way than anywhere else in the country. By next autumn Airin could be burning again.

A new man for the Blue House

NOVEMBER 7TH, SEOUL *Politics in South Korea has traditionally been a violent affair of riots and petrol bombs. But traditions change: it seems that under the government of Roh Tae Woo democracy was at last accepted*

NEXT month South Korea's voters will elect a new president, and for the first time in recent history he will not have a general's uniform hanging in his wardrobe. Do not assume, however, that their civilian choice will enjoy a carefree tenure: whoever, come February, inherits the presidential Blue House from Roh Tae Woo will take charge of a nation worried by its slowing economy yet eager for a costly reunification with the communist North.

The presidential campaign, barely started, already looks likely to be a race between Kim Young Sam, the candidate of the ruling Democratic Liberal Party (DLP),

and Kim Dae Jung, an opposition veteran who leads the Democratic Party (DP) and is making what is almost certainly his last plausible bid for the presidency. It would, however, have been more plausible still if Kim Woo Choong, the founder and chairman of the Daewoo conglomerate, had agreed to stand on behalf of the New (brand new) Korea Party. The reason is that the industrialist might have taken middle-class voters away from the government's candidate. Instead, perhaps pressed by President Roh, he declined the party's informal offer on October 29th, one day after his qualified Yes.

Whatever the odds, any contest between the two remaining Kims is likely to be bruising. Both are brave, having opposed the generals in the bad old days. But both are proud and stubborn. In 1987, when South Korea was on the brink of chaos, neither man would step aside to allow the other to be the "pro-democracy" candidate in the presidential election. The consequence was to allow Mr Roh, a former general, to become the handpicked presidential successor to the dictatorial Chun Doo Hwan.

In the event, the pro-democracy movement was lucky. History will probably judge Mr Roh more generously than most South Koreans do at present. Mr Roh has resisted the temptation to match his predecessor's style. Indeed, if anything, it is Mr

Roh presides; Dae Jung and Young Sam prepare

Roh who has edged the armed forces to the sidelines, although the generals are bound to remain a political force as long as the country is on a war footing against the North.

But though the permanence of democracy is no longer an issue in South Korea, its form is still unclear. The real question is whether in politics the country's industrialists will take the place of its generals. The answer will depend in part on the electoral fortunes next month of Chung Ju Yung, the rich patriarch of Hyundai, South Korea's largest *chaebol*, or conglomerate.

Mr Chung's Unification National Party, formed only last February, fared unexpectedly well in elections last March to the National Assembly, taking 31 of the 299 seats. Not bad for a fledgling. The National Assembly, however, holds little power. It is one thing for the middle classes to lodge a protest vote over their economic worries,

another to elect a political novice—shades of Ross Perot—to the presidency, no matter how strong his business credentials.

But Mr Chung could still hold the key in a tight election, and all the more so if the New Korea Party is also able to field a businessman candidate. If the key turned against Mr Kim Young Sam, it would not be on ideological grounds (Mr Kim Dae Jung has virtually the same platform as Mr Kim Young Sam), but because he is now the ruling party's man. He alienated many of his traditional supporters in 1990 by merging his party with President Roh's to form the Democratic Liberal Party.

In compensation, however, Mr Kim Young Sam reckons he will collect the conservative vote that in 1987 went to Mr Roh. In that election the president won 37% of the poll. By contrast, Mr Kim Young Sam took 28% and Mr Kim Dae Jung 27%.

The calculation may well be correct.

South Korea is an innately conservative society. As one election committee member of the Democratic Liberal Party puts it: "The people want change but they also want stability. Kim Young Sam represents both."

Not everything, however, is going Kim Young Sam's way. The DLP was modelled on Japan's Liberal Democratic Party in the apparent hope that it will match the LDP's longevity, but it also shares the Japanese party's vulnerability to factional splits.

The nucleus of the New Korea Party, for example, is drawn from DLP defectors. Also floating around dangerously is a former DLP power-broker, Park Tae Joon. Mr Park, formerly chairman of the Posco steel company, has refused overtures from the new party. But he is known to have harboured presidential ambitions and he could still pose a threat.

Meanwhile, it is ironic that Mr Kim Young Sam is the most vulnerable to the vote-splitting by the industrialists, since the DLP is big business's friend. Mr Kim Dae Jung, in contrast, mistrusts the industrial elite. If he became president, he might well fulfil his campaign pledge to distribute more widely the country's financial power, and the political power that goes with it.

On December 18th Kim Young Sam was elected with 42% of the vote; Chung Ju Yung got 16%; Kim Dae Jung received 34%—and the next day retired

A question of health

NOVEMBER 21ST, SINGAPORE   *For many years Singapore has run smoothly along the course prescribed by Lee Kuan Yew. But even the best laid plans of Mr Lee can sometimes go awry*

STABLE government has long been one of Singapore's biggest selling points. So it was hardly surprising that its stockmarket got the jitters when it was announced that Lee Hsien Loong, widely assumed to be Singapore's prime minister in waiting, has cancer.

On November 16th rumours of Mr Lee's illness had pushed the stockmarket down 2¼%. When a government statement was issued later in the day, it turned out that Ong Teng Cheong, a deputy prime minister like Mr Lee, also had cancer. Mr Lee's case, however, is more serious, if not medically then at least politically.

Fortunately, Mr Lee, who is undergo-

ing chemotherapy, is given a 90% chance of a complete cure. The present prime minister, Goh Chok Tong, has ruled out any immediate changes in the country's political leadership as "premature"—a statement that seems to have reasssured the stockmarket.

The whole scare, however, has renewed the fear that Singapore's stability rests on a political dynasty as much as a political system. Mr Lee is the 40-year-old son of modern Singapore's founding father, Lee Kuan Yew. Father and son (and mother) took first-class degrees at Cambridge University. When the elder Mr Lee stepped down two years ago, after 31 years in office, Mr

Goh took over. But most Singaporeans decided that Mr Goh was simply keeping the prime minister's seat warm until Lee *fils* was ready to take over the job. It is noticeable that the brightest lights in the ruling People's Action Party have tended to gather around the young Mr Lee, rather than Mr Goh.

Mr Goh himself has referred to Mr Lee as "my natural successor" and has talked of handing over power to him, perhaps at the end of the decade. But setbacks for the ruling party in last year's general election had led to speculation that Mr Lee might take over much sooner than that; hence the interest in by-elections due next March. Some believed that, if the party were to lose seats, Mr Goh might step aside in favour of Mr Lee. That may now have to wait.

A driving force

JULY 18TH **The 55m overseas Chinese are one of the world's great economic engines. They will become greater still as they pull forward China itself**

AS EARLY as the 17th century, European travellers described the Chinese living in South-East Asia as being like Jews. The parallels are many: long exile from a mother country to which a deep cultural attachment nonetheless persists, apartness at best and genocide at worst in many of the adoptive countries, a strong commercial bent. The difference is the mother country. Israel matters only because it slots into the interests of greater forces. China is a giant that could dominate the 21st century.

If so, the overseas Chinese—ethnic Chinese living outside China—will have had a big hand in the proceedings. This seems odd. Even if the 21m in Taiwan and 6m in Hong Kong are included, they number only 55m. They are politically powerless in most of the dozen Asian lands and handful of western ones through which they are sprinkled. How can they drive the modernisation of a poverty-ridden continental power with a population of 1.2 billion?

The first answer is that they command resources far beyond their numbers. Of Asia's four "tigers"—the poor world's fastest developers over the past 30 years—only South Korea is not Chinese. Almost all the citizens of Taiwan and Hong Kong are Chinese. So are three-quarters of Singaporeans. Another four South-East Asian countries have ambitions (of varying degrees of plausibility) to follow in the tigers' pawsteps. All four—Malaysia, Thailand, Indonesia and the Philippines—have Chinese minorities that account for an astonishing share of their economies.

Quite what that share is can only be guessed at. But all the guesses point the same way. A study of Indonesia in the mid-1980s reckoned that, of assets owned neither by foreigners nor by the government, 70-75% belonged to ethnic Chinese. A more recent study found that Indonesian Chinese, 4% of the population, controlled 17 of the 25 biggest business groups.

An observer of Thailand in the mid-1970s reckoned that ethnic Chinese, 8-10% of the population, owned 90% of commercial and manufacturing assets, and half the capital of the banks. The Philippines, no tiger yet, still has the stripes of one. Fewer than 1% of people in the Philippines are pure Chinese, but Chinese-owned companies account for two-thirds of the sales of the 67 biggest commercial outfits. Chinese dominate the smaller companies even more.

Malaysia's Chinese, who make up around a third of the population, have a much larger share of economic power than that. The Malay-controlled government tried for 20 years to whittle this down by forcing the transfer (often faked) of Chinese-owned company shares to Malays. Last year it threw up its hands, in practice if not in

principle. Too much investment was being lost to more hospitable Asian destinations, including China itself.

Overall, one conservative estimate puts the 1990 "GNP" of Asia's 51m overseas Chinese, Taiwan and Hong Kong included, at $450 billion—a quarter bigger than China's then GNP, and, per head, at about 80% of the level of Spain or Israel.

This performance rests on sturdy foundations. The Chinese are prodigious savers and investors. In the Chinese parts of Asia, savings rates run at 25-45% of GNP. The reasons are diverse: an ancient habit of laying aside money against frequent calamities, the high real interest rates available through informal Chinese networks, low income-tax rates, non-existent taxes on savings. The result is one of the world's deepest pools of liquid capital. Taiwan, with only 21m people, has foreign-exchange reserves of $83 billion. Bank deposits alone in Taiwan exceed $300 billion; add in gold and deposits in the underground financial system and the figure for ready capital is at least twice that.

Worldwide, the overseas Chinese probably hold liquid assets (not including securities) worth $1.5 trillion-2 trillion. For a rough comparison, in Japan, with about twice as many people, bank deposits in 1990 totalled $3 trillion.

The diaspora

This capital has been accumulated and is deployed through a distinctive form of social and business organisation. One Chinese writer described Japanese society as a block of granite and Chinese society as a tray of sand. Each grain in the tray is not an individual but a family. They are held together not, as in America, by law, government and public ideals, nor, as in Japan, by a concept of national solidarity, but by personal acquaintance, trust and obligation.

That was already true in China itself; it was intensified by the experience of the Chinese diaspora. The successive waves of emigration which, over the past 600 years, have carried people out of China often deposited them in places, or under circumstances (as in Hong Kong and Taiwan after 1949), where they felt besieged.

Except in Malaysia, the formal discrimination of the old days has disappeared. But

The diaspora	
Ethnic Chinese in:	**m**
Indonesia	7.2
Thailand	5.8
Malaysia	5.2
Singapore	2.0
Burma	1.5
Vietnam	0.8
Philippines	0.8
Rest of Asia and Australasia	1.8
United States	1.8
Canada	0.6
Latin America	1.0
Europe	0.6
Africa	0.1

Source: Overseas Chinese Economy Yearbook

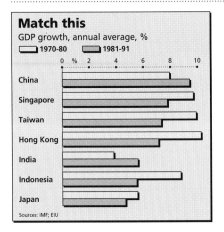

Match this

GDP growth, annual average, %

☐ 1970-80   ▨ 1981-91

China
Singapore
Taiwan
Hong Kong
India
Indonesia
Japan

Sources: IMF; EIU

Match that

Gross domestic savings, as % of GDP, 1991

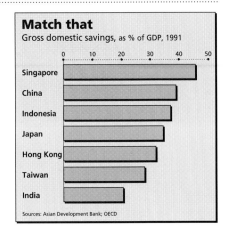

Singapore
China
Indonesia
Japan
Hong Kong
Taiwan
India

Sources: Asian Development Bank; OECD

makers who fled from communism to Hong Kong in the late 1940s and gave the British colony its first industrial boom. But most have come from southern China. By one reckoning, more than half of the entire diaspora can be traced to just two provinces, Guangdong, next to Hong Kong, and Fujian, across the strait from Taiwan.

Wary of governments and laws, the Chinese found that dialect, kinship, a common origin in a clan, a village or (at a pinch) a county gave a sure footing of trust for a business deal conducted even at great distance. However widely separated in the diaspora, Hakka tended to deal with Hakka, Chiu Chownese with Chiu Chownese. The certainty this gave and the informality it allowed shaped the loftiest transactions as well as the most humble. In the days when Taiwan had strict foreign exchange controls, it was possible (as it still is) for someone to deposit a large sum with a gold shop in Taipei and for a relative to withdraw the equivalent next day from an affiliated gold shop in Hong Kong.

The family rules

The knots in this worldwide net are family-owned firms. Even in listed companies, the founding family's control and accumulation of capital are principal aims; lines of authority are drawn to serve these aims. This accounts for the autocratic, "father-knows-best" management methods for which Chinese firms are famous.

It also explains the obsession with bringing younger family members into the firm: they can be expected to safeguard family interests. The sense of obligation is surprisingly strong. Heirs who have become doctors or physicists in America are summoned home to take over the family firm on the death of the founder. Even to-

as recently as 1960, 90,000 ethnic Chinese fled Indonesia over a three-month period fearing for their lives; five years later, at least 500,000 Indonesians, many of them ethnic Chinese, were slaughtered after the overthrow of President Sukarno.

Despite much intermarriage in Thailand, Indonesia and the Philippines, ethnic awareness there is never far below the surface. Thai Chinese, almost all of whom have Thai names and mixed blood, and few of whom speak a word of Chinese, assure visitors that assimilation is complete. Yet one Thai Chinese businessman, when asked to scrutinise a list of 100 top Thai business families, immediately identifies which are Chinese and which (only a handful of them) are not.

One way a rich but politically vulnerable minority can protect itself is by making mutually beneficial (and sometimes corrupt) bargains with those in power. Joint ventures between Chinese businesses and government enterprises, ruling parties, military interests and presidents' families are not uncommon in South-East Asia.

However, the main response of the overseas Chinese has been to avoid government and its nuisances (especially tax) as much as possible. Except in Singapore, which has an unusually intrusive government, this has been as true of countries with Chinese majorities as of those with Chinese minorities. The result has been a highly decentralised business structure based on secretive, entrepreneurial, family-owned firms that are run autocratically but co-operate smoothly and informally with each other, often across national borders which, for these purposes, might as well not exist.

The ties of kinship

The global network through which money, goods, ideas and occasionally people flow from one firm to another has been made possible by a peculiarity of the Chinese diaspora. Many of today's overseas Chinese originated in Shanghai, notably the textile-

day, they come. There is, as yet, no sign of the now familiar western pattern of founding families becoming coupon clippers, as they hand things over to professional managers and institutional investors.

Many of the biggest Chinese firms, like Li Ka-shing's empire in Hong Kong and Charoen Pokphand in Thailand, have successfully incorporated professional managers, but never at the cost of diluting family control. The most sweeping, and amusing, demonstration of the power of the family idea was the careful carve-up by Y.K. Pao, a Hong Kong shipping and property magnate, of his enormous empire before his death. His four sons-in-law—one a Shanghai-descended Hong Kong businessman, one an Austrian businessman, one a Singaporean-Chinese doctor, the last a Japanese architect—were each given a piece of the business to run.

The high, market-set real interest rates which (together with low taxes) encouraged the family firms' capital accumulation also helped to shape the structure of the overseas-Chinese economy. Throughout the Chinese diaspora—including North America and other remote outposts—there is a single informal market for capital. With none of the government allocation of low-interest credit that created (for example) South Korea's industrial behemoths, overseas-Chinese businesses have tended to be relatively small.

This has not stopped the occasional giant from popping up. The companies owned by Liem Sioe Liong's family are thought to account for 5% of Indonesia's GDP. Taiwan boasts a dozen billionaire families controlling large conglomerates, Hong Kong nearly as many. But these are merely the highest features in a wide landscape where thousands of small firms rise swiftly to success, fall and are replaced.

Problems of succession

A business system based on a multitude of autocratically owner-managed firms with intimate links to others like them has two big advantages: fast decision-making and

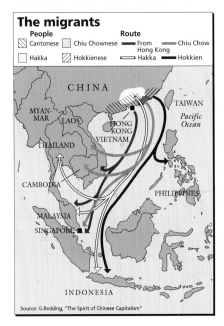

The migrants

People
☒ Cantonese   ☐ Chiu Chownese   ━ From Hong Kong   ▨ Chiu Chow
☐ Hakka   ▨ Hokkienese   ▭ Hakka   ━ Hokkien

Source: G.Redding, "The Spirit of Chinese Capitalism"

acute sensitivity to markets. The disadvantages are institutional. As the firm gets bigger, it will eventually outgrow the overseas Chinese network for the partners and capital it needs. How will decisions be made when personal connections cannot be relied on? How can the firm possibly be run by one or at most a handful of people, once it passes a certain size? How can a succession be achieved? Sons do not always have the founding father's touch.

Does this mean that, in a generation or two, Chinese firms will of necessity start to resemble the more institutionalised companies of the West, Japan or Korea? Some changes are already visible. Victor Fung, the chairman of Prudential Asia Capital and a scion of a Hong Kong business family, says that the days are gone when deals were done solely on the basis of a common birthplace or ancestor. Another network, that of second-generation overseas Chinese who got MBAS at the same American universities, is beginning to overlie the first.

The return of sons and nephews with MBAS is bringing at least an awareness of more systematic management to family firms. So too is the growing number of non-family, often expatriate, professional managers, especially in Hong Kong. But such things have brought no fundamental change. Nobody in Hong Kong imagines that the Stanford education of Li Ka-shing's two sons, both in their 20s, has much to do with their recently being given pieces of the Li empire to run, or with how they will be handling those businesses. Even those who foresee a sort of westernisation coming in, through the reluctance of heirs to put in the 16-hour days that their fathers did, cannot imagine families allowing their interest in a company to be reduced below 35-40%.

This means that both the size of the Chinese firms and the lines of business they go into could be limited. One observer who thinks so is Gordon Redding, a business professor at the University of Hong Kong. He points out that the businesses in which the overseas Chinese have done best—trading, property, commodities, shipping, mining, timber—are lines in which, even on a global scale, an instinct for the right price, time and place counts for more than complex management skills. One man can still make the important decisions on his own. An interesting test of a Chinese company's ability to move beyond this familiar ground will be Li Ka-shing's telecommunications and satellite-television ventures.

Yet why exactly, Mr Redding asks, should one expect the overseas-Chinese system to change? It may pose a problem for the individual firm, constrained by an inability to grow beyond a certain size or to arrange a smooth succession. But as a system, with entrepreneurial firms coming and going in quick response to market pressures, it works fine. The conditions that created it—the low-tax, high-interest, mostly little-regulated business environment—are still largely unchanged. If that continues, so may the ways of Chinese business.

Going home

Indeed, the old ways are being given a boost by the opening of a great new opportunity for the overseas Chinese: China itself. However distressing China's politics may be, the overseas Chinese have always felt the cultural, linguistic and often familial pull of the place they came from. "The family spirit elevated to national scale" is how one Hong Kong businessman puts it. Deng Xiaoping has managed to cultivate this spirit among the overseas Chinese, and it has already borne much fruit in the form of universities, hospitals and high-risk investments provided for the mainland by overseas-Chinese businessmen.

Now there is much more. Mr Deng's reformist policies have enabled China to enjoy one of the world's fastest rates of economic growth over the past 15 years. His recent go-for-broke push for a market economy promises even better.

The most striking element of the Dengist reforms—and the likely reason for their success—is their extraordinary dependence on foreign trade and foreign investment as engines of development. Foreign trade is now equivalent to more than a third of China's GDP. Foreign direct investment is pouring in: $11 billion in commitments last year, as much in the first half of this year. Probably uniquely, private foreign investment is even being used as a main way of building up infrastructure.

Though Japan is China's biggest source of foreign loans, far the largest part of direct investment is coming from the overseas Chinese. Hong Kong and Taiwan together account for two-thirds of the direct-investment flows. The Chinese of South-East Asia add another 10-15%. And it is direct foreign investment—with the technology, management skills and export potential that it brings—which is really transforming China's economy.

The investment is arriving through familiar channels. The overseas Chinese have started by doing business with people, provinces and even villages they are connected with.

Four-fifths of Hong Kong's investments have been going into neighbouring Guangdong province, where four-fifths of Hongkongers have relations. Most of Taiwan's money goes to Fujian. If the political hostility between Taiwan and the mainland makes this seem surprising, recall that the Chinese diaspora developed its particular methods of doing business not least to ensure that politics did not get in the way.

Western and Japanese firms can only watch enviously as the overseas Chinese exploit their contacts to snap up the safest and best of the opportunities which, by the estimate of one Hong Kong banker, yield average returns four times higher than investments in South-East Asia. China, for its part, enjoys a development resource that Russia, with essentially no ethnic Russian businessmen overseas, can only dream about, and India (with 11m overseas Indians) can only partially copy. If the recent enthusiasm of the overseas Chinese is anything to go by, the transnational Chinese economy, which in some ways already rivals Japan as a business influence in Asia, is poised for a great leap forward.

Or try capitalism. It's Chinese and it works

Contents

INTERNATIONAL

Novelty and nastiness

FOR many parts of the world it was a horrible year, a miserable half-way station between the ending of an old system and the beginning of a new one. The system that ended was the cold war, and its passing was a blessing. But in 1992 the new order had not yet come: not, at any rate, to millions of people in the developing world. There, too many unfinished conflicts, and too many fresh ones, overwhelmed hopes of peace and prosperity.

If one image summed up this year of disappointment it was those fragile black figures drawing themselves hopelessly in the Horn of Africa towards the latest rumour of food. Nobody really knows how many people starved to death in Somalia during 1992, but over the course of the year the total number of deaths probably climbed to 300,000. During the cold war the empty Horn had been deemed to possess immense geopolitical significance. This enabled Siad Barre, Somalia's dictator, to play the United States and the Soviet Union in counterpoint. When the cold war collapsed, so did he; and so, disastrously, did Somalia itself.

Clan fighting, too fractious and disorganised to be described as a civil war, tipped the country into anarchy. The world sent food, but men with guns stole it. The United Nations sent guards, but they were brushed aside by the warring clans. The Americans organised an airlift, but by the end of the year some 80% of the life-saving food was being pillaged before it could reach the starving. In mid-December therefore, under UN auspices, American marines stormed into a glare of television lights at Mogadishu, to intimidate the local warriors and oversee the relief effort. Nobody official said so, but Somalia's soverignty had in effect been abridged, and the country placed under the wardship of the UN.

The horror in Somalia was unique, or at least uniquely visible. It was far from being the only place where the old rules of national sovereignty were beginning to break down, and where the UN seemed in danger of being sucked into unfamiliar and sometimes dangerous new roles. In Yugoslavia and Cambodia, 1992 was the year in which the world body mounted some of its biggest peacekeeping operations. It tried, on a smaller scale, to oversee the end of civil wars in El Salvador, Angola and Mozambique. And it continued to invigilate the sanctions and inspections clamped on Iraq at the end of the Gulf war. Not all these ventures succeeded.

In former Yugoslavia the UN had neither the mandate nor the wherewithal to impose a political settlement. In Cambodia the Khmers Rouges refused to commit themselves to participate in the UN-monitored election. In Angola the election

Time to restore hope

went ahead, but when the loser, Jonas Savimbi of the UNITA movement, disavowed the result, the 16-year-old civil war seemed ready to reignite. The eruption in Angola set a dismal precedent for Mozambique, the next destination for UN peace monitors. Attempts to resolve the conflict in Western Sahara by means of a UN-supervised referendum came to nothing; so did an effort by Boutros Boutros-Ghali, the UN's new Egyptian secretary-general, to negotiate a settlement in Cyprus.

Mr Boutros-Ghali spent much of the year trying to coax, bully or shame the permanent members of the Security Council into giving the organisation clearer mandates, and more men and money to fulfil them. His main reward was a vague promise from George Bush to think harder about the kind of support the American armed forces might offer at times of emergency. With growing calls on the UN from all over the world, with a growing readiness to override national sovereignty, and with the beginnings of a campaign by Germany and Japan for permanent seats on the Security Council, it was possible to see 1992 as a turning-point in the organisation's history. But it was not the year it turned the corner.

The untidiness in the Gulf

It was an in-between sort of year in the Middle East, too. Saddam Hussein's eviction from Kuwait in 1991 had left the members of the American-led alliance glowing with success. But one little untidiness, the unexpected survival of Mr Hussein himself, refused to clear itself up. There was disappointment, too, that four ambitious objectives Mr Bush set himself at the Gulf war's end—control of the regional arms race, new security arrangements for the Gulf, wider economic co-operation and peace between Israel and the Arabs—were not achieved in 1992.

Arms control? Iran, emerging as a chief beneficiary of Iraq's defeat, set out to rebuild its armed forces and, said intelligence agencies, to buy or build itself nuclear weapons. New security arrangements? Saudi Arabia and the lesser Arab Gulf states made defence pacts with western powers, but squabbled among themselves and dropped a

Saddam still stirring it

Exile in no man's land

plan to bring Egypt and Syria into their defence plans. Economic co-operation? The Saudis and Kuwaitis, finishing the war in straitened circumstances, seemed more intent on punishing than helping their poorer brethren in Yemen and Jordan, who were considered to have been unfriendly during the Gulf war.

Progress on the Arab-Israeli front was a little more promising. Eight rounds of bilateral talks were held in Washington, and hope soared briefly after the defeat, in June's general election, of Israel's intransigent Likud government. By year's end, however, the hoped-for breakthrough had yet to come. Syria had promised "total peace" for "total [Israeli] withdrawal" from occupied lands. Israel replied that it was ready only for a partial withdrawal on the Golan Heights. The Palestinians said Israel's offer of interim self-governing arrangements in the West Bank and Gaza amounted to little more than a bantustan. Amid mounting violence in the occupied territories, Israel expelled more than 400 alleged supporters of Hamas, an Islamic underground group. The Palestinians threatened to break off negotiations until the deportees returned.

While Palestinians strove to achieve statehood by negotiation, Kurds tried to achieve it by stealth. The Gulf war had left a swathe of northern Iraq designated as a "safe haven" for Kurds. As the year went by, the Iraqi Kurds began at last to knit together their divided factions, and staged elections for a parliament. This creeping separation from Iraq earned the disapproval not only of Mr Hussein but also of Turkey, Iran and Syria, three other countries with large Kurdish minorities. Turkey, in particular, complained that its own Kurdish separatists had turned the safe haven into a base for their attacks. By the end of the year Turkish troops and aircraft were crossing into the haven at will, ostensibly in hot pursuit.

Anger at the humbling of Iraq and uncertainty about the Arab-Israeli conflict were only two of the tributaries that fed a growing stream of Islamic fundamentalism in the Arab world. In many Arab countries radical Islam appeared to offer an escape from corruption and economic distress. In Algeria at the beginning of 1992 the Islamic Salvation Front (FIS) was poised to overwhelm the ruling party, the National Liberation Front, in a parliamentary election. Certain of defeat, the government and army cancelled the second half of the election, and with it Algeria's brief experiment in democracy. When the FIS was banned and many of its supporters jailed, the fundamentalists hit back with bombings and assassinations. By December the country was under an indefinite night-time curfew.

The confrontation in Algeria caused turbulence in the Maghreb, and sent ripples as far away as Egypt. There, too, many people seemed to be turning back to Islam, either for personal solace or in the hope that faith could offer a collective solution in economics and politics. President Husni Mubarak and his regime had long ago learnt to live with the non-violent Muslim Brotherhood. But a number of armed Islamic underground groups—abetted, Egypt said, by Iran and Sudan—mounted a series of increasingly bold attacks, including the assassination of public figures and machinegun attacks on tourists. By December the government, stung into action, had sent tens of thousands of policemen on arrest sweeps through the slums of Cairo and the villages of Upper Egypt. In Arab countries as different as Egypt, Jordan and Saudi Arabia, 1992 was the first year for a decade in which radical Islam appeared to pose the principal threat to the survival of regimes.

Democracy, shamocracy

Away from the headlines, the collapse of communism produced a bounty for the world's poor places. In Africa and Latin America, if not everywhere in the Middle East, support for the big ideas of democracy and free markets continued to grow. Mexico continued on its reforming path; Brazil discovered that it could impeach a president without lurching back into chaos; Ghana, Kenya and others held their first free(ish) elections for umpteen years. Here and there came setbacks: President Alberto Fujimori's suspension of Peru's parliament, Nigeria's fumbling of its transition to civilian rule, the agonisingly slow transfer of power—and revelations of military dirty tricks—in South Africa. But at least the overall trend was the other way.

Impeachable Collor

Thursday 2nd
Israel said it intended to **expel 12 Palestinians** from the West Bank and Gaza, in response to attacks that had killed five Jewish settlers in the occupied territories. Four days later the UN Security Council unanimously condemned the expulsions as a breach of the Fourth Geneva Convention, and called on Israel to cancel them.

Wednesday 8th
A spokesman for Algeria's **Islamic Salvation Front** (FIS) claimed that army units were being deployed all over the country. Having won the first round of parliamentary elections in December, the Islamic opposition party was confident of victory in the second round on January 16th—unless the army stepped in.

Negotiators from the Organisation of American States, meeting in Caracas, worked out a deal to restore **Jean-Bertrand Aristide** to the presidency of Haiti, from which he was ousted in a military coup in September 1991. But the island's rulers later rejected the compromise. The OAS had imposed economic sanctions on Haiti shortly after Mr Aristide, the elected president, was overthrown.

Saturday 11th
Three members of an anti-Castro group that had landed from the United States with guns and ammunition were **sentenced to death** by a Cuban court, despite international pleas for clemency.

Sunday 12th
With support from the army, Algeria's leadership **cancelled the election** that had been due on the 16th, and which the opposition FIS had seemed certain to win. Chadli Benjedid, the president who had guided Algeria towards multi-party democracy, stepped down and ceded power to a body known as the High Security Council.

After protests, President Carlos Salinas of Mexico agreed at last to annul the results of the gubernatorial elections held in the state of Tabasco the previous November. This was the third time since the election that the president had acknowledged widespread **electoral fraud** and removed governors belonging to his own ruling Institutional Revolutionary Party.

Voters in **Mali** said they approved of a new constitution introducing multi-party politics. A fortnight later the government postponed legislative elections.

Monday 13th
Israelis and Arabs met in Washington for their second round of **bilateral negotiations** since the peace conference in Madrid the previous October. The Israelis and the joint Palestinian-Jordanian delegation sorted out a row about the structure of their negotiating teams, and tabled some ideas on Palestinian self-rule in the occupied territories. The talks adjourned after four days.

Tuesday 14th
Algeria announced that the country would be run until the end of 1993 by a five-man committee, headed by **Mohamed Boudiaf**, a 71-year-old veteran of the independence war who had chosen to live outside the country since 1963.

Wednesday 15th
Two right-wing parties, Tehiya and Moledet, indicated that they would **quit Israel's government** in protest at Israel's offer of self-government for the Palestinians of the West Bank and Gaza. Their departure, made formal four days later, deprived the ruling Likud Party of its majority in parliament and pointed towards early elections.

Thursday 16th
El Salvador's government and rebels signed a **peace agreement** in Mexico City. The left-wing guerrillas of the Farabundo Marti Liberation Front promised to disband and the government promised to halve the size of its army, end human-rights abuses and introduce reforms. A permanent ceasefire was set for February 1st. The 12-year civil war had cost an estimated 75,000 lives.

Sunday 19th
Five days after it had been allowed to resume work, **Zaire's national conference**, which was supposed to discuss political reform, was suspended by the government, prompting rioting in the capital, Kinshasa.

Tuesday 21st
the UN Security Council passed a resolution calling on Libya to respond fully to requests from Britain and America for the extradition of two intelligence agents suspected of planting the bomb that destroyed **Pan Am 103** over Lockerbie in Scotland in 1988.

Thursday 23rd
Crowds gathered outside Lusaka's radio station to celebrate what they believed to be the fall of **Mobutu Sese Seko**, Zaire's dictator for 27 years. The celebrations ended when the arrival of troops showed he was still in charge.

Friday 24th
In **Mauritania**'s first multi-party elections Colonel Moaouia Ould Sidu Taya retained the presidency, with over 60% of votes cast. Opposition cries of fraud were partially supported, to no avail, by observers from the European Parliament.

Tuesday 28th
A score of governments attended a two-day conference in Moscow on **Arab-Israeli peace**. It established a set of working groups on water, arms control, economic development, refugees and the environment. Syria, Lebanon and (after a row about representation) the Palestinians boycotted the meeting.

Police in South Africa arrested ten **white extremists**, leaders of the neo-Nazi AWB movement led by Eugene Terre'blanche. They were questioned in connection with a violent clash in 1990 in the town of Ventersdorp, in which three people died.

Wednesday 29th
Israel's main parties, Labour and Likud, agreed to bring the next **general election** forward to June 23rd.

Friday 31st
The **Big Five** countries with permanent seats on the UN Security Council, plus the non-permanent ten, held a summit meeting in New York. They called for measures to strengthen arms control and the peacekeeping role of the UN.

February

Saturday 1st

The civil war in **El Salvador** formally ended, under a plan negotiated by the United Nations.

The United States Coast Guard began shipping home the first 150 out of thousands of **Haitian refugees**, after the Supreme Court had ruled that they were fleeing poverty, not political repression. The UN commissioner for refugees said that, in her opinion, the returnees might be exposed to danger.

Tuesday 4th

Units of the Venezuelan army launched an **attempted coup** against the government of President Carlos Andres Perez. Their planning was poor and their motives obscurer.

Iraq cancelled talks with the UN about a plan that would allow it to sell a limited amount of oil, under international supervision. The Iraqis had argued that the plan, set out in a UN resolution the previous August, was an assault on its sovereignty.

Wednesday 5th

Several people were killed during **rioting in Algeria**. The main trouble was at Batna, 430 kilometres (260 miles) south-east of Algiers. It was the worst violence since the government's decision in January to cancel the second round of the parliamentary election, which the opposition Islamic Salvation Front had seemed sure to win.

Sunday 9th

The new government in Algeria introduced a **state of emergency**, to stop pro-democracy protests. A few hours later gunmen ambushed two police cars in the Algiers casbah, killing six policemen.

Friday 14th

Representatives of two feuding **Somali warlords**, Mohamed Farah Aydeed and Ali Mahdi Mohamed, agreed in New York to a ceasefire proposed by the United Nations. The announcement made no visible difference in Mogadishu, Somalia's capital, where more than 25,000 people were estimated to have died already in the civil war.

Saturday 15th

Palestinians armed with knives and axes attacked an army base in northern Israel. They **killed three soldiers** and carried off four machineguns. The Israeli army ordered an inquiry into security at the base.

Sunday 16th

Israel used helicopter gunships to **assassinate** Sheikh Abbas Mussawi, leader of Lebanon's Hizbullah, the "Party of God". The sheikh's wife and child were also killed in the attack. "Whoever opens an account with us will have the account closed by us," said Israel's defence minister, Moshe Arens.

Security forces opened fire on **demonstrators in Zaire**, killing at least 13 people. The demonstrators were marching, in defiance of a government ban, in support of democracy.

Wednesday 19th

Whites in the South African town of Potchefstroom shocked the ruling National Party by electing a candidate from the anti-reform Conservative Party in a by-election. Next day, President F.W. de

Klerk hit back by announcing that he would hold a **referendum** within five weeks. Voters (whites only) would be asked to give him a mandate to continue negotiations for a post-apartheid constitution. He said he would resign if he lost.

Yitzhak Rabin, a former chief of staff and prime minister, defeated Shimon Peres, his rival for 18 years, in elections to lead the Israeli Labour Party. Opinion polls gave Mr Rabin a better chance than Mr Peres of leading the party to victory against the ruling Likud Party in June's forthcoming general election.

Thursday 20th

Israeli forces moved **deeper into Lebanon** to stop the hail of rockets that had been descending on northern Israel and Israel's Lebanese "security zone" ever since Israel's assassination of a Hizbullah leader a few days earlier. The Israeli soldiers pulled back, after announcing success, about 24 hours later. But Hizbullah continued to fire some rockets.

Sunday 23rd

The exiled president of **Haiti**, Jean-Bertrand Aristide, signed an agreement with the Haitian parliament that would enable him to return to office. The apparent breakthrough, negotiated under the auspices of the Organisation of American States, would enable General Raoul Cedras, the army chief, to keep his job, despite the coup he organised.

Monday 24th

James Baker, the American secretary of state, said to Congress that the United States was willing to give Israel $2 billion a year in **loan guarantees** for five years, but only if Israel stopped building Jewish settlements in the occupied territories. On the same day, Israeli, Palestinian, Jordanian,

Syrian and Lebanese negotiators arrived in Washington for their third round of bilateral negotiation. Israel gave the Palestinians a ten-page proposal for limited self-government in the territories.

President F.W. de Klerk set March 17th as the date for South Africa's white referendum on constitutional reforms.

Tuesday 25th

Canada's finance minister announced in a budget speech that his country's **contribution to NATO** forces in Europe would be phased out by 1994. "The world has changed a great deal," he said. The American State Department expressed disappointment. Britain, afraid that the United States might one day follow the Canadian example, urged the Canadians to reconsider.

Thursday 27th

A French judge issued arrest warrants for four members of the **Abu Nidal terror group**, thought to be responsible for attacking a Greek ferry, the *City of Poros*, in 1988. The French said the group had bases in Libya. This was the second batch of warrants issued by France against suspects living in Libya. In late 1991 it had called for the extradition of four Libyans implicated in the bombing of a UTA airliner over Niger in 1989.

Friday 28th

One year after the Gulf war ended, Iraq failed to comply with a fresh **ultimatum** from the UN Security Council to begin destroying equipment for building missiles. The Iraqis said the equipment could be adapted for civilian use. The American ambassador to the UN, and current Security Council president, called the Iraqi position "totally unacceptable" and refused to rule out military action.

March

Sunday 1st
King Fahd of Saudi Arabia, one of the world's few remaining absolute monarchs, announced the creation of a **consultative council** and a bill of rights. He would appoint the council's 60 members himself.

Wednesday 4th
An Algerian judge ruled that the opposition **Islamic Salvation Front** was illegal. In January the party was on the threshold of winning power, until the government cancelled parliamentary elections.

Sunday 8th
In churches across Malawi, priests read out a letter from eight bishops criticising **President Kamuzu Banda**, who had ruled the country with an iron fist for 28 years. The letter sparked a wave of protests against the government; the priests went into hiding.

Monday 9th
A North Korean ship, believed to have been carrying **Scud missiles** destined for Syria, docked at the Iranian port of Bandar Abbas, despite American hints that it would be intercepted by the United States Navy. The hints had prompted furious criticism of America by President Hafez Assad.

Thursday 12th
After listening for two days to Iraq's deputy prime minister, Tariq Aziz, the UN Security Council said that **Iraq** had not destroyed the weapons and equipment it had promised to under the ceasefire resolution that ended the Gulf war in 1991. It warned Mr Aziz to do so immediately.

Tuesday 17th
In South Africa's **whites-only referendum**, 68.6% of voters voted in favour of continuing negotiations for a post-apartheid constitution. The referendum strengthened the hand of President F.W. de Klerk, whose reforms had run into fierce opposition from the right-wing Conservative Party.

Bombers **blew up** Israel's embassy in Buenos Aires, killing more than 20 people. Islamic Jihad, an offshoot of Lebanon's Hizbullah movement, claimed responsibility and said it was revenge for Israel's killing of their leader, Abbas Mussawi, the previous month.

George Bush made it clear that Israel would not receive a requested $10 billion in **loan guarantees** unless it stopped Jewish settlement in the West Bank and Gaza. The news marked a new low in Israel's relations with America. It coincided with reports that Israel had given China secrets about the American Patriot missile. A month later, after inspecting Patriot sites in Israel, the State Department said that the reports were apparently untrue.

Thursday 19th
Zimbabwe's parliament passed a **land-reform bill**, empowering the government to purchase large quantities of land owned by (mainly white) commercial farmers and redistribute it to black peasants. White farmers said the measure would damage the country's farm output.

Nigeria's census found that there were only 88.5m Nigerians, at least 20m fewer than had been expected.

Saturday 21st
Brazil's president, Fernando Collor, sacked his environment secretary, Jose Lutzenberger, ten weeks before the United Nations great Earth Summit was due to start in Rio de Janeiro. Mr Lutzenberger had said that third-world bureaucracies would squander money that rich countries gave them to **protect the environment**.

Sunday 22nd
The Arab League, meeting in Cairo, urged Britain and America not to take military or **economic sanctions** against Libya in their attempt to extradite the two men accused of blowing up Pan Am 103 above Lockerbie in December 1988.

Tuesday 24th
A committee from the Arab League flew to Tripoli after getting word that Colonel **Muammar Qaddafi** would hand over to them the two men accused by Britain and America of masterminding the Lockerbie bombing. The committee returned to Cairo empty-handed.

Wednesday 25th
An **open-skies treaty** was signed by 25 countries, including all 16 members of NATO, plus the five East European members of the (former) Warsaw Pact, and Russia, Ukraine, Belorussia and Georgia. The treaty gives signatories the right to conduct reconnaissance flights over other signatories' territories.

A UN team began to destroy **missile-production** equipment in Iraq. Earlier, Iraq's refusal to allow this to happen had drawn new threats of military action by America and its Gulf-war allies.

Sunday 29th
David Levy, Israel's foreign minister and unanointed king of its influential Moroccan community, threatened to **resign**. The ruling Likud Party, facing a general election in June, went into a tizzy. Mr Levy withdrew his threat a week later, in return for more party jobs for his supporters.

King Fahd of Saudi Arabia said in several newspaper interviews that western notions of **democracy** did not suit the Arab world. He thus ended speculation that the creation of a consultative council would lead on to freer politics inside the kingdom.

Monday 30th
The Brazilian president, Fernando Collor, asked for the resignation of all his ministers and assistants, in an attempt to stamp out **corruption**. A few of the better ones were later reappointed.

Algeria announced that it would **dissolve** 400 elected local assemblies controlled by the Islamic Salvation Front (FIS). The FIS was made illegal after the government decided in January to cancel a parliamentary election the opposition would have won.

Tuesday 31st
The UN Security Council passed Resolution 748, authorising **sanctions against Libya** unless Muammar Qaddafi handed over, by April 15th, two men accused by America and Britain of destroying Pan Am 103 over Lockerbie. Ten countries voted in favour of the resolution, but five abstained.

April

Wednesday 1st
A surge of violence in the Israeli-occupied **Gaza Strip** left four Palestinians dead, after a hand grenade was thrown at an army post.

Thursday 2nd
Libyans protesting at the threat of UN **sanctions** against their country mobbed embassies in Tripoli. Part of the embassy of Venezuela, one of the countries to have voted for the sanctions resolution on March 31st, was burnt down.

A **general strike** disrupted Nairobi, the Kenyan capital. It was part of a campaign by the newly legalised opposition to hasten the multi-party elections promised, for an unspecified date, by President Daniel arap Moi.

Sunday 5th
Peru's president, Alberto Fujimori, organised a **coup** against the country's Congress. Backed by the army, he dissolved the government and suspended the constitution. Mr Fujimori, frustrated by a fight against inflation, corruption and the Shining Path guerrillas, said he was trying to avert chaos.

Iran launched an **air raid** against the People's Mujahideen, an opposition guerrilla group based inside Iraq. One Phantom fighter-bomber was shot down. The next day, Iranian opposition groups stoned Iranian embassies in Europe, America and Australia.

Monday 6th
An opposition leader, Chakufwa Chihana, was arrested moments after returning to **Malawi** to argue for democratic change. The summary arrest at the airport dashed rising hopes of political reform.

Three Arab guerrillas in south Lebanon staged a daring **ambush** on an Israeli military convoy, killing two soldiers before being killed themselves. Israel said their aim had been to kill a senior Israeli general, probably in retaliation for Israel's assassination of the Sheikh Abbas Mussawi, the leader of Hizbullah, in February.

Tuesday 7th
An aircraft carrying **Yasser Arafat**, the chairman of the Palestine Liberation Organisation, went missing after a forced landing during a sandstorm in the Saharan desert. Palestinians everywhere went wild with relief when he was discovered alive. Three crew members died.

Friday 10th
Iran held elections for its Majlis (parliament). Supporters of the president, **Hashemi Rafsanjani**, a pragmatist by Iranian standards, did better than candidates who had advocated a line closer to that of Ayatollah Khomeini, his fiery predecessor.

Monday 13th
The Organisation of American States, meeting in Washington, deplored President Alberto Fujimori's **coup in Peru**. It called on him to restore the constitution, and sent a mission to Lima. James Baker, the American secretary of state, said Mr Fujimori had "destroyed democracy in the guise of saving it". The United States had already suspended all aid that was not for humanitarian purposes.

Citing "differences between ourselves on a number of issues", **Nelson Mandela**, president of the African National Congress, announced that he was separating from his wife Winnie. The couple had been married for 34 years. Later in the week Mrs Mandela resigned from her post as head of the organisation's social-welfare department.

Tuesday 14th
The **World Court** in The Hague refused a Libyan request for an order against Britain and America that would have stopped them trying to force Libya to hand over to them two men suspected of destroying Pan Am 103 over Lockerbie in 1988. Libya severed links with the outside world for a day, on the anniversary of the American air raids on Libya in 1986.

Wednesday 15th
An air embargo, a ban on arms sales and other **sanctions** came into force against Libya under the UN Security Council's Resolution 748. This called on Libya to hand over the Lockerbie suspects and prove by "concrete actions" that it was renouncing terrorism. Libya refused to comply with either request.

America, Britain and France warned Iraq to stop blockading the **Kurds' safe haven** in the north of the country, remove newly installed anti-aircraft batteries from the area and stop locking on to allied aircraft with radar.

Tuesday 21st
South Africa's Democratic Party lost five of its 33 members of parliament. The five said they were **joining the African National Congress**, the first members of the legislature to do so.

Thursday 23rd
President F.W. de Klerk proposed **early elections** for South Africa. He said citizens of every colour should elect a five-member council to run the country, under a rotating presidency, pending negotiation of a post-apartheid constitution. After reflection, the African National Congress rejected the idea.

Monday 27th
At another round of Arab-Israeli peace talks in Washington, Israel offered to let Palestinians in the occupied West Bank and Gaza hold **municipal elections**. Maybe, said the Palestinians, so long as they could first elect a body to take the place of the Israeli administration in the territories.

Tuesday 28th
In a **referendum**, Ghanaians voted by a huge majority to bring in a new constitution and restore civilian rule. This cleared the way for the unbanning of political parties and a presidential election in December. The intriguing question was whether the incumbent, Flight-Lieutenant Jerry Rawlings, would be a candidate.

Wednesday 29th
Sierra Leone's army staged a **military coup**, forcing President Joseph Momoh to flee to Guinea. Demonstrators in Freetown, the capital, supported the coup leaders. One of them, Captain Valentine Strasser, promised elections, plus "the resurrection of accountability, economic and social justice, and the dignity of Sierra Leoneans."

May

Saturday 2nd
Kenneth Matiba, one of Kenya's most popular dissidents, made a triumphal return to Nairobi. A former cabinet minister, he had spent nearly a year convalescing in London from the stroke he suffered as a political prisoner in Kenya. He announced plans to lead the Forum for the Restoration of Democracy, a newly legalised opposition party, to victory against the government of Daniel arap Moi.

Monday 4th
An Algerian court gave **death sentences** to 13 Islamic militants who attacked an army post in November. Two days later another three militants were condemned to death for raiding a naval post. The raids and trials were part of the continuing struggle between the government and the Islamic Salvation Front, forced underground after the government cancelled elections and jailed its leaders at the beginning of the year.

Islamic fundamentalists, using guns and knives, killed 13 **Coptic Christians** in Manshiet Nasser, a village in upper Egypt. The attack prompted a government crackdown on Islamic activists, and spread alarm among Egypt's 7m Copts.

Wednesday 6th
The **government of Lebanon resigned**, after the collapse of the currency had prompted widespread riots and looting. Predictably, the departing prime minister, Omar Karami, blamed his troubles on Israel.

Israel said it would **boycott** two out of five sets of peace negotiations planned for the following week. It said that by inviting Palestinians living outside the occupied West Bank to the meetings—on refugees in Ottawa and economic development in Brussels—the sponsors had broken the ground rules set forth when the peace talks began in October 1991.

Thursday 7th
In South Africa, a judicial report accused the Department of Development Aid, a government department that had since closed down, of presiding over the **filching** of millions of rand designated for projects in black areas. It was the latest in a series of financial and security scandals to rock President F.W. de Klerk's white administration.

Saturday 9th
More than 20 prisoners were killed when President Alberto Fujimori ordered that Peruvian soldiers should be sent in to end a **prison mutiny** in Lima. Most of the mutineers were jailed guerrillas of the Shining Path movement.

Monday 11th
The rich countries that give aid to **Malawi** began a three-day meeting in Paris. After discussing recent protests and strikes, during which at least 38 people were reported killed by police, the donors decided to suspend new aid until the country's dictator, President Kamuzu Banda, moved towards freer politics. Similar pressure, applied to Kenya in November 1991, had quickly persuaded President Daniel arap Moi to reinstate multiparty elections.

Wednesday 13th
Angry **riots** swept through Lagos, the Nigerian capital, when its petrol pumps ran dry. Nigeria, a large oil exporter, had kept the domestic price so low that it did not pay officials and businessmen to sell the stuff at home.

By pre-arrangement with Syria, Lebanon's parliament voted in a **new prime minister**. It was the 66-year-old Rashid Solh's second stab at the job. He was prime minister in 1975, when the country's civil war between Muslims and Christians started. His job now was to organise the first nationwide elections under the country's new power-sharing constitution.

Sunday 17th
Peru's president, Alberto Fujimori, flew to Nassau to tell the **Organisation of American States** that he intended to return his country to democracy by electing a constituent congress within five months. He had done away with Peru's existing parliament and constitution in a coup in April.

In **Ecuador** the Democratic Left government of President Rodrigo Borja finished fourth in the first round of the presidential election. That left two more right-wing candidates, Sixto Duran Ballen and Jaime Nebot, to fight a run-off election in July.

Tuesday 19th
About 1m Kurds living inside the "safe haven" in northern Iraq held an election in which the two main parties, Jalal Talabani's Patriotic Union of Kurdistan and Masoud Barzani's Kurdish Democratic Party, came out even. The inconclusive result mattered less than the election itself, which implied that **Kurdistan** was edging closer to independence from Iraq.

More than 100 Nigerians were reported killed in **communal fighting** between Christians and Muslims in the north of the country.

Sunday 24th
President Bush ordered the United States Coast Guard to start returning **Haitian boat people** directly to Haiti, instead of to America's Guantanamo naval base in Cuba as before. With 12,000 Haitians already at Guantanamo, the base was full, explained the White House.

A Palestinian from the Gaza strip **stabbed to death** an Israeli teenager in the town of Bat Yam, provoking widespread anti-Arab riots. In response the government sealed off the Gaza strip for two weeks, preventing the 50,000 or so Gazans with jobs in Israel from commuting to work.

Wednesday 27th
The UN Security Council voted to **renew the sanctions** on Iraq, imposed after the invasion of Kuwait in 1990.

Thursday 28th
The Sudanese army overran Kapoeta, the de facto capital of southern Sudan, sending thousands of refugees pouring across the border into Kenya. The government victory came just as peace talks, designed to end Sudan's **civil war**, got under way in Nigeria. Although the talks brought no agreement, the two sides promised to meet again.

June

Tuesday 2nd
The army in **Haiti** named a new prime minister, Marc Bazin, as head of a government of "national consensus". The decision was a setback for the Organisation of American States, which had been trying through sanctions to reinstate the elected president, Jean-Bertrand Aristide, ousted in a coup in 1991.

Wednesday 3rd
The 11-day **Earth summit** opened in Rio de Janeiro. Billed as the biggest-ever gathering of world leaders, it resulted in the signing of two treaties: on biological diversity (the preservation of species) and climate change (under which signatories promised to cut the emission of "greenhouse gases"). The summit also produced a declaration calling on rich and poor countries to act in partnership to protect the natural environment.

Friday 5th
Peace talks between the two sides in the civil war in Sudan adjourned in Nigeria, with both sides agreeing to continue negotiations. The talks came after a string of victories by government forces over the Sudanese People's Liberation Army, which had been weakened by an internal split.

Monday 8th
Farag Foda, an Egyptian writer and critic of **Islamic fundamentalism**, was shot dead near his office in the centre of Cairo. Police said his killers were from Islamic Jihad, the underground group that organised the assassination of President Anwar Sadat in 1981.

Wednesday 10th
Iran hanged four men, the first of a number of people accused of instigating **riots** in several Iranian cities, Mashhad, Shiraz and Arak, in May and June. Iranian opposition groups based in Iraq said they had organised the protests.

Wednesday 17th
More than 40 black supporters of the African National Congress at **Boipatong** township in South Africa were killed in clashes with Zulu hostel workers. The ANC said the police had helped to organise the killings. When President de Klerk visited the township himself three days later, angry demonstrators besieged his car.

Thomas Kemptner and Heinrich Strübig, the last of the western **hostages in Lebanon**, were released after nearly three years as prisoners of Hizbullah, the pro-Iranian Shia Muslim group. The release of the two Germans still left Israel holding hundreds of Lebanese prisoners, and four missing Israeli serviceman unaccounted for.

Friday 19th
Marc Bazin, a former World Bank employee, was sworn in as **Haiti's new prime minister**. The elected president, Jean-Bertrand Aristide, remained in the exile that began with an army coup in 1991. Mr Bazin's appointment was expected to increase American pressure on Father Aristide to negotiate a return to the island.

Sunday 21st
Despite the presence of international observers, elections for **regional assemblies** in Ethiopia (minus the breakaway province of Eritrea) brought accusations of fraud, and strained relations between the ruling Ethiopian People's Revolutionary Democratic Front and the Oromo Liberation Front, the second-biggest party. Two days after the vote, the Oromos pulled out of the coalition government in Addis Ababa.

Monday 22nd
The United Nations Conference on Disarmament produced a draft treaty banning the development, production and stockpiling of poison weapons. (The existing treaty merely outlawed their use.) Before coming into force, the draft had still to be approved by the 39 states participating in the conference, and ratified by 65 countries.

Tuesday 23rd
Labour stormed to power in **Israel's general election**, capturing 44 seats in the 120-member Knesset (parliament). After 15 years in power the Likud saw its representation slashed from 40 seats to 32. After the usual interval for haggling, Labour's Yitzhak Rabin formed a coalition consisting of his own party, the left-liberal Meretz party, and Shas, an orthodox religious party. Mr Rabin said his first priority was to negotiate an autonomy agreement with the Palestinians of the West Bank and Gaza.

Nelson Mandela's African National Congress **withdrew from talks** on South Africa's new constitution, citing the massacre at Boipatong. It said it would resume talks only when several conditions had been met. They included tighter control over Zulu migrant hostels, the disbanding of police hit squads, an inquiry into the killings at Boipatong and international monitoring of township violence.

Saturday 27th
Abassi Madani and Ali Belhadj, the two most prominent leaders of Algeria's banned fundamentalist party, the **Islamic Salvation Front**, were put on trial in front of a military court on charges of conspiracy. The trial was immediately suspended, after the defence lawyers staged a walkout.

Monday 29th
Muhammad Boudiaf, Algeria's president, was assassinated by one of his own bodyguards while giving a speech in the town of Annaba, in eastern Algeria. The assassin's motives were not immediately clear. The government said that it could have been the work of Islamic fundamentalists. Some Algerian newspapers thought it more likely that the president was the victim of members of the ruling party, the National Liberation Front, who felt threatened by his promised drive against corruption.

July

Saturday 4th
In voting for a new National Assembly, Nigerians gave the (leftish) Social Democrats a small majority over the (rightish) National Republican Party Convention. Both parties were created with the approval of the military government, as part of President Ibrahim Babangida's cautious plan to return Nigeria to **civilian rule** by January 1993.

Sunday 5th
In the final round of **Ecuador**'s presidential election (the first round was in May), victory went to Sixto Duran Ballen of the United Republican Party, a 70-year-old who had tried to become president twice before. Both he and his defeated rival, Jaime Nebot Saadi of the Social Christian Party, had campaigned for free-market economic reforms.

Tuesday 7th
Joe Clark, Canada's minister for constitutional affairs, announced that nine out of the country's ten provincial premiers had at last agreed on a set of **constitutional reforms** that would satisfy Quebec's demand for recognition as a "distinct society" within Canada. The tenth premier, Quebec's Robert Bourassa, was not a party to the agreement. He had already promised that Quebec would make up its mind by holding a referendum.

Sunday 12th
Mexico held elections in two states. President Carlos Salinas's ever-ruling Institutional Revolutionary Party (PRI) squeaked home in Michoacan but was defeated by the conservative National Action Party in Chihuahua. Some Mexicans were pleasantly surprised that the government did not once again rig the ballot so that the PRI won in both states, as it had in the past.

Monday 13th
Yitzhak Rabin presented a new government to the Knesset, Israel's 120-member parliament. The coalition comprised his own Labour Party (with 44 seats), the left-liberal Meretz party (with 12 seats) and the ultra-orthodox Shas party (with six seats). Mr Rabin, a former general, said his urgent task was to sign an interim "autonomy" agreement with the Palestinians of the West Bank and Gaza, adding: "No longer do we have to be a people that dwells alone and no longer is it true that the whole world is against us."

Sudanese government forces captured Torit, the southern headquarters of the rebel army led by **John Garang**. The rebels' military fortunes had been in decline since the collapse in Ethiopia of the regime of Halie Mariam Mengistu, which had provided arms and logistical support for the rebels.

Thursday 16th
In a unanimous resolution the United Nations Security Council passed a resolution calling for the resumption of constitutional negotiations in South Africa. It asked the secretary-general to send a **special representative** to help. Cyrus Vance, a former American secretary of state, was named for the job the following day.

Tuesday 21st
Israel's new prime minister, Yitzhak Rabin, paid a visit to President Husni Mubarak in Cairo. It was the first **Israel-Egypt summit** meeting to be held for six years. In the same busy week, his first in office, Mr Rabin announced a freeze in Jewish settlement in the occupied West Bank and Gaza, and met James Baker, the American secretary of state, who was on a tour of the region. Mr Baker later pronounced himself "really very satisfied" with the new Israeli government's attitude to the settlements.

Cyrus Vance arrived in South Africa on a fact-finding mission as a special representative of the United Nations. One day after he arrived came the collapse of an agreement that would have averted the national strike called for by the African National Congress.

Wednesday 22nd
UN inspectors who had been camping for 17 days outside the **agriculture ministry** in Baghdad withdrew to their hotel after harassment by Iraqi crowds. The UN said the inspectors had been looking for documents relating to Iraq's weapons programme.

Pablo Escobar, leader of the Medellin drugs cartel, escaped from the prison in Envigado where he had been living in luxury under an arrangement with the Colombian government.

Thursday 23rd
A three-day election in the **Seychelles islands** awarded the socialist ruling party, the Seychelles People's Progressive Front, a majority of seats on a commission set up to rewrite the constitution. A team of Commonwealth observers, on hand to watch the people vote, said afterwards that the election had in general been free and fair.

Monday 27th
A UN Security Council resolution called for an urgent airlift of **food to Somalia**, and gave warning of "other measures" if local factions failed to co-operate. Earlier, Boutros Boutros-Ghali, the UN secretary-general, had accused the council's permanent members of doing too little to alleviate Somalia's famine because of their preoccupation with the "war of the rich" in Yugoslavia.

Tuesday 28th
After a three-week stand-off, and the arrival of American naval reinforcements in the Gulf, UN **weapons inspectors** in Baghdad were allowed into Iraq's agriculture ministry. At Iraq's insistence, the team did not include any inspectors from the United States, Britain or France. Iraq and America said the other side had blinked first. Nothing incriminating was discovered in the building.

Thursday 30th
In a change of policy, South Africa's government said it would **welcome UN observers** inside the country. The request for the observers had come from the African National Congress, in the hope that they would prevent outbreaks of violence during a forthcoming campaign of "mass action".

August

Saturday 1st
Nigerians started to vote in **primary elections**, to pick presidential candidates for each of the two officially approved parties. Within days the voting had been cancelled because of fraud. The National Electoral Commission promised to try again in September.

Sunday 2nd
Iraqi newspapers celebrated the second anniversary of Iraq's **invasion of Kuwait** by declaring that the emirate would one day return to "its rightful [Iraqi] owner".

Monday 3rd
A two-day **general strike** organised by the African National Congress got under way in South Africa. By the time it was over, said the ANC, at least 4m people had stayed away from work. The minister of law and order said the strike had caused 40 deaths.

Tuesday 4th
American marines began **military exercises**, codenamed "Eager Mace", in Kuwait.

Jose Goldemberg, Brazil's education minister, resigned amid growing clamour to impeach President Fernando Collor on **corruption charges**.

Wednesday 5th
Up to 70,000 black demonstrators held a **peaceful march** through Pretoria to hear Nelson Mandela, president of the African National Congress, address them from outside the offices of President F.W. de Klerk. He called for the urgent formation of an interim government of national unity.

President Joaquim Chissano met rebel leader Afonso Dhlakama in Rome for **peace talks** to end the 17-year-old civil war in Mozambique. Two days later they agreed to implement a ceasefire, starting on October 1st.

Thursday 6th
Nine days after letting UN inspectors into its **agriculture ministry**, Iraq said that the UN would not be allowed to search government ministries in future. President Bush said the inspectors had every right to enter such buildings if they wished, "and we will help guarantee that right".

Sunday 9th
Israel's deputy foreign minister announced plans to repeal a "stupid" law barring private citizens from meeting members of the **Palestine Liberation Organisation**. But he said the government itself had no plans to talk to the PLO.

Monday 10th
Yitzhak Rabin, the newly elected Israeli prime minister, visited George Bush for a two-day meeting in Kennebunkport, Maine. The next day, Mr Bush praised Mr Rabin for having stopped new Jewish settlement in the occupied West Bank and Gaza. He said he would ask Congress to give Israel the $10 billion in **loan guarantees** which he had asked it to withhold from Yitzhak Shamir, Mr Rabin's predecessor.

Wednesday 12th
After more than a year of haggling, the United States, Canada and Mexico finalised a **North American Free Trade Agreement** (NAFTA). For the agreement to take effect it still needed to be approved by the three countries' legislatures.

A United Nations envoy signed an agreement on **relief for Somalia** with General Mohamed Farrar Aideed, one of the warlords who had been obstructing the distribution of food. Under the agreement 500 UN guards would be allowed to protect relief supplies in Mogadishu.

Sunday 16th
The *New York Times* published details of an alleged American plan to **bomb Iraq**, after provoking a confrontation over UN weapons inspections. President Bush denied trying to "pick a fight" for electoral reasons.

Monday 17th
Ten Southern African countries, with a combined population of 80m people, signed an **economic-co-operation treaty**. The treaty set up a new organisation, named the Southern African Development Community, but excluding South Africa.

The UN Security Council, acting on a recommendation from its special envoy, Cyrus Vance, voted to send a team of **international observers** to South Africa.

Wednesday 19th
After three postponements, a majority of voters in **Madagascar** said in a referendum that they favoured keeping the country as a unitary state. Many of the Imerina people, who live on the central plateau, had supported the case for a federal constitution.

Saturday 22nd
Brian Mulroney, the prime minister of Canada, reached agreement with ten provincial premiers on **amending the constitution**. The new constitution would recognise Quebec as a "distinct society", change the appointed upper house to an elected one (with equal representation for all provinces) and enlarge the House of Commons. It was not immediately clear whether all this would persuade Quebeckers to remain part of Canada. Their premier had promised to let them make up their own minds in a referendum.

Sunday 23rd
Lebanon held the first round of a three-round **parliamentary election**, the first for 20 years. Most Christians boycotted the voting, having argued that a fair election would not be possible while Syrian troops continued to occupy most parts of the country.

Monday 24th
Arabs and Israelis gathered in Washington for bilateral **peace talks**—the first since the election of a Labour government in Israel. The first week showed promise. Syria described the approach of the new Israeli negotiators as "constructive".

Wednesday 26th
America, Britain and France announced the creation of a **no-fly zone** in southern Iraq, ostensibly in order to stop Iraq's government from harassing rebels in the southern marshland near Basra. The Gulf war allies said that Iraqi aircraft and helicopters operating south of the 32nd parallel risked being shot down.

Under pressure from the army, prime minister Joseph Kokou Koffigoh of Togo agreed to **postpone elections** due to take place as part of the country's transition to democracy. He reluctantly agreed to restore some of the powers of Gnassinbé Eyadéma, the strongman president, which had been reduced at a "national conference" in 1991.

September

Tuesday 1st
A **tidal wave** up to 15 metres (50 feet) high crashed over the Pacific coast of Nicaragua, killing at least 150 people and leaving 16,000 without their homes or belongings.

Wednesday 2nd
Iraq's **nuclear-weapons programme** "stands at zero now," the head of a United Nations inspection team, Maurizio Zifferero from Italy, said during a visit to Baghdad. The next day, the International Atomic Energy Agency in Vienna issued a "clarification". It said that Mr Zifferero had not meant to rule out the possibility that more Iraqi nuclear goings-on, which the world did not yet know about, might be discovered in the future.

Friday 4th
In a **referendum in Morocco** 99.6% of voters were said to have approved some mild constitutional changes. Observers saw the exercise as a bid by King Hassan to make it clear that he would not relinquish control of the Western Sahara, due under a UN peace plan to hold a referendum of its own later in the year.

Sunday 6th
The third and final round of the **Lebanese elections** took place in the south of the country. As in previous rounds, most Christians boycotted the voting. With results in from all three rounds, the most notable victories had gone to Hizbullah, the pro-Iranian Islamic fundamentalist group. With its allies, it would control a score of seats in the 128-seat parliament.

Monday 7th
Police from the **Ciskei**, one of South Africa's nominally independent black "homelands", opened fire on a column of marchers from the African National Congress,

killing at least 28 and wounding nearly 200. The marchers, as part of an ANC campaign of "mass action" had planned to force the resignation of Ciskei's leader, Brigadier Oupa Gqozo.

Saturday 12th
Police in Lima captured Abimael Guzman, leader of the **Shining Path** terrorist group, along with his lover and several senior comrades. It was the biggest success the Peruvian government had ever scored in its war against the Maoist group, and gave a timely boost to the popularity of President Alberto Fujimori. He had cited the terrorist threat as one reason for having disbanded parliament and assumed dictatorial powers in April.

Monday 21st
After a break of more than 130 years, and just in time for the 500th anniversary of the church in the Americas, **Mexico** restored relations with the Vatican. Despite the lack of ties, most Mexicans had remained loyal Catholics.

The UN General Assembly received a promise from President George Bush that America wanted to train some of its soldiers for **peacekeeping** duties and make them available to the UN at short notice. Speaking the next day on behalf of the European Community, Britain's foreign minister, Douglas Hurd, put more stress on preventative diplomacy.

Wednesday 23rd
Two Damascus-based factions of the Palestine Liberation Organisation, the Popular Front and the Democratic Front for the Liberation of Palestine, created a **joint command** to challenge the policies of Yasser Arafat. They accused the PLO chairman of being too soft against Israel.

Thursday 24th
The sixth round of **Arab-Israeli peace talks** ended in Washington, without any clear sign of progress. Early hopes for a breakthrough between Israel and Syria came to nothing, after Israel asked Syria to clarify what sort of peace it was offering, and Syria's foreign minister said Israel could have "total peace" only in return for "total withdrawal". But the negotiators agreed to hold a seventh round on October 21st.

Sunday 27th
After a break of three months, South Africa's President F.W. de Klerk and Nelson Mandela of the African National Congress agreed to **resume negotiations** on a new constitution. Mr de Klerk promised to move rapidly towards creating an interim government, to release political prisoners, and to fence some of the Zulu migrant-worker hostels. A few hours later Chief Mangosuthu Buthelezi, leader of the mainly Zulu Inkatha Freedom Party, said he would withdraw from the constitutional talks.

A military-transport aircraft **crashed** in Nigeria, killing all of the 163 officers and men on board.

Tuesday 29th
The two-day **Angolan election**, organised as part of the agreement that ended a 16-year civil war, got under way. The main contestants were the former enemies in the war: Jonas Savimbi of the UNITA

movement and Jose Eduardo dos Santos of the (ex-Marxist) MPLA government. Although UN observers tried to ensure that voting was fair, there was scattered violence in many parts of the country.

The lower house of Brazil's Congress voted by 441 votes to 38 to **impeach the president**. Fernando Collor de Mello, in office since 1990, had been accused of receiving money in return for political favours. After the vote, Mr Collor was suspended for 180 days while the case went to the Senate for trial. In the meantime his duties as president were taken over by the vice-president, Itamar Franco.

Wednesday 30th
In South Africa an independent commission under Judge Richard Goldstone found that the **massacre** earlier in the month of ANC marchers on the border of Ciskei had been "morally and legally indefensible". The report discounted as "improbable" a claim that the marchers had opened fire first at the police.

Qatar accused Saudi Arabia of attacking a post on their disputed border. The Saudis said the gunfight took place between feuding bedouin tribesmen, and that all of it took place within Saudi Arabia's own national territory.

October

Thursday 1st
Qatar suspended a 1965 agreement on **border demarcation** with Saudi Arabia, following a military clash between the two countries.

In a voluntary poll, 30% of the electors of Uruguay said they wanted a national referendum on **privatisation**. The referendum was set for December. If it went against privatisation, the main plank of President Luis Lacalle's economic reforms would be broken.

Sunday 4th
A **peace treaty** for Mozambique was signed in Rome, putting an end to a 16-year-old civil war between the Frelimo government and the Renamo guerrilla movement.

Monday 5th
The government of Kuwait, fulfilling a promise it had made during the Iraqi occupation, held **elections** for the National Assembly it had dissolved in 1986. A majority of the 50 men elected (by an all-male electorate of "first-class" citizens) were opponents of the ruling family, and about 18 belonged to or were backed by Islamic fundamentalist groups.

Power changed hands in **Guyana**, in the first free election since 1964. Cheddi Jagan, a dentist and former Marxist, led his opposition party to victory against the ruling People's National Congress of President Desmond Hoyte. After the vote, there was rioting in the streets. Most of Dr

Jagan's supporters were of Indian descent; Mr Hoyte's party drew mainly on Guyanese.

Wednesday 7th
Scores of Palestinians were wounded by Israeli gunfire during protests in the **Gaza Strip**. The protest, in support of a hunger strike by Palestinian prisoners, was one of the biggest eruptions of violence since the start of Arab-Israeli peace talks in 1991. The hunger strike ended on October 11th, but one of the strikers died three days later.

Monday 12th
An **earthquake** hit Cairo, felling scores of buildings and killing nearly 500 people. In the ensuing days Islamic fundamentalists accused the government of having brought the calamity upon Egypt by pursuing ungodly ways and allowing shoddy workmanship in public buildings.

Friday 16th
The Armed Forces Ruling Council in Nigeria decreed that two attempts by the only two authorised political parties to **elect presidential candidates** had been chaotic and fraudulent. President Ibrahim Babangida dissolved the party leaderships and said the process would have to start all over again. That put a question mark over the military government's plan to hold a presidential election in December and return Africa's most populous country over to civilian rule in January 1993.

Saturday 17th
The government of Kuwait gave **cabinet jobs** to six of the "opposition" members of parliament elected at the beginning of the month. Although the ruling Sabah family kept control of foreign affairs, defence, the interior ministry and information, the appoint-

ments were taken as a sign of increasing democratisation in the emirate.

Sunday 18th
Kamuzu Banda, the "Life-President" of Malawi, astonished his countrymen by promising a referendum to decide whether they preferred **multi-party politics** to his single-party rule. But he set no date. In May, international donors had cut off new economic aid for Malawi until it showed signs of political reform.

Wednesday 21st
Islamic fundamentalists attacked a tour bus in **Egypt**, killing a British tourist. The attack was only the latest in a series of assaults targeting the Egyptian tourist industry. On October 2nd gunmen had opened fire on a tourist boat on the Nile.

Thursday 22nd
Rafiq Hariri, a self-made billionaire, was appointed the new **prime minister of Lebanon**. With the approval of Syria, and the backing of Saudi Arabia, the new man promised to rescue the Lebanese economy and return Beirut to its former glory.

Friday 23rd
The previously fractious Iraqi enemies of **Saddam Hussein** met in the Kurdish enclave in northern Iraq in a bid to sink their differences. They agreed to form a unified opposition in exile, under three leaders (a Kurd, a Sunni ex-army officer living in Syria and a Shia cleric living in London). They also picked an executive committee, led by Ahmad Chalabi, an Iraqi businessman in exile in London.

Saturday 24th
Gunmen in South Africa barged into the home of an Inkatha leader in Natal, killing 24 people. It was the latest

violent clash between the African National Congress and those supporting the Inkatha Freedom Party.

Sunday 25th
A **roadside bomb** planted by Hizbullah, a pro-Iranian group, killed five Israeli soldiers in south Lebanon, setting off two days of cross-border shelling and air raids. But the seventh round of Arab-Israeli peace talks, taking place in Washington, continued without interruption.

Monday 26th
In a referendum, Canadians **rejected** government proposals to change the constitution. The changes, negotiated in Charlottetown in August, would have recognised Quebec as a "distinct society", given the western provinces more seats in a reformed Senate and accepted the native peoples' "inherent" right to self-government. But six out of ten provinces, plus the Yukon territory, voted No. The overall No vote came to 54%.

Friday 30th
In fierce fighting in and around Luanda, the Angolan capital, soldiers loyal to Jonas Savimbi's UNITA movement came off worst. The clashes increased fears that the 16-year-old **civil war** could start all over again. Mr Savimbi had been refusing to accept that Eduardo dos Santos's MPLA government had won the election at the end of September.

Monday 2nd
An Iranian cleric announced that the bounty on the head of **Salman Rushdie**, a British novelist whom the Iranians accuse of blasphemy, had been raised above $2m.

Tuesday 3rd
Jerry John Rawlings, the flight-lieutenant who had grabbed power by force on two previous occasions, won a multi-party election to become **Ghana's president**. Opposition parties complained that Mr Rawlings's military junta had interfered in the voting, but observers from the (British) Commonwealth said that the election had been reasonably fair.

Wednesday 4th
Iraqis sang and danced in the streets at news that **George Bush** had lost the American presidential election. Iranians chanted "Death to America" in front of the former American embassy in Tehran. And Iran's government announced that it had arrested an American citizen, Milton Mayar, on spying charges.

Saturday 7th
Left-wing guerrillas in Colombia attacked a police post in the southern jungle, killing 26 policemen. Next day, President Cesar Gaviria imposed a 90-day **state of emergency**, banned the media from airing the views of the guerrillas, offered a reward for the capture of six senior guerrilla leaders and said that oil companies suspected of paying protection money to the rebels would be investigated.

Sunday 8th
Hizbullah guerrillas fired rockets into northern Israel, following an Israeli **air raid** on their bases. Israel reinforced its border. Undaunted, Israeli and Arab peace negotiators resumed talks in Washington the following day.

Nigerian aircraft attacked rebel positions in **Liberia**. Nigeria was the main contributor to a West-African expeditionary force striving to restore order in the strife-torn country.

Tuesday 10th
Jordan's State Security Court sentenced two members of parliament to 20 years in jail with hard labour. They had been accused of plotting, with Iranian help, to **overthrow the regime** of King Hussein and install an Islamic republic in its place. Both men denied the charges. The case had turned into a trial of strength between the king and the Muslim Brotherhood, which controlled one-third of the seats in parliament. A few days after the convictions, the king issued a pardon.

Thursday 12th
Five German tourists were wounded in southern Egypt, in the latest of a series of terrorist attacks by **Islamic fundamentalists**.

Saturday 14th
The foreign ministers of Iran, Syria and Turkey said after a meeting in Ankara that there should be no attempt to partition Iraq, or to make the "safe haven" for Kurds in northern Iraq into a **Kurdish state**.

Monday 16th
The head of the standing commission investigating political violence in South Africa accused the government of **dirty tricks**. Judge Richard Gold-

stone disclosed that in May 1991 military intelligence had recruited a team to entice members of the African National Congress into crime. The revelation was all the more embarrassing as it came two days after President F.W. de Klerk told a British television interviewer that all dirty tricks had ended.

One Arab was killed and 11 injured when attackers threw a hand grenade at them inside the Old City of Jerusalem. A **Jewish extremist group** claimed responsibility.

Kenya said the election due on December 7th would be postponed until December 29th. A court had ruled that opposition parties needed **more time** to organise.

Tuesday 17th
Nigeria announced that the presidential election due in December would be postponed until June 1993, and that the handover from military to civilian rule would take place in August 1993 instead of January 1993. The government blamed the delay on **pervasive corruption**, which had invalidated the presidential primaries two months earlier.

Sunday 22nd
Voters in Peru elected a new Democratic Constituent Congress to write a new constitution. The former constitution, together with the former congress, had disappeared in April when **President Alberto Fujimori**, with the backing of the army, abolished it. With the main opposition boycotting the election, the president's men won an outright majority in the new body.

Tuesday 24th
A conference in Copenhagen decided that **ozone-gobbling** chlorofluorocarbons (CFCs) would be phased out in the

industrial countries by the end of 1995.

Wednesday 25th
Yasser Arafat, chairman of the Palestine Liberation Organisation, said from Tunis that after more than a year the peace talks with Israel had reached a **dead end**. He said the Palestinian delegation might boycott the next round of talks.

Thursday 26th
The stand-off which had threatened **peace in Angola** since September's election appeared to end when members of the MPLA government and of the UNITA movement met under UN auspices. They agreed to a ceasefire, and UNITA's Jonas Savimbi, the election's loser, said he would join a cabinet if his men got senior posts. But UNITA members stayed away from an inaugural meeting of parliament, and launched fresh military attacks two days later.

The United States told the UN that it would be willing to offer up to 30,000 soldiers to help protect **famine relief in Somalia**.

Friday 27th
Soldiers in Venezuela mounted their second **coup attempt** of the year. The mutineers shot their way into the radio station and mounted air raids on the presidential palace. Several hundred people were killed before forces loyal to Carlos Andres Perez, the elected president, regained control.

Wednesday 2nd

Israel's government asked its parliament to **repeal** a 1986 law prohibiting Israelis from meeting members of the Palestine Liberation Organisation. The justice minister said the ban was "against the principles of liberty".

Algeria said it would impose an indefinite **night-time curfew** in its latest bid to crush opposition by the Islamic fundamentalists, whom the army robbed of an election victory in January. Since then about 9,000 people had been arrested, and some 300 killed in clashes with security forces.

Thursday 3rd

The UN Security Council approved a resolution allowing American soldiers to enter Somalia to create a **"secure environment"** for food aid.

A bomb in Medellin, Colombia, killed 14 people. Police blamed **drug traffickers** led by Pablo Escobar, still on the run after his escape from jail.

Sunday 6th

Fresh from surviving his second coup in a year, Venezuela's President Carlos Andres Perez saw his ruling Democratic Action party humbled in **local elections**. On a low turnout, the opposition won most of the state governorships at stake.

Monday 7th

Three Israeli soldiers were shot dead in the Gaza Strip by members of **Hamas**, the Palestinians' Islamic resistance movement. One of the most daring attacks on Israeli troops in recent years, it was followed a few days later by a similar ambush in the West Bank, in which another soldier was killed.

Boutros Boutros-Ghali, the UN secretary-general, reported that between 7,000 and 8,000 troops would be needed to supervise the **transition to peace** in Mozambique. They would supervise the demobilisation of the warring armies and oversee the election due in 1993. The Security Council approved a reduced version of this plan nine days later.

Wednesday 9th

Heavily armed and well-camouflaged **American marines** swarmed ashore in Somalia. The landing was unopposed, but the soldiers complained of harassment by television crews who had been waiting for them on the beach.

Egypt sent some 12,000 paramilitary police into Imbaba, a Cairo slum, in search of the **Islamic fundamentalists** who had been launching attacks on tourists since June. By the end of the week 600 people had been arrested. The government accused Iran and Sudan of inciting the troublemakers.

Thursday 10th

In the first lethal incident during Operation **Provide Comfort**, French troops in Mogadishu opened fire on a lorry, killing two of its occupants. The French said the lorry had crashed through a roadblock. Somali onlookers asked for a "better explanation".

Sunday 13th

Hamas, the Islamic movement in the Israeli-occupied territories, **kidnapped** an Israeli border-policeman and threatened to kill him unless Israel released Sheikh Ahmed Yassin, the movement's founder. The soldier's body was found in the West Bank two days later.

Monday 14th

In a ceremony marking the formal **end of the civil war** in El Salvador, 2,000 soldiers of the Farabundo Marti National Liberation Front (FMLN) handed their rifles to UN peacemakers. Under the peace plan the FMLN was to become a political party and the government was to reform the army, the government and the judiciary.

Thursday 17th

Israel's High Court brushed aside lawyers' appeals and allowed the government to **expel** more than 400 Palestinians suspected of supporting Hamas or other Islamic movements in the West Bank and Gaza. The deportees were dumped across the Lebanese border. The Lebanese government refused to take them in; the Israeli government refused to take them back. They pitched their tents in between the two armies.

Saturday 19th

President F.W. de Klerk announced a **purge** of army officers. He sacked or suspended 23 senior officers, including two generals and four brigadiers. "Some of the individuals", he said, "might have been motivated by a wish to prevent us from succeeding in our goals."

Monday 21st

King Fahd launched a rare public attack on **Islamic extremists** in Saudi Arabia. He criticised the circulation of cassette tapes containing political sermons and accused "foreign elements" of trying to destabilise the kingdom.

Saturday 26th

Prodded by Robert Oakley, the senior American diplomat in Somalia, the country's chief warlords, Mohammed Farah Aideed and Mohammed Ali Mahdi, promised to stop fighting each other and agreed to eliminate the "green line" that had divided Mogadishu, Somalia's capital, into two armed camps. Two days later the two men embraced each other at a **peace rally**.

Sunday 27th

American fighters **shot down** one of two Iraqi fighters which, the Americans said, had entered the "no-fly zone" the UN had imposed in southern Iraq in August.

Yitzhak Rabin, Israel's prime minister, refused a request from James Jonah, a UN official, to let relief supplies get through to the Palestinian deportees marooned in Lebanon. But the next day Israel said that ten of the deportees, victims of **mistaken identity**, would be allowed home.

Tuesday 29th

At talks in Geneva America and Russia agreed new cuts in strategic nuclear weapons. Under this **START-2 treaty**, long-range warhead stockpiles would be cut by two-thirds by 2003, and both sides would eliminate many missiles carrying multiple warheads.

Kenya held its first **multiparty elections** for 26 years. The two main opposition parties, sinking their own differences, accused the government of vote-rigging.

Brazil's disgraced president, Fernando Collor de Mello, **resigned** minutes after the Senate began to try him for corruption. The trial continued anyway. The Senate found him guilty, removed him from office and banned him from politics for eight years. Itamar Franco was sworn in as the new president.

As we reported then

Waiting for the other shoe

JANUARY 11TH *Algeria looked set to become the first Arab country to eject its leaders in a free election. An Islamic party was poised for victory. One week after this article was published, the army cancelled the vote*

LIKE Mikhail Gorbachev, Algeria's President Chadli Benjedid has ushered in more reform than he bargained for. Having prised his country democratically open, he finds his countrymen choosing a form of government that goes well beyond any plans that he might once have had. Yet, unless something nasty jumps out from behind mosque or barracks—and the Islamic fundamentalists have been hinting at the dire possibility of an army coup—the signs are that the president will stick by the democratic experiment he instigated.

The Islamic Salvation Front (FIS) is poised to win the run-off elections on January 16th, having triumphed in the first round on December 26th. For an absolute majority in parliament it needs to win only 28 of the 199 districts where there was no overall winner in December; since it already leads in three-quarters of these seats, it can probably do far better than that without much trouble. Even if the Constitutional Council, which on January 11th will pronounce on all the electoral fouls that the losing parties allege they have discovered, finds that some districts must hold their elections again, this is unlikely to affect the completeness of the FIS's victory.

The anti-Islamists are hoping for some democratic joy from the 5m Algerians (out of an electorate of 13m) who did not vote in the first round. The FIS, not yet three years old and a social and religious movement rather than an organised party, did a much better job than the secular parties in getting out the vote—and will continue to galvanise its followers with the fiery rallies planned for January 13th. Some of the earlier non-voters may now be haunted by the imminent spectre of an Islamic state, but there is no reason to suppose that many of them will gather behind what is now, in most districts, their only alternative: the corrupt, fossilised collection of chieftains and hacks, called the National Liberation Front (FLN), that has been running Algeria since independence.

The assumption must be that, by the second half of this month, Islamic fundamentalists will dominate Algeria's parliament and so have a logical claim on its government. Under the constitution, the president appoints the prime minister who then nominates his ministers, some of whom (for defence and foreign affairs) are directly responsible to the president. But it would cause deadlock—and subsequent chaos—to have a government antipathetic to the Islamic majority in parliament.

The FIS is expected to push for the appointment of its leader, Abbasi Madani, who remains locked up awaiting trial for conspiracy and subversion. It seems inevitable, and sensible, that Mr Madani and his fellow-prisoners are now swiftly released. But both sides, if they are anxious to avoid direct confrontation, will be striving for a temporary compromise. The search is on for a prime minister acceptable to both Islamic and secular forces; one of the better names to surface is Ahmed Talib Ibrahimi, a former foreign minister who belongs to the FLN's Islamic wing.

It is probable, though by no means certain, that the FIS will move in a restrained way towards its unrestrained aims. It believes, as its manifesto says, in an Islamic state in which "Islam is the ideological reference point embracing all aspects of life". But the party is roughly divided between those who believe that Algeria should find its own way to Islamic rule (the Djezara wing, which is currently in the ascendant) and the radicals (the Salafiya wing) who demand sweeping social changes.

The FIS pragmatists are talking of a period of *cohabitation* with the presidency. Their freedom to push for immediate reform is checked by constitutional constraints—and by the fact that they operate under the shadow of the Algerian army. Abdelkader Hashani, the FIS's acting leader, gave warning this week that the army and security forces, which intervened bloodily in October 1988 and again last June, were once more deployed in force throughout the country. The FIS has been careful, this time, not to provoke the kind of disorder that would give the president a pretext to bring the army in. A coup cannot be ruled out, dismal and retrograde though it would be.

Yet coexistence, at best, will be bumpy. Under the constitution, the president has the power to dissolve a defiant parliament and to call for new elections. A number of bodies are specifically empowered to protect constitutional rights. If the new parliament passes the kind of social laws that are expected of it—to restrict the right of women to work away from the home, to send girls to segregated schools, to ban contraception and to make all forms of alcohol illegal—these laws will be challenged.

There may be less controversy on the economic front, though nobody, at this stage, can really tell. The FIS is an economically liberal party, strongly supported by small businessmen and in favour of private enterprise. Mr Madani, when at liberty to do so, has gone out of his way to reassure foreign businessmen on questions of trade and investment. But other leaders sound a xenophobic note, perhaps warning away multinational companies that had been contemplating new forms of joint venture.

The party's headache, when its celebrations come to an end, will be how to keep its promises to the disinherited: the unemployed young, the urban families scrunched into a single waterless room, the hopeless and the angry. Banning some women from some jobs may provide a bit of work for some men. The FIS may win plaudits sharing out a little of the exaggerated wealth and property of Algeria's rich. But these reforms would be symbolic, at best. The only thing that would bring a quick change to the country's miseries—a rise in the price of oil and gas—is not in the hands of even God's messengers.

Algeria, says one of the FIS leaders, should become an Islamic state "inspired by the experiences of Iran, Saudi Arabia and Sudan". His words inspire the fear of many people. But Algerians have always seen themselves as leaders of the developing world, not as followers—let alone of such lamentable examples. They are unlikely to change. Besides, it is hard to isolate a people behind an Islamic veil when one-third of them have easy access to French culture and news from their satellite television sets.

De Klerk across the Rubicon

MARCH 21ST, SOUTH AFRICA **Two years after freeing Nelson Mandela in 1990, white South Africans showed, in a referendum, that the agonisingly slow retreat from apartheid had become irreversible**

IN 1985 P.W. Botha, then South Africa's president, promised but failed to lead his country across the Rubicon. This week his successor, F.W. de Klerk, succeeded. In the whites-only referendum on March 17th the wording on the ballot paper was woolly. Voters were asked whether they supported the government's reform process, which was "aimed at a new constitution through negotiation". But the meaning of the question was sharp as a pin. Whites knew that they were being asked to dump over 40 years of apartheid, along with all the privileges that went with it. Astonishingly, 68.6% of those who voted said "yes".

Two years ago, when Mr de Klerk let Nelson Mandela out of jail and began the retreat from apartheid, he promised to give whites a chance to vote on what he was doing. But the idea back then was that they would judge a new constitution after one had been negotiated. Instead, a string of setbacks—notably the Conservative Party's by-election victory in Potchefstroom in February—obliged him to go to the electorate early. This week's avalanche of assent gave Mr de Klerk more or less a blank cheque to take into his constitutional negotiations with Mr Mandela. He still needs to be careful how he spends it.

A good number of those who supported Mr de Klerk did so with mixed feelings: some out of fear that their beloved sports teams would otherwise be forced out of international competition, just when their cricketers had reached the World Cup semi-finals; others from dread

of renewed economic sanctions. But few look forward to black majority rule with anything other than foreboding.

A taste of the changes in store came one day after the referendum, in the form of a new budget. Barend du Plessis, the finance minister, said that it was designed to promote "stability and equity" in accordance with the needs of the new South Africa. More than 40% of state spending is to go towards social projects, many of which are designed to narrow the gap between black and white. Investment in public housing will double, and spending on health and education will rise by 22% and 24% respectively. Pensions will rise too, faster for blacks than for whites.

Some of the new spending will be financed by cuts in defence and sales of oil reserves: this is South Africa's post-apartheid version of the peace dividend. But the rest will come from borrowing, from taxes on petrol, tobacco and alcohol, and from the shifting of resources from whites to blacks. Most of the new education spending, for example, will go into black schools. White ones will be expected to cut costs.

Politically, the next step is likely to be the creation of a transitional "super-cabinet" to bring blacks into the cabinet for the first time in South Africa's history, and to prepare for the formation of a body that could serve both as a transitional parliament and as a constituent assembly responsible for drawing up a new constitution. This much was agreed on by the government and Mr Mandela's African National Congress before the referendum. But the exact nature of the transitional body is still in dispute. Mr de Klerk's National government, having resisted the idea of electing it via one man, one vote, seems now to have softened its objections—provided that all decisions about the new constitution are made with "sufficient consensus" and that all the main parties have a seat in the cabinet.

The referendum has not resolved the fear of Chief Mangosuthu Buthelezi's Inkatha Freedom Party that it is being elbowed out by government-ANC collusion at Codesa (the Convention for a Democratic South Africa), the 19-party forum in which the constitutional talks are taking place. Mr Buthelezi, aggrieved at the exclusion from Codesa of the Zulu monarch, King Goodwill Zwelethini, has threatened to take his case over Mr de Klerk's head to

the "very heart of Afrikanerdom", by which he seems to mean the Conservative Party.

Mr Buthelezi has vehemently denied that he intends to form a coalition with the Conservatives. But if he and his party feel excluded by the growing convergence between Mr de Klerk and Mr Mandela, some sort of co-operation cannot be ruled out. A "non-aggression pact" between Inkatha's Transvaal leader, Musa Myeni, and the neo-fascist Afrikaner Resistance Movement may be a straw in the wind, even though Mr Buthelezi disavowed it.

The white yes may encourage some Conservatives to end their boycott of

Codesa. Even before the referendum one prominent Conservative, Koos van der Merwe, argued for such a decision. He also incurred the enmity of party hardliners by insisting that the party should contest rather than boycott the referendum. That, it is now obvious, was a blunder, and Mr van der Merwe may be blamed for it. He has already broken with his party by repudiating apartheid and searching for "internationally acceptable and morally justifiable measures" to protect whites from the black majority. If the "New Right" faction he leads is forced out of the Conservative Party, it will probably head, like most groups in South Africa, for Codesa.

Reverses on every front

MARCH 21ST *For more than 20 years Arabs have complained that America's friendship with Israel obstructs peace in the Middle East. At the beginning of 1992, that friendship appeared to be fraying at the edges*

IT WAS a lousy week for Israel. Car bombers blew up the Israeli embassy in Buenos Aires, killing 20 people and burying more beneath the rubble. A Palestinian from Gaza ran amok in Jaffa, killing two people and wounding several others with a knife. But these events, though horrible, were in a way routine disasters. In Washington something less familiar was happening. This may have been the week when America, following the example of France in the 1960s, began at last to dissolve its special relations with the Jewish state.

The sudden change in Israel's fortunes is neatly illustrated by the fate of two callers on the American capital: Jordan's king and Israel's defence minister. One short year ago George Bush was heaping praise on Israel (for not firing back when Iraqi Scuds blitzed Tel Aviv) and cutting aid to Jordan (for publicly deploring the American bombing of Iraq). But when King Hussein visited the White House on March 12th all was beaming forgiveness. "He is my friend and I welcome him back," Mr Bush declared. The unsquashable king has somehow leapt from being *persona non grata* to the centre of the Arab-Israeli peace talks. He arrived in Washington bearing Yasser Arafat's power of attorney to put the case for a Palestinian-Jordanian confederation in the West Bank. And he got a right royal welcome.

A few days later Moshe Arens, Israel's defence minister, was given a different sort of welcome. He was greeted only with bad news—that Israel's hopes for $10 billion in Ameri-

can loan guarantees were as good as dead—and a roasting in the newspapers.

The roasting started even before Mr Arens had stepped off his aircraft. First the *Washington Times* accused Israel of giving a precious Scud-busting Patriot missile to China. Then the *Wall Street Journal* disclosed that a forthcoming report from the State Department would accuse Israel of transferring air-to-air missiles to China, anti-tank missiles to South Africa and cluster bombs to Ethiopia, Chile and other countries. Finally the *Washington Post* chimed in with a report that the accusations were based on firm intelligence.

Mr Arens, denying all, asked his hosts

Once this was an embassy

to quash the rumours. Instead, the State Department put out a frosty statement implying that there was indeed a fire beneath the smoke. Israel challenged the Americans to send a team to Israel to make sure that all of its Patriot missiles, and the associated technology, were still in the country. Slightly to Israel's surprise, the State Department took up the offer. Meanwhile Israelis back home denounced the series of leaks as deliberate: some members of the ruling Likud Party said Mr Bush's administration was out to sway Israel's general election, due at the end of June, in favour of the Labour Party.

It is no secret that Mr Bush and his secretary of state, James Baker, would prefer a Labour victory in June. Unlike Yitzhak Shamir's unflinching Likud, Labour accepts the idea of territorial compromise: if it gained power Mr Bush might make faster progress in the Arab-Israeli peace talks he inaugurated last October. The president's sharpest weapon against the Likud is to withhold the loan guarantees Israel needs for economic recovery, and he is using it. On March 17th Mr Bush dashed hopes of a compromise on the loans. "I've said over and over again that we want to help," Mr Bush told journalists. "But we're simply not going to shift and change the foreign policy of this country."

No freeze on Jewish settlement in the West Bank; no American loan guarantees. Although this outcome has enraged the Likud ("we will not crawl or beg," fumed Mr Arens) it was predicted many months ago by Zalman Shoval, Israel's ambassador to Washington, who was reprimanded for his prescience. The flap over the Patriots, on the other hand, blew up from nowhere and raises a new and more troubling question for Israel. Can its relations with America recover from their present trough, even after a putative Labour victory?

The answer is, at least, uncertain. Until this week Israelis liked to think that, no matter what ups and downs afflicted their friendship with America, military relations were secure. Israel, after all, is one of America's closest defence partners outside NATO. The two countries hold regular exercises, about 100 American warships a year visit Haifa, and three or four American generals a month pass through the American embassy in Tel Aviv. Technical interchange between the two defence establishments is intimate. Mr Arens himself was trained in America as an aeronautical engineer: the apple of his eye is the Arrow, a futuristic missile Israel is building under the American "star wars" programme.

Is it likely, Israeli defence officials ask rhetorically, that Israel would jeopardise all of that by passing America's secrets on to the Chinese and other shady customers? An answer may come when the Americans have made their inspection. But some Israeli military men suspect that, no matter what the inspectors discover, America has already determined that there will be no exoneration. Over and above charges that Israel has played fast and loose with secrets from the Patriot and Arrow missiles, the Americans are complaining about Israel's export of missiles it has made itself, on the ground that they contain American parts or ideas.

Israel acknowledges that a few of its missiles are modified or improved versions of American ones, but says that the Americans have known and approved of these sales for years. It is proud of its missiles, and promotes them vigorously in return for cash or, as in the case of China, political co-operation. A few Israeli officials blame the present fuss on envious American arms manufacturers who are feeling the pinch and eager to do down a thrustful competitor. But others fear that Patriotgate is the opening salvo of a campaign designed in the White House to reduce American military ties with Israel. Either way, the 25 year partnership between Israel and America is showing signs of collapse.

Peru's high-handed president

APRIL 11TH *The seemingly unstoppable march of democracy in Latin America came to a bumpy stop when economic muddle and the terrorism of Shining Path guerrillas pushed the president of Peru into a gamble*

ALBERTO FUJIMORI, a clever, determined, impatient man, and president of Peru, thinks he knows better than the rest of his country's politicians put together. In the night of April 5th, after careful preparation, he sacked the government, dissolved Congress, suspended the constitution and set about governing with absolute powers backed by the armed forces, which ran the country until the mid-1960s. In Spanish it is called an *autogolpe*, a self-coup.

Mr Fujimori says he intends to push through economic reforms, turn round the anti-terrorist war, write a new constitution, hold a plebiscite and bring his country through to a spruced-up democracy, all in less than a year. Authoritarians often make coups with similar good intentions. They less often live up to them.

Until Mr Fujimori smudged the picture, Latin America's politics had seemed transformed in the past decade. Traditional military dictators survived only offshore, in Cuba and Haiti. Democracy, peace, free trade and intimations of prosperity had replaced nationalism and military banners. Yet the most brilliant transformation was made in Chile, where the dictator Augusto Pinochet (in office 1973-90) ruthlessly built the economic foundations upon which Chile's decent democrats are now building. Mr Fujimori may see himself as an instant civilian Pinochet.

He has begun without brutality. Troops occupied party and newspaper offices, and detained opposition leaders and independent journalists (politely, it seems) in their homes. Schools and universities were closed. All was soon back to normal. The polls said 70% of the people approved.

Reaction abroad seemed unanimously hostile. Mr Fujimori has persuaded his clever economics minister, Carlos Bolona, to stay on (shamefaced, maybe) with most of the outgoing cabinet, to continue the economic reforms that the United States approves of. But the Americans have damned the coup, cutting off all save "humanitarian" aid to Peru. This has been welcomed by many Latin American leaders, still facing self-righteous soldiers who think a touch of discipline can set all right.

Peru, to be sure, is a hard case. Mr Fujimori, elected against expectations, started in July 1990 to run a country ruined by decades of civil and military misrule, riven by civil war, plagued by the traffic in drugs, and with a cumbrously detailed constitution. He had no real party behind him with which to muster a majority in Congress for his radical measures. He therefore pushed them through not by legislation but by presidential decree, subject not to parliamentary fixing but to the lesser risk of a post-hoc congressional veto. The prospect of such a veto prompted his coup.

The president's reforms were coherent. He cut tariffs and hacked his way through notorious restrictions (such as the labour regulations that made international shippers steer clear of Peru's ports). By raising prices and restraining liquidity he brought down inflation from 7,650% in 1990 to 139% last year. Loud street demonstrations, organised by trade unions and pressure groups, indicated his effectiveness as much as his unpopularity.

But the poor got poorer. The countryside is ravaged, by the guerrillas of the Shining Path and by the soldiers who hunt them. The capital is crammed with poor Indians fleeing that terror; about 2m of its 6m people were on the brink of destitution when Mr Fujimori was elected. Nobody knows how they survive the president's austerity. They cannot go back to the war-torn land.

Mr Fujimori rages against those (like Amnesty International) who criticise his troops for brutality in the anti-terrorist war. He condemns the judges and the legal restraints that safeguard the accused. More justifiably, he denounces the corruption that thrives on Peru's biggest export, which is coca for the United States drug market. The Americans have been helping his domestic war on drugs. They will have trouble continuing, since the army, now in control, tries to recruit coca farmers and the merchants who buy their produce, to resist the predators of the Shining Path.

Mr Fujimori seems to have tried to win friends abroad—notably in Japan—before staging his coup. He must, though, have known that his political rivals would not forgive him. He detests them, and complains loudly that the courts exonerated his predecessor, Alan Garcia, on charges of misappropriation of funds. Mr Garcia, who still leads the opposition American People's Revolutionary Alliance, Peru's largest party, had hoped to stand for the presidency at the next election. He has escaped arrest, and his friends speak of resistance to the new dictatorship.

Driving political opponents underground, in a country where terrorism is already rife, could be the worst consequence of Mr Fujimori's autocoup. Latin Americans still have to learn that democracy means obeying the rules, not breaking them to make them better.

The craving for kings

APRIL 25TH **For a time, after the ignominious failure of communism, the triumph of democratic ideas seemed inevitable. But early in 1992 we thought we saw a different trend**

AFGHANS, waving a delighted goodbye to President Najibullah, wonder whether ex-King Muhammad Zahir Shah might not be the man they need. Romanians, struggling to make sense of post-communist democracy, are allowing ex-King Michael home for the Orthodox Easter. In high society, monarchs never went out of fashion. In real life, too, they seem to be making a comeback. Why, and where?

Afghanistan has a hole where a government should be. An elected assembly would have to include old-fashioned Communists and fanatical Muslims, citified merchants and rustic chieftains, all talking together in at least four languages. Royalists say wistfully that a constitutional monarch with minimum explicit powers could unite the quarrelsome lot. But even if they offered him the job, the ex-king might turn it down. He succeeded his murdered father at the age of 19, in 1933, and was deposed in 1973 by a cousin who was duly murdered five years later. He lives as quietly as he can (after a recent knife attack) in Rome and Nairobi.

The Romanians have similar problems, in a longer historical tradition. King Michael is a Hohenzollern, a name that few history books omit. Like the Saxe-Coburgs (Bulgaria), the Romanovs (Holy Russia) and the Karadjordjevics (Serbia), they belong to the European cousinage that for centuries ran states for lesser peoples. Bourbons, Savoys, Braganzas and Oldenburgs have similar family trees to trim, in France, Italy, Portugal and Greece. They all have hopes that the monarchy business is ripe for expansion. Some families are already doing fine.

Restored, the Spanish Bourbons brilliantly eased their country from dictatorship to democracy. Queen Elizabeth (of Saxe-Coburg-Windsor and part Scottish too) moonlights over 15 realms as well as her United Kingdom—although the Mauritians fired her last year, and some Australians would like to do the same.

Monarchy is not just a deal that lingers on in Europe. Although five Muslim kings (in Iraq, Iran, Egypt, Libya and Zanzibar) have been kicked off their thrones in the past 40 years, nine still reign. Libya's exiled Sanousi dynasty is revelling in Muammar Qaddafi's troubles. There are 11 indigenous sovereigns in Asia (not counting Malaysia's multiple sultans), three in Africa (plus the Zulus' king and West Africa's emirs, fons and nanas) and two in Oceania. Apart from Afghanistan, at least three non-European republics—Ethiopia, Brazil and Cambodia—are wondering whether to invite old dynasties back.

Ethiopia's dynasty has been re-established several times since its foundation in about 2500BC, at a bedroom summit of Solomon, King over all Israel, and the Queen of Sheba. Today's pretender, ex-Crown Prince Asfa Wossen, was named heir by his grandfather, Emperor Haile Selassie. The old emperor inherited the throne in 1930, was deposed by Italian invaders in 1935, restored by the British in 1941, and deposed again in 1974 by a junta that turned communist and murdered as many as it could lay hands on. The reinterment of Haile Selassie's remains, in July, could be the occasion for declaring Asfa Wossen's succession.

Ethiopia's emperors, like Russian tsars, were supreme rulers of the (Coptic) Orthodox church, embodying the ancient Amharic culture. Most Ethiopians are not Copts, do not speak Amharic and remember the imperial system as reactionary, greedy and corrupt. The imperial title, if revived, would signify not much more than titular sovereignty in a Commonwealth of Independent Ethiopian States.

When Sheba met Solomon

Brazil sometimes remembers its branch of the European dynasty of Braganza. In 1822 Peter of Braganza, heir to the Portuguese throne, set up as emperor of an independent Brazil. His son Peter II ruled there for 58 years, until deposed by reactionary landlords in 1889. Brazil has since gone through two dictators, four deposed presidents, 19 military putsches and seven constitutions. Brazilians, who call their greatest footballer King Pele, may think a monarch would last longer. Dom Peter of Orleans, born in 1914, is in direct line, but disqualified because his grandmother was a commoner. His younger cousin Dom Louis of Braganza is a militant right-wing Catholic. Brazil may get a chance to choose in its forthcoming constitutional referendum.

Cambodia's Khmer dynasty goes back (with a few interruptions) to King Bhavavarman I before 600AD. Its current head, ex-King Norodom Sihanouk, became monarch under French protection in 1941, abdicated in 1955 in favour of his father, then served from time to time as head of state or as prime minister, with periods of exile in China. By all accounts, the Khmer people revere their subtle ex-monarch. Whatever regime finally emerges in Cambodia, he will be a leader, if not the sovereign.

The green legacy

JUNE 13TH, RIO DE JANEIRO **Greenery has become the conventional wisdom, subject to the flaws of conventional politics**

AS A galaxy of heads of state descended on Rio de Janeiro for the closing days of the Earth summit, their exhausted civil servants wondered how much of their labours would survive the flight home. Expectations had been so high: all those thousands of papers, books and television programmes that pinned hopes to what might happen when the world's leaders devoted the best part of a fortnight to discussing the world's environmental problems. The reality appeared so mundane: hours of sweltering negotiations, paragraph by paragraph, in yards of tortuous and heavily qualified text.

The conference tried to do too much: two treaties, 800 pages of green guidelines (called "Agenda 21"), a grandiose declaration of good green intent and a package of forest principles. Rio has involved nearly four times as many countries as founded the United Nations, and three times as many as devised the Montreal protocol on chlorofluorocarbons (CFCs), itself a prodigy of green diplomacy. In the sheaves of documents, there was something for everybody to object to: lines on territories under occupation that annoyed the Israelis, on population control that displeased the Vatican, on energy that irritated Saudi Arabia.

The planet will not be "saved", any more than it was after the last grand UN conference on the environment, in Stockholm 20 years ago. But just as Stockholm left a bureaucratic legacy of environment ministries and legislation that helped the rich countries to clean themselves up, so Rio's success will depend largely on the strength of the machinery that it leaves behind.

Quite a lot has been left, and some of it will have enduring effects. One such monument is the provision for national reports and plans that was embodied, with varying degrees of strength, in several conference documents. The climate treaty, with its obligation on signatories to draw up a plan to show how they intend to stabilise their output of global-warming gases, puts a powerful weapon in the hands of national green lobbies, as the cleverer ones are starting to realise. The Sustainable Development Commission, although modelled on the unpromising format of the UN Commission on Human Rights, also carries a rather vague obligation to submit national environmental reports.

Another legacy is the growing importance of the Global Environment Facility. This pot of cash, boosted at Rio, will pay for the climate treaty, and probably for the treaty on biological diversity (once the poorer countries have overcome their suspicion of the World Bank, which administers the GEF, and the fund has been reformed to give poor countries more say). Any future environmental treaties (the Africans want one on deserts, for instance) will probably draw from the GEF as well. International aid is likely to take on a greener hue.

Nostalgia, with a villain

A third bequest of Rio will be its influence on those who took part in it. Heads of state who rarely spare a thought for the environment have had to mug up on it to make their speeches and give their press conferences. The businessmen who assembled in Rio in the week before the Earth summit, under the chairmanship of Stephan Schmidheiny, a Swiss industrialist, went home full of good intentions to be cleaner and greener. Delegates from newly industrialising countries were, apparently, particularly inspired.

The jamboree had something of an old-fashioned flavour that did not come only from the presence of the Beach Boys and Bianca Jagger. There was also the 1970s-style confrontation between north and south (though mercifully not between east and west) that emerged. A nostalgic row broke out over the reluctance of some rich countries to reaffirm their aim to meet an aid target of 0.7% of GNP, so often pledged in those bygone days and so rarely achieved. "Give a number or a date, but never both," murmured delegates with long memories.

Old-fashioned, too, was the unofficial conference being staged at the other end of town by non-governmental groups. The Global Forum brought together an eclectic array of participants, ranging from Grandmothers Against Nuclear War to Greenpeace, with every gradation from sanity to nuttiness. Some sold psychedelic T-shirts and taught meditation at a sort of wholemeal trade fair; others held earnest negotiations on alternative treaties. The rows that these engendered were frequently more bitter than those at the official conference, even though the alternative treaties were usually trying to agree on the highest common factor rather than the lowest common denominator.

The final touch of nostalgia at the con-

The world answered

ference was the casting of the United States in the role of villain. The British, who were more sympathetic to the American position than most, thought that the Americans managed to attract the maximum amount of stick for the minimum amount of obstinacy. The American forestry initiative, George Bush's pet project, was launched ineptly and was soon bogged down in arguments over an accompanying list of forest principles with the Malaysians and Indians; their objections to the treaty on biological diversity, most of them reasonable, earned them only opprobrium; their objections to some of the sillier talk of the poor countries appeared arrogant.

The most awkward moment during the first week of negotiations was the leak of a classified memorandum sent by William Reilly, the head of the Environmental Protection Agency and of the American delegation, to the White House. The memo reported that the Brazilians had asked the United States to suggest ways in which they might "fix" the treaty on biological diversity, so that the Americans would be able to overcome their reluctance to sign it. Unfortunately the word for "fix" used by the Brazilian newspapers is generally applied in the context of parking fines.

In the second week America's public-relations wizards excelled themselves. An unnamed senior official at the White House told reporters that the Rio meeting was "a circus" where chaos prevailed. If America's allies supported measures, such as the bio-diversity treaty, that America disliked, it was only because they felt guilty and wanted to be "politically correct".

All this catapulted the conference from the inside pages of the American press to the front, thus drawing attention to the extent to which the summit had previously been ignored in America—in contrast to other countries. The legacy of Rio will not be truly secure until the United States revives its interest in the environment.

Labour's return

JUNE 27TH, JERUSALEM
The election of Yitzhak Rabin raised hopes of a dramatic breakthrough in the dismal politics of the Middle East

FOR nearly 30 years, from the birth of the state in 1948 until Menachem Begin swept to office in 1977, the Labour Party thought itself the master of Israel's fate. Over the next 15 years the pattern reversed itself. The Likud, having captured the almost tribal loyalty of the oriental Jews whom Labour neglected, came to seem invincible. So when Labour came back in this week's general election, it was no surprise that grown men in the party headquarters on Tel Aviv's seafront whooped and wept for joy.

Begin was not just another politician.

He was high priest of a particular form of Zionism that insisted on Israel's sovereign rights in the whole biblical patrimony: the West Bank, Gaza and Golan as well as the pre-1967 state. He and his successor, Yitzhak Shamir, strove to ensure that the territories taken in 1967 could not be given up. Except for Jerusalem and Golan, the land was not annexed, lest 1.8m Arab inhabitants demanded political rights. Instead came settlements: hundreds of Jewish towns and hamlets, sprinkled throughout the occupied areas to bind them eternally to Israel.

History may remember June 23rd as the day the whole mad scheme collapsed. Revitalised under Yitzhak Rabin (the prime minister Begin unseated in 1977), Labour increased its seats in the Knesset from 39 to 45, while the Likud's fell from 40 to 32. That meant that with his own seats, plus 12 from the lefter-wing Meretz and five from Arab parties, Mr Rabin appeared to have the necessary "blocking majority" of 62 sure anti-Likud votes in the 120-seat Knesset. He embarked at once on the business of choosing which of the smaller parties to invite into a ruling coalition. To the fury of his own left wing, he was refusing this week to rule out the possibility of inviting the Likud to join the coalition as a junior partner.

Having won the election mainly on the strength of his own reputation, Mr Rabin gave few clues about the shape of his preferred government, beyond announcing that he alone would decide on the appointment of ministers. It is plain that he intends to revolutionise Israel's foreign policy.

One day after the election he gave warning that government money would no longer pour into the Likud's "political settlements" in the West Bank (he is kinder towards front-line "security settlements", many of which were created under a Labour government after the 1967 war). The first priority, he said, was "the creation of autonomy and self-rule for the Arabs in the territories". A rapprochement with America is in the offing, along with renegotiation of the $10 billion loan guarantees the Americans had withheld from Mr Shamir. The peace talks that have staggered fitfully nowhere since last October in Madrid may now sprint ahead.

Before Mr Rabin's victory, Israelis had been deploring the dullness of the election. In general, the big issues of land and peace had taken second place, during the campaign, to more parochial grumbles: about government corruption, 11% unemployment, the undue influence of the religious parties and the Likud government's failure to sustain and absorb the massive immigration from the former Soviet Union. American disapproval of Mr Shamir's policies put a cloud over the government. But there was certainly no sense, as Israel voted, of the election being a referendum on the future of the territories. The change of government might have as much to do with the number of immigrant voters as with the debate on Greater or Lesser Israel.

The evidence for a change of mind on territorial matters is sketchy. But one suggestive surprise was the disappearance of the pro-annexation Tehiya Party, which lost all three of its vociferous members of

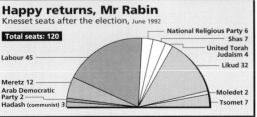

Happy returns, Mr Rabin
Knesset seats after the election, June 1992

Total seats: 120

Labour 45
Meretz 12
Arab Democratic Party 2
Hadash (communist) 3

National Religious Party 6
Shas 7
United Torah Judaism 4
Likud 32
Moledet 2
Tsomet 7

the previous Knesset. Another Greater Israel party, Rafael Eitan's Tsomet, it is true, performed exceptionally well, leaping from two seats to seven. The election may not have been a vote for territorial compromise, but neither was it a vote for sitting tight.

The Likud faces a painful post-mortem. The party knows that as the peace process moves forward, everything it has fought for since 1977 could be put in jeopardy. Mr Shamir is expected to step aside leaving perhaps five claimants—Ariel Sharon, Moshe Arens, David Levy, Binyamin Netanyahu and Benny (son of Menachem) Begin—to vie for the crown. Rank-and-file Likudniks are gloomily aware that by the next election, in four years' time, the "autonomy" period could be approaching an end, with negotiations about to begin on the final status of the territories.

Can Mr Rabin, a 70-year-old ex-general, really change things so fast? A huge gap separates his notion of border adjustments and security arrangements from the complete withdrawal that the Arabs continue to demand. But the important point to remember is that last time he was prime minister Egypt had not yet made peace, the cold war still existed and the Arab world was still refusing to talk to Israel openly and directly. Nowadays, anything could happen.

Murder in Annaba

JULY 4TH   *The murder of a president showed how low Algeria had sunk since abandoning its experiment in democracy*

AN OLD revolutionary hero, uncontaminated by the ruling party's long years of corruption and misrule, he might have been considered the right man for a bad time in Algerian history. But Muhammad Boudiaf, who was assassinated on June 29th, six months after he was brought back from self-imposed exile to give the respectability of a civilian head of state to a basically military regime, did nothing to heal his country's wounds. He was an honourable man but his job was too ambiguous to count for much. His savage death is expected to do little more than tighten the defensive rule to which he gave his blessing.

The motive of his murderers, one of whom is said to have been arrested alive, had not at mid-week been disclosed. The assassination was a planned operation. An explosion to the left of the stage in Annaba, a town in eastern Algeria where the president was speaking, caused a momentary agitation. Mr Boudiaf, who had just said, "We are all going to die. Why should we cling so much to power?" hesitated. The diversion was long enough for the gunman to move in from behind the curtain at the back of the stage and discharge two short bursts of automatic fire into Mr Boudiaf.

The government said later that one assassin was a secret-service officer. But the most likely suspects are still the Islamic fundamentalists, particularly as they are known to have infiltrated the police. Algerian policy, since the cancellation of the January election that the fundamentalist party, the Islamic Salvation Front (FIS), was all set to win, has been to try to squash the fundamentalists out of existence. The party was outlawed, its leaders are being tried (the trial of the top men, Abassi Madani and Ali Belhadj began last weekend but was post-poned until July 12th), and several thousand rank-and-file members are incarcerated in detention camps in the scorching temperatures of the southern Sahara.

The headless party declared in April that its members would take to the gun. Many obeyed; some 100 policemen and soldiers have been killed in ambushes and shoot-outs. Mr Boudiaf was heralded as a conciliator, but nothing that he said or did suggested he was advocating the sort of policy that might seek or lead to an accommodation with the frustrated movement.

Algeria's neighbours, with their own fundamentalist problems and obsessions, tend to take it for granted that the FIS or one of its extremist wings was responsible. The more imaginative Algerian press is indulging in an orgy of conspiracy-theorising. Although much of this is fantastical, there are non-fundamentalist suspects who are not wholly improbable. Mr Boudiaf came in as Mr Clean and his commendable zeal for purity in government won him many enemies. So far as he could, he set out to punish those who had dipped into the state's coffers during the 30 years of one-party rule by the National Liberation Front (FLN); one of his first victims was a senior general.

The army took its time to name Mr Boudiaf's successor. At mid-week it had not disclosed whether it would find another civilian to take Mr Boudiaf's place—and there are several admirable names on offer, probably including the prime minister, Sid Ahmed Ghozali—or whether General Khaled Nezzar, the defence minister, would become the regime's official, as well as its unofficial, leader. In any event the iron-fist policy towards the fundamentalists is unlikely to be interrupted. If this leads to civil war, say the policy's more fervent advocates, then so be it. After all, they add sombrely, 1m Algerians died in the long fight for independence from France.

It is not at all clear whether Mr Boudiaf's attempt at "direct dialogue" with the public will survive his death. With the FLN in disgrace, and the FIS hounded, Mr Boudiaf was encouraged by his army mentors to try to launch a non-party gathering called the National Patriotic Assembly, from which both fundamentalists and old-time politicians would be excluded.

The aim was to attract the people who abstained at the general election (where the turnout was low) by giving them a rousing alternative to Islam. They were encouraged to rally round the flag of "Algerian patriotism and modernity". Few were impressed: most Algerians are far too young to remember the revolution

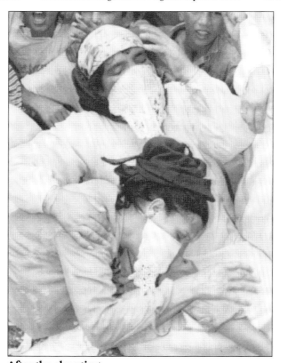

After the shooting

or, indeed, Mr Boudiaf; they correctly interpret "modernity" as economic reform. And what economic reform means, grumble Algeria's disaffected poor, is that they not only remain without jobs but also without the food subsidies that they enjoyed before the army's reformers took over.

Economic reform is vital to the regime, which is betting on an improvement in the country's broken economy to weaken the fundamentalists' hold on the loyalty of the unemployed young. Outside help is urgently sought. The finance team, under the direction of Mr Ghozali, has been striving to refinance Algeria's private and public

debt. It has done pretty well with the private debts, signing agreements with more than 100 banks, mainly in the United States and Japan. It has had a much tougher time in refinancing its public debt to France. Resentful Algerians like to claim that France wants to keep its former colony in a state of instability and dependence.

Imperturbably Saddam

AUGUST 1ST   *Though diminished, the man who towered over the Middle East in 1990 continued to make a nuisance of himself in 1992*

NEEDLESS to say, the cupboard was bare. Whatever it was the United Nations inspection team had been eager to look at inside the agriculture ministry in Baghdad had vanished once the team (minus, at Iraq's insistence, its American, British and French members) negotiated its way inside on July 28th. Three weeks had passed between the inspectors' first knock at the front door and their eventual entry. In the meantime, the world seemed to drift dangerously close to a new war in the Gulf.

That danger has receded, but it has not yet passed altogether. Perhaps unwisely, given the proximity of the presidential election in the United States, Iraqi leaders spent this week loudly congratulating themselves on their humiliation of the Americans. Although George Bush was at the same time insisting that it was Saddam Hussein who had caved in—the inspectors had, after all, got into the ministry—this looked other-worldly in Baghdad. There, demonstrators swarmed in the streets, celebrating the exclusion of UN inspectors drawn from the three western powers that had led the coalition in last year's Gulf war.

The showdown at the agriculture min-

istry was not the first time Mr Hussein had challenged the right of UN inspectors to do their job of defanging Iraq. A similar sequence of events followed last September's seizure, from Iraq's nuclear-energy agency, of reams of documents containing details of a clandestine atomic-weapons programme. In March a military strike had looked a hair-trigger away when Mr Hussein refused, for a time, to obey the Security Council's order to dismantle machinery that could be used to build missiles. On both occasions, as on this one, he drew back just before Mr Bush and his allies could agree upon, or deliver, a suitable military punishment.

This time, arguably, Mr Hussein sauntered closer to the brink. By the time Iraqi and UN negotiators had struck a last-minute bargain in New York, American reinforcements—a third aircraft carrier, the *John F Kennedy*, plus Patriot missile batteries for Kuwait (and later Bahrain)—had already started towards the Gulf. Only after the Iraqis granted access to the ministry did the White House concede that the situation had been "defused"—and then only "for the moment". The *John F Kennedy*

was called off, but American marines are to go ahead next week with a series of exercises inside Kuwait.

As the American election approaches, so Mr Bush's ability to tolerate another episode of Iraqi brinkmanship diminishes. One outcome of the latest affair may be that the president has at last armed himself with the necessary consents—from Congress and from his foreign allies—to strike without delay next time a UN inspection is disrupted. It is also possible that he will decide to act without waiting for a further Iraqi provocation. One tempting target could be the Iraqi military aircraft flying against Shia rebels in the southern marshes. Another is the Iraqi power grid, much of which could be dismantled from afar, without risk to Americans, by using cruise missiles.

Other methods, short of war, to increase the discomfort of Mr Hussein could include the reimposition of an air embargo, more stringent controls on the overland traffic through Jordan, the confiscation of Iraq's (frozen) foreign assets and a more muscular UN presence in the Kurdish haven in northern Iraq. A Saudi newspaper, *Asharq al-Awsat*, claims that a raft of such measures will shortly be discussed in the Security Council. One sign of new thinking in Washington was a meeting this week—the first since the war—between James Baker, the American secretary of state, and the exiled leaders of the Iraqi opposition.

Still, past experience suggests that stealing the initiative from a gambler as unpredictable as Iraq's president is no easy task. Indeed, a few usually sober analysts, watching the rapid reorganisation of the Iraqi army since the Gulf war, have even started to speculate about a second Iraqi invasion of Kuwait. The risks to Mr Hussein, from internal enemies as well as foreign ones, would clearly be enormous. But, in principle, Iraq still has enough military power to carry off an invasion.

Before occupying Kuwait in August 1990 Iraq had about 1m men under arms, 5,000 tanks, 5,000 artillery pieces and up to 800 combat aircraft. This August those numbers are down to about 350,000 men,

2,000 tanks, 2,000 artillery pieces and 300 aircraft (of which only 150 or so are operational). Although this is a huge reduction, the force that remains still towers over tiny Kuwait's. Iraq's elite Republican Guard is back to its pre-war eight divisions, the Iraqi air force has stepped up its flying hours and the air-defence network is thought to be back to its original strength.

Nobody seriously thinks Mr Hussein would be mad enough to use all this as a sword to force his way back into Kuwait. But as a shield it is a substantial one, from the protection of which his defiance is liable to grow. From the evidence of the agriculture ministry, the world's ability to scare him—never strong—is in danger of evaporating.

The Security Council's servant

AUGUST 8TH **New secretary-general, new world order, same old tussles at the United Nations' headquarters**

WHEN Boutros Boutros-Ghali was elected by the Security Council last November it was feared he might not be spirited or young enough to lead the United Nations into its more venturesome ways. The critics misjudged him: lack of spirit and stamina are not among his character failings. The new secretary-general has risen splendidly to the occasion. But his rise is upsetting those around him.

Ambassadors at the Security Council do not take kindly to being told home truths by the secretary-general. A crossness that has been festering for some time broke surface in mid-July when Mr Boutros-Ghali made a couple of sound points in an intemperate manner. He argued first that the UN, even though it has been defrosted from the cold war, can still do only as much as its members provide for and pay for. Then he complained, more controversially, that Security Council members allot disproportionate resources to the tragedies that affect them directly.

Poor countries were the first to declare themselves disappointed at the failure of an African to put third-world interests first. His streamlining of UN bureaucracy removed a slew of economic jobs that poor countries had put their faith in, though most duplicated work done elsewhere. Arabs thought him insufficiently dedicated to the resolutions on Palestine. As the humble servant of the Security Council, he came to be depicted as the too-humble servant of the United States.

As Mr Boutros-Ghali has responded to this third-world pressure, stresses have appeared between him and the bossy Americans and Britons at the Security Council (the French, who pushed for his election, have continued to give him their backing). He disliked spending so much time on the resolution imposing sanctions on Libya, which he felt had been clumsily handled, was directed largely at western audiences and had landed him with an ambiguous mandate. The failure of rich countries, particularly the United States, to pay their UN dues had flummoxed all secretaries-general, but became a particular irritant to this one as he was pressed to do more without the wherewithal to do it.

The snarling grew angrier over what the UN could, or could not, do to stop the carnage in Yugoslavia. In the late spring the Security Council instructed the secretary-general to break the siege of Sarajevo without giving serious consideration to the kind of force that would be needed to do so. Then, on July 17th, Britain's Lord Carrington got the three Bosnian factions to agree to put their heavy weapons under UN control. The Security Council met later the same day to agree that this should be done, asking the secretary-general, who was not at the meeting, to prepare a report on the logistics.

Mr Boutros-Ghali blew up. The Community, he said, should put its resources at the service of the UN, not the other way about. The Bosnian job would overstretch his resources when they were more urgently needed elsewhere, especially in Somalia where one-third of the population could soon be dead if the UN failed to act. It was reasonable that Europe should make the tragedy on its doorstep a priority; unreasonable that this order of priorities should be foisted on the UN, making it seem that the world body paid undue attention to crises where lobbyists have the ear of influential western leaders—and where refugees threaten rich countries rather than poor ones.

This needed saying. Yet the exchange revealed weaknesses in both the UN and its new secretary-general. Why, for a start, was he not at the Security Council meeting that had proposed rounding up Bosnian artillery? He was engaged, he said, in talks on Libya and on Cyprus, where he is trying to get the UN peacekeepers uninvolved so that Greek and Turkish Cypriots should at last be forced to make real peace with one another. Undoubtedly, the secretary-general should delegate more. He has done a fine job in getting rid of some of the UN's more formidable barons. But a fat inefficient bureaucracy survives, impeding the work of half-a-dozen excellent overstretched men. And the most overstretched of all is Mr Boutros-Ghali himself.

Also, though it is a relief that Mr Boutros-Ghali has shown that he is no photocopy of his emollient predecessors, he may, in a world of inflated egos, be going too far in the opposite direction, revealing more than a touch of arrogance. The British press, fed nasty and improbable leaks about his early retirement, had plainly got under his too-thin skin. But it was absurd of him to suggest recently that critics were yapping at him because he was a "wog".

With a single five-year stint in office in mind, Mr Boutros-Ghali does not mind making enemies. He has neither the time nor the patience to attend to all the self-important folk who cluster round the UN. Certainly his time is better spent saving the world. But he will accomplish nothing if the powerful governments of the world abandon their post-cold-war commitment to work through the world body.

Lochinvar goes west

Brazilians saw the humiliation of their president as a triumph for democracy

IF EVER a politician was impaled on his own sword, it was Fernando Collor de Mello. In 1990 the handsome young president from the obscure state of Alagoas swept into office promising to slay corruption and liberate Brazil from its self-isolating economic policies. To some degree, he succeeded. Thanks partly to his lectures, Brazilians will no longer put up with the venal politics of the past. So when they discovered their saviour's hand in the till, they showed no mercy.

On September 29th the Chamber of Deputies, the lower house of Brazil's Congress, voted by 441 votes to 38 in favour of impeaching Mr Collor. Technically he is now suspended for 180 days while the case goes to the Senate for trial. But his presidency is surely over. Though he refused at first to contemplate resigning, he may be hoping to do so in return for a pardon from his successor. Under the constitution, this must be the vice-president, Itamar Franco. Without a pardon, Mr Collor will probably soon face common criminal charges, in addition to his trial by the Senate.

The decisive vote in the Chamber of Deputies, which had to secure only a two-thirds majority, was greeted with jubilation. On the grassy esplanade outside the Congress building, tens of thousands of demonstrators, their faces painted in the national colours of green and yellow, set off a shower of fireworks. The capital erupted with the honking of cars and yells of joy.

Impeaching your president is not an obvious cause for delight. In this case the fateful vote was taken as a sign that Latin America's biggest democracy had come of age. The deputies had at last exercised the powers vested in them by the constitution of 1988. They had struck a blow for clean government, without fear that the generals who ran the country from 1964 to 1985 would come marching out of their barracks. Above all, they had listened to, and acted on, the wish of the people.

Mr Collor's downfall began in May as a family feud. His younger brother Pedro denounced him in the press as the "front man" for Paulo Cesar Farias, a businessman from Alagoas. "P.C.", as Mr Farias is known in Brazil, was accused of running a huge bribery ring inside the government.

Within three months a congressional investigation had confirmed the story. It found that Mr Farias had exploited his friendship with the president to extract millions of dollars in bribes from businessmen seeking government contracts. In return, Mr Farias passed money to Mr Collor through secret bank accounts. The president spent $2.5m of it sprucing up his family's gardens.

Ordinary Brazilians were unamused. Mr Collor had, after all, spent more than two years lecturing them on the virtues of belt-tightening. Since his election in

Collor unhorsed

March 1990, the real wages of federal employees have fallen by half, and the minimum wage is worth less than it has ever been since its creation more than half a century ago. Unemployment has soared and inflation has been running at more than 20% a month.

The evidence of presidential wrongdoing galvanised the press. Fearlessly, and often recklessly, the newspapers hounded the president and kept the story before the public. Hundreds of thousands of citizens, many of them students, sustained the pace of playful and peaceful mobilisation for two months. For them, the slow and difficult transition from 21 stifling years of military rule was at last over. Last time Brazilians turned out on the streets—to campaign in 1984 for direct elections to the

presidency—Congress closed its ears. This time it was the people who got their way.

After the party, Brazil needs to come to terms with the vastly different style of Mr Franco. Mr Collor, at 43, was a good-looking, telegenic reformer. Mr Franco, at 61, is a civil engineer and career politician from the mountainous mining state of Minas Gerais. He has a spotless reputation . But he also carries some of the pro-labour, anti-competition ideological baggage that many other Brazilians have abandoned.

In the Senate Mr Franco has been a bitter critic of the IMF. He has questioned the need for Brazil to repay its foreign debt. The new president's home state was one of the few regions to thrive during the past three decades of state-dominated, tariff-sealing policies. Recently, Mr Franco criticised the government for successfully selling off Usiminas, a big state-owned steel mill in Minas Gerais. It is not, he says, that he opposes privatisation in principle; only that it seems wrong to sell off first of all the handful of publicly owned companies that are truly profitable.

Yet it is far too early to assume that Brazil's change of president means an equally dramatic change of policy. For one thing, Mr Franco is in no position to make economic policy all on his own. He will have to bend to the will of the opposition coalition that organised Mr Collor's impeachment. And (in an ironic tribute to Mr Collor's achievements) all members of this coalition, including the parties of the left, say they want to persist with reforms to cut state spending and expose the economy to foreign competition. "The name of the next finance minister", said Orestes Quercia, the head of the Brazil Democratic Movement Party, the biggest party of all, "is tax and structural reform."

Besides, Mr Franco's own views may recently have altered. "I'm not the only one who has changed. The world changed," he said last weekend. The extraordinary circumstances in which he became president will guarantee him some goodwill in Congress. How peculiar it would be—and how excellent for Brazil—if Mr Franco, a reluctant bystander during many of Mr Collor's reforms, became the man who put them properly into practice.

Mr Collor resigned on December 29th.

Down on the farm

All over the world, farming is on the defensive. We visited the pampas of Argentina

ABUNDANT, fertile land, worked by hard-grafting migrants from the farms of Spain and Italy, made Argentina briefly one of the richest nations in the world, and the gaucho, the caped cowboy of the pampas, the symbol of that wealth. Today, as the country struggles to catch up after decades of economic malaise and mismanagement, the farmers are lagging behind.

The farmers' associations say that at least one-third of those who work more than 50 hectares (125 acres) of land do not make a living. The land is, as ever, ideal for raising cows, wheat, maize, soyabeans and sunflowers. But economists agree that the men and women of the pampas face more obstacles than ever.

The farmers are angry about President Carlos Menem's programme of economic reform. With the Argentine peso fixed against the dollar, cheap imports flow in from Brazil, where the currency keeps on falling; the government, by fiddling with charges on imports and exports, is trying to achieve a de facto devaluation. But borrowing in Argentina costs more than twice as much as in neighbouring countries.

It may be that farmers would not update their equipment, even if credit were cheaper. But the high cost of money guarantees they will not invest. So far, only those who own the largest farms have been able to get credit at foreign rates. Mr Menem's economy minister, Domingo Cavallo—in most things a true believer in letting markets work by their own rules—is ordering lenders to lower their rate for farmers.

In late October the three largest farmers' organisations got fed up with lobbying, and decided to send "a political message to the president" by striking on November 2nd and 3rd. For those two days their members duly withheld deliveries of livestock and grain to the markets. But because milk spoils (and cattle suffer if they are not milked), deliveries continued as usual.

Blaming Mr Menem is easy. Argentine farmers' long-term problems lie far beyond his control. The European Community and the United States have for decades competed to sell what their farmers grow, well under their cost of production. China's recent agricultural success has meant that it buys less food. The Soviet Union's collapse means that its ex-citizens can no longer afford what they used to buy.

There are plenty of excuses on offer, and plenty of faults in Argentina too. Moving crops and livestock from the fields to the customers has always been expensive. Export routes, and domestic customers, are concentrated in the immense city of Buenos Aires. The capital was well served by the country's early railway builders but the transport system has barely been improved since the 1940s. Prices in city supermarkets swing wildly up and down.

When farm profits were big, farmers grew lazy. Between 1910 and 1940, many became absentees, spending their money in the capital while nobody took decisions about the farm. The government of General Peron deliberately imposed levies on farm exports, to subsidise its supporters in the urban trade unions and the army. Periodic bouts of raging inflation hit farmers especially hard; by the time they were paid, the money was almost worthless. With future receipts uncertain, there was little incentive to plan years ahead.

Nowadays, it seems that fewer people want to work on the land. The number of farmers has dropped from about 525,000 to 400,000 in the past 25 years. Sales of tractors fell from 22,000 in 1977 to under 4,000 last year. It is reckoned that just one in five farm children will keep up the family tradition.

Farming optimists are looking forward to Mercosur, a free-trade group that is supposed to embrace Argentina and Brazil in 1995, creating a market of 150m, and another 7.5m when Paraguay and Uruguay join a year later. If Argentina's farmers on their excellent, empty acres are to meet their neighbours' demand for food, they would do well to learn from their parents' mistakes, and start investing now.

Sins, ancient and modern

In 1992 the Catholic church made it as easy as ever as ever to be really bad

AT ALMOST 700 pages, it bears no resemblance to those dog-eared little red books, stained with ink and repentant tears, that used to be kept in the schooldesk of every Catholic child. But it is just as formidable in its intent. The old Catholic catechism, drawn up by the Council of Trent in the mid-16th century, was aimed at the errors of Protestants; the new Catholic catechism, six years in the making and just released in Paris, takes on the world.

Pope John Paul II is anxious about both the struggling eastern church and the carelessly secular western one. Cardinal Jean-Marie Lustiger of Paris says the new catechism aims at "real universality", the sort of market penetration achieved "by blue jeans or foreign-exchange markets, which can ruin a country in two days".

Translations and pocket versions will appear next year. Catholics will read the text with trepidation, knowing the answers already but hoping, as usual, for a modification here and a softening there. They will find a few. Homosexuals, for example, "do not choose their condition; for most of them, it is an ordeal". They should be treated with compassion and not discriminated against. Homosexual acts are "disorderly". Masturbation, however, is "gravely disorderly". Less a matter of hope for homosexuals than despair for teenage boys.

The old sins are firmly restated: divorce, abortion, suicide, euthanasia (though not necessarily removal of life-support systems) and prostitution. Birth control is forbidden when technical and effective, not when natural and haphazard. War is accepted as a last resort, but chemical and nuclear weapons are "a crime against God and man". Capital punishment is acknowledged as a way for the state to protect itself, "but it should be avoided".

Sins once indulged in seldom go out of style, but new ones have been discovered. "Thou shalt not steal" now covers tax evasion, embezzling company assets, paying unfair wages and speculating. Genetic engineering and drug-taking, if not therapeutic, are sins. Rich countries sin if they turn away "the foreigner in search of security and vital resources". Drunken driving and joy-riding are added to the list. Oh, and women priests: "The Lord Jesus chose men . . . and the church is bound by this choice." Clear enough?

Contents

BUSINESS

O harsh new world

SOME hangovers last longer than the celebrations which cause them. In 1992 businessmen everywhere began wondering whether a few joyous years of excess in the late 1980s were going to have to be paid for with years of suffering in the 1990s. Recession in America, Britain, Canada and Australia in 1991 was bad enough. But 1992, contrary to what businessmen hoped, brought no relief. Price wars raged in a number of industries: steel, cars, computers, consumer electronics, household appliances, air travel, fast food and retailing, to name just a few. Some former high fliers, such as computer maker Wang, Macy's department stores and Olympia & York, the world's biggest property developer, went bust. Recession spread to Japan and Germany.

The canary is grounded

Much of this pain was, indeed, the result of 1980s excess: too much borrowing, too much investment, too much capacity. The recession, and the 1980s hangover, will end some day, as it already looked like doing by the end of 1992 in America. But the increase in competition which many companies faced in 1992 may not. The globalisation of business, so long foretold, is now a reality for tens of thousands of firms.

Many of the big firms which preached the virtues of globalisation assumed it meant a brave new world of easy opportunities. What they began to discover in 1992 was that it is more likely to mean a harsh new world of endless competition. This was most evident in America, the world's biggest, most open and most fiercely contested national market. But companies everywhere were affected. A paroxysm of self-doubt gripped German companies, which suddenly discovered that their costs were far higher than those of foreign competitors. Japanese car makers, struggling to cope with a downturn at home in 1992, found that they could no longer rely on easy profits in America and Europe, where local rivals have copied their techniques to raise quality and productivity. Japanese computer firms found their domestic market under attack from lower-priced, better products from American and other rivals. Cracks began to widen in the officially-sanctioned cartel propping up many international airlines, as British Airways, Air France, Alitalia and KLM all bought stakes in foreign airlines. As this new world emerges, consumers will benefit enormously. But running a company will be a tougher, and riskier, task.

Japan's recession came as the biggest shock of the year. Until its arrival became undeniable, most Japanese businessmen tried to pretend it did not exist. Many firms did not begin cutting capital-spending budgets until the spring, well after it became obvious that Japan's economy was headed for more than a mere slowdown. The bursting of the so-called "bubble economy" of 1987-90 had a devastating effect on corporate profits, which plunged an average 36% in the six months ending in September. Many of the biggest names in Japanese business suffered far worse. Pre-tax profits at Matsushita, the world's largest maker of consumer electronics, crashed by 66%, at car maker Mazda by 72% and at Nippon Steel by 74%. Nissan, Japan's second-biggest car maker, lost ¥14.2 billion ($114m) before tax. That sounds like peanuts compared with the billions lost by General Motors, but it is the first loss ever for Nissan. The revenues and profits of Japan's five biggest computer manufacturers—Fujitsu, NEC, Hitachi, Toshiba and Mitsubishi Electric—fell for the first time in nearly two decades. By one estimate, 30% of small businesses in Japan lost money in 1992 and corporate bankruptcies were double those of 1990.

The government rightly received much of the blame for this, especially for causing the bubble in the first place by letting monetary growth get out of control. But businessmen admitted that they were also at fault. Flush with what seemed like cheap money from a soaring stockmarket, Japanese companies of every stripe over-indulged in new factories, lavish offices and dormitories—and speculation in property and shares. And, dare it be said, many Japanese manufacturers became bloated, rather belying their reputation for obsessive cost-cutting.

But Japanese business is rightly famous for coping with sudden and dramatic changes. When the yen more than doubled against the dollar between 1985 and 1988, Japanese manufacturers responded by moving some production abroad and learning how to become multinationals. In 1992 they were scrambling to adjust to a harsh new climate. Ironically, many firms were doing this by diluting or revers-

Japan's bubble bursts

Germany stalls

ing practices which American and European firms have tried so hard to imitate. Car makers and electronics firms slashed the bewildering number of products and features which they offered, and talked of introducing fewer new products less frequently in future. Many firms also seemed to shift their focus from market share to the bottom line. And big firms grew restive under the restraints of life-time employment, cutting overtime and bonuses and, often none-too-gently, pushing older or less productive workers into early retirement. Yet another paradigm of Japanese management is certain to emerge from such changes. But in 1992 its outlines were not yet clearly visible.

German companies also suffered in 1992 from an earlier investment binge which turned out to be unjustified. In their case, the disappointment came from eastern Germany, which did not boom as businessmen once foolishly expected it would. High interest rates, higher taxes and lower demand all produced the usual headaches for companies. But the biggest worry of German companies remained their high costs. German labour costs in manufacturing were the highest in the world, more than a third higher than Japan's and almost 50% higher than America's. It was hardly surprising, then, that BMW, a luxury car maker, pushed ahead with plans to make some of its cars in America. Daimler-Benz's Mercedes unit, another firm which had long exploited Germany's reputation for quality and craftsmanship, is considering an American factory of its own.

For some industries 1992 brought a confusing mix of triumphs and tragedies. The most notable example was the computer industry. Brutal price wars drove down the price of personal computers, and with them the price of bigger, more powerful machines such as workstations, minicomputers and mainframes as well. For the first time price-cutting also swept through the personal-computer software market. Though lower prices kept personal-computer sales buoyant, industry profits tumbled. Nevertheless, amid this carnage some firms, such as Apple and Compaq, staged spectacular comebacks. Others, such as Microsoft, Novell and Dell, continued to post huge increases in sales and profits.

In contrast, older computer makers, the giants of the industry, had a terrible year. The biggest victim was IBM, which cut 40,000 workers from its payroll and said another 25,000 would have to go in 1993. Big Blue also announced more than $11 billion in special charges to pay for job losses and other cuts. Coming on top of the awful year it had in 1991, IBM's woes in 1992 heralded either the birth of a smaller, more decentralised firm capable of surviving the changes sweeping the industry, or the death of one of the world's greatest companies.

Even while big companies struggled to adjust to harsher times, their shareholders were growing more impatient. The debate about how to make big public companies more accountable—known as corporate governance—rumbled on throughout the year. In Britain the Cadbury report recommended splitting the titles of chairman and chief executive into two separate jobs as well as appointing more board directors from outside the firm and giving them clearly defined powers. Most big American firms already have such directors.

But militant institutional shareholders in America have not been content to rely on directors, who they feel are often too friendly to a firm's managers to act as disciplinarians. Such institutions want a more direct say themselves. To make that easier, America's Securities & Exchange Commission proposed to ease insider-trading rules restricting discussions between powerful institutional shareholders, and to force companies to delineate the pay of top managers more clearly in their annual reports.

In fact, for American bosses 1992 proved to be a bruising year. Their pay, which soared in stark contrast to their companies' profits, scandalised the public and put many bosses on the defensive. In a move that shocked corporate America, angry shareholders forced outside directors on the board of General Motors to first demote and then sack the company's chairman, Robert Stempel. A number of other American bosses were ushered out of the door earlier than they expected: Time Warner's Nick Nicholas, DEC's Ken Olsen, American Express's James Robinson. In Britain Robert Horton, BP's hard-driving boss, also got the order of the boot.

There was, at least, one break in the clouds of 1992. Japan-bashing, that inane sport of feeble businessmen, seemed to go out of fashion, at least in America. The number of collaborative deals, from simple licensing agreements to ambitious joint ventures, between Japanese and American firms grew rapidly. Perhaps the well-publicised tribulations of Japanese firms shattered the myth of their invincibility and so made them more congenial partners. Perhaps it finally dawned on the managers of big companies that the hordes of smaller firms learning to compete globally represented more of a threat than supposed "cheating" by their Japanese rivals.

OPPORTUNITIES UNLIMITED.

In a borderless world, one **GLOBAL CITY** can advance your **STRATEGIC INTENT**. Against shifting forces. Creating strategies to steer businesses ahead of their competition. Already it is the world's **LARGEST HARD DISK DRIVE PRODUCER** and **THIRD BIGGEST OIL REFINING CENTRE**. It manufactures the world's **BEST SELLING PRESCRIPTION MEDICINE**, and over US$15 billion of electronic products a year. A leading user of **SURFACE MOUNT TECHNOLOGY** and rated the top location for **INTERNATIONAL BUSINESS HEADQUARTERS** in Asia. This '**INTELLIGENT ISLAND**' offers sophisticated IT and telecommunication networks, and business linkages to plug you into the booming Asia-Pacific region and beyond. **A TOTAL BUSINESS HUB** aligned with the corporate goals of over 3,000 MNC investors. This is **SINGAPORE UNLIMITED.**

CALL SINGAPORE ECONOMIC DEVELOPMENT BOARD, FRANKFURT (069) 23-3838, LONDON (071) 839-6688, MILAN (02) 799-277, PARIS (01) 4500-1183, STOCKHOLM (08) 663-7488.

January

Monday 6th

A big American telecommunications carrier, **Sprint**, became the first foreign firm to apply for a licence to compete against BT and Mercury in Britain by providing domestic and international telecommunications services.

Sales of **new cars in America** dropped to 8.2m in 1991, down by 12% from 1990 levels. Japanese manufacturers suffered least.

Japan's cross-border M & As

¥bn	1989	1990	1991
Japanese takeovers overseas	3,691	3,206	684
Of which: USA	2,677	2,051	382
foreign takeovers in Japan	51	21	177

Source: Daiwa Securities

Foreign **mergers and acquisitions** by Japanese companies collapsed in 1991, it was reported. They were down by almost 80% by value compared with 1990, with the biggest falls in America and Britain. But spending by foreigners on Japanese companies rose by 700%, albeit from a minuscule base.

Tuesday 7th

Prompted by George Bush's visit to Japan and his moans about American exports, Japan promised it would **increase imports**. Japanese car makers agreed to try to sell their American rivals' products, and the prime minister, Kiichi Miyazawa, promised to boost domestic demand.

One of **America's largest retailers**, Sears, Roebuck, said it would spend $60m on computers for its sales floors, cutting 7,000 jobs and saving around $50m a year. Another big retailer, Woolworth, announced plans to sell or revamp 900 stores, cutting up to 10,000 jobs.

LSI Logic became the first member to pull out of Sematech, an American **semiconductor consortium** set up in 1987 to do battle against Japanese competition. LSI Logic decided its money was better spent on its own research than on shoring up American semiconductor-equipment companies.

A consortium headed by **Air France** announced that it was buying a 40% stake in CSA, Czechoslovakia's state-owned airline, for $60m. The French airline became the first western carrier to take a stake in an existing East European airline.

Tuesday 14th

News of the resignation for health reasons of **John Kerridge** as boss of Fisons boosted the firm's share price, battered by negative comments from America's Food and Drug Administration.

America's AT&T and Holland's state-owned PTT Telecom said they were forming a joint venture with the government of Ukraine to modernise and handle that country's long-distance and international **telecommunications system.**

Monday 20th

Switzerland's Nestlé and France's Banque Indosuez made a FFr13.4 billion ($2.5 billion) hostile bid for **Perrier**, which the bottler of the eponymous mineral water promptly rejected. The bid came soon after the Agnelli family's bid for Exor, the French wine and food group that controls at least 35% of Perrier, was cleared by stockmarket authorities in France.

It was revealed that America's Securities and Exchange Commission was considering changes which could give shareholders a clearer view of **directors' pay.** Under the new rules, firms would have to use a standardised method of valuing executives' share options. Shareholders would also be allowed to vote on questions of remuneration.

The debts of companies going **bankrupt in Japan** soared to ¥8.15 trillion ($61.3 billion) in 1991, quadrupling 1990's figure.

Tuesday 21st

United Technologies, an American aerospace and building-products group, took a pre-tax charge of $1.53 billion against fourth-quarter earnings, resulting in a $1.22 billion net loss for the quarter. With a loss for the year of $1.02 billion, the group announced it would cut 14,000 jobs over two years and close over 100 plants.

Wednesday 22nd

Boeing sold its ailing **de Havilland** subsidiary, which makes small propeller-driven aeroplanes, to Canada's Bombardier group and the province of Ontario. Europe's trustbusters had blocked a previous deal to sell it to Italy's Alenia and France's Aerospatiale.

Monday 27th

One of America's largest chains of department stores, **R.H. Macy**, filed for protection from creditors under chapter 11 of the bankruptcy code. It could no longer service its $3.7 billion of debt, a legacy from the 1986 management buy-out that took it private.

Jean-Luc Lagardère, chairman of both Hachette, a French publishing group burdened with the bankrupt television station La Cinq, and Matra, maker of missiles and electronics, said he planned to merge the two firms to allow cash flow to circulate more freely between them. Mr Lagardère's holding company owns controlling stakes in both firms.

Tuesday 28th

The French government picked **IBM** as a partner for its loss-making computer maker, **Groupe Bull**. The government said that the alliance, when details were finalised, would cost IBM $100m-120m for a 5-7% stake in Bull, making Big Blue its biggest non-French shareholder.

Eight months after Hanson bought a 2.8% stake in Britain's biggest chemicals firm, **Lord Hanson** intoned that "we have never said we would bid for ICI . . . and we have no plans to do so now." The statement ruled out a bid for several months under Britain's takeover code. Lord Hanson also chose a successor, but would not name him.

The Swedish government rejected a SKr38.7 billion ($6.7 billion) plan by **Pehr Gyllenhammar**, head of Volvo, to merge his industrial group with Procordia, a Swedish food and drugs conglomerate whose main shareholders are Volvo and the state.

Wednesday 29th

America's loss-making **Bethlehem Steel** said it would shed 6,500 jobs, a quarter of its workforce.

February

Saturday 1st
A $7.5 billion plan to build a pipeline to carry **Iranian oil to Ukraine** was agreed by the two governments. Ukraine, trying to reduce its dependence on Russian oil, said it hoped to receive 10m barrels of oil a year from Iran by 1995.

Monday 3rd
Russia's **economic reforms** were watered down as criticism mounted all over the country and Boris Yeltsin warned donors in the West that time was running out. Taxes on some foods were cut and payments to the poorest were raised.

The scope of GATT should be widened to include a strong role in formulating and enforcing **international competition rules**, said Sir Leon Brittan, the EC commissioner for competition.

Bill Gates, boss of Microsoft, America's top computer-software firm, made big management changes. Out went Mike Hallman, the company's president for almost two years. He should have been flattered: no fewer than three people from within the company replaced him.

After 15 years **IBM** said it was returning to a liberalising India to join forces with Tata, India's biggest industrial group. IBM said that the joint venture, initially costing 850m rupees ($33m) in equity and loans, would make computers and develop software. At one time, Big Blue refused to share ownership of its overseas subsidiaries with anyone.

Friday 7th
Outrage followed a Tokyo court's decision to clear the Japanese government of responsibility for **Minamata disease** after an outbreak of mercury poisoning in the 1950s. More than 100,000 people were poisoned after eating fish affected by mercury pumped out by Chisso, a chemicals firm.

After three years of over-production, sharp spring frosts in 1991 cut output of **French wine** by 35%, to 42.7m hectolitres, with better wines suffering the steepest falls.

Monday 10th
One of America's biggest airlines, **United**, said it would cut back on spending on new aircraft over the next four years, reducing its bill by a third to $12.2 billion.

America's **Dow Corning**, at the centre of the controversy over leaking silicone breast implants, replaced its chairman and chief executive after it was revealed that the firm had known about medical problems for years. As far back as 1980 one salesman had written: "To put a questionable lot of mammaries on the market is inexcusable."

In a big cellular-telephone deal, **Motorola** and **Northern Telecom** formed a joint venture to develop and sell equipment in the Americas.

Tuesday 11th
Microsoft said it was being sued by **Apple** for $4.4 billion in damages for alleged infringements of Apple copyrights involving Windows software.

Friday 14th
Leopoldo Pirelli, the 66-year-old head of Italy's struggling Pirelli tyre and cables group, handed his job to his son-in-law, Marco Tronchetti Provera. The group has suffered since its costly and failed hostile bid for Germany's Continental in 1991.

A management shake-up at **Time Warner** left its president, Nick Nicholas, without a job. He was replaced by Gerald Levin, the group's chief operating officer.

With concern for the ozone layer mounting, the European Community's environment ministers decided that the use of chlorofluorocarbons (CFCS), used extensively in refrigerators, aerosols and fire extinguishers, and other ozone-eaters should be phased out by 1995, 18 months earlier than planned.

A German chemicals giant, Bayer, said it would pay £10m ($18m) for a **genetically engineered sheep called Tracy**, created by Edinburgh-based Pharmaceutical Proteins. Her milk includes AAT, a protein in which one in 2,000 people is deficient.

Monday 24th
Rupert Murdoch took direct control of Fox, **News Corporation's biggest earner**, after the surprise resignation of Barry Diller, who had been head of the Hollywood studio and television network since 1984. Mr Murdoch also said News Corp would raise up to $1 billion in order to reduce bank debt. In 1991 the group successfully restructured $8.2 billion of debt.

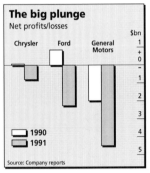

The big plunge
Net profits/losses

Chrysler | Ford | General Motors

□ 1990
▓ 1991

Source: Company reports

America's **big three car makers** suffered badly in 1991. General Motors, the world's largest car maker, announced a loss of $4.5 billion, the biggest in corporate history, and said it was restructuring. Among other things, it said it would reduce the $1.2m pension paid annually to Roger Smith, its former chairman.

Wednesday 26th
Silvio Berlusconi, an Italian media magnate, said he planned to bid for Britain's new commercial-television franchise, Channel 5, which is to be awarded by competitive tender. He already owns stakes in German, French and Spanish television, as well as dominating Italy's commercial-television industry.

Thursday 27th
British Airways and Holland's **KLM ended merger talks** after the two sides failed to agree on the size of each other's stakes in what would have become Europe's biggest airline. America's Northwest, in which KLM has a stake, would also have joined the group. The collapse of the talks was a big setback for the expansion plans of all three airlines.

March

Monday 2nd
American customs officials deemed **Canadian-built Hondas** ineligible for duty-free status under America's free-trade pact with Canada. This left Canada annoyed and the Japanese car maker owing nearly $17m in back duties.

The **Wellcome Trust** said it planned to sell a large chunk of its 73.6% holding of Wellcome, the British drug firm that makes AZT, a top-selling anti-AIDS drug. At some £4.4 billion ($7.7 billion), it would be London's largest private offering.

Tuesday 3rd
A six-year partnership between ITT, an American telecommunications giant, and **Alcatel Alsthom**, a French telecommunications equipment group, ended when ITT sold its 30% stake in their jointly owned subsidiary back to its former partner for FFr18.7 billion ($3.3 billion).

Sun Microsystems hired Boris Babayan, a **Russian computer expert**, and 50 of his colleagues at a research institute in Moscow. Sun said the Russians would carry out research for the company in exchange for a grant and equipment.

Friday 6th
The United States fined six companies a total of $550,000 for violating **sanctions against Libya**, which were introduced in 1986 to punish alleged terrorist acts in Europe by Libya.

Tuesday 10th
In a change of tactics, America's **IBM** planned to sell a cheap "IBM-compatible" computer made by an Asian producer but not under the IBM brandname, initially in Europe.

A French food group, **BSN**, took a 24% stake in San Mi-guel, a Spanish brewery, for an undisclosed price. Europe's second-largest beer producer, BSN already owned brands such as Kronenbourg, Kanterbräu and Peroni and a 33% stake in Mahou, another Spanish beer firm.

The **big German chemicals companies** felt the recession for the second year running, as their 1991 results showed. Hoechst reported pre-tax profits down by 20% to DM2.56 billion ($1.54 billion) and BASF a fall of 23% to DM2.11 billion. Both firms cut their dividends. Bayer did better. Its profits slipped by just 4.8% to DM3.2 billion, and the firm maintained its dividend.

Brazil's deeply divided **coffee exporters** reluctantly decided in favour of worldwide coffee quotas. The previous quota agreement collapsed in 1989.

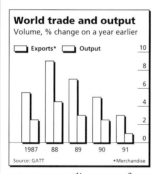

World trade and output
Volume, % change on a year earlier

Exports* / Output

1987 88 89 90 91
Source: GATT   *Merchandise

1991 was a mediocre year for **world trade**. A 3% gain in volume was the smallest since 1983, with a 1½% gain in value, the smallest since 1985. America became the leading exporter, overtaking Germany. Japan was third.

Thursday 12th
California's **Mips Computer Systems** announced it would merge with Silicon Graphics, a maker of workstations, in a $334m share swap. The accord was a blow to ACE, a computer-industry association dedicated to turning Mips's powerful processor chip into a market standard.

Monday 16th
A group of investors led by Investcorp, a bank that channels Arab money into western industry, agreed to pay around $450m for **Circle K**, a big American convenience-store chain which is in chapter 11 protection from its creditors.

France ordered an independent inquiry into the methods used by **Glaxo** to promote Imigran, a new and costly migraine treatment. The government believed Glaxo had been encouraging demand among patients before the drug was cleared for use in France.

America's Chrysler named **Lee Iacocca's successor**. Robert Eaton, 29 years with General Motors and recently the successful president of GM Europe, became vice-chairman and chief operating officer of Chrysler. Mr Eaton was promised Mr Iacocca's posts of chairman and chief executive by the end of the year.

Monday 23rd
After a takeover battle of extreme complexity, Switzerland's Nestlé wrested control of **Perrier**, a French mineral-water firm, from the Agnelli family in a deal that valued Perrier at around FFr15.3 billion ($2.7 billion).

Friedrich von Hayek, economist and philosopher, scourge of socialism and leading light of classical liberalism, died. His ideas were unfashionable for decades—but, with the collapse of communism in his final years, he was triumphantly vindicated.

Another candidate dropped out of the race to bring a new system of **high-definition television** to America. That left five of the original 23. The David Sarnoff Research Centre dropped its idea of improving the present analogue signals; the Federal Communications Commission has made it clear it wants a digital system.

Tuesday 24th
La Cinq, a bankrupt French television station operated by Hachette, lost its saviour. **Silvio Berlusconi**, an Italian media magnate with a 25% stake, abandoned his FFr1.5 billion ($266m) rescue plan after failing to find enough adventurous French investors.

South Africa, freeing up the skies, granted Richard Branson's **Virgin Atlantic** the right to start flying the Johannesburg-London route. South African Airways and British Airways, Mr Branson's arch-rival, had had the lucrative route to themselves.

Thursday 26th
In what looked like a bad omen for reforming Eastern Europe, America's **General Electric** said it would cut its planned investment in Tungsram, its Hungarian light-bulb maker, this year because the country's inflation was boosting costs.

Saturday 28th
After months of speculation, **Volkswagen**'s supervisory board picked Ferdinand Piech to succeed chief executive Carl Hahn in January. The company also announced that it would cut its 130,000-strong workforce by 12,000 over the next five years to lower costs, especially in Germany.

April

Wednesday 1st
Three of the four biggest companies listed in *Fortune* magazine's famous list of the 500 biggest industrial firms were also among the list's **biggest loss-makers**. General Motors, Ford and IBM lost a total of $9.6 billion in 1991.

Sunday 5th
Sam Walton, one of the richest men in the world and founder of the Wal-Mart chain of retail stores, the biggest retailer in America, died in Arkansas aged 74. Robson Walton, his eldest son, became chairman.

The Belgian government approved a partnership between its state airline, **Sabena**, and **Air France**, France's state-owned carrier. Under the deal, Air France and its Belgian financial partners would acquire a 37.5% stake in Sabena.

Monday 6th
The European Community lifted its ban on the sale of **oil to South Africa**.

Following its $4.5 billion loss in 1991, the board of directors at **General Motors** delivered a stunning rebuke to Robert Stempel, the company's chairman, by replacing Lloyd Reuss, a friend of Mr Stempel, as president and chief operating officer with Jack Smith, once in charge of GM's Euro-

pean operations. GM's share price rose.

Although America made the largest number of **investments in Eastern Europe** in the last quarter of 1991, by far the biggest spenders were Germany and Italy. They accounted for, respectively, $3.7 billion and $2.1 billion of the $6.9 billion total.

Tuesday 14th
The cost-cutting programme of **Michelin**, a French tyre maker, helped reduce its 1991 net loss to a mere FFr699m ($124m), it was announced. This result was a good FFr4 billion better than in 1990.

Monday 20th
America's **Caterpillar** declared a first-quarter net loss of $132m as a five-month strike at the world's biggest maker of heavy earth-moving equipment came to an end.

Tuesday 21st
Both Toyota and Nissan saw sales of cars and light trucks in Japan drop in the year to end-March because of **Japan's faltering economy**. It was Toyota's first decline in Japan for over ten years, with sales down by 5.5% to 2.34m vehicles. Nissan's sales fell by 4.4% to 1.32m vehicles, its second annual decline in a row.

IBM, an American computer giant, and **Thomson-CSF**, a state-controlled French defence-electronics group, announced a technology and marketing pact giving Thomson-CSF access to a new chip, developed jointly by IBM and Motorola, used in high-speed RISC computers.

America's Intel, which spent millions developing **flash memory**, a Japanese-invented chip, slashed its price to compete with conventional memory chips. Flash memories can store data almost indefinitely

and be reprogrammed with ease, but they are slower than conventional memory chips.

Capital flows* into America

* Foreigners' purchases less sales
Source: US Commerce Department

New foreign direct **investment in America** continued to slide in 1991, when the total was less than a third of its peak in 1989. Lower inflows of direct investment from Western Europe and Japan explained much of the fall. However, foreign investors' interest in American government bonds revived.

Friday 24th
America's second-biggest computer maker, **Digital Equipment Corporation**, said it was going to take a $1-billion charge in its fiscal year beginning July 1992 in order to cut 10,000-15,000 more jobs. That was on top of the 10,000 jobs that the company already planned to shed by the end of this fiscal year.

Monday 27th
For the first time in 18 years, **Germany's public-sector unions went on strike**, bringing chaos to airports, public transport, roads, postal services, rubbish collection and much more. Workers sought a 9.5% pay rise to help offset higher taxes and inflation due to unification; employers offered only 4.8%.

The Group of Ten industrialised countries gave the go-ahead to a $6 billion fund to **stabilise the rouble**. The decision came as Russia and 13 other ex-Soviet republics were

voted into the International Monetary Fund, opening the door to more aid. The UN's International Labour Organisation gave a warning that unemployment in Russia could reach 10m by the end of 1992.

After years of dispute, Canada agreed to **remove barriers** that had long hindered trade in the North American beer market.

In a drive to revive its flagging personal-computer sales, **IBM** said it was entering the mail-order market so it could deal with customers direct rather than through its hard-pressed dealers. IBM also said it intended to buy Northgate, a small maker of computers, in order to sell that company's cheaper clones in the American market.

Compaq Computer pulled out of ACE, a consortium set up to produce new industry standards for powerful personal computers. The Texas computer maker, struggling to compete with lower-cost rivals, also reported a 60% plunge in 1992's first-quarter profits.

Wednesday 29th
Within a week all three of **America's car makers** announced a long-awaited, though still feeble recovery. The biggest, General Motors, ended a run of six quarterly losses of nearly $8 billion to make a net profit of $179.3m in 1992's first quarter. The news followed an announcement that GM would launch a $2.9 billion share issue. Ford made a $338m first-quarter profit compared with a massive $884m loss in 1991's first quarter. Chrysler's first-quarter oss of $13m included gains from accountancy changes, but its results pleased the market. In the previous first quarter its loss was $598m.

May

Friday 1st
Hungary became the first former Warsaw Pact country to be axed from a list of nations subject to strict export controls by America and its allies.

Monday 4th
After a bitter and unsuccessful takeover bid for **Continental**, a German tyre company, Italy's **Pirelli** put its own non-tyre-making operations up for sale as part of a restructuring. Continental promptly joined the bidding.

Tuesday 5th
Russia's nuclear industry struck its first major deal to supply radioactive material to the West. Mayak, a production centre in the Ural mountains, announced a joint venture with Britain's Amersham International to supply radioactive isotopes for non-military applications like nuclear medicine and research.

Thursday 7th
IBM was reported to be talking to **Time Warner** about taking a 12.5% stake in the firm's film and television businesses. IBM wanted help in winning a stake in the emerging market for computer-based home entertainment. IBM also ended an earlier diversification into telecoms with the sale to Germany's Siemens of its 50% stake in Rolm, a firm which makes telephone exchanges.

Monday 11th
General Dynamics, America's second-largest defence contractor, sold its **missile business** to Hughes Aircraft, owned by General Motors, for $450m. Spending cuts were forcing a shake-out in the industry.

Tuesday 12th
PepsiCo and General Mills announced they will merge their **European snack-food businesses**. The average

American eats 14lb of snacks a year, the average Briton 9lb and a Spaniard a mere 3lb. Combined, the firms hope to bring Euro-snacking up to American levels.

California's supreme court rejected a challenge to the state's **unitary taxation system**. If a certain percentage of a company's sales, property and payroll arises in the state, the state taxes the company on the same percentage of worldwide profits.

America saw the first trade of **pollution licences** under the 1990 Clean Air Act. Wisconsin Power and Light sold to the Tennessee Valley Authority, another power generator, the right to emit 10,000 tons of sulphur dioxide. The price paid was $300 per ton.

Wednesday 13th
An American telephone company, Nynex, said it will lay the world's longest undersea **fibre-optic cable**, linking Britain and Japan via the Indian Ocean.

Friday 15th
A Swedish drug maker, Astra, said it had found a new treatment for **peptic ulcers** that would badly hurt Glaxo's money-spinning Zantac, often used for treating ulcers. Astra's treatment works by attacking a bacterium that is believed to cause recurring ulcers.

Sunday 17th
A 5.8% pay settlement for 4.7m

metal and construction workers in **Germany** averted trouble after disruptive strikes by public-sector unions won them an average 5.4% pay increase. Germany's labour unrest, fuelled by the high costs of unification, increased fears that the country's workers were making themselves too expensive for many manufacturing companies.

Monday 18th
Deutsche Aerospace, with France's Aerospatiale and Italy's Alenia, began negotiations to take joint control of **Fokker**, a Dutch aircraft manufacturer.

Taiwan Aerospace put forward fresh plans for its venture with America's McDonnell Douglas. It proposed to set up a leasing company to channel orders and loans to the American aircraft maker. But McDonnell said it needed equity capital to develop its MD-12 jumbo jet.

Wednesday 20th
Italy's **Fiat** said it would invest about $2 billion in FSM, a Polish car maker. It was the biggest foreign investment in Poland to date.

Thursday 21st
After meeting all night, the European Community's farm ministers agreed a reform of the EC's **common agricultural policy**. Though less than radical, it did improve the chances of a deal in the Uruguay round of GATT talks.

Saturday 23rd
Bernard Tapie resigned from the French cabinet on news that he would appear in court over allegations that he embezzled a business partner's share of FFr13m ($1.4m) of revenues from the sale of a company to Toshiba in 1985.

Two big Japanese camera makers, **Nikon** and **Minolta**,

reported poor results for the year to end-March. Minolta blamed its troubles on the payment of ¥16.9 billion ($131m) to America's Honeywell to settle a dispute over an auto-focus patent. It made a ¥8.5 billion pre-tax loss, its first in 26 years. At Nikon, pre-tax profits took a 62.4% dive, to ¥7.2 billion.

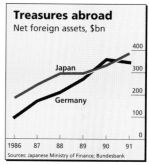

Treasures abroad
Net foreign assets, $bn

Sources: Japanese Ministry of Finance; Bundesbank

Tuesday 26th
Japan's net foreign assets rose by 16.8% in 1991 to a record $383.1 billion, putting Japan back in first place ahead of Germany as the world's largest net holder of foreign assets.

Japan's computer and computer-chip manufacturers reported gloomy results for the year to end-March. Fujitsu took the biggest drop in pre-tax profits, down 68.6% to ¥40 billion ($300m). Profits at Toshiba, NEC and Mitsubishi Electric were down respectively by 59.7%, 43.1% and 54.9%. Sharp managed a drop of only 11.9%.

Japan's **Honda** announced it will invest $17.6m in the first joint venture in China to produce motorcycles.

Wednesday 27th
Sprint, America's third-largest long-distance telephone company, said it planned to acquire Centel, a local and mobile operator, in a share swap worth about $2.85 billion. The deal received an immediate thumbs down from both firms' shareholders.

June

Monday 1st
The finances of America's airline industry remained as dire as ever. A credit-rating agency downgraded the credit worthiness of **four big America airlines**, American, Delta, Northwest and USAir. Standard & Poor's said that only American had a chance of making a profit in 1992.

Detroit's **Big Three** car makers said they planned to collaborate on the research needed to meet stringent clean-air standards in America.

Tuesday 2nd
Britain's **Rolls-Royce**, maker of aero-engines, and **Westinghouse**, an American power-systems group, signed a 15-year partnership to take on America's General Electric, the world's leading maker of power generators.

Arab states lifted a ban on **Coca-Cola** for investing in Israel. After a 40-year absence in Jordan there was a run on stocks—cheap, locally bottled Pepsi notwithstanding.

Two Australian airlines, both government-owned, said they would merge. **Qantas**, which flies internationally, announced it would take over **Australian Airlines**, a domestic carrier. The merged airline would then be privatised for some A$1 billion ($760m).

Monday 8th
Loaded with cash from the disposal of peripheral companies, America's **General Dynamics** said it would spend as much as $975m buying back 30% of its shares.

America's Supreme Court ruled against **Eastman Kodak** in an antitrust suit that could have serious repercussions for large firms. The ruling reinstated a lawsuit barred by lower courts that had been filed in 1987 by 18 independent companies which repair Kodak copiers and printers. The plaintiffs had sued Kodak because the company had refused to supply them with spare parts for Kodak machines.

The biggest mining group in the world, **RTZ**, said it was selling its 51.5% stake in Rio Algom, a big Canadian mining company and metals distributor, to financial institutions for £118m ($216m).

Wednesday 10th
TI Group, a British engineering company, won a bitter battle to take over Dowty Group, an aerospace and information-technology firm.

Bosses' pay in Europe
Chief executive of company with sales over $130m, May 1992
Net pay,* Switzerland=100

	40 50 60 70 80 90 100	
Switzerland		220
Spain		223
Germany		196
Austria		182
France		175
Italy		187
Britain		155
Portugal		155
Holland		164
Belgium		148
Ireland	Gross pay $'000	116
Denmark		166

*After tax and adjustment for cost-of-living differences (excluding housing)
Source: European Remuneration Network

Thursday 11th
Measured by purchasing power, the Swiss still have the **best-paid bosses** in Europe, according to a report by the European Remuneration Network. But Spanish bosses have the biggest gross salaries.

Friday 12th
A quarterly report by Japan's central bank showed business confidence in Japan at a five-year low. A few days later pessimism over Japan's economy drove Tokyo stockmarket to its lowest close for six years.

Canadian telecoms regulators ended Bell Canada's **long-distance telephone monopoly** when they approved a ten-year-old application by Unitel, a joint-venture of Rogers Communications, Canada's biggest cable operator, and Canadian Pacific, a railway company.

Monday 15th
After two years of trying, **British Telecom** sold its stake in Mitel, a loss-making Canadian telecoms switchboard manufacturer, to a group of nine unidentified investment partnerships—at a loss of over C$250m ($210m).

Tuesday 16th
Germany's Lufthansa and Japan Airlines increased their stakes in **DHL International**, the world's biggest air courier, from 5% to 25% each. Nissho Iwai, a Japanese trading house, will take its stake from 2.5% to 7.5%. The three holdings represent an investment of around $500m.

A group of 38 companies, broadcasters and programmers would receive as much as 850m ecus ($1.1 billion) from the European Community to help them prepare for **high-definition television**, it was announced.

IBM, which had always kept all of its semiconductor production strictly for its own use, said that it planned to sell $500m-worth of chips to other companies in 1992.

Thursday 18th
The planned flotation of **GPA**, an aircraft-leasing company, was abandoned just hours before it was due. The company blamed weak stockmarkets.

Monday 22nd
Wellcome Trust announced that it would float around 330m of its 632m shares in **Wellcome**, the British drugs company that makes AZT, an AIDS-combating drug.

The EC agreed to **open up its skies**. From January 1st 1993 every EC-based airline would be able to set its fares freely and fly between any EC countries.

Tuesday 23rd
In America, **Hoffmann-La Roche** benefited from the FDA's new accelerated-approval process when its ddC drug, for use in combination with AZT against AIDS, was approved. It is only the third AIDS drug to be approved.

Sweden's **Electrolux**, a leading maker of white goods, and Germany's **AEG**, a division of Daimler-Benz, announced plans to pool production of products common to both companies, and to take minority stakes in each other.

Wednesday 24th
America's Supreme Court ruled that **cigarette health warnings** do not protect manufacturers from personal-injury lawsuits.

Thursday 25th
British Petroleum's chairman, Bob Horton, **resigned** abruptly at the behest of the company's outside board directors, who cited "personality clashes", not disagreements about strategy, as the reason for his departure.

July

Tuesday 7th
In a deal worth DM621m ($417m), Pentland, a British consumer-products company, bought the remaining 80% that it did not already own of **Adidas**, a big German maker of sporting goods, from Bernard Tapie and other minority shareholders. A decade earlier, Pentland had helped launch Reebok, Adidas's arch-rival.

Wednesday 8th
Airbus Industrie won a $5 billion order for up to 100 A320 jets from America's United Airlines. It was a breakthrough for the European consortium because United had been a traditional customer of arch-rival Boeing.

Monday 13th
In an unprecedented $1 billion alliance, Germany's **Siemens**, America's **IBM** and **Toshiba** of Japan said they would share the escalating costs of developing a 256-megabit dynamic random access memory chip, two generations ahead of present capacity. The same day Fujitsu, Japan's biggest computer company, and Advanced Micro Devices of America announced a 50-50 joint venture to manufacture flash memory chips for a rapidly expanding market.

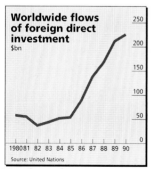

Worldwide flows of foreign direct investment
$bn

Source: United Nations

Tuesday 14th
Foreign investment is booming, said a UN report. The flows of direct investment soared during the second half of the 1980s, 2½ times faster than exports did. But developing countries' share of this cash fell, from 25% in 1980-85, to 17% in 1986-90.

Dawn raids were made on **chemicals companies** throughout the European Community by commission officials investigating allegations of price-fixing in the unprofitable PVC market.

Wednesday 15th
Europe's airlines began a campaign for a unified **air-traffic** control system to solve congestion in the air. They pointed out that an average 2,600 flights were being delayed every day in Europe. The continent's air-traffic system, organised around national boundaries, uses 31 different systems and over 70 assorted computer languages.

Thursday 16th
Robert Palmer took a step up to become the new boss of America's second-biggest computer maker, **Digital**, whose founder and president, Kenneth Olsen, announced his retirement. Digital had been in trouble for some time and was trying to restructure itself. Insiders said Mr Olsen was pushed out.

Tuesday 21st
British Airways fulfilled its long-held ambition to find an American partner. It said it would pay $750m to buy a 21% voting stake in **USAir**, the maximum allowed under foreign-ownership rules. The deal offered British Airways entry to the America's huge domestic market and a share in the world's biggest airline alliance.

Britain's **Rover Group** opened a revolutionary new £200m ($380m) car factory at Cowley, combining three sprawling sites into one. The highly flexible plant, with its Japanese-style working practices, has the ability to produce entirely different cars on the same production line.

The German government accelerated its privatisation programme by announcing the gradual sell-off of **Deutsche Telekom**, the state's vast telecoms system, worth up to DM70 billion ($47 billion). The government said it also planned to sell its remaining 51% stake in **Lufthansa**, the loss-making state airline.

A French company won a contract to **export vodka to Russia**. Caves Byrrh, a subsidiary of Pernod-Ricard, said it had just delivered a third of the 3m litre bottles on order—but only after collecting its payment first.

Wednesday 22nd
The European Commission cleared **Nestlé**'s acquisition of France's **Perrier**, on condition that it shed the equivalent of 20% of total mineral-water production capacity in France. The commission's decision annoyed Nestlé and BSN, its ally; they claimed that, after the deal, an 82% market share between them would not amount to a duopoly.

Compaq, one of America's biggest personal-computer makers, reported a 43% year-on-year increase in its second-quarter net profit to $29m on sales up 15%. The company abruptly changed strategy at the beginning of the year and slashed prices on most of its machines.

Almost half the men in France aged 55-64 are **out of work**, reported an OECD study, and elsewhere numbers are almost as high and rising quickly. The OECD blamed the trend on cushy redundancy packages and pension and sickness schemes that encourage people to opt out of work.

Monday 27th
In a big step towards a **borderless Europe**, finance ministers agreed to set minimum value-added and excise tax rates across the EC.

Wellcome Trust completed its flotation. It raised £2.2 billion ($4.2 billion) rather than the £4 billion initially hoped for. The fact that the issue was completed won admiration, given the recent collapse in world stockmarkets.

Tuesday 28th
IBM raised its forecasts of job losses in 1992, from 20,000 to at least 32,000. The extra $1 billion in redundancy costs would be recouped in 18 months, said Big Blue.

France's state-owned electronics company, **Thomson-CSF**, gave up its joint $260m attempt with Loral, a defence-electronics company based in New York, to buy the missile division of America's LTV.

The fortunes of **America's big car makers** improved in the second quarter of 1992 compared with the same period in 1991. Ford's reversed a loss of $324m to earn $502m. Chrysler's loss of $212m became a profit of $178m. General Motors stayed in loss, but cut it from $784m to $357m.

Thursday 30th
ICI, Britain's chemicals giant, said it planned to split itself up, putting drugs and agrochemicals, its more profitable businesses, into a new firm called ICI Bio.

August

Monday 3rd

Two of **America's biggest airlines**, Delta and American Airlines, objected to British Airways taking a stake in USAir. Bob Crandall, American's boss, said the deal should not be approved unless American airlines are allowed greater access to Britain.

World semiconductor market shares

US producers

Japanese producers

Rest of world

1980 81 82 83 84 85 86 87 88 89 90 91
Source: Dataquest

Tuesday 4th

Carla Hills, America's trade representative, warned Japan that action would be taken unless Japanese companies bought more **foreign semiconductors**. America had expected that foreign-made chips would take 20% of the Japanese chip market, but they only accounted for 15% and their market share showed no signs of rising.

Adelaide Steamship is to sell Australia's second largest retailer, Woolworths, in the country's largest public offering. The flotation, due in October, could raise A$2 billion ($1.5 billion), which would cut Adsteam's debts by a third.

Monsanto, a big American chemicals firm, announced the sale of its control-valve unit to Emerson Electric, an electronics-products maker, for $1.28 billion, declaring that it would now concentrate on its core chemicals business.

Wednesday 5th

Shareholders in **WPP**, the world's biggest advertising agency, overwhelmingly approved a £520m ($1 billion)

refinancing package. Fidelity Investments, a large American shareholder, had earlier agreed to support the package after it became clear that WPP would otherwise go into receivership.

Friday 7th

A big American telecommunications group, **GTE**, sold its worldwide lighting business in two separate deals to Osram, a subsidiary of Germany's Siemens, and a consortium of unnamed international investors for a total of $1.1 billion.

A lawsuit brought by **Apple** against Microsoft and Hewlett-Packard lost much of its bite. An American court threw out most of the remaining claims by Apple that software produced by its two rivals violated copyrights that protect the Macintosh computer's "look and feel".

Monday 10th

Another round in the **computer industry's savage price wars** was sparked by Intel's announcement of a new high-speed microprocessor. Dozens of personal-computer makers immediately said they would incorporate the new chip. They then promptly began undercutting each other's prices on the yet-to-be launched machines.

Tuesday 11th

Administrators for **Polly Peck**, the collapsed fruit-to-electronics conglomerate, sold Del Monte Fresh Produce for $499m to a consortium of Mexican companies eager to expand into the United States. **Saatchi & Saatchi**, a cash-

strapped advertising giant, hauled itself back into the black in the first half of the year with a pre-tax profit of £11.1m ($19.9m), compared with a loss of £32m in the first half of 1991. Meanwhile, Martin Sorrell's WPP, a rival advertising and marketing group, saw pre-tax half-year profits collapse to £1.8m from £16m in the previous year.

In one of Poland's biggest privatisations, America's **International Paper** paid $120m for 80% of Kwidzyn, Poland's second-biggest paper maker and owner of Eastern Europe's largest integrated bleached-paper mill. International Paper said it would invest a further $175m in the company over four years.

Wednesday 12th

After 14 months of bargaining, George Bush announced that America, Mexico and Canada had agreed to end trade barriers and sign a **North American Free Trade Agreement** (NAFTA). The agreement, claimed Mr Bush, would create a single market of 360m people producing goods and services of $6 trillion a year—if Congress agreed to ratify it.

Monday 17th

Two American giants, **IBM and Sears Roebuck**, announced that they will merge their data-networking businesses into a company called Advantis, in which IBM will hold the majority stake. The joint venture is expected to generate $1 billion a year in sales.

Tuesday 18th

Best known for transforming office life by inventing computerised word-processing, America's **Wang Laboratories** filed for protection from its creditors under chapter 11, with debts of around $540m. With 5,000 jobs to be cut, the workforce, which once stood

at 31,500, would fall to only 8,000.

Two drugs groups, Anglo-American **SmithKline Beecham** and America's **Marion Merrell Dow**, said they were going into partnership to exploit America's lucrative over-the-counter drugs market. Both companies had drugs that could do well when prescription rules are relaxed.

Friday 21st

Because of sluggishness in the semiconductor market, **LSI Logic**, a Silicon Valley chip maker, said it would close its German plants and some American ones and shift most of its manufacturing to Japan and other Asian countries.

Tuesday 25th

America announced an "**open skies**" agreement with KLM, a Dutch airline, giving it permission to fly to any American city. In return American carriers would be allowed to serve any Dutch city—not much of a concession. But the Americans hoped that the deal would begin to prise open the entire European market.

Wednesday 26th

News Corporation, the international media group headed by Rupert Murdoch, saw its net profit soar by 65% to A$531m ($409m) in the year to June. The company said it planned to raise $1 billion in long-term debt.

September

Tuesday 1st
Japanese vehicle exports fell by 5% in July, year-on-year, thanks mainly to a 25% drop in exports to America, its biggest market. Domestically, August saw a 16% fall in sales, the sharpest year-on-year slide for ten years.

Saturday 5th
To end a crippling nine-day strike, **General Motors** said it would delay closing a tool and die shop and take measures to save jobs. But GM said it would still shut down 21 other plants and slash 74,000 jobs.

Monday 7th
Russian **diamond smuggling** was wreaking havoc on world trade in rough (uncut) diamonds, said De Beers, which controlled 80% of the market.

Friday 11th
In a big step nearer to restoring its investment-grade rating, Rupert Murdoch's **News Corp** announced plans to raise A$2 billion ($1.5 billion) through debt and share offerings.

Tuesday 15th
Germany's economics minister, Jürgen Möllemann, predicted the total collapse of eastern Germany's social and economic system unless steps were taken to restore **Germany's competitiveness**. He proposed the relaxation of labour laws, the overhaul of educa-tion and welfare, restraints on public spending and a reduction in the top rate of income tax.

Australia's biggest company said it would take control of **Foster's Brewing**. BHP said it planned to pay A$1.5 billion ($1.1 billion) for a 32% stake, plus options, in the ailing brewer, which declared a loss for the year to June, its third annual loss in a row.

Thursday 17th
Britain's Reed International and Holland's Elsevier said they planned to merge to form one of the world's biggest **publishing and information** groups, with a combined turnover of $4.5 billion.

Friday 18th
Philips, Holland's huge manufacturer of consumer electronics, and **Lotus**, an American software maker, said they were contemplating a joint venture to develop a new generation of computer telephones with display screens.

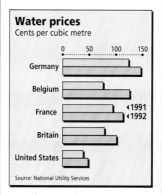

Water prices
Cents per cubic metre

	0	50	100	150
Germany				
Belgium				
France			◀1991 ◀1992	
Britain				
United States				

Source: National Utility Services

Tuesday 22nd
The **price of water** was revealed to have soared in Britain by almost 50% since 1987. But Belgians suffered an increase of 48% in 1991 alone.

British Aerospace, one of Britain's biggest manufacturers, said it planned to cut 3,000 jobs and shift the manufacture of its loss-making re-gional jets to Taiwan, where it was signing a $500m joint venture with Taiwan Aerospace. The announcement came as BAe declared a £129m ($231m) pre-tax loss for the first half of 1992, compared with a profit of £86m in the same period of 1991.

Wednesday 23rd
Air France confirmed a strategic alliance with **Air Canada** that will increase the number of flights between the two countries and will mean expansion for both airlines into new routes.

Monday 28th
IATA, the airline industry's trade association, said it would try to rationalise accounting procedures among the **world's airlines**, following a survey by IATA and KPMG, an accounting firm, that showed big disparities. More accounting harmony should make it easier for airlines to take stakes in each other and form partnerships, claimed IATA.

Two big American firms chased after Scandinavia's biggest maker of sweets and chocolate, Freia Marabou. **Jacobs Suchard**, part of Philip Morris, made an offer of $1.5 billion, which was accepted, after a failed bid by **Hershey Foods**, a chocolate maker with an 18.6% stake in the Norwegian firm.

After protracted negotiations, **Glaxo** and French authorities reached an agreement over the pricing of the injected version of Imigran, a new migraine treatment. The deal looked like a blow to the efforts of drug firms to establish Europe-wide prices to stamp out parallel imports from countries where the drug is sold more cheaply. France, the fifth-biggest user of drugs in the world, wanted to keep prescription prices low.

In a determined effort to keep increasing its share of the personal-computer market, **Apple** cut the prices of its Macintosh range by up to 36%.

Tuesday 29th
IBM said it would take a $2.8 billion after-tax charge in the third quarter of 1992. The move, although alleviated by a change in accounting methods, put the world's biggest computer maker into loss in those three months. IBM also said it would cut its workforce by 40,000 in 1992, double its original estimate.

Sears Roebuck, the world's second-largest retailer, abandoned a decade-old diversification strategy and announced that it would sell most of its non-retail businesses to cut its corporate debt. Among the planned disposals was Dean Witter, a financial-services group, together with its profitable Discover credit-card operations.

Wednesday 30th
A proposed swap of **ICI**'s nylon business for **Du Pont**'s acrylic business (and some cash) was approved by the European Commission—but with some important strings attached. Du Pont was required to sell a chunk of ICI's carpet-fibre capacity to a competitor. It also had to agree to sell an entire R&D facility to the same firm.

October

Monday 5th
America's Congress overrode George Bush's veto of a bill designed to regulate the **cable-television industry**. The new law curbs prices charged for basic cable services.

The European Commission said **Air France** could take a 37.6% stake in Belgium's **Sabena**, so long as rivals were allowed on certain routes to maintain competition.

Friday 9th
China at last agreed to open its markets to more American goods, after pressure, then threats, from Carla Hills, America's trade representative. America's trade deficit with China in the first half of the year was $7.2 billion.

Monday 12th
Through its subsidiary, Kraft, America's Philip Morris beat Hershey to win control of Norway's Freia Marabou, **Scandinavia's biggest chocolate maker**. It made a friendly offer that valued Freia at $1.5 billion. Freia was to become a part of Jacobs Suchard of Switzerland, a subsidiary of Kraft.

EC finance ministers agreed to a minimum 15% VAT rate across the Community and standardised minimum rates of excise duty on alcohol. The accord was a big step towards a **single-market Europe**.

Tuesday 13th
The **Nobel prize for economics** was won by a 61-year-old American, Gary Becker, for explaining social behaviour in economic terms. He became the University of Chicago's sixth winner of the prize.

Alan Greenspan, chairman of the Federal Reserve, said **worldwide price stability**, in which "households and businesses do not base their decisions on expectations of con-

tinued inflation", was close to being achieved.

Germany's loss-making **Siemens** said it would cut jobs in its semiconductor division by nearly 25% over five years, citing weak demand. But America's leading chip maker, **Intel**, said its business was booming. Third-quarter income was up a record 19% over the same period last year, largely because the price war among personal computer makers had boosted demand, and so sales of Intel's microprocessors. **Microsoft**, a big American maker of software, also benefited.

Bring and buy
Cross-border acquisitions
Jan 1st–Sept 30th 1992, $bn

	$bn	Number of deals
United States		249
France		151
Hong Kong		9
Italy		73
Britain		219
Switzerland		59
Germany		112
Mexico		7
Japan		63
Australia		31

Source: KPMG

Although **cross-border acquisitions** worldwide were down slightly, to 1,367, their value rose from $36 billion in the first nine months of 1991 to $57.4 billion in the same period in 1992.

Thursday 15th
Britain's Pentland Group called off its agreed takeover of Germany's BTF after a review of the company and its subsidiaries. They include **Adidas**, a company that makes sports goods.

Friday 16th
South Africa's Royal Foods joined Anglo American Corporation in paying £360m ($585m) for **Del Monte Foods International**, a tinned-fruit company sold to management during the 1990 break-up of RJR Nabisco.

Tuesday 20th
EC countries could ban imports of **hazardous waste** for disposal, environment ministers decided. The idea that toxic waste should be dealt with near its point of production overrides the principle of free circulation of goods.

Wednesday 21st
Big differences in **telephone charges** between EC countries were found by the European Commission to be unjustified. The most expensive three-minute call in the EC—from Portugal—was about 2½ times the cost of the cheapest—from Luxembourg.

Thursday 22nd
PepsiCo signed a joint-venture deal with two Ukrainian partners and Fram Shipping of Bermuda to market $1 billion-worth of Ukrainian-built commercial ships over the next eight years. The foreign exchange earned would be used to create a chain of Pizza Huts across Ukraine.

Monday 26th
Robert Stempel, chairman of **General Motors**, the world's biggest car maker, resigned after accusations of inaction in the face of a deepening crisis. A few days later GM announced a third-quarter loss of $753m, compared with a $1.06 billion loss in the same period of 1991. Ford's third-quarter losses shrank from $574m to $159m. But Chrysler

moved into net profit, of $202m, after a previous third-quarter loss of $82m.

Britain's Storehouse, a retailer, sold for £78m ($123m) its 76 **Habitat** furniture and household-goods stores in Britain and France to SIF, a charitable foundation that owns Sweden's highly successful Ikea chain of furniture outlets.

Negotiations between Germany's Treuhand privatisation agency and Krupp over the sale of Eko, eastern Germany's biggest steel maker, fell through. In an oversupplied **steel market**, Krupp was demanding too large a government subsidy.

Tuesday 27th
Russia's economic mess meant the country would pay only about 10% of its debts to foreign creditors in 1992 and 1993, said Pyotr Aven, the government's chief debt negotiator.

The big **Japanese electronics companies** announced miserable half-year results and more cuts in capital spending as weak demand, lower margins and a stronger yen took their toll. Drops in pre-tax profit varied from Toshiba's 39% to Fujitsu's 87%.

Thursday 29th
Tomkins bid £952m ($1.45 billion) for **Ranks Hovis McDougall**, a British milling and baking firm, thus topping rival conglomerate Hanson's offer by £172m. RHM recommended shareholders to accept the new bid.

November

Monday 2nd
Following a boardroom shake-up at **General Motors** in which Robert Stempel was ousted as chairman and chief executive. Jack Smith, who brought record profits to GM's European operations in the 1980s, was named as chief executive. John Smale, a former chairman of Procter & Gamble, became chairman.

Daimler-Benz dropped its plans to build a DM1 billion ($640m) commercial-vehicle factory in eastern Germany because of poor lorry sales in Western Europe.

Allied-Lyons, a British food and drinks group, put **Château Latour**, one of the top Bordeaux vineyards, up for sale in an effort to reduce its net debt of £1.9 billion ($2.9 billion). In October it sold two large German wine businesses.

Tuesday 3rd
Oil prices were depressed by confirmation that supplies of OPEC oil rose sharply in October, topping 25m barrels per day for the first time since 1980. There was also a big rise in American crude stocks.

Wednesday 4th
AT&T agreed to spend $3.8 billion on a 33% stake in McCaw, the operator of **America's biggest cellular-telephone network**, which covers 40% of the country's population. AT&T also bought an option to buy majority control of McCaw later, positioning itself to play a dominant role in what is expected to be a huge market in mobile telephoning.

Thursday 5th
Founder Alan Sugar bid £113m ($175m) to **buy back Amstrad**, the British consumer-electronics firm, from other shareholders after 12 years on the stockmarket.

Monday 9th
A $1.2 billion bid led by Robert Bass, a Texan billionaire, for the American end of **MCC**, the late Robert Maxwell's group of companies, was turned down by the administrators, who valued the bid at only $725m. The administrators said that they preferred to break up the companies, which included publishers Macmillan and Official Airline Guides.

Air Canada's $450m bid for **Continental**, an American airline in chapter 11 bankruptcy, was accepted.

Wednesday 11th
Following complaints from competitors, America's Gillette was ordered by the European Commission to dispose of its stake in the parent of Wilkinson Sword of Holland, its main competitor in the **wet-shaving market**.

Friday 13th
Italy gave details of its **ambitious privatisation plans**. The government said it wanted to reduce drastically its stakes in banking, finance, insurance, energy, engineering and food. The government said it hoped to raise 27 trillion lire ($20 billion) and that it also planned to combine its three telecommunications services into one operating company.

Monday 16th
Kraft, the American food division of Philip Morris, agreed to pay $450m for **RJR Nabisco**'s cold-cereal business, which includes Shredded Wheat and Shreddies.

Following its investment in McCaw, **AT&T** announced alliances with three Japanese electronics makers, NEC, Matsushita and Toshiba, that will give it a head start in the race to provide "personal communicators".

Richard Branson's **Virgin Group** announced a joint venture with **Blockbuster Entertainment**, a video-rental company based in Florida, which will jointly own Virgin's music and computer-games megastores in Europe, Australia and Los Angeles and develop a big American music and entertainment chain.

Tuesday 17th
Pre-tax profits at **British Airways** fell in the second quarter by 23%, compared with the same period a year earlier, to £136m ($259m). Recession, currency fluctuations and a price war were blamed.

Monday 23rd
One of America's biggest defence contractors, with annual sales of $11 billion, was formed when **Martin Marietta**, a defence-electronics group, agreed to pay $3.1 billion for **General Electric**'s aerospace business.

Continuing its $1 billion five-year drive into the Spanish market, **PepsiCo** announced that it was buying Kas, a beverage company, and Knorr Elorza, a bottling firm and distributor, for $320m, almost doubling its share of the fizzy-drinks market in Spain, to 13%.

The Nissan Micra became the **first Japanese car** to win Europe's "car of the year" award.

Tuesday 24th
Moody's downgraded the debt of **General Motors**, humiliating America's biggest car maker and raising the cost of its future borrowings.

The French government said that its sale of shares in **Rhône-Poulenc**, a chemicals and drugs company, would take place by February 1993. The sale, of at least 6m shares, would raise up to FFr4 billion ($735m) and reduce the government's direct voting rights from 77.5% to 45%, though control would be maintained through other state-controlled shareholders.

Group net third-quarter profits at **Volkswagen** dropped by 47% from a year earlier, to DM104m ($71m), as Europe's leading car maker suffered from a slumping domestic market in Germany and devalued currencies.

Sir Leon Brittan, the EC competition commissioner, said he was going to demand detailed **prices from car makers** so that consumers would be able to compare the large discrepancies in Europe. It followed a crackdown on Citroën and Alfa Romeo, which had found ways to discourage cross-border sales.

Wednesday 25th
An EC panel recommended a 3.5 billion ecus ($4.3 billion) programme to help **European supercomputer makers** catch up with their American and Japanese rivals.

December

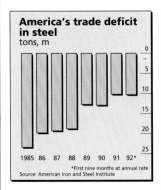

America's trade deficit in steel
tons, m

1985 86 87 88 89 90 91 92*
*First nine months at annual rate
Source: American Iron and Steel Institute

Tuesday 1st
America risked a trade row by slapping temporary duties of up to 59% on **imports of steel** from 12 countries, including six EC members. This followed complaints from American steel makers about unfair competition from government-subsidised EC steel producers. Observers thought this strange as steel imports had fallen and exports had boomed.

Friday 4th
Italy's privatisation programme came in for criticism when Britain's **United Biscuits** complained that Pai, a maker of crisps and snacks, was sold hurriedly to Unichips, an Italian rival, for 30.2 billion lire ($22m). UB had been pondering making a bid.

Monday 7th
Northwest Airlines cancelled orders for 74 aircraft worth $3.5 billion from Airbus Industrie. That was a blow to the European consortium and its new A340 long-range widebodied jet, for which Northwest was its biggest customer. The airline also delayed delivery of $2.7 billion-worth of Boeing aircraft.

Carl Icahn agreed to give up control of **TWA** and provide $200m in short-term loans, increasing the chances of saving the American airline which had long been in chapter 11 bankruptcy.

Tuesday 8th
In an unusually harsh move, EC competition officials slapped restrictions on a joint venture between Ford and Volkswagen to produce minivans in Portugal. Brussels fears the two firms will carve up the market between them.

Wednesday 9th
Months of wrangling over the **European Fighter Aircraft** ended with the announcement that the project would go on, after all. The $38 billion multi-country programme had been threatened when Germany said it would pull out.

America's **General Dynamics** sold its military-aircraft division, responsible for producing F-16 jet fighters, to Lockheed for $1.5 billion.

Alan Sugar lost his bid to buy back **Amstrad**, the company he founded. Shareholders snubbed his offer, which had valued the British computer and consumer-electronics company at £113m ($180m).

Tiny Rowland, the long-time boss of Lonrho, an international trading conglomerate based in London, said he planned to sell half of his 15% stake in the firm to Dieter Bock, a German financier for £50m ($78m), well above the market price. Mr Rowland indicated he would retire in three years.

Friday 11th
America's big three car firms, General Motors, Ford and Chrysler, said that they would collaborate on the development of **electric vehicles**. GM said it had shelved plans to mass-produce its own electric car, the Impact, by the mid-1990s.

Monday 14th
Time Warner, an American media and entertainment group, said it aimed to cut its debt by a third by selling around $3 billion of assets. The company's 21% stake in Turner Broadcasting was said to be up for sale.

Tuesday 15th
British Petroleum said it would cut 9,000 more jobs over the next three years, bringing the total announced by the company in 1992 to more than 20,000—a fifth of its workforce. And America's **Ford** announced it would cut almost 10,000 jobs at its European plants.

International Lease Finance Corporation, a Californian **aircraft-leasing company**, placed a $4.1 billion order for 82 airliners. Boeing won 53 of the orders; all but one of the rest went to Europe's Airbus Industrie. ILFC took advantage of a recession in the airline business to snap up aircraft at bargain prices.

John Akers, chairman of **IBM**, said the world's biggest computer maker would cut a further 25,000 jobs in 1993, 8% of its workforce. Over 100,000 jobs had already been lost at the company since the mid-1980s. IBM also said it would take a $6 billion charge in the fourth quarter of 1992, and hinted that it might cut its dividend. The company blamed recession and a dwindling market for its mainframe computers.

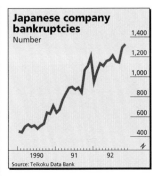

Japanese company bankruptcies
Number

1990 91 92
Source: Teikoku Data Bank

Wednesday 16th
Japan's **corporate pain** got worse. Official figures revealed that 1,328 businesses went bust in November, more than double the monthly average in 1990.

Thursday 17th
British Airways bought 25% of Qantas, an Australian airline. And, despite protests by Air France, the French government gave the acquisitive BA permission to take a 49.9% stake in TAT, a French regional airline.

Sunday 20th
Steven Ross, the 65-year-old chairman of Time Warner and one of the highest paid executives in the world, died of cancer. Only hours after his death, the debt-laden company he created in a controversial 1989 merger announced a board shake-up.

Wednesday 23rd
British Airways **abandoned its plan** to take a 44% stake in USAir after American and British authorities failed to agree a relaxation of rules governing air travel between the two countries.

Tuesday 29th
Carla Hills, America's outgoing trade representative, lobbed a **hot potato** into the lap of President-elect Bill Clinton by complaining that Japanese companies were not living up to their agreement to import 20% of the microchips they consume.

*D*esigning your competitive edge with Singapore.

Singapore offers more than superb infra-structure, excellent IT and telecommunications networks, worldwide distribution linkages, and a total value chain to support a diversity of manu-facturing and service businesses.

With our total business capabilities, we can be your strategic partner. To develop and capitalise on new business opportunities, especially in the world's fastest growing market: the Asia-Pacific.

Banking on 30 years of successful economic planning, and the testimony of over 3,000 MNCs operating here, Singapore is the business architect that can enhance your competitive edge.

You can leverage our strategic alliances with other economies, our familiarity with regional markets, and not least our expertise in distributing and configuring businesses to stay ahead.

So use our value-added solutions to your advantage now, call the Singapore Economic Development Board today.

Europe: Frankfurt (69) 233-838 • London (71) 839-6688 • Milan (02) 799-277 • Paris (01) 45001183 • Stockholm (08) 6637488 **North America:** Boston (617) 261-9981 • Chicago (312) 565-1100 • Los Angeles (310) 553-0199 • New York (212) 421-2200 • San Francisco (415) 591-9102 • Washington DC (202) 223-2571 **Asia-Pacific:** • Hongkong (852) 810-0036 • Jakarta (21) 520-1489 • Osaka (06) 261-5131 • Singapore (65) 336-2288 • Tokyo (03) 3501-6041

SINGAPORE
YOUR GLOBAL BUSINESS ARCHITECT

As we reported then

Can America compete?

JANUARY 18TH **A prolonged recession and George Bush's humiliating trip to Tokyo lent an air of credibility to pundits bewailing the decline and fall of American industry. We argued that this was dangerous and unjustified**

INTROSPECTION and self-doubt have rarely been synonymous with Hollywood. But shortly after George Bush returned from his ill-conceived trip to Japan this month, the "Third Decade" council of the American Film Institute held a private conference. The subject: whether Hollywood, like a complacent Detroit in 1965, is about to lose its hegemony over the world's entertainment industry to hungrier, nimbler foreign rivals. If even the dream merchants of Tinseltown share the nightmare view that America is in inexorable decline, perhaps it really is time for drastic action to save American business?

"Declinism" has been persistent in America ever since the first oil shock in 1973 shook the self-confidence which had characterised the country after the second world war. Since then, the success of Japanese companies in highly visible markets such as consumer electronics and cars, together with a flood of imported products from dozens of other countries, have seemed to add support to those forecasting America's economic decline. In the 1980s doom-mongering became not just the speciality of a few vocal jeremiahs, but positively fashionable.

Now, with recession dragging on longer than expected and an election looming, to say that American business can no longer compete and that Americans have lost their ability to innovate is no longer controversial—it is the conventional wisdom. All five Democrats seeking the presidency have, at one time or another, blamed foreign powers, especially Japan, for at least some of America's decline. And Mr Bush himself now seems to be abandoning his commitment to free trade in favour of the managed variety. There are even strong hints in Washington that the administration may be about to ditch its long-held opposition to the overt interventionism of an "industrial" or "technology" policy.

The problem is that the belief that American business is no longer competitive is wrong. Thousands of American firms, both big and small, remain among the most competitive and innovative in the world. The danger is that remedies designed to cure a supposed decline in competitiveness will actually help bring one about.

American firms lead in a slew of technology-based industries such as computer software and hardware of all types, microprocessor chips, aerospace, pharmaceuticals, biotechnology, new materials, energy and environmental control. Listing American companies that are world-beaters in many of these fields is easy: General Electric, Microsoft, Apple, Motorola, Cypress Semiconductor, Intel, Cray Computer, Compaq, Exxon, Dow, Merck, Eli Lilly, Bristol-Myers Squibb.

Even the Japanese agree that America remains ahead in many leading high-tech industries. When the Japanese government's Economic Planning Agency surveyed 110 critical technologies in 1991, it concluded that American firms dominated 43 of them, Japanese firms 33, while European and others the remaining 34. Clearly American firms continue to innovate. Whether they will stumble in the future is another matter.

Outside such high-tech industries, it is also possible to identify plenty of world-beating American firms among consumer-goods companies: Procter & Gamble, Philip Morris, and Johnson & Johnson are among the world's best. Walt Disney is another American "brand" that can hold its own against any entertainment company. Time-Warner, squeezed as it is by self-inflicted debts, makes plenty of money exporting Madonna records and re-runs of American soap operas. In fact, American firms dominate the world's entertainment industry, and only a loss of self-confidence looks capable of shaking their grip. American films and television programmes are finding new markets in Eastern Europe and South-East Asia, as well as new media outlets, such as satellite television.

Ironically, nothing proves America's competitive advantage in entertainment more conclusively than Sony's $3.4 billion purchase of Columbia Pictures in 1989 and Matsushita's $6 billion purchase of MCA in 1990. Both firms could have built movie studios from scratch for a fraction of those sums and then challenged Hollywood directly, just as Toyota and Honda took on Detroit. Instead, they tried to buy their way into Hollywood with mountains of cash. America's film makers have always been happy to take anybody's money. They nevertheless remain American.

Service industries are another area in which America has world-class companies, though many services are not internationally traded, making international comparisons difficult. But where they are, such as the fast-food industry, America reigns supreme. There are no European or Japanese fast-food chains to rival McDonald's, Pizza Hut or Kentucky Fried Chicken.

One big international service industry in which America remains a clear leader is construction engineering—the building of sophisticated factories. Well-trained workforces have made Bechtel, Fluor, Parsons and Jacobs successful around the globe. "Whenever there is an open competition overseas, an American firm tends to win," says Joseph Jacobs, the founder of Jacobs Engineering.

Merely listing America's many successful companies may be missing a genuine average decline, as well as avoiding an important point: some of these firms now import as much as they make at home. The worry about America's loss of competitiveness tends to centre on its trade deficit. In fact, this has shrunk significantly (from $160 billion in 1987 to an estimated $72 billion in 1991). In any case, a trade deficit, by itself, says nothing about a country's "competitiveness". That requires deeper examination.

Start with exports. America's excellent export performance in the past five years hardly suggests that American goods are uncompetitive (see chart). Since 1986 the volume of America's manufactured exports has risen by around 90%, compared with average growth in the rest of the OECD industrialised countries of 25%. Even in 1991, as the world economy slowed sharply, exports of American manufactures rose 7%, compared with an average increase of just 1½% in other OECD countries. This increased America's share of the industrialised world's manufactured exports to an estimated 18% by the end of 1991, up from 14% in 1987, not only restoring America's share to its level in 1980, but also pushing it ahead of Japan's current 17% share.

The star performer was the iron and steel industry: its exports quadrupled in the five years to 1991 in dollar terms. Exports of aircraft, electrical machinery, pharmaceuticals, telecoms equipment and clothing all more than doubled over the same period. Capital goods (ie, machinery and transport equipment) have risen from a third of total exports in the early 1980s to almost a half last year.

Far from being "uncompetitive" in manufacturing, America is actually one of the industrial world's cheapest producers of many goods. This is due partly to the cheap dollar, which has fallen by half from its 1985 value against the yen and the D-mark. But just as important has been the fact that America has the highest level of productivity of the big OECD economies.

Data on absolute productivity are always years out of date, but a study using OECD figures shows that in the mid-1980s America produced amost twice as much for every man-hour worked, across the entire economy, as Japan. One reason for this is Japan's notoriously inefficient service and distribution industries. But even in manufacturing America's output per man-hour was roughly the same as Japan's; it was 50% higher than Germany's.

But, claim the doom-sayers, even if this is true, America's productivity is growing more slowly than that of other countries, so Japan is now pulling ahead and Germany is rapidly closing the gap. False. America's productivity growth for its entire economy (the figures most commonly waved around) has been the slowest of the big industrial economies in each of the past three decades, but productivity is difficult to measure in services, which account for more of America's output than that of other countries. Figures for manufacturing alone tell a different story. America did have slower productivity growth in manufacturing than Japan and Europe in the 1960s and 1970s, but America's productivity spurted in the 1980s, growing by an average of 3.4% a year, faster than the growth in both Japan and Germany.

Not only is America's productivity relatively high, but its labour is also cheap. America's bosses may be taking home the world's fattest pay packets, but American workers are paid less per hour than in most other rich countries. In 1990, average labour costs (including non-wage costs) per hour in manufacturing were $15 in America, compared with $23 in western Germany and $16 in Japan.

So part of the price of America's competitiveness has been paid by factory workers. Real wages per hour have fallen by 13% in America since 1973, compared with increases of 30% or more in Japan and western Germany. Many use these figures as evidence of the falling standard of living in America—and hence the ultimate test of America's falling competitiveness. But fears about falling living standards are exaggerated. Once the figures are adjusted for changes in the number of hours worked and increases in fringe benefits and bonuses, and then adjusted correctly for inflation, real family incomes in America have risen over the past two decades.

More to the point, one reason why real hourly wages have not risen faster has been America's steady stream of immigrants who have been more than willing to take low-paying jobs, as well as women joining the labour force. Employment has jumped by a phenomenal 50% since 1970. The growth in low-wage jobs has dragged the figure for average wages down. However, America's remarkable ability to absorb such a huge influx of new workers is surely evidence of the flexibility and strength of its economy, not a weakness.

But what of the future? The biggest reason to doubt whether America can stay so competitive is its low level of investment. Last year capital spending by American businesses accounted for only 9% of the country's GNP, compared with almost 20% in Japan and 13% in Germany. Part of the gap between America and Japan reflects the heavy investment by Japanese firms in labour-saving machinery because of their fears about a labour shortage, now and in the future. American firms, with an ample pool of labour, probably do not need to invest as much to sustain output. Yet that accounts for only part of the gap. American businesses are clearly investing too little. The American government is also investing too little in infrastructure: 1½% of GNP, compared with Japan's 5%.

So Americans should not be complacent. If a shortage of public and private investment continues throughout the 1990s, it could eventually sap the country's economic strength. Americans should also worry about the deterioration in the quality of their elementary schools. America

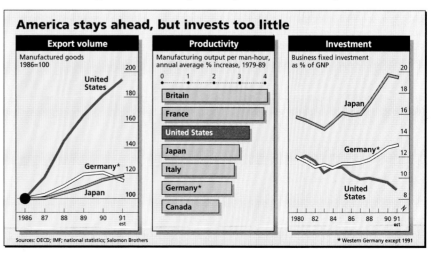

America stays ahead, but invests too little

Export volume — Manufactured goods 1986=100 — United States, Germany*, Japan — 1986, 87, 88, 89, 90, 91 est — 200, 180, 160, 140, 120, 100

Productivity — Manufacturing output per man-hour, annual average % increase, 1979-89 — Britain, France, United States, Japan, Italy, Germany*, Canada — 0 1 2 3 4

Investment — Business fixed investment as % of GNP — Japan, Germany*, United States — 1980, 82, 84, 86, 88, 90 91 est — 20, 18, 16, 14, 12, 10, 8

Sources: OECD; IMF; national statistics; Salomon Brothers   * Western Germany except 1991

still has one of the best university systems in the world, but basic skills such as reading have declined sharply among shopfloor workers. As the spread of computers encourages companies to devolve more and more responsibility to lower-level workers, declining reading standards could take a heavy toll. Already companies like Motorola and Ford are spending vast sums just teaching their workers to read. Simon & Schuster, a publisher, reckons that there is a growing market in America selling remedial-reading textbooks to employers. The market is already worth $500m a year.

But expressing concern about low investment rates and declining educational standards is not the same as claiming that America can no longer compete. If Americans heed the alarmists' cries, then frantic government efforts to prop up weak industries with trade protection or subsidies will almost certainly be the result.

Such measures would not only provoke retaliation from America's trading partners, they would damage the American economy's flexibility and openness, virtues which have always been its greatest assets. For example, the best and brightest of other countries have regularly sought to make their fortunes in America. Skilled immigrants from Europe and Asia have played a big part in building many of America's high-tech industries. An estimated one-third of the engineers working in Silicon Valley were born in Asia. Growing numbers of these Chinese, Korean and Indian engineers are now establishing their own firms in California, with the help of money from family and contacts abroad.

If such firms succeed, they will help keep America competitive. In any high-tech rivalry with Japan or other East Asian countries, predicts one Wall Street banker, "America will win because our Asians will beat their Asians." There is no reason to be alarmed about that.

The anti-brand brand

MARCH 14TH, TOKYO *The power of established brands had been declining for years everywhere but Japan, where cash-rich consumers paid for labels as much as products. We spotted a sign of change*

TRY TO imagine (if you are not one already) that you are a 22-year-old woman office worker living at home with your parents in Japan. You spend most of your ¥160,000 ($1,200) monthly pay packet on yourself. Elegant in your Jean Paul Gaultier dress, Hermès scarf draped casually around the neck, gold Cartier watch on your wrist and Chanel handbag dangling from the shoulder, you step jauntily into the office lift. Seconds later the doors open and—horrors—in steps another lady decked out in precisely the same designer-brand uniform, then another, and yet another. Many Tokyo office buildings are now full of young Japanese women who dress exactly alike.

Jaded by the ubiquity of fancy brand names, many of Japan's conspicuous consumers are now turning to "no-brand" goods in what looks like a forlorn attempt to display some individuality. The trendsetter has been Seibu, a department-store chain that goes after the affluent young. Inside Seibu's flagship store in Tokyo, one section sells only Mujirushi ryohin ("no brand/good quality") products. Their labels say only what materials are used and the country of origin—mostly China, Hong Kong, South Korea, Thailand or India. The products are easy to spot because of their simple design, plain colours, high quality and reasonable pricing.

Seibu's parent, the Saison group, originally developed the no-brand idea for tinned food and household items for its Seiyu supermarkets. Two years ago the group established a separate company, Ryohin Keikaku, to handle an expanded line of Muji goods, which today includes 1,800 items.

Ryohin Keikaku now has 201 outlets in Japan and two overseas. One of its foreign stores is a joint venture with Wing On in Hong Kong. Another is a joint venture with Liberty in London's Carnaby Street, where the firm's no-brand goods sell for an astonishing 70% more than they do in Japan, where prices for most products are usually higher. Ryohin Keikaku plans to open 20-30 more outlets in East Asia over the next few years, if Muji products prove as popular abroad as they have been at home. Many fashionable young Japanese would not be caught dead in anything else.

Basta

MARCH 28TH, PARIS *France's business establishment closed ranks against the Agnellis in a bitter battle for control of Source Perrier, France's bottled-water group. But the Agnellis also bungled their attack*

AFTER several months spent in battling Nestlé, a Swiss food group, for control of Source Perrier, a French producer of sparkling water, Italy's Agnelli family has had enough. On March 24th Giovanni Agnelli, the head of the Italian dynasty, admitted defeat. Nestlé said that it would lift its own bid for the firm by 15% to FFr15.4 billion ($2.7 billion). Though the European Commission will examine Nestlé's acquisition on competition grounds, the deal will almost certainly go ahead in some form. As for the Agnellis, they should make a tidy profit on their Perrier stake. But the defeat is a blow to their plans to diversify into the food business and into France. Worse, it is a blow that was partly inflicted by one Agnelli holding company on another.

The Agnellis' desire to enter new industries has grown as the performance of Fiat, their core car and engineering business, has deteriorated. Fiat's operating profits plunged 70% to 636 billion lire ($500m) in 1991, mainly because of stiff competition in cars. Although its costs are among the lowest in Europe, Fiat depends on its home market for two-thirds of its sales. This

Does Giovanni talk to Umberto?

makes it vulnerable. Over the past four years its market share in Italy has shrunk from 60% to around 45%, as rivals like Ford have increased sales there.

Fiat will soon face even tougher competition as restrictions on Japanese car im-

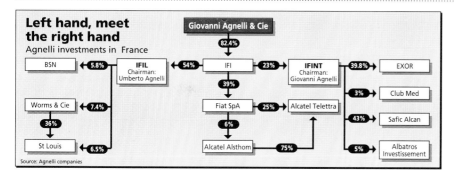

Left hand, meet the right hand
Agnelli investments in France

Source: Agnelli companies

ports are eased in Italy. No wonder, then, that the Agnelli family has been diversifying fast. It has done so via two holding companies, IFIL and IFINT. IFIL, which has $2.2 billion-worth of assets, concentrates on long-term investments in food and tourism. It operates mainly in Italy, though it has also taken stakes in a handful of French companies such as BSN, a food group, and Saint Louis, a food and paper firm.

IFINT, with $1.5 billion of assets, is an opportunistic investor in a variety of fields including car components, engineering and property. Its main aim is to diversify geographically. Some 40% of its assets are in America, and another 30% in Europe. In

France it bought into Albatros Investissement, an industrial holding firm, and a trading company, Safic Alcan. Fiat has also diversified into France, where it has swapped shares and some businesses with Alcatel Alsthom, an engineering company.

Until the Perrier spat, the Agnellis had always worked closely with leading bankers and industrialists in other countries, especially France. And they were content to take small stakes in companies on a friendly basis. Indeed, Umberto Agnelli, Giovanni's younger brother and the chairman of IFIL, is said to want to create a form of Japanese-style *keiretsu* group in which European companies co-operate closely

without having to buy large stakes in one another.

The snag, according to one French industrialist close to the Agnellis, is that IFINT, which is chaired by Giovanni Agnelli and managed by Gianluigi Gabetti, has a more aggressive, short-term strategy which can conflict with IFIL's long-term view. Mr Gabetti admits that the two units may compete, particularly in France (see chart), but says that "what [the Agnellis] don't want is for competition to become conflict".

Yet by bidding for Exor, the holding company which controls 29% of Perrier's shares, IFINT sparked off a row whose repercussions will make it harder for IFIL to forge long-term alliances in France, which had looked like a promising market. To underline this, BSN, which sided with Nestlé during the bid battle, stressed again this week that it did not want the Agnellis to raise their stake in it.

Why do the Agnellis need two holding companies? Mr Gabetti says that the Italians "don't want to look like a monolithic group", rigid and bureaucratic. But the Perrier débâcle suggests that a little more co-ordination back in Turin might not be such a bad thing after all.

When copying gets costly

MAY 9TH, TOKYO *A spate of successful suits against Japanese firms highlighted the differences in America's and Japan's patent regimes*

AS AMERICAN and European companies inspect their patent portfolios to see whether they are earning proper returns in these straitened times, Japanese bosses are scurrying for their lawyers. Several western firms expect to collect $1 billion or more for infringements of their intellectual property in Japan.

Earlier this year Japan's Minolta agreed to a $127m settlement with Honeywell after a six-year wrangle over patents for the auto-focusing technique used in modern cameras. The American company is now taking action against five other Japanese camera makers and is threatening to start proceedings against Japanese manufacturers of video camcorders as well. Industry analysts reckon Honeywell could eventually collect more than $1 billion for infringements of its auto-focusing patents.

It is not alone. Loral Fairchild, a subsidiary of Loral, an American defence contractor, is seeking "several billion dollars" from Sony, Matsushita, Sharp, Canon, Toshiba, NEC and around two dozen other companies that either manufacture or use charge-coupled devices (CCDs) in their products. The New York-based firm owns

the patents covering CCDs—the "electronic-eye" microchips used in camcorders, photocopiers and fax machines—and is demanding royalties of up to 10% of sales.

But the biggest royalty prize of all looks like going to Texas Instruments (TI). Back in the late 1950s, a TI employee called Jack Kilby patented the basic principles behind the integrated circuit. Any chip maker without a licence from TI—costing typically 3-5% of sales—is vulnerable to a suit. The Dallas-based firm is believed to have earned nearly $1 billion in patent royalties between 1987 and 1991. That was before it put the squeeze on Japanese chip makers. Since then TI has signed up Hitachi, Toshiba, Ricoh and Sharp. Mitsubishi Electric will probably be the next to buy a TI licence to carry on making chips. Fujitsu, for now, has chosen to fight. That could be costly.

The irony for Fujitsu and other Japanese microchip makers is that Mr Kilby's cornerstone patents are valid in Japan until 2001. They would have expired long ago but for bureaucratic delays caused when TI first tried to patent the invention in Japan

in 1960. Determined to protect the country's fledgling semiconductor firms of the day, the Japanese government had TI's patent application repeatedly turned down for being "too comprehensive". It was not until 1989—with the threat of American trade sanctions—that TI eventually got its Kilby patents registered in Japan.

Like the majority of original concepts patented in the United States, the Kilby patents cover broadly defined ideas. In America, for instance, Grid Systems has managed to patent the concept of a laptop computer as a hinged flat box, with the underside of the lid forming a screen when opened and the base containing a keyboard. Elsewhere, Grid would have been laughed out of court. But for Toshiba, NEC, Sharp, Epson and other Japanese manufacturers selling laptops in America, the Grid patent is a persistent headache.

Japanese manufacturers have even greater difficulty dealing with the way patents are granted in the United States on the basis of first-to-invent rather than first-to-file, the rule in force everywhere in the world except America and the Philippines. The first-to-invent principle favours the small entrepreneurial inventors who were common in America when its patent laws were formulated in the 1830s. The first-to-file approach favours large companies—especially Japanese behemoths with their well-endowed patent departments and corporate laboratories churning out improvements to existing products.

The American patenting system keeps the inventor's idea secret until the patent is granted. In contrast, the Japanese Patent Office publishes the inventor's idea 18 months after the application is made, so competitors can challenge its claims. It then takes anything up to seven years for the Japanese authorities to examine the claim, hear the objections and decide whether to grant a patent or not—in some cases, even longer. As TI found to its cost when it first tried to patent Mr Kilby's invention in Japan, determined opposition can delay an application for decades, giving rivals ample chance to examine the original claim in detail and "invent around" it. In the meantime, competitors are free to carry on using the inventor's ideas without permission.

A far narrower definition of what is patentable and a propensity to make incremental improvements to existing ideas have long encouraged Japanese firms to is-

sue flurries of patents that differ only marginally in their claims. The approach shows up in the numbers of patents recorded. The Japanese Patent Office accepted more than 720,000 applications in 1990; the comparable figure for the United States was around 150,000. Even in America, Japanese companies account for one

out of every five patents actually granted. Four of last year's top five patent holders in America were Japanese firms—Toshiba, Mitsubishi Electric, Hitachi and Canon (Eastman Kodak came fourth).

The Americans think that the Japanese patenting system is sound in principle but prone to abuse—especially in the way competitors are allowed to delay applications almost indefinitely. But harmonisation talks under the auspices of the World Intellectual Property Organisation, a body affiliated to the United Nations in Geneva, are slowly bringing the Americans into line with the Europeans and the Japanese. Policy-makers in Washington say they are ready to adopt the first-to-file principle, provided Japan slashes the time taken to process patents to just two years.

Easier said than done. Though the most automated in the world, the Japanese Patent Office has fewer than 1,000 qualified examiners trying to do five times as much work as America's 1,500 inspectors. Japan will have to train a lot more examiners if patent parleying is not to turn into patent war.

Going for broke

MAY 16TH, PRAGUE   *In the biggest sale of companies ever seen, Czechoslovakia launched a bold mass-privatisation scheme, auctioning shares in 1,200 state-owned firms.*

AMONG Eastern Europe's economic reformers, the Czechoslovaks have always been considered the wild-eyed extremists. Like every other country in Eastern Europe, Czechoslovakia has eagerly sought to sell many of its state-owned companies to western firms. But recognising that only a small proportion of its firms would attract a foreign buyer, the Czechoslovaks have spent nearly two years preparing a plan that will virtually give away most of the country's firms by distributing shares in them to millions of its own citizens using vouchers. As other countries have also struggled to privatise thousands of state-owned firms, rumours about Czechoslovakia's voucher scheme have swirled through Eastern Europe. Most reformers called it crazy. Many thought it would never get off the ground.

Czechoslovakia is about to confound the sceptics—or those, at least, who scoffed that its scheme would never fly. On May 18th, after repeated delays, the government is due to publish a final list of 1,200 firms whose shares will be sold in a series of com-

puterised auctions over the next few months. The first auction is scheduled to start a week later and continue until June 8th. By the time the auctions finish in the autumn, corporate assets with a "net book value" of about 270 billion koruna ($9.3 billion) will have been distributed to millions of new shareholders.

Many expect the latest deadlines to slip yet again, but this time the delay will probably be for only a few days. National elections on June 5th are unlikely to derail the voucher scheme. The right-wing party led by Vaclav Klaus, Czechoslovakia's finance minister and the driving force behind the scheme, is leading in the polls.

Even if Mr Klaus's party does worse than expected, his opponents will find it difficult to suspend voucher privatisation for one simple reason: three out of every four adult citizens have already paid 1,035 koruna, equivalent to one week's average wage, to take part. The voucher scheme will probably go ahead even in hard-hit Slovakia, where increasingly vocal separatists have always argued that mass privatisation

would immediately produce mass unemployment. But 2.5m Slovaks are participating in the scheme, which makes it hard for politicians of any stripe to oppose it.

Almost overnight Czechoslovakia will boast the biggest private sector in Eastern Europe–and one of the highest rates of individual shareholding in the world. A second round of auctions is already being prepared for early next year. Another batch of 1,200 firms is due to be selected by mid-August. Other East Europeans will be watching with fascination. Russian officials are already formulating a mass privatisation scheme modelled on Czechoslovakia's.

They will not find it easy. Czechoslovakia's scheme continues to puzzle even the people who have chosen to take part. After paying what was meant to be a nominal sum to participate, each citizen received a booklet of vouchers (known locally as coupons). Each booklet contains slips permitting the participant to bid a total of 1,000 "points" in the first auction for all the shares on offer. Initially every share in every company will be priced at the same fixed number of points. The price of unsold shares will be lowered in each subsequent auction until they are all sold. Those shares attracting too many bids will not be distributed. Bidders will retain their points and the shares will be offered again at higher prices until an equilibrium price is found that satisfies all bidders.

Individuals can either bid themselves or give all or some of their points to privately run investment funds in exchange for shares in the fund, whose managers will bid the points they collect and then manage the resulting portfolio of shares. By the time shares are handed to investors in January, bourses in Prague and Bratislava, as well as a computerised over-the-counter market, are supposed to be operating.

Though the voucher scheme now looks unstoppable, it is far from clear that it will deliver economic gains quickly. Privatisation on such a scale has never been attempted before. If it works, many firms suddenly cut off from soft bank credit and government subsidies in the middle of a severe recession will promptly go bust. But the uncertainty of mass privatisation has been increased even further by two big changes to the scheme since it was first worked out in detail last year: few of the firms in the plan are having all their equity sold via vouchers, as originally planned, and private investment funds will dominate the auctions–a development that has taken the government by surprise.

The first change was a concession forced on the government by company managers. They argued that stakes in most companies should be kept out of the scheme on the dubious grounds that this would make it easier to negotiate joint ventures with foreigners and to motivate their own workers with share distributions. The size of the stake to be sold in the voucher programme now varies from less than 10% to 97% (with 3% of every firm retained to meet restitution claims). Across all 1,200 firms, the average stake to be sold is 50%.

This is unfortunate. One of the great attractions of the original scheme was that it allowed the government to sidestep the time-consuming and politically fraught process of reviewing each firm's privatisation plans. As it is, the need to review each plan, however hastily, has delayed the programme for months and inevitably laid some government officials open to accusations of corruption.

Critics also fret that many firms, with less than a majority of their equity privatised, will hardly be compelled to change their behaviour. But if the government sticks to its guns and treats such firms as private rather than state-owned, as it has pledged to do, this last worry may not matter that much. Already managers at many big firms are behaving as if the government means what it says, informally courting investment-fund managers who they guess could soon be among their shareholders. If Mr Klaus wins impressively in next month's elections and so is given a freer hand, speculates one official at the Czech Republic's privatisation ministry, he will revert to the original plan in the second round and privatise firms wholesale.

The second change to the scheme—the dominant role of investment funds—could prove to be a much wilder card. An advertising blitz in December 1991 by the as-

tutely named Harvard Capital and Consulting, a little-known financial conglomerate run by a young Czech emigré, saved the entire voucher scheme from oblivion. The Harvard fund pledged to pay people at least ten times their original 1,035 koruna investment for their voucher points a year after shares began trading. Since each voucher booklet represented a claim on assets worth 25,000-80,000 koruna, this was not a nonsensical offer–provided, of course, that the scheme worked, that the shares became tradable, and that the asset valuations meant something.

Nevertheless Harvard's guarantee alarmed officials. It also caught the eye of a public bored and confused by the government's own clumsy promotion of the voucher scheme. Sales of voucher booklets soared. A horde of other funds followed in Harvard's footsteps, including those run by state-owned commercial banks, nearly all offering similar, or even more generous, guarantees. Now 437 funds have collected two-thirds of all voucher points issued.

There are two ways to view the success of the funds: either as the appearance of western-style financial institutions which will eventually evolve into a genuine capital market, capable of trading, valuing and financing companies; or a recipe for fraud and the immediate collapse of the planned stockmarket. In other words, capitalism or bust.

The auctions proceeded smoothly. But, by the end of the year, it was still not clear how the shares were to be distributed or traded.

Double or quits

MAY 30TH, TOKYO   **Sony, the world's most innovative consumer-electronics company, decided to defy the rest of the industry yet again with its unique Mini Disc format**

WHEN the chips are down, the gambler in Sony invariably comes to the fore. Even by the standards of Japan's battered consumer-electronics industry, Sony has just reported some horrendous results for the year to March 1992. Though its sales worldwide were up by almost 6% to ¥3.8 trillion ($28.5 billion), its operating profit plunged 44% to ¥166 billion. Arch rival Matsushita, in contrast, managed to contain the drop in its profits to just 18%. Worse, Sony suffered a humiliating ¥18 billion operating loss in its final quarter as it slashed prices ruthlessly to shift its mounting stocks of unsold goods. What better time, then, for a high-roller like Sony to announce a spectacular new gadget?

Sony's Mini Disc, long publicised but shown to the public for the first time only

on May 26th, is both an impressive feat of engineering and an enormous gamble. It is to be marketed as a recordable version of today's compact discs (CDs)—and one that, like a tape cassette, does not skip beats when jolted in the pocket or on the dashboard of a car. As such, Sony is out to position the Mini Disc as a direct rival to the tape-based Digital Compact Cassette (DCC) announced recently by Matsushita and Philips. But it is also trying to sell the handy little Mini Disc machines as strictly for use on the move, while the bulkier CD player remains at home. The thinking behind this strategy is to stimulate new sales without killing demand for CDs and CD players; Sony is a big supplier of both.

Some might praise Sony's ageing bosses, chairman Akio Morita, 71, and

president Norio Ohga, 62, for yet another bold stroke. Under their direction Sony has sometimes thrived by taking the electronics industry, and consumers, by surprise. But it has also spent a fortune in Hollywood which may take years to earn a decent return, if it ever does. And the company's marketing strategy for the Mini Disc looks worse than merely risky—it looks nonsensical. Perhaps Sony now needs somebody more prudent, or more calculating, at the top, though no successor to either Mr Morita or Mr Ohga is in sight.

Consumers are already dazed by the proliferation of new formats and products offered by the electronics industry. Sony's plans for the Mini Disc threaten to so bewilder customers that they could stop spending money on such gadgets entirely.

To ensure the success of the new format, the company believes that it must make plenty of prerecorded music titles available quickly. Some 500 Mini Disc albums—mostly pop music and jazz—are scheduled to go on sale on November 1st in Japan, when the new machines reach the stores. Yet stressing prerecorded discs will only reinforce the Mini Disc's image as strictly a playback medium—in short, a direct replacement for the CD.

The same is true for Sony's emphasis on the Mini Disc's portability. The machines that Sony, and 21 other manufacturers which have licensed the technology from it, will offer initially will be Walkman-like players, car stereos and portable "boom-boxes". Unfortunately, the market for portable hi-fi has proved to be almost exclusively for playback-only equipment. Most consumers make their recordings at home.

If Sony produces a Mini Disc machine for the home, where its recording facilities are more likely to be used, the company

will be asking consumers to scrap their new and pricey CD players along with their collections of CDs. Many consumers will not be amused. Most could prefer the DCC format offered by Matsushita and Philips. DCC machines will play conventional tapes, though not with the same pristine sound when new digital tapes are used, and will be marketed simply as a better type of cassette player. Consumers will not have to junk any of their existing music collections or their new CD players.

One reason Sony is pushing its Mini Disc so hard may be that the company badly needs a new money-spinner. Its current problems have less to do with the worldwide slump, stiffer competition, the strengthening yen and the prolonged depression in Tokyo's stockmarket (all cited by the company's managers) than with its

own over-reliance on the slow-growing market for video equipment and its forays beyond consumer electronics.

Sony's music business, which it bought for $2 billion in 1988 from CBS, suffered a 7% decline in sales last year. Sony's movie business, acquired when it bought Columbia Pictures for $3.4 billion in 1989, is probably still failing to cover the cash lavished on it. Movie revenues did grow by 28% last year, thanks to such box-office hits as "Terminator 2" and "Hook". But the movie industry is notoriously fickle. This year, or next, Sony could have more flops than hits. For the longer term, Sony's rationale for buying CBS Records and Columbia was to reap gains from the "synergy" between entertainment software (records or movies) and electronic hardware. No such gains are yet visible.

Chip diplomacy

JULY 18TH, TOKYO **A spate of joint-venture deals, most between American and Japanese firms, to develop and manufacture microchips marked a turning point for the world's electronics industry**

THE announcement on July 13th by Toshiba, IBM and Siemens that they would collaborate in the development of advanced memory chips made headlines around the world. But this deal is only the latest, and most visible, of a series of recent joint ventures that are reshaping the semiconductor industry. On the same day Fujitsu and Advanced Micro Devices said they would jointly manufacture "flash" memories, a new kind of chip destined to replace disk drives in personal computers.

More than a dozen similar announcements have been made over the past year. Most of them bring together American semiconductor makers with a flair for design and development and Japanese firms with impressive manufacturing skills. The majority of the tie-ups have been in the memory-chip business, but some deals

also include microprocessor chips, the "brains" of today's computers.

The electronics industry is at last going global in much the same way, and on a similar scale, as the motor industry did a decade ago. In both cases the huge cost of developing the next generation of basic components—gearboxes and engines in the motor industry, memory chips and microprocessors in electronics—has made it less attractive for even the biggest companies in the business to do it on their own. Developing each new generation of DRAM (dynamic random-access memory) chips now costs $1 billion or more. Building a factory to make the new chips costs about the same.

At the same time, going it alone brings fewer and fewer advantages. New chips, especially the memory chips common to all

electronic products, have to be compatible with the industry standards now demanded by consumers and software suppliers, making them little more than commodity items. And people who buy electronic machines—whether fax machines, televisions or personal computers—do not care who makes the chips inside them. What counts is how well the product uses such components.

So, like the car makers before them, electronics firms see less and less sense in trying to compete on the components which are common to all their products. Instead, they are trying to differentiate their products by other means. Some manufacturers (Matsushita and Apple) now specialise in making their electronic gizmos easy to use. Others (Hewlett-Packard, Compaq, Xerox and Sony) go for innovation, quality and performance. Still others (IBM, Hitachi and AT&T) stress reliability and service.

As the big car companies have come to

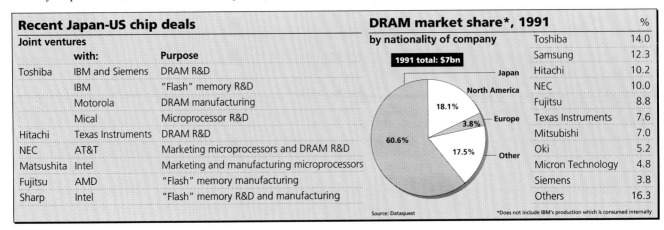

Recent Japan-US chip deals			DRAM market share*, 1991	%
Joint ventures			**by nationality of company**	
	with:	Purpose	Toshiba	14.0
Toshiba	IBM and Siemens	DRAM R&D	Samsung	12.3
	IBM	"Flash" memory R&D	Hitachi	10.2
	Motorola	DRAM manufacturing	NEC	10.0
	Mical	Microprocessor R&D	Fujitsu	8.8
Hitachi	Texas Instruments	DRAM R&D	Texas Instruments	7.6
NEC	AT&T	Marketing microprocessors and DRAM R&D	Mitsubishi	7.0
Matsushita	Intel	Marketing and manufacturing microprocessors	Oki	5.2
Fujitsu	AMD	"Flash" memory manufacturing	Micron Technology	4.8
Sharp	Intel	"Flash" memory R&D and manufacturing	Siemens	3.8
			Others	16.3

1991 total: $7bn — Japan 60.6%, North America 18.1%, Europe 3.8%, Other 17.5%

Source: Dataquest

*Does not include IBM's production which is consumed internally

adopt similar production techniques and to use the same components, they have competed less on hardware and more on styling, packaging, marketing and offering the mix of features that consumers want most. The same trend will make an even bigger impact on the electronics industry.

Powerful new memory chips will blur the boundaries between the computer, telecoms and consumer-electronics businesses. New pocket-sized appliances promise to replace the personal computer. Many industry specialists predict that, within a decade, a single hand-held machine will combine a mobile telephone, pen-based computer and fax machine. It will tap into databases from anywhere, run all day off a single charge of batteries and will be as ubiquitous as pocket calculators.

To make such products easy for consumers to use, despite their technical complexity, powerful memory chips will be needed to store and manipulate massive amounts of data. Many of the electronics firms making and marketing these machines will regard these chips as simply the rivets holding their products together. Most will buy them from the cheapest or the most reliable supplier.

Yet the biggest consumers of memory chips—like the leading manufacturers of computers—will want to retain some say in their design, price and delivery dates. That is why IBM, Toshiba and Siemens have decided to collaborate on the next-but-one generation of 256-megabit DRAMS.

They are not the only ones working on such an advanced DRAM design. Hitachi has been collaborating with Texas Instruments for several years on future memory chips. Japan's number-two computer company, NEC, and the American telecoms giant AT&T have been doing the same.

Years of collaboration will be needed to create a 256-megabit chip. The tools for making it will have to be created too.

Cramming 256m memory cells on a sliver of silicon the size of a finger nail will require the ability to etch lines on the material's surface a mere quarter of a micron wide—400 times thinner than a human hair. That is three times narrower than what can be achieved commercially today.

The problem lies with the optical "steppers" used for laying down the chip's microscopic wiring pattern. Steppers are highly accurate lithographic machines that step across the surface of an eight-inch wafer of silicon, repeatedly printing a tiny image of the memory device ready for etching. The trouble is that optical steppers, which use ultraviolet light, are approaching the limits of their resolution. They can probably be adapted to produce the 64-megabit DRAMS that will follow today's most advanced chip, the 16-megabit DRAM.

For 256-megabit chips, however, the only answer is to use an x-ray machine. And that means rethinking—for the first time since the DRAM's earliest days—the entire lithographic process for making microchips. Japanese firms fear they could be left behind in the race to cross this technological barrier, which is one reason they are so eager to find American partners.

Collaboration between American and Japanese firms should end the long-running quarrel between America and Japan over chip trade. The new alliances make a nonsense of the long-cherished view that maintaining an indigenous semiconduc-

tor industry is necessary for the survival of any one country's industry, a common excuse for government handouts to high-tech firms. Interestingly, America's Sematech—the government-supported consortium that became a monument to such economic nationalism—is now discussing collaboration with JESSI, its counterpart in the European Community. A link with the Japanese looks possible too.

The big question is whether firms such as IBM and AT&T, by teaming up with rivals in Japan, are surrendering one of the few advantages that their immense size confers: the ability to pay the enormous costs of developing new chips and building the factories to make them. Would a Japanese manufacturing giant that dominated its industry ever do the same? Japan's largest car maker, Toyota, has so far stood aloof from similar link-ups in its industry.

IBM's answer is twofold: no matter how big its own resources are, making memory chips with Toshiba and Siemens is cheaper; and it is sharing only its process technology with its rivals, not its know-how for designing the chip's logic. The company will continue to design certain types of chips itself. "First we become partners and then we become competitors," says Mike Attardo, IBM's general manager for technology products.

IBM may be big enough to look after itself. For other American firms, collaboration could be riskier. Japanese companies have a knack of profiting more from joint ventures than their foreign partners. Some Japanese firms—Fujitsu is a good example—are fond of taking a stake in any joint-venture partner and then, later, gaining control of the other firm. In signing their joint venture, Fujitsu and AMD agreed to take a 5% stake in each other. The Japanese chip maker has sales 20 times larger than the hotshot little American firm. Hardly a marriage of equals.

America builds a trade block

AUGUST 15TH, WASHINGTON, DC, AND MEXICO CITY **The governments of America, Canada and Mexico signed a draft North American Free Trade agreement. Mexico celebrated. But the deal was greeted with mixed feelings in both America and Canada**

A LITTLE over two years after Mexico convinced the United States of the benefits of a North American Free Trade agreement (NAFTA), and 14 months after negotiations for one began, George Bush was at last able

to announce a draft accord on August 12th between America, Mexico and Canada. That this would create a market, in output and population, to match the size of the European Community ought to be a boon

for Mr Bush, who can now wave his foreign-policy credentials more confidently at next week's Republican convention in Houston. But will it be a boon for the three economies?

Yes—if it ever happens. Make no mistake: NAFTA has many hurdles to leap before it is ratified, at the soonest, early next year. Take the deal that Mr Bush struck with Congress to win approval to negotiate. The "fast-track" procedures granted to the administration commit Congress to voting a straight yes or no on NAFTA—they may not fiddle with the treaty. In return, however, the administration is bound by strict rules in presenting NAFTA to Congress.

Once an agreement is "initialled" by Mr Bush, Mexico's Carlos Salinas de Gortari and Canada's Brian Mulroney, a minimum of 90 days must elapse before it may be signed by those leaders. During this time Congress is able to propose changes. This initialling will probably now not take place until September, which means the signing will not happen until December. Once the signed treaty is sent to Congress for ratification, 90 legislative days will then be taken to consider it. And that takes ratification perilously close to the expiry of the fast-track deal, in June 1993.

It would be nice to see more enthusiasm for a free-trade agreement in the two northernmost countries. Canada, which does not do much business with Mexico, joined the NAFTA talks with little joy. It wanted mainly to protect the concessions Canada had won in the free-trade deal it had already struck with America. That earlier deal is now being blamed by many Canadians for aggravating their economic slump. The unpopular Mr Mulroney tries not to mention NAFTA in public.

In America, the administration seems to have trouble recalling why it thought NAFTA was such a good idea. True, the larger part of the economic benefits will be reaped only well into the next century, as Mexico graduates from the third world to the first—but policies for long-term growth often have this drawback of working in the long term.

Also true, in the short term a NAFTA deal will provide a comparatively modest boost to American employment. Gary Hufbauer and Jeffrey Schott at the Institute for International Economics (IIE) think that after five years NAFTA might have created 325,000 new American jobs and have destroyed about 150,000, for a net gain of 175,000. That is small in relation to the size of the American economy. And it is politically awkward, because the losses will be concentrated in certain industries (eg, farming, bulk-steel production and textiles) whereas the gains will be more widely dispersed (processed foods, plastics, pharmaceuticals, capital goods and high-grade steel). Even so, a policy that can be relied upon to create jobs overall is rare enough to warrant no apology.

Messrs Hufbauer and Schott reckon that, again after five years, America's exports to Mexico could be $17 billion a year higher than without a NAFTA; Mexico's exports to America might be $8 billion a year higher. Now use a rule of thumb: for coun-

A lot at stake

United States	% of total trade	Canada	% of total trade	Mexico	% of total trade	NAFTA members	% of total trade
Canada	17.1	United States	69.2	United States	72.9	GDP	$6,450 bn
Japan	15.3	Japan	6.1	Japan	5.2	Intra-NAFTA trade	$245 bn
Mexico	7.0	Germany	2.1	Germany	3.6		
Germany	4.7	France	1.4	Canada	3.1	Extra-NAFTA trade	$801 bn
Britain	4.4	South Korea	1.4	Spain	2.1		
World total	$931.2bn	World total	$246.6bn	World total	$85.3bn	Population	360 m

Source: IMF

tries previously separated by quite high trade barriers, the gain in welfare due to trade liberalisation equals about one-fifth of the expansion in trade. The total gain in welfare, given an increase in trade of $25 billion a year, is therefore $5 billion a year, to be shared between the two countries. Express that permanent flow of income as a discounted present value and you get to a once-for-all prize of about $50 billion. What other policy to create $50 billion of real wealth out of nowhere does Mr Bush have on his agenda?

Perhaps it is a sign of the times that Mexico is the most enthusiastic member of this arrangement. In 1985 it reversed decades of protectionism and massive state intervention in its economy, embarking on trade liberalisation and a tight, anti-inflationary monetary policy. Since then it has sucked in American goods and capital. Between 1987 and 1991 American merchandise exports to Mexico grew by more than a fifth each year, to $33 billion. Between 1986 and 1991, exports of heavy industrial machinery grew by 150%. Today 70% of Mexico's imports are from America.

Mexico is the biggest foreign market for exports of American clothes, textiles and foreign airline travel. It is the second-biggest market for chemicals and plastics, steel output, machine tools, car parts and consumer durables, among others. Only a small fraction of these are re-exported to America from the duty-free *maquiladoras* that line the Mexican border. This surge in exports (or imports, if you live south of the border) has occurred despite a welter of non-tariff barriers and an average Mexican tariff of 10%, which NAFTA would phase out.

Is Mexico therefore terrified of a further wave of imports? On the contrary, it seems to be looking forward to it. NAFTA, says Mr Salinas, is "inevitable because we already have a very intense trade relationship and the agreement will bring order to that relationship. The longer it takes, the more it will benefit our competitors; the less time it takes, the more it will benefit Mexico, the United States and Canada."

Much of Mexican business is already feeling the rigours of freer trade. Because of

the recent surge, imports now account for a third of Mexico's domestic market in textiles, plastics, chemicals, paper and machinery. Mexican companies have been feeling the squeeze: some 500 engineering firms in Mexico City alone have crumbled. Thousands more small- and medium-sized firms are threatened. Big, vertically-integrated companies are breaking themselves down, spinning off parts and closing unprofitable lines. And the need to modernise to prepare for even freer trade under NAFTA has sparked an investment boom.

Some Mexican companies are buying up American competitors, to get new technologies, protect their domestic markets and reap economies of scale. In 1989 Vitro, a glass-maker in the thriving northern city of Monterrey, bought Anchor Glass in Florida. Cemex, a cement producer, has a string of ready-mix plants and terminals along the American border. On August 11th a group of Mexican investors bought PPI Del Monte, a distributor of fresh fruit. A Mexican, Alfredo Brener, has bid $385m for Continental Airlines. Mr Brener's family is already the largest shareholder in Mexican de Aviacion, a newly privatised Mexican airline.

If America wants a good reason to be churlish about an agreement that brings decades of political and economic hostility to an end, there is one. Deals like NAFTA can threaten progress towards multilateral free trade—the best sort—unless the partners take care. Most pro-trade economists are happy with NAFTA because the trade it will create is likely to dwarf the trade it will divert (ie, from efficient suppliers outside the agreement to less efficient insiders). As a result, outsiders are unlikely to lose much, while the insiders will gain a lot. But doubts about NAFTA's trade-creating virtues would be far less if America seemed committed to the Uruguay round of global trade talks. Instead of regarding NAFTA and the Uruguay round as complements, which they could be, the administration has often seemed to think of them as alternatives. That, unlike the draft signed this week, really is worrying.

From Pampers to Pontiacs

NOVEMBER 7TH, DETROIT **The resignation of Robert Stempel as chairman and chief executive of General Motors marked the end of the old order at GM. The new, generally younger, executive team inherited a colossal task**

FOR generations it has been a gerontocracy, with promotions based more on seniority and golf partnerships than merit. Now much of the old order has been swept away at General Motors (GM). A new, younger team is trying to save the world's biggest car maker. Many of them learnt their business away from the stifling and parochial bureaucracy of America's motor city.

They also have a mentor: John Smale, who helped transform another hidebound company, Procter & Gamble, which makes soap and detergent as well as Crest toothpaste, Pampers nappies and other personal-care products. As an outside director of GM, the 65-year-old Mr Smale led a boardroom coup in April that eventually forced the resignation of Robert Stempel as chairman and chief executive. On November 2nd Mr Stempel's job was split between Mr Smale, who became non-executive chairman, and Mr Smale's handpicked lieutenant, Jack Smith, who was appointed chief executive.

Mr Smith, 54, led a successful turnaround at GM's European operations in the mid-1980s. He has replaced some of GM's older directors with colleagues from overseas. Louis Hughes, 43, one of Mr Smith's successors in running GM's profitable European business, becomes responsible for all of the firm's international operations outside America. Richard Waggoner, 39, is chief financial officer. He ran GM's operations in Brazil and was a finance director in Europe.

The task they face is colossal. Last year GM's core North American car business made an operating loss of $7 billion. For the time being, at least, Mr Smith plans to stick with a plan to cut 74,000 jobs and close 21 plants in North America. But he also has to transform the company in other ways. His experience in Europe suggests how he should set about this.

Mr Smith reversed chronic losses at GM Europe by driving down costs and developing dashing new models. As a result, its share of the West European car market increased from 8% in 1981 to more than 12% last year. GM Europe (which includes Vauxhall, Opel and Saab) has now nipped into second place behind Germany's Volkswagen. It has kept Detroit afloat with cumulative net profits of $8.5 billion since 1987.

The strategy included establishing a

Jack the lad

small headquarters staff of about 200 people in Zurich in 1986. The aim was to get away from manufacturing fiefs and their ingrained habits and to make executive decisions in a neutral location. The same could happen in America, with Detroit losing power. Mr Hughes intends to run GM's international operations from Zurich. Mr Smith has also been holding meetings of his kitchen cabinet not in GM's sprawling headquarters, but at the firm's technical centre at Warren, Michigan.

The sun also sets

NOVEMBER 21ST, TOKYO **After the oil shock of the 1970s and the rise of the yen in the 1980s, Japan emerged stronger than ever. As its financial bubble burst, we asked whether Japanese industry would again find strength in adversity**

HOW the mighty have fallen. The results reported by Japanese companies over the past few weeks show the devastating effect that the bursting of the bubble economy has had on business in Japan. During the six months ending in September, companies' pre-tax profits plunged by an average of 36%. Manufacturing firms have fared worst. Matsushita, the world's largest maker of consumer electronics, saw its pre-tax profits tumble 66%. NEC's crashed 71%. Mazda's fell 72%. Nippon Steel's were down 74%. Japan's second-biggest car maker, Nissan, lost ¥14.2 billion ($114m) before tax, its first loss since it listed on the stock exchange in 1951.

Across Japan, production lines are being mothballed, wages frozen and bonuses paid in unsold goods instead of cash. Even the unmentionable—sacking lifetime employees—is being discussed. The word "restructuring" is on everyone's lips.

For the third time since the second world war, Japanese business is facing massive and painful readjustment. On the two previous occasions, it benefited enormously from the experience. The oil shock in 1973 got Japan out of smokestack industries and into more profitable electronics and office automation. The high-yen shock—when the yen more than doubled in value against the dollar between 1985 and 1988—spurred productivity to new heights and turned stay-at-home Japanese manufacturers into eager multinationals. Now Japanese business is facing the "post-bubble" shock. The betting is that the experience will make Japan more competi-

tive still—especially in areas such as services and high technology, where until now it has lagged behind America and Europe.

Japanese firms invariably blame the rising yen and the economic downturn worldwide for their troubles. For top Japanese exporters, that may be so—but only partly. The real origins of Japan's current difficulties stem from changes that were under way in the mid-1980s. The abundance of capital that could be raised virtually free as the Tokyo stockmarket soared between 1987 and 1990 only helped to mask the problem. Much of the money was wasted on prestige property developments, empty research centres and more factories for producing a bigger surplus of unwanted goods.

The consumer-electronics firms and motor manufacturers were among the worst offenders. As the twin engines of Japanese manufacturing, they account for over one-fifth of the country's industrial output and one-third of its manufactured exports. Both have invested heavily in shortening product cycles and building additional factories. Nothing wrong with that—except that their respective markets were fast approaching saturation.

Every household in Japan, America and Europe that is ever likely to own a colour television, hi-fi and video recorder now has at least one. No other "must have" gizmo is expected until the late 1990s, when Japan's consumer-electronics firms ought to have learnt how to make HDTV (high-definition television) sets for reasonable prices. Until then, they have four or five lean years to get through.

More of the consumer-electronics industry's second-tier manufacturers are expected to go out of business. Pioneer's share price took a dive last month when rumours circulated that one of its subsidiaries was heading for bankruptcy. Investors are also jumpy about JVC, a subsidiary of Matsushita. It is expected to report a pre-tax loss of ¥21 billion for the year to March 1993. The firm will probably have to suspend its dividend, for the first time since being publicly listed in 1960. JVC blames its overdependence on video recorders for its woes. With ¥10 billion accruing annually from its VHS patents, JVC has viewed its video business as an annuity for life, so has done little to prepare itself for the product's demise. In August JVC announced that 3,000 of its 14,000 jobs would have to go.

Japanese car makers have been equally blind to the saturation of their markets at home and abroad. Car ownership in Japan stopped growing in double-digits in the late 1980s, as the country ran out of road space and parking slots. Meanwhile, sales by Japanese car firms overseas—never as lucrative at the best of times—became even less so as motor manufacturers in America and Europe caught up with Japanese levels of quality and productivity. Japanese car makers used to make an average profit of ¥83,000 on every car that left their factories. Now they count themselves lucky if they get ¥15,000 a car.

Belatedly, Japanese motor firms are adjusting to a replacement market that is growing at no more than 2-3% a year, instead of the 10-15% for which they are geared up. Toyota has shelved plans for a new factory in Miyagi prefecture and cut production at its big assembly line in Tahara City from two shifts to one. Mazda has cancelled two new luxury models, along with plans for a new sales network in

Samurai of the new Japan

America. Over the next three years, Nissan intends to cut 4,000 jobs from its 57,000-strong payroll.

The retrenchment now under way among Japan's hard-pressed manufacturers is only the beginning. Few of the production lines that are being mothballed during the present recession are likely to be switched on ever again. None of the workers sent home or to subsidiaries on reduced

The fall		
Japanese company results, 1st half 1992, % change from a year earlier		
	Sales	Pre-tax profit
Construction	+9	+2
Pharmaceuticals	+4	+3
Transport	+2	-1
Shipping	+1	-16
Telecommunications	-2	-34
Motors	-2	-60
Textiles	-4	-36
Chemicals	-4	-38
Electronics	-5	-60
Precision machinery	-6	-69
Steel	-7	-61
Machinery	-8	-48
Property	-10	-23
Manufacturing	-4	-41
Non-manufacturing	-1	-11
Source: Wako Economic Research Centre		

pay, can expect to get his old job back. Once again, the shock of adjustment is being borne almost entirely by Japan's long-suffering salarymen.

Not all Japanese businesses are faring as badly as its motor makers or consumer-electronics firms—or other bombed-out businesses in shipbuilding, steel, machinery, mining, chemicals, plastics and textiles. It is no coincidence that, even during the present recession, most of Japan's best-performing firms are in retailing, transport and various forms of services.

A recent OECD study* on structural change suggests that Japan has already outstripped Europe, and even America, in its drive to become a predominantly high-tech and service-based economy. Japan has boosted its high-growth industries (communications and retailing, for example); maintained little or no expansion in its medium-growth industries (such as chemicals and aerospace); and begun to abandon its low-growth areas. According to the OECD, Japan has been going high-tech twice as fast as America, its closest rival. America still has more high-growth output than Japan, but it also has more low-growth activity (eg, petroleum, timber and textiles), which pulls its overall performance down.

Services are going high-tech. Restaurant chains have adopted the just-in-time tricks used in the car industry for delivering individually prepared meals. The Seven-Eleven convenience stores operated by Ito-Yokado, Japan's second-largest supermarket chain, do not label their shelves. Instead, the goods on each shelf vary with customer tastes. A read-out of what is selling well is fed to the nearest warehouse, from which stock is delivered throughout the day to match the store's changing sales pattern. The myth of antiquated Japanese distribution is about to be exploded.

Perhaps as a foretaste of things to come, the best half-yearly results announced in Japan this month have come from the country's top video-game maker, Nintendo. While other Japanese firms were seeing sales slip and earnings tumble, Nintendo's pre-tax profits for the six months to September rose by more than 5%, to ¥80 billion, on sales that were up 13%, to ¥277 billion. The post-bubble shock has introduced a brand new game—one based on services and high-tech—that Japanese business is determined to win.

*"Structural Change and Industrial Performance", OECD, Paris, 1992.

The big break

NOVEMBER 14TH, NEW YORK AT&T's purchase of a 33% stake in McCaw, America's biggest mobile-telephone operator, heralded a telecommunications revolution

THE SEVEN regional "Baby Bells", spun off from Ma Bell eight years ago, have grown used to a quiet life of steady profits, fed by their local monopolies. They have watched with equanimity the battle for market share between American Telephone & Telegraph (AT&T) and its competitors for long-distance telephone traffic. Two big deals announced this month, along with a new president, could ruin their peaceful existence. The Baby Bells—more formally known as the regional Bell operating companies—ought to be hard at work on a reassessment of their future role. Few industry observers see much sign of this happening.

Yet even the least imaginative Baby Bells must have felt the ground wobble on November 4th, when AT&T announced plans for a big move into cellular telephones. AT&T intends to correct a strategic error made during the earliest days of the cellular market, when it took only a limited role as an equipment supplier.

To put that right, AT&T has agreed to buy a 33% stake in McCaw Cellular Communications—the biggest firm in the wireless market—with an option to take majority control of the firm at some time in the future. The $3.8 billion deal gives AT&T access to a cellular network covering 40% of America's population and almost all its big cities. Overnight, the Baby Bells' cellular subsidiaries will be faced by a far deadlier competitor, with the financial muscle to match McCaw's proven marketing skills.

For AT&T a big attraction of the deal is that it will be able to use cellular technology to connect local customers directly to its long-distance lines. (To do this now, AT&T has to pay the Baby Bells 50 cents out of each $1 of revenue for access through their wire-based local networks.) Bob Allen, AT&T's chairman, insists the McCaw deal is not an attack on the local exchanges. He just wants AT&T to present as wide a choice of products as possible, and it happens that many of its best customers "don't want to be tethered by wired services". But how many can be untethered before the traditional market of the regional Bells begins to shrink?

The AT&T announcement knocked 5-10% off the shares of the regional Bells. More interestingly, Wall Street also applauded AT&T for promising to invest in a company that has never made an operating profit in its (short) life. The stockmarket

plainly agreed with Mr Allen's assessment: with the cellular industry increasing its revenues by 40% a year—and expected to notch up 10m subscribers by the end of this month—AT&T could not afford to risk staying out of the cellular market any longer.

One of AT&T's two main rivals for the long-distance market has come to the same conclusion. In another deal with far-reaching consequences for the regional Bells, MCI announced on November 9th that it aims to establish a national consortium of companies to launch a new wireless network. As MCI virtually created the mobile-telephone market in the first place, its new initiatives tend to get noticed.

If it can get the regulatory go-ahead, MCI says that by 1994 it could offer a "personal communications system" (PCS). This would use a higher frequency than existing cellular networks and a technology better suited to a high traffic density. According to its champions, PCS (known elsewhere as PCN, for "personal communications network") could thus herald a mass market for cheap pocket telephones.

MCI is not the only company interested in developing such a system. By November 9th, the closing date for submissions, the Federal Communications Commission received over 100 rival proposals. Bert Roberts, MCI's chairman, thinks there could be scope for the regional Bells' subsidiaries to participate in a national consortium; others would exclude the Bells and all the independent cellular operators, in the interests of creating more competition. Either way, the prospect of personal networks ought to be alarming the regional Bells—"they should be petrified," says Mr Roberts.

The reason? Not only would personal networks be a threat to the Bells' local voice traffic; they could open up a new era of cross-industry alliances to compete for the bit of the telecoms industry where the real growth lies—in video and data services.

To provide these goodies, MCI—along with AT&T and the third main long-distance operator, Sprint—has its eye on the prospect of collaboration with the regional Bells' arch-enemy, the cable-television industry. Its coaxial cables could provide access to millions of homes for what analysts at Goldman Sachs, an investment bank, call a "communicopia" of telecoms products. The long-distance companies, with their computer allies, would build the

products and ensure the long-distance transmission quality—perhaps eventually with optical fibre—to allow national distribution.

Meanwhile, where would the regional Bells stand? With their own products priced too high and their technology too primitive, they might find it hard to compete for this glamorous business. Even in the more humdrum world of the ordinary telephone they could face a nasty squeeze. George Dellinger, an analyst in the Washington, DC, office of County NatWest, a stockbroker, estimates that one-quarter of their revenues come from payments by long-distance companies for access to local networks. He thinks that, by the end of the century, enough wireless gadgetry could be in place to wipe out much of that.

All this adds up to a stiff challenge for the Baby Bells. One or two, however, have begun to think about radical responses. California's Pacific Telesis, for instance, is studying the possibility of floating off its cellular subsidiary. At least one regional Bell has already met MCI to talk about its PCS ideas. For the most part, though, the Bells have gone through the old routines—bullying the regulators for higher local tariffs, and lobbying in Washington for access to service markets beyond their monopolies.

The regional Bells might be wise to tread carefully in Washington. For the third big change this month is the election of a Democratic president with an explicit (if vague) commitment to giving the country better telecommunications.

Leaving this up to the regional Bells is the most obvious option. But they have cut their annual capital spending by more than 40% (in real terms) since 1980, which has reduced their credibility as champions of high-tech. Vice-president-elect Al Gore and his allies want to promote high-tech ventures; they may prefer to open the Baby Bells' monopolies to competition.

This could mean that if the regional Bells continue to make their familiar plea to be allowed into long-distance telephony, they just might find themselves taken at their word. The corollary, though, would be a forced opening of the local marketplace. "You could see an unbundling of the regional monopolists' services as well as a pricing of those services in a way that fairly and transparently reflected their underlying costs," says Goldman Sachs's Robert Morris. And that would open the floodgates to all sorts of competitors.

Contents

FINANCE

The might of markets

POLICY-makers who for the best part of a decade had talked up efficient markets were surprised—nay, aggrieved—in 1992 when those markets turned upon them and made a nonsense of their policies. The crumbling of Europe's exchange-rate mechanism (ERM), once speculators realised that its semi-fixed parities were not necessarily a prelude to full economic and monetary union, was by far the most important financial development in that part of the world. It was also, or should have been, a healthy reminder to those in authority everywhere of the limits to government and central-bank intervention in currency markets.

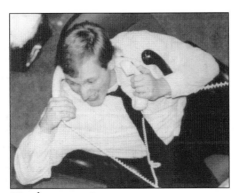

Manic moment

More volatile than at any time since the demise of Bretton Woods in the early 1970s, currencies provided the main excitement in a year, for most, of frustration, uncertainty and slog. Against a background of generally dreary economic growth, financial markets overall were no less glum. Japan, Britain and Scandinavia remained crippled by deflating real assets and heavy debt, from which America was only beginning to recover. Borrowers were reluctant to borrow and lenders—with an eye on the new risk-capital ratios coming into effect in 1993—to lend. The corpses of property companies (Canada's Olympia & York the biggest of them) littered the landscape.

Falling short-term interest rates outside continental Europe provided some cheer. They helped banks survive their bad old loans, widening their margins and encouraging them to buy government bonds rather than make bad new loans. They also spurred companies to issue securities. Yet, though feebler returns on cash pushed more money into equities, share prices worldwide went nowhere. American equities were their least volatile in living memory. Morgan Stanley's World Index fell by 6.8%, mostly because Japan's 26% decline

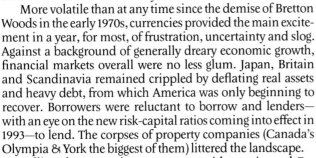

More losses at Lloyd's

more than offset Britain's 14% gain and a 4% rise in America's Dow Jones Industrial average. Bonds did better in many places, but rising government deficits subdued bond prices too. To escape a growing suspicion that the 1990s might be a decade of unpalatably low returns, investors fled to emerging markets.

Insurers, too, had a heavy year. Clever or lucky currency plays boosted investment returns for many, but years of underwriting underpriced risks, and buying overpriced property, continued to take their toll. Lloyd's, London's insurance market, reported the biggest loss (over £2 billion, or $3.4 billion, for 1989) in its 304-year history: law suits increased and outside investors declined. Slowly-rising non-life premium rates rose faster after Hurricane Andrew struck; the cost of this improvement for insurers was the $20 billion-worth of damage done by the worst storm ever.

Financial markets looking for a lead were obsessed for most of the year by three questions. Was America about to see sustainable economic growth? Was Japan's financial system heading for terminal melt-down? Would Germany's Bundesbank ease monetary policy enough to keep slowing Europe's currencies and interest rates converging? By year-end only one answer was clear: America, which with Britain had led the world into recession, was finally heading out of it.

At last, growth

America kept its fans waiting. Not until the third quarter did signs of economic recovery seem solid, and share prices near record highs. Trading was heavy: by December 8th the New York Stock Exchange had seen as many shares bought and sold as in all of 1987. Unsurprisingly, securities firms saw their second straight year of unprecedented profits. Salomon Brothers, tainted in 1991 by Treasury-bond fiddling, settled with the government and returned to normal life. A final symbol of Wall Street's public rehabilitation from its greed and loathing image of the 1980s was president-elect Bill Clinton's appointment of Robert Rubin, co-chairman of Goldman Sachs, as his special assistant on economic affairs.

America's banks, too, mostly managed to mend their balance sheets, helped by lower interest rates. Only 278 national banks reported losses in the first nine months, the Comptroller of the Currency reported, compared with an average of 681 banks in the same period of the previous five years. Though fewer banks than before failed, their numbers were cut by continuing mergers: the biggest, BankAmerica's effective takeover of Security Pacific, was completed. Unless presidential politicking had postponed big bad news for a new administration, American banks—unlike those in Japan and much of Europe—looked ready to pick up their beds and walk.

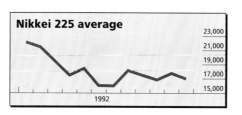

Nikkei 225 average

How differently things turned out in Japan. In January share prices seemed to have regained their equilibrium, after a 40% fall in 1990. The Nikkei share average was near 24,000, about where it had been a year before. Property values had clearly fallen, but the illiquidity of the market masked by how much. Both shares and property were to drop sharply.

Throughout the year the markets were buffeted by growing fears that Japan's financial system was in serious danger. In April shares plunged, led by bank stocks. More bad news—falling property prices, the problems of housing-loan companies, banks' bad loans—had pushed down shares further by the middle of August to 14,309, their lowest in six years. After politicians said they would help, the Nikkei gained 4,500 points—only to slump again from mid-September as scandal paralysed the ruling party. The promised expansive supplementary budget languished until late December. The bank bail-out proved no more than hat-passing among the banks themselves. The Nikkei ended the year at 16,925, and shares still looked expensive. For corporate earnings were in decline, along with consumer demand and key export markets.

All this hurt Japan's financial institutions. Hardly any securities firms were making money. As the value of their equity and property investments declined and new business slowed, insurers suffered too. Banks, which had lent heavily on property, had even bigger problems. Estimates of dodgy credits ranged from ¥20 trillion ($160 billion) to ¥60 trillion. Bad-debt reserves were slim, for the tax code did not encourage banks to provide against duff loans; yet the cushion of unrealised profits on banks' shareholdings was losing air. Restrained by the finance ministry, banks lent a bit less than they had the year before; to preserve scarce capital, many pared foreign operations. Even so, several looked unlikely to meet the new capital ratios in 1993.

The deconstruction of Europe

America's stop-go economic recovery and Japan's slow-to-surface financial problems almost paled into insignificance next to events in Europe, however. As 1992 opened, the most controversial Euro-topic was where to locate the new central bank that would eventually run the Community's single monetary policy. By its close, deepest doubt surrounded that whole project. Yet the exchange-rate crisis had, with hindsight, been building since before the beginning of the year.

Wage increases and the fiscal cost of unifi-

The listening Bundesbank?

cation had put a heavy burden on German monetary policy. Germany's interest rates—the highest since the second world war—kept those of its ERM partners above what their flagging economies required. America's "benign neglect" of its dollar let that currency weaken, thus increasing upward pressure on the D-mark. Then the Danish vote in June against the Maastricht treaty, coupled with the risk (in the event, unrealised) of a similar outcome in France's referendum in September, called into question the closer union towards which the ERM is meant to lead.

Once the diceyness of monetary union became clear, no amount of political posturing, unsustainable interest-rate hikes or central-bank intervention could hold back speculators who scented a one-way bet against Europe's weaker currencies. From September currencies in the ERM or pegged to the ecu were one by one prised away: the Finnish markka, the pound, the lira, Sweden's krona and Norway's krone. The peseta and the escudo were devalued; Spain and Ireland reimposed exchange controls temporarily. France, with Germany, managed to beat off attacks on the franc and there was talk of closer union between the two. But by the end of the year the franc remained fragile, and with it the whole concept of an ERM broader than the D-mark and its hangers-on.

The effects of the turmoil were felt well beyond the currency markets. After sterling left the ERM, Britain cut interest rates by three percentage points, to 7%. Buoyed by the pound's new competitiveness and signs of renewed economic growth, British share prices gained 20% between mid-September and the end of the year. One of the best performers was HSBC Holdings, parent of Hongkong and Shanghai Bank, which had muscled into big-league British banking by buying Midland Bank in June. Investors stampeded out of high-yielding ERM-currency bonds (Spanish, Italian) and into safer German and Dutch ones. Ecus wilted. Futures blossomed.

More broadly, a crucial lesson was relearnt: that central banks committed to defending unsustainable parities only hand fat profits to speculators. Another was perhaps unlearnt: leaders who were tiring of the fight against inflation in a world of slow or no growth started to look for other stars to steer by. "There can be no hard currency without hard measures," said Karl Blessing, first president of the Bundesbank. The lasting legacy of a year in which hard measures conspicuously outnumbered hard currencies may prove to be Europe's abandonment of both.

January

Thursday 2nd
Shaking off indications of faltering economic recovery, **American blue-chip shares** rose to their fifth record close in as many sessions.

Friday 3rd
The **Korea Stock Exchange** became the last big Asian stockmarket to open its doors to foreign investors, at least part-way. South Korean shares rose by 6.5% in two days.

Saturday 4th
Western creditor countries agreed to let eight **former Soviet republics** defer some $3.2 billion in debt repayments until the end of the year.

Tuesday 7th
Russia applied to join the IMF.

Thursday 9th
Heralding a round of generally better results for America's banks, **J.P. Morgan** showed net earnings up 41% in the fourth quarter of 1991, to $269m. Profitable bets on currencies and bonds helped.

Sterling/D-mark

Continuing pressure on **sterling** pushed it, after hours, below its effective floor against the D-mark in the exchange-rate mechanism of the EMS.

Monday 13th
Tokyo shares fell by more than 3% for the second trading day in a row. Fears of a new **Japanese political scandal** were confirmed by the arrest later that day of a former cabinet minister who was charged with taking bribes.

America's biggest bank, **Citicorp**, saw its share price shoot up almost 14% on news that it expected to announce a loss of $450m-475m for 1991, about what it earned in 1990. The markets had feared even worse.

Tuesday 14th
At the Bank of England's request, a British judge ordered the **Bank of Credit and Commerce International** to be wound up, speeding the tentacular bank's worldwide liquidation.

An American brokerage, **Smith Barney**, part of a financial-services firm named Primerica, announced record profits for the fourth quarter, and indeed all, of 1991. Other brokers followed suit.

Wednesday 15th
A task force at **Lloyd's of London** urged cutting costs, revamping management, admitting corporate members and limiting members' future losses. Lloyd's ruling council immediately rejected the proposals affecting its own existence. That, plus the fact that the report did not address the rising total of past losses, meant that the report failed to restore confidence in the troubled insurance market.

Thursday 16th
Britain's **TSB Group** reported a £47m ($83.2m) loss for 1991, due mostly to bad commercial loans by its merchant bank, Hill Samuel. Later, the results of several bigger bank rivals were to prove fairly horrible too.

Measures to tighten **financial regulation in Germany** were announced. Germans were pushing to make Frankfurt the home of a future European central bank; its reputation had been tarnished by the revelation in the summer of 1991 of widespread insider-dealing.

Monday 20th
EC partners' hopes that Germany would soon cut interest rates were killed by news that its **money supply** had grown by 7% between May and November 1991, far more than it was supposed to do.

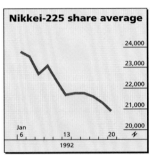

Nikkei-225 share average

Japan's **Nikkei share average** dropped below 21,000, raising fears that Japanese banks, which are allowed to count some of their unrealised share gains towards capital, might soon find they had too little of it and lend even less.

Tuesday 21st
Proof that America's banking recession had finally hit its most important state: California's **Wells Fargo** and **Security Pacific** reported large net losses for 1991.

Wednesday 22nd
America's Treasury and Federal Reserve whacked another nail into the coffin of the government-bond market's clubby **primary dealers**. They decided to abolish the rule requiring dealers do at least 1% of all customer transactions to qualify for club membership.

The French government said it planned to raise from 25% to 49% the stake which private investors could take in France's three **state-controlled insurance companies**. The shares of all three promptly fell.

Saturday 25th
Leaders of the **G-7** big industrial countries agreed to reinforce long-awaited economic

recovery and keep exchange rates stable, but to do nothing more specific. On President Bush's unilateral pledge to spur America's economy, the dollar rose by 1.4% against the yen, on Monday. The D-mark and sterling fell too.

Monday 27th
Moody's, a credit-rating agency, downgraded debt of **Crédit Suisse** and put that of **Swiss Bank Corporation** on review. The banks were holding too many dicey debts, and greater competition at home meant that they could no longer expect to coin their previous profits, the agency reckoned.

Wednesday 29th
American **stock and bond prices** plunged when Alan Greenspan, chairman of the Federal Reserve, suggested that the central bank would not cut interest rates further for a while.

Thursday 30th
Politicians approved a law giving greater independence to **Italy's central bank**. Alongside a newly reorganised Treasury, the law looked likely to improve economic management in a country badly in need of it.

Loans to collapsed Maxwell companies helped push **Paribas** into a net loss of FFr200m ($35.4m) in 1991, after making profits of FFr2.5 billion in 1990. Credit-rating agencies put the French investment bank's debt under review.

Friday 31st
Americans continued their three-year streak of **foreign share purchases**. They bought, net, $25.3 billion-worth in the first nine months of 1991, the Securities Industry Association said: nearly double the previous record of $13.1 billion in 1989.

Monday 3rd
In its biggest fund-raising exercise in years, troubled **American Express** said it planned to raise up to $1 billion by floating as much as 45% of its credit-card processing subsidiary.

Tuesday 4th
The **D-mark** strengthened and German share prices fell on Monday's news of a higher-than-expected 6.4% wage increase for German steel workers. The pay settlement dealt another blow to hopes of a cut in German interest rates.

Wednesday 5th
Finland's biggest bank, Kansallis-Osake-Pankki (KOP), posted its first loss since 1894. To the recession that had heaped woes on other Nordic banks, KOP added losses from investments and foreign-exchange trading.

Thursday 6th
While the rest of Wall Street reported booming earnings, **Salomon Inc** showed a net loss of $29m for the fourth quarter of 1991. Its Phibro Energy unit was more to blame than fall-out from the firm's Treasury-bond fiddling revealed in August 1991.

Friday 7th
Gilt-edged market makers in London made operating profits of £49m ($86.7m) in 1991, only the second year since Big Bang in 1986 that it had happened, a report said. It helped that the British government had begun to borrow again.

An American court ruled that national banks could not sell **insurance** in small towns. Many banks had seized on a loophole in the general prohibition against selling insurance to launch nationwide sales efforts from small-town bases. The ruling seemed unlikely to prove the last word.

Tuesday 11th
The perpetrator of one of Britain's biggest financial frauds was sent to jail for ten years. The collapse in 1988 of Barlow Clowes caused the government to pay out more than £150m ($239m) to investors from whom **Peter Clowes** had stolen millions of pounds.

A British judge dismissed the jury in another fraud trial, the second arising from **Guinness**'s takeover of Distillers in 1986. One of the defendants was beginning to crack up, he said.

A $211m out-of-court settlement with disgruntled members of loss-making Outhwaite syndicates ended one of the biggest legal suits hanging over the **Lloyd's of London** insurance market—at the cost of encouraging still more.

Wednesday 12th
Commercial-property problems pulled down 1991 earnings at two **American insurers**, it was revealed. Travelers managed a profit nonetheless, but Aetna made a loss.

Friday 14th
More than a year after the **Blue Arrow** trial began, a British jury convicted four financiers from prominent firms of conspiring to defraud in their handling of a big rights issue in 1987. The delay fuelled criticism of Britain's legal procedures against fraud.

Monday 17th
In a preliminary settlement to dispose of hundreds of civil suits, junk-bond fraudster **Michael Milken** agreed to hand over $900m. He still had more than $500m left. Who says crime doesn't pay?

Tuesday 18th
Three **European insurers**— Britain's Royal, Germany's AMB and Italy's Fondiaria— said they planned to pool all their European operations outside their home bases, to take advantage of the emerging pan-European market in insurance. One hitch: France's AGF had already built up a hostile 25% stake in AMB, to the German insurer's dismay.

Wednesday 19th
German bank workers walked out after employers refused to better a 5% pay increase.

Thursday 20th
Germany's **Allianz** said it planned to raise more than DM1 billion ($607m) in a rights issue. Expanding into eastern Germany was costing Europe's biggest insurer dear.

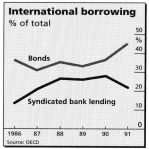

Friday 21st
Borrowing on the world's international financial markets reached a record $518 billion in 1991, the OECD said, despite slumping economies. Bonds boomed; bank lending dropped.

Britain's **Lloyds Bank** reported a 9% increase in pre-tax earnings, despite much higher provisions for bad debts. Where Lloyds led, others did not follow. The next

week saw horrible slumps at Barclays and National Westminster banks but improvement at troubled Midland.

Monday 24th
ABN Amro Bank said it would buy **Hoare Govett**, a large London securities firm that Californian Security Pacific Bank was trying to sell before its own merger with BankAmerica. It was part of its expansion across Europe and into investment banking, the Dutch bank said.

A Canadian rating agency downgraded some securities guaranteed by **Olympia & York**, an international property developer. The raters worried about a 44% fall in the value of the firm's listed investments, the slump in North American property prices, and financial troubles at London's Canary Wharf.

German share prices rose to a record high, after climbing for several weeks. The DAX Index gained 11½ points to hit 1,729. Bits of good company news were the only obvious reason.

Wednesday 26th
The only big British composite insurer to report profits in 1990, **Commercial Union** kicked off the results season by reporting a pre-tax loss of £68.6m ($121.4m) for 1991. It blamed recession.

Thursday 27th
Brazil and its creditor countries agreed to reschedule most of its $21 billion-24 billion Paris Club debt. The deal included previously-rescheduled debt, which had long been a Paris Club taboo.

Bank Austria, that country's largest, fired three senior executives for making bad loans and investments abroad. An example that banks elsewhere might profitably have followed.

Monday 2nd
Shares in **Wellcome**, a British drugs firm, fell on news of what looked likely to prove Britain's biggest private-sector share offering. The trust that owns 73.5% of Wellcome said it wanted to reduce its stake to as little as 25%, reaping up to £4.5 billion ($8.2 billion).

Tuesday 3rd
Bertelsmann, a German publisher, agreed to buy a **Manhattan office building** for $119m—less than half what it had cost to construct in 1989-90. More evidence that property prices there were nowhere near recovery.

Wednesday 4th
Defying Moody's, which downgraded its debt in January because greater competition looked likely to trim **Swiss banks**' profits, Swiss Bank Corporation reported net earnings for 1991 of SFr1.03 billion ($684m), up 25% over the previous year. Crédit Suisse announced a 57% growth in profits, to SFr848m, a few days later.

Thursday 5th
America's Securities and Exchange Commission (SEC) said the American Stock Exchange could launch a new market for **very small companies**. Tighter bank lending had made it hard for firms to raise money elsewhere.

Monday 9th
Britain's National Westminster Bank asked the Department of Trade and Industry (DTI) to reopen its investigation of the bank's role in the 1987 **Blue Arrow** share issue, looking especially at whether Natwest and its chief executive, Tom Frost, had misled the original investigators. On March 12th the department reopened the inquiry; on March 30th Mr Frost resigned.

Wednesday 11th
The president of **Daiwa Securities** stepped down after Japan's second-largest securities firm reported that it had lost ¥72 billion ($642m) settling legal disputes. These arose from the practice, called *tobashi*, of shifting assets around among clients to window-dress accounts. More firms were expected to announce big *tobashi* losses.

Thursday 12th
Pessimism about America's economic prospects pushed yields on 30-year **Treasury bonds** back above 8% for the first time in five months. The optimism after the Federal Reserve cut interest rates in December dwindled fast.

Monday 16th
Tokyo shares fell by 3%, pushing the Nikkei below 20,000 for the first time in more than five years. The fall increased fears that their shrinking capital would further restrict Japanese banks' lending.

Despite the recession, **American securities firms** earned at least $5.8 billion before tax in 1991, it was reported. The record exceeded even the most bullish estimates.

Tuesday 17th
Midland Bank, Britain's third largest, agreed in principal to merge with the parent of **Hongkong and Shanghai Bank**, to create one of the world's top 15 banks by assets and its largest transcontinental one. Hongkong's later formal bid valued Midland at £3.3 billion ($5.68 billion).

In the second day of steady selling, the price of **gold** fell to a five-year low, at $336.75. The usual suspects—in Eastern Europe and the Middle East—were rumoured to be dumping the metal.

Wednesday 18th
Japanese securities firms cut their earnings forecasts for the year to March 1992, as share prices continued to slide and scandals to mount. All the big four except Nomura said that they expected net losses, for the first time since the mid-1960s, and nine of the second-tier ten did too.

The **Paris Bourse**'s bosses voted to make would-be acquirers of publicly traded companies offer for 100% of the targets. A series of controversial takeover bids had made France's minority shareholders increasingly unhappy.

South African securities soared on news that whites there had voted overwhelmingly for reforms making possible a non-racial government.

Friday 20th
America's largest stockbroker, **Merrill Lynch**, which made its highest-ever earnings in 1991, revealed that it had given its chairman compensation of $16.8m for 1991 and had rewarded others lavishly as well. Merrill's looked the plumpest of Wall Street's newly burgeoning pay packets.

Monday 23rd
Confirming fears that Japan's economy was stalling despite three interest-rate cuts in nine months, the Bank of Japan reported that **Japan's broad money** (M2 plus CDs) grew at its slowest annualised rate on record, 1.6%, in February.

Tuesday 24th
A management shake-up at **Olympia & York** and the appointment of well-known advisers to help renegotiate its $19 billion or so in bank debt spurred worries that the property developer's problems were more serious than had been thought. Fears were not allayed when Thomas Johnson, O&Y's new president, quit a few weeks later.

Wednesday 25th
A clerical error at **Salomon Brothers** made the Dow Jones plummet in the last two minutes of trading on the New York Stock Exchange. Clerks misread a customer's electronic instructions to sell $11m-worth of shares and keyed in instead an order to sell 11m shares, worth up to $500m. The SEC added this to its list of unfortunate events to pursue with the beleaguered Wall Street firm.

Friday 27th
Property woes deepened. Heron International, a British property developer, said it had asked its bankers to reschedule its debt. Speyhawk, another, announced a £216.8m ($383.5m) net loss for 1991. In Toronto, Olympia & York asked bankers to roll over maturing debt until a broader restructuring could be discussed. France's Paribas, a *banque d'affaires*, blamed much of its first net loss on property lending.

Tuesday 31st
The IMF agreed the terms on which Russia was to join: a 3% quota, entitling the new member to draw about $4 billion from Fund resources.

April

Wednesday 1st
Tokyo share prices plunged despite a cut in Japan's **official discount rate**, from 4½% to 3¾%, and the announcement of other measures to bolster Japan's flagging economy. The Nikkei average fell 3.9% to 18,582, its lowest in five years.

American equity and bond issues totalled $216 billion in the first three months of 1992, said Securities Data Company, a research firm—87% higher than a year earlier. Wall Street's bumper profits looked set to continue.

The Group of Seven rich industrialised countries unveiled a **Russian aid package** worth $24 billion in credits, loan guarantees and money for a rouble stabilisation fund.

Thursday 2nd
Allianz, Europe's largest insurer, said it would resist an order by Germany's cartel office that it reduce its 22.3% stake in Dresdner, Germany's second biggest bank.

Friday 3rd
Gerald Ronson, who had recently completed a spell in jail for his part in the Guinness fraud, asked banks and bondholders to reschedule almost £1 billion ($1.7 billion) of the £1.35 billion owed by Heron International, his privately owned property group.

Monday 6th
Joining the European main-stream, **Portugal** became the 11th country to join the EC's exchange-rate mechanism. It then had to cut interest rates and sell escudos to stay within its 6% band.

Tuesday 7th
After five years of planning and $70m in costs, June 25th was fixed as the launch date for **Globex**, the international after-hours system for trading derivatives developed by Reuters for the Chicago Board of Trade and the Chicago Mercantile Exchange.

Foreign selling of **Japanese bank shares** helped push down the Nikkei to 17,791. It fell to 16,598 the next day, before rising again. Falling shares in Tokyo pushed down other markets too.

Thursday 9th
Worried by a shrinking money supply, America's **Federal Reserve** cut its key federal-funds interest rate by 0.25%, to 3.75%. Share and bond prices rose; the dollar gave ground.

Friday 10th
British share prices soared after the Conservatives won a fourth term in office. The FT-SE 100 jumped 5.6% in the heaviest trading the London Stock Exchange had ever seen. Sterling gained too. Later, a terrorist bomb devastated several buildings in the City of London, killing three people and injuring dozens.

Monday 13th
Trading on **Chicago's futures markets** was suspended and thousands of people were evacuated when a construction accident sent the Chicago River pouring through downtown basements.

For the first time in five months, **sterling** moved off the bottom of the European exchange-rate mechanism.

The election result helped, but not for long.

Tuesday 14th
Alan Bond, an Australian entrepreneur once worth around $270m, was declared bankrupt by a court in Sydney.

Four big **American securities firms**—Merrill Lynch, Paine-Webber, Charles Schwab and Dean Witter—reported record first-quarter earnings, as retail investors and new-issue underwriting kept Wall Street profits surging. Share prices rose too, and the Dow Jones closed at 3,306, a record.

The parent of Hongkong and Shanghai Bank finally spelt out its agreed offer for **Midland**, Britain's third-largest bank: £3.1 billion ($5.5 billion) in shares and bonds. Investors had expected more, and Midland's shares fell.

Thursday 16th
Carlo De Benedetti, an Italian industrialist, was sentenced by an Italian court to more than six years in jail for his role in the collapse of Banco Ambrosiano in 1982. Like most of the other 32 defendants, he appealed.

Monday 20th
The heads of the Federal Reserve and the Securities and Exchange Commission told Congress that the collapse of **Japanese stock and property** prices was not affecting America's economy much. American shares and bonds fell.

Tuesday 21st
Big American banks reported surprisingly strong first-quarter earnings, thanks to fewer problem loans and tighter cost controls. **Citicorp**'s profits were nearly double those of a year earlier.

Thursday 23rd
News of surprising growth in the **German money supply** disappointed those who had hoped that the Bundesbank would ease interest rates. Germany's broad-money measure, M3, increased by an annualised 9.7% in March, up from 8.6% in February.

Japan's finance ministry unusually previewed **Japanese bank performance** in the year to March 1992. Officials said the big banks were sound despite rising bad debts, which they put at ¥7 trillion-8 trillion ($52 billion-59 billion), and falling share prices. The next day banks said they had suffered ¥1.3 trillion in share-valuation losses in the 12 months to March. Investors sold bank shares.

Monday 27th
The **IMF** voted formally to admit Russia and 13 other former Soviet republics.

Tuesday 28th
Lloyds Bank, Britain's fifth largest, said it might make a £3.7 billion ($6.6 billion) counter-bid for **Midland**, beating the offer from Hongkong and Shanghai Bank that Midland's board had recommended to shareholders. Lloyds said its offer depended on both bids getting equal treatment from competition authorities.

Thursday 30th
Britain's Office of Fair Trading opened an inquiry into whether investing institutions were operating an **underwriting cartel** by setting standardised fees for their services.

Monday 4th
Shaking off the Los Angeles riots, **American share prices** hit a new high. The Dow Jones Industrial average jumped 42 points, to close at 3,378.

Tuesday 5th
Two days before local elections were held, Britain cut **base rates** by ½%, to 10%. That put interest rates at their lowest in four years, reducing the difference between German and British rates to its smallest in 11 years, ¼%.

To capitalise on the capital weakness of big American and Japanese banks, Germany's **Deutsche Bank** said it planned to expand its lending to big American companies.

Thursday 7th
Olympia & York, a Canadian property developer, offered its bankers up to 20% in the company and 30% of its Canary Wharf development in London in exchange for new money, a five-year freeze on repaying almost $12 billion in debt and suspension of interest on part of it. Banks were unimpressed. On May 14th O&Y filed for protection from its creditors in Canada and (on part of its operations) in the United States.

After France's central bank nudged interest rates lower, **French shares** jumped to their highest level in nearly two years, to close at 2,063.

Friday 8th
Runaway loan losses forced Sweden's government into the second big bail-out in less than a year of **Nordbanken**. The state said it would spend SKr22 billion ($3.73 billion) to buy what it does not already own of the country's second biggest bank and deal with some SKr60 of dubious loans.

Tuesday 12th
Moody's, a credit-rating agency, downgraded Britain's **Barclays Bank** and **Swiss Bank Corporation**, mainly because of their dubious property loans. That left only a handful of banks worldwide with a triple-A rating.

California's supreme court rejected a challenge to the state's **unitary tax**, which assesses a company according to how much of its world sales, property and payroll is in California. Barclays, which brought a suit that many multinationals supported, said it would take the case to the Supreme Court in Washington.

Thursday 14th
EC ministers cleared the way for a single market in **European life insurance**, allowing EC firms licensed by their home authorities to offer life insurance throughout the Community. With full agreement likely in June, the new system seemed set to start in most countries in mid-1994.

Friday 15th
Three of the four big **Japanese securities firms** managed to make money before tax in the year to March 1992, they said, though profits fell sharply. The fourth, Yamaichi, reported a pre-tax loss.

Harshad Mehta, a stockbroker, was suspended by the **Bombay Stock Exchange** after his assets had been frozen by the authorities. Mr Mehta was implicated in what proved to be a billion-dollar scam in India's interbank securities market.

Sunday 17th
The **Swiss** voted in a referendum to join the IMF and the World Bank, it was announced. The next day the government said it would apply for membership of the EC. The Swiss franc soared.

Monday 18th
The **London Stock Exchange** launched a broad review of its trading system, which differs from that in most other markets. Market makers' privileges were to be its focus.

Tuesday 19th
A German court ruled that **AMB**, a large German insurer, was entitled to refuse to let AGF, its unwelcome French suitor, vote its entire 25% stake in the company. AGF kept up the pressure, and in July won full voting rights and a deal to co-operate from the Germans.

Wednesday 20th
Salomon Brothers settled civil charges arising from its false bids at Treasury auctions. It agreed to pay $290m—and sought to put behind it a scandal that had rocked all Wall Street. A week later Deryck Maughan was named chairman and chief executive of the firm. Warren Buffett, acting chairman of the securities house's parent, later resigned in favour of lawyer Robert Denham, a close associate.

The rout of British bankers in America continued. Britain's **Barclays** sold the rest of its retail-banking operations there to Bank of New York.

An Arizona jury ordered **Price Waterhouse**, an accounting firm, to pay $338m to Standard Chartered for negligence in its auditing of a bank which the British bank later bought. It was believed to be the largest award ever levied against an accounting firm. Price Waterhouse said it would seek a new trial.

Friday 22nd
Michael Heseltine, Britain's trade and industry secretary, decided to refer Lloyds' bid for **Midland Bank** to the competition authorities. Though that left rival bidder Hongkong Bank with a clear field, Lloyds said it would battle on. And did, for a bit.

Monday 25th
Another property bust: receivers were called in at **Mountleigh**, one of the biggest British property firms and owner of Spain's second-largest department-store chain. Among its creditors were Barclays and Citicorp.

Wednesday 27th
Britain's **Cadbury report** on corporate governance suggested splitting the roles of chairman and chief executive, and recommended making companies give more responsibility to non-executive directors and more information both to them and to shareholders. It provoked debate on both sides of the Atlantic.

Thursday 28th
Olympia & York's east London development, **Canary Wharf**, went into administration under Britain's bankruptcy laws. Bank creditors faced losses of up to $500m on Europe's largest commercial-property project.

Big **Japanese commercial banks** reported a decline in annual profits before tax for the third year running.

June

Tuesday 2nd
Hongkong and Shanghai Bank's parent improved its offer for Britain's **Midland Bank**. Rival bidder Lloyds decided three days later to throw in the towel. Hongkong bought Midland.

Wednesday 3rd
On the day after the Danes voted against the **Maastricht** treaty, casting into doubt the future of Europe's economic and monetary union, European stock and bond prices fell. The D-mark surged against most currencies.

The biggest agency group at **Lloyd's of London**, Sturge Holdings, cut its interim dividend for the six months to March, and saw its share price fall by a third.

Thursday 4th
America's Securities and Exchange Commission (SEC) filed one of the biggest **insider-trading** cases ever brought. Among the seven prominent financiers and businessmen named was Edward Downe, a former director of stockbrokers Bear Stearns.

Monday 8th
The British government announced emergency grants to help those worst hit by the plundering of **Maxwell companies' pension funds**. It also pledged a review of pensions law and an official inquiry into the affairs of Mirror Group Newspapers, especially its flotation in 1991. Many pensioners were unimpressed.

Aetna, a large American insurer, agreed to sell its reinsurance unit to Kohlberg Kravis Roberts for $1.4 billion. It was the largest-ever leveraged buyout of an insurance company.

Tuesday 9th
EC finance ministers laid the base for a **single securities market** in Europe. They reached preliminary agreement on rules to harmonise capital requirements for securities firms and banks dealing in securities. On June 29th the capital-adequacy directive was approved, together with one allowing a securities firm licensed in one EC country to do business in all of them.

Thursday 11th
Standard & Poor's, a rating agency, downgraded the debt of Barclays Bank, Britain's largest, blaming recession, and bad property and commercial loans.

Britain's law lords ruled that its Serious Fraud Office had the right to compel an arrested person to give evidence in complex fraud cases, by-passing the traditional **right to silence**.

Monday 15th
The $150 billion **foreign debt** that Eastern Europe and the former Soviet Union were struggling to pay did not constitute a threat to the world's financial system, said the Bank for International Settlements. Much of the commercial-bank debt was guaranteed by western governments, and banks had already made substantial provisions.

Commercial and industrial **bank lending** in America has been infiltrated by foreign suppliers more than have the car or computer markets, suggested a study published by the Federal Reserve Bank of New York. Foreign banks raised their share of outstand-ing loans from 18% in 1983 to 45% at the end of 1991, as America's capital-constrained banks held back.

Tuesday 16th
The **Swedish bank crisis** deepened. Gota Bank announced a bad-loan insurance scheme and an operating deficit for the four months to April. Svenska Handelsbanken revealed a 35% drop in profits. Earlier Skandinaviska Enskilda Banken, Sweden's largest bank, had announced its first financial operating loss, and state-controlled Nordbanken told of its own problems.

Wednesday 17th
An emergency meeting of the council of **Lloyd's of London** ruled out proposals to give serious help to the insurance market's external names. Some reckoned that 4,000 outside investors faced losses averaging more than £300,000 ($492,000) for 1989 alone.

A crop of dismal corporate-earnings forecasts pushed down **Tokyo share prices**. The Nikkei fell 508 points to close at 16,446.

Thursday 18th
A privately-owned Irish aircraft-leasing company, **GPA**, scrapped a planned $800m global flotation at the last minute. Falling world stockmarkets and airline-industry troubles had made institutional investors unkeen, GPA said. The news helped push down share prices further.

Two sons of the late **Robert Maxwell**, the shady media magnate, were arrested in connection with the plundering of the Maxwell companies' pension funds. Kevin and Ian Maxwell, with a third Maxwell employee, faced a total of 15 charges of conspiracy to defraud and theft involving £135m ($258m).

Monday 22nd
As investors lost faith in the government's willingness to revive Japan's flagging economy, the Nikkei fell 599 points to close at 15,921. This was the first time since October 1986 that **Tokyo shares** had closed below 16,000.

Tuesday 23rd
America's Securities and Exchange Commission proposed a series of changes to improve both the way companies disclose **executive pay** and communication among shareholders. An earlier version was withdrawn the year before when companies objected.

Wednesday 24th
More than 5,000 names attended the six-hour annual general meeting of **Lloyd's of London**. Outside investors attacked the insurance market's council for failing to control what some termed gross negligence and even fraud, which contributed to 1989 losses of £2.06 billion ($3.4 billion).

Monday 29th
Aetna said it would reduce its 46,000-strong workforce by about 10% within 18 months, continuing its search for more profitability in America's troubled insurance market.

Tuesday 30th
A new law reduced the required minimum par value of **Swiss shares** to SFr10 ($7.30) from SFr100. It prompted at least 20 companies—including Ciba-Geigy, Union Bank of Switzerland and Nestlé—to announce share splits.

July

Wednesday 1st

As part of its broad economic reforms, Russia floated the **rouble**, but made it less convertible than expected.

Sheikh Khalid Bin Mahfouz, chief operating officer of Saudi Arabia's biggest private bank, the National Commercial Bank, was indicted in America for scheming to defraud in relation to the **Bank of Credit and Commerce International (BCCI)**. He later resigned.

The council of **Lloyd's of London** voted to change the insurance market's structure and make regulation more autonomous. The vote came in response to a report by Sir Jeremy Morse, chairman of Lloyds Bank.

Thursday 2nd

America's Federal Reserve responded to new signs of economic weakness by cutting the **discount rate** by ½%, to 3%—its lowest level since 1963.

Monday 6th

Rich-country central bankers in Basle issued new **banking-supervision rules** in the wake of BCCI. The main change: requiring the authorities of a bank's home country to take responsibility for supervising its operations worldwide.

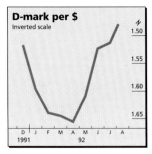

D-mark per $
Inverted scale

1.50
1.55
1.60
1.65

D J F M A M J J A
1991   92

Tuesday 7th

Nicholas Brady, America's Treasury secretary, said he wouldn't be bothered if the **dollar** fell to less than DM1.50. It did, as markets reflected that Germany's short-term interest rates were 6½ points higher than America's.

Thursday 9th

A decade after Mexico kicked off the sovereign-debt crisis, **Brazil** was the last big Latin American debtor to announce agreement in principle with its commercial-bank creditors on a Brady-style rescheduling of $44 billion of its foreign debt. Then Brazil's worsening problems delayed ratification.

Friday 10th

Unease in the **foreign-exchange markets** continued. Britain's Chancellor, Norman Lamont, spoke against realignment of the European exchange-rate mechanism and said sterling would move to the narrow fluctuation band in due course. Sterling lost 2¼ pfennigs against the D-mark.

Standard & Poor's, a rating agency, downgraded the previously top-rated long-term debt of Britain's **National Westminster Bank**, citing Britain's depressed economy.

Monday 13th

Helped by falling interest rates, several big **American banks** announced higher-than-expected second-quarter net profits. Investors reckoned it was the last good news they might hear for a while and sold J.P. Morgan, Chase Manhattan and First Chicago.

Tuesday 14th

Earnings reported by three big **American brokers** for the three months to end-June showed only modest gains on a stratospheric first quarter, prompting fears that Wall Street had peaked.

Wednesday 15th

For the first time in 50 years, **Hong Kong**'s hidden reserves were disclosed. They amounted to $29 billion—the biggest in the world, per head, after Singapore's.

Thursday 16th

Worried that money growth was overshooting its target, the **Bundesbank** raised its discount rate from 8% to 8¾%. Stock and bond prices fell heavily the next day in Europe, America and Japan. Sterling and the dollar dropped against the D-mark. Economic malaise deepened.

The convictions of four City advisers found guilty of conspiring to mislead the markets in the 1987 **Blue Arrow** rights issue in Britain were overturned on appeal. Costs of the long trial, some £40m ($75m), would fall to taxpayers.

Friday 17th

Italy's government announced a freeze of up to two years on debt repayment by **EFIM**, a state holding company. Foreign bankers, owed a third of EFIM's 8.5 trillion lire ($7.5 billion) in debt, yelled foul.

Monday 20th

Central banks bought **dollars** and sold D-marks in the first concerted exercise to prop up the American currency for more than a year. They gained four pfennigs for the dollar, but failed to keep share prices around the world from closing sharply lower, for the second trading day in a row.

Tuesday 21st

Though still battling bad commercial-property loans, **Citicorp**, America's largest bank, announced net second-quarter profits of $171m, up from $11m a year before.

Thursday 23rd

Another patient showed signs of rising from its sickbed. Less than a year after its Treasury-bond scam was revealed, **Salomon** reported its highest quarterly earnings (after tax, but before special charges).

Monday 27th

Britain's largest private-sector share flotation closed with reasonable success. **Wellcome Trust** said it had sold some £2.2 billion-worth ($4.2 billion) of shares in the drugs company of the same name. That was less than the Trust had originally hoped but more than many thought troubled markets would bear.

Falling together

7
%
6

5

4

Nikkei 225 average ▶

◀ Japanese 3-month money market rate

25,000
23,000
21,000
19,000
17,000
15,000

1991   92

Japan's central bank cut its discount rate, from 3¾% to 3¼%, as had been widely leaked before the election on July 26th. As after previous cuts, the Nikkei share average fell nonetheless. It closed at 15,373, its lowest in six years.

Tuesday 28th

The shares of Europe's largest insurer, **Allianz**, fell 3% when it said that its 1991 profits (DM1.05 billion, or $633m, up 4% from the previous year) had been depressed by a large underwriting loss due mostly to acquisitions in America and eastern Germany.

Wednesday 29th

BCCI paid huge bribes to bank regulators around the world to cover up its deceitful banking practices, according to sweeping indictments brought by Manhattan's district attorney against scores of the bust bank's former executives, shareholders and associates. Among those indicted was Clark Clifford, once America's defence secretary.

Share prices rose sharply in America and Britain for the second day running. Japan's then followed suit, bouncing back from a six-year low.

August

Monday 3rd
Salomon, the Wall Street house that for its misdeeds had been suspended from bidding on behalf of customers at Treasury-bond auctions, quietly resumed that business as the sanctions against it came to an end.

Wednesday 5th
Britain's Treasury cut the interest it paid to individuals on many of its **National Savings** products. The move was intended to placate building societies, which threatened to put up their mortgage rates if the government lured away depositors. It looked likely to work—for a couple of weeks.

Germany's biggest bank, **Deutsche**, reported first-half operating profits down by 3.2%, to DM3.1 billion ($2 billion). It blamed expansion in eastern Germany and a slowing domestic economy. Dresdner and Commerzbank, in contrast, announced strong profits growth for the period. Pessimists concluded that their stumble had yet to come.

Citing his "model" behaviour and co-operation with prosecutors, an American federal judge cut the ten-year prison term to which junk-bondster **Michael Milken** had been sentenced in November 1990. Mr Milken seemed likely to serve only 24 months in jail.

Thursday 6th
Barclays, Britain's largest bank, announced a £1.06 billion ($1.9 billion) addition to credit-risk reserves. This pro-duced a first-half loss of £30m after tax, the bank's second reported loss in three centuries. Earlier, National Westminster reported earnings almost double those of the same period in 1991, and Lloyds' profits rose 8.4%. All gave a warning that a sagging British economy would wreak further damage on loan portfolios.

German shares slipped again, as news of falling manufacturing orders rekindled concern about economic performance. The 30-share DAX index ended the week at 1,610, some 11% off its 1992 high of 1,812 on May 25th.

Friday 7th
America's troubled **Citicorp** said it planned to strengthen its capital base by raising about $650m through a hybrid kind of convertible preferred stock that allows investors to share in the common stock's price gains up to an agreed limit. Citicorp was the first bank to issue these so-called Percs.

Monday 10th
Misery in Japan sent European **share prices** tumbling, too. In its third straight day of losses, the Nikkei fell 2.9% to close at 15,066. Lack of confidence in Japan's stalling economy kept investors selling. The Nikkei plunged to 14,823 the next day—the first time it had closed below 15,000 since March 1986.

Tuesday 11th
Concerted intervention by central banks halted the decline of the **dollar** against the D-mark but failed to strengthen it much.

Rioting subsided as thousands waited in disorderly queues for lottery tickets giving them the chance to subscribe to shares that were to be floated on the **Shenzhen Stock Exchange** in southern China.

The exchange suspended trading.

Wednesday 12th
UBS Phillips & Drew, a securities firm, suspended the head of its British research department when he refused to withdraw from publication a book he had written that criticised the **accounting techniques** of big British firms.

Thursday 13th
For the first time since it joined Europe's exchange-rate mechanism, **sterling** fell below DM2.82.

Friday 14th
America's **Citicorp** said that it had signed a memorandum in February agreeing to closer regulatory scrutiny because of its bad loans and slim capital. No other money-centre bank was known to be subject to this regime.

Monday 17th
Ten years after Mexico's threatened default precipitated a worldwide crisis in sovereign debt, **Chile** became the first Latin American country to receive an investment-grade rating from a big credit-rating agency. Standard & Poor's assigned a triple-B to Chilean government debt.

Tuesday 18th
The **Tokyo stockmarket** fell by 4.2% in a day, apparently prompting Japan's finance minister to unveil a package of palliatives to prop up both shares and the banks that own them. Prices then rose.

Thursday 20th
The costs of doing business at **Lloyd's**, London's insurance market, have risen sharply, according to its members' association. Syndicate expenses increased by 45.3% in 1989, and by 40% the year before.

Friday 21st
The **dollar** reached a new low against the D-mark, closing below DM1.44. This put pressure not only on American share prices, but also on sterling and other weak members of the European exchange-rate mechanism. Repeated central-bank intervention that day and the following Monday failed to halt the dollar's decline, to about DM1.40.

Monday 24th
A man who was once in charge of **fraud prevention** at Belgium's state-owned Crédit Communal said he had stolen $23.8m over 35 years.

Tuesday 25th
The parent of **Hongkong Bank** reported a 51% increase in first-half profits, to HK$5 billion ($646m). They would have been higher still but for a 63% increase in charges for bad and doubtful loans, many of them to Olympia & York, a tottering property firm.

Wednesday 26th
The Bank of England's biggest intervention in six years helped steady **sterling** against the D-mark and prevent an interest-rate rise. Leaked remarks by a member of the Bundesbank council that European currencies needed realignment later undid much of its effect.

Thursday 27th
Reports of the government's planned measures to stimulate the Japanese economy, announced the next day, sent **Tokyo shares** soaring. The Nikkei closed at 17,555, 6.1% up on the day.

September

Tuesday 1st
The **dollar** touched a new low against the D-mark of DM1.3895, as investors fretted over America's slow growth and low interest rates. The switch into D-marks hurt weaker European currencies.

Thursday 3rd
Kevin Maxwell, son of the crooked media mogul who was once one of Britain's richest men, became Britain's biggest bankrupt, with £407m ($812m) in debts.

Friday 4th
To defend the **lira**, Italy's central bank raised its discount rate by 1¾ percentage points, to 15%—its highest since 1985. This did not help long.

Tuesday 8th
In the run-up to France's referendum on the Maastricht treaty, **Nordic currencies** too came under strain. Its reserves depleted, Finland cut loose the markka from the ecu. A run on Sweden's krona prompted its Riksbank to put up its marginal lending rate, first to 24% and then to 75%.

Low interest rates and cheap deposits helped **American banks** earn record profits for the second straight quarter, the Federal Deposit Insurance Corporation said.

Thursday 10th
On the campaign trail, **President Bush** proposed an economic pick-me-up, including a large cut in income taxes. American shares and the dollar soared.

Holland's **ING Group** said it would launch a $2 billion takeover bid for Belgium's Banque Bruxelles Lambert, of which it already owned 10%. Such a merger would produce a banking and insurance giant, with assets totalling some $265 billion.

The **lira** slipped back to its floor in the European exchange-rate mechanism, a day after the Italian government announced emergency measures to reform public finance. Elsewhere in the ERM, Britain's prime minister, John Major, called realigning sterling "a betrayal of our future".

France's private-sector **Société Générale** was the latest big bank to lose its triple-A credit rating from Moody's.

In Japan, the **Nikkei share average** closed at 18,908, 32% up from its August low of 14,309. Investors were cheered by government promises the previous month to help banks and the economy. It proved the market's peak. The next day a survey showed Japanese business confidence at its lowest level in 15 years.

Sunday 13th
Italy devalued the lira by 7% against the rest of the European exchange-rate mechanism. To alleviate tensions within the system, **Germany cut interest rates** the next day, by a meagre quarter of a percentage point. Pressure on **weaker currencies**—notably sterling—built up during the days that followed.

Monday 14th
Britain's Takeover Panel at last censured the **Fayed brothers** for making potentially misleading financial statements during their successful contested bid in 1985 for the House of Fraser stores group (which includes Harrods).

Tuesday 15th
Published reports that **Helmut Schlesinger**, head of Germany's Bundesbank, favoured further currency realignment in Europe enraged British Treasury officials and spurred sales of sterling.

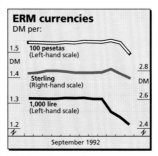

ERM currencies
DM per:
100 pesetas (Left-hand scale)
Sterling (Right-hand scale)
1,000 lire (Left-hand scale)
September 1992

Wednesday 16th
When hiking the minimum lending rate from 10% to 15% and spending between a third and a half of its foreign-exchange reserves failed to halt **sterling**'s plunge, Britain "temporarily" took the currency out of Europe's exchange-rate mechanism and put interest rates back where they started. Later on Black Wednesday, the lira was floated and the peseta devalued by 5%.

Friday 18th
London shares jumped 3.4% on hopes of lower domestic interest rates. The pound ended the week 6% below its previous floor against the D-mark and lost another 3.4% during the month.

Monday 21st
The day after French voters narrowly approved the **Maastricht treaty**, the D-mark climbed against major currencies, French shares fell by 3%, and Italy said that it might be a while before the lira re-entered Europe's exchange-rate mechanism.

Tuesday 22nd
Britain slashed a percentage point off interest rates, bringing them below short-term German rates for the first time

in 11 years. A meeting between Germany's Chancellor Helmut Kohl and France's President François Mitterrand fuelled talk of a **two-speed Europe**. The yen soared against the dollar and the D-mark, as Japanese investors pulled out of Europe.

The first big French bank to report first-half results, state-owned **Crédit Lyonnais**, announced net group profits down 93% from the same period a year earlier. The bank blamed bad loans, mainly to corporate borrowers.

Wednesday 23rd
Another day of crisis for European currencies saw France and Germany concert a massive defence of the **French franc**. Spain reintroduced capital controls to halt the peseta's slide; Ireland reinstituted them the next day.

Thursday 24th
A big American firm, **Dow Chemicals**, said its European operations would begin invoicing in D-marks rather than local currencies.

Even before September's currency turmoil, central-bank surveys revealed, the volume of **foreign-exchange trading** around the world had increased by 50% in three years, to $1 trillion a day.

Friday 25th
Greece chose an odd time to say that the **drachma** would join the European exchange-rate mechanism in 1993.

Tuesday 29th
The liquidators of the Bank of Credit and Commerce International (**BCCI**) said they would sue the bust bank's auditors, Price Waterhouse and Ernst & Young, for about $8 billion. The damages, for alleged negligence, were believed to be the largest ever claimed in Britain.

October

Thursday 1st

An American Senate investigation into the bust Bank of Credit and Commerce International (**BCCI**) found the Bank of England's supervision of it "wholly inadequate". The spirit of that criticism was echoed on October 22nd in a better-informed report by Britain's Lord Justice Bingham, who suggested improvements.

The chairman and four directors of **Westpac**, Australia's biggest bank, resigned after criticism of the bank's bad loans, heavy losses and halved share price. Bosses of badly-run banks elsewhere found their example easy to ignore.

Monday 5th

Share prices fell sharply in Europe and Japan—in Britain, by the most in a single day since 1987—on fears of worsening economic stagnation.

The president of Citicorp, **Richard Braddock**, resigned, shortly before America's biggest bank announced a big third-quarter write-off of bad debts in the consumer division, with which Mr Braddock had been closely associated. Citicorp's shares fell 4.8%.

Wednesday 7th

Agreement on the creation of a centralised **German stock-market** was announced by the Frankfurt Stock Exchange, the largest of eight in Germany. The move was expected to increase Frankfurt's attractions as a financial centre.

Friday 9th

In one of its most creative offerings, **Walt Disney**, an American entertainment company, launched a $400m Eurobond on which returns were pegged to revenues on a portfolio of films.

Tuesday 13th

American securities firms reported unexpectedly high third-quarter earnings, boosted by gains in trading, investment banking and retail broking. Merrill Lynch's after-tax income leapt 44% from the same period a year earlier, to $230m. An exception, Salomon, was hit by trading losses on its own account and reported a meagre $6m in earnings on October 22nd. Its shares fell by 12% that day.

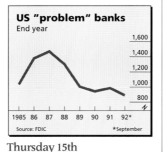

US "problem" banks
End year

1985 86 87 88 89 90 91 92*
Source: FDIC   *September

Thursday 15th

Big American banks reported generally healthy third-quarter earnings, with **J.P. Morgan**'s up 7% from the same period in 1991, to $400m. Most spoke of wider interest-rate margins, gains on trading during Europe's currency turmoil and lower bad-debt provisions.

As the **Nordic financial crisis** deepened, three of the region's biggest banks—Finland's Kansallis-Osake-Pankki (KOP) and Unitas (Union Bank of Finland), and Sweden's Skandinaviska Enskilda Banken—revealed pre-tax for the first eight months.

America's Securities and Exchange Commission approved long-mooted reforms aimed at publicising **bosses' pay packages** and boosting shareholder democracy.

Friday 16th

A cut of one percentage point in **Britain's base rate**, to 8%, boosted share prices a bit and bond prices a lot. Sterling fell two pfennigs against the D-mark, to below DM2.45.

Monday 19th

On the fifth anniversary of the October 1987 stockmarket crash, **American shares** rose modestly. The Dow Jones Industrial average closed 14 points higher, at 3,188.

As Britain's government struggled to make public sense of a decision to close more than half the country's coal mines, **sterling** fell 1½ points to its lowest trade-weighted level, 79½, since the index was started in 1975.

Tuesday 20th

Nomura, the biggest of Japan's struggling stockbrokers, pulled out of market-making in continental European shares and fired 50 people in London. Later, with two other big firms, it reported slim pre-tax profits for the half-year to September while a fourth, Yamaichi, showed a loss.

Wednesday 21st

American insurance companies raised the figure they expected to pay in claims to victims of **Hurricane Andrew** from $7.8 billion to $10.2 billion. Even at the lower estimate, Andrew was the costliest catastrophe ever to hit the country's insurers.

Lira against the D-mark
Inverted scale

700
lira
800

900

1,000

Sep   Oct
1992

Friday 23rd

The **Bank of Italy** cut its discount rate by one percentage point, to 14%, as parliament made progress on an austere budget package. The bank's governor, Carlo Ciampi, later said the lira, down 14% since leaving Europe's exchange-rate mechanism in September, needed to bounce back a bit before re-entering it.

Monday 26th

As troubles continued at **American Express**, the travel and charge-card company announced a third-quarter loss of $205m. Included in the red ink was a $342m charge for restructuring its card business and a $25m operating loss at Shearson Lehman Brothers, its stockbroking subsidiary.

Invesco MIM, a British fund-management company, said it would pay £9.5m ($15m) to shareholders in Drayton Consolidated Investment Trust, because it had failed to disclose a sizeable investment it made for Drayton that later went bad. It was the first such payment by a fund manager.

Tuesday 27th

Germany's five leading economic research institutes urged the **Bundesbank** to relax interest rates to halt the country's economic decline.

Wednesday 28th

Britain's Accounting Standards Board said it would require firms to re-state their **profit-and-loss accounts** radically from June 22nd 1993. The biggest change was the abolition of extraordinary items.

Friday 30th

A report by the Bank for International Settlements in Basle concluded that although banks had worked hard to control the risks in **financial derivatives** (futures, options, swaps and the like), these still had the potential to jolt the financial system.

Japan's banks announced plans to set up an industry-financed body to buy dodgy loans from overburdened banks. Meanwhile, the finance ministry said the country's 21 biggest banks had non-performing loans totalling ¥12.3 trillion ($100 billion) at September 30th, 54% more than in March.

November

Monday 2nd
The Bank of France lowered its benchmark interest rates by one-quarter of one percentage point. Economics minister Michel Sapin declared victory in the "battle of the **franc**".

Tuesday 3rd
Britain's foreign-exchange reserves fell by an underlying $3.02 billion in October, reported the Treasury, after losing the battle for **sterling**.

Wednesday 4th
American shares fell on the expected news that Bill Clinton had been elected president. Long bonds slumped too but the dollar rose, on rumours of a Russian coup.

Thursday 5th
New Zealand's bitterest bid battle ended when the National Australia Bank won approval for its NZ$1.5 billion ($781m) purchase of the **Bank of New Zealand**.

The Swedish government, which had already bailed out three banks during the previous year, announced details of a sweeping plan to underwrite **Sweden's banking system**.

Sunday 8th
Rumours that **GPA** faced a liquidity crisis were denied by the Irish aircraft-leasing company, the world's largest buyer of aircraft. GPA had failed to raise $725m from the sale of bonds backed by 18 aircraft leases after withdrawing a $1 billion international equity issue in June.

Tuesday 10th
Britain's most prestigious merchant bank, **S.G. Warburg**, said its pre-tax profits had fallen 44% in the six months to September 1992 from the same period a year earlier, to £51.2m ($91.6m). Though specific factors, such as Europe's currency crisis, were partly to blame, disgruntled investors

pushed down its share price by nearly 10%.

France's state-owned **Crédit Lyonnais** announced that agreement had been reached on its hotly-negotiated purchase of 50.1% of BfG Bank, for DM1.42 billion ($889m). The French bank wanted better access to the German market.

Wednesday 11th
Pressed by regulators anxious to improve control over the $200 billion market in **junk bonds**, the National Association of Securities Dealers (NASD) said it would start showing prices on its electronic marketplace for the most actively-traded issues.

Thursday 12th
In a series of **European interest-rate reductions**, Britain unveiled an economic recovery package that included a one percentage-point cut in interest rates, to 7%; France, Italy, Denmark and Sweden also lowered rates. The Bundesbank left Germany's unchanged.

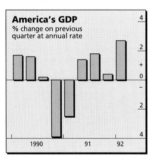

America's GDP
% change on previous quarter at annual rate

Friday 13th
For the first time, **institutional investors in America** owned directly more publicly quoted shares than did individual investors, the Securities Industry Association said—though if mutual funds were included, individuals still owned 55.9%.

Monday 16th
In the wake of a warning by the German government's independent Council of Eco-

nomic Advisers that Germany faced **no growth** in 1993, the D-mark slid nearly 2½ pfennigs against the dollar, to DM1.59.

Italy's government revealed its much-leaked **privatisation plans**. These included the sale of stakes in three large banks— 67% of Credito Italiano, 57% of Banca Commerciale Italiana and 35% of Banca di Roma— and a majority stake in Istituto Nazionale delle Assicurazioni, a large insurer.

Tuesday 17th
Standard & Poor's, a credit-rating agency, downgraded a raft of **American insurers**, including the Prudential. The insurer's capital base was weaker than it should have been to justify a triple-A claims-paying grade, said the agency, and reduced it to double-A.

Wednesday 18th
Japanese shares gained 4.9%, for no obvious reason, as the Nikkei rose from 15,993 to 16,779. Some credited official pressure on institutions to buy. Hong Kong shares, meanwhile, fell by 3.9% on fears about the growing row between China and Britain over the latter's plans to give the colony more democracy.

Thursday 19th
After an attack on its currency threatened to wipe out foreign-exchange reserves, Sweden abandoned its 18-month-long campaign to peg the **krona** to the ecu. Investors in droves bought D-marks, renewing pressure for further realignment of European currencies and forcing down even the previously ebullient dollar.

ING, a Dutch banking and insurance group, said shareholders in Banque Bruxelles Lambert, Belgium's second-largest bank, were asking too

much and dropped its planned bid.

Saturday 21st
For the third time since early September, Europe's **exchange-rate mechanism** (ERM) was realigned. Spain's peseta and Portugal's escudo were devalued by 6%. In trading the following week, the weaker among the remaining currencies—the Irish punt, the Danish krone, even the French franc—were under pressure. So was Germany—to cut its interest rates.

Monday 23rd
In America, **Ernst & Young** agreed to pay the Federal Deposit Insurance Corporation $400m to settle lawsuits arising from its audits of thrift institutions that went bust. In Britain, the Auditing Practices Board, financed by the accounting profession, recommended wider duties for auditors.

Norway revealed a NKr5 billion ($775m) rescue plan for its three biggest banks.

Germany's money supply
M3, % increase on a year earlier
Source: Bundesbank

Tuesday 24th
Figures showing a leap in Germany's money supply in October dashed hopes of an early cut in **German interest rates**.

Monday 30th
Felled by a property slump that had halved London office values in three years, one of Britain's most successful property developers in the 1980s, **Rosehaugh**, went into receivership. It owed its bankers about £350m ($529m).

December

Tuesday 1st
The president of Germany's Bundesbank, **Helmut Schlesinger**, insisted that Germany had no room to cut interest rates at present. He criticised as a gift to speculators the requirement that central banks intervene without limit to defend weak currencies in Europe's exchange-rate mechanism. The D-mark soared.

Wednesday 2nd
France's largest insurer, Union des Assurances de Paris (UAP), agreed to give Winterthur 3% of its own shares in exchange for the Swiss insurer's 37.4% stake in **Nordstern**, a German insurance company. UAP had been fighting Nordstern's indirect French shareholder, Compagnie de Suez, for a foothold in Europe's largest insurance market.

Thursday 3rd
Hong Kong shares fell by 8%, to 4,978, as the row intensified between Britain and China over how democratic the colony's immediate future should be. Prices were 23% below their peak on November 12th.

Sunday 6th
James Robinson, boss of American Express, the troubled travel and credit-card giant, said he would resign as chief executive in 1993, as soon as a successor could be found. The company's share price gained 6%.

Monday 7th
The day after the **Swiss** voted

not to tighten ties to the European Community by joining the European Economic Area, Swiss share prices rose.

Tuesday 8th
Although its two main rivals saw operating profits increase comfortably in the first ten months of the year, **Deutsche Bank**, Germany's largest, reported a 5% fall, to DM4.94 billion ($3.17 billion). The bank blamed fluctuations in foreign-exchange rates, but promised undiminished full-year net results.

Thursday 10th
On the eve of the EC summit in Edinburgh, **Norway** cut loose its krone from the ecu. It was the third Nordic country in three months to do so. The Bundesbank's council, meanwhile, left Germany's high real interest rates unchanged, adding to pressure on Europe's weaker currencies.

Monday 14th
The apparent rescue of the Maastricht treaty at the EC summit in Edinburgh failed to convince the currency markets. In the days that followed, the **French franc** continued weak against the D-mark, amid speculation that the franc might be devalued before France's parliamentary elections in the spring.

The number of loss-making **banks in America** dropped to its lowest level in years in the first three quarters of 1992, said the Office of the Comptroller of the Currency. Only 8% of all national banks reported losses, compared with an average of 16% for the previous five years. Falling interest rates boosted net interest income and profits from the sale of investment securities.

Wednesday 16th
An American judge threw out a $338m jury award in May to Standard Chartered, a British

bank, which claimed that **Price Waterhouse**, an accounting firm, had been negligent in auditing a bank that Standard later bought.

Moody's downgraded triple-A **Banque Nationale de Paris** and bumped lower-rated **Crédit Lyonnais** down a notch too, blaming France's worsening economy and an increasingly competitive banking scene.

Thursday 17th
In one of the largest single write-offs in British banking history, **Barclays** provided £240m ($378m) against its loans to property group Imry.

Monday 21st
On better economic data, **London shares** set a new record when the FT-SE 100 closed at 2,807.7. Stockmarkets in France and Germany also rallied.

Tuesday 22nd
Bundesbank president Helmut Schlesinger predicted that Germany's long-term interest rates could fall below 6% before long. The dollar surged against the **D-mark**, and share prices rose in London and Paris. Italy cut official interest rates by a point, to stave off deep recession.

Japan's finance minister, Yoshiro Hayashi, said the **Osaka Securities Exchange** would replace the Nikkei 225 share average with a new weighted average as a basis for its popular futures contract. The aim was to reduce arbitraging and volatility in the cash market.

Wednesday 23rd
Banco Santander was accused by Spain's highest monetary court judge of inducing clients to commit tax fraud in the late 1980s and required to post bail of Ptas8 billion ($71m). The bank appealed.

Tuesday 29th
Spain's cabinet approved draft legislation giving the **Spanish central bank** autonomy in defining monetary policy to ensure price stability.

Boosted by increasing confidence in the American economy, the **dollar** touched its highest point against the D-mark since the summer, DM1.6235. Its strength pushed sterling briefly to $1.4988, a level last seen in January 1987.

Wednesday 30th
Shareholders of **Aachener und Münchener (AMB)**, a German insurer, voted to sell a 25% stake in BfG Bank to Crédit Lyonnais, giving the French bank control of Germany's sixth-largest bank. They also agreed to give full voting rights to the 25% stake in AMB owned by Assurances Générales de France, ending a titanic struggle for corporate control.

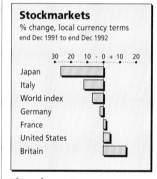

Stockmarkets
% change, local currency terms
end Dec 1991 to end Dec 1992

Thursday 31st
Shares ended 1992 in mixed mood. Britain's FT-SE 100 closed just off the year's highs, at 2,846.5—14% up over the year. America's Dow Jones gained 4% over the 12 months, closing at 3,301.11. German shares lost about 2%; trading stopped on December 30th with the DAX at 1,545.05. French share prices edged up less than 2%, to 484.49. Japanese shares were the most dramatic: the Nikkei closed on December 30th at 16,924.95—down 26% on the year.

As we reported then

Myths and dividends

JANUARY 25TH *Most British investors hate dividend cuts. Yet others say that companies which maintain dividends while their profits dwindle risk running short of capital. Both are illogical*

THEY mock recession. They defy the low-inflation discipline of Europe's exchange-rate mechanism. In 1991 the dividends paid out by Britain's industrial companies rose by 5.3%, even though profits fell by 10.5%. This year has begun in similar fashion: on January 16th the TSB group, Britain's sixth-largest bank, maintained its dividend despite a large loss. No other big economy behaves like this. In America's recession, dividends have been as dull as profits. In Japan and Germany, dividends account for a far smaller proportion of company earnings.

Some find the British anomaly alarming. In November the governor of the Bank of England suggested that companies might be wise to cut their dividends during recession. "The more companies pay out in dividends," declares a recent paper from Kleinwort Benson Securities, a British investment firm, "the less they have to plough back into other corporate activity." High dividend pay-outs are cast as the counterpart of credit crunch: shareholders, like bankers, demand a growing proportion of corporate profits during recession.

A look at the cash flow of industrial and commercial companies supports these worries. In each of the 25 years to 1987, according to S.G. Warburg Securities, British

firms retained at least two-fifths of their earnings, using the money to invest or build up reserves. By 1990-91, retentions had fallen to less than a third, because dividends and interest had each grabbed a bigger share. Bigger interest payments were inevitable, as real interest rates were high and earnings were falling. Equity, on the other hand, is risk capital. If shareholders accepted their share of recession, borrowing might be restrained or capital expenditure suffer less, softening the economic cycle. Is it coincidence that fat-dividend economies have performed disappointingly?

In the 1970s worry over inflation prompted governments in Britain and America to impose a cap on the proportion of earnings paid to shareholders. This time, sacrificed growth is the main anxiety. Yet theory suggests that dividends have little effect on either inflation or growth.

Shareholders can be rewarded in two ways: with dividends, or with capital gains. In theory, more of one means less of the other. If a company pays no dividend, the retained cash will strengthen its balance sheet and boost its share price, from which shareholders can benefit by selling stock. A big dividend should drive the shares down.

In theory, again, dividends are equally

irrelevant from the firm's perspective. It can increase its equity capital either by retaining earnings or by selling new shares. Britain's big dividends are matched by its frequent rights issues. It is firms' ability to exploit good projects, not the size of dividends or retentions, that determines their rate of growth. British firms retained over half their earnings in the dividend-capping 1970s, hardly a decade of miraculous growth.

Few finance directors or investors can bring themselves to believe this. Dividends are worth more to the shareholder than cash on the balance sheet, goes one popular argument: money in the company is money at risk. Actually, this is true only of money that the firm puts into a business project, since such projects may not bring the hoped-for return. Money in the firm's bank account is not especially risky.

Or again: big dividends, accompanied by occasional rights issues to finance large projects, give shareholders more say. If all spare cash were paid out in dividends, investment managers would collect all profits, then decide (by supporting or cold-shouldering rights issues) how they should be spent. In practice, however, British institutions almost never refuse to underwrite an issue. If they are unimpressed by a firm's investment plans, they simply sell its shares.

Yet even weak arguments can be self-fulfilling. British companies know investors hate them to cut dividends. They therefore raise them only when they feel confident of being able to sustain the new level. A rising dividend signals a firm's optimism—and is therefore a good reason to buy its shares. As a result, share prices usually fall following a dividend cut, even though a cut should strengthen the balance sheet. Last year the hint of a dividend cut, together with gloomy talk about profits, caused the share prices of two British blue chips, British Steel and Trafalgar House, to drop 30%.

For some investors, special circumstances may harden the soft line between dividends and capital gains. A family trust may entitle one beneficiary to dividends generated by a fund, while consigning the capital to his heir. Income unit trusts (mutual funds), sold to investors who want income plus security of capital, lay down that the return must come from dividends, not from selling shares. Britain's huge pension funds also have a reason to seek dividends: since the 1970s actuaries have regarded a fund's dividend income as the best measure of its ability to meet future liabilities. Tax breaks, in some cases, reinforce the bias. Pension funds, for example, which are tax-exempt for most purposes, may reclaim the advanced corporation tax that the company pays the taxman on all dividends.

Modest problem recedes

Does the British appetite for big dividends matter? Certainly they are less important than is sometimes suggested. There is no evidence, for example, that fat dividends entail low earnings growth. Research by GMO Woolley, a fund manager, shows that, in the 1970s and 1980s, Britain's high yields have meant slower capital appreciation (as theory would suggest); but real company earnings have grown faster than those in Germany and America.

Nor is there much evidence that big dividends exert a temporary squeeze on company balance sheets during recessions. For, as the chart shows, 1991's big pay-outs coincided with bumper issues of new equities. If you subtract last year's £3.7 billion ($6.5 billion) raised by FT-SE 100 compa-

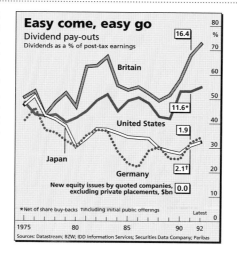

Easy come, easy go
Dividend pay-outs
Dividends as a % of post-tax earnings

16.4
Britain
11.6*
United States
1.9
Japan
Germany
2.1†
New equity issues by quoted companies, excluding private placements, $bn 0.0

*Net of share buy-backs †Including initial public offerings Latest
1975 80 85 90 92
Sources: Datastream; BZW; IDD Information Services; Securities Data Company; Paribas

nies through rights issues from the dividends that they paid, the adjusted pay-out ratio falls by a quarter.

The real case for worry over dividends is therefore modest. A few companies, obliged by shareholders to pay big dividends, may have trouble issuing new equity. The transaction costs involved in paying dividends, then issuing rights, may add slightly to the cost of capital. At its most basic, the case for change in Britain is that companies should be freer to choose which

dividend policy suits them best.

The good news, however, is that change may be on the way. As recession drags on and bad debts mount, British banks are beginning to press their debtors to retain more earnings. Meanwhile, monetary integration in Europe, and the prospect of permanently low inflation, may dent Britons' long-time reluctance to buy bonds, so pulling income-hungry investors from equities. The shift towards fixed-interest holdings is likely to be be encouraged by the revival of government-bond issues in Britain.

At the same time, the value of dividends as signals may be fading. Though it could just be a cyclical effect, companies have grown so anxious to maintain their dividends that these have ceased to be a real mark of optimism: investors increasingly look beyond the dividend at dividend cover (the ratio of spare cash to dividends). Meanwhile computers and sharper competition have raised standards among stock analysts, providing investors with more reliable information about companies' operations. And if Britain's promised accounting reforms do produce clearer balance sheets, investors' reliance on the vague signals given out by dividends will be reduced still more.

The wiring of Wall Street

FEBRUARY 22ND, NEW YORK *As competition culls low-quality, high-cost producers, Wall Street is doing what inefficient metal-bashers have been at for a decade: re-engineering itself*

THEY pour through the doors of America's biggest securities firms these days, the consultants and computer wizards who claim responsibility for reorganising the country's car makers, chemicals firms, steel mills and drugs companies. Main Street has much to teach Manhattan, claim Andersen Consulting, Coopers & Lybrand and IBM. To improve productivity, profitability and quality in a fundamental way, companies must strip out underlying operating inefficiencies, not just sack the odd employee. This means redesigning completely the way work flows through an organisation: in a word, "re-engineering" the business.

Wall Street is listening, and well it might. Repeated attempts to cut costs since the stockmarket crash in 1987 have reduced the number of employees in the securities business by 17% but made little impact on operating costs. Moody's, a rating agency, reckons that these are still more than three times as high in real terms as in 1980.

The heart of the task is to reorganise information systems. The increase in com-

puting power over the past ten years created new products and markets by the bucketful. These prompted huge increases in investment in computer systems and supporting infrastructure.

Wall Street's spending on technology grew by almost 20% a year through the 1980s, to some $7.5 billion last year. That is more than the combined pre-tax profits of securities firms in any year. Costs and systems spiralled without providing commensurate productivity gains. Re-engi-

neering promises to impose order on both.

For securities firms, it means integrating front and back offices (rather as car makers have tried to bring design and assembly closer together). It also implies lowering processing costs by eliminating repetitive paper-based tasks. The result: getting closer to customers, the biggest of whom will otherwise be increasingly inclined to bypass securities firms, investing directly or through electronic off-exchange networks.

Investment banks like Salomon Brothers, Goldman Sachs and Morgan Stanley have been spending hundreds of millions of dollars to integrate their diversified, far-

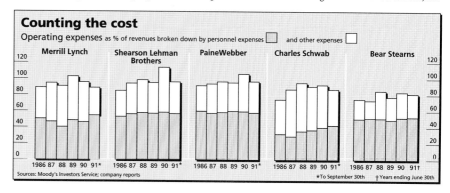

Counting the cost
Operating expenses as % of revenues broken down by personnel expenses ☐ and other expenses ☐

Merrill Lynch Shearson Lehman Brothers PaineWebber Charles Schwab Bear Stearns

1986 87 88 89 90 91* 1986 87 88 89 90 91* 1986 87 88 89 90 91* 1986 87 88 89 90 91* 1986 87 88 89 90 91†
Sources: Moody's Investors Service; company reports
*To September 30th †Years ending June 30th

flung businesses, and still have much to do. Only then will it be clear whether the money was well spent.

At the big retail brokerages, where margins are under pressure and there are heavy processing costs to attack, the benefits of re-engineering are likely to be seen first. Merrill Lynch, Kidder Peabody, PaineWebber and Shearson Lehman Brothers are all overhauling their operations. None dares hang back, lest it be left at a permanent cost disadvantage to its rivals. Nor can discount brokers like Charles Schwab (one-third of the way through a six-year project), if they want to stay competitive.

Merrill Lynch has stolen a technological march on the others with its Advanced Order Entry (AOE) system, which went on stream in November. All the firm's 10,500 American brokers can now enter orders for listed stocks directly from their workstations. Brokers used to pass a ticket to a wire operator, who keyed in the order to the processing system that sent it to an exchange. Instead, AOE now sends the order directly to the exchange and brings it back once it is executed.

This achievement has big implications. The one the customer sees is better service. A Merrill broker can execute and confirm a trade in the course of a telephone call: a deal which used to take up to ten minutes, during which time prices could move, can now be processed in less than one. While rivals like Shearson and PaineWebber rush to catch up, Merrill is preparing to extend its system to over-the-counter stocks and derivatives. Kidder Peabody, too, has started to automate over-the-counter deals. Meanwhile, the electronic exchange NASDAQ is redesigning its software to help

firms enter orders automatically.

The new systems should reduce not only the time but the cost of trading. Merrill Lynch spent $200m over three years developing AOE, and predicts that it will start to pay for itself within another two.

Some of the savings will come from eliminating back-office jobs. Merrill got rid of 500 wire-room clerks, and broke with Wall Street tradition by requiring brokers to do the clerical work themselves. More savings should stem from another idea borrowed from manufacturing: "zero-defect" production. The software behind the screens will be able to check for entry mistakes, like mistyped account numbers. It can also be made to run compliance checks, to verify that a transaction meets investor-protection rules. Real-time risk-management measures could be run on individual traders. All this should weed out much duff, illegal and unnecessarily risky business.

Opening new accounts is in for the same speedy face-lift. At Merrill Lynch, a salesman enters the necessary information into a workstation. This transmits the data

to a processing centre, where an "expert system" draws up a document sent to the client to sign and return. The signed form is scanned and stored in an electronic archive; the paper is thrown away. What used to take a week can now be handled overnight.

Merrill Lynch has secured a competitive advantage that rivals have no choice but to try to duplicate. Charles Schwab is one that is exploring another avenue: standardising systems that have developed over the years but cannot talk to each other, and extracting advantage from it once they can.

It was common in the 1980s for firms to build separate back-office systems for, say, futures and options. Re-engineering removes duplicated costs. The application of new technologies like relational databases makes it possible to extract information from customers' accounts, real-time pricing feeds and firms' inventories, for example, to create new reporting and risk-management tools. Schwab is now able to check in the course of the day on the collateral positions of customers who are trading on margin, for example, thus reducing the risks it runs.

Tomorrow's technology promises even more. Improved versions of computer-aided software engineering (CASE), for example, which can help applications to improve themselves automatically, are starting to appear. Wall Street's seers also expect artificial intelligence to start making the inroads in their industry that it has already made in insurance and manufacturing. Shearson is experimenting with expert systems that will replace traders themselves. The ultimate re-engineering?

Beta beaten

MARCH 7TH *In continued pursuit of the Philosopher's Stone, financial theorists cast doubt on a central tenet of modern portfolio management*

A BATTLE between some of the top names in financial economics is attracting attention on Wall Street. Under attack is the famous capital-asset pricing model (CAPM), widely used to assess risk and return. A new paper by two Chicago economists, Eugene Fama and Kenneth French, explodes that model by showing that its key analytical tool does not explain why returns on shares differ.*

According to the CAPM, returns reflect

risk. The model uses a measure called beta—shorthand for relative volatility—to compare the riskiness of one share with that of the market, on the basis of past price changes. A share with a beta of one is just as risky as the market; one with a beta of 0.5 is less risky. Because investors need to earn more on riskier investments, share prices will reflect the demand for higher-than-average returns on shares with higher betas.

Whether beta does predict returns has

long been debated. Studies have found that market capitalisation, price/earnings ratios, leverage and book-to-market ratios do just as well. Messrs Fama and French are clear: beta is not a good guide.

The two economists look at all non-financial shares traded on the NYSE, AMEX and NASDAQ between 1963 and 1990. The shares were grouped into portfolios. When grouped solely on the basis of size (that is, market capitalisation), the CAPM worked—but each portfolio contained a wide range of betas. So the authors grouped shares of similar beta and size. Betas now were a bad guide to returns.

Instead of beta, say Messrs Fama and French, differences in firm size and in the ratio of book value to market value explain differences in returns—especially the latter. When shares were grouped by book-to-market ratios, the gap in returns between the portfolio with the lowest ratio and that with the highest was far wider than when shares were grouped by size.

So should analysts stop using the CAPM? Probably not. Although Mr Fama and Mr French have produced intriguing results, they lack a theory to explain them. Their best hope is that size and book-to-market ratios are proxies for other funda-

mentals. For instance, a high book-to-market ratio may indicate a firm in trouble; its earnings prospects might thus be especially sensitive to economic conditions, so its shares would need to earn a higher return than its beta suggested.

Advocates of CAPM—including Fischer Black, of Goldman Sachs, an investment bank, and William Sharpe of Stanford University, who won the Nobel prize for economics in 1990—reckon the results of the new study can be explained without discarding beta. Investors may irrationally favour big firms. Or they may lack the cash to buy enough shares to spread risk completely, so that risk and return are not per-

fectly matched in the market.

Those looking for a theoretical alternative to CAPM will find little satisfaction, however. Voguish rivals, such as the "arbitrage-pricing theory", are no better at explaining actual share returns. Which leaves Wall Street with an awkward choice: believe the Fama-French evidence, despite its theoretical vacuum, and use size and the book-to-market ratios as a guide to returns; or stick with a theory that, despite the data, is built on impeccable logic.

"The Cross-Section of Expected Stock Returns", by Eugene Fama and Kenneth French. University of Chicago Centre for Research in Security Prices, 1991.

When bears run wild

APRIL 4TH, TOKYO *Tokyo's long bear market turned from a cub into a grizzly in one week. Those predicting that share prices had touched bottom were proven horribly wrong. The Nikkei ended 1992 at just 16,925*

DESPITE more than two years of plunging share prices, until this week many people still believed that official Japan had the power to support the Tokyo stockmarket. No longer. Even the most credulous investors are now questioning their faith.

The stockmarket's response to the Japanese authorities' fiscal and monetary easing announced on March 31st and April 1st was worse than even the grizzliest bears had predicted. The spending package, under which ¥5 trillion ($38 billion) of public spending is to be brought forward into the first half of the 1992-93 fiscal year, had been so widely leaked that it was already absorbed into market prices. But the cut in the official discount rate, from 4½% to 3¾%,

was unexpectedly large. Even so, the Nikkei-225 average fell on April 1st-2nd by 1,060 points (a two-day drop of 5½%) to 18,286, the first time since 1987 that it has gone below 19,000. The wider Topix index fell 97 points to 1,322.

Worst hit were bank shares, which are suffering from mounting worries over bad debts. Some city (large commercial) and long-term credit bank shares plunged by 10% on All Fools' Day. Worryingly, volume has not risen enough to suggest that selling has reached its peak.

The Nikkei has now fallen by 53% from its all-time high at the end of 1989. Normally such a decline would suggest the end of a bear market and a good buying opportunity. It might not do so this time, because the speculative mania that gripped Japan in the second half of the 1980s was so feverish. Historical parallels suggest that when a boom such as this goes bust, a decline of closer to 80% can often be expected (see table). That could mean the Nikkei falling to 10,000 or less. As Barton Biggs, Morgan Stanley's chief investment strategist, notes with fine understatement, such a decline would depress prices in many of the world's markets.

It would also depress foreign investors, who last year bought a net ¥6 trillion of Japanese shares when the Nikkei was averaging 25,000. They are desperately clutching at contrarian arguments.

Sinking sun

Nikkei-225 average

They say, for instance, that the uniformity of bearish sentiment among Japanese investors is a sign of an imminent turnaround. That is unlikely. When Japanese investors are all bearish it suggests a lasting consensus has been reached—and that they will be cautious about rushing back into shares. The life insurers, the biggest institutional investors, have said publicly that they want to cut the proportion of their assets invested in Japanese equities by 1995 from 25% to 20%, so they are not likely to be net buyers. They may even be net sellers, depending on how fast their assets grow.

Foreign investors also delude themselves when they argue that falling interest rates will push Japanese institutional investors back into the equity market in search of decent returns. The institutions will probably prefer Japanese corporate bonds. These will be issued in growing amounts as companies have to refinance some $170 billion-worth of bonds with equity warrants attached. Thanks to the slumping stockmarket, most of these warrants will expire worthless in the next few years.

Once they realise their mistake, foreign investors might also start selling. That

Booms and busts

	% rise bull phase	Length of bull phase (months)	% decline peak to trough	Length of bear phase (months)
Tulips Holland (1634-37)	+5,900%	36	−93%	10
Mississippi shares France (1719-21)	+6,200%	13	−99%	13
South Sea shares Britain (1719-20)	+1,000%	18	−84%	6
American stocks US (1921-32)	+497%	95	−87%	33
Mexican stocks Mexico (1978-81)	+785%	30	−73%	18
Silver US (1979-82)	+710%	12	−88%	24
Hong Kong stocks Hong Kong (1970-74)	+1,200%	28	−92%	20
Taiwan stocks Taiwan (1986-90)	+1,168%	40	−80%	12
Japanese stocks Tokyo (1965-?)	+3,720%	288	*	*

Source: Morgan Stanley Research   *-53% over 27 months to date

could be disastrous, since they have been the main buyers supporting the market over the past year. Curiously, the *gaijin* show no sign of rushing to get out. Some are even said to be contemplating more buying. Yet the Tokyo stockmarket is still far from cheap.

The Nikkei now trades on a price/earnings ratio of 37, with a dividend yield of 1%. That gives it a higher rating than almost all other markets. It is also well above what the Japanese stockmarket commanded before 1986, when speculative fever began to send share prices soaring. The banking industry, which accounts for a quarter of the stockmarket, still sells on a p/e ratio of nearly 50. Even after its shares fell by 20% in two days, the Industrial Bank of Japan (IBJ) continues to sport a p/e ratio of 57.

Nor is there much hint of high earnings growth to support such frothy ratings. Company earnings are expected to fall in the year to March 1993, the third consecutive year of earnings decline. If they were to fall by 15%, as some securities firms suggest, the stockmarket would still be on a historic p/e ratio of 20 even if the Nikkei fell to 10,000. This thought should make pension-fund trustees shudder as they see their fund managers putting money into the Tokyo stockmarket simply because it represents a certain percentage of the world's stockmarket capitalisation; such policies ignore the fact that percentage shares can quickly decline.

There is also evidence that Japan's cosy *keiretsu* system of cross-shareholdings may be unravelling. Many companies own bank shares thanks to their business relationships. One reason that these shares collapsed on April 1st may have been that such companies did not want their selling to be revealed in the accounts that closed on March 31st. So they dumped them the next day instead. In any case, a growing number of firms are admitting to sales of bank shares brought on by their own financial difficulties.

The stockmarket fall could take on a momentum of its own because of the significance to banks and life insurers of unrealised capital gains on their shares. For banks, these are almost the only reserve they have to set against rising bad debts. They are also crucial to the 8% capital ratios that banks are supposed to meet under the international Basle agreement. After this week even the big names are troubled. Also, small life insurers such as Yamato, Saison, Toho and Tokyo may already be facing unrealised losses, which raises questions about their ability to pay up on their policies.

It all adds up to a decidedly bearish outlook which could quickly turn into a cathartic dumping of Japanese equities. Despite this week's market fall, such a dumping has yet to happen.

Not there yet

MAY 16TH, WASHINGTON, DC *The world in which the World Bank moves changed beyond recognition with the collapse of the Soviet Union. The institution itself has been slower to change*

A YEAR ago the World Bank had put the Latin American debt saga behind it. It began to look forward to what it ought to have been concentrating on all along: helping more than a billion people out of chronic poverty. Then came the Soviet collapse and the request by Russia and 14 other republics to become members. The Bank has seen nothing comparable in scale or nature to the challenge that these command economies now present. Can it cope?

The positive points first. The arrival in September of Lewis Preston, recently retired from a long stint as chairman of J.P. Morgan, America's only big AAA-rated commercial bank, has worked undoubted good. The new World Bank president is a competent manager, if not an exuberant one.

Almost immediately, Mr Preston set about cleaning up the top layers of the bank. "I find the structure of the Bank quite uncomfortable in its hierarchical rigidities," he says. He has replaced a layer of decision-trapping managers with an inner cabinet of three. It meant the loss of talented and visible people, and the occasion allowed personal scores to be settled. But few deny that the streamlining is an improvement.

Mr Preston is also setting up a workable budgeting system, which scarcely exists. He is changing the incentives for loan officers, who have been keener to launch new projects than to see them through. Around $50 billion of the Bank's loans—equal to a quarter of all those it has ever agreed to—has been committed but not paid out.

These changes and more will be needed to cope with the Bank's new members. Nobody knows how much they will need in World Bank loans over the coming decade, but estimates start at an annual $4 billion-5 billion, beginning two years from now. The Bank's private-sector arm, the International Finance Corporation (IFC), says that their accession will increase its pace of new investment by half, from a growth rate of 10% a year to as much as 15%. The IFC's head, Sir William Ryrie, calls the rise in investment and staff "really almost scary". Outside the IFC, the World Bank says it will need to dedicate 180 people to looking after the Commonwealth of Independent States, and its estimate is probably low. Despite assurances to the contrary, other poor regions fear that talent will be diverted to the CIS.

For all the former Soviet Union's compelling needs and attractions, the World Bank's central purpose is to pursue policies that help to alleviate poverty. For more than a decade the Bank has concentrated on policy-based adjustment lending. Pov-

A long way to New York state

erty plans have been grinding along with painful slowness. A report on the subject came out two years ago, but it was not until May 11th that guidelines implementing its recommendations were issued. In the foreword to the directive Mr Preston said that reducing poverty was the Bank's "overarching objective". Yet such is the bureaucratic machine that it will be years before actual lending practices reflect the shift.

Bored on the board

The twin challenges of helping Eastern Europe and attacking world poverty require, more than ever, clear policy-making at the top of the Bank. This is, by and large, lacking. Mr Preston feels uncomfortable leading philosophical debate. And the Bank's most important policy-setting body, its board, has long ceased to function in a way that any commercial company would recognise.

The board's 22 members are divided into those from poor-country borrowers and those from rich-country donors. The latter have the most votes, and the power. But power has often been used for self-serving ends. The United States, the biggest shareholder, long blocked a much-needed capital increase for the IFC. The money was voted through this month, but the United States squandered so much goodwill during the delay that the board has lost what little cohesion it had. One example: board meetings broke up in bickering last week over how to admit the new republics to the IFC.

The Bank's board routinely rubberstamps specific projects but rarely discusses broad policy. On May 12th it approved $130m to build an Indian road; it has never debated the huge and fundamental changes taking place in India's economy at large. "We were talking about 175 miles of highway," says a board member, "as if it were being laid down in upper New York state."

Mr Preston himself shows brusque impatience with board meetings—unsurprising, maybe, but dangerous. He rarely asks a director for an opinion. And directors are "pusillanimous", as one of them puts it. Rich-country directors, mostly upper-middle-ranking civil servants, know they have little to gain from confronting a Bank president who can get through on the telephone to their bosses, the finance ministers, at any time of the day or night. And poor-country directors hesitate to confront top managers if they think they might jeopardise capital flows to their countries or compromise their comfortable compatriots inside the Bank.

The board's paralysis means that little clear guidance on policy is handed down to line managers. The board does not supervise them, or demand accountability. It does not help make senior appointments, nor is it informed, except very broadly, of managerial pay. The board does not even look at the creditworthiness of the Bank's loan portfolio. For too long it has chosen not to challenge the Bank's top management. Even if that management is now more effective than before, a board with the energy to involve itself could still make the Bank work better. With new challenges to be faced, will things soon change, of necessity?

There are signs that they are doing so already. The board fought to strengthen the directive on poverty. A group within the Bank is looking into reforming board procedures; its recommendations should be bold and swift. This autumn the World Bank needs $18 billion-21 billion to replenish its soft-loan affiliate for the next three years. It will be in no position to quarrel if, in return, its shareholders insist on greater control.

Taming the derivatives beast

MAY 23RD, NEW YORK   *Regulators and financial folk are increasingly concerned that the risks in financial derivatives are neither measured nor priced correctly. What chance have either to change this?*

IF ARISTOTLE is to be believed, Thales started it all in the 6th century BC with an option on olives. But it was only after academic options-pricing theory of the 1960s and 1970s met the volatile financial markets of the deregulating 1980s that options took off. So did futures, warrants, swaps, swaptions, collars, caps, floors, circuses and scores of other products known collectively as derivatives. Nothing today is transforming financial markets as rapidly and completely as what their inventors like to call tools for the management of financial risk. Nothing now gives so many financial regulators so many nightmares.

America's Federal Reserve and Securities and Exchange Commission (SEC) are increasingly worried about derivatives. So are European regulators, including the Bank of England and Britain's Securities and Investments Board, as newer varieties spread from America. Japanese regulators want to slow the growth of derivatives there.

What especially worries most of them is that banks are the biggest traders and counterparties, and neither banks nor anyone else understand the risks well enough to price them properly. A derivatives disaster could overwhelm the world's financial system, as third-world debt, highly leveraged transactions and property lending have not managed to do.

What are the chances of such a disaster? Maybe not big, but nobody really knows. That is what is frightening. For derivatives have exploded in recent years. A recent study by the Bank for International Settlements (BIS) puts banks' outstanding exchange-traded derivatives at $3.5 trillion at the end of 1991, up from $583 billion five years earlier. Interest-rate futures accounted for three-fifths of the total. Banks' over-the-counter derivatives (two-thirds of them interest-rate swaps) were $4.1 trillion last June, compared with only $500 billion at the end of 1986. Trading in derivatives often exceeds transactions in the markets for the underlying securities or currencies.

Banks and securities firms, companies and investors use derivatives to hedge risks, to gain access to cheaper money, to make profits. The products are likely to get even more popular, for three reasons.

Derivatives are proving cheaper to trade than the bonds, currencies, commodities and equities from which they are "derived". Exchanges have rushed to provide new standardised contracts to meet this demand. Over-the-counter trading has also soared with the increasing volume of products tailored to the needs of particular customers.

Another reason is simple familiarity, and more sophisticated ways of pricing and managing derivatives' risks. Fischer Black and Myron Scholes, academic economists who were hired by Goldman Sachs and Salomon respectively, developed the options-pricing model that gave derivatives a theoretical foundation—and their Wall Street employers a competitive edge. They are now revising their model.

A third spur is that in many countries legal, fiscal and regulatory restrictions on the use of derivatives have been eased. In Britain unit trusts are now allowed to invest in futures and options. Most importantly, the new Basle bank-capital rules weight derivatives more lightly than assets that appear on banks' balance sheets. Banks need less capital to hedge or speculate through derivatives than to carry the underlying assets.

While derivatives zoom, regulators and even financial folk are panting behind in their attempts to assess their risks. The first

is posed by the volatility of the underlying markets. A market participant's exposure can change rapidly if, say, interest rates or share prices suddenly change. Derivatives are often highly geared, and a small movement in share prices, for instance, can trigger a big change in the value of a stock-index option. Hedging secondary-market positions is difficult; anyway, it is by taking risk that a trader makes money.

Measuring just the value of a derivative can be difficult enough. Many are arcane or unique, with no benchmark to determine their worth. Positions often stretch across several markets, through, say, an option on a combined interest-rate and currency swap (a swaption on a circus, in the jargon).

The second big risk is managerial. The increasing complexity of derivatives makes it difficult for managers to keep track of their traders. In 1987 Merrill Lynch lost $377m trading mortgage-related derivatives, in part because of unauthorised transactions. Merrill, and other firms, have tightened internal controls but it is always a struggle to keep up. A firm's managerial control is only as good as its mathematics. It is the derivatives desks that have the MIT PhDs, not the chairmen's offices.

Credit quality is another problem. Although exchanges are the counterparty in exchange-traded derivatives, the growing volume of over-the-counter products requires financial firms to judge the creditworthiness of their partners accurately. And derivative positions are becoming longer-term. Traditionally, those who traded securities, foreign exchange and commodities were skilled at taking short-term risks. As that changes, the chances in-

crease that even a prudent firm will end up as counterparty to a naive risk manager. Wise firms are monitoring more carefully their exposures to specific counterparties.

A fourth risk is that of illiquidity. Some secondary markets for derivatives have plenty of buyers and sellers. The more tailored and long-term the derivative, however, the scarcer active traders become. Positions that cannot easily be liquidated are harder to value and to hedge.

Then there are legal risks. The legal aspects of derivatives are hazy, as banks were shocked to find after entering into swaps with British local authorities. The contracts were voided by the courts because the authorities had no right to enter into them.

Regulators know that all this adds up to potential trouble. Tighter control of derivatives seems inevitable. American regulators have started to rein in what they consider excessively risky products. The SEC has stopped mutual funds from buying some municipal-bond derivatives and is restricting the issue of hybrid bond-cum-derivatives to large companies. Yet regulators are still far from knowing how to measure the risks, still less deal with them.

In the meantime, regulators will look more closely at the banks' off-balance-sheet assets. The BIS says that these assets (which include derivatives) are more than seven times as large as balance-sheet items at some American banks. Gerald Corrigan, president of the New York Fed, recently told bankers that they "had all better take a very, very hard look at off-balance-sheet activities, including the payments, clearance and settlement risks associated with many of those activities. I hope this sounds like a warning, because it is."

Write-off

JULY 11TH, LOS ANGELES *Regulatory battles being waged in California do not bode well for America's insurance industry*

"INJURED? Work, accident, job stress? Attorneys who care available 24 hours . . ." The classified advertisements in the *Los Angeles Times* often terrify insurers even more than the front-page news about the state's earthquakes, fires and floods. In southern California, birthplace of the "Hit me, I need money" bumper-sticker, insurance fraud is popular sport. Now insurers have a new *bête noire*: the state's first elected insurance commissioner, John Garamendi.

Mr Garamendi is an extreme example of the strange way that America regulates insurance. A remarkable number of Americans believe that insurance cannot be treated like a normal business, because it

often provides products mandated by law (car insurance) or essential to normal living (home insurance); and because it is so complicated. In fact seat belts are also mandated by law and provided by private firms; plenty of businesses are complicated. Never mind: America's insurers are sometimes like state monopolies, and at other times asked to be public servants.

The result is often messy. California, in 1988, passed Proposition 103, a voter initiative on insurance. This ignored the causes of rising rates, such as fraud, tort law or medical costs. Its chief selling point was that it promised a 20% refund of recent premiums paid by consumers. It also made Mr Garamendi's job electable—and

gave him wide-ranging powers. The commissioner can halt rate changes and "redlining" (discriminating against places or types of people). A populist with barely concealed ambitions to become governor, Mr Garamendi aims to make a splash in office. California's insurers have treated their customers so badly for so long that they present a tempting target.

The Supreme Court, for its part, has tempered the commissioner's power by insisting that insurers should make a "reasonable rate of return". The result is endless legal argument. Mr Garamendi has refused to grant rate increases unless the insurers give refunds. So far only a few have taken the bait. The rest have gone without rate increases—despite sharply rising costs.

This is big news, because California is a

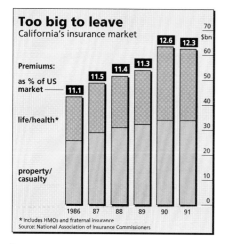

Too big to leave
California's insurance market

Premiums:
as % of US market

life/health*

property/casualty

11.1 · 11.5 · 11.4 · 11.3 · 12.6 · 12.3

1986 87 88 89 90 91

* Includes HMOs and fraternal insurance
Source: National Association of Insurance Commissioners

big place. It is America's largest insurance market, and its share of total premiums is increasing. Yet insurers claim their industry is at breaking point. The number of independent insurance brokers has declined from 5,500 in 1985 to fewer than 4,000 today. In June Ohio Casualty, which has not made an underwriting profit in the state since 1981, announced that it was quitting California. This month Aetna, which has been clobbered in the Californian casualty market as well as in property elsewhere, said it was laying off 10% of its workforce. Other insurers scrape by on investment income and profits from life insurance.

To insurers, Mr Garamendi's sins extend beyond refusing rate increases to bureaucratic meddling. In 1990 Farmers Group sought permission to offer discounts to customers who buy insurance for both car and home; the idea was not approved until this year. "The rules of the game change arbitrarily in California," argues Ohio Casualty—pointing to Mr Garamendi's insistence that insurers pay the full value of homes destroyed in the Oakland fire last winter (rather than their insured value).

The most awkward area of the debate is red-lining. Good insurers have always made money by choosing which risks to insure and which to avoid. Technology, such as computer programs that can tell an insurer which area a consumer lives in and even predict his likely route to work, is in-

creasing that power to discriminate. Yet politicians like Mr Garamendi are adamant that insurers play a social role, by doing business in communities like South-Central Los Angeles whether or not it is profitable. Such social policy—worthy though it is—looks like a job for the taxpayer rather than the insurance industry. As technology opens up fresh ways for insurers to choose between different risks, those conflicts will increase. The gap between business logic and public service will become more noticeable.

Cry regulator, cry wolf

Mr Garamendi pooh-poohs such moaning. After all, the law (incredibly) now guarantees insurers the opportunity to make a "reasonable profit"—which seems to mean a return on capital of between 10% and 15%. Besides, a few insurers have proved it is possible to prosper in California: outfits such as Mercury General and 20th Century have been stars on Wall Street. One of Mr Garamendi's advisers, Steven Miller, reckons that over the past five years Ohio Casualty's average return on capital in California was 7.9%—not great, but not the stuff of bankruptcy. Are the insurers crying wolf?

Over the past four years the state's average loss ratio (ie, the value of non-life claims divided by the value of premiums) has gradually risen, from 66% to 70% in 1991. In California an insurer's expenses are typically around 35% of its premiums, yielding a combined-loss ratio of 105%, not far off the national average. Thanks to the Oakland fires, the loss ratio before expenses for homeowners' insurance (usually one of the most profitable lines) soared to 118%.

The loss ratio for workers' compensation was a less dramatic but still hefty 79% last year. Steven Gavios, an analyst at Kidder Peabody, admits that California's market for workers' compensation insurance

has become noticeably less profitable, but says it is still no worse than a cluster of other states, including Texas, Louisiana, Massachusetts and Rhode Island. Moreover, California's size allows for big regional differences. Selling workers' compensation insurance in litigious Los Angeles is not profitable, but it is in less fractious Fresno.

Litigiousness makes car insurance dicey too. The Insurance Research Council says that 60% of all accidents in California involving successful car-damage claims also lead to the payment of a bodily-injury claim—almost double the average for states with similar liability laws. In Los Angeles the figure may be closer to 80%. Last month two people died in a freeway crash that was allegedly staged to collect insurance.

There is one small hope for change: cheap "no-fault" insurance. This covers motorists against minor injuries in accidents, so relieving the need to sue the other party. Mandatory no-fault insurance could reduce the industry's costs—and cut the cost of basic liability insurance to $220 a year, roughly a third of normal cheap motor insurance. Both Mr Garamendi and the insurers support the concept (though they disagree over details). But the

Governor Garamendi?

legislature, where trial lawyers have a fearsomely powerful lobby, will not pass the measure.

Arguably, insurers could do well enough, despite Mr Garamendi and the politicians. Their biggest problems are at least partially self-inflicted: the national slump in property and casualty insurance rates is caused more by over-capacity than by bureaucratic meddling. Still, any system that guarantees an industry "a reasonable return" and allows bureaucrats to set prices seems a little, well, socialist. The odds are that Mr Garamendi and the insurers will continue squabbling until he runs for governor or they start making decent profits.

A ghastly game of dominoes

SEPTEMBER 19TH **While Europe dithered over its exchange-rate future, speculators took matters into their own hands. Are the ERM's days now numbered?**

A STERLING crisis, a big jump in British interest rates, and Britain's prime minister cancelling a trip abroad, all on the eve of the IMF's annual meeting: it brings back memories of September 1976, when Brit-

ain's chancellor of the exchequer turned back at Heathrow airport to sort out an economic crisis. For Norman Lamont, the current chancellor, history seemed to repeat itself this week. Despite repeated

pledges not to devalue, he was forced to withdraw sterling temporarily from Europe's exchange-rate mechanism (ERM) on September 16th. Later that night, Italy pulled out the lira, too, and Spain devalued its pcscta by 5%.

The markets have pre-empted this Sunday's French referendum on the Maastricht treaty, which set out a path to European economic and monetary union (EMU). Worries that the French would vote No had been a big reason for the strains within the ERM. A No vote could deal a fatal blow to EMU, and hence to hopes that countries would be forced to reduce inflation and budget deficits to meet the convergence criteria agreed upon at Maastricht. The recent weakness of the dollar as a result of the enormous interest-rate gap between Germany and America had also put the ERM under the hammer. As investors switched from dollars into D-marks, the markets began to desert sterling and other currencies perceived as fragile.

On September 14th Germany's Bundesbank agreed to trim its interest rates for the first time in almost five years, in exchange for Italy's commitment to devalue the lira by 7% against other European currencies. The bank knocked half a percentage point off its discount rate, but just one-quarter of a point off the more important Lombard rate. This was supposed to ease tensions in the ERM. The relief was short-lived.

Fresh from their victory against the lira, the markets decided to have a go at sterling. The dollar's rebound against the D-mark, from DM1.39 to DM1.52 during the week to September 16th, should have boosted the pound. Instead, Britain's currency kept sliding. Reports that Helmut Schlesinger, the Bundesbank's president, had said he thought the pound should have been devalued too, triggered heavy selling of sterling.

On September 16th massive intervention by the Bank of England failed to prevent the pound from dipping below its permitted floor against the D-mark of DM2.778. The lira, peseta and escudo also came under heavy selling pressure. Britain's government was forced to raise interest rates, initially from 10% to 12%, and then, in a second desperate act, to 15%. This pushed rates back to their level before Britain entered the ERM in October 1990. Some wondered whether Mr Lamont was prepared to go as far as the Bank of Sweden, which raised its overnight lending rate to 500% to support its currency.

In just one day, the Bank of England may have spent $15 billion-20 billion, up to half its total foreign-exchange reserves, to support the pound. To no avail; sterling remained below its floor in the ERM. That evening, the hapless Mr Lamont had the humiliating task of announcing that sterling was to be allowed to float outside the ERM—ie, devalued—and the rise in interest rates from 12% to 15% was to be cancelled. A day later he cut interest rates back to 10%. The pound tumbled almost immediately, to DM2.70, and fell further in overnight trading. In an all-night meeting of

Who's next?

	Currency's ERM position Sept 15th *	Currency's over/under valuation, % †	Reserves, import cover**	Budget deficit as % of GDP, 1992 ‡	Inflation rate %, latest	GDP growth, %, 1992‡	Devaluation risk ††
Italy	27	2	0.5	-11.3	5.2	1.3	1
Britain	-90	3	2.6	-4.6	3.6	-0.8	2
Spain	16	11	8.2	-4.9	5.7	2.0	3
Portugal	-3	11	11.7	-5.4	9.5	2.8	4
Denmark	-22	-2	2.5	-2.1	2.2	2.1	5=
Belgium	31	-18	1.3	-5.5	2.1	1.6	5=
Holland	30	-16	1.5	-3.4	3.5	1.6	5=
France	-36	-12	3.1	-2.3	2.7	2.0	8
Ireland	-6	-10	2.9	-1.9	3.6	2.4	9
Germany	35	—	1.7	-3.4	3.5	1.3	—

Sources: OECD; IMF; government statistics; NatWest; *The Economist* poll of forecasters   * % of permitted divergence from central rate
† Central rate against DM relative to PPP   ** Foreign-exchange (mid September estimates), number of months' imports   ‡ Forecast   †† 1=greatest risk, 9=least risk

monetary officials in Brussels, Britain lobbied in vain to suspend the ERM until after the French referendum. Stiffened by, among others, the French, whose overriding aim has been to keep the franc lashed to the D-mark, the majority resisted.

And after the referendum?

If the French vote Non on September 20th, it will trigger a further flight to "quality" currencies. The pound's likely resting place is anyone's guess. At midday on September 17th it was languishing at DM2.65; the lira was 3% below its ERM floor; and the peseta was heading for its new floor. What now for Europe's other currencies?

In the table, *The Economist* has made a stab at ranking currencies, starting with those that looked most at risk of devaluation at the close of trading on September 15th (ie, before sterling and the lira floated). The first column shows the position of each currency within the ERM, measured by its divergence from its central rate. A large negative figure means the currency was weak.

Column 2 shows whether a currency was over- or undervalued, by comparing its central ERM rate against the D-mark with its PPP (purchasing-power parity). Most looked undervalued. The exceptions were the peseta and escudo (both overvalued by around 10%), the lira (still slightly overvalued even after its 7% devaluation) and sterling (overvalued by 3% at its central rate in the ERM, but 7% undervalued at DM2.65).

Column 3 shows the level of foreign reserves in terms of the number of months of imports they could buy. The fourth and fifth columns track budget deficits and inflation: the bigger these numbers, the greater the market pressure on a currency if the French vote against the Maastricht treaty. The sixth column is the forecast rate of economic growth in 1992: the slower the growth rate, the more domestic pressure

there is likely to be for a devaluation. Britain is the only country currently in recession, with GDP expected to shrink by 0.8% this year. The French economy, by contrast, is holding up well, with 2% growth predicted.

The final column suggests a ranking for currencies according to their overall risk of devaluation against the D-mark, taking into account all the individual factors. Most at risk was the Italian lira. Before its 7% devaluation, the lira was clearly overvalued; Italy, moreover, has severe budgetary problems and high inflation. Sterling was next in line, though the economic arguments for its fall from grace were less obvious. The currency was not overvalued. Unlike Italy, Britain's inflation is little higher than Germany's. Furthermore, British reserves were almost six times as large as Italy's—thanks partly to the 10 billion ecus that the Bank of England recently arranged to borrow and will now have to repay in devalued pounds. This week, however, the financial markets cared not a jot about economic fundamentals. The British Treasury's seemingly comfortable reserves were as nothing compared with speculators' firepower.

There were two other prime candidates for devaluation: the Portuguese escudo and the Spanish peseta. Portugal and Spain boast large reserves in relation to the size of their trade. But they also have the highest inflation rates in the ERM, and their currencies are overvalued.

The other five currencies look relatively safe. The French franc is in the bottom half of its ERM band and came under pressure on September 17th. But France's inflation is low, its budget deficit modest, and its currency undervalued against the D-mark. The same is true of the Irish pound and the Danish krone, and also of the Dutch and Belgian currencies, which keep within 1% of the D-mark rather than within the 2¼% band which most ERM members observe.

These are the core currencies that seem likely to slog on together regardless.

As *The Economist* went to press, only the peseta looked under immediate threat, but markets remained in turmoil. The only question was whether French voters would endorse Maastricht with enthusiasm, thus helping weaker currencies bounce back. Even that outcome, however, could provide only a short-lived tonic. For the markets now know that exchange rates are once again adjustable, ERM or no.

In the weeks ahead, Europe's exchange-rate mechanism will face even sterner tests than this week's terrible turbulence. Its survival in anything like its current form must be in doubt. Italy says it wants the lira to rejoin the ERM after the French vote; sterling's float looks likely to be longer. But what sort of ERM will there be to join?

Europe's weak-currency countries—albeit against their will—have done much to harm the exchange-rate mechanism. But blame must also rest with Europe's stron-

gest. The Bundesbank's grudging interest-rate cut gave critics cause to claim that the legendarily independent inflation-fighters had caved in to political pressure, without providing enough headroom to save the system's more fragile currencies. Perhaps Germany's central bankers had no choice. Yet they made things worse by gossiping about future devaluations, so sealing sterling's fate. The ERM can survive many things, but not sabotage by its strongest member.

A funny thing happened

OCTOBER 10TH *Throughout the turmoil in Europe's exchange-rate mechanism (ERM), the French franc seemed to have nine lives. We suggested why*

ON OCTOBER 5th the dollar fell to within a whisker of its all-time low of DM1.38; sterling fell briefly to less than DM2.40; and Europe's weaker currencies continue to hang on to the ERM by their fingernails. Throughout the crisis, the French franc has fared better. It is fragile, but for now looks out of danger.

The chart suggests why. It plots two interest-rate differentials: the gap between three-month domestic money-market rates and the corresponding Eurocurrency rate, and the gap between the domestic money-market rate and the rate banks charge their prime borrowers.

Since France has supposedly abolished its capital controls, arbitrage should ensure that the first of these gaps (measured by the white line) is roughly zero—as it was until the crisis of mid-September. Once the trouble began, the Euromarket rate exceeded the domestic rate by a big margin for nearly two weeks, before falling below it. This sign of friction in arbitrage across the two mar-

kets shows that implicit barriers to capital flows remain.

The other differential (the black line) is even more striking. Before the pressure on the franc built up, prime lending rates slightly exceeded money-market rates—as you would expect, for money-market rates influence the banks' cost of funds. In May, however, money-market rates moved higher than bank rates. At the end of September, when the run on the franc was at its worst, the gap widened to more than

four percentage points.

Conclusion: the banks were being told to hold their lending rates down and operate at a loss. Thus, market rates defended the currency, while bank rates were held down to spare the domestic economy. Such "moral suasion" is out of fashion—and probably unworkable—in Britain. Even in France it surely cannot last. But so far it has done its bit for franc and country.

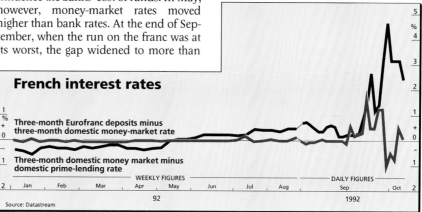

French interest rates

Three-month Eurofranc deposits minus three-month domestic money-market rate

Three-month domestic money market minus domestic prime-lending rate

WEEKLY FIGURES   DAILY FIGURES
Jan Feb Mar Apr May Jun Jul Aug Sep Oct
92   1992

Source: Datastream

A leap into the unknown

DECEMBER 26TH *A week before Europe's single financial market opened we looked at why, in practice, active retail cross-border trading seems years away*

THE sceptics seem to have been routed. As January 1st 1993 looms, most of the measures needed to create a single European market in financial services are in place, though some will come into effect only later. Since finance accounts for about 7% of the European Community's GDP, bulldozing national barriers (mainly in retail finance) that preserve inefficiencies should deliver big economic gains. A report for the European Commission by Paolo Cecchini in 1988 reckoned consumers might save more than 20 billion ecus ($25 billion) a

year. Yet those gains are to come at the expense of powerful financial intermediaries. No wonder many doubted the single financial market would ever be built.

The commission's plan to free financial services fell into two parts. The first, scrapping restrictions on capital movements, was implemented in 1990, though several EC countries were allowed to keep their barriers a bit longer. Recent troubles in Europe's exchange-rate mechanism may have reversed the momentum—both Spain and Ireland temporarily reimposed

capital controls. But the principle of free capital flows is now entrenched.

The second part was a series of "passport" directives to let financial intermediaries offer services across borders without setting up local subsidiaries. This went smoothly for banking: the directives were adopted in 1989. Insurance and stockbroking proved trickier. Insurance was held up by Germany, keen to maintain detailed product regulation. The investment-services directive was blocked by a battle between liberalising "North Sea" countries like Britain and France's "Club Med" group, anxious to protect local bourses.

Thanks to fast last-minute footwork by

the commission and by Portugal and Britain (which successively held the EC presidency in 1992), compromises have been found for these directives. Their implementation will now be later than January 1st 1993. Some countries have still longer derogations: foreign banks will not gain direct access to stock exchanges in Spain, Portugal and Greece until 1999, for example. But when the measures at last come into effect, firms should be able to compete across borders on reasonably equal terms.

Plenty of hurdles to a genuine single market will remain, however. The first is translating directives into national law. This can take time: Belgium and Spain, for instance, have missed the banking-directive deadline of January 1st. The commission also has to make sure that implementation is whole-hearted. Will Italy, for example, permit the investment-services directive to overturn its 1991 SIMS law, requiring brokers who sell shares to Italian nationals to be incorporated in Italy?

Then there are areas that still need EC action. Bank deposit-insurance schemes vary widely; a directive on the subject seems to be languishing. Cross-border payments systems work badly and slowly; the commission is looking at how to speed them up. A directive is promised on the exchange of information among national financial supervisors. Work continues on the harmonisation of insolvency and winding-up practices. The biggest gap of all is freeing pension funds to invest across borders; a draft directive may be presented next year.

The next frontier

Even if these gaps are filled, three other obstacles to a single market remain:

• **Tax.** This is by far the biggest. At a recent conference at the Centre for European Policy Studies in Brussels, a Belgian law professor, Marc Dassesse, suggested that if nothing were done to smooth out tax differences there might be less, not more, cross-border trading in financial services after 1992. Sales of financial products like life insurance and pensions are usually influenced by the tax treatment they receive, and are designed accordingly. Tax regimes differ from country to country. Another problem arises when taxes are withheld on income from securities. In theory, double-taxation agreements between EC countries should make it possible for an investor to buy foreign bonds without fear of disadvantage; in practice, refunds of excess tax can take years.

Tax barriers may prove particularly difficult to blow up, for two reasons. The first is a weird judgment handed down in 1992 by the European Court of Justice. In the Bachmann case, the court upheld Belgium's restriction of income-tax relief on life insurance premiums to policies bought from Belgian firms. Its rather odd grounds were that allowing tax relief on policies bought elsewhere would threaten the "cohesion" of Belgium's tax system. This decision could encourage other countries to use their tax systems to protect local firms. The commission is looking for a test case to reverse the Bachmann precedent. The alternative is legislation, but this is tricky. For the second reason why tax barriers may prove hard to budge is that tax measures, unlike financial-service directives, require unanimous approval by member countries.

• **The general good.** Another barrier is the flexibility that most directives give countries to apply local conduct-of-business rules to foreign firms, if some broad general good is invoked. The let-out is backed by case-law. A judgment by the European Court in 1986, for instance, let Germany impose restrictions on insurance products sold by foreign firms. But the court laid down that such measures must be non-discriminatory, must not duplicate rules to which foreigners were subject at home and must be no more stringent than required to produce the desired general good. Some fear nonetheless that countries will invoke the general good to justify restrictions which protect domestic markets. Relying on litigation to overturn such rules is chancy.

• **Culture,** the most pervasive barrier of all. Most retail customers are naturally conservative about which institutions they use. That tends to favour local firms over foreign ones, especially when foreigners find it hard to rival domestic distribution networks. There are also plenty of intangible blockages to foreign competition. State-owned banks, for instance, may have a head-start over foreigners. Cross-ownership between banks and industrial firms (especially widespread in Germany) entrench relationships and keep foreign institutions at bay.

Two other uncertainties may slow the spread of retail financial services. The first is currency risk. Until the autumn of 1992, this seemed to be disappearing, thanks to the success of the exchange-rate mechanism and the prospect of monetary union. Now it is back with a vengeance.

The second is the role of national regulators. The various directives, the commission and the courts should among them stop national regulation from being overtly discriminatory. But, as concerns about tax and the general good suggest, there may still be ways for national authorities to protect local firms. One solution may be to switch some regulation from domestic to Community institutions. That is working in competition policy, and the Maastricht treaty suggests a role in bank supervision for the European Central Bank. Today, though, even the most zealous Euro-enthusiasts jib at handing more powers to Brussels. True market-building is a mighty intrusive enterprise.

Passports to freedom		
EC directives	**Date agreed**	**Date applies†**
Banking	December 1989	January 1993
Insurance: non-life	June 1992	July 1994
life	November 1992	July 1994
Investment services	November 1992*	January 1996

*Common position agreed † Later, in some countries

Ride the wave

JUNE 20TH *The rich world's ageing population will affect international competitiveness as well as the structure of financial markets. It need not mean the end of growth*

DEMOGRAPHY has been kind to the rich world just recently. The baby boom that ran from peace in 1945 to the pill in the early 1960s created a big cohort of workers now in their prime. Roughly half of all workers are already in that phase of life—age 35 to 55—when they save most in order to buy homes, educate their children and, above all, anticipate old age. With plentiful labour and plentiful savings, economies can hardly fail to grow. And with relatively few old people, the burden of social-security taxes has been relatively light.

This bonanza will soon run out. Early next century the boom generation starts retiring. Each worker will have to support more elderly dependants. He will therefore be poorer, unless higher productivity permits wages to rise. Savings rates will fall, as retired baby-boomers consume their nest eggs. Fewer workers, less abundant capital: growth may no longer be taken for granted. Indeed, demography may depress growth just as growth is most needed, to meet the rising cost of pensions and health. Higher taxes to pay for grandparents may dampen incentives, so making the baby bust worse.

Troubled Japan, then troubled Europe

This pattern will affect just about all the rich economies, but at different times and with varying force. It will therefore shake up international competitiveness. Some countries are especially vulnerable, for they have no savings set aside in pension funds. Those that do have funds are protected, but not as completely as they hope.

As the Japanese have grown rich, they have become healthier and less fertile. Their life expectancy overtook that of Americans in 1982; it lengthens still. The result of this marvellous achievement is a marvellous crunch.

In 1990 11% of Japan's population was aged 65 and over, making it younger than America or Western Europe. By 2010 18% will be 65-plus, making Japan the greyest part of the rich world. Japan's diminishing workforce faces rising taxes to pay for multiplying grandparents. Recently Akio Morita, the chairman of Sony, has made much of the light social burdens on Japan's economy. They grow weightier all the time.

A 1986 IMF study reckoned that Japan's social-security costs, at 15% of GNP, were the lowest of the OECD's seven largest economies. By 2010, however, the study expected Japan's costs to have risen to 26% of GNP, around the middle of the pack. Japanese firms do not have long-established pension funds, so meeting these costs will cut into profits and wages all the more. Already pension contributions add $87 to the cost of each Honda car.

In America, by contrast, roaring markets have left many pension funds with more than enough money to meet their future liabilities. As a result, firms have taken "contribution holidays"; pensions add nothing to the cost of an American-built Ford or GM car. Meanwhile Japan's dramatic ageing hurts competitiveness in another way as well. In the past, the country's system of pay by rank, and rank by years of service, kept down labour costs because the workforce was young. Now it has the opposite effect.

After Japan the pension crunch will hit Europe, between 2020 and 2040. The OECD expects the EC's population (minus eastern Germany) to peak in 2000, at around 330m. Thereafter it may fall to 290m by 2050. Some reckon the decline will be steeper, because the OECD assumes that EC fertility will rise to the replacement rate of 2.1 children per woman of child-bearing age. In 1990 it stood at 1.57.

Worse, the EC (with the exception of Britain and Holland, which have large private-sector pension funds) has put aside even less than Japan for tomorrow's grandparents. A higher proportion of the cost of retirement—pensions and health—is paid for through public schemes than in Japan or America. In 1985 social-security pensions as a percentage of GDP came to 11.8% in continental Europe, compared with 7.2% in America, 6.7% in Britain and 5.3% in Japan.

France, Italy and Spain currently pay pensions to the old directly out of money earned by the young. Ageing will make this unsustainable. A French government paper recently predicted that, if the value of pensions remains unchanged, contributions will leap from the current 19% of payroll to between 31% and 42% by 2040—much worse than anything predicted for Japan. Italy is still more vulnerable. It spends nearly 14% of GDP on pensions now, up from 5% in 1960. With a budget deficit at 10.5% of GDP, its pensions are already unaffordable.

Shrinking funds

Rich economies that do have well-established pension funds—America, Britain,

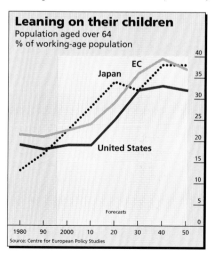

Leaning on their children
Population aged over 64
% of working-age population

Canada, Holland—may be tempted to feel smug. Yet they too are vulnerable. Capital will become scarcer, and—unless demand for it drops—more expensive to raise.

The median baby-boomer is now in his mid-30s; he will carry on saving hard for the next two decades. As a result, private-sector pension funds will grow rapidly. According to Michael Howell and Angela Cozzini of Baring Securities, each percentage-point rise in the share of the population over 45 years old results in a roughly equivalent rise in the ratio of institutional savings to GDP. In 1990 pension funds in Japan, the EC and North America amounted to $4.2 trillion. By 2000 they are expected to swell to as much as $11 trillion. Japan's funds are growing especially quickly; many were founded recently, and require large contributions to catch up with their liabilities.

These burgeoning funds plough their expanding riches into stockmarkets, pushing up share prices, making equity finance cheaper to firms. At the same time, the funds have contributed to dramatic financial innovation. That makes equity more convenient and, again, cheaper for firms.

It is no coincidence that this new sophistication is concentrated where there are funded pensions. Rich economies without funds—Germany, Italy—have primitive stockmarkets, never mind designer derivatives. Big German and Italian firms have got round this by raising money in New York or London. For smaller ones, the cost of equity finance has been higher than it might otherwise have been.

The funded economies will soon lose this advantage. For one thing, others will catch up, as states' inability to sustain unfunded pensions compels the private sector to do more. Mr Howell thinks the shift will transform Europe's smaller stockmarkets. Italy's market capitalisation-to-GDP ratio could rise by as much as 1,000% over the 1990s, Germany's by more than 300%. That compares with a projected 17% rise for Britain's established stockmarket.

More seriously, the funded economies will see their funds shrink, as ageing workers retire and spend their booty. When pension funds stop growing, some of the bounce and innovation in financial markets may fade. If the demand for capital remains the same or grows, duller equity prices—ie, higher equity yields—will push bond yields higher, and returns on cash. Real interest rates, which are already high in many countries, will rise. And demand for capital might well grow, for companies' first response to a shrinking workforce is often to replace labour with capital.

Call up the reserves

The greying of the baby-boomers and the potential pressure on capital costs present

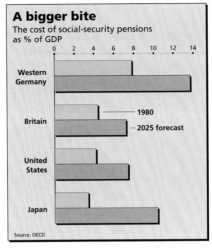

A bigger bite
The cost of social-security pensions as % of GDP

1980
2025 forecast

Source: OECD

special problems for Germany and Japan, too. Tax rules in both countries have encouraged firms to promise pensions without creating special funds to pay for them. Instead, firms save for their employees' retirement by making reserves. German firms can deduct their contributions from taxable profit; Japanese firms can write off part of them.

Reserves have one great attraction for companies: the employers themselves can decide how to use them. German and Japanese firms have invested pension savings in ways that further their business aims, rather than entrusting them to an investment manager who merely tries to earn a good return on them. One frequent use is to buy stakes in friendly companies, so both Germany and Japan are dominated by families of firms that hold stakes in one another. This web of cross-shareholdings shields firms from hostile takeover. It has bred strong relationships between producers and suppliers.

Outsiders complain that these family economies are hard to break into. That will change with demography. As retired workers multiply and active workforces shrink, firms will run down their pension reserves and find it harder to hang on to their friendly shareholdings.

Even before the baby-boomers retire, demography will punish Germany for its pension habits. Accounting rules there permit firms to set aside a smaller share of each worker's wages than do their British counterparts, until the worker reaches 55. For the ensuing decade, Germans have to contribute more: for a 64-year-old, Germans set aside 34% of pay compared with 26% in Britain, according to Hubert Peters of Coopers & Lybrand, an accounting firm. This will prove expensive as the workforce ages.

Beyond retirement, German firms are required by law to raise pensions in line with inflation. This liability is unaccounted for in their reserves. (Funded schemes, by contrast, set contribution rates high enough to cover inflation-proofing promises.) As German unification pushes up inflation, indexation is getting dearer.

Crunch medicine

For countries with unfunded pensions, population trends suggest a fiscal crisis. Others may face costlier capital and slower growth. Yet the history of extrapolation should temper the conclusion that calamity cannot be escaped. Malthus predicted demographic disaster: he feared too many people, not too few. In 1971 the Club of Rome warned that the world risked exhausting its resources: in real terms, commodity prices have declined steadily since.

The rich world may adapt remarkably well to the shock of falling numbers. Dwindling workforces and savings rates may turn out to stimulate innovation—the invention, refinement and application of technologies and business techniques. This is an uncertain area of economics; but most studies suggest that advances in knowledge account for just over half of total growth.

Equally, workers face higher taxes to pay for grandparents. But it does not inevitably follow that they will be worse off. The supply of labour is likely to contract more than the supply of capital: this increase in labour's relative scarcity should raise its price. Higher social-security taxes may also be offset by lower consumption taxes per worker, since the consumption base will expand with the growing ranks of old people. One econometric study* suggests that, in the period from 1985 to 2050, the wedge that tax and social-security contributions drive between pre-tax and after-tax wages will expand and then shrink in Japan and America, while widening in Germany (see chart on next page). If governments adopt policies to ease the shock of ageing, including later retirement, workers may actually find themselves better off in all three countries.

The need for government action presses most in continental Europe, because of the absence of funded pensions. Fortunately, Europe has plenty of scope to spread the burden of grandparents by putting more people to work. In 1990 just 60% of the EC's people in the 15-64 age band had jobs, according to Jorgen Mortensen of the Centre for European Policy Studies in Brussels; that compared with 71% in America and 73% in Japan. If Europe increased its employment ratio by ten percentage points, it would cancel out the 20m drop in its workforce due to demogra-

*"The Economic Dynamics of an Ageing Population". Alan Auerbach, Laurence Kotlikoff, Robert Hagemann, Giuseppe Nicoletti. National Bureau of Economic Research, No 1268. Reprinted from OECD Economic Studies

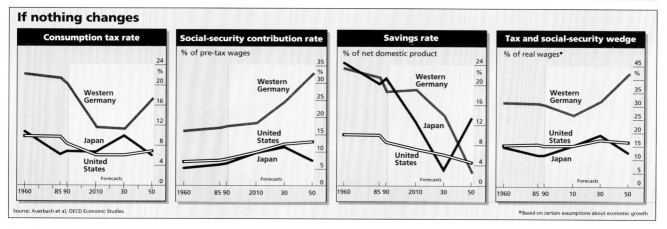

If nothing changes

Consumption tax rate	Social-security contribution rate	Savings rate	Tax and social-security wedge

Source: Auerbach et al, OECD Economic Studies

*Based on certain assumptions about economic growth

phy. This is not an impossible target. Over the past three decades, America has achieved that sort of rise.

Europe's low employment ratio reflects the large numbers of people who cannot find work and of women who choose not to work. As demography takes its toll on the labour supply, unemployment may come down—provided that the unemployed have the education and skills that firms are looking for. A drop in EC unemployment from, say, 9% to 6% would mean 6m extra people in jobs and contributing towards the health care and pensions required by the elderly.

Europe would still need to find another 14m workers to defeat demography. Young immigrants could help, but are sadly unpopular. Around 6m new workers could be recruited by raising female participation rates from the current roughly 50% to America's 60% (not to speak of Japan's 70%). Governments could encourage this, if it is possible to do so without discouraging child-bearing. The growing demands of the elderly will make it hard to find extra cash for creches, for example. And if grannies' needs push up taxes, women may grow less, not more, inclined to work.

Next, something could be gained from raising the retirement age. Here the scope for absorbing the demographic crunch is not confined to Europe. America's government has made mandatory retirement and discrimination on the basis of age illegal. Japanese firms are pushing the retirement age up from 55 to 60.

In Britain many firms, ordered by the European Court to equalise retirement ages for men and women, have seized the opportunity to equalise upwards: women will no longer collect a full pension at 60. Germany raised its retirement age to 65 in 1989. Denmark commendably makes both men and women struggle on to 67. Italy is the laggard. It has not got around to implementing plans to raise the retirement age to 65—up from 60 for men and 55 for women.

The other way to ease the crunch is to encourage saving. This is best done with a mixture of tax breaks and loud warnings that the state cannot be relied upon to provide for old age. Here, again, America and Japan show continental Europe the way forward.

Towards funding

In 1980 Japan reduced tax breaks for reserves that companies made to pay for pensions; this encouraged them to fund pensions. By 1988 the proportion of Japanese workers in private funded plans had risen from 31% to 38%. Japan's pension assets will grow by 16% a year in the near future, reckons Asset Strategy Consulting, a Californian firm. The more Japan keeps saving, the more easily it will absorb the cost of ageing. In parts of Europe this lesson has been learnt. Spain, Portugal and Belgium recently cancelled tax breaks for pension reserves. Germany has yet to do so.

In 1983 America's federal government laid down that, between 2000 and 2022, social security would pay out a smaller percentage of pre-retirement earnings. In theory this should goad Americans to participate more enthusiastically in private pension schemes. Not all the evidence so far is encouraging. The percentage of American workers in company pension plans has fallen from its peak of 49% in 1979 to 43% last year. That reflects declining unionisation and lower wages among less skilled workers. Big, union-dominated firms seem unlikely to regain their old share of the economy, so traditional occupational pensions may not recover either.

More flexible schemes, not based on the assumption of a lifelong career with one employer, may fill the gap. Tax-privileged company savings plans, which do not promise a fixed proportion of salary on retirement, are gaining ground in both America and Britain. So are personal pensions. In America the number of individual retirement accounts has shot up by more than 3m since 1981, when Congress opened them to workers who were also participating in company plans. Since 1988 over 4.5m Britons have started personal pensions. Similar schemes have been started recently in France and Switzerland.

To make the most of the new savings, governments must allow them to be invested freely. American and British pension schemes are already free to chase the best mixture of risk and return; other countries are slowly easing curbs on "risky" investments like equities and foreign securites.

Once freed, money may well flow disproportionately to developing economies. For this is the surest way to beat demography. The old world will buy a stake in the productive energies of the young one, so supplementing its income from the diminished cadre of young workers at home. This has happened before. Between 1890 and 1911 the French labour force was relatively static. Half of French savings went abroad, but only a quarter of British and a tenth of German savings. The current fashion among first-world money managers for investing in third-world markets is usually seen as reward for the developing countries' economic liberalisation. It also reflects the rich world's needs.

Tomorrow's providers

Contents

ECONOMICS

The dangers of disappointment

EVERY downturn in the world economy puts the liberal, non-interventionist school of policy-making on the defensive. When times are hard, popular opinion insists that governments must do something about it. In this respect, the downturn that continued in 1992 was no different from earlier recessions. In other respects, however, it was quite unusual. These peculiarities have not been well understood; they are causing the familiar demands for government-led solutions to be made with unfamiliar vigour; and for this reason the past disappointing year may prove more than ordinarily dangerous.

The main oddity about the present downturn is that it has lasted so long. In December 1991 forecasters at the OECD predicted that the American economy would grow by 2.2% in 1992; even that would have been unexciting, given that the economy grew by only 1% in 1990 and contracted by 0.5% in 1991. According to the most recent estimates, however, America's economy grew by only 1.8% in 1992—too slowly to reduce unemployment. The coming year will be better and the mood of disappointment may be lifting—but business and consumer confidence remain fragile.

In the other big economies, 1993 will probably be worse, not better, than 1992. Japan was expected to grow by 2.4% last year; its actual growth was 1.8%. The OECD's forecast for growth in 1993 has already been scaled back from more than 3% to 2%, and many domestic forecasters regard that as too optimistic. Germany was expected to grow by 1.8% in 1992; it managed only 1.4%. Growth in 1993, a year ago predicted to be more than 2%, is now expected to be less than 1%.

Slow growth and persistent or rising unemployment suggest to many a failure of government policy. The charge of "inaction" on the economy weighed heavily against George Bush during the campaign for the presidency, and may well have cost him victory. Elsewhere, almost throughout the rich, industrialised countries, voters seem equally dissatisfied with their governments. And the charge is not simply one of neglect or a reluctance to stimulate demand where necessary. In several areas governments have undertaken bold economic initiatives: to liberalise world trade by bringing the GATT talks to a successful conclusion; to stabilise Europe's currencies by means of the exchange-rate mechanism (ERM) of the European Monetary System; to promote economic transformation in the former Soviet Union with aid and co-operation on trade and finance. In each case, they have failed.

At the end of 1992, the GATT talks remained on the brink of collapse, with France threatening to veto a crucial farm-trade deal between America and the EC, and many

Gatt's conjuring Dunkel

Americans demanding that their new president should renegotiate many other aspects of the draft agreement. Riven by high interest rates in Germany and economic weakness elsewhere, the ERM had all but fallen apart, following a series of involuntary currency realignments and the humiliating withdrawal of sterling and the lira from the system. And, as the year drew to a close, Russia's principal architect of economic reform, Yegor Gaidar, was forced to resign as the country's prime minister; one reason for this setback, it is argued, was the failure of the West to deliver its promised aid.

All of a piece?

Some see these failures as connected—and charge western governments with a lack of purpose, born of a decade of liberal economics. Slow growth: because of a reluctance to apply "Keynesian techniques" of "demand management". Chaos over trade policy: because of a failure to see that the future lies not with the GATT, but with bilateral or multilateral deals among like-minded governments (deals, please note, that allow for the "activist" trade and industrial policies that the GATT frowns upon). Chaos in the currency markets: because Europe's governments abdicated their sovereignty over monetary policy—ceding it to Germany's Bundesbank, only to find, after all, that the markets would not allow them to duck their responsibility. Impending collapse in Russia: because the West's insistence on fiscal orthodoxy prevented it from helping Mr Yeltsin's government fast enough.

At every turn, it can thus be argued, conservative economics is to blame. But, the argu-

Calls for Keynes

ment continues, things are changing, with America leading the way. Where conservative economics shrugs its shoulders, Bill Clinton promises action to get the economy moving. Soon, if the GATT talks fail, governments will be free to design trade policies that are more "relevant" to their countries' needs. The unravelling of the ERM has brought activist macroeconomic policy back into fashion, especially in Britain. And Russia will benefit, it is argued, if reform slackens to a more manageable pace. At every turn, in other words, it is possible to draw precisely the wrong lessons from the disappointments of 1992.

Causes and remedies

The recession of the early 1990s was indeed, in one sense, a by-product of conservative economics. But the cause was not the abandonment of Keynesian policies of fiscal and monetary stimulus. For one thing, especially in America, it is debatable whether such policies were ever abandoned (witness Ronald Reagan's deficits). More important, recourse to such policies in the 1960s and 1970s showed, in country after country, that governments get it wrong. Typically, they stimulate demand after the economy has begun to recover, thus adding to inflation and preparing the way for the next recession. It would be a shame if the lesson has to be learned afresh. If Mr Clinton is as fiscally active as many of his supporters hope, just this fate may await America in the mid-1990s.

For a connection between conservative economics and the recent downturn, look not to any lack of macroeconomic activism, but to financial deregulation. During the past decade a process that started much earlier accelerated out of control. Throughout the capitalist world, the barriers between different sorts of financial institution—barriers of function, as well as of nationality—crumbled. This financial revolution was driven by innovation rather than by policy; in many cases, deregulation merely acknowledged that, thanks to new techniques, the old barriers no longer worked. The result was intense competition among banks and other institutions for new business—and much easier borrowing for firms and consumers. America's slow recovery, Britain's deep recession and the slowdown in Japan can all be blamed at least partly on debt, and on the strains it has imposed on those countries' financial systems.

Was financial deregulation therefore a mistake? Doubtless, with hindsight, it could have been done better. America's savings-and-loan fiasco showed, for instance, the perils of combining deregulation in one respect (ie, weaker supervision) with heavy intervention in another (ie, deposit insur-

High-tech money

ance). However, since the transformation in finance was driven ultimately by cheap computer power and advances in telecommunications, radical change was inevitable. So, in turn, was a difficult period of transition, as economies learned to live with their new financial freedoms, and made mistakes in the process.

Financial change, and the over-rapid accumulation of debt that went with it, were a huge economic disturbance all by themselves. But the world economy is also having to cope with another: the collapse of communism. The countries of the former Soviet block are engaged in an enormously difficult transition from state control to market economics. In some cases, as many have argued, the West can and should do more to help. The best way is not to pour in cash, but to open the West to the reforming economies' exports; this is only one reason why the Uruguay round of trade talks must succeed. But just as macroeconomic fine-tuning is one interventionist illusion, so it is another to suppose that western help will be decisive in Eastern Europe. Success or failure rests largely with the countries themselves, and with their determination to embrace capitalism once and for all.

Meanwhile, however, this change has imposed further strains on the West—chiefly through the effects of German unification on German economic policy. Because Germany's government chose not to finance unification through higher taxes, its budget deficit ballooned; that, together with big wage rises on both sides of the vanished border, led the Bundesbank to raise, and keep high, German interest rates. This happened at a time when other European economies (especially those with lots of debt) needed low interest rates: hence the crisis in the ERM. In 1993, however, as inflationary forces abate in Germany, interest rates there will fall, and the tensions in the ERM will subside. Faced with the difficulty of managing monetary policy outside the system, Britain's government may even remember why abdicating its "monetary sovereignty" (another illusion) seemed such a good idea.

In 1992 it became clear that two momentous transformations are going on in the world economy: one in global finance, the other in the former communist countries. In the long run, neither raises fundamental doubts about liberal capitalism; on the contrary, both are aspects of its historical success. In the short run, though, they have given the opponents of free enterprise their first real sustenance for more than a decade. With the GATT round at a critical juncture, the revival is badly timed. It remains to be seen how much harm will be done.

As we reported then

Explaining the mystery

JANUARY 4TH *Mainstream economics has had little to say about economic growth. Conventional methods beg as many questions as they answer. New ideas look more promising*

LITTLE to say about growth? Surely economists talk of nothing else? Forecasters argue indefatigably about growth this year (even this quarter) and next. Economic advisers tell ministers that this tax cut or that increase in public spending will be good for growth. To some critics, indeed, the trouble with economics is precisely that its obsession with growth leaves issues such as sustainability out of account. True enough: economists are interested in growth. The trouble is that, even by their standards, they have been terribly ignorant about it. The depth of that ignorance has long been their best-kept secret.

What has kept it hidden is the distinction between short-term growth and long-term. To predict whether an economy's output will increase from one year to the next, no proper theory of growth is required—nor is one used. Economists look first at the gap between an economy's current output and its capacity for production, then at the forces (consumer confidence, the stockbuilding cycle, the state of other economies and what have you) that will affect this gap in the months ahead. Out of that comes a forecast of growth.

Such forecasts are informative enough to be taken seriously by governments and financial markets. But they merely predict fluctuations around a trend, in the course of one business cycle. For long-term forecasting—estimating how far output will increase from one decade to the next—this approach is no use, because what matters here is not the gap between output and capacity, but the long-term trend of capacity itself.

Why has growth in productivity slowed in America in the past two decades? Did the reforms of the Thatcher years raise Britain's long-term rate of growth? Why have the economies of Japan, South Korea, Taiwan and the other Asian dragons expanded at an astonishing pace in the past 40 years, while much of Africa has stagnated or declined? How long will the ex-communist countries of Eastern Europe and the Soviet Union take to catch up with the West? To answer these questions needs something that economics has so far been unable to provide: an understanding of the forces that drive long-term growth.

Mainstream economics does have a theory of long-term growth. It was devised by Robert Solow, of the Massachusetts Institute of Technology, in the 1950s, and has been much modified and improved since then. But this so-called neoclassical theory is patently inadequate—so much so that its teachings have had virtually no influence on policy-makers. Only now are there signs of a change. The defects of the theory are the starting-point for new ideas which, with luck, may end the short-termism of economics and push long-term growth to the front of policy-makers' minds.

Assume better mousetraps

The heart of the neoclassical theory is an equation, called the production function, which says that the output of an economy depends on the amount of capital and labour employed. The theory also made some linked assumptions about this relationship. First, if you double the amount of both capital and labour, you will get twice as much output. This is the assumption of constant returns to scale. Second, if you add more capital to any given labour force, or more labour to any given stock of capital, you will get successively smaller increases in output: for each factor of production, holding the other fixed, there are diminishing returns.

These assumptions seemed plausible. Reassuringly, they were also consistent with the imagined world that economists call perfect competition. But they have a striking implication. In an economy where the stock of capital is rising faster than the labour force, the return to new investment (ie, to a further increase in the capital stock) should fall with time. For today's industrial countries, this has not happened: the returns to investment have been higher in the past few decades than they were in the late 19th and early 20th centuries.

In the same way, the theory implies that poor countries should find it easy to grow much faster than rich ones: investment in a country with little capital should spur output more powerfully than a proportionate amount of investment in a country with plenty. Again, the facts do not bear this out. The chart shows how GDP per head grew between 1960 and 1985 in 114 countries, ranked (poor-to-rich, left-to-right) by their GDP per head at the start of the period. If poor countries had found it easier to grow faster than rich ones, the points on this scatter-graph would cluster along a downward-sloping line, from top left to bottom right. Take the Asian dragons and the rich countries alone, and that seems to be so. Add in the rest of the world, however, and the trend vanishes.

To both these difficulties, the neoclassical theory has an answer: technological progress. Though returns diminish as more capital is added to the economy, that effect is offset by the flow of new technology. This could explain why rates of return have stayed high in the industrial countries and, arguably, why most poor countries have not grown faster than rich ones.

Yet the theory still looks odd. For instance, it implies that a sustained increase in investment will not, of itself, raise an economy's long-term rate of growth. As the capital stock grows, more of each year's investment must be set aside to replace old

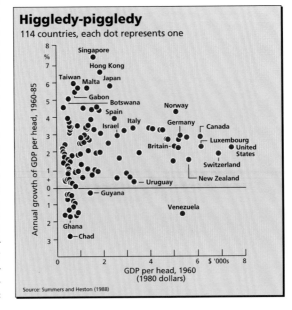

Higgledy-piggledy
114 countries, each dot represents one

Annual growth of GDP per head, 1960-85

Singapore
Hong Kong
Taiwan · Malta · Japan
Gabon
Botswana
Norway
Spain
Italy · Germany
Israel · Canada
Britain · Luxembourg
United States
Switzerland
New Zealand
Uruguay
Guyana
Venezuela
Ghana
Chad

GDP per head, 1960
(1980 dollars)

Source: Summers and Heston (1988)

machines as they wear out. An increase in investment, says the theory, will cause the capital stock to grow—but only until investment is again exactly sufficient to hold the amount of capital steady. So a permanent increase in investment—say, from 10% of GDP to 12% of GDP each year—will cause only a transitory increase in the capital stock, and hence in output. Ultimately, therefore, technological progress, not investment, is the engine of growth.

That makes it crucial to understand what technological progress is, and how it happens. Neoclassical theory has no convincing answer. It supposes, in effect, that new technologies rain down from heaven as random scientific breakthroughs. In statistical terms, technological progress is simply "the residual"—the thing that accounts for any growth that cannot be accounted for in other ways. When economists apply the theory to real economies, they get a poor fit. Typically, studies find that increases in capital and labour account for half or less of the growth in output. The rest is put down to technological progress or, as the residual is also known, "total factor productivity". The neoclassical theory can explain only half of what it purports to explain.

The endogenous innovator

For 30 years the larger part of economic growth was thus consigned to a black box; the best that mainstream economics could do was to offer a choice of fancy labels for it. Outside the mainstream, and in a disconnected way, economists worked for years on how to look inside the box and make sense of the contents. Only recently have these strands of work begun to be drawn together into a radically new theory of growth.

With hindsight, intellectual historians will probably date the revival of growth theory to 1983 and a University of Chicago doctoral thesis entitled "Dynamic Competitive Equilibria with Externalities, Increasing Returns and Unbounded Growth". Its author was Paul Romer, now a professor at the University of California at Berkeley and a fellow of the Canadian Institute for Advanced Research. Since then, he and a growing band of economists have built parts of a theory that seems likely to fit the facts. The work is still providing as many new questions as answers to old ones, but the outline of the next orthodoxy is now discernible.

Recall that the neoclassical theory takes into account just two factors of production: capital and labour. In effect, Mr Romer and his colleagues add another: knowledge. This makes the theoretical production function much more plausible, in several ways.

First, the new theory recognises that

From this . . .

knowledge (eg, about how to make things) can raise the return on investment. This accounts for the evidence on rates of return over time, and the non-convergence of growth rates among countries. Second, whereas in the neoclassical theory technological progress just happens, in the new theory knowledge is a factor of production which, like capital, has to be paid for by forgoing current consumption. Economies have to invest in knowledge in the same way that they invest in machines. Third, since past investment in capital may make it more profitable to accumulate knowledge, the new theory admits the possibility of a virtuous circle in which investment spurs knowledge and knowledge spurs investment. This in turn implies that a sustained increase in investment can permanently raise a country's growth rate—an idea that the traditional theory denied.

In short, the new theory is capable of explaining the world as it actually is. In his most recent work, Mr Romer has elaborated it, to take four factors of production into account: capital, unskilled labour, human capital (measured by years of education, for instance) and ideas (which might be measured by patents). Not everyone thinks that an improvement. But whether with three factors or four, Mr Romer's theory has one most uncomfortable consequence. It is flatly inconsistent with the idea of perfect competition—the theoretical underpinning not just of the neoclassical theory of growth but of a good part of modern economics. No wonder the old theory, despite its obvious drawbacks, survived so long.

Why is the new theory inconsistent with perfect competition? Because perfect competition means that firms are price-takers: they accept the price that rules in the market and cannot change it. Under constant returns to scale, as assumed by the old theory, this can be so. If firms cut their prices to win a bigger share of the market, they achieve no further economies of scale

and therefore risk losing money.

With three (or more) factors, the assumption of constant returns to scale no longer stands up. Taking all the factors together, the production function shows increasing returns: if you double all the factors, output more than doubles. In this theoretical world, firms can cut prices, raise output and—thanks to lower costs—make a bigger profit than before. With increasing returns, therefore, competition is imperfect—another way of saying that firms are price-setters, not price-takers. This change may seem insignificant. In fact it turns economic theory inside out.

Despite that, Mr Romer's approach is likely to form the basis of mainstream thinking on growth during the coming years. Many recent advances in economic theory have started from, or ended up at, the idea of imperfect competition. This is partly because economists now have the mathematical techniques that are needed to explore it.

Abandoning the assumption of perfect competition no longer means abandoning most formal analysis of economic systems. In this respect, the new growth theory is in tune with the times. The new theory is attractive in another way too. Because it simply brings new factors into the neoclassical production function, it can be seen—despite its far-reaching implications—as an extension of the existing orthodoxy. That makes it easier to digest.

Don't patch it up, chuck it out

If Mr Romer's approach is to be the new orthodoxy, its principal challenger will probably be a theory developed by Maurice Scott, of Nuffield College, Oxford. Though appealing, his theory is less digestible. The differences between the two shed light on the questions that the new generation of growth theorists will have to grapple with.

Mr Scott agrees that the neoclassical production function is no use. But rather

. . . to this . . .

than modify it, he wants to abandon it entirely. The core of his argument echoes an old debate in economics. He says that the measure of capital that appears in the production function is fundamentally incorrect.

The production function is concerned with the change in the net stock of capital—ie, with gross investment less depreciation. This implies that depreciation is a physical process that reduces the productivity of capital; as it were, a reduction in the number of machines in the economy. Wrong, says Mr Scott. Machines that are properly maintained can run at their designed capacity for years—long after the production function regards them as having evaporated. That is why some economists prefer a different measure of change, gross investment less scrapping. Wrong again, says Mr Scott. Machines are mostly scrapped when they become profitless. They may still be making things, but they are not adding to net output. So no productive capital is lost when they are scrapped.

This suggests that simple gross investment, without deductions, is the best measure of change in the capital stock. Yes—but there is a problem, says Mr Scott. It does not follow, as you might think, that the sum of all past gross investment provides a good measure of the stock, because there is no way of knowing how much each bit of old capital is contributing to total output. Regrettably, the idea of a production function that links the level of output to the level of capital must be abandoned. The best one can do is use changes in capital—gross investment—to explain changes in output.

Like Mr Romer, Mr Scott regards technological progress as crucial for understanding growth. In his theory, though, technological progress does not appear as a separate influence: he treats gross investment and technological progress as one and the same thing. At first sight, this view may seem puzzling, but there is plenty of evidence to support it. In a classic study,

"Invention and Economic Growth", Jacob Schmookler analysed nearly 1,000 major inventions in four industries (farming, railways, oil-refining and paper-making) around the world between 1800 and 1957. Where a stimulus for the invention could be identified, it was in nearly every case an economic one (ie, the invention was needed for some industrial purpose); in not a single case was the stimulus a particular scientific discovery.

Clearly, scientific progress broadens the possibilities for useful innovation. But the evidence suggests that, as Mr Scott says, "inventions are motivated and caused by similar factors to those which cause investment, that is, by their expected profitability". Innovation does not pour down from heaven, as in the neoclassical world. Nor is technological progress, or "knowledge", a commodity distinct from new capital, one that has to be separately invested in, as in the Romer models. Knowledge and investment, Mr Scott argues, are inextricably bundled up together.

In his most recent work, Mr Romer, in contrast, insists that the analytical effort of separating the two is worthwhile. Why have decades of heavy investment yielded so little in India and so much in South Korea and Taiwan? Perhaps because India's investment happened behind trade and foreign-investment barriers that kept out knowledge of new techniques and products, whereas the dragons' investment was mixed with a copious supply of new ideas. If nothing else, the debate over the new growth theories has revealed how bad economists have been at thinking about the national and global transmission of economic knowledge—production methods, designs for products and other forms of intellectual property.

Pure and applied

Much of the new work on growth has so far been abstract and theoretical; non-economists can fairly wonder whether the effort will prove worthwhile. It will. Already the new growth theory is yielding results.

Studies by Robert Barro, of Harvard University, and others have used Mr Romer's approach in empirical studies that compare growth rates in many different countries. In statistical terms, the approach seems to work. In economic terms, its results are striking: lack of human capital (ie, education), not lack of investment in physical capital, is what prevents poor countries from catching up with rich ones. In a similar vein, Daniel Cohen, of CEPREMAP in Paris, has estimated feasible long-term growth rates for the reforming economies of Eastern Europe (where standards of education are comparatively high); he arrived at growth rates of income per person that ranged between 3% and 3.5% a year.

Richard Baldwin, of Columbia University, has used a Romer model to estimate the effects of the EC's single-market programme on growth. Traditional growth theory simply could not address such a question: it contained no mechanism by which trade liberalisation (or indeed anything but "technological progress") could raise the long-term rate of growth. In the Romer framework, trade liberalisation is likely (though not certain) to raise the long-term rate of growth, by stimulating investment. The European Commission's Cecchini report concluded that the 1992 programme would raise the EC's output once and for all by between 2.5% and 6.5%, with no permanent effect on growth. Using the Romer framework, Mr Baldwin predicted not only a bigger one-off gain but also a permanent increase in the annual growth rate, of 0.25-0.9 of a percentage point.

As such studies multiply, the value of the new growth theory will become clearer. But it is to be hoped that its biggest effect will be to reorder the economic-policy agenda. This is influenced more than most politicians would admit by debates that they barely understand—witness Keynes and demand management after 1945, or Milton Friedman and the monetarism of the 1970s. The new growth theory confirms that governments are mistaken to concentrate so exclusively on the business cycle. If, however indirectly, it leads them instead to think harder about education, investment, research and development, trade reform, intellectual-property rights and so on, it will be a breakthrough indeed.

. . . to get this

Why a queue?

FEBRUARY 8TH *Queuing often seems as much a part of capitalism as it was of communism. Why make people queue when you can raise prices instead? Here is one answer*

ANYWHERE in the world where young Italians gather, you will find a black-market in Swatch watches. Buy one of the most sought-after models, the Chrono, the Scuba or the Automatic, for around £45 ($82), and you will have no trouble selling it again for twice as much. Take the watch to Italy, and it might fetch £300. Unsurprisingly, such Swatches are hard to come by. When stocks arrive they sell fast. Jewellers in London's Oxford Street limit sales of these models to one a customer. Some expect punters also to buy a second, less fashionable, model as part of the deal.

The people at Swatch know all about this black market; indeed, some observers think they encourage it. Each Swatch model is sold at a fixed price throughout the world. The price is deliberately low—and supply is restricted. Only a few of each popular model will go to any particular shop, or area, at a time. Production of these models tends to be limited, sometimes to as few as 150, but more typically to between 5,000 and 15,000.

This is puzzling: queues and black markets are usually signs of under-pricing. Swatch, it seems, could make more money either by raising its prices or by expanding supply. What reason might there be for a producer to let queues form? How could that possibly maximise the company's expected profits?

Gary Becker, of the University of Chicago, chewed this over while dining out. Why, he pondered, did one restaurant refuse reservations and have a queue outside at peak times, when a similar one across the street seemed never more than half-full? Why did the restaurant with the queue not charge more? Being a fine economist, Mr Becker decided not to ask, but to

work it out from first principles.

The answer, he argues, is that certain goods are demanded partly, if not primarily, because other people demand them, too. These are not "Giffen goods" (where the relationship between demand and price is peculiar because the good makes up a large part of the consumer's budget). Mr Becker is concerned with otherwise ordinary goods, that are preferred for their popularity. A queue is an indicator of this. People want to eat at restaurants that are "in", go to the "big" game, see the new block-busting movie, pretend to have read the latest best-selling novel. It need not be that the queue is a mark of quality: as far as Mr Becker is concerned, what is in or out may be entirely arbitrary. But once something has been designated as "in" (a cheap wristwatch, "A Brief History of Time"), people want it for that reason alone.

Perhaps this seems obvious. But next Mr Becker draws the demand curve for such a product, and suggests some striking properties. To begin with, Mr Becker surmises, the demand curve might slope downwards in the normal way: the cheaper the good, the greater the demand. But after a certain point, the good's popularity itself generates further demand, allowing the producer to raise the price and still sell more—that is, the demand curve slopes upwards. But eventually another turning-point is reached, where price rises begin to outweigh the good's popularity. Beyond this point, to achieve further increases in sales, prices must be cut again: in this third phase, the demand curve slopes downwards once more.

Consider the chart. Suppose it plots a restaurant's price per head against the number of would-be customers—and suppose, for the sake of argument, that this (small) restaurant can feed only 20 customers a night. In the first phase, where the demand curve slopes down, a price of £10 attracts 20 customers. This is the market-clearing price (supply equals demand). Further assume that this is the profit-maximising price: a higher one would deter too many customers, and a lower one would be pointless, because extra diners cannot be accommodated.

Now look across to the second phase, where the demand curve is sloping up again, thanks to the crowd effect. A price of £10 a head, together with its new "in" status, enables the restaurant to attract 60

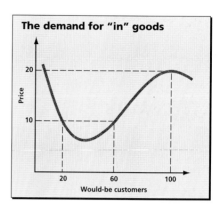

The demand for "in" goods

would-be customers—most of whom are turned away. Note, however, that unlike the combination of £10 and 20 customers, the combination of £10 and 60 would-be customers is not a profit-maximising one. Why? Because the demand curve is now rising. The curve says that if there were 100 would-be customers, each would be willing to offer £20 to be one of the lucky 20 to get in. Since the curve slopes down again beyond that point, the combination of £20 and 100 would-be customers is precisely the one that will maximise profits.

So the chart suggests that there may be pairs of profit-maximising equilibriums for each producer of crowd-effect goods: a "bad" equilibrium with unused capacity, and a "good" one with queues. The question is, if you are in a bad one, what do you need to push you to a good one? Plausible answers might be a willingness to gamble on enough promotional spending to start a bandwagon, and luck.

In theory, as in life, you would expect bad equilibriums to be extremely common, and good ones extremely rare. To see why, return to the chart. Consider what happens when a restaurant in a good equilibrium raises its prices to trim its queues a little: at a price just pennies higher than £20, demand crashes back to almost nothing. A good equilibrium is highly unstable. The £20 price had been supported by a bubble of popularity, which then popped, sending demand down to its "real" level. This could explain why producers of "in" goods often choose not to increase supply: investing in extra capacity is risky.

For a firm in a bad equilibrium, a small change in price causes only a small change in demand—the normal case. In a bad equilibrium, at least you are secure. Owners of fashionable restaurants with apparently silly pricing policies may well have economic theory on their side—and Mr Becker outside queuing to get in.

A short history of inflation

FEBRUARY 22ND
Today inflation is accepted as an unavoidable fact of life: if politicians promise stable prices, they must be insincere. Yet, historically, inflation is not at all normal

Consumer prices
1820=100
(Germany rebased twice: 1924*=100 and 1948†=100)
Log scale

Germany   United States

1,000
500
250
100
50

1820 30 40 50 60 70 80 90 1900 10 20 30 40 50 60 70 80 90
* Reichsmark introduced   †D-mark introduced, second half 1948

SINCE 1933 consumer prices have risen by 950% in America and by 4,000% in Britain. To put this another way, the dollar is today worth only 10 cents in 1933 money, and the pound is really worth a paltry 2½p. Even the supposedly cast-iron D-mark has lost two-thirds of its value since it replaced the worthless Reichsmark in 1948.

Since prices have risen almost continuously since 1933, most people today expect that prices will continue to rise every year. In fact history shows that inflation is far from "normal".

The charts show consumer prices from 1661 in Britain and from 1820 in America and Germany. Official figures do not exist that far back, but various series (of admittedly varying quality) can be linked together to give a broad picture of price movements over the centuries. Typically, the older indices covered only food and housing, and excluded services.

In the years before 1933, prices fell in Britain and America in more years than they rose. The longest unbroken period of rising prices in both America and Britain lasted only six years. Germany's hyperinflation in 1922-23 (when the inflation rate was over 1 billion %) is well known. More interesting is the fact that unlike America and Britain, where prices drifted downwards during the 19th century, in Germany prices doubled.

After falling by 40% between 1820 and 1900, American prices more than doubled during the first world war. But by the early 1930s the average price level had fallen back to its level in 1820.

The British figures, covering the longest period, are the most revealing. During the three centuries to 1933, there were only six occasions when prices increased for more than three years in a row, mostly during wars, when government borrowing soared. Prices peaked in 1813, during the Napoleonic wars, but by the end of the 19th century had more than halved again. As in America, prices surged during 1914-20 but then fell back. By 1933 prices in Britain were hardly changed from their 1660s levels.

Although it is true to say that Britain's general price level was broadly stable over the three centuries as a whole, the annual inflation rate was highly volatile from one year to another, with rates of plus or minus 10% quite common. Today, when economists talk about price stability being the only sensible goal for central banks, they mean that the price level should be stable from one year to the next, not just over a decade or so.

So far as economic growth is concerned, the volatility of inflation matters as much as its level. An inflation rate which averages 0%, but which swings from plus to minus 10%, is as damaging as one that swings between 10% and 30%—the more volatile inflation is, the more uncertainty it creates, and this discourages investment. Moreover, even if prices are broadly stable over a period as a whole, falling prices are bad for investment and growth. Nominal interest rates cannot fall below zero, so falling prices result in painfully high real interest rates.

Price stability, however, is not necessarily the same as zero inflation as measured by consumer-price indices. These indices, which measure the weighted average of price changes for a fixed basket of goods and services, tend to overstate the true rate of inflation for two reasons.

• First, they do not adjust fully for im-

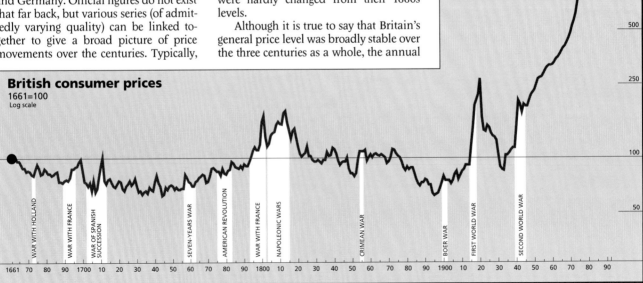

British consumer prices
1661=100
Log scale

2,500
1,000
500
250
100
50

WAR WITH HOLLAND   WAR WITH FRANCE   WAR OF SPANISH SUCCESSION   SEVEN-YEARS WAR   AMERICAN REVOLUTION   WAR WITH FRANCE   NAPOLEONIC WARS   CRIMEAN WAR   BOER WAR   FIRST WORLD WAR   SECOND WORLD WAR

1661 70 80 90 1700 10 20 30 40 50 60 70 80 90 1800 10 20 30 40 50 60 70 80 90 1900 10 20 30 40 50 60 70 80 90

provements over time in the quality of goods and services. Some of the rise in a price index may reflect better-quality hi-fi equipment, say, rather than general cost pressures.

• Second, in many countries the weights used to combine the different goods are often out of date. Britain updates its weights every year, but in America they are revised only every ten years (the current index is based on 1982-84); Germany's index is based on 1985. This exaggerates price rises over time, as it does not allow for changes in consumption patterns in response to changes in prices—consumers shift away from goods that are becoming compara-

tively more expensive towards cheaper alternatives.

So would you recognise price stability today if you saw it? Central banks, such as the Reserve Bank of New Zealand, define price stability as 0-2% inflation. A zero inflation rate reported by officialdom may in fact imply falling prices.

In praise of Hayek

MARCH 28TH **In 1992 one of the giants of 20th-century economics and political philosophy died. We paid homage to a staunch defender of liberalism and lifelong scourge of communism**

LIKE Maynard Keynes, Friedrich von Hayek achieved fame less for what he wrote than for what others said he wrote. The economic philosophy he developed over six decades, and especially during the 20 years he spent at the London School of Economics after 1931, was not, as so many now suppose, "neo-conservatism". Still less was it the underlying rationale for Thatcherism or Reaganomics, whatever those might be. And as it happens, the supposed "godfather of monetarism" had no time whatever for the assumptions on which that narrow, technocratic doctrine is based. None of these labels fits the great man. Call him instead an original thinker in the tradition of classical liberalism—perhaps the century's finest.

Much of Hayek's work is difficult; all of it is idiosyncratic. His writings seem especially peculiar to economists trained in the modern Anglo-American way, because Hayek rejected that school's paradigm: the idea of a static system in which certain stable properties (many buyers, many sellers, perfect information, homogeneous goods) yield certain stable results (an optimal allocation of resources). Hayek was interested in markets and economies as systems in flux. In his scheme, sequences of events, not states of affairs, were the object of study. Anglo-American economics starts by abstracting from change and time—and is then obliged to reintroduce them, with difficulty, to make its analysis more informative. Hayek, and others of the so-called Austrian school, put change and time at the centre from the outset.

Other themes seem to follow naturally from that perspective. They recur in almost everything Hayek wrote.

The most crucial is the notion of a market as a process of discovery. Modern economies are vastly complicated. Somehow they must process immense quantities of information—concerning the tastes and incomes of consumers, the outputs and costs of producers, future products and methods of production, and the myriad in-

terdependences of all of the above. The task of gathering this information, let alone making sense of it, is beyond any designing intelligence. But it is not beyond the market, which yields "spontaneous order" out of chaos. Hayek looked on the miracle of the invisible hand with the same delight as

Adam Smith. He celebrated it anew, and made it his mission to understand it.

A related idea from his early writings reappeared, after a pause, with new clarity in his later works—and especially in his last book, "The Fatal Conceit", published in 1988. Hayek was always at pains to emphasise that civilisation did not come about by design: rather, it is human actions, with consequences both intended and (more often) unintended, that yield another sort of spontaneous order. Systems of human interaction are in competition with each other. Some thrive; others fail. With time, and many a reversal, history chooses the winners. (Perhaps that sounds familiar: Francis Fukuyama, au-

thor of a best-seller, "The End of History and the Last Man", owes a debt to Hayek as well as to Hegel.)

Hayek brought these ideas—the market as a processor of information, natural selection as a filter for systems of interaction—together in his critique of socialism. Like Smith, he took a kinder view of human nature than other writers in the liberal tradition. He asserted that, within small groups, co-operation is the instinctive mode of human interaction. Such groups depend on altruism and loyalty to survive; at that level, those traits are successful. But as the range of interaction extends, this sort of co-operation is no longer feasible. The socialist fallacy—the "fatal conceit"—is to try to stretch small-group virtues such as loyalty and selflessness too far.

Co-operation makes impossible demands on the ability of large groups to gather and process information; competition is the only way to regulate interaction on this scale. The attempt to extend co-operation beyond its natural limits is not just doomed to fail, it is also extremely dangerous. Competition requires no designer; co-operation on the large scale does. Socialism, the most ambitious and misguided form of large-scale co-operation, cannot be implemented without a strong central authority. Hence another Hayekian theme: economic and political freedom are tied together.

Hayek carried his distrust of the state to an implausible extreme. He argued, in effect, that governments could never legitimately pursue goals of their own—not even on behalf of "society" (a term he disliked). Goals and values are for individuals themselves to choose. The state ought not to be a policy-maker with an agenda, but an arrangement of rules that allow people to go about their business in peace. Hayek was especially worried about the appearance of legitimacy that majoritarian democracy lends to the interventionist state. Where, he asked, is the minority's defence against the power of the majority? On Hayek's view, most of the economic powers that modern governments take for granted—from industrial policy to redistribution of income—are not merely ill-advised but immoral.

Few could find that position satisfactory. The modern state may presume too much—but to deal with some economic ills, collective action (and hence the coercion that Hayek detested) is almost universally agreed upon. In some cases, moreover, it is simply inescapable. Hayek's greatest weakness was that he had almost

nothing to say about market failure. This justification for state action is often falsely invoked—but sometimes the argument is convincing. In cleaning up the environment, for instance, the state must indeed intervene on behalf of society: externalities mean that free markets are unable to discover the outcomes that individuals seek.

If there is one label that Hayek would have accepted with pride, it is this: scourge

of socialism. For decades his tireless attacks on what he saw from the beginning to be a profoundly evil system won him little praise from fellow economists. In the 1960s and 1970s he was a hate-figure for the left, derided by many as wicked, loony, or both. How marvellous it is that he lived to see communism collapse, as he said it would, with all its corruption, insanity and injustice laid bare.

Big MacCurrencies

APRIL 18TH *How do you know when a currency is "overvalued" or "undervalued"? One answer is to examine its purchasing power over a basket of commodities, available internationally. A Big Mac, for instance*

THE ECONOMIST'S Big Mac index was first launched in 1986 as a ready reckoner to whether currencies are at their "correct" exchange rate. It is time for our annual update.

The case for munching our way around the globe on Big Macs is based on the theory of purchasing-power parity. This argues that the exchange rate between two currencies is in equilibrium when it equalises the prices of an identical basket of goods and services in both countries. Advocates of PPP argue that in the long run currencies tend to move towards their PPP.

Our basket is simply a Big Mac, one of the few products that is produced locally in a great many countries. Many of our readers ask why we do not simply derive our PPPS from different cover prices of *The Economist*. But because the magazine is not printed in every country, local prices would be distorted by transport and distribution costs.

The Big Mac PPP is the exchange rate that leaves hamburgers costing the same in each country. Comparing the current exchange rate with its PPP gives a measure of whether a currency is under- or overvalued.

For example, the average price of a Big Mac in four American cities is $2.19. In Japan our Big Mac watcher had to fork out ¥380 ($2.86) for the same gastronomic delight. Dividing the yen price by the dollar price gives a Big Mac PPP of $1=¥174. On April 10th the actual dollar exchange rate was ¥133, which implies that on PPP grounds the dollar is 24% undervalued against the yen.

On similar sums, the dollar is 20% undervalued against the D-mark, with an estimated PPP of DM2.05. The dollar has moved further away from its PPP over the past

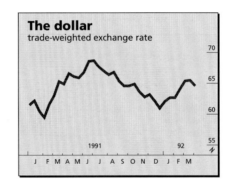

The dollar
trade-weighted exchange rate

year: in April 1991 it was undervalued by only 13%. How can the dollar have become more undervalued when its actual exchange rate has barely budged? The answer lies in price movements. Big Mac prices have fallen by an average of 3% in America over the past 12 months; in Germany they have risen by 5%.

As the table shows, the dollar seems to be undervalued against most currencies. The exceptions are the currencies of countries where Big Macs cost less in dollars than in America: the Australian dollar, the Brazilian cruzeiro, the Chinese yuan, the Hong Kong dollar, the Hungarian forint and last, but by no means least, the rouble. Moscow is the best place for burger-bargain hunters: a Big Mac costs only 59 cents at the market exchange rate. In other words, the rouble is undervalued by 73% against the dollar.

An addition to our table this year are three Latin American currencies. The Big Mac index signals, for example, that the Argentine peso is overvalued against the dollar (though much less so against other currencies). Brazil's cruzeiro, however, looks cheap.

Looking at cross rates within Europe suggests that most of the ERM currencies are overvalued against the D-mark on PPP grounds. For example, sterling's PPP is DM2.59, compared with its central rate of DM2.95. This supports those who argue that sterling joined the ERM at too high a rate. Other estimates, however, put sterling's PPP at up to DM3.10.

Some readers find the Big Mac index hard to digest. To be sure, hamburgers are primitive predictors of exchange rates. Local price differences may be distorted by taxes, property costs or trade barriers. Nevertheless, the Big Mac can provide a rough and ready guide to how currencies might move over the long term. Experts who calculate PPPs by more sophisticated means

The hamburger standard

Country	Prices* in local currency	Implied PPP** of the dollar	Actual exchange rate 10/4/92	% over(+) or under(-) valuation of dollar
Argentina	Peso3.30	1.51	0.99	-34
Australia	A$2.54	1.16	1.31	+13
Belgium	BFr108	49.32	33.55	-32
Brazil	Cr3,800	1,735	2,153	+24
Britain	£1.74	0.79	0.57	-28
Canada	C$2.76	1.26	1.19	-6
China	Yuan6.30	2.88	5.44	+89
Denmark	DKr27.25	12.44	6.32	-49
France	FFr18.10	8.26	5.55	-33
Germany	DM4.50	2.05	1.64	-20
Holland	Fl 5.35	2.44	1.84	-24
Hong Kong	HK$8.90	4.06	7.73	+91
Hungary	Forint133	60.73	79.70	+31
Ireland	I£1.45	0.66	0.61	-8
Italy	Lire4,100	1,872	1,233	-34
Japan	¥380	174	133	-24
Russia	Rouble58	26.48	98.95†	+273
Singapore	S$4.75	2.17	1.65	-24
S.Korea	Won2,300	1,050	778	-26
Spain	Ptas315	144	102	-29
Sweden	SKr25.50	11.64	5.93	-49
United States††	$2.19	–	–	–
Venezuela	Bs170	77.63	60.63	-22

Source: McDonald's *prices may vary locally, **purchasing-power parity: local price divided by dollar price, † Market rate, †† New York, Chicago, SanFrancisco and Atlanta

come up with results that are not radically different. Indeed, many of them suggest that the dollar is even more undervalued than the hamburger standard indicates.

The message, therefore, is that the greenback should rise in the future. But when? Exchange rates can deviate significantly from PPPs for long periods.

Yet other economic fundamentals now seem to point in the same direction. Most currency-watchers expect interest rates to rise in America over the next 12 months as the economy picks up steam. Germany's interest rates may fall as its economy continues to stall. If so, interest-rate differentials will move in favour of the dollar and the greenback will rise. It has already gained almost 10% against the yen and the D-mark since January, and most forecasters are betting it will climb further this year.

The snag is that forecasters used the same arguments about relative interest rates a year ago, and that expectation helped to push the dollar up by 27% against the D-mark in the five months to July. As America's recovery faltered, the Fed cut interest rates again, and inflation fears caused Germany's Bundesbank to raise its rates further. The dollar slid, to end the year little higher than it began.

Forecasts of a firmer dollar are therefore only as firm as forecasts of economic recovery. Wise investors will not hold their breath—and will grab those cut-price Big Macs while they can.

Summers on sustainable growth

MAY 30TH **In the spring we ran an article which discussed the claim that economics and the environment do not mix. We disagreed—but too mildly for Lawrence Summers of the World Bank, who wrote this letter in reply**

SIR—You accept too credulously the arguments of those who criticise economic approaches to the environment. Certainly, the idea of sustainable development has drawn attention to environmental problems that were ignored for too long. But there is no intellectually legitimate case for abandoning accepted techniques of cost-benefit analysis in evaluating environmental investments, either by using abnormally low discount rates or, worse yet, by invoking special criteria regarding sustainability.

The argument that a moral obligation to future generations demands special treatment of environmental investments is fatuous. We can help our descendants as much by improving infrastructure as by preserving rain forests, as much by educating children as by leaving oil in the ground, as much by enlarging our scientific knowledge as by reducing carbon dioxide in the air. However much, or little, current generations wish to weigh the interests of future generations, there is every reason to undertake investments that yield the highest returns.

That means holding each investment, environmental and non-environmental, to a test of opportunity cost. Each project must have a higher return (taking account of both pecuniary and non-pecuniary benefits) than alternative uses of the funds. Standard public non-environmental investments like sewage-treatment facilities, education programmes, or World Bank transport projects have returns of more than 10%. Most private investors apply even higher "hurdle rates" in evaluating investments, generally 15% or more, because higher-return alternatives are available.

Once costs and benefits are properly measured, it cannot be in posterity's interest for us to undertake investments that yield less than the best return. At the long-term horizons that figure in the environmental debate, this really matters. A dollar invested at 10% will be worth six times as much a century from now as a dollar invested at 8% (see table).

The premise that our first priority should be to do more for our descendants is, anyway, debatable. Surely it is ethically relevant that our grandchildren will in all

Miraculous interest		
The value over time of $1		
	invested at:	
for:	8%	10%
10 years	2.2	2.6
20	4.7	6.7
30	10	17
40	22	45
50	47	117
75	321	1,272
100	2,200	13,781

likelihood be much better off than we are. While nobody can accurately predict long-term growth rates, remember that standards of living are three times higher than 60 years ago in the United States, seven times higher in Germany and almost ten times higher in Japan. Should my American grandparents have reduced their standard of living, when life was considerably more nasty, brutish and short than now, to leave raw materials in the ground for my benefit?

To think so implies an odd morality. What is the better course for rich countries: to put more aside for a posterity that will be far richer than we are, or to do more to help the world's poor now? I, for one, feel the tug of the billion people who subsist on less than $1 a day in 1992 more acutely than the tug of future generations.

Some environmentalists talk about stewardship. They say we have an obligation to pass on to our children what has been passed on to us. Of course, we all wish our children to be better off than we are. But any investment that would make the difference between rising and falling living standards would pass a cost-benefit test at standard discount rates.

The reason why some investments favoured by environmentalists fail such a test is that their likely effect on living standards is not so great. Take the most serious global problem—climate changes from greenhouse gases. In the worst-case scenario of the most pessimistic estimates yet prepared (those of William Cline of the Institute for International Economics), global warming reduces growth over the next two centuries by less than 0.1% a year. More should be done: dealing with global warming would not halt economic growth either. But raising the spectre of our impoverished grandchildren if we fail to address global environmental problems is demagoguery.

Some suggest that whatever happens to an economy's productive potential, it is always wrong to damage any part of its natural patrimony irreversibly. But what is irreversible damage? Clearly, cutting down some trees and burning some scarce natural gas is all right, because sufficiently close substitutes are available. At the other extreme, no sane person would favour causing the extinction of hundreds of species to build a dam, if other poverty-reducing strategies were available. In every case, the question returns to trade-offs between costs and benefits. Chanting the mantra of sustainability is not enough.

In applying the standard cost-benefit paradigm to the environment, however, two issues do come up.

First, some advocate treating environmental investments differently, on the grounds that they are alternatives to consumption, not to other investments. This partly depends on how additional environmental spending is financed. But that is essentially a political judgment. Honest analysts should not endorse projects if proposals yielding higher returns are available. And given the extremely high interest rates at which most of the world's consumers are willing to borrow, consumption should not in any case be lightly sacrificed.

Second, it is argued that environmental damage is both uncertain and possibly irreversible. The right way to allow for the unusual riskiness of environmental decisions is to estimate the benefits of environmental investment generously, making special allowance for the value of options that they preserve. However plausible it may seem to reduce the discount rate to allow for risk, this reflects an elementary fallacy. To apply a specially low discount rate merely increases the weight attached to risks in the distant future as compared with risks in the near future—which makes no sense.

Environmentalists who point to the damage done by dams, power plants and roads evaluated according to standard economic criteria have a point. The answer does not lie in blanket sustainability criteria, or in applying special discount rates, but in properly incorporating environmental costs into the appraisal of projects. The grim fact is that no careful analysis was done of many of the projects which environmentalists condemn. The world's problem is not too much cost-benefit analysis, but too little that is done well. Plenty of environmental improvements can pass rigorous cost-benefit tests. There is no need to cook the books.

LAWRENCE H. SUMMERS
WORLD BANK

Future imperfect

JUNE 13TH *Economic forecasters had a bad year in all the industrial countries—but nowhere more so than in Britain. Are forecasts growing less accurate? Actually, we argued, no*

WHILE Albert Einstein is queuing to enter heaven, he meets three men. He asks about their IQs. The first replies 190. "Wonderful," exclaims Einstein. "We can discuss my theory of relativity". The second answers 150. "Good," says Einstein. "I look forward to discussing the prospects for world peace". The third mumbles 50. Einstein pauses."So what is your forecast for GDP growth next year?"

This old joke sums up most people's view of economic forecasters. Their reputation has been severely dented of late, not least because they failed to predict the strength of the world economic boom in the late 1980s and then, worse still, failed to warn of the consequent recession.

Are forecasts becoming less accurate? Financial deregulation and globalisation have made it harder to track the economy, so you might expect the answer to be yes. The facts, however, suggest otherwise.

The first table judges the forecasting record of Britain's Treasury over the past 13 years. It shows the mean absolute error (ie, adding up the differences between forecast and outturn each year and ignoring its sign) of forecasts made each March for growth, inflation and the current account in the year ahead. During 1985-91 the average error for growth was 0.7 of a percentage point, compared with 1.2 points in the previous six years. The Treasury's forecasts of inflation and the current account also seem to have improved.

But such tests depend upon the time horizon. Looking at the forecasts which the Treasury made in the previous November of each year, its GDP forecasts for the period since 1985 seem to be more off beam than before, though it has got better at predicting inflation.

Victor Zarnowitz, an economist at the University of Chicago, has studied a large number of American forecasts over the past 30 years. Taking the mean absolute error of predictions made at the end of each year for the year ahead, he finds that the accuracy of growth forecasts has hardly changed (see lower table). Inflation forecasts have become less accurate since the 1960s—but that is not surprising, given the surge in inflation in the 1970s.

Mr Zarnowitz also compared the average error of these forecasts with the error from forecasts using a crude extrapolation of four-year moving averages of output and inflation. Professional forecasters will be relieved to know that the extrapolations proved much less accurate.

British economic forecasts

Mean absolute error of forecasts, % points

Treasury forecasts* made in:	1979-84	1985-91
March		
GDP	1.2	0.7
Inflation	1.4	1.2
Current account†	1.0	0.9
November		
GDP	0.5	1.4
inflation	2.7	1.4
Current account	1.0	1.2

* for year ahead † as % of GDP
Sources: S.G Warburg; updated by *The Economist*

American economic forecasts

Mean absolute error of forecasts*, % points

	1959-67	1962-76	1969-89
GDP	1.2	1.2	1.1
Inflation	0.6	1.0	1.1

* Selection of private and government forecasts   Source: Zarnowitz

Further evidence that American forecasters have improved their aim comes from *Blue Chip*, an American newsletter, which polls about 50 economists each month. The mean absolute error of October forecasters for GDP growth in the following year fell from 1.1 percentage points in 1977-83 to 0.9 of a point in 1984-91.

Forecasters may be no worse than they used to be, but that is still not good enough. In particular, their biggest blunders tend to be at turning points, when the economy dips into recession—the very time when forecasts are most needed.

Conventional forecasting relies upon a computer model built from the economist's favourite theory about how the economy works. Using past data, he tries to get the best fit for hundreds of equations that attempt to explain the relationships between economic variables. Assumptions about such things as tax rates, which cannot be forecast because they are decided by governments, are then plugged in and the computer cranks out an economic forecast.

Disappointment with such models has encouraged some economists to test different kinds of crystal balls. Two developments pursued in America over the past decade have attracted growing interest.

• The first is **vector auto-regressive models** (VARS). These are much simpler, with far fewer variables than standard macroeconomic models. The process makes virtually no use of economic theory to establish causal links. Each variable is "explained" largely by detecting patterns in its own statistical history; to make a prediction, the forecaster extrapolates this history into the future. Experience in America suggests that VAR models may be helpful in predicting turning points.

• A second development is the use of **financial-spread variables** (eg, the gap between short- and long-term interest rates) and **business-confidence surveys** as leading indicators of activity. Past experience suggests that financial indicators are also good at spotting turning points. For example, if short-term interest rates rise relative to long-term rates, this typically heralds an economic slowdown.

More recently, several British economists have gone down the same road. Gavyn Davies, an economist at the London branch of Goldman Sachs, has attempted to incorporate both of these techniques into forecasts for the British economy. Almost all standard economic models completely missed Britain's latest recession. But, claims Mr Davies, his new model, which uses both VAR and financial-spread indicators, would have given at least 12 months' warning of recession, if it had been available. It would also have predicted each of the previous two recessions and would have given no false alarms of recession during the past two decades.

Only time will tell whether VAR methods will continue to beat standard models. Their weakness is that they work only for as long as statistical relationships hold true, and in the past such models have often broken down almost as soon as they were used. In fact, this is just an extreme case of a general difficulty with all models based on past experience: they cannot cope with structural changes in the economy. Unprecedentedly high levels of debt in America and Britain, for instance, may have weakened the benefits of lower interest rates, which may explain why recovery has taken longer to happen than most economists predicted.

It is probably best to see VAR models and financial indicators not as alternatives to macroeconomic models, but as complementary, above all in helping to spot turning points. Economic forecasting will never be 100% accurate, except by luck. But armed with every tool available, an economic forecaster just might earn his keep.

Poor odds, high stakes

JUNE 27TH **The GATT talks resumed after their pause in the winter, but made painfully little progress during the year. During the summer, we paused to reflect on what was at stake**

"FATIGUE, frustration, disenchantment." That is how Arthur Dunkel, director-general of the General Agreement on Tariffs and Trade (GATT) recently described the mood in the Uruguay round, the most ambitious attempt in history to liberalise trade. "Totally and utterly blocked . . . on its knees or dead", was the verdict of one of his officials last week.

The pity is that a deal on trade is there to be had. Indeed, though the odds lengthen daily, an agreement is yet possible before the leaders of the world's seven big industrial economies meet for their annual economic summit in early July. Such a deal would deliver big economic gains to all involved, especially America, and would surpass expectations at the launch of the Uruguay round almost seven years ago. It is in America's power to call an end to the talks and realise these gains. Instead it is gambling for more, risking the round's collapse.

Once before, at the end of 1990, the talks faltered. Since then America has won further concessions in three areas it regards as crucial. The European Community is ready to make specific cuts in its subsidies to farmers. Measured by the yardstick of free trade in farm goods, these cuts are feeble; but they go far beyond the empty generalities on offer in 1990. An agreement protecting intellectual property, valuable to America's high-tech and entertainment industries, now contains a mechanism to punish transgressors. And for trade in services, where America ranks as the world's biggest exporter, rules that were imprecise have been tightened and a loophole that would let countries protect their services for "cultural reasons" has been closed.

Still dissatisfied, America is betting that it can win more concessions. This is a reckless gamble. Any further winnings seem quite out of proportion to the stake—the progress already made in the Uruguay round and possibly the future of GATT itself. Also, further winnings are mostly unlikely to be grasped. For the moment, the EC has little scope to extend its reforms of the common agricultural policy. And Asian and Latin American governments are unwilling to shift their positions on intellectual property and services—positions they were reluctant to adopt in the first place.

If the round falls apart, a marvellous opportunity will have been squandered. Measured against America's goals in the mid-1980s, when the Uruguay round was launched, the negotiations have been remarkably successful. Compare one indication of what a deal struck now might look like—the 438-page draft of the final text prepared by Mr Dunkel last December—with a wish-list presented to the Senate's finance committee in 1985 by Clayton Yeutter, then the country's trade representative.

In 1985 Mr Yeutter told the senators that "the GATT is in urgent need of repair". Mr Yeutter also expressed a desire to increase "confidence in the GATT as an institution"—difficult though it is to reconcile that view with the administration's actions thereafter. In three areas, Mr Yeutter called for urgent reform: settlement of trade disputes; rules allowing countries emergency protection; and rules governing non-tariff barriers to trade. If America said yes to the Uruguay round as it now stands, all these ambitions would be met, and more.

The Uruguay draft text contains an impressive list of new or improved rules for global trading. They cover the manipulation of technical standards; subsidies, and protection against them; government procurement; manipulation of import li-

cences and rules on the origin of goods; discriminatory behaviour of customs officials; restrictions on inward investment that interfere with trade; protection of intellectual property; and anti-dumping actions.

In 1985 Mr Yeutter also said that America needed progress in two areas entirely new to GATT: agriculture and services. Again, if America declares victory now, both will have been brought into the GATT's book of trade rules. Yes, the EC's agreement to cut farm subsidies by roughly 30% falls far short of America's original target of 70%. Yes again, countries are unwilling to open their markets to foreign service companies, even though most have given their blessing to rules that will make such concessions possible. But a great victory would still have been won. In future, negotiations about agriculture and services will be about how much to cut protection, not whether to cut it.

Count your blessings

Trade reform is a time-consuming business. It has taken eight rounds of talks, starting in 1947, to cut tariffs on goods to today's average of 4.7%. The long-term benefits justify the effort—witness the industrial countries' economic growth and the expansion of world trade since 1945. But to forgo even the short-term benefits of the Uruguay round would be costly.

The table, from a study by three Canadian economists, compares two possible

Much better than nothing

Gains from a successful Uruguay round ($bn)	Compromise	Radical
United States	35.3	73.5
Japan	27.6	50.1
EC	27.5	60.4
Ex-Comecon countries	6.6	23.6
Rest of world	5.6	13.3
Canada	4.4	9.3
Middle-income agricultural importers	4.2	7.6
Other West European countries	4.0	9.3
Middle-income agricultural exporters	2.5	12.1
Australia & New Zealand	0.9	3.2
World	118.6	262.4

Source: Nguyen, Perroni and Wigle in World Economy

outcomes of the Uruguay round. One, which the authors call the radical outcome, represents a really ambitious deal that all countries (including America) say is now beyond reach—cuts of 70% in agricultural support, cuts of 20% in the protection of services, and quick, deep cuts in the protection of textiles. The second, a compromise, is closer to Mr Dunkel's plan. It assumes only a 30% cut in agricultural support. On other contentious areas the authors are conservative; they underestimate gains already promised by the Uruguay round. They assume no progress on trade in services (a modest, worthwhile deal is on the table) and little progress on textiles trade

(total liberalisation, albeit phased in over ten years, has been agreed to).

America's government has often said that no deal is better than a weak deal. What can this mean? According to the cautious Canadian study, America would gain $35 billion a year from the compromise deal (as compared with no deal). When the authors looked at the effect of the compromise in particular industries they found that, though farmers and their suppliers would suffer, America's light and high-technology industries would do well. The biggest winner was services—despite the authors' unduly pessimistic assumption that there would be no progress in the services negotiations. (The reason is that as trade in other industries expands, the demand for intermediate inputs, many of which are supplied by producers of services, rises too.) Yet America's service companies have lately muted their support for the round, saying they must have more.

Many Americans believe they can survive without this round of multilateral trade talks or, for that matter, any other. Instead of multilateral trade, companies and politicians look to America's unilateral section-301 trade rules and the emerging North American Free Trade Agreement. By these means, they hope to secure gains that will dwarf the $35 billion that might come from the Uruguay round. That is a dream that could easily become a nightmare. In the meantime, America will have kissed $35 billion a year goodbye.

Anyone for snakes and ladders?

AUGUST 1ST *As pressures on Europe's exchange-rate mechanism mounted, we put the case against a realignment*

TIME was when only the most hardened Eurosceptics reckoned that European exchange rates needed overhauling. In recent weeks, however, speculation has been mounting that a realignment of Europe's exchange-rate mechanism (ERM)—the first since January 1987—is imminent. The lira is dangerously close to its permitted floor within the system, and some fear that Italy may be unable to resist devaluing it. A few economists and politicians go further. They argue that all the non-German countries should devalue against the D-mark to boost their flagging economies.

The ERM has come under strain for several reasons. The lira has been savaged by Italy's political troubles and by growing worries about its government's ability to cut the huge budget deficit. The weakness of the dollar has pushed money into D-marks, strengthening the German currency within the ERM. And lastly, markets have

been unnerved by the uncertain future of European economic and monetary union (EMU) after the Danes' rejection of the Maastricht treaty in June.

For the past couple of years financial markets have acted almost as if EMU had already happened and exchange rates had been fixed. It was assumed that Italy and other spendthrifts would be obliged to cut their budget deficits and reduce inflation to meet the convergence conditions set down in the Maastricht treaty. So Italy and others paid a smaller risk premium to persuade investors to hold their currencies than would otherwise have been necessary. With EMU now in doubt, realignment is again on the agenda. Since the Danish referendum, the lira, the peseta and sterling have fallen most.

France's Maastricht referendum on September 20th will be crucial. A "yes" vote will help to put EMU back on track

and ease market pressure to realign. A "no" will do the opposite. The Italian government, along with all other EC members, has ruled out devaluation. But if Italy caves in, others may do the same.

The intriguing question is whether it would be in the interests of the non-German members to devalue against the D-mark, to loosen the Bundesbank's grip on their monetary levers. Although Germany's inflation rate fell to 3.3% in July from 4.3% in June, as indirect tax increases in July 1991 dropped out of the year-on-year change, inflationary pressures are still too strong for the Bundesbank's taste. The central bank is unlikely to cut interest rates soon. This means that interest rates elsewhere in Europe will remain high, cramping growth.

If an individual country devalues its currency against the D-mark, its interest rates are more likely to rise than to fall, for future devaluation will seem more probable. Higher interest rates will offset the benefits of (temporarily) improved competitiveness. The interest-rate gap between two currencies reflects expected movements in the exchange rate. As long as the markets rule out a devaluation of the D-mark, German interest rates will set the floor for interest rates in the ERM.

Some economists, however, argue that a general devaluation of all currencies against the D-mark would help to loosen monetary policy in Europe. A lockstep realignment would not in itself enable other countries to push their interest rates below Germany's. But a stronger D-mark would help to squeeze inflation in Germany, and so allow the Bundesbank to cut its own interest rates sooner.

The chances of a general realignment are remote. France is committed to a strong franc, in order to keep down inflation. Belgium and Holland would almost certainly move with Germany. They already keep their currencies within 1% of the central rate against the D-mark, rather than exploiting the full official 2¼% band.

Nor does a general realignment seem justified on the basis of relative competitiveness. Economists at National Westminster Bank have calculated purchasing-power parities (PPPs) for ERM currencies against the D-mark. (PPPs are the exchange rates which equate the prices of an identical basket of goods and services in two countries.) Comparing actual rates with PPPs provides a rough guide to whether currencies are correctly valued.

NatWest's figures show that the curren-

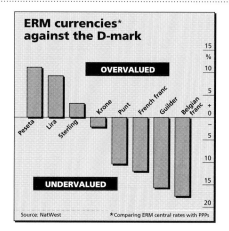

ERM currencies* against the D-mark

OVERVALUED

UNDERVALUED

Source: NatWest   *Comparing ERM central rates with PPPs

cies of Belgium, France, Holland and Ireland are undervalued against the D-mark (on the basis of their ERM central rates) by 10-18%. The Portuguese escudo is not included in the chart, but most economists reckon that it too is undervalued. The Danish krone and sterling are almost spot on their PPPs. Only the lira and the peseta are overvalued, both by about 10%. This fits with the fact that Italy and Spain have the biggest current-account deficits.

Those who argue for a general devaluation against the D-mark do so on the presumption that monetary policy in all non-German countries is tighter than domestic economic conditions warrant. If this is true, it suggests that countries should move towards EMU as fast as possible. Europe's monetary policy would then be set not by

the Bundesbank but by the European Central Bank. Because the ECB would be required to ensure price stability in the EC as a whole, it could be more tolerant of German inflation. From this point of view, it is curious that those who are most critical of the current tightness of monetary policy in Europe are also those who oppose EMU.

How much lower might European interest rates now be if there were a European central bank—assuming, as its designers intend, that the bank is given as tough a mandate to fight inflation as the Bundesbank has today? The average inflation rate in the EC is now 4%. With a medium-term goal of 2%, say, it would not be unrealistic to aim for 3% inflation over the next 12 months. Combine this with an average potential growth rate for economies of 2½%, and monetary policy should aim to accommodate annual growth in nominal GDP of 5½%. In the year to the first quarter of 1992, nominal GDP grew by an average of 6.2% in the whole of the EC, slightly faster than Germany's 5.9%. In most countries, nominal GDP expanded by at least 5%. The exception is Britain, where it increased by only 3.9%.

These figures cast doubt on the conventional wisdom that monetary policy in Europe as a whole is too tight. The only grounds for arguing that policy is too restrictive now is if price stability is rejected as a long-term goal. Yet, for most EC countries, price stability is precisely what the ERM was intended to achieve.

Torn beyond repair?

SEPTEMBER 26TH   *Less than two months later sterling had left the ERM and the system seemed on the point of collapse. What went wrong?*

A WEEK is a long time in economics. On September 16th sterling was withdrawn from the European exchange-rate mechanism (ERM) after extraordinary waves of selling overwhelmed the British authorities; later Italy suspended the lira and Spain devalued the peseta by 5%. Startling as all that was, however, the victims were currencies recognised by the markets as "weak"—candidates, on one test or another, for devaluation.

Since then the markets have looked elsewhere. Intense pressure has fallen upon the French franc—despite, or because of, the country's weak endorsement of the Maastricht treaty on September 20th. In contrast to earlier events, the franc is a "strong" currency. And, instead of tossing it to the speculators, Germany's Bundesbank has staked its own reputation and resources on resisting a franc devaluation.

On September 23rd France raised a benchmark short-term interest rate from 10½% to 13%, and intervened heavily in the markets. A joint statement by the French and German governments promised no realignment. Later, talk of a secret pact on monetary union for the franc and the D-mark lent further support. Yet the franc struggled to stay above its ERM floor of DM0.2915. This turn of events has brought the very survival of the ERM into doubt.

What has gone wrong? And what, if anything, can be done about it? The first question, with the power of perfect hindsight, is easy. German unification is the main cause. It would be hard to imagine a bigger shock to the fixed parities of the ERM than the absorption of the eastern *Länder* into the German economy. German producers saw demand surge; this fuelled inflation. The government's budget deficit expanded, adding to the

Bundesbank's alarm. So interest rates were pushed up.

Because the D-mark anchors the ERM—ie, because nobody expects it to be devalued—no country can expect to hold its interest rates below German ones for long. So the question the markets asked of Britain, France and the others was this: are interest rates at German levels—or somewhat higher, supposing a devaluation scare begins—sustainable in your country? This is a political judgment as much an economic one. When the answer is No, devaluation looks a good bet. When the answer is very firmly No, central-bank intervention is powerless to resist the sheer weight of capital in the market.

This explains why assertions that a given exchange rate keeps producers competitive in trade are beside the point. For the moment, the markets could not care less about that. It explains why the "strong" franc has taken nearly as brutal a beating in recent days as the "weak" pound: Mr Mitterrand's government

promised lower interest rates if France voted Yes in its referendum. It explains why the improved arrangements for central-bank intervention agreed upon in 1987 were impotent during the crisis: the resources at the central banks' disposal are simply too puny. And it makes clear what, above all, needs to happen if the ERM is to return to any semblance of stability: Germany must cut its interest rates.

The pressure on the Bundesbank to do just that is now intense. Helmut Kohl, it appears, is unwilling to see France forced to endure the humiliation of a realignment. (Britain was another matter.) Undoubtedly he is urging the bank to do everything in its power to rescue the franc—and, with it, the ERM. But the bank has no grounds, it reckons, for lower interest rates: new money-supply figures show that M3, the bank's chosen portent, grew 8.8% (too fast) in the year to August. A cut in interest rates could not be presented as anything but an expedient to rescue the franc.

Peering back with even sharper hindsight, might anything have been done to avoid this mess? John Major, Britain's prime minister, talks of "fault lines" in the ERM. By this he means the Bundesbank's reluctance, up to now, to help ERM-victims such as Britain off the hook. Odd that he did not notice it before. The ERM's success in curbing inflation in Europe has been chiefly due to this very intransigence. Paradoxically, German "flexibility" on interest rates might yet save the ERM—but quite possibly at the cost of emasculating it.

The Bundesbank has long favoured a different sort of flexibility for the ERM: greater willingness to realign the system's parities. That would have allowed it to stamp firmly on domestic inflation without being interrupted by squeamish bystanders. Most economists would now agree (and many said so at the time) that German unification called for a substantial appreciation of the D-mark against most of the other ERM currencies. A dearer D-mark would have tightened monetary conditions in Germany and perhaps have allowed the Bundesbank to cut its interest rates sooner.

The Bundesbank wanted this; the other countries did not. By 1990 the system had not been realigned for three years, a matter of great Euro-pride; partly for that reason, monetary union was coming into sight; and governments and markets alike had come to expect no further changes in parities. Reportedly, the Bundesbank nonetheless offered the same deal—lower German interest rates in exchange for a realignment—at a meeting of EC finance ministers last August.

Officials speaking for Norman Lamont, Britain's chancellor of the exchequer, deny this story (in suspiciously careful terms). It would now look pretty silly to have turned the proposal down. At the time, though, the dilemma would have seemed acute: governments would have had to break their promises not to devalue their currencies, without being forced to do so by the markets. Such U turns are hard to defend, and damage more than pride: long before this summer, the credibility of governments' promises had become what held the ERM together.

That is why, if the markets force further realignment, the ERM may be torn beyond repair. In the mid-1980s the character of the system changed. Originally it exerted little pressure on countries with high inflation; instead, frequent realignments accommodated that divergence. In the late 1980s the system hardened. Governments believed it could deliver stability in exchange rates together with low inflation. In this new ERM the disciplinary role of the Bundesbank was crucial. So too, most recently, was the prospect of monetary union, which served to confirm expectations of no realignments. The momentum of this evolutionary process was a stabilising factor in its own right. Now, whatever happens to the franc, this momentum has been checked.

To restore credibility, it would make economic sense to hasten EMU. Politically, that looks difficult—even if the core countries, led by Germany and France, decide to go it alone. If the ERM endures its present troubles, the question will be: how long can the system stand still and survive?

Central banking on the cheap

AUGUST 8TH *Do central bankers provide value for money? We made a stab at picking the best bargains among central-bank governors*

PERFORMANCE-related pay for company managers is all the vogue. Is it unreasonable to suggest that central bankers be paid according to how well they beat inflation? The chart looks at the relationship between the two. We asked the central banks of 15 countries how much their governors were paid. Nine answered; central bankers in Belgium, Germany, Holland, Japan, New Zealand and Spain prefer to keep their salaries secret. For the chart, however, we used an unofficial estimate of $450,000 for the salary of Helmut Schlesinger, president of Germany's Bundesbank.

Converting the salaries into dollars at current exchange rates reveals a wide variation. The world's most powerful economy pays its central-bank governor the least: Alan Greenspan, chairman of America's Federal Reserve, receives a bargain-basement salary of $129,500. Only a bit better off, at $130,000, is Bengt Dennis, head of Sweden's Riksbank. The top earner is Maria Schaumayer, president of the Austrian central bank, who makes an adequate $575,000.

The chart suggests that performance-re-

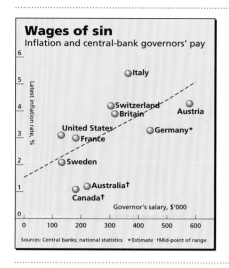

Wages of sin
Inflation and central-bank governors' pay

Sources: Central banks; national statistics *Estimate †Mid-point of range

lated pay has taken on a new meaning in central banking. By and large, the higher a country's inflation, the higher seems to be its central-bank governor's pay. Italy is a prime example.

Shoppers' choice
When New Zealand was drawing up the act that made its Reserve Bank independent of politicians in February 1990, the drafters considered tying the governor's salary to his success in conquering inflation. Had they done so, Donald Brash would be in line for a lot of money. He is ahead of schedule in achieving the Reserve Bank's inflation target (0-2% by the end of 1993) and New Zealand's inflation rate of 1% is the lowest of any industrial economy.

Mr Brash's salary is unknown, but the bank has told *The Economist* that the positive relationship between inflation and governors' salaries "is not invalidated by the New Zealand case". Does he do it for free?

The big salaries of some European central bankers will raise tricky questions if an enlarged European Community moves towards economic and monetary union. Can central-bank governors in Germany and Austria keep earning so much more than their counterparts in France or Sweden? How will they all justify their fat pay packets once the European central bank is set up, leaving them little to do? And who should be the president of this new European central bank? Take home a bargain while stocks last.

In the valley of debt

NOVEMBER 7TH **Heavy borrowing by households and firms fuelled the economic boom of the 1980s. In the 1990s these debts are prolonging the slowdown**

SOME economists have nightmares that the world recession will turn into a 1930s-style depression. In fact, the OECD countries, taken together, are not yet even in recession, in the strict sense of the word: their total output is still growing. But the current economic slowdown is different from previous recessions since the second world war, and more worrying. In country after country, the slump has been longer, and recovery feebler, than in the past.

It is no coincidence that the most protracted recessions have been in places where households and firms have piled up the biggest debts. The larger English-speaking countries, plus Japan and Scandinavia, are all suffering from nasty debt deflation. Huge borrowings and falling asset prices are hindering recovery.

Financial liberalisation and lax monetary policies in the 1980s encouraged households and firms to buy property and equities with borrowed money. The consequent surge in asset prices made households feel wealthier, so they saved less and borrowed even more to keep acquiring. Debts soared to record levels in relation to income, after remaining broadly stable in the 1970s. The change was greatest in Britain, where households and firms doubled their debts as a percentage of GDP between 1980 and 1991. In America the ratio rose by one-third, in Japan by two-fifths.

In many countries households accounted for the lion's share of the new debt. But the value of property and equities rose even faster than personal debt, so households' balance sheets still looked healthy. In Japan, for example, the price of

urban residential land tripled in the ten years to 1990, lifting net household wealth (assets minus debts) from five times disposable income in 1985 to 8.5 times in 1990.

The snag is that whereas the value of debt is fixed in nominal terms, that of houses and shares is not. Once central banks tightened monetary policy at the end of the 1980s, asset prices tumbled. The value of residential land in Japan has dropped by about a quarter from its peak and is still falling. London house prices have fallen by more than a third.

Worries about their shrinking wealth and ability to service debts have encouraged consumers to save and repay what they borrowed. This explains why big cuts in interest rates in America and Britain have done little to revive consumer demand. People have used the savings from

lower interest payments to pay off principal, rather than to service new borrowing or go on a spending spree. Only when households have cut their debt to acceptable levels in relation to their income will they start chatting up their bank managers and haunting the high streets again.

Alan Greenspan, the chairman of America's Federal Reserve Board, recently argued that debt-burdened economies would need to go through a lengthy period of adjustment to repair debt-laden balance sheets. Despite two years of such adjustment in America, the process, says Mr Greenspan, is only about half-complete. Economic growth could therefore remain subdued for a while.

This is bad news for Britain and Japan, which have even bigger debts than America. The amount owed by Britain's households and firms has barely budged from its peak of around 160% of GDP; Japanese debt is more than 200% of GDP. In America it has fallen slightly, from 149% to 145%

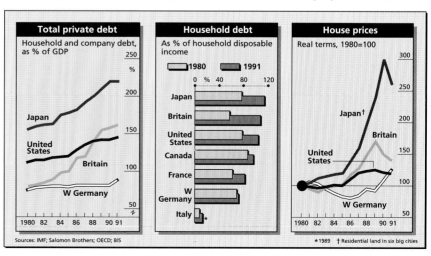

of GDP. American companies have made good progress in whittling down their debts by issuing record amounts of equity this year; households, however, still owe a lot.

The economies of Western Germany and the rest of continental Europe have slowed sharply in recent months. Are they, too, heading for a debt recession? The answer is probably no. The middle chart at the bottom of page 261 compares the level of household debt in the seven big industrial economies. Japan, America, Britain and Canada all have household debts in the range of 96-117% of disposable income. In both France and Germany the ratio is around 75%, and in Italy a paltry 13%.

Outside the Nordic countries, conti-

nental Europeans did not overborrow in the 1980s. In 1980 German and French households were actually bigger debtors than the British, but they have since been left far behind. Continental home-buyers typically borrow only 60-70% of the value of a property, compared with 90-95% in Britain. Another difference is that real house prices fell in Germany for most of the 1980s. Although they have rebounded since 1990, they are not hugely out of line with historical levels.

But what of those countries which are suffering from debt deflation? The risk is that debt-servicing difficulties will force households to sell their homes to repay debt, pushing house prices even lower and depressing consumer confidence and

spending still further. To prevent this from turning into a depression, policy-makers can do only two things. Interest rates must be reduced to lighten debt service, as America, Britain and Japan have all done. And central banks must stand ready–as they did not in the 1930s–to support the financial system if banks or other lenders fail.

Aside from this, policy-makers can only be patient, ignoring those who urge a "little dose of inflation" to cure debt deflation. Inflation would certainly bail out borrowers more quickly, by eroding their real debt burdens. It would also sow the seeds of the next cycle of boom and bust. Inflation was the policy of the 1970s. It was more than a little to blame for the borrowing excesses of the 1980s.

Before the flood

NOVEMBER 28TH *Europe's governments are worried about migration from east to west. What are the risks, and what should governments do to reduce them?*

THE EC has announced anti-dumping duties on imports of steel from Czechoslovakia. Even Euro-sceptics were impressed by this: the same EC that sends money and teachers of market economics to Eastern Europe slaps a fine on producers striving to make money from trade, not charity. Since the collapse of communism, where else could you find economic ignorance, political incompetence and moral turpitude so neatly combined?

The governments of Western Europe, it seems, need to think hard about the choices that confront them in their policies toward the East. A good place for ministers to start would be a new book. "East-West Migration: The Alternatives" is a joint effort by four distinguished economists*. In Eastern Europe and the former Soviet Union, they point out, the average wage is less than $1 an hour. The average in Western Europe is $10. Already Eastern Europe's governments allow their people to come and go as they please; in 1993 Russia and other former Soviet republics will do so as well. The pressure of migration is therefore likely to increase.

Are there precedents? Between 1970 and 1988 more than 3m Mexicans moved (legally or otherwise) to the United States—about 4% of Mexico's population. In the 1950s and 1960s a movement on a similar scale took place between southern and northern Europe: net migration northward from Yugoslavia, Turkey, Spain, Portugal and Italy amounted to 5m, or 3% of their population. (About as many southern

Europeans moved to America.) Then, in the 1970s, trans-European migration slowed. Northern unemployment began to rise, jobs for immigrants grew scarce and governments tightened the rules for new work permits.

Reviewing such cases, the authors conclude that migration reflects not just restrictions on movement nor disparities in wages, but other factors. One is the probability of finding work at home or abroad. Because of this link to employment, migration has often proved self-regulating: it happens most when the host country is best able to absorb newcomers (ie, when unemployment is low). For the same reason, history suggests that migration has been beneficial not only to the migrants but also to the host countries—though not, of course, to particular groups of host-country workers, who have to compete with foreigners for jobs.

Another finding is that migration has usually been a long-term process—a shift of people over many years, not a sudden burst (which is what wage differentials, taken in isolation, might lead you to expect). Again, this pattern reflects not just the extent of controls, but the fine balance of pros and cons perceived by potential migrants. And there is another long-term factor at work: the people most likely to move (young adults with good job prospects) are only a segment of the population—one that is replenished each year by new entrants.

Eastern Europe may be different. Migration was forbidden for so many years that there may be a lot of pent-up demand. Barring economic catastrophes, however,

the authors guess that Western Europe might have to deal with about 10m would-be immigrants over the next decade—about 4m from Eastern Europe and another 6m from the ex-Soviet republics. (This is on top of the expected movement of 3m ethnic Germans to Germany.) This trend might continue at a similar rate for many years beyond.

Under its current law, America accepts 750,000 immigrants a year. The authors argue that Western Europe, with its bigger population, could comfortably absorb a flow of 300,000 a year—though even that figure will strike many EC governments as much too high.

The study points out that, left to itself, Western Europe's labour force will soon start to shrink, and the decline will accelerate. Western Europe is short of children to support today's workers in retirement. The age structure of Eastern Europe and the former Soviet Union is not skewed in this way; immigrants will tend to come equipped with future taxpayers. Greater migration from the east could help the west to deal with its emerging shortage of young workers, and with the fiscal pinch which that shortage would otherwise cause.

Even a managed flow of 300,000 East European immigrants a year would leave a lot of would-be movers behind. So the authors say it is essential for the rich countries to supply conditional aid to the region. And, they say, the EC should bring Eastern Europe into a pan-European free-trade area. Trade, as much as flows of capital and people, can help living standards in east and west to converge. Unless there are signs soon that this is starting to happen, the EC may find its immigration pressures surging out of control.

* Richard Layard, Olivier Blanchard, Rudiger Dornbusch and Paul Krugman. The book is published by MIT Press.

How low is low enough?

NOVEMBER 7TH **Almost everybody agrees that double-digit inflation is bad for economic growth. But how far down should inflation be pushed? Right to zero?**

DURING the past few years, inflation has tumbled throughout the industrial world. In most countries it is now back at its 1960s level of about 3%. Not content with this, some policy-makers want to eliminate inflation completely. Price stability, they argue, will lay the best foundation for faster growth. In the opposite corner, a growing number of critics claim that central banks are overdoing it. Today's problem, they argue, is recession, not inflation, and a "little dose of inflation" is exactly what economies need now to reduce real debt burdens and so get moving again. Who is right?

Most governments now accept that low inflation is essential for sustainable growth, and not, as was once thought, an alternative to it. The trade-off between a bit more inflation and a bit less unemployment can still be made in the short term. But experience has shown that attempts to apply it in the long term do not work. They simply result in ever-rising inflation. So keep inflation low. But how low? Is 5% inflation acceptable? Is 3% better than 5%? Is zero inflation best of all?

Several governments are setting inflation targets of 2% or less. The Reserve Bank of New Zealand, probably the world's most independent central bank, is aiming for 0-2% by the end of 1993. The Bank of Canada's target is 2% by 1995. The Bank of Japan and the Bundesbank both have medium-term goals of no more than 2%. Britain's Treasury recently announced a target of 1-4% for the next few years and 2% or less in the long term. The governor of the Bank of England plans to give a speech on November 11th in favour of price stability.

These ambitions may sound strange to modern ears. Since the early 1930s, prices in industrial economies have risen almost every year; by a total of about 1,000% in America and 4,000% in Britain. Yet, through history, inflation—in the sense of continuously rising prices—has been the exception, not the rule. Bursts of sustained inflation occurred during the Roman Empire, the Middle Ages and the reign in England of Queen Elizabeth I; but, in between, prices remained broadly stable over long periods. Short periods of rising prices were interspersed with years of falling prices. The average price level in Britain in the early 1930s was no higher than in the 1660s.

Those who favour a return to price stability argue that it would make possible the fastest long-term growth. Their critics either believe that a little inflation is healthy or argue that the costs of reducing inflation to zero are greater than the costs of inflation itself.

What's wrong with inflation

What are those costs? If the rate of inflation were perfectly predictable, then most of the ill-effects could be avoided. Contracts, wages, interest rates and the tax system could take future inflation into account, and it would make little difference to economic performance whether the rate was 0% or 5%. It is because inflation is not predictable that it damages economies.

Unforeseen inflation stunts growth because it distorts the price mechanism, by making it difficult to distinguish changes in relative prices from changes in the general price level. If apples are rising in price relative to other fruit, this ought to attract new apple-growers and encourage consumers to buy plums instead. But general inflation obscures that relative movement: neither housewife nor fruit-grower takes much note of a 20% jump in apple prices, when even plums have gone up 15%. So resources are misallocated, and growth is consequently slower. Even with just 5% annual inflation, prices double every 14 years, swamping most relative price changes. If the general price level were stable, the market economy would function better.

The second effect of inflation is uncertainty, the enemy of investment and growth. If businessmen are unsure about the future level of prices, and hence of real interest rates, they will be less willing to take risks and to invest, especially in long-term projects. Inflation encourages a preoccupation with short-term profits at the expense of longer-term returns. Furthermore, uncertainty about inflation pushes up real interest rates, as lenders demand a bigger risk premium on their money.

These arguments suggest that—in a real world that cannot foresee the future—the best inflation rate is the one that plays the least role in decision-making. This must be zero; anything higher will generate unnecessary uncertainty and inefficiency.

Yet some people don't worry

Some economists disagree. They argue that if uncertainty is the real trouble with inflation, then the volatility of inflation is more important than its level. An inflation rate that averaged 0% but fluctuated between plus 5% and minus 5% would be just as damaging, they argue, as one that averaged 10% and swung between 5% and 15%. Their conclusion is that policy-makers do not need to eliminate inflation but merely to stabilise the rate, to make it easier to predict and so less harmful.

In fact, however, over the past 30 years the countries with the lowest inflation have also had the most stable inflation rates (see chart 1). It seems to be easier to stabilise inflation at low levels, partly, perhaps, because this creates a virtuous circle of low inflationary expectations.

Larry Summers, the chief economist at the World Bank, argues that 2-3% inflation is best. His first reason is that it leaves open the possibility of negative real interest rates, which could help to pull an economy out of depression. With zero inflation, real rates cannot be negative: lenders would be paying borrowers to borrow. Second, a little bit of inflation acts like a lubricant, helping relative prices and wages to adjust more efficiently. Trade unions in declining industries may resist a cut in nominal pay, yet be prepared to allow inflation to erode their real wages. With zero inflation this safety valve would be blocked, resulting in job losses and possibly greater labour unrest.

A counter-argument to this is that, while inflation keeps ticking, the inevitability of annual (or, at best, triennial) pay-bargaining rounds strengthens the position of trade unions. Were prices stable, wage increases would be justified only by a rise in productivity or by individual performance. So unions would play a weaker role, making industrial unrest less likely. Chart 2 confirms that high-inflation countries are more strike-prone: the higher the inflation rate, the more frequent wage negotiations need to be, so increasing the risk of strikes.

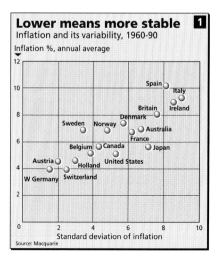

Lower means more stable **1**
Inflation and its variability, 1960-90
Inflation %, annual average
Standard deviation of inflation
Source: Macquarie

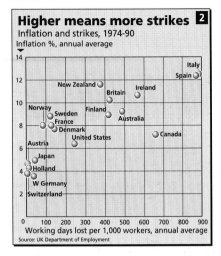

Higher means more strikes **2**

Inflation and strikes, 1974-90

Inflation %, annual average

Working days lost per 1,000 workers, annual average

Source: UK Department of Employment

Arguments for zero inflation, however, ignore one basic statistical point: the most commonly used measure of inflation, the consumer-price index (CPI), is often inaccurate. It tends to overstate the true rate of inflation. So could a bit of inflation, as measured by the CPI, be acceptable?

There are two reasons why the CPI exaggerates inflation. First, it fails to adjust fully for improvements in quality. A typical 1992 car costs much more than did a 1982 car. But it is a much better vehicle. Second, and more technical, the weights used to add together the prices of the different goods and services that go into the index are often out of date. This exaggerates the increase in the cost of living, since it does not allow for the fact that consumers shift from goods which become relatively expensive to cheaper alternatives. If apple prices, say, multiply twentyfold, few apples will be eaten. Apples should then barely figure in the index at all. But they will, often for many years. The weights used today in America's CPI are based on the spending patterns of 1982-84.

Robert Gordon, an economist at Northwestern University, Illinois, estimates that America's CPI has overstated the rise in the prices of consumer durables by an average of 1.5% a year over the past couple of decades. Thus the 2.2% rise in the price of goods in the year to this September may imply that America is close to price stability, so far as goods are concerned. In other big economies too the CPI has shown the prices of goods up by only 2-3% over the past year.

The exact size of the upward bias will vary from country to country. But it is one reason why central banks tend to define price stability as an annual rise in the CPI within the range of 0-2%, rather than zero.

If policy-makers aim for literally zero inflation, as measured by the CPI, they may end up pursuing an overly tight policy, for this would—in practice—imply falling prices. And these too have damaging ef-

fects. Just as the expectation of rising prices encourages people to buy now, not later, so falling prices cause consumers to spend less, because the return from holding money exceeds the return from holding goods. In periods of inflation, there is a self-correcting mechanism: nominal interest rates rise with prices, encouraging consumers to hold money. But the process cannot work in reverse when prices are falling, because interest rates cannot, in practice, be negative. So it will remain more attractive to hold money than goods, and the demand for goods—and hence their prices—will continue to fall.

Governments should not conclude from this, however, that, because an apparent inflation rate of 2% really means price stability, they can turn a blind eye to it. The CPI itself influences wage- and price-setting. If it continues to rise, countries will be denying themselves the full benefits of price stability. The lesson for governments is that they must devise more accurate price indices.

From theory to fact

Despite all the theoretical reasons why inflation is bad for growth, the empirical evidence is rather sparse. True, the global slowdown in growth in the 1970s coincided with a surge in inflation. But was the rapid expansion in the 1950s and 1960s due to the modesty of inflation at the time? It can also be explained by other factors, such as the post-war catch-up in industrial investment and the liberalisation of world trade.

Do countries with high inflation have slower or faster growth than those with low? The answer is not clear-cut. Charts 3 and 4 plot the relationship between growth in GDP per head and inflation in 20 industrial economies during two periods. In 1955-73 (ie, when inflation was modest, see chart 3), it looks as if growth and inflation went together: countries with the highest inflation tended to have the strongest

growth in GDP per head. That correlation, however, depends heavily on Japan, which had both the highest average inflation rate (5.8%) and the strongest growth (8.6%). Excluding Japan, there is little relationship between inflation and growth.

Since 1973, in contrast (see chart 4), low-inflation countries have tended to enjoy slightly faster growth. In countries where inflation averaged less than 6%, growth per head averaged 2.1%; in those with inflation of 6-10%, that growth was 1.9%; and where inflation was above 10%, it averaged 1.7%.

There were four main exceptions to this rule: Ireland, Italy, Spain and Switzerland. The latter grew by a paltry 1.1% a year in 1974-91, despite having the second-lowest inflation rate of the 20. At the other extreme, Italy, Spain and Ireland all enjoyed strong growth, despite inflation rates of more than 10%. Herein lies a clue to why the link between inflation and growth appears to be weak. Among the 20 countries, Italy, Spain and Ireland at the start of the 1970s had by far the lowest income per head. So they had plenty of room to catch up, and enjoyed faster growth in their "productive potential" than other countries—just as Japan did in the 1950s and 1960s. Switzerland, the richest country, had less scope for growth.

Another factor which may have blurred the relationship between growth and inflation is the way that expectations of inflation lag behind events. After decades when prices were expected to remain broadly stable over long periods, future inflation was persistently underestimated between the 1950s and 1970s. This resulted in abnormally low real interest rates. In theory, countries with high, and hence more variable, rates of inflation should have had higher real interest rates; in practice, their average real interest rates were lower, which boosted their growth rates.

For example (see chart 5), if industrial economies are split into three groups according to their rates of inflation, then dur-

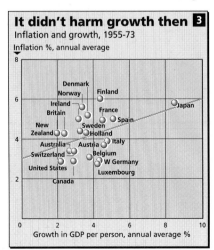

It didn't harm growth then **3**

Inflation and growth, 1955-73

Inflation %, annual average

Growth in GDP per person, annual average %

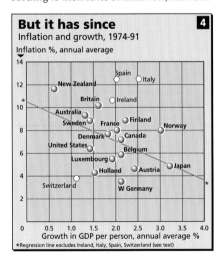

But it has since **4**

Inflation and growth, 1974-91

Inflation %, annual average

Growth in GDP per person, annual average %

*Regression line excludes Ireland, Italy, Spain, Switzerland (see text)

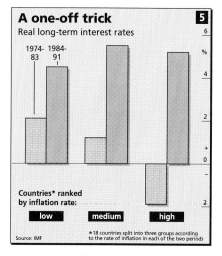

A one-off trick `5`

Real long-term interest rates

1974-83   1984-91

Countries* ranked by inflation rate: low · medium · high

Source: IMF

*18 countries split into three groups according to the rate of inflation in each of the two periods

ing 1974-83 real long-term interest rates averaged 2.1% in the countries with the lowest inflation, 1.2% in those with medium rates of inflation, and were actually negative in those with the highest inflation.

But this trick could not be repeated, for financial markets will not be cheated a second time. From 1984, as the chart shows, high-inflation countries have had higher real interest rates than low-inflation countries, making the adverse consequences of inflation far more severe than they were in earlier years.

The link between inflation and unemployment is a much clearer story. During 1974-91, countries with low inflation had the lowest jobless rates (see chart 6). This is not to deny that the process of reducing inflation pushed unemployment temporarily higher in some countries. But, for the period as a whole, low inflation was not achieved through high unemployment; if anything, it favoured job creation.

Some more sophisticated econometric studies have tried to disentangle the effects of the many factors that influence growth. One study by two economists at the Bank of Canada, covering 62 countries over 25 years, concludes that a reduction in the inflation rate by one percentage point increases the annual growth rate by one-tenth of a percentage point. A recent OECD study reaches a similar result. That may seem piffling, but it adds up. If a country cuts its inflation rate from 5% to 0%, say, then in 20 years its output should be 10% higher than it would otherwise have been.

Assuming that the benefits of moving from 3% to 0% inflation are no less than those of moving from 6% to 3% (they should in fact be bigger, since price stability will eliminate many unproductive activities), then the issue of whether it is worth aiming for price stability boils down to whether the long-term benefits exceed the short-term costs.

Price stability may, in theory, maximise economic growth, in a long-run steady state. But there are short-term costs in getting from here to there. To reduce inflation, unemployment must temporarily be held above its so-called natural rate (the rate consistent with stable inflation), and the short-term loss in output and jobs will initially offset the benefits. For example, growth might need to be reduced by one percentage point for one year in order to reduce inflation by one point. Applying those estimates from the Bank of Canada economists, in this case it will take ten years before output reaches the level where it would have been if nothing had been done. If the cut in growth needed is only half as great, it will still take five years.

Over a 20-year period, the economy as a whole would certainly gain. The snag is that governments are in power for only four or five years, and today's workers care far more about jobs today than prosperity in 20 years' time. The risk is that policy-makers will conclude that a bit of inflation is not so bad after all—as the British government now appears to have done.

The transitional costs of moving to price stability arise because expectations are slow to change, and because large parts of the economy are built on the assumption of continuing inflation. Workers expect annual pay increases roughly in line with last year's inflation rate. Home-owners may have borrowed heavily to buy a house in the expectation that inflation will erode the real weight of their mortgage; if inflation suddenly falls, they are stuck with a burden of debt bigger than they had expected.

Likewise, just as some of the damage to economic growth from inflation was muted in the 1970s by negative real interest rates, as expectations lagged behind actual inflation, so the 1990s could see the reverse. As inflation falls, real long-term interest rates will rise and stay high until investors believe price stability has come to stay.

A recent study by Stephen King, an economist at James Capel, a London stock-broking firm, concludes that zero inflation is currently an impossible goal for some countries. The short-term costs of disinflation, he argues, will prove too great, and a prolonged slump will force policy-makers into reverse. Attempts at achieving price stability will fail, unless certain preconditions are met: in particular, private-sector debt must be at a sustainable level, and the labour market must work efficiently, with flexible wages.

Mr King ranks the six big industrial economies according to whether they meet these preconditions. He concludes that only two of the six, Germany and Japan, can cope with disinflation. Elsewhere, he fears that excessive zeal in crushing inflation could prove self-defeating. Britain looks least able to cope, thanks to its rigid labour markets, high debt burden and stubborn inflationary expectations.

Yes, if governments cut the cost

The real lesson from this, however, is not that governments should immediately abandon their fight against inflation, but that they must put more effort into reducing the short-term costs of the fight. Tight monetary and fiscal policies are not enough: to reduce the cost of disinflation, governments must wean firms and workers off their inflationary habits and tackle the institutional rigidities that keep inflation going.

This also underlines the importance of making anti-inflationary policies fully credible, to reduce inflationary expectations and thereby minimise the loss of output needed to carry them through. The first priority is to remove from politicians the temptation to give the economy a short-term stimulus, by removing the means: ie, by making central banks independent. There is evidence that the greater independence won by central banks in New Zealand and Canada in recent years, combined with explicit inflation targets, has helped to dampen inflationary expectations and to hold down wage demands. Both countries have reduced inflation to around 1%, albeit at the cost of deep recessions. New Zealand is at last starting to enjoy the rewards: output has grown by almost 4% over the past 12 months and most economists are forecasting rapid growth over the next few years.

Zero inflation is not the instant, miracle cure that some proclaim; its benefits are long-term in nature. Unless governments reduce the short-term cost of inflation-fighting by attacking supply-side rigidities, the goal will remain elusive. But the sooner governments can convince individuals and firms that they are committed to price stability, the sooner the economic rewards will follow.

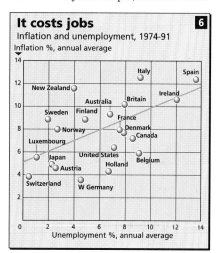

It costs jobs `6`

Inflation and unemployment, 1974-91

Inflation %, annual average

New Zealand · Italy · Spain · Australia · Britain · Ireland · Sweden · Finland · France · Norway · Denmark · Canada · Luxembourg · Japan · United States · Belgium · Austria · Holland · Switzerland · W Germany

Unemployment %, annual average

Contents

SCIENCE AND TECHNOLOGY

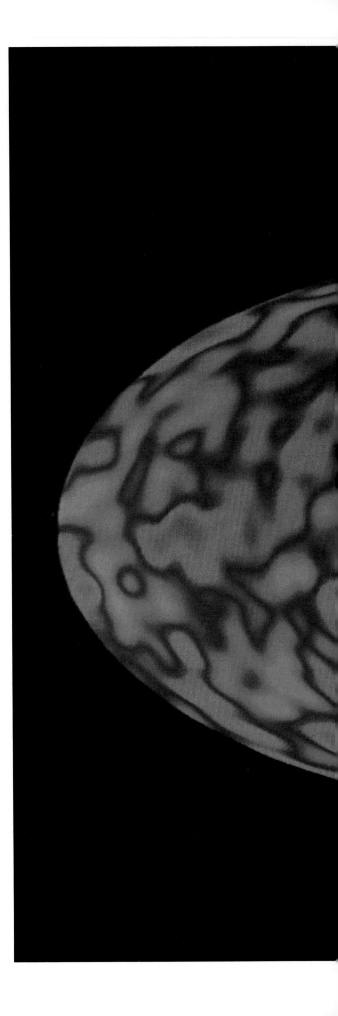

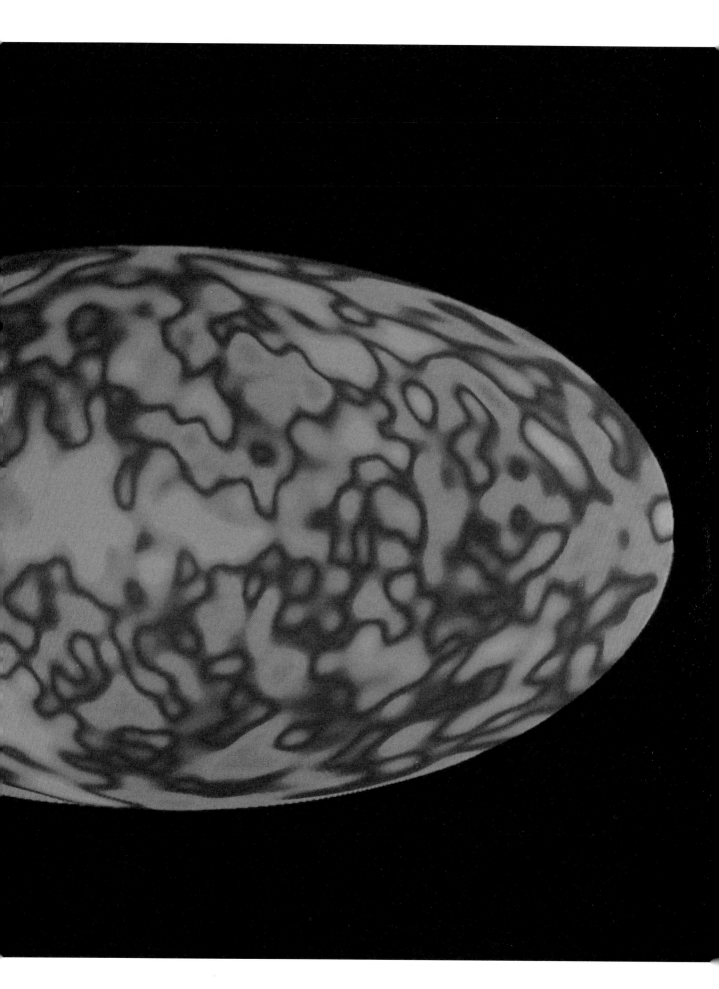

Frontiers

THERE are limits to everything: frontiers that have not been, sometimes cannot be, passed. The map on the previous page shows the background radiation that hangs behind everything the eye—even the eye that gazes through the greatest telescopes—can see. Look at this cosmic microwave background, as mapped in 1992 by COBE, an American satellite, and you are looking back 15 billion years, to a time only a few hundred thousand years after creation. And you will never see further, in space or time. You are looking back to a time when the whole universe was a dense ball of gas like the sun, and you can no more look further back than you can peer below the surface of the sun. You can make inferences about things that happened before, just as you can make inferences about what happens deep in the sun. But you will not see it directly. There are limits.

Every year, scientists try to push back the limits that can be pushed back, and try to circumvent those which the universe refuses to be flexible about. 1992 was no exception. The tiniest electric circuits were made, so small that the electrons inside them move around one at a time. Bones were found that may have belonged to humanity's earliest direct ancestor. Neutrinos from the sun's core were counted, revealing secrets that would otherwise remain forever hidden behind the bright solar surface. Nerve cells were made to divide, suggesting that the limits imposed on life by nerve degeneration may not be unbreakable.

Of all these, though, the COBE results garnered the most attention, perhaps because of the long chain that connects the blotchiness of the microwave background to the existence of people and newspapers. If the universe had started perfectly smooth, it would have gone on so, pristine and featureless. The tiny fluctuations in the earliest universe revealed by COBE allowed irregularities such as galaxies, stars, planets and, in the end, people to develop. It is inspiring to be made aware of this grand sweep: inspiring, but humbling. If the frontier is grand, it is also all but ineffably distant.

Was this what Vannevar Bush, of the Massachusetts Institute of Technology, had in mind in 1946 when he called science "the endless frontier"? The phrase, coined in a report of the same name made to Harry Truman, was used to justify government's role in the great adventure of science:

It has been basic United States policy that Government should foster the opening of new frontiers. It opened the seas to clipper ships and furnished land for pioneers. Although these frontiers have more or less dis-

New limits in the making

appeared, the frontier of science remains. It is in keeping with the American tradition—one which has made the United States great—that new frontiers shall be made accessible for development by all American citizens.

Pushing back the frontier, Mr Bush believed, meant prosperity, health and security. They would flow from it as surely as they flowed from the land that America had opened up in the west. The new ideas would give bright minds new ways to make money, and good governments new ways to improve the lot of their citizens. The idea that the frontier of science might move so far from the realms of everyday concern as to be of questionable utility was not really broached. Vannevar Bush had just seen an obscure fungal substance called penicillin become a lifesaver; he had overseen some of the world's loftiest minds as they turned the minutiae of electromagnetic and atomic physics into war-winning radar and war-ending nuclear weapons.

In 1992 America's National Science Foundation, created from the enthusiasm which greeted Mr Bush's report, averred that its future would be as resolutely exploratory as its past, and that it would continue to work at the pure sciences of the frontier. Yet elsewhere, frontiersmanship was already giving way to the urge to homestead—to making research useful to technologists. President George Bush gave America an explicit "technology policy", albeit a modest one—a few policy documents, a small programme in the Department of Commerce, increased industrial access to national laboratories. And, in 1992, as America chose a president keen to echo John Kennedy, a new mood could be discerned in Washington: "Ask not what you can do for science—ask what science can do for you." The Clinton administration seems likely to try to yoke public R&D expenditure ever more closely to the nation's technological competitiveness.

New frontiers

Of course publicly funded research should serve the nation—and around the world, in Germany and Japan and elsewhere, it has and does. It has done well by America, too, despite the gainsayers. All the countries concerned could doubtless improve their situations by cleverer, not necessarily costlier, policies. But there is more to scientific service than the promotion of economic growth. Science provides new possibilities, new potentials for all sorts of endeavour; acting on them may make pots of money, but it also changes society more deeply than a percentage point on GDP can. Consider the pre-eminent science of this and many recent years: genetics. Even against a background of impressive achievement, genetics and the sciences allied to it stood out in 1992. The human genome programme, an attempt to list and decipher all the genes that humans carry, went from strength to strength; hitherto obscure techniques and laboratories came into their own—a French laboratory sprung to the fore, and may be widely imitated elsewhere. Researchers are now optimistic that they may have a handle on all the genes within five years.

This, of course, has huge implications for medical science. A gene in hand is worth something, to be sure, but it is worth far more if you know what it does. The impending flood of genetic data presents a daunting challenge to the other researchers who must try to piece the genetic fragments into pictures of how cells and bodies work. Yet already, some are rising to it with a new technology that was barely dreamt of—at least in reputable places—until a few years ago: that of genetic therapy. The progress towards practical gene therapy has been, if anything, even more impressive than the forward motion of the genome programme. The idea of stitching new genes into the cells of people who are not doing too well with the ones they have has gained currency and feasibility; there are new gene therapies suggested every few weeks. As yet, there is little clinical data to suggest that they work particularly well. Yet biologists are sure that they should work, and are determined to prove themselves right: and they will succeed, somehow.

Genetic therapy provides opportunities and risks of far greater importance than the economic role it will be able to play in the near future. It raises questions about how people should live, what they should aspire to, how they should regulate their lives that are as profound as the questions raised by the technological control of fertility. As the genes associated with an ever greater number of illnesses are found, direct genetic remedies are bound to be tried more and more. Here is the frontier, with risk and promise galore.

Not all technologies that change the world are so obviously identifiable in advance, though. Many come about almost by chance—a side-effect of living at the frontier. As they fulfil the unique requirements of scientific research, technologists are given reasons to make things that they would otherwise not have made. Once made, the recently-impossible may turn out to be useful for all sorts of things. The way in which the de-

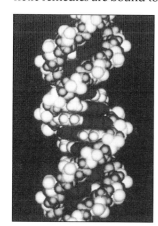

Designer genes

mands of laboratory life turned the laser from a quasi-military curiosity to one of the basic tools of the 20th century is a good example. Others can be found in materials science, electronics or anywhere you care to look. It is because they believe in this and other links between the cutting edge and the applied—more

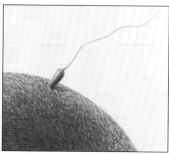

The limit of life

subtle than simply looking for new products—that the Japanese are ever more intent on basic research, wherever in the world it is done.

There is a caveat here, though. Not all science drives technology equally. The new gravity-wave observatories given the go-ahead in 1992 in Europe and America, which may find ways to guess at the goings-on behind the veil revealed by COBE, will undoubtedly drive laser technology forward by demanding things no other user could possibly need—yet. But will the multi-billion dollar international mission to Saturn? Or huge new particle accelerators? Probably not. Programmes which do something old in a bigger way should always attract the hardest questioning. The Superconducting Super Collider and the international space station provide good examples. One of the advantages of a shift towards a policy pursuing technology itself will be that such giants will find it harder to justify themselves in terms of their mediocre technical spin-off. Ideas and technical challenges are the meat of scientific progress; size alone is no guarantee of either.

There is more to the frontier than a place to live and produce wealth. In his famous essay "The Significance of the Frontier in American History" (1893) the historian Frederick Jackson Turner articulated the romance of the frontier, and assured his compatriots that it was over:

> That coarseness and strength combined with acuteness and inquisitiveness; that practical, inventive turn of mind, quick to find expedients; that masterful grasp of material things, lacking in the artistic but powerful to effect great ends; that restless, nervous energy; that dominant individualism, working for good and for evil, and withal the buoyancy and exuberance that comes from freedom—these are the traits of the frontier . . . Since the days when the fleet of Columbus sailed into the waters of the New World . . . the people of the United States have taken their tone from the incessant expansion which has not only been open but which has been forced upon them . . . But never again will such gifts of free land offer themselves . . . the frontier has gone.

The traits he lists are those of the best science, and they need not ever be in short supply. If they are shackled too closely to short-term returns, though, Vannevar Bush's frontier will close, as Turner's did. A limit will be reached.

January to June

January

On January 9th, Aleksander Wolszczan, an astronomer at the Arecibo Observatory in Puerto Rico, reported that he had found two **planets orbiting a pulsar**. This followed the discovery, announced the previous July, of a single planet revolving around a different pulsar. Unfortunately, the earlier discovery was retracted on January 16th.

Gene therapy for cystic fibrosis was brought a little closer. Working copies of the gene that makes the protein which, when faulty, causes the disease, were successfully inserted into cells lining rat lungs. The agent used to smuggle them in was the virus that causes colds.

Angling threatened to become an even duller sport with the discovery of a **chemical fish bait**—a combination of amino acids which proved irresistible to catfish.

A primitive desert shrub called "Mormon tea" yielded clues to the **origin of flowering plants**. Endosperm, which nurtures seedlings in the way that yolk nurtures a chicken, is found only in seeds that come from flowers. But Mormon tea, a non-flowering plant, shows the beginnings of endosperm formation.

Strange scars discovered on the landscape of Argentina were said to have been gouged out by a **bouncing meteorite**.

The heavenly visitor had arrived about 2,000 years ago, hit the earth, and skipped across Patagonia like a stone skimming over the ocean.

February

Page Caufield, a dentist at the University of Alabama, used DNA analysis to show that the bacteria which cause **tooth decay** are given to children by their mothers. If they are not passed on in the year following the arrival of the baby's milk teeth, the child will be caries-free.

A team of NASA scientists said that a hole in the northern hemisphere's **ozone layer** was likely to develop within ten years. Previously, only Antarctica had been affected.

Satellite-borne radar discovered the **lost city of Ubar**, in Oman. It was once a hub of the frankincense trade.

Data gathered by research groups in America and Germany showed that **young children grow in bursts**, sometimes remaining the same height for a couple of months and then putting on up to a centimetre in a day.

The ancient remains of the **largest landslide on earth** were reported from below the Atlantic Ocean. The discoverer, Brian Tucholke, reckoned that the wave generated would have been about 700 metres high.

Two groups of computer-oriented biologists challenged the nationality and **age of Eve**. The putative female ancestor of everyone alive today had been reckoned to be an African lady who lived 200,000 years ago.

The sites for a **gravity-wave observatory** were announced. The two detectors (working together, but well separated to stop random signals from affecting both) will be built in the states of Washington and Louisiana. Gravity waves are predicted by the General Theory of Relativity, but have not yet been recorded.

March

By transplanting "stem cells" for human blood into sheep embryos, the animals were induced to make human blood cells alongside their own. Performing the same trick on human embryos may be a way to **treat blood disorders**.

Broccoli, so loathed by certain former American presidents, was found to contain a powerful **anti-cancer agent**, suggesting that it's a good idea to eat up your greens after all.

April

Workers at the Harwell Atomic Energy Laboratory in England set their super-computer the task of finding the **biggest prime number** yet discovered. It took 19 hours.

A United Nations report on **soil erosion** said that 3 billion acres of agricultural land had been damaged by human activity and might prove costly or impossible to reclaim.

A **series of small earthquakes** in southern California gave geologists something to ponder. Other inhabitants of the area pondered when the "Big One" would hit them.

May

Results from **COBE**, an American astronomy satellite, pushed politics off the front pages. They showed that the early universe was lumpy, to the relief of cosmologists who had said it should be.

James Watson, co-discoverer of the structure of DNA, resigned as director of the American National Centre for Human Genome Research, part of the international project to map and sequence all the genes in the human body.

The announcement of the discovery of an ancient mine in Turkey helped shed light on the source of **bronze-age tin**. Though copper is abundant, bronze's other ingredient is rare. Tin used in Anatolia was previously thought to come from Afghanistan.

June

Two **fossil human skulls** found in China threw another spanner into the human evolutionary works. Palaeontologists argued whether they were *Homo sapiens* (modern man) or *Homo erectus* (his immediate predecessor).

America's House of Representatives voted not to build the **Superconducting Super Collider**, a big machine for looking at small particles of matter. But the Senate later voted to keep the project (estimated cost $8.25 billion) alive for another year.

A russo-american collaboration yielded a **lens that focuses neutrons**. The sub-atomic particles—useful for jobs such as killing tumours—should now be easier to guide to their targets.

The **Rio Conference** on the global environment took place. Thousands of tonnes of carbon dioxide were injected into the upper atmosphere by the jets that carried the world's politicians, scientists, journalists and green activists to Brazil. Treaties on global warming and biodiversity were duly signed, or not, according to national interest.

July to December

July

Six years after the soccerball-shaped molecule was first isolated in a laboratory, Semeon Tsipursky, a Russian geochemist, found **naturally occurring buckminsterfullerene** in some rocks from northern Russia.

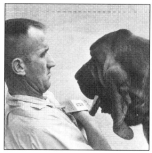

There was more comfort for those who profess to believe that dogs are people too. Like their masters, canids sometimes seem to suffer from **obsessive-compulsive disorder**. Frequent paw-licking appears to be the canine equivalent of Lady Macbeth handwashing.

August

Precision dating (to 64.98m years ago, give or take 50,000) of a crater in Mexico suggested that the explosion which formed it **wiped out the dinosaurs**. The impact of a 10km-wide asteroid would have plunged the earth into years of darkness, and the skies would have rained battery acid.

Judith Hall, a Canadian geneticist, proposed a new theory to account for the **origin of identical twins**. She suggested that they might not quite be identical after all—small mutations occurring shortly after fertilisation could cause some cells to secede from the main embryo and grow into a separate one.

Karen Wynn, a psychologist from Arizona, showed that **babies can count**. Children as young as five months are able to work out whether subtrac-

tions (done with cuddly toys rather than written numbers) have been done correctly or not.

Another space-shuttle mission failed. An attempt to launch a **tethered satellite** resulted in it unreeling only 256 metres from *Atlantis*, rather than the planned 20km.

Using a machine called a scanning-tunnelling microscope, engineers from California created the **world's tiniest battery**. It supplied one fiftieth of a volt.

A **uranium-eating bacterium** was reported. It was able to accumulate nine times its own weight of the stuff, and may find a job helping to clean up radioactive pollution.

Farmers who want weed-free fields without herbicides were recommended to **plough at night**. Even a brief exposure to daylight triggers the germination of many types of seeds. If clods are turned in darkness, this does not happen.

September

Following the fate of **40,000 pairs of Nikes** helped plot the currents of the Pacific Ocean. The trainers were washed overboard from a freighter in 1990 and have been turning up on beaches ever since.

Two American astronomers announced the discovery of the first object in the **Kuiper Belt**, a hitherto-theoretical reservoir supplying comets to the inner solar system. They called it QB1.

In a small blow for animal welfare, a researcher designed **an artificial dog** to help breed fleas for medical research. Each "dog", which supplies the insects with cow's blood, should be able to replace about 25 real ones.

October

Geneticists announced that they had **mapped two human chromosomes**. Chromosome 21, which is associated with Down's syndrome, and the male-sex-determining Y chromosome, had yielded to the sub-cellular cartographers.

A Dutch group reported that they had found **intact proteins in dinosaur bones**. The bio-molecules had held out against decay for 150m years.

Discoveries in the Sahara suggested that **African agriculture** originated there around 8,000 years ago, and not in northern Egypt, as had previously been thought.

Sealions joined the growing list of **animals capable of abstract reasoning**. Made to play a version of Kim's game, they were able to work out what was missing from a group of objects when it was shown to them again.

November

A spider-like robot designed to explore the interiors of volcanoes ran into trouble well before it reached the gates of hell. **Dante broke four of its legs** trying to negotiate a slag-heap in Pittsburgh.

A comet, recently rediscovered after an absence of 130 years, caused a bit of a stir. One astronomer reckoned there was one chance in 10,000 that **Comet Swift-Tuttle** would hit the earth in 2126. Since Swift-Tuttle is about 10km across,

this could cause humanity the sort of trouble suffered by the dinosaurs.

Dating of a skeleton dug up by archaeologists in the 1950s confirmed that the Texan was the **oldest known American**.

A comparison of the rates of marital break-up in identical and non-identical twins suggested that there is **a genetic propensity to divorce**.

There was good news for moderate topers. A study done in California added weight to the idea that **drinking wine** reduces heart disease.

December

Southern Californians flocking north to the safety of Seattle were disturbed to discover that their haven had suffered a **huge earthquake**. Admittedly it happened around 1,000 years ago. But no-one knows when the next one will be. . .

People are getting **more depressed**. Analysis of data from all over the world showed that the rate of clinical depression has risen in each successive generation since 1915.

One of nature's little mysteries, the **heavy neutrino**, was shown not to exist after all. Theoretical physicists breathed a sigh of relief.

Eco-worriers were given something else to think about. Studies of old ice in Greenland showed evidence of **rapid climate change** in the recent past. Glacial conditions could turn to warm weather in as little as two years.

There was more **evidence for other solar systems**. The Hubble Space Telescope photographed discs of dust surrounding 15 infant stars. Given a few million years, these will probably condense into planets.

As we reported then

Pity the typists

JANUARY 18TH *Baron Cuvier, the great 19th-century French biologist, used to work on half a dozen papers at once, each on a separate desk. Even he would be amazed, though, at the productivity of some of today's scientists*

JAMES BROWN bills himself as the "hardest-working man in showbusiness". The rather less funky Yury Struchkov, a Russian chemist at the Institute of Organoelemental Compounds in Moscow, may feel in a position to emulate him, and refer to himself as the hardest-working man in science. Between 1981 and 1990 Dr Struchkov was named as an author on 948 scientific papers. On average, he was producing one every 3.9 days.

Dr Struchkov's industriousness has not made his name a household word. In fact, until recently, it would have been flattering to describe him as obscure. He has come to the public eye as a result of research by David Pendlebury, of the Institute for Scientific Information, a concern devoted to analysing the scientific literature for publication trends. Mr Pendlebury decided to find the scientists in the world who published most. He ended up with a list of 20 people who published, in total, 9,365 papers over the decade in question, getting their names into print, on average, every nine hours 20 minutes.

There are different reasons for the apparent productivity of the top 20. Some of them are specialists in particular techniques, who collaborate with people on a large number of different projects. Some of them are chemists, able to divide one research topic into lots and lots of papers. Ferdinand Bohlmann (5th, 572 papers) is the author of "Naturally occurring terpene derivatives, part 462" and other classics. Others are the heads of large, productive laboratories, who help plan a great deal of research. Given how quickly the papers come out, they cannot have done a lot of work on all of them; one hopes they have at least read them, though.

Some of the scientists are well known. Robert Gallo (9th, 428 papers) and Anthony Fauci (17th, 338 papers) are both famous AIDS researchers. Donnall Thomas (18th, 328 papers) got the Nobel prize for his work on bone-marrow transplants. By and large, these well-known scientists write worthwhile papers—papers that get cited often by other people. Dr Gallo's papers are, on average, cited 86 times each; two of them have been cited over 1,000 times. Even those right at the top of the output table can be widely cited. Stephen Bloom (2nd place, 773 papers) gets, on average, 21 citations for each of his papers on gastroenterological research. Only

15% of them are never cited, in a field where, on average, perhaps 25% of papers are not cited within five years of publication.

For the four Russians in the list, though, this is not the case—perhaps because, despite Robert Maxwell's efforts, the rest of the world pays little attention to Russian academic journals. Whatever the reason, though, half Dr Struchkov's 948 papers have never been referred to once. Not even by himself.

Truly messed up

FEBRUARY 22ND *The first astronaut to run America's National Aeronautics and Space Administration was ejected*

THE finale was precipitous and somewhat messy, but the preceding drama was long drawn-out, and the effects may be felt for even longer. On February 10th President Bush asked Admiral Richard Truly, who runs the National Aeronautics and Space Administration (NASA), for his resignation. He got what he wanted; the resignation was announced two days later. But while the White House was saying what a fine public servant the admiral had been, he was telling reporters that he had been fired.

An embarrassing end to a job that, by some lights, Admiral Truly performed quite well. When Mr Bush chose him for the top job at NASA in 1989, he had just nursed the space-shuttle programme out of its post-Challenger malaise and back into orbit. As administrator, he saw to it that the shuttle got as close to routine operation as it is ever likely to get. He also presided over an increase in NASA's budget from $10.4 billion in 1989 to $14.3 billion this year, and spent much of that money on the grand space station the agency has been designing since the mid-1980s.

This growth, though, is not a tribute to Admiral Truly's salesmanship. He is not a particularly charismatic or expansive man,

nor is he overburdened with vision. He has reaped the benefits of running NASA at a time when the president, the vice-president and the director of the budget are all keen on spaceflight. Such benefits carry a cost: true believers, in space as on earth, are apt to try to shake things up. Admiral Truly is a spaceflight enthusiast, too. He has experienced its realities as a shuttle astronaut. However, like many others in NASA, he sees little if any difference between a commitment to space travel and a commitment to NASA's space shuttle and space station. In the eyes of other believers, most notably those of the National Space Council, a policy body run by Dan Quayle, things look less straightforward. To the space council, NASA is a tool with which to execute the president's policy—a sometimes clumsy tool.

The space council saw a clear distinction between the bureaucracy's interests and the national interest, and felt that Admiral Truly did not. Its main complaint was that whenever NASA was asked to do something—like prepare plans for a return to the moon and a trip to Mars—it would come back with a set of projects it already had going or in a file, rather than with fresh ideas. The council tried various ways of chivvying NASA, the most public of which was a commission to ponder the agency's future. This reported a little over a year ago.

The situation got worse, and more personal, when Admiral Truly's deputy, J.R. Thompson, resigned last year because of family problems. Admiral Truly wanted to appoint a replacement from within NASA. The space council wanted an outsider who might see things differently. There was no shortage of names, but none of them was willing to take the number two job. So thoughts turned to removing the admiral. According to council sources, last December Mr Quayle suggested other jobs that Admiral Truly might take, but he appeared not to respond. From then on, apparently, it was only a matter of time until his resignation was demanded.

The manner of Admiral Truly's going has made the differences between the administration and NASA quite public. Now the gap will have to be closed—and the movement will likely come from NASA. The new administrator and his or her new deputy may shake NASA up quite thoroughly. As Mr Thompson pointed out in a

Thanks, Dan

report just before he retired—a report that Admiral Truly appeared to be about to act on—NASA's research centres duplicate each other's work. Some should be reorganised, merged or closed. New procurement practices are under discussion, though despite reports to the contrary they seem not to have played a crucial part in Admiral Truly's departure. There is always the possibility of staff cuts—made easier by the fact that a lot of NASA management is nearing retirement. Some senior staff may leave in Admiral Truly's wake.

Perhaps the most intriguing of the mooted new brooms is James Abrahamson, who ran the shuttle programme in the early 1980s. As the first head of the Strategic Defence Initiative Organisation, General Abrahamson proved himself good at selling ideas. The SDIO has a reputation for coming up with clever, even whacky, notions in abundance, though it has no

record of turning them into full-scale programmes. A former SDIO man, Michael Griffin, recently took over NASA's tiny manned-exploration office, and is making gratifyingly innovative noises. General Abrahamson is now with Hughes, an aerospace company, where he might have hoped to succeed the current chief executive, Malcolm Currie. He might take the NASA job if offered it. That offer might not come, though; some say he would have a hard time getting confirmed by the Senate.

There are doubtless many other people on the list—but whether they would want the job is another question. Aerospace industry leaders lose a lot of money by choosing public service; why should they do so for an unpleasant job? NASA's budget is unlikely to grow much, so to get exciting new things done the new chief will have to cut others. At present, the administration supports the space station and the shuttle; their budgets may be hard to trim. So the new head might well end up unable to do much more than Mr Truly did, while making himself unpopular by cutting many smaller programmes. The smart thing for a candidate to do would be to take the job provided he be allowed to rethink the space station from scratch, an offer the administration would be wise to accept. Whether such wisdom will prevail is anyone's guess.

Dan Goldin, a senior manager with TRW, an aerospace firm, took the job on with reforming zeal.

The embryo's canary

APRIL 4TH *Morning sickness may not be much fun for the mother, but could be good for the baby*

THE fact that many women spend the first three months of their pregnancies vomiting and feeling rotten has always been a little baffling to scientists. Their explanations, and the solutions that flowed from them, have been unimpressive. Some Freudians thought morning sickness reflected an (anatomically unlikely) urge to expel the fetus and reject motherhood. Women with severe cases were locked up without receptacles so that they wallowed in the consequences of their own unmaternal natures. In modern times, the drug that proved best at eradicating the symptoms of morning sickness was thalidomide, which dreadfully deformed fetuses.

That could be a terrible irony; a new theory has it that morning sickness exists to stop women from eating things that might

deform their fetuses. The suggestion is put forward by Margie Profet, a scientist at the University of California at Berkeley. Ms Profet's idea is that morning sickness is a way of avoiding toxic food.

Most people do not need any extra inducement to avoid poisons, except if the poison is pleasurable or the dose negligible. But an embryo is sensitive to small doses that a healthy woman takes in her stride. When it is 20-56 days old it undergoes the delicate process of organogenesis, in which bland all-purpose cells are told that they must become parts of the fetus's limbs, brain, heart, genitalia and the like. At this point the embryo is especially vulnerable to deformation by tiny doses of chemicals that can cause havoc among its impressionable, quickly growing cells.

Morning sickness, which peaks at exactly that period, does not take the form of overt vomiting in all women; in some it is manifested as an aversion to certain foods, tastes and smells, which can provoke nausea. Typical nauseators are coffee, meat and bitter or spicy vegetables. Ms Profet believes the smells given off by the toxins with which vegetables fight off herbivores, and those which bacteria produce in rotting meat, are those that most revolt pregnant women.

Vegetables are loaded with toxic chemicals, put there to stop animals from eating them. When they do not succeed in this deterrence, the effects, particularly for the unborn, can be dire. On one farm in California, a boy, some goat kids and a litter of puppies were all born deformed because of milk from a goat that had been eating lupins. In Ireland, anencephaly-spina-bifida is a relatively common condition;

Enough of the nausea, bring on the Valium

Ms Profet points out that this might be because of potato toxins.

Various factors suggest that morning sickness is a way of avoiding such things. During the early stages of pregnancy, women's sense of smell—better than men's—becomes yet more acute; food tends to linger longer in their stomachs, as if being gingerly tested for toxicity, to be got rid of if anything suspicious is found; and the part of the brain that triggers vomiting is made more sensitive by the ratio of the hormone oestradiol to the hormone progesterone, which quintuples. All this, says Ms Profet, looks like an evolved ability to sense food that might be dangerous to embryos. A telling piece of evidence, perhaps, and one that doctors use to reassure their patients, is that a pregnancy is three times more

likely to end in miscarriage if the mother does not feel sick.

In practice, few foods contain enough toxins to be of danger, but that is because mankind invented agriculture and tamed the plants it eats, greatly reducing their toxic contents by selective breeding. Cooking, too, can help: bake a potato in clay and the alkaloid toxins within are drawn out. Back in the Pleistocene epoch, when people were hunter-gatherers and all food was wild, the risk of eating something that might damage a fetus was probably quite high. In some societies people make deliberate use of these toxins to terminate pregnancies. The fact that few pregnant women develop an aversion to alcohol, though it can damage fetuses, would be nicely explained if morning sickness was tuned to

the dangers faced by long-ago hunter gatherers, who did not have the wherewithal to produce liquor.

Ms Profet is not alone in offering a new explanation for morning sickness. David Haig at Oxford University believes that the nausea is the result of the early embryo's efforts to prevent its own abortion—an idea which might supplement, rather than contradict, Ms Profet's. Dr Haig's argument is that during the weeks when morning sickness is at its worst, the embryo produces a hormone called chorionic gonadotropin. This makes the mother's ovaries produce progesterone, and progesterone keeps the pregnancy going, but may make the mother sick. All this is good for the fetus, but not necessarily for the mother. It may well be better—in evolutionary terms—for her to have an early miscarriage if she is too undernourished or sick to carry a pregnancy to term, or if her fetus is abnormal. So morning sickness is a symptom of a power struggle between the fetus and the mother.

Dr Haig sees other examples of this struggle. Later on in pregnancy, the fetus secretes hormones into the mother that make her hungry and liable to build up her mammary tissue. After birth, the mother strikes back. According to scientists in Sweden, breast milk contains enough benzodiazepines (the family of chemicals that includes Valium) to soothe a baby for a few hours. Whether that is in the baby's interests is hard to tell. It certainly helps everyone else.

Silicon cilia

APRIL 18TH, TOKYO
The technology used for making silicon chips can do a lot else, if you use a little imagination. Here is one example

THERE is more to making microscopic machines than simply shrinking the parts of ordinary ones. At small scales, the world behaves differently. Things that normally matter, such as gravity, become negligible; other things, such as electrostatic forces, take on a new significance. These forces make friction a terrible nuisance. Gears and joints, the stuff of everyday machinery, become harder and harder to engineer as you shrink. However, natural selection has provided nature with alternative solutions, and Japanese researchers have been learning to imitate one of them: ciliary motion. In future, tiny plastic hairs on a silicon chip could move light objects around in the same way that minute hairs in your lungs rhythmically sweep away mucus.

Using the same standard techniques with which silicon chips are made, Hiroyuki Fujita and colleagues at Tokyo

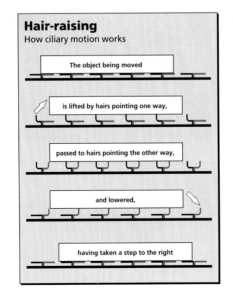

Hair-raising
How ciliary motion works

The object being moved

is lifted by hairs pointing one way,

passed to hairs pointing the other way,

and lowered,

having taken a step to the right

University's Institute of Industrial Science have made arrays of tiny hairs, each about half a millimetre long, on a piece of silicon. Each hair is made of two different types of plastic, with a minute wire sandwiched between them. To begin with, the hairs lie flat; after being cured at a high temperature, they curl up. Then, when a current is run through the wire, making it warm, the two types of plastic expand, but to a different degree: the hair uncurls until it is almost flat again.

The fact that they depend on warming up and cooling down to do anything might make you think that these "bimorph thermal actuators" would be slow. Here, though, is one of the advantages of smallness. As objects shrink, their volume gets smaller more quickly than their surface area does. Since the rate of cooling depends on the surface area, but the amount of heat stored depends on the volume, microhairs cool much more efficiently than the large parts of a normal machine would. So they can be made to curl and uncurl more than ten times a second.

It is easy to produce arrays of thousands of hairs wired up in such a way that the heating can be computer-controlled. The simplest such arrays, like Dr Fujita's, have the hairs arranged in rows, with successive hairs in each row pointing in opposite directions. By heating the two types of hair in the right sequence, it is possible to move an object along the direction of the hairs (see diagram opposite).

Though the individual hairs are minute, they can do a good deal of work when acting in unison. Dr Fujita's prototype can support aluminium foil. More robust versions now being developed should be able to move a silicon wafer. By inter-

weaving rows of hairs at right angles to each other, it will be possible to control the exact position of an object anywhere on the hairy surface. One obvious application would be to make a surface that automatically moves a chip into exactly the place it has to be in, in order for automatic tests to be done.

In large arrays with millions of hairs, trying to send messages to each individual hair would be a logistical nightmare. So the hairs will have to be given some autonomy. Since the hairs are already on a silicon chip, it is quite simple to give each one some computing power. Then, as long as each hair can communicate with its nearest neighbours, the surface can work out what needs to be done all on its own.

Imagine an array with microsensors dispersed among the hairs, with the sensors designed to detect certain chemicals on biological cells, and tell the hairs about them. Such a device might well be able to sort out cells, moving one type one way and one type the other way, a useful trick for biological laboratories.

Even more ambitious would be to mimic one of nature's applications of microhairs. Ciliates are micro-organisms that move themselves around by undulating the hair-like protrusions on their surfaces. If robots are ever to get really small, they might be obliged to do the same thing, swimming around the world—or around the human body—on a layer of rippling, intelligent fur.

Almost in the beginning

MAY 2ND   *Cosmologists, astronomers and physicists have found new evidence for their picture of the early universe—but there are still gaps to fill in*

ON A clear day, you can see the tail end of the big bang—a warm, comforting glow of microwaves. Until last week, that glow seemed to be spread evenly across the sky. Then, on April 23rd, George Smoot of the University of California at Berkeley announced to the American Physical Society that it was subtly warped. Cosmologists were cock-a-hoop. They had had trouble reconciling the picture of early smoothness painted by the microwaves with today's lumpy universe. A little youthful acne was just what they wanted.

Dr Smoot's modest lumps, the cosmologists think, are the seeds from which today's galactic agglomerations, strewn across the heavens like foam on a beach, have grown. Though such lumps were expected, their discovery—not startling, but impressive— gave the theoreticians a warm, comforting glow of their own.

The radiation from the cosmic microwave background that reaches earth—or, in the case of this latest work, a NASA satellite called the Cosmic Background Explorer (COBE) in orbit around it—has been travelling since just after the beginning of time. Its discovery, in 1965, was evidence for the big bang. It showed that, fairly early on, the universe was a uniformly hot cloud of gas not unlike the sun. Like the sun, this cloud gave off light. That light has been stretched into microwaves during 15 billion years of travel across an ever-expanding universe.

The big bang was the start of this expansion: the bursting into existence of space itself, as well as matter. After the initial turmoil had settled down, the particles in the early universe began to combine. Quarks— among the most basic particles known— linked up to form protons and neutrons; later some of the protons joined neutrons to create atomic nuclei; later still things got so cool that electrons, which had remained aloof in the previous kerfuffle and were rushing around unattached, abandoned their frivolity and settled down with the nuclei to form atoms.

At this point (between 100,000 and 1m years after the beginning) the universe, hitherto opaque because light could not move any appreciable distance without hitting something, became transparent. It is the radiation released then that COBE sees.

Observations like COBE's mark the limit of astronomy. Nothing earlier can be seen; astronomy in an opaque universe is a fruitless task. So everything before the release of the microwaves—which means almost all the most significant developments in the history of the universe—can only be inferred. Dr Smoot and his team believe they have found suitable material for inference: the traces of "inflation".

According to theoreticians an inflationary fit seized the universe soon after the big bang. At the point when it was the size of an atom and growing sedately, it suddenly sped up its expansion enormously and became billions of times bigger. Thus enlarged, it slowed back to its previous rate of growth.

Theoreticians like this model because it explains why the initial bubble of space and matter ended up as today's relatively even universe, rather than immediately collapsing in on itself or expanding so quickly that no structures at all could form. It also allows the big bang to co-exist happily with modern particle physics. Older versions of the big bang predicted the release into the universe of some of the more upsetting things that live in physicists' imaginations. Inflation kept most of them confined.

Inflation was so abrupt that the post-inflation universe retained many of the pleasant attributes of its former, microscopic self, such as smoothness. But nothing is perfectly smooth—quantum mechanics introduces a fuzzy uncertainty that brooks no perfection, so a slight unevenness was left in the fabric of space. It is this unevenness, reflected in the microwave background, that Dr Smoot believes he has mapped.

The people who developed the idea of inflation (it was thought up by Alan Guth, of the Massachusetts Institute of Technology, but others have added to it substantially) are delighted to have had their ideas borne out. Only inflation can explain how structures could have grown so big when the universe was still small. And inflation predicts mild density fluctuations, all the same depth but on a wide range of scales. That is what seems to have been seen, so their theories look good. But they are not the only ones interested in the new map.

Particle physicists adore hot environments where their subjects can be made to whizz around at high speeds. Today's big particle accelerators can heat things up and bang them together forcefully enough to recreate the conditions that held sway a trillionth of a second after the big bang. A trillionth of a second may not sound very long, but in the early history of the universe, it was an eon. By the time it had reached that ripe old age, the universe was already a hundred trillion trillion times older than it had been at the end of inflation, and commensurately cooler and more sedate.

The really early stuff is far beyond the reach of any earthly accelerator imaginable. It was during this period that the fundamental forces of the universe—gravity, electromagnetism and the forces that hold atomic nuclei together—sorted themselves out. The two clans of elementary particles—the quarks, and the electrons and their relatives—also asserted their identities at this time. Studying the faint echoes of the big bang is the most realistic hope of understanding how this happened.

As well as shedding light on the smallest things around, the COBE data, and the research which will follow on from them, should provide those who study the large structures in the universe—clusters and superclusters of galaxies, and mysterious barren voids between them—with much assistance. Most of these researchers think that these structures are pulled together by gravity, which means that there must have been an uneven distribution of matter at the beginning. If matter were evenly spread, such structures would never form; nothing would have any reason to fall one way rather than another. So there must have been denser and thus more attractive regions to act as seeds for later structures to form around. The anomalies seen by COBE look like such seeds.

Although knowing what the seeds are like helps a lot, more is needed to explain the structures. The anomalies seen by COBE cannot be the ancestors of the galaxies and clusters observed today in the local neighbourhood. They are much too big.

COBE can see nothing that stretches across less than 7° of the sky (a full moon is ½° across). The largest features in the sky today, vast though they are, would take up about 1° if seen from the perspective of 15 billion light years—the distance to the features COBE is seeing. Theory says that if there are density fluctuations on the scale COBE can see, there must be similar ones on smaller scales; it is these that would actually explain galaxies. As yet, they have still to be glimpsed.

Even so, more might soon be known about the seeds than about the things they grew into. Astronomers have only a shaky grasp of the extent and nature of the large-scale structure around today. Some ways of looking at the sky reveal huge structures; others reveal less. To say how the density fluctuations evolved, it would help to have

a clearer picture of what they evolved into. Huge new surveys of the sky planned for the next few years should help with that.

A few beasts escape

There is another problem. Although the features seen by COBE are wide, they are not terribly deep. The highs are only a thousandth of a percent higher than the lows; the density differences are tiny. Though these are the only possible seeds for structures to form from, they seem too small to do the job.

Theorists exist to find answers and they have an answer for this one—invent a new form of matter. They reckon that the gravitational effects of the visible seeds are amplified by the presence of something that otherwise barely interacts with "normal" matter of the sort from which the earth is made.

This idea—that there is much more to the universe than meets the eye—can be arrived at by other paths. Inflation specifies

the density of the universe quite precisely. If the visible stars and galaxies were all there was to it, its density would be much too low. But, by watching the movements of the galaxies, astronomers infer that there is lots of invisible mass around, pulling at the visible. Invisible matter can still be normal matter—the earth is invisible from any significant distance. Other arguments, though, suggest that the missing mass is not in the form of planets and dust clouds.

One way to peer around the veil of opacity that hides the earliest universe is to study the elements created in the big bang by the combination of protons and neutrons—a method on which most ideas about the post-inflation big bang are based. The abundance of these elements depends on how densely the protons and neutrons were packed together in the fireball. It turns out that the density of protons and neutrons in the fireball could at most have been about 10% of what is needed for inflation to be true. Since almost all of the mass of normal matter is in the form of protons and neutrons, this implies that something else, probably something unlike any type of matter ever seen, makes up 90% of the mass of the universe.

The COBE results back this extraordinary idea up in various ways. They argue strongly against a "lumpy" big bang. Lumpiness was one suggested way of cooking up the observed primordial distribution of elements with a lot more protons and neutrons around. This would eliminate the need for new sorts of matter to satisfy inflation. COBE has also shown that the only things that could be seeds for structure are too small to do the job unaided. There must be some odd extra matter to amplify them. That last part of the argument may not be elegant. To say that the fluctuations are the seeds, but then that they are not deep enough to be the seeds, is not terribly satisfying. The lack of other possibilities does, however, give it strength.

The most popular current mechanism for turning seeds into structures invokes "cold dark matter". The theory does not specify what this matter is, but the imaginations of the physicists can provide a wide, not to mention weird, range of possibilities. Cold dark matter theory is hard pressed to produce structures as large as those that many now seem to see in the night sky from fluctuations as weak as those that COBE has found. On the other hand, it can turn such fluctuations into almost the right sort of structures. If the seed fluctuations were twice as pronounced as they appear, all would be clear. As it is, the argument will be hard fought. Some theorists welcome the new results as vindications of cold dark matter, others see them as the final nail in its coffin.

Perhaps there is more than one sort of

dark matter. Or perhaps the seeds are more complex than these first results suggest. At scales smaller than those that COBE sees—corresponding to patches of sky only a degree or less across—the fluctuations may be more pronounced (though canonical inflation says they should not be). Or there may be extra sources of structure at such scales. Experiments on balloons and in Antarctica, where the air is dry and clear, are already measuring the background at these scales and are almost as sensitive as COBE's detectors. As yet, the groups making these measurements have reported seeing no structure at all.

For the moment cosmologists have every right to feel happy about the COBE results. But they should not give the impression that everything is sewn up. Leaving aside the risk of hubris, there is also the problem of using up some excitement best left for later, yet more dramatic, findings. Otherwise, what will there be left to say when someone manages to find some of the presumably ubiquitous but curiously elusive dark matter, and mankind finally sees what most of the universe is made of?

By December results from balloons seemed to confirm COBE's findings.

Drift-nets for data

APRIL 4TH *Oceanographers around the world are trying to bridge the gulfs between them. On their success may hang any chance of predicting climatic change*

LOOKED at from space, the earth is largely a tranquil blue, smeared with a few swirling clouds. On the surface, it is a wet and windy place. The oceans rage as powerfully as the atmosphere. Their stirrings, though, are poorly understood. Compared with oceanography, weather forecasting is an exact science.

This might seem surprising, since the two disciplines have a lot in common. They are both concerned with the behaviour of large bodies of thinly spread fluid. The difference is that whereas the oceans cover 70% of the planet's surface, the atmosphere covers 100% of it, including the bits where people live. That means people are interested in the weather. Few, apart from sailors, pay much attention to the sea.

That is changing, at least among scientists. Fishermen and their friends are given to describing the seas as a vast storehouse. As well as storing food, they also store large amounts of heat and carbon dioxide (CO_2)—both of which matter to climatologists. Tracking the movement of these two things has given oceanography the stimulus, and the money, it needed to bloom. New equipment is being designed, satellite launches planned, and cans of alphabet soup (WOCE, the World Ocean Circulation Experiment; JGOFS, the Joint Global Ocean Flux Study; and, ultimately, GOOS, the Global Ocean Observation System) are being stirred into the currents.

As the acronyms suggest, the emphasis is on collecting data from all over the world. The old way of doing oceanography with a few expensive cruises is giving way to a new "drift-net science", in which huge amounts of data are gathered from as wide an area as possible. Floating probes are being thrown into the ocean by the hundred. Satellites scan all seven seas, listening to the probes or monitoring things themselves.

The probes are oceanography's weather balloons—they go with the flow in a global game of Pooh-sticks. Some float on the surface. Others, of carefully calculated density, sink to a particular level and then drift with the deeper currents—poorly understood and often at odds with their superficial siblings.

There are two sorts of sinking probe: cheap and simple; not-so-cheap and clever. Both sorts have to overcome an obstacle which physics has put in their path. Water is opaque to radio waves and, for that matter, to light. The ocean depths are dark and silent. To reveal what it has learnt in those Stygian currents, a probe must surface.

A cheap, simple probe is essentially an alarm clock and a radio transmitter. The clock is set for anything from six months to five years. When it goes off, the instrument

jettisons a weight and bobs to the surface. The radio transmitter then starts up, announcing to a passing satellite—normally one of America's weather satellites—where the probe is. Toss enough probes overboard, at $1,700 a throw, and with time you can get some idea of whither, and how fast, the undersea currents are flowing.

Clever probes tell you more. They use sound waves, which travel extremely well underwater, to communicate with beacons fixed to the sea floor. In some cases the beacons broadcast and the probes work out where they are every few days by listening to the nearest beacons. They then store the information until it is time to surface and reveal, not just where they are, but also how they got there. Other probes talk to the beacons and rely on them to pass the word on; these probes need never surface at all.

All these fancy probes cost a lot ($3,700-15,000) but yield much more data. They can map "mesoscale eddies", which are to the oceans what storm systems are to the atmosphere. A few hundred kilometres across, eddies are the things from which larger ocean currents are made. These currents are responsible for about half of the heat-flow from the equator to the poles. That "about half" could be a quarter; it could be three-quarters. With figures as basic as these in doubt, it is impossible to make plausible forecasts of the planet's climate. One of the goals of WOCE, which supervises most of today's probe-dumping, is to get a better grip on these figures.

Source for the GOOS

Satellites can do much more than listen for the chirpings of probes. Though physics conspires to stop them looking into the ocean deeps, they can study its surface in many different ways. WOCE is about to launch a satellite to do just that. TOPEX/Poseidon is a Franco-American effort due to lift-off from French Guiana in July. The radar it carries should be able to map the level of the sea to within 2cm; that should be good enough to pick up the

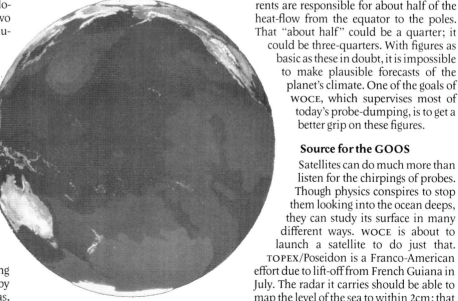

A wet world

slight variations caused by the currents.

Floating probes and satellites like TOPEX/Poseidon should help to discover how heat moves around. Another trick will enable scientists to take the ocean's temperature and see whether the overall amount of heat is increasing. The speed of sound in water depends upon how hot the water is; so measuring how long a noise takes to get from A to B is like sticking a thermometer in the sea—or, rather, like stringing a line of thermometers through the depths and taking the average.

In 1991 a group of scientists, led by Walter Munk of the Scripps Institution in La Jolla, California, tried this out in a big way. They broadcast noise from Heard Island in the southern Indian Ocean to 18 receiving stations around the world, the farthest being 18,000km (11,000 miles) away near Seattle. All the stations heard the signal loud and clear. A series of such reports would, in theory, allow the measurement of temperature changes of a few thousandths of a degree a year, enough to pick up global warming. The group now hopes to start a decade-long experiment, beginning in 1993 with broadcasts from California to New Zealand, and eventually incorporating a worldwide network of stations. Some scientists interested in marine mammals have worried that this may deafen their charges. To lessen their fears, Dr Munk is turning down the volume.

The other climatic variable at the mercy of the oceans, CO_2, moves in and out of the sea at the whim of the creatures that breathe and photosynthesise near the surface. JGOFS exists to study these whims. At the moment it uses ships to study plankton but it, too, should soon get a satellite. In

Follow that seal

1993 the Orbital Sciences Corporation, based in Virginia, will launch a satellite called SeaStar. This will carry an instrument called SeaWiFS (Sea-viewing Wide Field Sensor) which will monitor the colour of the sea, showing scientists where plankton are growing. OSC has agreed to sell the SeaWiFS data to NASA for $43.5m—an intriguing new way for governments to catch data.

So far JGOFS has mainly studied the north Atlantic, though it is now extending its net to the Pacific and Antarctic. Scientists co-ordinated by Michael Whitfield of the Plymouth Marine Laboratory in England have studied how the amount of CO_2 in the top few metres of the ocean varies. In the spring, small plants called diatoms bloom and grow, using up CO_2 as they do so and making room for more of it to dissolve from the atmosphere. Diatoms are eaten by fish, so some of this CO_2 ends up being removed from circulation, dropping to the bottom of the ocean as—well, as

droppings. JGOFS has provided new detail on this, and turned up a surprise. Coccolithophores (more small, floating plants) bloom at more or less the same time; they use CO_2 to make their shells and were thus expected to reduce its level still further. But their shell-making leaves the water near the surface slightly more alkaline. CO_2 does not dissolve well in alkaline water. So the growth of coccolithophores, unlike that of diatoms, reduces the amount of gas the oceans absorb.

WOCE, JGOFS and their like are intermediaries. They pave the way for GOOS and its atmospheric partner, the Global Climate Observing System. These should be flying, floating and drifting into existence in about ten years' time. John Woods, of Britain's Natural Environmental Research Council (NERC), hopes GOOS will net about 100 times more data than are landed today—enough to test supercomputer models of how the oceans work. It will require better equipment and more money, perhaps $2 billion a year.

At NERC, they have already laid their plans. They are designing DOLPHIN (Deep Ocean Long Path Hydrographic Instrument), a robot submarine powered by a fuel cell, which will be capable of crossing an ocean, of diving as deep as 6km, and of resurfacing every 30km to talk to satellites. Much of DOLPHIN is still at the design stage, but the transmitter is already finished. Casting around for something to test it on, NERC turned to its zoologists. They had just the thing—as large and ocean-going as DOLPHIN is hoped to be, though a little more difficult to handle. So elephant seals are the latest recruits to the grand alliance of cceanographers.

The paradigm shift hits the particle fans

JUNE 27TH   *After years of argument, the House of Representatives voted to cancel the Superconducting Super Collider*

THOMAS KUHN invented the notion of the paradigm shift to explain what happens in scientific revolutions. A revolution happens, his theory goes, not because of startling new facts, but because of a change in the overall way that the universe is seen. This may be for some reason that has little to do with the internal logic of science, and a lot to do with the society in which scientists live and work. After this shift, old knowledge suddenly takes on new meaning: the sight of the rising sun becomes evidence for the turning earth.

Something like a paradigm shift seemed to take place in June—not among scientists, but among a group that has enormous influence over them. America's

House of Representatives voted to cancel the Superconducting Super Collider. The facts about the SSC had not changed much since it was endorsed by the House in 1991; but old knowledge had taken on new meaning.

The plan was as follows. The SSC, a loop 86km (54 miles) in circumference, would house two counter-rotating beams of protons, accelerated to inordinately high energies. These beams would meet each other head-on inside massive detectors. So much energy would be released in these collisions that particles never before seen anywhere on earth would parade before the detectors' all-seeing eyes.

Physicists think a study of these parti-

cles—there may be only one, a "Higgs boson", but most expect nature to be more bountiful—will explain why the electromagnetic force and the weak nuclear force, which theory describes as two faces of one coin, look so different. Electromagnetic forces exert their influence at great distances; the weak force can barely make itself felt outside the confines of atomic nuclei.

That understanding would go some way to explaining the masses of subatomic particles, and perhaps the nature of mass itself. And, said its proponents, the SSC might also produce any number of other novelties, since its collisions would provide 20 times the particle-making energy available in today's most powerful machine, the Tevatron at Fermilab in Illinois.

As well as particles, the SSC would produce jobs and prestige. Most of the jobs are for physicists and Texans—the collider was to be built below the fields of Waxahachie, south of Dallas—but some would be found farther away. General Dynamics, for example, which still hopes to build many of the superconducting magnets needed, plans to do so in Louisiana, represented in the Senate by Bennett Johnston, a keen ssc supporter and chairman of the Senate appropriations committee. The prestige is felt important because, in the past decade, the most impressive discoveries in particle physics—a field in which America was once world leader and which the ssc would dominate—happened in Europe.

Balanced against these benefits is the project's cost. When the ssc was first planned, by a group of physicists who were not going to have to build it, the cost of the machine and its two detectors was estimated at around $4 billion (in 1986 dollars). Inflation and changes to schedule and design had raised this to $8.25 billion. In big science, what goes up keeps going up.

A new mood in the House of Representatives gave the arguments over cost added weight. The debate over the balanced-budget amendment raised temperatures and pricked consciences. Loud Texan support for the amendment left some thinking that a big cut that hurts Texas is no more than just deserts. Texan opposition to aid for Los Angeles and Chicago may not have helped, either. The Illinois and Californian delegations both showed a strong swing against the ssc.

As it happens, these are the home states of America's two big particle-physics laboratories, Fermilab and the Stanford Linear Accelerator Centre (SLAC). When the

ssc was first proposed, it was on the understanding that its budget would be "new money", not taken from the existing particle-physics budget. That proved not to be the case. The cost of the ssc threatened the proposed upgrade of Fermilab's Tevatron—which will be essential for preparing scientists to work on the ssc. SLAC is in a more parlous state. Without money for a modest new machine, it may have to close. Physicists in other areas supported by the Department of Energy (DOE) have similar complaints. After hearing them, the secretary of energy, James Watkins, is reported to have said that "the level of unhappiness is about equal, and that makes me feel good". However gratifying its even distribution, though, the level of unhappiness was high, and likely to climb. Advisers to the DOE said that non-ssc particle physics might be cut in half to pay for the ssc.

Despite the fact that it seems to blight their present, American particle physicists are still supporting the ssc as their future.

Even physicists who doubt the wisdom of spending every last penny on a mammoth proton accelerator—often those with more experience in accelerating electrons—will not speak out against it. For six decades they have wanted more powerful accelerators, and governments around the world have paid up. It is hard to call a stop.

Now that the stop appears to have been called, many will despair. If there is no reprieve, some will leave for Europe, where a similar though smaller machine is planned. Others will busy themselves with lesser machines designed to study the already-known in greater detail, rather than to push back the frontiers, or with experiments to detect particles provided by nature, not made by man. If, that is, any of the money saved by cutting the ssc is spent on particle physics.

It may not come to that. The Senate may seek to restore the ssc's money. But it is hard to believe that President Bush's request of $650m will be sent to Texas in 1993. A big cut would set back schedules, drag out the programme and increase the total cost—meaning that next year's request will have to be even larger.

The House may merely have been venting its frustration and anger against Texas; next year, or even next week, could be business as usual. That is the hope of those backing the space station, another big programme with a large Texan component that now looks less secure than it did. But perhaps, having killed once, the House will kill again. If the space station, in its turn, is brought low, then the big-science paradigm could be gone for good.

....

The Senate saved the ssc, and the space station lived on, too; both now face a new Congress.

The defences

AUGUST 1ST, AMSTERDAM *In the effort to understand AIDS, attention is moving from the virus to the immune system that the virus attacks. Within that system the virus may find allies as well as enemies*

A FEW people die of AIDS within a year of being exposed to the human immunodeficiency virus (HIV). Most of those infected suffer a slower decline, but with the same sad end. A study in San Francisco shows 65% dying within 12½ years of antibodies against the virus being detected in their blood. Some, though, have lived healthily with the virus for more than ten years. And

others, it seems, have been exposed to the virus but have suffered no subsequent infection at all. No one knows what distinguishes these groups—but at the eighth international AIDS conference, in Amsterdam last week, researchers were backing the immune system as the likeliest candidate. The body's response to the virus is getting more and more attention, and

not before time.

One reason for the increase of interest in the immune system is the ever more pressing need to make use of it. Large clinical trials are already being designed to test vaccines that might produce a protective immune response. The snag is that nobody yet knows which vaccine should be tried, because nobody knows which immune response might turn out to be protective.

Vaccines that encourage the production of antibodies, large proteins secreted by immune cells, have received most atten-

tion to date. Some antibodies can stick to HIV's protein coat, stop the virus from getting into its target cells—those which carry a cell-surface protein called CD4—and call down upon the invader the wrath of other parts of the immune system. But antibodies may not be the best thing for the immune system to make. After all, people with antibodies to HIV do get sick. Jaap Goudsmit of the University of Amsterdam, summing up the conference's basic science, put it like this: there is little evidence that antibodies that can neutralise all the different strains of the virus that exist, whereas there is evidence that small viral mutations can make hitherto-effective antibodies useless, or even harmful.

Some cells in the immune system, rather than producing antibodies to attack invaders, go after the enemy themselves. These vigilantes recognise and kill any cells they find infected with viruses. They can be primed by vaccines just as antibody responses can. Nobody knows quite how important it is for an AIDS vaccine to bring forth this sort of cell-mediated immunity, but in a fascinating if speculative talk at the conference, Jonas Salk argued that it is vital.

Dr Salk's ideas date back a long way, but he has linked them to one of the most exciting new findings in immunology. The immune cells that carry the most CD4, and which HIV attacks most severely, aid and abet the killers and the antibody producers. These "helper T-cells" may sound secondary, but they are no more subservient than senior civil servants, whom they resemble in many ways. They look after the immune system's old records, implement its new programmes and stop things from grinding to a halt. Unfortunately, there is another similarity between civil servants and helper T-cells; it can be hard to tell one from the next, and thus difficult to know

which can help you.

This confusion is now being sorted out. Since the mid-1980s work on mice has shown the existence of two job-specific sub-groups of helper T-cell, called TH1 and TH2. TH1 cells appear to be involved in cell-mediated immunity, TH2 in antibody responses. In the past couple of years, evidence has grown for the existence of distinct TH1 and TH2 cells in people, as well as mice, though there are probably other sub-groups as well, as yet undefined.

Using various studies as support, Dr Salk argues that a TH1 response is the key to fighting the virus. He points out that, in his laboratory, vaccines designed to protect monkeys against a related virus, SIV, were useless even when they produced lots of promising-looking antibodies. (Other groups have managed to protect monkeys with vaccines.) Moreover, there are other diseases in which small doses of vaccine or of the disease-inducing organism provoke no production of antibodies, but still leave a protective immune response.

Dr Salk suggests that the body's first reaction to an invader which passes from cell to cell—as some viruses and parasites do, and as HIV well might—is to use the TH1 system. TH2, he thinks, kicks in later, and is not a good thing, since the TH2 system suppresses the activities of the TH1 system. A TH1 response which never escalated into antibody-producing TH2 might work better.

As evidence, he cites the work of Gene Shearer and Mario Clerici at America's National Cancer Institute. Dr Shearer presented this research to an enthusiastic audience. The study looked at people whom one might expect to be infected but are not—men who have had unprotected receptive anal sex with a number of partners; intravenous drug users; children of HIV-positive mothers; and health workers ex-

posed to infected blood. In all these groups, half or more of those tested had cell-mediated responses to proteins associated with HIV—but their bodies held no trace of the virus, nor any antibodies against it. In control groups of people at no particular risk of infection, only about one in 20 showed a similar response to the proteins.

Those background reactions may well be caused by cells attuned to something else reacting to the HIV proteins by mistake—there is no reason to think that all those people have been exposed to HIV. But the fact that those who might have been exposed show a ten-times higher frequency of response suggests that some of them have indeed been exposed to the virus, and that their TH1 cells have orchestrated a successful defence without the TH2 system ever being turned on.

This idea excites Dr Shearer, Dr Salk and many others. Dr Shearer ended his talk by suggesting that, in studying antibody-positive people, most of whom eventually die, scientists have been devoting their time to immune systems that have failed. Look for uninfected people with a cell-mediated response, and you will see systems that have succeeded. That is why Dr Salk, working on the principle that success is the thing to emulate, suggests that a protective vaccine should be designed to bring forth the TH1 response, not an antibody response.

This is not an idea that applies only to AIDS. Work on leprosy and tropical parasites has also shown that TH1 responses can be the best available, and that TH2 and other similar responses can facilitate the course of disease. The most widely used vaccine in the world, BCG, which protects children against tuberculosis, produces a TH1 response—though its effectiveness is notoriously variable. Dr Salk thinks that questions about the feasibility of an HIV vaccine that produces a TH1 effect could largely be answered by tests in mice and monkeys before anything was tried on humans. There is, of course, no guarantee of success. People who show a cell-mediated response to HIV might still become infected if they encountered the virus again. And the fact that some antibody-positive people remain healthy for a long time suggests that a successful response need not spurn TH2 and antibodies.

After the damage is done

What of preventing disease in those already infected? Here the picture becomes even more complex. The mechanisms by which HIV causes its depredations are far from understood—a point that the few who doubt the virus's causal role are keen to stress.

A fair number of scientists still believe—as most used to—that the virus does its damage simply by killing the cells it infects. Early work showed little virus and few infected cells in the blood, which made this "direct killing" hard for some to imagine. Now more sensitive tests have revealed higher levels of infected cells and virus particles. And researchers have found yet more HIV—ten times as much—in the lymph nodes, the redoubts to which immune cells flock for reinforcements, new commands and anything else they need. Anthony Fauci, who runs the AIDS programme at America's National Institute of Allergy and Infectious Diseases, devoted much of his talk to new studies of the complex goings-on in lymph nodes. (The man who donated the nodes in question had his say too, talking about ways in in which infected people could help research. Only at AIDS conferences are such partnerships seen.)

Dr Fauci's pictures provided further fuel for an idea that many researchers are now starting to embrace: that something more subtle than direct killing is going on. AIDS bears little resemblance to diseases caused by run-of-the-mill viruses, but in some ways it looks like an auto-immune disease. Other viruses like HIV do their damage by setting a confused immune system upon itself. So the idea that HIV does at least some of its damage by getting the immune system to malfunction and attack itself has much to be said for it. That might explain why, as Australian research has shown, the body is able to deal with large amounts of virus straight after infection, but fails to control smaller amounts later.

The conference in Amsterdam heard as many different theories about what HIV does to the immune system as the city has canals. Broadly speaking, by disrupting the helper-cell bureaucracy and perverting other CD4-bearing cells, the virus might: activate various types of immune cell uncontrollably, or allow other micro-organisms to do so; turn large parts of the immune system off; get parts of the immune system to lay waste to other parts; or somehow persuade uninfected cells to kill themselves. The last idea exploits a sort of built-in obsolescence for cells called "apoptosis"; it is very trendy at the moment, particularly in France.

For all the discussion, none of these ideas was ruled firmly in or out. That may be because of too little data. But it may also be because the virus tries its hand at every

method, and that, like the city's canals, these are all connected.

Various ways in which the virus might cause disease by affecting cells it does not infect have intrigued Dr Shearer and Dr Clerici over the years. Their latest research may help to reveal some of the connections among them, especially those which lead back to the TH1/TH2 story. Immune cells give off chemicals called cytokines in order to influence each other. One of the things TH1 cells give off is interleukin-2 (IL-2), which suppresses TH2 cells. TH2 cells give off IL-4 and IL-10, among other things, which suppress TH1. In people infected with HIV who get sicker, Dr Shearer sees initially high levels of IL-2 drop; then IL-4

Too late for this cell

levels rise; lastly IL-10 levels climb, too.

That looks like TH2 replacing TH1, but things may be a little more complicated. In their studies of leprosy, Barry Bloom, of the Albert Einstein College of Medicine in the Bronx, and his colleagues have seen TH1 suppressed not by CD4-carrying helper T-cells but by cells carrying a different marker, CD8. However, the active agents still seem to be the interleukins associated with TH2 cells. Dr Shearer and Dr Clerici have shown that CD8 cells are responsible for suppressing normal T-helper function in seemingly healthy people infected with HIV.

These findings may matter to researchers experimenting with therapeutic vaccines—vaccines given to help the body cope after infection rather than to protect it from infection in the first place. Various trials are going on, so far without any conclusive evidence of an effect. Dr Salk thinks that the aim should be to return the body to a strong TH1 response. Dr Bloom and his colleagues have had success trying some-

thing similar. They took people with leishmaniasis, a tropical disease, and injected them with TH1-inducing BCG and dead leishmania parasites. Damaging TH2 responses were turned into successful TH1.

Dr Salk's therapeutic-vaccine trial, which uses a vaccine that does not elicit the normal anti-HIV antibodies, might produce the TH1 effect he wants. The other therapeutic vaccines are designed to boost antibody responses against the virus's protein coat, which would normally mean a TH2 response. In this case, though, the two do not seem to be mutually exclusive. Fred Valentine, of the New York University Medical Centre, finds that the therapeutic vaccine he is working with produces responses typical of TH1—cell-mediated immunity and sensitivity to skin tests—as well as antibodies.

All this immunology is intriguing, but is it fruitful? Few cytokines have been turned into even moderately successful therapies for any disease. This is hardly surprising. If you do not know what a chattering group of civil servants is doing, or even what the words you overhear mean, then shouting at them is unlikely to do much good. Drugs that act against the opportunistic infections which come with AIDS, and drugs against HIV itself—AZT, ddC and ddI—remain the only treatments available.

As knowledge of cytokines improves, and it becomes easier to tell different sorts of CD4 T-cells apart, things should improve. The next step is to find cell-surface markers, like CD4 or CD8, that distinguish TH1 and TH2 cells—a step the grapevine says is imminent, and perhaps already taken. At present the cells can be told apart only by the cytokines they produce. Molecular markers would make studying them far easier—like the introduction of name badges for clerks. Successful immune responses could be better analysed, and the effects of all sorts of vaccines, immune-therapies and old-fashioned drugs could be compared with them. Such developments, spurred by amply financed AIDS research, could improve the treatment and prevention of many diseases. Eventually they might benefit even more people than the ever-growing tally infected with HIV.

In September, America's Congress set aside $20m for trials of a particular therapeutic vaccine. After an outcry from other researchers, plans were made to use the money on a trial of various such therapies. The results will be a while coming.

Strange and unusual plants

AUGUST 8TH   *"Dog bites man" is not a story; nor is "Fish eat plankton". "Plankton eat fish", on the other hand...*

VENUS fly-traps chomp the odd insect, vegetables generally eschew violence. But there are exceptions. To supplement their photosynthesis, certain dinoflagellates (single-celled algae which make up a big part of the oceans' plankton) attack and eat things their own size, or even slightly larger. Some of them go further: they kill full-grown fish by the million.

It has been known for a while that "red tides" (coloured springtime algal efflorescences) can be poisonous. They sometimes kill fish in large numbers and, if the poisons get into shellfish that are harvested for the table, they can hurt people, too. Dinoflagellates produce the toxins that make red tides poisonous. Until now it has been assumed that the algae used poisons to protect themselves against her-bivorous fish. This plea of self-defence will no longer do, however. In North Carolina an as-yet-unnamed species appears capable of murder with malice aforethought.

JoAnn Burkholder and her colleagues at the North Carolina State University in Raleigh described the dino-flagellates' *modus operandi* in *Nature*. The algae lurk dor-mant in the mud of tidal riv-ers until excited by schools of fish swimming by. They are not fooled by crabs or scal-lops, but in response to things with fins, they pop out of the mud and swim to the surface, secreting a powerful nerve-poison when they arrive. As

Dinner for two, please

the fish succumb, the poison causes their skin to peel off and disintegrate. The dino-flagellates then batten on to small scraps of this carrion and gorge themselves. After that the creatures mate and their offspring sink back to the river bed.

These orgies of gluttony and sex may ex-plain some of the mass fish-kills observed in American es-tuaries ever more frequently over the past 20 years. But why is the carnage on the rise? The reason could be pollu-tion—the piscivorous dino-flagellates are stimulated by the phosphates poured into rivers. Bleeding-hearts may say that makes the algae help-less victims of their environ-ment. Nonsense. They are born killers, and they will strike again.

The end of life's long childhood

OCTOBER 10TH   *Did the break-up of a vast ancient continent make it possible for complicated animal life to evolve?*

THE geological past is measured in fossils, from the bones of mammoths that have scarcely had time to petrify to the tiny mys-terious shells that clutter the sediments of the early Cambrian period, 540m years ago. Each epoch is identified by its charac-teristic fossils; the history of life is the index to the history of the earth. Before the Cam-brian, though, the writing in the index is barely visible. The Cambrian was marked by the first appearance of complex bony animals; though there was life aplenty in earlier days, it was almost all single-celled, and what fossils it left were all-but-feature-less blobs.

When they gaze into the poorly mapped abyss of the Precambrian, billions of years deep, most palaeontologists quail and quickly return to the 540m years of re-corded history. An increasing number, though, are fascinated by life's Precam-brian pre-history. They are like psychoan-alysts, seeking in ill-remembered child-hood the forces that shape the adult mind. And like Freudians, they tend to have few facts to go on. The defining feature of the Precambrian, after all, is its lack of useful fossils.

This scarcity, though, has its liberating side. While some palaeontologists wrap themselves in the details of a particular type of fossil or a particular region, those who are trying to make sense of life in the Precambrian have to take a broad view. Though detailed field work is vital to them, they cannot look at only one place or only one type of fossil. To make sense of their sparse data, they must look at all sorts of evidence—from geochemistry to the tec-tonic history of continents to models of the climate—from all over the face of the planet. Looking at the Precambrian means looking for the big picture; it is simply too far away for anything else to be visible.

The painter of one such big picture is Andrew Knoll of Harvard. He has been looking at the end of the Precambrian and wondering why, given that life on earth dates back at least 3.5 billion years, compli-cated animals chose that point at which to make their first appearance. From his own research and that of others, he has put to-gether a plausible story. And unlike the plausible stories told by Freudians, it can be supported or knocked down with hard facts—the sort of facts that can be chiselled from cliffs with geological hammers.

One prerequisite for complex lifeforms, it has long been agreed, is a cer-tain amount of free oxygen in the atmo-sphere. Free oxygen comes from photosyn-thesis, but that has been around for far longer than animals have. By the late Pre-cambrian it had been going on for billions of years. So if you want to explain the emer-gence of animals in terms of increased oxy-gen availability, you have to find some fea-ture of the late Precambrian which explains why oxygen levels should have risen then, and not before. That is what Dr Knoll has tried to do, with the help of sedi-mentary rocks from Spitsbergen that range from 600m to 800m years in age.

Imagine life in a Precambrian sea. Al-gae are making oxygen and carbon com-pounds from carbon dioxide (CO_2) and water; other creatures are breathing the oxygen and exhaling CO_2. The processes can balance each other almost perfectly, but they do not have to. If carbon is taken out of the cycle—by creatures dying and falling into the depths where there is noth-ing to eat them, there to be buried in sedi-ment—then the system can produce a sur-plus of oxygen, leading to a net increase in the amount of oxygen around. The Spits-bergen rocks and other contemporaneous sediments suggest that lots of carbon was being taken out of the cycle and buried, and thus that oxygen was produced.

Even in the Precambrian, though, there was no free lunch. The carbon lost to the sediments had to be replaced if the cycle was not to run down. That was not a prob-lem in itself, since the Precambrian atmo-sphere was thick with carbon dioxide. But by pumping CO_2 from the atmosphere into the sediments (stripping it the while of its oxygen), the carbon cycle might have had a bad effect. To those worried about global warming today, a decrease in atmospheric CO_2 might sound good—but in the late Precambrian the sun was younger and cooler. If life thinned that greenhouse it could have made the world much colder.

That it became cold is not in doubt. The period saw the first global glaciations for over a billion years, and the worst ice age the earth has ever undergone. Its cause is not yet known for certain, but the idea that decreased CO_2 and increased oxygen are part of the same process is attractive.

To make the story completely satisfying, though, you need to know why so much carbon got buried in the depths of the Precambrian oceans at this particular time, and to explain the fact that the carbon burial, and thus the oxygen production, seems to start 250m years before the animals appear. The answer lies under the oceans. Oceans expand as new ocean crust is formed in volcanic rifts at their centres. Those volcanoes produce, among other things, an unusual amount of the lighter isotope of the element strontium. The Spitsbergen rocks, and others, are enriched in this lighter strontium.

Light strontium means underwater volcanism and rifting—the opening up of new ocean depths suitable for storing organic sediments. It also means that there were lots of "reduced" minerals around—those, like iron, eager to react with oxygen. So large amounts of rifting in the late Precam-

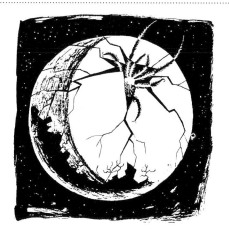

brian could explain where the carbon went and also use up some of the oxygen produced. At the end of the period, though, after the biggest ice age, the strontium levels even out—which would allow, at last, the dramatic oxygen build-up needed for the first animals.

Where were these new oceans? Over the past two decades geologists have traced the paths of the continents further and further back into history, watching them come together and separate again in a planet-wide square dance. There is now a general consensus that 1 billion years ago the continents were gathered up into a single supercontinent, and that by the dawn of the Cambrian that continent had split up. Such a break-up would have been accompanied by just the sort of deep-ocean volcanism the strontium isotopes suggest.

In late October specialists will gather for a conference at the edge of Death Valley to try and firm up their picture of the late-Precambrian continental dance—which bits of the supercontinent broke away when. They have every hope of eventually putting together a pretty accurate picture, and (with the help of advances in dating techniques) discovering the pace of the dance, as well as its pattern. With a clear tectonic picture, it will be possible to ask new detailed questions about the late Precambrian. How did the ocean currents flow, and what effect would that flow have had on the ice ages? How did the continents erode, and how does that change the rate at which carbon is buried and atmospheric carbon dioxide is used up? Matching the inanimate cycles of continents and oceans to the cycles of life should eventually provide a detailed history, showing how the different processes sometimes reinforced each other and at other times cancelled each other out.

As a spur to research, nothing beats questions that are interesting and answerable, and questions about the late Precambrian are now both of those things thanks to new conceptual frameworks and new tools. It is quite possible that, after a few decades during which big pictures will inevitably change in the face of hard facts, the late Precambrian will be as well understood as the fossil-strewn periods that follow it. The span of recorded geological history would then be half as long again—a great achievement. But 80% of life's history would still remain tantalisingly uncharted, lost in the earth's long childhood.

Viral chaff

DECEMBER 11TH *Sometimes it seems that evolution has pre-empted mankind's cleverest ideas*

PEOPLE can pick up new genes from viruses; viruses can pick up new genes from people. When an infected cell makes new copies of the virus that has invaded and enslaved it, it sometimes sends them out into the world with a few of the cell's own genes packed in, too. This will normally be a hindrance, but sometimes the extra genes can work to the virus's advantage.

When researchers first analysed the gene for the protein that picks up tumour necrosis factor (TNF), one of the immune system's molecular messengers, they hurried to their databases to see if anyone else had seen anything like it. To their surprise, they found almost the same gene in a type of pox virus, its function unknown.

The difference between the pox gene and the normal TNF-receptor gene is that the pox gene describes a version of the protein which is secreted; normally, the protein is kept anchored to the surface of the cell. By secreting its version of the receptor, the virus interferes with the immune system's signals. A TNF-receptor on the surface of a cell is less likely to pick up its molecular messages if there are lots of free-floating receptors around, intercepting the TNF before it reaches the cell.

This is not the only cellular gene that viruses have hijacked and turned to their own end. Many slow-acting viruses contain genes that cause the cell they have taken over to reproduce itself more often than is necessary: growth genes, which, introduced into the wrong place, become cancer genes. Pox viruses have hijacked a gene for a protein that stops other proteins from cutting up the virus, a gene for proteins that stick primitive parts of the immune system together and genes for growth factors. The newest addition, described in Science by Grant McFadden and his colleagues at the University of Alberta, is a soluble version of the interferon-gamma receptor. It seems to stop infected cells from responding to the interferon, another immune-system messenger, by intercepting the messenger before it gets to the cell. Dr McFadden dubs this and the soluble TNF-receptor "viroceptors".

A similar tactic has been tried by doctors—against a virus. They have made various attempts to tackle HIV, the AIDS virus, with soluble versions of CD4, the molecule on the surface of immune-system cells that HIV recognises and sticks to. The idea was to swamp the virus with soluble CD4, so that it could not latch on to the target cells. It has not worked; but it is humanity's first attempt at such a thing. Natural viroceptors have developed over billions of generations of trial and error.

Contents

BOOKS AND ARTS

Sneers, cheers and tears

IT WAS not until long after the turn of this century that "Eminent Victorians" was published. Written by Lytton Strachey, it gracefully denigrated the reputations of the great and the good of the 19th century. The 20th century is not yet over but the reappraisal has already begun, and not just of British pillars of respectability. The intellectual giants of our age, people whose thinking has had an enormous influence, have in 1992 been the subject of critical, irreverent and even rude books.

Several authors have sought to consign to the dustbin of history the thoughts of Karl Marx and Vladimir Lenin. The most powerful salvo of the year was an indirect one. In "Ecocide in the USSR", Murray Feshbach and Alfred Friendly described the degraded state of the land and the people of the former Soviet Union more than 70 years after the revolution inspired by Marx and led by Lenin.

Sigmund Freud was also rubbished. Several books have tried to persuade their readers that Freudian psycho-analysis will eventually be viewed as quackery—the 20th-century equivalent of phrenology in the 19th century. But none has attracted more attention than this year's "Freudian Fraud: The Malignant Effect of Freud's Theory on American Thought and Culture". Its author, E. Fuller Torrey, a psychiatrist specialising in schizophrenia, was appalled by how Freudian ideas had swept all before them in the universities, the media, and even Hollywood. "Talking to one's therapist about your mother has become virtually a national pastime."

Even Charles Darwin, an eminent Victorian whose influence has expanded mightily in the 20th century, was under fire. The core of his evolutionary theory survived scrutiny in "The Ant and the Peacock" by Helena Cronin. But in their biography, "Darwin", Adrian Desmond and Jane Moore portrayed the great scientist as asserting "middle-class Malthusian values" in the application of his theories to human beings. These biographers implied that Darwin, like Thomas Malthus, opposed help for the poor lest it encourage them to breed and so add to their misery.

Not all biographers were as jaundiced. Victoria Glendinning deserved all the praise she got for "Trollope". The year also saw fine biographies of Harold Wilson by Ben Pimlott, of Harry Truman by David McCullough and of Henry Kissinger by Walter Isaacson ("a fascinating book about an overrated man", said the critics; "an overrated book about a fascinating man", said Mr Kissinger). The publication of the letters of Philip Larkin demonstrated, once again, that wonderful poetry can be written by a putrid person. Tony Harrison's poem about the Iraq war, "A Cold Coming", seared everybody who read it.

Religious, or rather anti-religious, books attracted much attention, notably a slick study of Jesus by A.N. Wilson and a novel of breathless blasphemy by Gore Vidal. Both seemed juvenile when measured against P.D. James's "The Children of Men", an unusually spiritual book from a writer of thrillers.

Another powerful novel with a spiritual bent was Ian McEwan's "Black Dogs", which pitted an atheist husband against a believing, and estranged, wife. The wife is irritated by what she sees as her husband's dreary, spiritual impoverishment and "fundamental lack of seriousness", his blinkered reasonableness and by his arrogant insistence, "against all the accumulating evidence", that sensible social engineering will deliver mankind from its miseries. The husband is irritated by what he sees as his wife's betrayal of her social conscience and her "self-protecting fatalism".

Many tipped "Black Dogs" to win the Booker prize for fiction. In the event it was beaten, in a tied result, by two even better novels: Michael Ondaatje's "The English Patient" and Barry Unsworth's "Sacred Hunger". American fiction also enjoyed a strong year and some of the best women writers appeared prominently on the bestseller list compiled by the *New York Times*: Toni Morrison, Susan Sontag and Alice Walker among them.

The most talked-about novel was Günter Grass's "The Call of the Toad", a humorous but sad satire by a wise German of how love for one country so often goes along with insensitivity towards another. The most hyped (and most overpriced) book of the year was Madonna's "Sex"; the most shocking "Laogai: The Chinese Gulag", in which Hongda Harry Wu revealed the part played by exploited prison labour in China's surge into the international market economy.

In the visual arts Documenta IX was the event of the year. Now recognised as the Olympics of contemporary art, this occasional exhibition in the otherwise undistinguished German town of Kassel presented an amazing compendium of the best—and most outrageous—work of established masters and the avant-garde. The most controversial, and some said most moving, exhibit this year was Ilya Kabakov's "Die Toilette". It looked from the outside to be just that, a standard outdoor public convenience. But inside it had been converted into living quarters for a family, who had arranged their shabby furniture in the space opposite the latrines. Mr Kabakov described the work as a metaphor. "The general situation in my country [Russia] is frightening and totally unbearable, but people get used to it . . .".

As usual the bourgeoisie were outraged when the works of the finalists for the Turner prize for best youngish British sculptor went on show at the Tate Gallery. But this year even avant-garde critics found it hard to admire sculptures that showed so little imagination. The public responded more warmly to a magnificent Matisse retrospective in New York, where ticket touts sold $12.50 tickets for $50, and to a disorientating show of Magritte's paintings which moved on from London to go on to New York, Houston and Chicago. A showing of the work of 11 hitherto almost-unknown artists in the "Out of Africa" exhibition at the Saatchi gallery in London astonished all with its irrepressible idealism. Some of these paintings were as powerful in their way as the comprehensive collection of Benin sculptures which was displayed at New York's Metropolitan Museum. The art world was left poorer by the deaths of Francis Bacon and Sidney Nolan.

Recession dogged the stage. Most producers at commer-

Bacon's horror survives on canvas . . .

cial theatres in London's West End and on Broadway shied away from putting on plays that were challenging, and so financially risky. To save money, London producers preferred plays with three or four actors (like John Osborne's "Déjàvu", Ariel Dorfman's "Death and the Maiden" and "The Complete Works of Shakespeare: Abridged") or better still with only one or two (like Alan Bennett's "Talking Heads" and Willy Russell's "Shirley Valentine"). In central Europe there was a retreat into theatrical nostalgia, not just to operettas which cheerfully recalled the days of the Habsburgs and Hohenzollerns but also, worryingly, the revues of Berlin and Vienna in the 1930s.

Opera witnessed an extraordinary rise in the popularity of Leos Janacek, a 20th-century Czech composer. His "The Cunning Little Vixen" and "From the House of the Dead" seemed suddenly to be as popular as the operas of Mozart and Verdi.

A televised production of "Tosca" in Rome took place in "real time". It was staged at the exact locations, at the exact times of the day and night, specified in Puccini's opera. Dance was depressed by the dry-rot suffered by some of the great companies in the former Soviet Union. Even the sets and the costumes of the Bolshoi began to look shabby.

Fine films were produced outside the United States. The Grand Prix at the Tokyo international film festival was deservedly won by "White Badge", a South Korean critique of that country's participation in the Vietnam war. At 26 hours, Edgar Reitz's "Die Zweite Heimat", the Odyssey of a young German through the 1960s, was the longest European film ever made. It won rapturous critical acclaim, with some saying they could easily have sat through a further 26 hours.

"Den Goda Viljan" ("The Best Intentions"), the winner of the Golden Palm for the best film at the Cannes Film Festival, was another strong European offering. Directed by Denmark's Bille August, it was a portrait of the parents of Ingmar Bergman in the early 1900s and told the story of their complex and passionate relationship. As the Cannes festival came to an end a golden chapter in the history of cinema was brought to a close in Berlin. Marlene Dietrich, the Prussian screen diva and husky singer most famous for her roles in films directed by Josef Von Sternberg, including "The Blue Angel", "Morocco" and "Shanghai Express", was returned to her home town to be buried.

Despite the critical success achieved by some Asian and European pictures, the film world was more than ever dominated by Hollywood. After a couple of poor years, Tinseltown rediscovered its touch and produced a batch of movies that for once pleased the financiers and the critics as well as the public. Spike Lee's "Malcolm X", Robert Reiner's "A Few Good Men", Robert Redford's "A River Runs Through It", Robert Altman's "The Player", Gary Sinise's "Of Mice and Men" and Clint Eastwood's "Unforgiven" all had their admirers. A film adaptation of a sharp play by David Mamet, "Glengarry Glen Ross", was mentioned in the same breath as Oscars.

Only one thing was lacking this year—optimism about the years to come. Like the writers, the film-makers looked back several decades for their inspiration, not to the present, let alone the future. This was a year of reappraisal, not of renewal.

. . . Dietrich's charm on film

As we reported then

Destination where?

JANUARY 11TH *Many a post-mortem was published on how communist governments had impoverished the economic, cultural and religious lives of their citizens. One of the best, and least po-faced, "How We Survived Communism and Even Laughed" (Hutchinson), was written by Slavenka Drakulic, a Yugoslav novelist*

LAVATORY paper, it seems, is what doomed communism in Eastern Europe. Once people discovered that a kinder, gentler alternative existed, it was the end for Honecker, Ceausescu and co. Of course, communism failed to provide all kinds of other things in proper quality or quantity; but as Slavenka Drakulic points out, women turned against the old regimes for just such delicate reasons.

Talking to women in Czechoslovakia, Poland, Bulgaria and East Germany at the beginning of 1990, Miss Drakulic, a Yugoslav novelist, found similar complaints and survival techniques throughout Eastern Europe. To live under communism was a process of everyday dehumanisation, and she captures it sharply. At the Post Office, for example,

> it was perfectly normal not only to have to wait in line pressed tightly together, but to peer at each other's documents, accounts, letters and bills quite shamelessly ... Asking for the right to privacy meant you had something to hide. And hiding something meant it was forbidden. If it was forbidden, it must have been against the state. Finally, if it was against the state, you must have been an enemy.

Apart from the inevitable problems of shortages, women were united by a con-stant hankering after anything regarded as western. Even drinking from a Coca-Cola bottle became a symbolic gesture. Watching a young man eating a banana, Miss Drakulic becomes almost lyrical: "It was not a banana he was eating, but the promise, the hope of the future."

When the Berlin Wall finally broke, and items from the West flooded into Eastern Europe, women were both delighted and confused. The new order brought not only fruit and tampons but also pornographic posters, which were proudly displayed in buses, taxis and private homes as trophies of free expression. This was rather shocking to feminists, who are now busy trying to sort out sexist oppression from the old communist kind. "It's hard", Miss Drakulic writes,

> to see [men] as an opposite force, hard to confront them as enemies. Perhaps because everyone's identity is denied, we want to see them as persons, not as a group or category, or a mass ... we are not able entirely to distinguish *us* from *them*, and all of us together from *it*. So, in our kitchens, while the soup is boiling, what we talk about is identity.

Which must make for a lot of spilled soup.

Many East Europeans refuse to surrender their unrealistic hopes for capitalism, and Miss Drakulic is one of them. Her idea of living standards in the West is still hugely inflated. She appears to believe that only under communism do women recycle things out of economic necessity. "A nice, strong shoe box can have several purposes," she informs the reader, as though no woman in the West would realise that.

Similarly, Miss Drakulic still clings to a cloudy and romantic view of democracy. She can understand why telephone booths and parking meters were vandalised in the East—obviously, it was because people were frustrated with socialism—but she is shocked and bewildered to find the same thing in the West, where there seems no reason for it. She is shocked, too, to encounter beggars in New York. Perhaps, she reasons, westerners cannot see them there; perhaps only those people from the East, who possess a "communist eye", are alert to the presence of vagrants in the street. "Like a third, spiritual eye placed in the middle of one's forehead, this eye scans only a certain type of phenomenon; it is selective for injustice."

Old communist habits die hard, not least sanctimony. Despite her infatuation with the West and all its consumer goodies, Miss Drakulic has a strong inkling that freedom can be terrible; she concedes that, for all its destruction, communism offered her native Yugoslavia (and other countries) some sort of cohesion, and a brutal guarantee against tribal warfare.

On a more humdrum level, too, she is never far from the piety of the old order. "I am not tempted to buy a dryer," she declares. "I think I will always hang my clothes outside for the sheer poetry of it." She goes on to tread imperiously on modern western sensibilities: "Before [East European women] give up their fur coats, they certainly want to have them, at least for a while." In her opinion, ecologists have no right to force "a green totalitarianism on us, telling us what to eat, wear and think."

In short, Miss Drakulic believes that the emerging democracies have earned certain allowances for what they suffered in the past. They cannot be expected to become politically correct overnight. And the long-suffering housewives of Eastern Europe surely deserve to take pride in their triumphs, before capitalism breeds a new kind of sourness in them.

Show-it-yourself

FEBRUARY 1ST, SYDNEY **A lingering economic recession hurt the market for art and artists almost everywhere. But it is an ill-wind . . .**

WHEN Australian bankers threw billions of dollars at property developers in the boom years of the late 1980s, they were sure they had found a way to coin money. The skyscrapers they financed would, they reckoned, quickly be let to corporate and professional clients, the speculative builders would all make fat profits, they would pay back their loans to the banks with interest and everybody would live profitably ever after.

Instead the Australian economy went sour, property developers went into receivership or liquidation, and banks were left with surplus property on their hands. They slashed the rents they were asking for in a desperate effort to find tenants for their skyscrapers. Small businessmen, lawyers, consultants and accountants rushed to take advantage of the low rents in the central business district, leaving behind the low-rise buildings they had previously occupied in grubbier parts of town. In their wake, artists have come in, and have persuaded the owners of the vacated space to let it out for art exhibitions that are organised and run by the artists themselves, not by art dealers.

These do-it-yourself galleries have opened in Melbourne as well; but they are thickest on the ground in Sydney, and especially around Oxford Street, a bohemian district similar to New York's SoHo. The financial arrangements the artists negotiate with the landlord and among themselves are sometimes as creative as their artworks. Ty Townsend, an arts graduate in his mid-20s who is trying to make his mark with models of monsters, is a case in point.

Mr Townsend could not afford the typical terms demanded by landlords: a rent of A\$150-200 (\$110-150) a week for the hire of a ground floor and basement off Oxford Street. So in mounting a recent showing of his monsters he persuaded his flatmate, Sue Vardy, to sign up as a co-renter of space in a small dilapidated building and to show her artworks alongside his. She makes bowler and straw hats that are painted in almost incandescent colours and decorated with witty charms. The hats ought to have looked odd beside "Graveyard Muppet 3", "Dance Party Wolfman" and "Doonside Vampire Insect", but somehow they proved compatible neighbours.

Michael Minglis, a maker of wooden artworks that could serve as hangers for the hats, was then brought in as a third co-tenant. He was even poorer than the other two, but got a rent rebate from the landlord in return for painting the basement an eerie mauve. The three artists took turns manning the gallery and cleaning the premises. In return, the landlord reduced her commission on each work sold from the typical 25-30% to 15%. The three artists combined forces to draw up an invitation

Townsend's monsters

list for the opening of their exhibition.

At another d-i-y art gallery in the neighbourhood, inquirers are handed a card that invites them to call a telephone number and ask for Keith or Mooreen. Artists who take up the invitation are told that they can rent wall space to show their paintings for a remarkably low price— A\$10 for three miniatures for a fortnight at a recent exhibition—so long as they agree to go on a roster that commits them to put in several one-day shifts at the gallery for nothing.

Not all the artists-cum-dealers make tenants as reliable as the consultants and accountants who used to rent the buildings. But these are hard times in Australia, and landlords cannot afford to be choosy.

The bamboo curtain

MARCH 21ST **Political repression eased in many parts of the world but tightened in China. Film-makers were among those to suffer**

A VILLAGE teacher has been murdered. Everybody knew he would be, because the killers had made no secret of their plan, but for various reasons nobody tried to stop them. "Chronicle of a Death Foretold"? Wrong. This is the plot of a Chinese film, "Bloody Dawn", which takes Gabriel Garcia Marquez's story and reinterprets it in terms of the legacy of puritanism, and of the Chinese concept of gaining and losing face.

It is a tour de force. And yet this picture, and almost every other film of quality made in China since the Tiananmen Square killings in 1989, remains unseen by the audience for which it was intended.

Most of them cannot officially be shown abroad. Five of the banned films, however, were seen on video at London's Institute of Contemporary Arts in circumstances best left unexplained. They were a revelation.

Films are banned now in China not because they are critical of communism but because somebody fears that some day someone might take exception to them. This makes for extreme caution. "In Their Prime", now five years old, is still unseen in China because it deals frankly with the Chinese-Vietnamese border war of 1979, in which, in the space of a few weeks, China is believed to have lost a third as many men as America lost in the whole of its own part

of the Vietnam war. "In Their Prime" rams home the humiliation this brought to China. Its picture of an ill-equipped, badly trained army was anathema to the army's generals, so into limbo went maybe the most moving account of war since "All Quiet on the Western Front".

"In Their Prime" was made by the generation of film-makers who graduated from the Beijing Film Academy in 1982. These were the men and women who, in the years before Tiananmen, put Chinese cinema on the world map with films such as "Yellow Earth" and "Red Sorghum". Yet those films, set mostly in the past and dealing with remote rural communities, are regarded as irrelevant to contemporary life by their successors.

One of the most instructive of the films

shown in London comes from one of these successors. Zhang Yuan's "Mama", the story of a retarded child, was detested by officialdom, probably because it points to holes in the Chinese welfare state. Yet the film escaped the central controllers. In China the state is the sole supplier of film stock. Zhang Yuan got round that by buying up film in job lots from various film studios. And because his film by-passes the normal state distribution system he is free, at the moment, to sell it abroad. It is a genuinely independent production.

Other ways in which Chinese film makers can express themselves include co-productions (responsible for "Raise the Red Lantern", which is in line for an Oscar this

Too quiet on the eastern front

month) and the use of the cheaper and widely available video form. China has no formal distribution system for independent videos, but neither has it an apparatus for banning them.

So a work such as "The Last Dreamers", which was shot on video, slips through the net and has been shown both in London and at the Hong Kong film festival. A documentary about artists who have opted out of the system and become illegal squatters in Beijing, this could be the most subversive movie yet made in China. It says that people have managed to live and work in the capital without a resident's permit and without belonging to a "work unit". If that is so, even China's powerful system of control is cracking up. The people of Hong Kong certainly hope so. The prospect of a takeover of the British colony by a dictatorship threatens to have a chilling effect on the press as well as the arts in Hong Kong.

Darwin evolves

APRIL 4TH *Old scientific certainties continue to crumble as revisionist books, like Helena Cronin's "The Ant and the Peacock" (Cambridge University Press), make a wider public aware of dissension within the Darwinist ranks*

THIS is a book about the evolution of beauty, goodness and intelligence, three things that especially puzzled Charles Darwin. It is part history, part science-reporting, part philosophy, and though it is footnoted like an academic book it reads much too well to be left to the professionals. Nobody with an interest in how the human mind has come to work the way it does can

fail to be gripped by it.

The peacock stands for beauty. How can natural selection have produced such an extravagant and useless ornament as the tail of the peacock? The ant stands for goodness. How can the altruism of the worker ant, sterile and toiling for its fertile mother, have been produced by natural selection's utilitarian imperative? Man, though missing from the book's title, stands for intelligence. How can it possibly have been of benefit to early man to have developed the latent abilities of an Einstein or a Mozart?

These were telling arguments against Darwin a century ago, and for too long his followers got away with dodging them. They said peacocks had tails to frighten other males, not to seduce females. They said ants worked for their mothers because it was good for the group (which it is, but why should ants be charitable?) They said man developed a big brain to make complicated stone tools, as if that needed relativity.

Then, lest anybody inquire more deeply, they retired to safer ground, like the evolution of ear bones from reptile jaw bones. It is misguided, they said, to think too much about the evolution of social

behaviour. To which their colleagues in the social sciences heaved a hearty sigh of assent, and got back to dreaming up Freudian explanations of beauty, or Marxist ones of altruism, or Skinnerian ones of intelligence.

News travels slowly across the divide between scientists and other academics, and it has not yet dawned upon the social scientists just how much their evolutionary colleagues have changed their tune since the arrival of selfish-genery in the 1960s. This is the notion that animals behave as if they were mere vehicles for the transmission of genes between generations. With the aid of this notion those questions have been answered.

Nobody would now disagree that the peacock's tail is the product of an arbitrary preference among peahens for gaudy, seductive tails on their menfolk. Quite why peahens have such a preference remains a subject of debate. One idea is that it enables them to pick the healthiest male to father their offspring. Another is that it enables them to pick the male most likely to father a son that will prove attractive to females in his generation. Either way, aesthetic fashion makes evolutionary sense.

Altruism has also been solved. Because of the way their genes mix, ants are more closely related to their sisters than to their daughters; so working to help their mothers rear more sisters is, genetically, more selfish than altruistic. Because apes live in small groups, doing a good turn can bring a reward of help from the beneficiary. Society is built on reciprocity, which is why it

Not the altruist you thought he was

requires laws when it gets large and anonymous.

As for the mind, Helena Cronin fearlessly treads where not many dare. She insists (as Darwin did) that evolution has little to say about why certain kinds of behaviour—murder, say, or liking music—evolved. To think it did was the mistake of sociobiology's brief flourish a decade ago. But sociobiology can say much about the mentality that lies behind behaviour, about morality and politicking, logic and thought.

Take murder. Far more people are killed, with different weapons, as a proportion of the population in Chicago than in England, yet the killings are done by exactly the same proportions of men, rather than women, and by the same proportions of different age groups. The murder tendency peaks at 25 for all men everywhere, then tails off at exactly the same rate—and always has.

Why? Other culturally determined things like age of first marriage show no such similarity. But the notion that a young man's reputation as he tries to ascend a dominance hierarchy depends on a credible threat of violence is easily borrowed from studies of animals, and is easily accepted by common sense. So young men are murderers more than women or older men are. Why they should do it more in Chicago than in England is another matter.

Perhaps the biggest insight from evolution is that in a reciprocating society it is essential to detect cheats and enforce social contracts. It seems to be something human minds are instinctively good at, as some powerful recent experiments have shown. Most Darwinians now agree that human intelligence developed so luxuriantly because it was needed for amateur psychologising: for deceiving, manipulating, detecting deception, resisting manipulation and generally outmanoeuvring. That, not logic, is what people are good at.

As a history of science, this story could easily have been told in the fashionable manner, by pointing out that Darwin's revival has come at the expense of good-of-the-species Utopianism, just as the free market's revival has come at the expense of good-of-society socialism (Darwin = Adam Smith, Julian Huxley = Marx, Richard Dawkins = Friedrich Hayek). But Dr Cronin is not in the relativist school of science history. In "The Ant and the Peacock", she refuses, as John Maynard Smith puts it in the foreword to the book, to throw away the baby of science and keep only the bathwater of the scientists' politicking. Sometimes, people are wrong as well as wrelative.

Francis Bacon

MAY 2ND *One of England's—and the world's—greatest painters died. But his paintings continue to haunt and to horrify*

THE trauma of our age, after Auschwitz, after Hiroshima, haunts so many of his pictures. Francis Bacon, who died aged 82 on April 28th, was the greatest British painter since Turner but also something more. His works, like Picasso's, have left their mark on everyman, not just the art public.

He nearly always painted the human face and figure, stripped bare of civilised niceties, set against backgrounds of stark colour and a terrifying clinical vacancy. "I hate a homely atmosphere," he once said, and there is nothing cosy or illustrative about his figures: screaming prelates; manically grimacing businessmen; naked men vomiting, defecating, wrestling (or making love) with each other. He compressed reality to the claustrophobia of the interrogation chamber, the screaming cell, the slaughterhouse.

Nothing about Bacon, a descendant of the Elizabethan English philosopher of the same name, was conventional. He suffered from asthma in his childhood in Dublin and had little schooling. Despaired of by his family, the adolescent Bacon set out for London, then to Paris and Berlin. During the wandering years that followed, he worked sometimes in nightclubs, and was always a keen gambler. He never attended art school, in his case a saving grace. A 1927 Picasso exhibition opened his eyes to the imaginative possibilities of distorting the human face.

In 1944 he painted "Three Studies for Figures at the Base of a Crucifixion", in which humanoid creatures, grotesquely phallic in proportion, emit ineffable primal screams. The human cry, inspired by images such as that of the bloodied nurse in Eisenstein's 1925 film "Battleship Potemkin", obsessed him. He always denied, however, being a visual terrorist out to shock gratuitously. "I've always hoped in a sense to be able to paint the mouth like Monet painted a sunset."

His first London exhibition in 1949 shocked and riveted the art public. Its iconoclasm and gallows humour broke every

A tragic view of man

taboo, but, as always, with tremendous assurance of composition, acute sense of the figure in space and beautiful qualities of paint. Figures were depicted mid-howl: a pope in a transparent box, like a hunted specimen; a monstrous man with opened umbrella under suspended animal carcasses.

By the late 1950s Bacon was internationally famous. In 1962 and 1985, he had retrospectives at London's Tate Gallery. His 1988 Moscow retrospective was among the few of a living, western artist to be held in the Soviet Union. His pictures commanded prices in seven figures. But he remained an elusive figure, avoiding interviews. "I'm just trying to make images as accurately off my nervous system as I can. I don't even know what half of them mean. I'm not saying anything." Yet as Cecil Beaton, a famous society photographer, described him in 1960, Bacon provided lively, humorous company for his friends, gay and straight. His studio was incredibly dishevelled; he enjoyed heavy late-night drinking in London clubs; he was indifferent to the opinions of others.

He lived and worked like this almost to the end. In his art, he desperately exorcised the ravaging tensions within. He described his portraiture as a kind of injury inflicted on the subject, and spontaneously applied paint almost as a physical assault on the viewer's sensibilities. A flayed human body on a bed under a rude electric light bulb: this is Bacon's tragic view of man. His are 20th-century icons, without a glimmer of redemption or release from horror.

American trouble-makers

JUNE 6TH The agitators in the struggle for civil rights in America are beginning to acquire the status of heroes—and the saintly patina that goes with it. An oral history edited by Eliot Wigginton, "Refuse to Stand Silently By" (Doubleday), de-mythologises them

THE men and women in this oral history of grass roots social activism in America between 1921 and 1964 are introduced as people who at last said: "That's it. Enough. That's all I can stand." And then, instead of quitting, went into action. All of which makes them heroes in the American tradition, or at least candidates for heroship.

Throughout its history the United States has venerated its trouble-makers. Not, it is true, always at the time of their trouble-making, but anyway in retrospect. Studs Terkel, the most famous contemporary writer of oral history (ie, history based on interviews with participants), invites those who doubt it to reflect on the American Revolution. There was not a majority for the revolution. The majority sat by. "It was Sam Adams causing trouble. Sam Adams was a rabble-rouser." If he had chosen to, he could have added the names of Patrick Henry ("Give me liberty, or give me death!"), Ben Franklin ("We must indeed all hang together, or, most assuredly, we shall hang separately."), and, above all, Tom Paine, an agitator too radical for most revolutionaries in both the American colonies and monarchist France.

In the Civil War, the trouble-makers are again lionised: Dred Scott, a rebellious slave; Frederick Douglass ("Slaveholders ...tyrants and despots have no right to live"); William Lloyd Garrison, who burnt a copy of the United States Constitution on the Fourth of July and denounced it as a covenant with death. But not, surprisingly, Harriet Beecher Stowe, even though her incendiary "Uncle Tom's Cabin" so angered the editor of a leading southern newspaper that he instructed his reviewer to write "the review as hot as hellfire, blasting and searing the reputation of the vile wretch in petticoats who could write such a volume."

It is fascinating to see in this oral history how the reputations of some latter-day agitators are on the rise while the once-inflated reputations of their tormentors, especially Joe McCarthy, J. Edgar Hoover of the FBI and Walter Winchell, the most influential gossip columnist of his day, continue to suffer a calamitous fall. It is also fascinating to see how the agitators are beginning to acquire the status of heroes, and the myth-making patina that goes with it.

A notable case in point is Rosa Parks, the black woman whose name is synonymous with the 1955 bus boycott in Montgomery, Alabama—the event that propelled Martin Luther King to the helm of the civil-rights movement. As the story is now so often told, on uplifting television documentaries and to American children in classrooms, Mrs Parks was a black seamstress who felt so worn out after a hard day's work she decided that she just could not, and would not, obey an order from the driver of the bus to give up her seat to a white passenger.

This is a long way from the truth and it converts Mrs Parks from a real person into a symbol of resistance to injustice. In short, she is on her way to becoming the secular version of a plaster saint. It is a fate that has already befallen Martin Luther King, who is so venerated it is politically incorrect even to acknowledge his human failings, like his womanising and his plagiarism.

As Mrs Parks herself makes plain in this book, she was not just a put-upon black menial but a veteran at trouble-making who had spent years agitating against racial segregation in Dixie. She says she first started questioning the morality of the colour bar as a precocious seven-year-old when she read a book called "Is the Negro a Beast?"

Much the same can be said of Edgar Daniel Nixon, another experienced agitator who has been mythologised as a simple Pullman-car porter who was stung into upbraiding a white passenger who screamed at him: "Get that bag, boy!"

And not only black agitators are mythologised in this way. It is also happening to Pete Seeger, America's favourite folk singer and a courageous but naive trouble-maker. For he too is devalued when he is turned into a plaster saint: a devoted disciple of Woody Guthrie and a singer of protest songs like "We Shall Overcome" and "Where Have All the Flowers Gone?"

When in the "frightened fifties" he was summoned to a hearing before Senator McCarthy's by now notorious committee, Mr Seeger refused to be cowed, and made his defence on the basis of the First Amendment rather than the Fifth Amendment to the United States Constitution. As Mr Seeger (rather crudely) puts it, the Fifth Amendment in effect says: "You have no right to ask me this question." The First Amendment, he says, is more like: "You have no right to ask *anybody* such questions." The emphasis is his.

So when he presented his testimony to the committee that gave its name to McCarthyism, Mr Seeger said: "I don't think any American should be forced to answer such questions, especially under the threat of reprisal if he or she gives the wrong answer." For his impudence he was cited for contempt of Congress, indicted by the Justice Department and sentenced to a year in jail. Characteristically, Mr Seeger reacted to the sentence by taking out his banjo in court and asking the judge if he could sing a song inspired by Tom Paine's famous phrase at a low point of the American Revolution—"These are times to try the soul of man."

It is Americans like these, like Martin Luther King, Studs Terkel, Pete Seeger, Rosa Parks and Edgar Daniel Nixon, who help make the United States the land of the free and the home of the brave.

Rosa Parks as an old saint . . .   **. . . and a young radical**

All over the map

JULY 11TH *The need to redraw the world's maps after the collapse of the Soviet empire had cartographers working overtime*

JOKES about "keeping the map makers busy" are not popular with publishers of atlases. With the collapse of the Soviet empire, cartographers are having to change the names of towns and the borders of countries as well as their colour schemes and, in many instances, the spelling and alphabet they use. Along with increasing the demand for maps, the most radical changes in geography since at least the first world war are also increasing the cost of map publishing and drastically reducing the lead time available for production and distribution.

Times Books, which also publishes Bartholomew and Collins, is among those groaning about the extra costs. Thanks to the unification of Germany, last year's reprint of the "Times World Atlas" cost the company £50,000 ($95,000) for colour corrections and a revised index. Moreover, the reprint schedule for the new version—commonly used by international conferences as the definitive geographical source—has had to be speeded up in 1990, from every five years to every two years. George Philip, another map publisher, tells a similar story.

How do map makers cope with the turmoil? Publishers of atlases say that they are meticulous in their research and diplomatic in their choice of names. The name of a country or its borders are changed only when its independence has been recognised by the European Community, the

United Nations or another international authority of similar standing.

They are wise to be cautious. It is hard to avoid offending somebody with a new map. The looming dissolution of Czechoslovakia is a case in point. Although Slovakia has long existed as a region, the Czech half was not formed until after the first world war and has yet to declare a proper name. The Royal Geographical Society suggests that Britain's Foreign Office, and those map makers who cannot wait until the dust settles, should opt meanwhile for the bland but reasonably safe name of Czech Lands.

Boundaries are still more tricky, especially in the Balkans. Once the European Community recognised Slovenia, Croatia and Bosnia & Hercegovina as independent states, publishers got ready to redraw the borders of old Yugoslavia. A question mark still hovers over Macedonia. The EC has agreed to recognise it, but insists that it must change its name.

The disintegration of the Soviet Union presents an even greater challenge for map makers. Although no borders have yet been redrawn, the refutation of communism is causing lots of changes in the names of cities, towns, villages, mountains and rivers. According to the Royal Geographical Society's Permanent Committee on Geographical Names (PCGN), 4-5% of the 300,000 names of places or geographical features in the most detailed maps of the former So-

viet Union are politically communist in nature. Thus map makers face the prospect of 12,000-15,000 adjustments. Even the detailed addresses on letters to friends are likely to require drastic revision as they are decommunised. Paul Woodman, the secretary of the PCGN, makes the point by quoting a typical household address in the former Soviet Union: Flat 24, Socialism Apartment, Lenin Prospect, Car Factory Suburb, Electoral Town.

Also under threat, if they have not been changed already, are the names of places called after political dinosaurs (Kirov, Kalinin); politically incorrect organisations (Young Communist League, Proletarians); important Marxist dates (Red October; May 1st); and any names that owe their origin to the "perceived quality of Soviet life" (Truth, Freedom, Glory, Progress, Path of Lenin and so on).

Map makers sigh too over what spelling and what alphabet to use. Before 1990, spelling in the Soviet Union was laid down by the central government, and all official documents had to be standardised in Russian Cyrillic. Ukraine now insists that as many as 30,000 names be translated into Ukrainian. Armenia and Azerbaijan are returning to Roman script. Other similar changes are threatened or pending.

Inaccurate records complicate matters. From 1953 to 1990, Soviet maps—sometimes printed without latitude or longitude readings—were regularly falsified. Militarily sensitive places were moved, or left out altogether. For instance, Nevel, a strategic railway junction in north-western Russia, was shifted by several miles in each successive edition of the official map of the area. The purpose of these attempts at deception puzzles Mr Woodman. Western cartographers, he says, have had access to accurate maps of the former Soviet Union since at least 1945, when the western powers captured them from the Germans at the end of the second world war—not to mention satellite reconnaissance.

At the moment the PCGN and its American counterpart, the United States Board on Geographic Names, are divided on certain matters of language and dialect. British map publishers are, for example, opposed to the use of Belarus for Belorussia and Moldova for Moldavia (it is like referring to Germany as Deutschland, they say). A compromise applied in other parts of the world suggests itself: some publishers are willing to place Myanmar in the index beside Burma, but not on the map.

With all this work in hand, some map makers are talking, hopefully, about persuading the United Nations to create a fund to subsidise cartographers. Their cheek is astonishing. By the end of this year, every atlas that still contains the Soviet Union will be obsolete, and map sales will presumably see a big increase. And with continuing troubles in the Balkans, the division of Czechoslovakia, the absorption of Hong Kong by China in 1997, growing demands for Quebec to leave the Canadian confederation and the possibility that South Africa will get another name, map makers look set to be recession-proofed.

He knew he was right

AUGUST 15TH *The publication of "Trollope" (Hutchinson and Knopf), a biography by Victoria Glendinning, was perfectly timed. The revival of the Victorian novelist's reputation reached new heights*

THE best of Trollope's biographies, it has often been said, is his autobiography. Published after his death, it set the pattern: a paranoiac and under-achieving father and a courageous, bustling mother, a miserable childhood and hobbledehoy young manhood, and then a late blossoming that led to a contented marriage and a prosperous career both as an administrator in the Post Office and as a popular novelist.

The autobiography is carefully crafted, to convey the impression that Trollope wished it to convey. It has its reticences. There is little about his wife, Rose, and only a fleeting, anonymous reference to his infatuation with a young American, Kate Field. But, granted those Victorian limits, it is startlingly candid and honest. So honest, indeed, that its publication led to a slump in Trollope's popularity, revealing, as it did, the methodical way he set about writing his novels, so that they were damned as mechanical and pedestrian.

Yet all that Trollope, honest to a fault about himself, was seeking to show was that everything had its due time and place: his novel writing, his work at the Post Office, his social and domestic life, his hunting and even his brief, unsuccessful attempt to enter politics (in the Liberal interest, of course).

Trollope wrote to earn money, fully aware of the market he was serving. It is all of a piece with his jogtrot prose and jogalong plots. He produced exactly the stuff that the subscribers to Mudie's Li-

brary wanted. He was the most practical, the most workmanlike of all the Victorian novelists, the least Angst-ridden or daemon-driven.

Only fairly recently have these virtues been recognised in their proper light—as virtues. Trollope is back in fashion. At long last, he has a commemorative plaque in Westminster Abbey. And, quite suddenly, there has been a crop of biographies: three by American scholars and now this intimate portrait by Victoria Glendinning. She makes a few trifling historical slips, but these fade into insignificance in the warm glow she brings to her subject. Her theme is the outer and inner man in Trollope.

The outer man was loud-mouthed, sometimes brusque and occasionally touchy, very masculine and, in the round, a successful man of the world. The inner man was moral, compassionate, susceptible, feminine and, in the round, a man of delicate conscience. In writing about social, sexual and human relationships, there are no blacks and whites for Trollope, but a series of grey tones, good and evil being mixed together in both conduct and motive. Ms Glendinning draws extensively on Trollope's novels to illuminate his life as well as to pinpoint those of his experiences and emotions that served as sources for his imaginary people and plots.

In his novels, Trollope dug his soil over assiduously. But, aware of his own limitations, he never drove his spade more than a spit deep. His characters are always credible; Dickens's, by comparison, are often grotesque and incredible. But Trollope lacked Dickens's incandescent insights.

He wrote, for example, in "The Way We Live Now", about the same money-conscious, money-grubbing society that Dickens pilloried in "Little Dorrit", but it was quite beyond Trollope's power to depict, as Dickens did, society as a prison. Trollope was no genius. Fortunately for his readers then and now, he knew it. He, unlike Dickens, was at ease with his own temperament. He was, to quote Ms Glendinning, a "most worthwhile and lovable man" who "needed to have his worth and his lovableness proved to himself and to the world over and over again". So much so that he has inspired a loving and lovable biography.

Maestro deflated

SEPTEMBER 5TH *For many years Herbert Karajan was above and beyond criticism as a great condutor. Not any more*

WHEN the new director of the Salzburg Festival, Gérard Mortier, declared that the "Karajan era" was over, he seemed to be repeating an evident truth. Herbert von Karajan was once Europe's most powerful conductor, reigning over the Philharmonic Orchestras of Berlin and Vienna as well as a plethora of musical festivals. But his reputation has shrunk in the three years since his death.

Indeed, one of Karajan's last tries to form a festival, a Pentecost concert series, also at Salzburg, has fallen through this year for lack of money. The conductor's widow, Eliet von Karajan, says she will try to handle the fund-raising herself to keep the idea alive. What has happened in three years to change the way people see Karajan?

Part of the answer comes from such books as Roger Vaughan's "Karajan"

(Belfond Publishers; 339 pages; FFr148) and Werner Thürichen's "Furtwängler ou Karajan" (Bernard Coutaz Editions; 196 pages; FFr99). More people now know how the gifted young musician born Herbert Karajan (the "von" he added himself as elevator shoes to nobility) rushed to join the Nazi Party in 1933 in Austria and how, when that group was outlawed the next year, he went to Germany to join the Nazi Party there. Karajan remained affiliated to the Nazi Party throughout the war.

Musicians now tell how Wilhelm Furtwängler tried to prevent his Jewish players from being exiled. There are no such anecdotes about Karajan. After the war many Jewish musicians refused to perform with him. When Richard Tucker, a tenor who began singing as a synagogue cantor, was asked to record "Aida" with Maria Callas, he demurred so long as Karajan was the scheduled conductor. Another conductor was found for the recording. When Mischa Elman was a guest artist in the 1960s with the Berlin Philharmonic, the great violinist said he would accept the engagement only if he did not have to play with Karajan.

Walter Legge, an EMI producer, put music before politics. He collaborated in a series of recordings that may prove Karajan's most lasting legacy. Part of their greatness is in the meticulous casting and preparation of the orchestra. Mozart's "Cosi fan tutte" with Elisabeth Schwarzkopf, Nan Merriman and Léopold Simoneau (EMI CHS 7696352) is one outstanding example. Mozart's "Magic Flute", with Erich Kunz as Papageno, is another (EMI CHS 7696312). Other 1950s recordings with the young Miss Schwarzkopf, such as Verdi's "Falstaff" (EMI CDS 7496682) or Humperdinck's "Hansel and Gretel" (EMI CMS 7692932) are further evidence of the expert team-

Karajan deflates

work between Karajan and Legge. At this time in his career, with soloists like Dinu Lipatti playing Mozart's 21st Piano Concerto (EMI CZS 7671632A) or Maria Callas in Verdi's "Il Trovatore", (EMI CDS 7493472), Karajan seemed to justify all the hoopla surrounding his ever-expanding career.

But the reasons for his fame help also to explain why Karajan's music is currently out of fashion. He liked to compare his conducting ideal to driving a great sports car. Strength and control were all. As Sir Colin Davis, a leading British conductor, says: "Karajan's career was all about seeing how much power one can have over an orchestra, over people in general. That doesn't interest me in the slightest."

Once Karajan stopped working with Legge, he lost his balance. His Italian opera recordings, for instance, became occasions for exaggerated sonic experiment, piling on the bass, reducing the pianissimi to near-inaudibility, taking tempi at voice-breaking slowness, and casting the young voices he preferred in roles far too heavy for them.

In the 1960s there were still seductive moments: Bizet's "Carmen" has a cigarette girls' chorus of the majesty of Wagner's Valhalla, even if it has nothing to do with Bizet or Mérimée (RCA GD 86199). Similarly, Puccini's "Madam Butterfly" (Decca 4175772) has an entrance for Cio Cio San that is magnificently shaped by the maestro, to the point where it seems to belong more to Bruckner than to Puccini's teenage heroine.

By the 1980s Karajan's ability to make human contact was so limited that his repeat performances were rarely better than his past efforts. His concert career and recording activity had outlived his genius and he influenced several young conductors in unfortunate ways, Semyon Bychkov and Michel Plasson among them. A number of conductors, with noticeably lesser orchestras than Karajan worked with, still seem to hanker after the controls of an expensive sports car.

As well as his wilfulness and his abhorrent politics, an additional explanation for the eclipse of Karajan may be the advance of music technology. Thanks to the CD, Karajan has lost the dominance he had when, say, his version of the Beethoven symphonies was the only one available in recordings of the highest current quality.

Today people can hear reissues on CD of Toscanini and Furtwängler conducting Beethoven and Wagner. Richard Strauss, another Karajan favourite, is conducted on re-releases by Fritz Reiner, Willem Mengelberg and Strauss himself. Puccini and Verdi are available from numerous Italian maestros like de Sabata, Serafin and Gavazzeni.

With the competition so intense, it is perhaps no wonder that even a massive discography like Karajan's has lost a bit of its lustre. There are just too many superb conductors who left magnificent performances for a single Kaiser of Music to be wanted—or needed.

Is Hollywood anti-American?

OCTOBER 31ST, LOS ANGELES *The way films and song lyrics glamorise violence has led the entertainment industry to think aloud about a return to self-censorship*

"NO PICTURE shall be produced which will lower the moral standards of those who see it," ran the first General Principle of the Hays Code of 1930, Hollywood's self-censorship system. One wonders what crusty old Jack Warner would have thought of two recent Time Warner products: Madonna's tawdry photograph collection, and "Cop Killer", Ice-T's infamous paean to "dusting some cops off".

"The dream factory has become the poison factory," is how Michael Medved puts it in a provocative new book, "Hollywood vs America" (HarperCollins). Newspapers in the United States have bristled with comment on "Cop Killer". Los Angeles's Roger Cardinal Mahony even suggested the reintroduction of some form of the Hays Code. And Dan Quayle's charge that the "cultural elite" lauded single-motherhood in "Murphy Brown", a television sit-com, has rippled through the presidential campaign.

Some of this criticism is right-wing posturing. Many Americans found the relentless trumpeting of family values at the Republican Party's convention much less American than "Murphy Brown". Nonetheless Americans increasingly dislike what they see in their homes and cinemas—and Hollywood itself senses something is wrong. It is hard to find a movie mogul who thinks Time Warner should have released the recording "Cop Killer"; many are ashamed of films like "Basic Instinct". Rupert Murdoch invited Mr Medved to address his company; Cardinal Mahony has been lunched by Hollywood power-brokers.

Consider also a speech by Jeffrey Katzenberg, Disney's studio boss:

> When our critics charge that we show violence that is too graphic, sex that is too gratuitous, or feature lyrics that are too inflammatory, we're all too quick to offer the defence that it's only a movie or piously invoke the First Amendment.

As Mr Katzenberg indicated, Hollywood is starting to reject a canard it has long promulgated: that the entertainment industry does not influence its audience. A similar view was expressed by Brandon Tartikoff in a recent forum of movie moguls organised by *Premiere* magazine. Mr Tartikoff, who ran the NBC television network before heading Paramount studios, admitted that he did not agree with the "social scientists that my network was hiring from places like Yale to provide data that violence on TV does not lead to acts of violence." The Yale men are indeed disingenuous: the networks spew out data to show that the (short) advertisements shown during their "commercial breaks" influence people to buy things.

The music industry is caught in a similar trap. On the one hand, it never tires of boasting about the positive social effect of concerts like Live Aid and campaigns like "Rock the Vote". Yet it has also denied that the anti-Semitic, homophobic and sexist messages of many rap bands have any effect.

If Hollywood is prepared to discuss its responsibilities, are its values really out of line? Underneath the accusations and counter-accusations, there are two different debates: whether Hollywood is too liberal in the political sense ("the Murphy Brown debate"); and whether Hollywood's enthusiasm for sex and violence is irresponsible (the "Terminator" debate).

Among many misses, Mr Medved's book sinks a few good blows in Holly-

The basic instinct is greed

wood's liberal bias—most noticeably in its contempt for religion (when was the last time a good priest or rabbi appeared in a film?). Other conservatives railed against this year's Emmy awards for television, where speaker after speaker made (increasingly boring) jokes about Mr Quayle.

By European standards, American prime-time television is remarkably tame. "Murphy Brown" would have provoked little comment in the European citadels of family values so cherished by American conservatives. In the cinema, big-budget films with a strident liberal message are hard to find—"JFK" being the one notable exception. Liberals groan that Hollywood's infinitely larger crop of violent films probably encourages a conservative "shoot first, ask questions later" attitude.

The "Terminator" debate is likely to last much longer. Films have got gradually more brutal. New sorts of heroes, played by the likes of Arnold Schwarzenegger and Steven Seagal, not only exterminate people, they dispatch them with jokes that imply life is cheap. And, as Mr Medved points out, the Rolling Stones' "Let's Spend the Night Together" sparkles with romance when set aside rap songs by 2 Live Crew and Niggers With Attitude.

Yet the dilemma remains: the only thing worse than 2 Live Crew is censorship. Some critics think that the moguls should sign a statement of principle (a little like the Hays Code, but much vaguer and more politically correct). This looks dangerous ground. Good art cannot be defined by morality: "The Birth of a Nation", Hollywood's first great film, celebrated the Ku Klux Klan. Mr Medved criticises "Silence of the Lambs" for its gory content; yet the film also had a strong moral message.

The more likely approach will be some form of mild, informal self-censorship by the leading film studios. A British film producer, David Puttnam, argues that there is a new "sensitivity and unease" among the upper echelons of Hollywood. Perhaps. But profit remains Hollywood's main motive, and "violent films about peace"—as the director of "Terminator 2" once described his *oeuvre*—make money.

Joe Roth of Twentieth Century Fox explained that he rejected a gang film called "Juice" because "it seemed wrong to make a $5m or $7m profit" when there was a risk of people getting shot at the opening. But when he asked himself whether he would do it for a $50m or $100m profit, he decided "that is a really hard question".

America's shame

NOVEMBER 7TH   *After amusing, and shocking, the world with her account of the American way of death, Jessica Mitford has done the same with "The American Way of Birth" (Gollancz/EP Dutton)*

"STOUT brown paper, boiling water and a competent doctor." According to Jessica Mitford, who had all these to hand in her own bedroom in Bermondsey in 1937, not much more is needed for a normal delivery, and improvements since are illusory. The 1930s seem, in retrospect, a high point in birthing practice. Puerperal fever had been eliminated; anaesthesia was established (although the awful technique of Twilight Sleep, requiring huge doses of scopolamine and morphine, was enjoying a vogue among the rich); and the more intrusive devices, such as ultrasound and electronic fetal monitoring, had not yet been invented. Miss Mitford feels sorry for modern mothers, and proceeds in brisk hockey-sticks fashion to try to stir them up.

If labour has miseries, in Miss Mitford's view it is all men's fault. Medieval churchmen and doctors started the persecution of midwives, hounding them as witches. The inventor of the forceps, Peter Chamberlen, and their chief exploiter, Hugh Chamberlen, used to blindfold the labouring woman and bar relations from the chamber to keep the invention secret. It was men who liked women to be strapped down in labour, men who gave them fever (by proceeding to births directly from dissecting corpses), and men who drew up ludicrous time-charts for the various stages of birth. And they still wreak havoc.

In the United States, the main target of Miss Mitford's book, men still make up 80% of obstetric/gynaecological departments. There, they have fun punctuating their slide lectures with pictures from "Playboy"; and, according to Miss Mitford, ambitious young doctors haunt the wards of hospitals, hoping for the chance of a Caesarian which will improve their surgical technique and get them more money. One in four births in America is now a Caesarian, most of them performed, it appears, out of sheer impatience with the course of normal labour.

Miss Mitford's tract seems out of date in Britain, where the battle against regimented hospital births has been largely won, where midwives are respected and the rate of Caesarian sections is low. It is an effective indictment of methods in the United States. There, almost all births happen in hospitals. Doctors go in terror of malpractice suits, and midwives, where they exist, cannot afford the insurance premiums: in Alabama, these are now $50,000-60,000 a year. Many poor women in rural America and in inner-city slums do not get prenatal care until the moment before birth, and are shunted from one emergency room to another as doctors refuse to take them. Infant mortality rates are around 10 per 1,000. Fear of "socialised medicine" means that the most basic kinds of care are neglected, and the cost of having a baby is crippling for almost everyone.

The book's argument would be more effective, however, if it were better put. Miss Mitford enjoys the history, and is entertaining about such matters as administering chloroform on a folded handkerchief, as was done for Queen Victoria. But her modern sections, which are

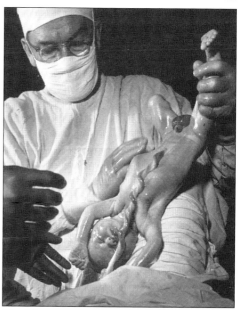

Pity his mom

much more important, read like the unsubbed copy of an untrained reporter. To seize the ear of those overweening male doctors, something steadier and more professional should be prescribed.

Reitz's Odyssey

NOVEMBER 28TH *The longest European film ever made was so good that many wished it had been longer*

AT 26 hours, it takes more than a day and a night of anyone's life to see. Yet, as the final credits roll, many wish there were 26 hours more. It is "Die Zweite Heimat", the sequel, seven years later, to what was then the longest film in European history—Edgar Reitz's 16-hour "Heimat", the story, through a close-knit family of characters, of German history from 1918 to 1960. The sequel covers only one decade, the 1960s, but in other respects dwarfs its parent. It has 71 main roles and took 552 days to shoot.

Self-indulgent? Only if you regard Proust or Balzac as self-indulgent. What Mr Reitz has done, in "Heimat" and now in "Heimat II", is to make the cinematic equivalent of a *roman fleuve*, like "A la recherche du temps perdu" or "La Comédie humaine"—a vast river of a film that sweeps up everything into a portrait of an age. It is a movie that needs special handling. The London Film Festival recently unspooled it in great chunks over two weekends. On television it will be shown in 13 weekly instalments, where it will seem, like "Heimat" itself, a soap opera transformed into a work of art.

"Die Zweite Heimat" does not just mean "Heimat II". Literally it means "The Second Homeland"—the search for a place or a way of life of one's own, different from the world in which one grew up. It is a quest for personal identity.

Edgar Reitz traces this Odyssey through the son of the leading character in "Heimat". Hermann Simon, son of Maria Simon, leaves his native village at the start of the film to seek fame and fortune as a composer in Munich. The 26-hour journey charts his career and the people he befriends and falls in love with along the way. Each of the film's 13 chapters centres on one character, though all thread in and out of the story as friends and acquaintances do in life. One leading character is encountered briefly in chapter one and only re-enters the story in a big way seven episodes later. Others seem to be important in the early scenes only to fade away as the story moves on. But life is like that.

Mr Reitz's film is the chronicle of a generation—the era that led, all over Europe, to the student revolution of 1968. It is a film that does not supply answers but asks questions—about life, love, politics, music, film, big business, the whole damned thing. More than any other movie, it seems to embrace the entire compass of life, while staying anchored to the human factor.

In a film of this length, not everything is on the same level. There are weaker episodes, naturally, but nobody can agree on which they are. Which may be one definition of universality. What nobody disputes is Mr Reitz's virtuosity. In "Heimat II" he shoots all the daytime scenes (scenes of the everyday struggle for survival) in black and white and all the night scenes (the world of dreams and hopes) in colour. Only twice does he break the "rules": at the start and at the end are daylight scenes shot in colour.

Mr Reitz says he does this in order to lead the audience away from a world with which it is familiar and back to it again at the end with all the questions that the film raises uppermost in the mind. Does growing up, for example, mean losing something (the ideals of youth) or gaining something (the wisdom of maturity)?

Not addressed at all in the two "Heimat" films is the future of Germany. They consider the past (the Nazi legacy) and the 1960s revolutionary era. Still awaited is a third panel in the triptych, bringing the saga up to the reunified present. A 52-hour "Heimat III" perhaps?

Underground poetry

DECEMBER 5TH *People rushed to buy a book of poetry after reading verses on their journeys to and from work by train*

SOMETIMES publishers do unexpected things. And sometimes the public picks up on a book that no book dealer in his right mind would have regarded as a potential best-seller. An outstanding example is "Poems on the Underground" (Cassell): an anthology of the poems that have been appearing on posters in the London Underground railway system since 1986, some of them with illustrations, like Spike Milligan's sketch for his poem "Teeth".

Since it was launched last year in paperback with an initial print run of 7,000 copies (large for a book of poems), the publishers have been unable to keep it in print, such has been the public demand. Some 45,000 copies have been sold in less than a year. Now the publishers have brought it out again, in hard covers this time (the reverse of what usually happens) and with an extra ingredient that should bring it an even larger readership.

Cassell & Co dipped into the archives of London Transport and discovered that many of the great Underground posters of the past—from 1911 to 1941—had not only been fine works of art in their own right,

but had used poems to complement the illustrations. Twenty of these posters, many with poems or parts of poems by Wordsworth, Shelley, Shakespeare, Browning and others, have been reproduced in full colour and dispersed throughout the book. "Poems on the Underground" is not a new idea, but the revival of an old one.

The posters themselves are a marvellous evocation of their times. One, produced as war was breaking out in 1939, shows an illustration of daffodils in bloom, beneath which runs a quotation from Shakespeare ("When daffodils begin to peer/With heigh! the doxy, over the dale"), and beneath that, the glorious banner headline: "The daffodils are out— What about you?" Such innocent public exhortation is quite unimaginable today.

The finest of all the old posters is Dora McLaren's "Pied Piper" of 1914, which shows the piper leading his merry band of young innocents past the station entrance and down into that "joyous land" beneath the ground. A snatch from Browning's "Pied Piper of Hamelin" runs beneath.

The book also includes the 15 poems

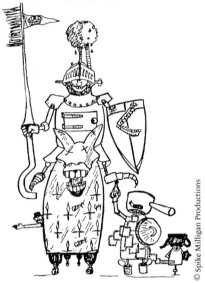

English teeth

© Spike Milligan Productions

that have been used since the paperback was first published. They are, as before, a mixture of the traditional and the unexpected. It all goes to prove that poetry and popular success can go together provided that the public is not browbeaten by too much self-conscious obscurity.

A mess of parables

DECEMBER 5TH *Tom Peters is as famous as a business adviser in America as John Harvey-Jones is in Britain. But he ignored his own teachings in writing "Liberation Management" (Knopf/Macmillan)*

MOST people call Tom Peters a "management guru", a term suggesting those brainy theorists who sit on academic pedestals handing down pronouncements on how businesses are, or should be, run. This is unfair to Mr Peters. He is no austere spiritual teacher, but rather an evangelist who passes among his flock. He becomes intimately involved with their problems, shouting "you too can be saved". On the platform at his seminars (which are really rallies), he does not spout theories or present data but instead tells stories, usually parables about companies just like yours which saw the light and were saved.

This book is a collection of those parables. The great thing about it is that it does not pretend to reduce management to a series of abstract theories or even practical formulae. Mr Peters does not claim to have all the answers. But he has worked with many companies which are thriving in

their different industries and countries, and which share one, rather general, characteristic: they are discarding their old bureaucratic, hierarchical habits.

Such firms, typified by Alfred Sloan's GM and Harold Geneen's ITT, used hierarchies and rule-books to solve their basic problem: how to harness hundreds of thousands of erratic, selfish humans into an organisation with a common purpose and to manage it in a predictable or even scientific way. Mr Peters hates such firms, which have become buried under their manuals and their committees, and are being left behind by their rivals.

To Mr Peters, the fact that companies are made up of erratic, selfish humans is not something to be shackled but rather to be exploited. Hence the title of this book: managers need to be liberated from their structures and rules if their firms are to be dynamic, to provide what customers want

and to keep pace with technological and market change. Big firms can act like small ones if they cut out committees and break themselves into tiny units; dying firms can revive if they allow people to take decisions rather than simply follow orders; managers should think in terms of projects that need their own unique groupings of people rather than committees which try to fit tasks into their fixed teams and categories.

Mr Peters's message cannot be summed up in a paragraph as simple as that one. But the trouble is that his great strength— his refusal to offer a simple theory—also leads to this book's downfall. Mr Peters teaches by telling stories. But he also wants his lessons to be comprehensive, to cover as many different circumstances as possible and thus to avoid the danger of drawing conclusions from a few carefully selected anecdotes.

That spirit is fine, but the result is that he goes way over the top, including hundreds of anecdotes in a sprawling book of more than 800 pages. In such a thicket the reader quickly gets lost, so entangled in the undergrowth that each fresh anecdote detracts from others rather than adding to them. A man who wants firms to "think small" and to be accessible has ended up writing an inaccessible book.

This is odd because Mr Peters is, like Ronald Reagan, a great communicator. His seminars work because he keeps things simple, he strides around talking like an ordinary mortal rather than a stuffed shirt at a lectern, and he conveys his own enthusiasm. People enjoy attending them even if they have heard him tell the same story before (which they often have). But they will not enjoy reading this book; it is a safe bet that few will read more than 100 pages.

Put it more charitably: somewhere in this book there is something for everybody. To Mr Peters, all organisations can be liberated, so his stories include a prison, several hospitals and even his own publisher. His observations are straightforward, and he does not feel silly when making basic but sensible recommendations about dealing with people and bonding them into teams: holding a barbecue is, in his view, at least as worthwhile a management technique as setting the right formula for performance-related pay.

The result is that most people can learn something even when reading just a few pages of this book. That something will not be a revelation; it is more likely to be of the sort that goes "yes, I agree; I must remember to do that next week." When that happens, stop reading immediately. Otherwise you will get so bogged down that you forget what it was you meant to do. And you may never find that point again.

Parthenon puzzles

DECEMBER 18TH, NEW YORK
An American professor's new theory about the Parthenon put the cat among the archaeological pigeons

SOME archaeologists will see it as confirming the misogyny of the ancient Greeks; others as an indication that they regarded women as just as capable as men of behaving heroically. Still others will dismiss it as nonsense. Whatever the reaction, controversy is certain over a new interpretation of the Parthenon frieze by Joan Breton Connelly, a professor of archaeology at New York University.

The conventional explanation for the so-called "peplos scene" in the Parthenon frieze, which is now part of the Elgin Marbles in the British Museum, dates back to the studies of two 18th-century British travellers, James Stuart and Nicolas Revett. After examining the frieze they concluded that it represented the Panathenaic procession, which was part of the regular celebrations of the birthday of Athena, the patron goddess of Athens.

Miss Connelly disagrees. Her theory connects figures from the peplos scene with part of a play by Euripides that was found about 20 years ago on papyrus wrapped around a Hellenistic mummy in the Louvre. The play, which has been dated to 423-421BC, is set in the mythical days of Erechtheus, the legendary king of Athens, when Eumolpos, king of Thrace, rallied a large force of Thracians to attack the city.

In the fragment, Erechtheus consults the oracle at Delphi to find how he can protect Athens from an impending siege, and learns that he must sacrifice a daughter to save the city. But his three daughters have made an oath that if one should die the others will die as well. The king breaks the sad news to his wife, Praxithea, who says:

The ruin of one person's house is of less consequence and brings less grief than that of the whole city. If there were a harvest of sons in our house rather than daughters, and a hostile flame came to the city, would I not have sent my sons into battle, fearing for their death? I hate women who, in preference to the common good, choose for their own children to live.

With Praxithea's permission, Erechtheus sacrifices his daughters and the battle ensues. As promised by the oracle, the Athenians are victorious, although Erechtheus is killed in the course of combat by Poseidon.

Miss Connelly identifies five figures from the play by Euripides in the peplos scene (see picture): one is Erechtheus dressed as a priest and about to slay his youngest daughter, who stands beside her father unfolding her death shroud. Next to Erechtheus is the queen, Praxithea. A second daughter hands down a sacrificial table to her mother. The end figure is the third princess, who carries a basket in her left arm, perhaps containing a knife.

This reading of the frieze, says Miss Connelly, has "enormous implications" for understanding the role of women in Greek myth and, perhaps, in Greek culture as well. Conceding that some might see the sacrifice of virgins as misogynistic, she disagrees:

Valiant and heroic women go willingly to death, and are proud of their critical roles in saving the populace. These women are the equals of men who die in battle for their cities.

Sir Hugh Lloyd-Jones, professor of Greek at Oxford, describes Miss Connelly's theory as "very seductive". Homer Thompson, professor of history at the Institute for Advanced Study in Princeton, says: "The great argument in favour of this new interpretation is that it does give us a mythical motivation for the frieze; it is much more in keeping with the language of sculptural adornment of Greek temples."

Sir John Boardman, Lincoln professor of classical archaeology at Oxford, is more circumspect, saying he awaits Miss Connelly's full treatment. In the meantime he holds to his own theory that the Parthenon frieze commemorates the Athenian victory over the Persians in the battle of Marathon. Miss Connelly has been invited to present her paper at Oxford University. She is now preparing a final draft. Rows are likely. As Mortimer Wheeler, a famous British digger, once said: "Archaeology is not a science, it's a vendetta."

Contents

SPORT

As we reported then

Fishing for prizes

JULY 11TH *Angling claims to be Britain's most popular sport. And sport it is: The compleat angler can be a competitive fellow*

"ENGLAND International newcomer Alan Scotthorne brushed aside nerves to win his section and finish fifth overall in the four nation Ostallato Canal Challenge in Italy. And his club mate, 1989 world champion Tom Pickering, surged back to form . . . " No, this is not golf or snooker or anything involving a ball. The paragraph is from a British weekly magazine called *Angler's Mail*.

Anybody who imagines the catching of fish is just a tranquil pastime is in for a rude surprise. *Angler's Mail* devotes pages to matches and leagues and team performances and even gossip: "Canal ace Dave Berrow has made a shock split from Drennan Super League finalists Browning Starlets and signed a lucrative contract to promote Maver poles."

Angling is among the most popular participant sports in Britain, where the number of anglers has risen from a smidgen over 3m in 1981 to about 4m today. The national championships have six divisions. Each division has 90 teams and each team 12 anglers: 6,480 competitors in all, picked from tens of thousands of match-playing club members all over the country.

A fishing competition works like this. A week before the event, the water is put out of bounds to competitors. The bank is divided into 12 sections, with one angler from each team in each section. On the Saturday morning, at about 10am, the competitors take up their positions and, at a signal, begin fishing. There are strict rules about the techniques they may use. "No wasp grub, bloodworm, joker or steak," said one match prospectus. (Bloodworms and jokers are the red-blooded larvae of midges, which thrive in polluted water

and make catching fish too easy. Most anglers use maggots.)

The competitors retain all the fish they catch in a "keep net" suspended in the water. Then, at the end, the umpires come along the bank and weigh the fish in the net before returning them to the water. Points are awarded according to the total weight of fish in the net. Most are roach, bream, perch and chub. (The only fish that do not count are game fish, ie, trout and salmon, and crustaceans. Most game fishermen kill and eat their catch, and insist theirs is not a competitive sport.)

The winner of each section gets 90 points. Others receive points according to their finishing place, with zero for those who catch no fish. The team with the most points wins and the man with the heaviest bag is the individual champion. In the national championships, which are held all over the country between July and October, there is one match per division; the 15 bottom teams are relegated to the next division, replaced by the 15 best teams from it, just as in the soccer league.

Last year the league champion was a team by the name of Izaak Walton Preston. The England team, picked from the best individual anglers, won gold medals in both the team and individual events in the world championships in Hungary in 1991, in competition against anglers from a score of countries.

Although anglers are not professionals, money and sponsorship are an integral part of the sport. A match costs only £8,000 ($15,000) or so to stage (to rent the water, bus the competitors there, pay the officials and so on), but an angler can run up large bills for groundbait (thrown into the water

to attract the fish) and tackle—unless he catches the eye of a sponsor like Sensas, a French producer of groundbait.

In the past decade rods have been decisively replaced by "poles". The average angler now sits astride a gigantic, 11-metre pole, assembled in sections and costing at least £1,500. From its tip dangles a short stretch of line straight to the float and hook, so that when a fish takes the maggot, the fisherman slides the pole back on to the bank quick as a flash and plops the fish into his net: it is faster than reeling the fish in on a short rod. The only drawback of a pole is that a strong fish has no chance to take line off the reel and therefore snaps the line. Kevin Ashurst, the runner-up to Bob Nudd, the British winner of the individual gold medal, suffered this sad fate in the world championships, when he hooked a big carp.

There are many other forms of competitive fishing. Carp fishermen try to beat records for size of fish. American bass fishermen take part in two-day tournaments, with entry fees of perhaps $200 and prizes of $50,000 for the angler who catches the heaviest bag of bass. But to be enshrined in America's National Freshwater Fishing Hall of Fame as a "legendary angler" requires more than just winning such tournaments; you must also make a contribution to the sport, like invent a new lure.

All this is rather frowned on by fly fishermen. True, they sometimes compete in championships to cast the longest and most perfect line to an exact spot. But most fish for diversion or to get something to eat. In the *Daily Telegraph* recently, Hugh Falkus, doyen of salmon fishermen, deplored the habit of catch-and-release precisely because it would turn their pastime into a competitive sport.

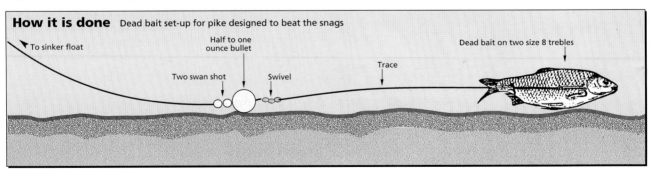

How it is done Dead bait set-up for pike designed to beat the snags

To sinker float

Half to one ounce bullet

Dead bait on two size 8 trebles

Two swan shot

Swivel

Trace

Europe jinxed

AUGUST 8TH **Why cannot a European golfer win the United States PGA championship?**

THE United States PGA championship, one of the last redoubts of American dominance in golf, is being contested from August 13th-16th over the Bellerive Country Club course in St Louis. Will it prove for European players another frustrating and insufferable experience, another unsuccessful attempt at mastering the peculiar and distinctly American brand of championship golf?

Britain's Tony Jacklin won the American Open in 1970. But it is more than 60 years since a European player won the PGA. Among the four major championships—the others are the Masters, the American Open and the British Open—the PGA is the one that is as American as McDonald's.

What is it about the PGA that keeps it out of the European grasp? The ball, after all, remains 1.68 inches (4.3 cm) in diameter, the hole is 4.5 inches across and there are 14 clubs in each player's bag. There are 18 holes on the course and, aside from the increased number of raucous and inebriated spectators shouting, "You the Man!" the tournament is conducted in much the same fashion as the other majors.

Several different things inveigh against Europeans. First, a dearth of competitors. This year, there will be just 11 Europeans in a field of 156 players, and several will be suffering from jet lag. The weather also handicaps Europeans. This is ironical, since one of the acknowledged strengths of the stars from Europe is their ability to compete in differing types of inclement weather—as the Scots are fond of pointing out, "nae wind, nae cold, nae rain, nae golf". But for the PGA, the frightful heat must be factored in: not the moderate heat of the English summer, but 90°F (32°C) heat with 60% humidity.

Nick Faldo himself pointed to just this difficulty when he was in the midst of his victory celebration at the British Open at Muirfield. "The next one's going to be the PGA and it's going to be stinking hot. I'm going to have to practise in the bathroom to get ready for that one." One would think that the top two Spanish players, Seve Ballesteros and Jose Maria Olazabal, would not have problems with excessive heat since their country has an abundance of it. But neither of these players has fared well at the PGA.

Where another sort of heat is applied to Europeans, and where short-game artists such as Mr Ballesteros lose their edge, is in the way golf courses are set up for the PGA. In America the game is played in the air. A premium is placed on hitting the ball high and carrying it into greens surrounded by rough and bunkers and, sometimes, water. There really is no ground game, no bump and run, and the heavy rough that surrounds the greens and borders the fairways presents a number of situations which golfers from Europe generally do not face.

"The heavy rough and narrow fairways take away the driver," says Bernhard Langer, the German who won the Dutch Open in July. "The rough around the greens eliminates chipping. This is why the tournaments are often boring and almost always produce the same kind of winner—the player who can drive it straight, hits many greens and two putts."

Mr Langer's observation is an accurate criticism of the philosophy of course design adopted by the United States Golf Association and shared by the PGA of America, the umbrella organisation for club pros that oversees the PGA championship. This philosophy—designed to make par hard to beat—is sometimes taken to absurd lengths. At Shoal Creek, Alabama, in 1990, for example, the Bermuda grass rough was so thick and gnarly that it prompted Ian Woosnam, the tiny Welsh wizard, to threaten never to return.

To examine a roster of the most recent

Faldo leads the charge

winners of the PGA is to see a vivid illustration of Mr Langer's critique. From 1987 to 1990, the winners were Larry Nelson, Jeff Sluman, Payne Stewart and Wayne Grady. All those players are relatively short but straight hitters off the tee and are usually among the best at getting their balls on to the greens without mishaps on the way. The obvious exception to the rule is last year's winner, "Long John" Daly, the longest driver in golf, the player whose fast and loose approach to all things—golf and otherwise—have earned him the popular monicker "Wild Thing."

Somewhere among the 11 Europeans due to play next week at Bellerive, there could be a surprise lurking—a player who can break the American stranglehold. There is at least a precedent associated with the site that could serve as a harbinger: the last and only time a major championship was contested at Bellerive, the American Open in 1965, the Americans were shut out. South Africa's Gary Player defeated Australia's Kel Nagle in a play-off. There is hope yet for Europe.

The European challenge faded again. Nick Price from Zimbabwe won, Britain's Nick Faldo came second.

Major victories													
UNITED STATES · AUSTRALIA · EUROPE													
	1980	1981	1982	1983	1984	1985	1986	1987	1988	1989	1990	1991	1992
Masters	US	US	US	EUR	US	EUR	US	US	EUR	EUR	EUR	EUR	US
US Open	US	AUS	US	US	US	US	US	US	US	US	US	US	US
British Open	US	US	US	US	EUR	EUR	AUS	EUR	EUR	US	EUR	AUS	EUR
US PGA	US	US	US	US	US	US	US	US	US	US	AUS	US	?
Source: PGA													

Forever at the crease

AUGUST 29TH *In most sports, the stars come and go in a few short years of glory. Cricket continues to be a wonderful exception. Why?*

WHEN Australia's cricket team did badly in the world cup in March, the critics said that its 36-year-old captain was past it. He ignored them, and is at the moment leading the Australian side on a tour of Sri Lanka. England's captain is going to take his team on a two-month tour of India this winter—enough to test the spirit, and the stomach, of the fittest—and he is 39. Yet neither Allan Border nor Graham Gooch is unusually old for a top-class cricketer.

At first glance, that is odd. After all, cricket is played with a small, hard ball, sometimes travelling at over 100 miles an hour (160kph). It involves long hours in the field, where players need quick reflexes, fast legs and a strong arm. Yet it has always attracted a disproportionate share of middle-aged maestros. So experience matters above all? No, because cricket has been just as notable for its pimply-faced prodigies. At a time when sporting success seems to come younger, and last shorter, than ever before, a "career in cricket" is still a phrase with some resemblance to the truth.

Down the years, many of the game's legendary figures carried on at the top long after their counterparts in other sports had peaked. Jack Hobbs started playing first-class cricket in 1905, at the age of 22. He was still appearing for his county, Surrey, in 1934. For most of that time he was in the England team, making his first appearance in 1907, his last in 1930. His most successful season was in 1925, when he scored 16 centuries; he was 42. Had it not been for the first world war, he would surely have broken every record there was, and still be holding on to many of them today.

The carnage of that war left several cricketing nations with great gaps where the young players would have been. This explains some of the oddities of the 1920s and 1930s, when seven men made their test-match debuts after their 40th birthdays. And Wilfred Rhodes bowled his last ball for England in 1930, when he was 52.

Even in recent years, however, some less-than-young men have flourished. Brian Close made his last appearance for England when he was 45, David Steele his first one at 33. And some famous names have been called back to the highest levels when it seemed they were long past their best. Tom Graveney played regularly for England between 1951 and 1962, then withdrew to the quieter world of county matches. But he had a renaissance for England in 1966-69, scoring centuries and playing his last test when he was 42.

The game is kind to young men too, particularly in India and Pakistan. Those two countries have had some precocious talents: Mushtaq

Old Hobbs

Mohammad, the youngest of all test players, who had barely turned 15 on his debut for Pakistan in 1958; little Sachin Tendulkar, who was 16 when he first played for India and, at the age of 19, has just had a season with Yorkshire in the county game; and the three Pakistani fast bowlers who cut their way through England this summer were only 16 (Aqib Javed), 17 (Waqar Younis) and 18 (Wasim Akram) when they first played for their country.

This spread of ages does not happen at the top of other sports. Take baseball, which is arguably the closest equivalent to cricket. As the chart shows, the 18 players who were in the American League's 1992 All-Star team had an average age of 28, and nearly all of them were clustered within four years either side of it. Their average was only a little higher than that of Pakistan's victorious world-cup squad in Australia; but the Pakistanis' ages ranged far wider, from 18 up to 39.

With this spread of ages goes another feature of cricket: as in many other sports, the passion, and the skill, tend to run in families. The Cowdreys, father and son, both played for England, and only ten

years apart. The Nourses of South Africa were separated by 11 years. But the most extraordinary family feat belongs to a pair of New Zealanders: Lance Cairns played his last test match in 1985, only four years before his son Christopher began his international career. That could not happen in tennis. Or football, or any of the varieties of rugby, or squash. So why is cricket different?

The answer, once upon a time, would have included the fact that you did not need to be particularly athletic to be a good cricketer. England used to field teams who were carrying perhaps 100 kilos of excess weight between them. In the mid-1960s its test sides included Colin Cowdrey, Tom Graveney, Colin Milburn, Basil d'Oliveira: geniuses, all four of them, but jellies over a hundred metres. Today's top cricketers are mostly fine athletes, who train in the gym as often as they practise in the nets. At this year's world cup, the only old-style belly to be seen among nine national teams belonged to England's Ian Botham.

So the best in cricket are now as fit as the best in most other ball games, yet the cricketers still span a wider age range. The puzzle remains: why is cricket different? The answer, painful for other sportsmen to accept, may be profound. It starts with the fact that top cricketers tend to be good at other ball games. Ted Dexter, who captained England in the early 1960s, might have been a professional golfer. At about the same time, out in South Africa, young Roy McLean was having to choose between cricket and rugby union. Denis Compton, perhaps the most elegant of England's batsmen, played first-division football in the winter. The list could go on, down the decades and across the continents. Give a great cricketer a ball and some way of striking it, and the chances are he will do it well.

A talent for ball games is not something that really can be taught. If you have it, it is there from the beginning: hence cricket's teenage prodigies. And it does not suddenly disappear: hence the magical 40-year-olds. Cricket, more than any other sport, requires that talent, and lets it flourish. It is the true ball game, the greatest there is.

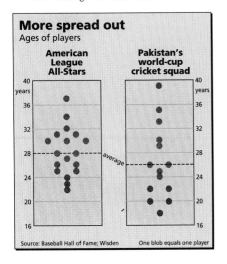

More spread out
Ages of players

American League All-Stars	Pakistan's world-cup cricket squad

Source: Baseball Hall of Fame; Wisden   One blob equals one player

Stud poker

The decline in bloodstock prices is not all bad news

JAMES JOYCE set "Ulysses" on Ascot Gold Cup day in a year when Lord Howard de Walden's horse was much fancied. In those days, patrician owners dreamed only of breeding the world's perfect thoroughbred. They rarely dwelt upon the little Leopold Blooms who stuck weekly pin money upon their racers. But times have changed. World over, the punter is increasingly being asked to underwrite the hobby of rich owners, and this does not stop the latter from complaining. "You can't win enough," the current Lord Howard de Walden complains. "You're jolly lucky if you can make it pay."

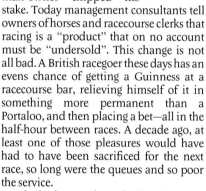

Beloved Ardross

Making it pay has become an obsession in a sport that began when horses raced for a pot into which Charles II and each gentleman-owner chipped his stake. Today management consultants tell owners of horses and racecourse clerks that racing is a "product" that on no account must be "undersold". This change is not all bad. A British racegoer these days has an evens chance of getting a Guinness at a racecourse bar, relieving himself of it in something more permanent than a Portaloo, and then placing a bet—all in the half-hour between races. A decade ago, at least one of those pleasures would have had to have been sacrificed for the next race, so long were the queues and so poor the service.

The bad news about the "service revolution" in racing is twofold. First, the po-faced owner's assertion that the racegoer can get "value" from the product only if the owner makes money and therefore stays in the game. The main chance for that to happen, the owner claims, is for a bigger percentage of a gambler's stake to be returned to the sport in the form of prize money. Barely a week goes by in Britain without a landed politician calling for a state-run monopoly that more efficiently bilks the punter in favour of the owner. The Stuart kings, arch-purveyors of monopolies, would have been impressed at the elegance of this suggestion.

At far greater risk than the punter from the corruption of profit and product is the thoroughbred itself. Look back to the beginning of the 1980s, when bloodstock prices began to swell (see chart). Since the 17th century, breeders of racehorses have known that a thoroughbred's value is only

as great as its ability to perfect its descendants' bloodline. Translated into the language of the greedy 1980s, this meant that a three-year-old colt's worthiest attribute was its ability to transform an original cost as a yearling into a sale price that reflected the value, discounted back to the present, of its future stream of semen.

Three hundred years ago, the only measure of bloodline value was a sire's ability on the racetrack—ie, his track record. Over the past decade, however, the overriding measure has been what an Arab prince or an American mogul was prepared to pay. Horses became, literally, too valuable to race.

So the fabulous price inflation of top thoroughbreds came to be based upon racecourse careers which, though often dazzling, lasted preferably fewer than ten minutes. Secreto and El Gran Senor, first and second in the 1984 Epsom Derby, were too valuable ever to be risked on a racetrack after the June of their three-year-old season. It remains a mystery whether these two horses were flashes-in-the-pan or truly great horses, for they ran just seven races between them.

These horses at least won. Once others that were bought for more than $10m proved racecourse disasters, bloodstock prices were bound to collapse. This they started to do in 1985, and they are still falling. According to *Racing Update* in Lexington, Kentucky, stud fees for the top American sires fell by 18% in 1990, by 14% in 1991 and by another 20% this year. Sale prices have followed suit. The average price of a yearling at last month's great

Keeneland select sale, at $260,331, was the lowest since 1981.

The continuing collapse of bloodstock prices internationally is good news. For a start, good horses are once again becoming affordable for people whose love of racing exceeds their love of profit. Better still, owners of the top horses have begun to race them again. The racegoer, once again, is being offered good sport.

The new willingness of owners to race their horses more often is sensible. In 1967 one English horse, Busted, won his first race at the age of four. He then went on to win the Coronation Stakes, the Eclipse, the King George VI and Queen Elizabeth Stakes, and the Prix Foy. A victory in any of those races is a noble achievement. The brave Ardross could never have won two Ascot Gold Cups and been pipped in the 1982 Arc de Triomphe had he not still been in training as a six-year-old.

Meanwhile, three-year-old horses not fully proven on the racecourse can become horses of uncertain potential in the stallion shed—with offspring of unproven robustness. The market now seems to sense this. El Gran Senor was in his time reckoned to be the greatest horse of the 1980s. But a visit by a mare to this barely fertile nag now costs just $30,000, which represents a huge loss on his owners' $30m-40m investment. Secreto's stud value has fallen tenfold in the past two years: $7,500 gets your mare a ride. The well-raced heroes of the 1970s—Lyphard, Mr Prospector, Seattle Slew—still command stud fees several times that.

Ardross was the last flat horse truly to win the affection of the British racing public. Far better horses have since cantered past the grandstand. You would be lying if you claimed to know which they all were.

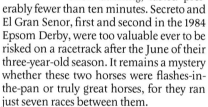

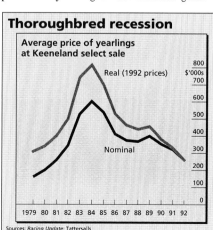

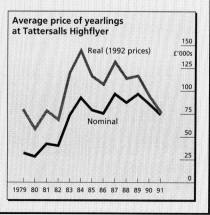

Thoroughbred recession

Average price of yearlings at Keeneland select sale

Real (1992 prices) $'000s

Nominal

800 700 600 500 400 300 200 100 0

1979 80 81 82 83 84 85 86 87 88 89 90 91 92

Average price of yearlings at Tattersalls Highflyer

Real (1992 prices) £'000s

Nominal

150 125 100 75 50 25 0

1979 80 81 82 83 84 85 86 87 88 89 90 91

Sources: *Racing Update*; Tattersalls

Ladies at deuce

Women's tennis is not the same as men's—but does that mean it is any worse?

"EIGHTY per cent of women in the top 100 are fat, lazy pigs," declared Richard Krajicek, a politically incorrect Dutchman at this year's Wimbledon. When reprimanded for his male chauvinism, he confessed to exaggeration: "What I meant to say is that 75% are fat pigs." Clearly Mr Krajicek is not the apologising sort—but, insulting metaphors apart, does he have much to apologise about?

Critics of women's tennis make two complaints: that the women's game is not as good as the men's, and that the women's game has too few good players. Their logic is that women therefore play less entertainingly than men and so should be paid less than men. As with all good sporting arguments, reason and fact matter less than opinion and judgment.

What cannot be disputed is that a male player will beat his female equivalent: he will hit harder, cover the court faster and endure longer. True, in a much-hyped "battle of the sexes" in 1973 at the Houston Astrodome, Billie Jean King humiliated Bobby Riggs—but Mrs King, then aged 30, was the reigning Wimbledon champion and Mr Riggs was a hustler 26 years her senior. A better example was the contest two months ago at Caesars Palace, Las Vegas: 40-year-old Jimmy Connors gave away 4ft (1¼ metres) of extra court-width and his second serve, and still strolled to victory against 35-year-old Martina Navratilova, who is ranked fourth in the women's game. When men say their 100th-ranked player—someone like the hard-serving Kevin Curren or Haiti's Ronald Agenor—would beat the best of the women, they are surely right.

But does the fact that men are better players mean the women's game is not as "good"? The answer depends less on the players than on the spectators. The men's game, especially on fast courts, is all about power. On Wimbledon's grass, a rally of more than three strokes is a rarity in a men's match. Goran Ivanisevic served 206 aces in this year's tournament, including 37 in the final (which he lost). By contrast, Steffi Graf, who has one of the best serves in the women's game, served a mere 26 aces, including only three in the final (which she won).

In the 1970s, the women's game was all too often a boring pat-a-cake affair that palled beside the men's. In the 1990s, carbon-fibre racquets may have made the men's game oppressively powerful—but they give physically weaker women the strength to play fast and exciting tennis. For the spectator, the see-saw matches between Miss Graf, Monica Seles, Miss Navratilova, Gabriela Sabatini and Arantxa Sanchez Vicario are every bit as good to watch as those between the men.

The problem comes when those stars play against their inferiors. One attraction of the men's game is its depth: the player ranked number 100—or even 200—occasionally defeats the number one. In 1974 Chris Evert went undefeated for 55 matches; in 1984 Miss Navratilova went for 74 matches without defeat. Between June 1989 and May 1990, Miss Graf had a winning streak of 66 matches. There have been impressive sequences in the men's game, too (Ivan Lendl had 44 consecutive victories in 1981-82). But where the top men may lose to the lowly, the top women lose only to each other.

One consequence is that, although women's tournaments normally offer less prize money than men's (the United States Open is one exception), the top women win as much as the men. Before the Virginia Slims Championships that began on November 16th, Miss Seles, ranked number one, had this year won almost $1.9m, compared with the $1.6m won by her male counterpart, Jim Courier. A second consequence is that the top women take a bigger slice of the prize-money cake than their male equivalents. Miss Seles has won six times more than the sixth-ranked woman, Jennifer Capriati;

Seles earns more off court

Mr Courier has won not even twice as much as sixth-ranked Petr Korda.

A third consequence is that the earnings gap between the women's élite and the rest is even greater off-court than on. Miss Seles gets paid even to have her hair cut; her income from endorsements is around $7m a year. Miss Sabatini has a perfume named after her. The only top woman player not to have multiplied her on-court millions into off-court ones is Miss Navratilova. Advertisers apparently worry about her lesbian image.

Such concentrated wealth is a symptom not just of the top players' success but of their sport's weakness. If the same few women cruise through to the semi-finals, some fans will wonder, what is the point of watching the no-hopers in the early rounds? Fewer followers will mean less sponsorship, which in turn will mean fewer tournaments—especially if the top players demand still more prize money. The pessimists are always ready to say that the sport is being throttled by greed.

Their argument misses the point. It is not the players' greed that determines sponsorship, but the forces of the market. Paradoxically, the financial dominance of the top-rankers could be not the downfall of the women's game but its salvation, since it will encourage more young players to seek their fortune on the circuit. That way the "fat, lazy pigs" will either have to shape up or retire. Meanwhile, just wait until Venus Williams—12 years old, American and black—joins the pro game. Then the sponsors will sit up, and women's tennis will find a new audience.

Mixed doubles

Career prize-money, $m

	Women		Men	
1	Martina Navratilova	18.0	Ivan Lendl	18.2
2	Steffi Graf	9.6	John McEnroe	11.6
3	Chris Evert	8.9	Stefan Edberg	11.0
4	Gabriela Sabatini	5.6	Boris Becker	9.4
5	Monica Seles	5.6	Jimmy Connors	8.3
6	Pam Shriver	4.8	Mats Wilander	7.4
7	Helena Sukova	4.1	Guillermo Vilas	4.9
8	Zena Garrison	3.4	Andre Agassi	4.3
9	Hana Mandlikova	3.3	Andres Gomez	4.3
10	Arantxa Sanchez Vicario	2.9	Anders Jarryd	4.0

Sources: WTA; ATP

Basket cases

Why are basketball players such dunces at American colleges, and what can be done about it?

HOW big is the basketball in college basketball? Well, when the University of Kentucky held its first official practice of the 1992-93 season, at one minute past midnight on a November night, 8,000 spectators crowded in, and another 8,000 were turned away. How small is the college in college basketball? Only 22% of the basketball players who entered the North Carolina state university system in 1986 graduated within five years.

At many colleges the lectures hall has always taken second place to games for students admitted mainly for their sporting prowess. But when it comes to college basketball, the education of the players, especially the black players, is scandalously neglected. A recent study by the National Collegiate Athletic Association (NCAA) of its 297 Division I colleges and universities showed that 47% of the sportsmen who enrolled in 1984 and 1985 received their bachelor's degrees within five years. But only 38% of the male basketball players graduated within that period, and only 29% of the black ones (see chart).

Scandals over the behaviour of their star players, who appear on police blotters with some regularity, have always vexed colleges. These low graduation rates are also a serious matter but are often treated lightly; academics joke about their jocks experiencing difficulties with the harder letters of the alphabet. The National Basketball Association (NBA) cheats students when it views colleges as a sort of minor league, a recruiting-ground for its professional basketball teams. There is stiff competition for the few slots in professional basketball and many students who concentrate on the sport at college have to settle for menial jobs when they leave.

Even a degree is not necessarily proof that a student has learnt anything. When Elden Campbell, a centre for the Los Angeles Lakers, was asked if he had earned his degree from Clemson University, he replied: "No, but they gave me one anyway." But it is probably better for a student to go through the motions of learning than to do nothing.

Professor Gary Funk, at Southwest Missouri State, the author of "Major Violation: Unbalanced Priorities in Athletics and Academics" (Human Kinetics), says:

> As long as the big carrot, money, is out there, college athletics is a complete hypocrisy, and basketball is by far the worst example. The rewards for success on the court are far too great, and the rewards for success in the classroom far too small. The NCAA will claim that it is making progress in academics, but I haven't seen it.

The money at stake is staggering. A team earns as much as $2m for its college, mainly from television, for making basketball's Final Four (ie, the semi-finalists in the national championship tournament), and that is not counting the increased donations the college gets from pleased (and wealthy) alumni and from boosters. Victory not only improves a coach's job security; it also boosts his shoe contract, his television show, his basketball camp . . . And when a player sees that the average NBA salary is over $1m a year, what is the point of Economics 101?

Still, some schools do manage to win and educate. Duke, an academically distinguished university in Durham, North Carolina, has won the past two NCAA tournaments even though its coach, Mike Krzyzewski, persuades almost all his seniors to study hard enough to graduate. Two years ago, when Duke beat the University of Nevada, Las Vegas, it was not just a victory of the Blue Devils over the Runnin' Rebels. It was a victory for education and Duke's high graduation rate versus UNLV's low one (100% compared with 25% in 1983-84).

Who, after all, makes the more successful college coach? Is it Dale Brown of Louisiana State University, whose players get to the NCAA tournament every year but rarely to the graduation podium? Or is it Bruce Parkhill of Penn State University, who may never make the Final Four but who has seen all 25 seniors he has coached in his nine years there get a diploma?

College presidents are forever revamping their rules, with the expressed purpose of improving education. But for every new reform there is a

Duke also scores in class

new loophole. When, several years ago, they instituted Proposition 48, which established minimum academic standards for freshmen, some schools got around that by finding two-year junior colleges for the athletes who could not qualify, and then—hey presto!—admitting them two years later as juniors.

Some suggest that colleges dispense with the hypocrisy and just hire the players on "athleticships". If they want to study, fine; if they do not, they can be paid like the kitchen or maintenance staff. But that would probably make matters worse. Although many college basketball players neglect their education, enough of them stay on at college for another year or two to earn their degrees to make any further relaxation of standards undesirable.

What can be done to put the college back in college basketball? The answer may be as simple as tying the number of scholarships a college is granted by the NCAA to its graduation rate. If the basketball team's rate is below a certain level, the college would be granted fewer scholarships.

Cynics say that such a rule would turn certain institutions into diploma mills offering such challenging courses as basketball theory and practical sun-tanning, but a basic monitoring system could prevent that from happening. Perhaps college basketball could then begin to eliminate its double standard. A few years ago the NBA ran some public-service announcements for its worthy "Stay in School" campaign. The only trouble was that seven of the NBA players who did the spots—Karl Malone, Michael Jordan, Charles Barkley, Clyde Drexler, Isiah Thomas, Doc Rivers and J.R. Reid—had all dropped out of college early, to join the NBA.

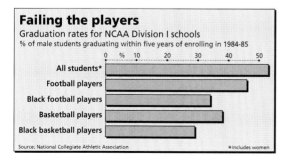

Failing the players

Graduation rates for NCAA Division I schools
% of male students graduating within five years of enrolling in 1984-85

	0 %	10	20	30	40	50
All students*						
Football players						
Black football players						
Basketball players						
Black basketball players						

Source: National Collegiate Athletic Association   *Includes women

Contents

GOVERNMENT

AFGHANISTAN

After the overthrow of the Najibullah government in May a self-proclaimed Leadership Council formally abolished the structure of the former regime and an Islamic state was officially established. Power in the new state would rest in the hands of the 51-member Islamic Jihad Council. The last presidential election was held in November 1987; the next is due in 1994. The last general election was held in April 1988; the next is due in 1993.

President (interim) Burhanuddin Rabbani (replaced in Jun Senghbatullah Mujjaddedi, who had replaced Najibullah Ahmadzai in Apr)
Prime minister (interim) Ustar Farid (replaced Fazl Haq Khalequiar in Apr)

ALBANIA

Parliamentary republic. Two rounds of voting in a general election in March produced a victory for the Democratic Party and gave an overall majority of 92 seats in the People's Assembly. In April the new 140-member unicameral People's Assembly elected the president and the Council of Ministers.

President Sali Berisha (replaced Ramiz Alia in Apr)
Prime minister Alexander Meksi (replaced Vilson Ahmeti in Apr)

ALGERIA

Presidential republic. The National Liberation Front has had control of the 281-seat National Assembly since 1962. Other parties have been legal since 1989. The last presidential election was in December 1988. The first round of a multi-party general election was held in December 1991. The second round planned for January 1992 was cancelled. The next election will not be called before the end of 1993.

President Following the resignation of Col. Chadli Benjedid in Jan a five-member High Committee of State (HCS) was created, chaired by Mohammed Boudiaf. After the assassination of Boudiaf in July Ali Kafi assumed the position of president of HCS.

Prime minister, economy minister Belaid Abdesselam (replaced Sid Ahmed Ghozali in Jul)

PRINCIPAL MINISTERS
Foreign affairs Lakhdar Brahimi
Defence Maj.-Gen. Khaled Nezzar
Interior Mohamed Hardi (replaced Maj.-Gen Larbi Belkheir in Feb)

ANDORRA

Parliamentary monarchy, with the president of France and the Bishop of Urgel (in Spain) holding joint suzerainty. These two heads of state are represented in Andorra by the Veguer de Franca and the Veguer Episcopal. A 28-member General Council of the Valleys is elected on a restricted franchise. The last general election was in 1989; the next is due by January 1994.

Co-prince François Mitterrand (since 1981)
Co-prince Joan Marti Alanis, Bishop of Urgel
Permanent French delegate Joan Keller
Permanent episcopal delegate Maj. Ramon Vilardell Mitjaneta
Veguer de Franca Enric Benoît de Coignac
Veguer Episcopal Francesc Badia-Batalla

ANGOLA

Presidential republic. Following independence from Portugal in 1975, the Popular Movement for the Liberation of Angola-Workers' Party (MPLA-PT) was the sole legal political party until a multi-party system came into effect in May 1991. The first multi-party election took place in September 1992. As expected, the ruling Popular Movement Party won a majority of seats. In the presidential election President Jose dos Santos won 49.57% of the votes, just short of the 50% needed to avoid a second round. The presidential run-off was arranged for January 1993, but was postponed due to fighting.

President Jose Eduardo dos Santos (since 1979)
Prime minister Fernando Jose Franca van Dunem (since 1991)

ANTIGUA AND BARBUDA

Parliamentary monarchy. The head of state is the United Kingdom sovereign, represented by a governor-general. The Antiguan Labour Party has controlled the 17-seat House of Representatives since 1976. The last general election was in 1989; the next is due by March 1994.

Governor-general Sir Wilfred Ebenezer Jacobs (since 1981)
Prime minister Vere C. Bird Sr (since 1981)

ARGENTINA

Federal republic. The ruling Justicialist Party (PJ – popularly known as the Peronists) controls the 300-member Congress. The last general election was in 1989; the next is due by May 1995.

President Carlos Saul Menem (since 1989)
Vice-president Eduardo Menem

PRINCIPAL MINISTERS
Defence Antonio Erman Gonzalez
Economy Domingo Cavallo
Foreign relations Guido di Tella
Interior Gustavo Beliz (replaced Jose Luis Manzano in Sep)
Secretary-general of the presidency Eduardo Baua
Justice Cesar Arias (replaced Leon Carlos Arslanian in Sep)

ARMENIA

Former republic of the Soviet Union and a founder member of the Commonwealth of Independent States. In August 1990 the Armenian Supreme Soviet adopted a declaration on sovereignty. In September 1991 a referendum on independence took place, and Armenia became an independent state. In October 1991 the first presidential election was held.

President Levon Ter-Petrosyan (since 1991)
Prime minister Khosrv Arutyunyan (since 1992)

AUSTRALIA

Federalist parliamentary democracy. Head of state is the United Kingdom sovereign, represented by a governor-general. The lower house of the bicameral legislature, the House of Representatives, is elected for three years on the basis of proportional representation. Since 1981 it has been controlled by the Australian Labor Party (ALP) which was elected for a record fourth consecutive term in March 1990, winning 78 of the 148 seats. The next general election is due by March 1993.

Governor-general Bill Hayden (since 1989)
Prime minister Paul Keating (since 1991)

PRINCIPAL MINISTERS
Health, housing and community services Brian Howe
Treasurer John Dawkins
Industry, technology and commerce John Button
Foreign affairs and trade Gareth Evans
Finance; vice-president Ralph Willis
Defence Robert Ray
Immigration, local government and ethnic affairs Gerry Hand
Arts, sport, environment and territories Ros Kelly

AUSTRIA

Federal republic with parliamentary democracy. The Socialist Party of Austria (SPÖ) and Austrian People's Party (ÖVP) have ruled in coalition since January 1987. The last general election was held in October 1990; the next is due by 1994. The last presidential election was held in April 1992.

Federal president Thomas Klestil (ÖVP) (replaced Kurt Waldheim in Jul)
Federal chancellor Franz Vranitzky (SPÖ) (since 1986)

PRINCIPAL MINISTERS
Vice-chancellor Erhard Busek (ÖVP)
Foreign affairs Alois Mock (ÖVP)
Finance Ferdinand Lacina (SPÖ)
Interior Franz Löschnak (SPÖ)
Defence Werner Fasslabend (ÖVP)

AZERBAIJAN

Former republic of the Soviet Union and a founder member of the Commonwealth of Independent States. In August 1991 the Azerbaijani Supreme Soviet announced a declaration of independence. In November 1991 Turkey became the first country to recognise Azerbaijan. In June 1992 a presidential election was held.

President Abulfaz Elchibei (replaced Ayaz Mutalibov in June)
Prime minister Gasan Gasanov (since 1991)

THE BAHAMAS

Parliamentary monarchy. The head of state is the United Kingdom sovereign, represented by a governor-general. The elected 49-seat House of Assembly has been controlled by the Progressive Liberal Party since 1968. The last election was in 1992; the next is due by mid-1997.

Governor-general Sir Clifford Darling (replaced Sir Henry Taylor in Jan)
Prime minister Hubert Ingraham (replaced Sir Lynden Pindling in Aug)

BAHRAIN

Absolute monarchy ruled by the emir who appoints a cabinet.

Head of state Sheikh Isa bin Sulman al Khalifa, Emir (succeeded 1961, took title of Emir 1971)
Heir apparent Sheikh Hamed bin Isa al Khalifa
Prime minister Sheikh Khalifa bin Sulman al Khalifa (since 1973)

BANGLADESH

Parliamentary republic. The Bangladesh National Party (BNP) controls an absolute majority in the National Assembly. The last general election was in February 1991; the next is due in 1996. The last presidential election was held in October 1991.

President Abdur Rahman Biswas (since 1991)
Prime minister Khaleda Zia (since 1991)

PRINCIPAL MINISTERS
Foreign affairs A. S. M. Mustafizur Rahman
Finance and planning Saifur Rahman

BARBADOS

Parliamentary monarchy. The head of state is the United Kingdom sovereign, represented by a governor-general. The Democratic Labour Party has controlled the 28-seat House of Assembly since 1986. The last general election was in 1991; the next is due in 1996.

Governor-general Dame Nita Barrow (since 1990)
Prime minister Erskine Sandiford (since 1987)

BELGIUM
Parliamentary monarchy. Parliament comprises a 212-member Chamber of Representatives and a 181-member Senate. The Flemish Christian People's Party (CVP), the Walloon Social Christian Party (PSC), the Flemish Socialist Party (SP), the Walloon Socialist Party (PS) and the Flemish nationalist People's Union (VU) governed in coalition from May 1988 until the VU withdrew in September 1991. The government resigned in October and a general election was held in November. A coalition government was finally formed in March 1992. The next election is due by 1995.

Head of state Baudouin, King of the Belgians (since 1951)
Prime minister Jean-Luc Dehaene (CVP) (replaced Wilfried Martens in Mar)

PRINCIPAL MINISTERS
Foreign affairs Willy Claes (SP) (replaced Mark Eyskens in Mar)
Finance Philippe Maystadt (PSC)
National defence Leo Delcroix (CVP) (replaced Guy Coeme in Mar)
Interior Louis Tobback (SP)

BELIZE
Parliamentary monarchy. The head of state is the United Kingdom sovereign, represented by a governor-general. The People's United Party has controlled the 28-seat House of Representatives since 1989. The last general election was in 1989; the next is due by September 1994.

Governor-general Dame Minita Elmira Gordon (since 1981)
Prime minister George Price (since 1989)

BELORUSSIA
Former republic of the Soviet Union and a founder member of the Commonwealth of Independent States. In July 1990 Belorussia's Supreme Soviet adopted a declaration of sovereignty. In September 1991 the republic was renamed and became officially independent.

President Stanislav Shushkevich (since 1991)
Prime minister Vyacheslav Kebich

BENIN
Presidential republic. In line with decisions made by a policy-making National Conference, a presidential election was held in March 1991 following an 11-month period of transitional government. The next election is due in 1996.

President Nicéphore Soglo (since 1991)
Prime minister Désiré Vieyra (since 1991)

BHUTAN
Constitutional monarchy. Political power is shared between the king (assisted by a Royal Advisory Council), the council of ministers, the National Assembly (the Tsogdu) and the monastic head of the kingdom's Buddhist priesthood. Of the 150 members of the Tsogdu, 100 are directly elected.

Head of state Jigme Singye Wangchuk, Druk Gyalpo (Dragon King) (succeeded in 1972)

BOLIVIA
Presidential republic. A coalition of the centre-left Movement of the Revolutionary Left (MIR) and the right-wing Democratic Nationalist Action Party (ADN) controls the 157-member Congress. The last general election was in May 1989; the next is due by June 1993.

President Jaime Paz Zamora (MIR) (since 1989)
Vice-president Luis Ossio Sanjines (PDC) (since 1989)

PRINCIPAL MINISTERS
Foreign affairs Ronald Maclean Abaroa (ADN) (replaced Carlos Iturralde Ballivan in Mar)
Interior Carlos Saavadera Bruno (MIR)
Finance Pablo Zegarra (ADN)
Defence Alberto Saenz (ADN)

BOSNIA & HERCEGOVINA
Presidential republic. Former republic of ex-Yugoslavia, officially recognised as an independent state in April 1992. But then war erupted between its Serb, Muslim and Croat communities, leaving Bosnia's future status uncertain. The formal legislative body is a bicameral 240-seat assembly with a seven-member collective state presidency.

President of the state presidency Alija Izetbegovic (since 1990)

BOTSWANA
Presidential republic. The Botswana Democratic Party has been the ruling party since independence in 1966. It holds 31 of the 34 directly elected seats in the 40-member National Assembly. The last legislative and presidential elections were held in October 1988; the next are scheduled for 1994.

President Quett K. J. Masire (since 1980)

BRAZIL
Federal republic. The National Reconstruction Party (PRN) won the presidential election of December 1989 but does not command a majority in the Congress whose size (487 in 1992) varies in proportion to the population. The next general election for president, state governors and government is scheduled for October 1994.

President Itamar Franco (replaced Fernando Collor de Mello in Dec)
Vice-president vacant (Itamar Franco until Dec)

PRINCIPAL MINISTERS
Foreign affairs Fernando Henrique Cardoso (replaced in Sep Celso Lafer, who had replaced F. H. Cardoso in Apr)
Finance Gustavo Krause Goncalves Sobrinho
Chief of staff of armed forces Gen. Antonio Luiz Rocha Veneu
Army Gen. Zenildo Gonzaga Zoroastro de Lucena (replaced Gen. Carlos Tinoco Ribeiro Gomes in Sep)

BRUNEI
Absolute monarchy. The sultan has supreme executive authority and presides over an advisory Council of Ministers, a Privy Council and a Religious Council.

Head of state Hassanal Bolkiah, Sultan (since 1968)

BULGARIA
Parliamentary republic. Under the constitution of July 1991 the unicameral 240-member National Assembly is elected for a maximum five-year term by universal adult suffrage and in turn elects the president and the Council of Ministers. A general election in October 1991 brought the Union of Democratic Forces (UDF) to power, replacing the former communist Bulgarian Socialist Party. A presidential election was held in January 1992. On December 30th after a two months' cabinet crisis and a no-confidence vote, a new government was formed.

President Zhelyu Zhelev (since 1990)
Vice-president Blaga Dimitrowa (replaced Col.-Gen. Atanas Semerdzhiev in Jan)

PRINCIPAL MINISTERS
Prime minister Lyuben Berov (replaced Filip Dimitrov in Dec)
Foreign affairs Slavi Pashovski (replaced Stoyan Ganev in Dec)

Finance Stoyan Alexandrov (replaced Ivan Kostov in Dec)
Defence Valentin Alexandrov (replaced Aleksandar Staliyski in Dec)
Internal affairs Col. Viktor Mihailov (replaced Yordan Sokolov in Dec)

BURKINA FASO
Presidential republic. Thirteen years of military rule ended in June 1991, following a national referendum on a draft constitution. On June 11th a new constitution allowing for multi-party politics was brought into effect. The president was re-elected unopposed in December 1991. Legislative elections were held in May 1992.

President Capt. Blaise Compaore (since 1987)

PRINCIPAL MINISTERS
Defence Yarga Larba
Foreign affairs Thomas Sanon
Finance Rock Marc Christian Kabore

BURUNDI
Republic, ruled by a military council. The Military Council for National Salvation took power in a bloodless coup in 1987. The last elections were in 1982.

President Maj. Pierre Buyoya (since 1987)
Prime minister Adrien Sibomana (since 1987)

CAMBODIA
A peace agreement ending the 13-year civil war was signed in October 1991 and provided for a UN Transitional Authority in Cambodia (UNTAC) to oversee the transition to multi-party democracy. Under the previous regime in Phnom Penh, which was recognised by virtually none of the UN member states, elections to a 117-member National Assembly were last held in 1981.The next general election is planned for March 1993 at the earliest.

Interim president Prince Norodom Sihanouk (since 1991)
Chairman of the council of ministers Hun Sen (since 1991)

CAMEROON
Presidential republic. The first multi-party legislative elections since 1964 were held in March 1992. The ruling Cameroon People's Democratic Movement won 88 seats, 3 seats short of an absolute majority. The country is in effect a one-party state.

President Paul Biya (since 1982, re-elected)
Prime minister Simon Achidi Achu (replaced Sadou Hayatou in Mar)

CANADA
Federal parliamentary democracy, with the United Kingdom monarch as head of state, represented by a governor-general. It has a bicameral legislature, comprising an elected House of Commons (the lower chamber) and a Senate appointed by the governor-general. The Progressive Conservative Party (PCP), elected in 1984, was returned to power in 1988 with 170 of the 295 seats in the House; the next election is due by November 1993.

Governor-general Ramon John Hnatyshyn (since 1990)
Prime minister Brian Mulroney (since 1984)

PRINCIPAL FEDERAL MINISTERS
Constitutional affairs Joseph (Joe) Clark
Deputy prime minister; finance Donald Mazankowski
Secretary of state Robert de Cotret
Industry, science and technology; international trade Michael Wilson
Minister of state; government leader in the House Harvie Andre

National revenue Otto Jelinek
Indian affairs and northern development Thomas Siddon
Agriculture William McKnight
Defence Marcel Masse
External affairs Barbara McDougall
Forestry Frank Oberle
Government leader in the Senate Lowell Murray
Justice and attorney-general Kim Campbell

CAPE VERDE
Presidential republic. Until constitutional changes in 1990 the sole legal political party was the African Party for the Independence of Cape Verde (PAICV). In the first multi-party elections, held early in 1991, the opposition Movement for Democracy (MPD) gained 65% of the votes in the elections for the National People's Assembly, and the MPD candidate defeated the incumbent PAICV president.

President Antonio Mascarenhas Monteiro (since 1991)
Prime minister, minister of defence Carlos Veiga (since 1991)

CENTRAL AFRICAN REPUBLIC
Presidential republic. The present ruler seized power in a bloodless coup in 1981. In November 1986 a referendum approved the establishment of a one-party state, the sole party being the Central African Democratic Rally, set up in February 1987. In April 1991 the president promised the adoption of multi-party democracy.

President Gen. André Kolingba (since 1981)
Prime minister Edouard Frank (since 1991)

CHAD
Republic, ruled by a military council since December 1990. In February 1991 it was announced that a referendum on a new constitution would be held after a 30-month period. An interim government was appointed in March 1991.

President Idriss Déby (since 1990)
Vice-president Maldoum Bada Abbas (since 1990)
Prime minister Jean Alingue Bawoyeu (since 1991)

CHILE
Presidential republic. The 17-party Coalition for Democracy (CPD) has controlled the 167-member National Congress since March 1990. The last general election was in 1989; the next is due by December 1993.

President Patricio Aylwin (since 1990)

PRINCIPAL MINISTERS
Interior Enrique Krauss
Foreign affairs Enrique Silva Cimma
Finance Alejandro Foxley
Defence Patricio Rojas

CHINA
People's republic. Effective political control rests with the Chinese Communist Party (CCP), directed, since 1978, by Deng Xiaoping. The last, indirect, elections to the National People's Congress (the unicameral legislature) were held in 1988; the next are due in 1993.

President Yang Shangkun (since 1988)
Vice-president Wang Zhen (since 1988)

PRINCIPAL STATE COUNCIL MEMBERS
Premier of the state council Li Peng
Vice-premiers Yao Yilin, Tian Jiyun, Wu Xueqian, Zhu Rongji, Zou Jiahua
State councillor (national defence) Qin Jiwei
State councillor (finance) Wang Bingqian
State councillor (public security) Tao Siju
State councillor (foreign affairs) Qian Qichen

Secretary-general Luo Gan
Minister in charge of the state commission for restructuring the economy Chen Jinhua
Justice Cai Cheng
Minister in charge of the state family planning commission Peng Peiyun

COLOMBIA
Presidential republic. The Liberal Party (PL), which had controlled the 311-member Congress since 1986, dissolved it in June 1991 but regained control in legislative elections in October 1991. The last national election was in May 1990; the next is due by May 1994.

President Cesar Gaviria Trujillo (since 1990)

PRINCIPAL MINISTERS
Interior Humberto de la Calle Lombana
Foreign affairs Nohemi Sanin Posada
Finance and public credit Rudolph Hommes Rodriguez
Defence Rafael Pardo Rueda

COMOROS
Federal republic. The last presidential election was in March 1990, the next is due in 1996. Elections to the Federal Assembly were last held in March 1987 when all 42 seats were won by the Union for Comorian Progress. The next Federal Assembly elections were due in October 1992, but after a military rebellion the first round of legislative elections was postponed.

President Said Mohammed Djohar (since 1990)

CONGO
Presidential republic. The country was dominated by the Marxist Congolese Labour Party from 1970, with the chairman of the party's central committee as the head of state. In February 1991 a national conference began to prepare the country for multi-party elections. A presidential election was held in August 1992, but a date for the legislative elections has not been decided yet.

President Pascal Lissouba (replaced Denis Sassou-Nguesso in Aug)
Prime minister Stephane Bongho-Nouarra (replaced André Milongo in Sep)

PRINCIPAL MINISTERS
Defence Gen. Raymond Damase Ngollo
Interior Martin Mberi
Foreign affairs Benjamin Bounkoulou

COSTA RICA
Presidential republic. The Social Christian Unity Party (PUSC) has controlled the 57-seat Legislative Assembly since 1990. The next general election is due by February 1994.

President Rafael Angel Calderon Fournier (since 1990)
First vice-president German Serrano Pinto (since 1990)

COTE D'IVOIRE
Presidential republic. The Democratic Party of Côte d'Ivoire, under Félix Houphouët-Boigny, has been in power since independence in 1960. The first contested presidential election was held in October 1991, with multi-party elections for the National Assembly the following month. The ruling party retained 163 of the 175 seats.

President Félix Houphouët-Boigny (since 1960)
Prime minister Alassane Ouattara (since 1990)

PRINCIPAL MINISTERS
Minister-delegate to the prime minister for economy, commerce and plan Daniel Kablan Duncan
Defence Léon Konan Koffi

Foreign affairs Amara Essy
Interior and security Emile Constant Bombet

CROATIA
Presidential republic. Former republic of ex-Yugoslavia, officially recognised as an independent state in January 1992. The first post-independence presidential and legislative elections were held in August 1992. President Franjo Tudjman and his ruling Croatian Democratic Community won and he was re-elected.

President Franjo Tudjman (since 1990)

CUBA
People's republic. Legislative power formally lies with the National Assembly of People's Power, composed of 510 members indirectly elected by popularly elected local assemblies; it was last elected in 1986 and normally was due for re-election in 1991. The sole and ruling party, the Cuban Communist Party (PCC), is the major focus of power.

President Fidel Castro (since 1976)

CYPRUS
The island is de facto divided between two administrations: the (Greek-Cypriot) republic of Cyprus and the (Turkish-Cypriot) Turkish republic of northern Cyprus. The latter was declared in November 1983 and has not received international recognition. The republic of Cyprus is a presidential republic. Of the 80 seats in the House of Representatives, the 24 which are reserved for Turkish Cypriots remain unoccupied. Following the last general election in May 1991 the Democratic Rally continued as the predominant party. The next general election is due by May 1996. The next presidential election is due by February 1993.

President George Vassiliou (since 1988)

PRINCIPAL MINISTERS
Foreign minister George Iacovou
Defence Andreas Aloneftis
Finance George Syrimis

CZECHOSLOVAKIA
Czechoslovakia was a federal state consisting of the Czech Lands and Slovakia, each having its own government. The bicameral Federal Assembly, elected by universal adult suffrage, elects the president who in turn appoints the federal government. The first multi-party elections, held in June 1990, were won by Civic Forum in the Czech Lands and Public Against Violence (PAV) in Slovakia. A general election was held in June 1992. A presidential election was held in July 1992, but no candidate was elected. After negotiations between the Civic Democratic Party and the Movement for a Democratic Slovakia, Czechs and Slovaks agreed on separation from January 1st 1993.

President vacant (after Vaclav Havel's resignation in July)
Prime Minister of the Federal Government Jan Strasky (replaced Marian Calfa in Jun)

PRINCIPAL FEDERAL MINISTERS
Foreign affairs Jozsef Moravcik (replaced Jiri Dienstbier in Jun)
Interior Petr Cermak (replaced Jan Langos in Jun)
Defence Imrich Andrejcak (replaced Lubos Dobrovsky in Jun)

PRIME MINISTERS OF THE REPUBLICS
Czech Lands Vaclav Klaus (replaced Petr Pithart in Jun)
Slovakia Vladimir Meciar (replaced Jan Carnogursky in Jun)

DENMARK
Parliamentary monarchy. The Conservative People's

Party has ruled in a minority coalition with the Liberal Party (Venstre) since December 1990. The last general election was held in December 1990; the next is due by the end of 1994.

Head of state Margrethe II, Queen of Denmark (succeeded 1972)
Prime minister Poul Schlüter (Con.) (since 1982)

PRINCIPAL MINISTERS
Foreign affairs Uffe Ellemann-Jensen (Lib.)
Finance Henning Dyremose (Con.)
Defence Knud Enggaard (Lib.)
Interior, Nordic affairs Thor Pedersen (Lib.)

DJIBOUTI
Presidential republic. The legislature is a 65-member Chamber of Deputies. At the last general election in April 1987 all candidates were elected, by universal suffrage, from a single list put forward by the Popular Rally for Progress, which since October 1981 has been the sole legal party. In September a constitutional referendum was held. As a result a multi-party system was adopted. In the first multi-party election in December 1992 the ruling party, the People's Rally for Progress, won nearly 75% of the vote.

President Hassan Gouled Aptidon (since 1977)
Prime minister Barkat Gourad Hamadou (since 1978)

DOMINICA
Parliamentary republic. The Dominica Freedom Party has controlled the 30-member House of Assembly since July 1980. The last general election was held in 1990; the next is due by May 1995.

President Sir Clarence Henry Augustus Seignoret (since 1983)
Prime minister (Mary) Eugenia Charles (since 1980)

DOMINICAN REPUBLIC
Presidential republic. The Social Christian Reformist Party (PRSC) has controlled the 147-member National Congress since May 1986. The last general election was held in 1990; the next is due by May 1994.

President Joaquin Balaguer (since 1986)

ECUADOR
Presidential republic. The Democratic Left (ID) has controlled the 71-member Congress since August 1988. The last general election was held in May 1992 and the next is due in 1996.

President Sixto Durán Ballén (replaced Rodrigo Borja Cevallos in Aug)

PRINCIPAL MINISTERS
Defence Gen. Jose Gallardo Roman (replaced Gen. Jorge Felix in Jun)
Foreign affairs Diego Paredes (replaced Diego Cordovez in Jun)
Finance Mario Ribadeneira (replaced Juan Falconi in Jun)
Interior Roberto Dunn Barreiro (replaced Pablo Better in Jun)

EGYPT
Presidential republic. The National Democratic Party won 348 of the 444 elected seats in the People's National Assembly in elections (boycotted by the three main opposition parties) in November-December 1990. The president is nominated by the assembly, and by popular referendum for a six-year term. The next general election is due by November 1994; the next presidential election is due by October 1993.

President Husni Mubarak (since 1981)
Prime minister Atef Sidki (since 1986)

PRINCIPAL MINISTERS
Defence and military production Lt.-Gen. Mohammed Hussein Tantawi Sulayman
Deputy prime minister; financial and economic affairs; planning Kamal Ahmed Al-Ganzouri
Foreign affairs Amer Mohammed Moussa
Interior Mohammed Abdel-Halim Moussa
Finance Mohammed Ahmed Al-Razaz

EL SALVADOR
Presidential republic. The ruling National Republican Alliance (ARENA) has no absolute majority in the 84-member Legislative Assembly. The last presidential election was in 1989 and the next is due by March 1994; the last legislative elections were held in 1991; the next are due by 1994.

President Alfredo Felix Cristiani Burkard (since 1989)
Foreign affairs minister Manuel Pacas Castro

EQUATORIAL GUINEA
Presidential republic. The ruling Supreme Military Council (composed of both military and civilians since December 1981) took power in August 1979. Elections to a 41-member House of Representatives last took place in July 1988, when all candidates were elected unopposed for a five-year term. The president was elected unopposed in June 1989 for a seven-year term.

President Brig.-Gen. Teodoro Obiang Nguema (since 1979)
Prime minister Capt. Cristino Seriche Bioko (since 1982)

ESTONIA
Parliamentary republic, which became independent from the Soviet Union in September 1991. On September 20th in the first post-independence elections, the right-wing nationalist Fatherland group won a strong position in the Parliament. In the presidential election no candidate gained an overall majority, so parliament was required to choose between the two leading candidates.

President Lennart Meri (replaced Arnold Ruutel in Oct)
Prime minister Mart Laar (replaced in Oct Tiit Vahi, who had replaced Edgar Savisaar in Jan)

PRINCIPAL MINISTERS
Defence Hain Rebas (replaced Uno Veering in Oct)
Foreign affairs Trivimi Velliste (replaced Jaan Manitski in Oct, who replaced Lennart Meri in Mar)
Finance Madis Uurike
Interior Lagle Parek (replaced Olev Laanjan in Oct)

ETHIOPIA
Presidential republic. Following the overthrow of President Mengistu in May 1991 a transitional government was formed under the leadership of the Ethiopian People's Revolutionary Democratic Front (EPRDF). In the 87-member Council of Representatives which was elected by a national conference in July 1991 the EPRDF, with 32 seats, was the best-represented group. A general election is scheduled for 1994.

President Meles Zenawi (since 1991)
Prime minister Tamirat Laynie (since 1991)

FIJI
Parliamentary democracy, prior to the two military coups of 1987 which overthrew a newly elected left-wing government supported by Fijians of Indian extraction. Civilian government was nominally restored in December 1987, but was dominated by Fijians of Melanesian descent, on whose behalf the coups had been staged. A new constitution was promulgated in July 1990. In May 1992 the first general election since the two military coups of 1987 was held. The Fijian Political Party won 30 of the 37

House of Representative seats reserved for ethnic Fijians.

President Ratu Sir Penaia Ganilau (since 1987)
Prime minister Maj.-Gen. Sitiveni Rabuka (replaced Ratu Sir Kamisese Mara in Jun)

FINLAND
Parliamentary republic. The Centre Party has ruled in coalition with the conservative National Coalition Party, the Swedish People's Party and the Finnish Christian Union since April 1991. The last general election was held in March 1991; the next is due by 1995. The next presidential election is due in 1994.

President Mauno Koivisto (since 1982)
Prime minister Esko Aho

PRINCIPAL MINISTERS
Foreign affairs Paavo Vayrynen
Defence Elisabeth Rehn
Interior Mauri Pekkarinen
Finance Ilkka Kanerva

FRANCE
Presidential republic. Executive power is vested in a president who is directly elected every seven years, most recently in 1988. The president appoints the prime minister, who is responsible to the bicameral parliament comprising the 321-member Senate and the 577-member National Assembly. The Socialist Party (PS), in power since 1988, has no absolute majority in the National Assembly. It has relied at times on support, or at least abstention, from some members of the centrist UDF, or from Communist deputies. The last general election to the National Assembly was in June 1988; the next is scheduled for March 1993.

President François Mitterrand (since 1981)
Prime minister Pierre Bérégovoy (PS) (replaced Edith Cresson in April)

MINISTERS OF STATE
National education and culture Jack Lang (PS) (replaced Lionel Jospin in Apr)
Foreign affairs Roland Dumas (PS)
Civil service and administrative modernisation Michel Delebarre (PS) (replaced Jean-Pierre Soisson)

MINISTERS
Defence Pierre Joxe (PS)
Interior Paul Quilés (PS) (replaced Philippe Marchand in Apr)
Overseas departments and territories Louis Le Pensec (PS)
Environment Ségolène Royal (PS) (replaced Brice Lalonde in Apr)
Keeper of the Seals, justice Michel Vauzelle (replaced Henri Nallet (PS) in Apr)
Economy and finance Michel Sapin (replaced Pierre Bérégovoy in Apr)
Agriculture and rural development Jean-Pierre Soisson (replaced Louis Mermaz (PS) in Oct)
Capital works, transport and housing Jean-Louis Bianco (replaced Paul Quilés (PS) in Apr)
Industry and foreign trade Dominique Strauss-Kahn (PS)
Labour, employment and vocational training Martine Aubry
Relations with Parliament, government spokesman Louis Mermaz (PS) (replaced Jean Popereu (PS) in Oct)
Budget Martin Malvy (replaced Michel Charasse (PS) in Apr)
Social affairs and integration René Teulade (replaced Jean-Louis Bianco in Apr)
Health and humanitarian policy Bernard Kouchner
Research and space Hubert Cunieu (PS)
Postal services and telecommunications Emile Zuccarelli

Youth and sport Frédérique Bredin (PS)

GABON
Presidential republic. The Gabonese Democratic Party (PDG), formed in 1968, was the only legal party until a national conference in March-April 1990 approved the introduction of multi-party politics. In legislative elections in November 1990 the PDG retained an overall majority in the 120-seat National Assembly, and eight opposition parties gained representation. A government of national union was formed at the end of November 1990, including 24 members of the PDG and eight members of the five largest opposition parties. The last presidential election was held in November 1986; the next is due in 1993. Legislative elections are due in 1995.

President Omar Bongo (since 1967)
Prime minister Casimir Oye Mba (since 1990)

GAMBIA
Presidential republic. The Progressive People's Party of President Jawara secured 25 of the 36 directly elected seats in the 50-member House of Representatives in the presidential and legislative elections held in April 1992; the next are due in 1997.

President Sir Dawda Kairaba Jawara (since 1970)

GEORGIA
Former republic of the Soviet Union, not a member of the Commonwealth of Independent States. In April 1991 the Georgian Supreme Soviet declared independence and instituted an executive presidency. In October 1992 elections were held for a new parliament and parliamentary chairman.

Parliamentary chairman Eduard Shevardnadze (since Oct) (new post after abolition of presidency in Jan)
Prime minister Tenghiz Sigua (acting) (replaced Vissarion Gugushvili in Jan)

GERMANY
Parliamentary republic. Under the 1949 Basic Law (constitution) the parliament comprises the Bundestag (lower house), which is directly elected every four years, and the Bundesrat (upper house), in which sit representatives from the *Länder* (states). The president is elected by both houses every five years, most recently in May 1989. The Christian Democratic Union (CDU) together with its Bavarian sister party, the Christian Social Union (CSU), and the Free Democratic Party (FDP) have ruled in coalition in West Germany since 1982 and in the united Germany since 1990. The last general election was held in December 1990; the next is due by December 1994.

Federal president Richard von Weizsäcker (since 1984 in West Germany)
Federal chancellor Helmut Kohl (CDU) (since 1982 in West Germany)

MEMBERS OF THE CABINET
Head of chancellery Friedrich Böhl (CDU)
Foreign affairs Klaus Kinkel (FDP) (replaced Hans-Dietrich Genscher (FDP) in May)
Interior Rudolf Seiters (CDU)
Finance Theo Waigel (CSU)
Economy Jürgen Möllemann (FDP) (resigned early Jan 1993)
Agriculture Ignaz Kiechle (CSU)
Defence Volker Rühe (CDU) (replaced Gerhard Stoltenberg in Mar)
Health Horst Seehofer (CSU) (replaced Gerda Hasselfeldt in May)
Transport Günther Krause (CDU)
Environment Klaus Töpfer (CDU)
Education Rainer Ortleb (FDP)
Justice Sabine Leutheusser-Schnarrenberger (FPD) (replaced Klaus Kinkel in May)
Labour Norbert Blüm (CDU)

Women and youth Angela Merkel (CDU)
Family; the aged Hannelore Rönsch (CDU)
Post vacant (Christian Schwarz-Schilling (CDU) resigned Dec)
Construction Irmgard Adam-Schwätzer (FDP)
Development aid Carl-Dieter Spranger (CSU)

PREMIERS OF THE LÄNDER
Baden-Württemberg Erwin Teufel (CDU)
Bavaria Max Streibl (CSU)
Brandenburg Manfred Stolpe (SPD)
Hesse Hans Eichel (SPD)
Lower Saxony Gerhard Schröder (SPD)
Mecklenburg-Western Pomerania Berndt Seite (CDU) (replaced Alfred Gomolka (CDU) in Mar)
North Rhine-Westphalia Johannes Rau (SPD)
Rhineland-Palatinate Rudolf Scharpin (SPD)
Saarland Oskar Lafontaine (SPD)
Saxony Kurt Biedenkopf (CDU)
Saxony-Anhalt Werner Münch (CDU)
Schleswig-Holstein Björn Engholm (SPD)
Thuringia Josef Duchac (CDU)

MAYORS
Berlin Eberhard Diepgen (CDU)
Bremen Klaus Wedemeier (SPD)
Hamburg Henning Voscherau (SPD)

GHANA
Republic, ruled by military council. The Provisional National Defence Council (PNDC) took power in December 1981. Political parties are banned. Executive power is vested in the PNDC, which rules by decree. There have been no elections at national level since 1981, but a presidential election was held in December 1992. Elections to district assemblies with executive powers were held in 1989.

President Flt.-Lt. Jerry Rawlings (since 1981)
Chairman of the committee of secretaries P. V. Obeng (since 1982)

GREECE
Parliamentary republic. The New Democracy Party has held a majority in the 300-member parliament since a general election in April 1990. In July 1990 the ND's single-seat majority was confirmed when a deputy from a smaller party joined the ND. The next general election is due in May 1994.

President Constantine Karamanlis (since 1990)
Prime minister Constantine Mitsotakis (since 1990)

PRINCIPAL MINISTERS
Foreign affairs Michalis Papaconstantinou (since Aug) (post had been held by prime minister after dismissal of Antonis Samaras in Apr)
National defence Yannis Varvitsiotis
Interior Nicolaos Kleitos
Finance Stefanos Manos (replaced Yannis Palaiokrassas in Mar)

GRENADA
Parliamentary monarchy. The head of state is the United Kingdom sovereign, represented by a governor-general. The National Democratic Congress remains the largest party in the 15-member House of Representatives but does not command a majority. The last general election was held in 1990; the next is due in 1995.

Governor-general Sir Paul Scoon (since 1978)
Prime minister Nicholas Brathwaite (since 1990)

GUATEMALA
Presidential republic. The National Congress has 116 members, 87 elected directly and the rest by proportional representation, for a five-year term; it is dominated by three right-wing parties, the National Centrist Union (UCN), the Christian Democratic Party (PDCG) and the Social Action Movement (MAS). The MAS formed a minority coalition government in

January 1991. The last general election was held in 1990 (with a second round in January 1991); the next is due by November 1995.

President Jorge Serrano Elias (since 1991)

PRINCIPAL MINISTERS
Foreign affairs Gonzalo Menendez Park
Interior Fernando Hurtado Prem
Economy; finance Juan Luis Miron Aguilar
Defence Gen. Luis Mendoza Garcia

GUINEA
Republic, ruled by military council. The Military Committee for National Recovery has been in power since 1984 when it suspended the constitution which provided for an elected National Assembly. All political parties are banned. A new constitution, providing for an end to military rule and the creation of a two-party system of government within five years, won overwhelming support in a referendum in December 1990. A full multi-party system was introduced in April 1992. There have been no recent elections.

President Gen. Lansana Conté (since 1984)

GUINEA-BISSAU
Presidential republic. Under the constitution of 1974 the African Party for the Independence of Guinea and Cape Verde defines policy in all fields. The last elections (unopposed) of the president and of the 150-member National People's Assembly were held in June 1989.

President Brig.-Gen. Joao Bernardo Vieira (since 1980)
Prime minister Carlos Correia (since 1991)

GUYANA
Presidential republic. A general election held in October 1992 ended the rule of the People's National Congress (PNC) which has controlled the 65-member National Assembly since 1968. The People's Progressive Party (PPP) won narrowly.

President; foreign affairs Cheddi Jagan (replaced Desmond Hoyte in Oct)
Prime minister Sam Hindis (replaced Hamilton Green in Oct)

HAITI
Presidential republic. General elections were annulled in 1988 and 1989 by military coups. The National Front for Democracy and Change (FNCD) formed a minority government in the bicameral 110-member Legislative Assembly, after presidential and legislative elections in December 1990–January 1991. The next election is due in 1995. In September 1991 the military Front National (FNCD) staged a coup and drove President Aristide into exile. The Organisation of American States has imposed a trade embargo to try to force the restoration of the elected president Aristide.

President Jean-Bertrand Aristide (in exile)
Provisional president Joseph Nerette
Prime minister Marc Bazin (replaced Jean Jacques Honorat in Jun)

HOLLAND
Parliamentary monarchy. The Christian Democratic Appeal has governed in coalition with the Labour Party (PVDA) since November 1989. The last general election was held in September 1989; the next is due by May 1994.

Head of state Beatrix, Queen of the Netherlands (since 1980)
Prime minister Ruud Lubbers (CDA) (since 1982)

MINISTERS
Deputy prime minister; finance Wim Kok (PVDA)
Home affairs Ien Dales (PVDA)

Foreign affairs Hans van den Broek (CDA)
Development co-operation Jan Pronk (PVDA)
Defence Relus ter Beek (PVDA)
Economic affairs Koos Andriessen (CDA)
Justice; Netherlands Antilles and Aruba Ernst Hirsch Ballin (CDA)
Agriculture, nature management and fisheries Piet Bukman (CDA)
Social affairs and employment Bert de Vries (CDA)
Education and science Jo Ritzen (PVDA)
Transport and public works Hanja May-Weggen (CDA)
Housing, planning and environment Hans Alders (PVDA)
Welfare, health and culture Hedy d'Acona (PVDA)

HONDURAS
Presidential republic. The National Party (PN) has controlled the 128-seat National Assembly since January 1990. The last general election was held in November 1989; the next is due by November 1993.

President Rafael Leonardo Callejas Romero (since 1990)
Defence minister Claudio Lainez
Foreign affairs minister Mario Carias Zapata

HUNGARY
Parliamentary republic. The highest state body is the 386-seat National Assembly which serves for a five-year term and elects the president. Multi-party elections were held in March-April 1990 and won by the Hungarian Democratic Forum (HDF), which gained 165 seats. The next general election is due by March 1994.

President Arpad Goncz (since 1990)
Prime minister Jozsef Antall (since 1990)

PRINCIPAL MINISTERS
Defence Lajos Fur
Interior Peter Boross
Foreign affairs Geza Jeszenszky
Finance Mihaly Kupa

ICELAND
Parliamentary republic. The Independence Party (IP) has governed in coalition with the Social Democratic Party (SDP) since the last general election in April 1991. The next election is due by 1995.

President Vigdis Finnbogadottir (since 1980)
Prime minister David Oddsson (IP)
Foreign affairs Jon Baldvin Hannibalsson

INDIA
Federal republic. The Congress party was returned to government in June 1991, some 17 months after losing power to a coalition led by the Janata Dal. The last general election to the 545-member Lok Sabha (lower house of parliament) was in June 1991; the next is due by June 1996. The number of pro-government members in the Lok Sabha after June 1991 was 243.

President Ramaswamy Venkataraman (since 1987)
Prime minister Narasimha Rao (since 1991)

PRINCIPAL MEMBERS OF THE COUNCIL OF MINISTERS
Finance Manmohan Singh
External affairs R.L. Bhatia (replaced Madhavisinh Solanki in Mar)
Defence Sharad Pawar
Home affairs Shankarro Chavan
Parliamentary affairs Ghulam Bani Azad
Law, justice and company affairs B. Shankaranand (replaced K. Vijaya Bhaskara Reddy in Jan)
Water resources V. C. Shukla

INDONESIA
Presidential republic. The government-sponsored

Golkar has won an absolute majority of seats in elections to the House of Representatives since 1971. The last general election was held in June 1992; the next is due by April 1997. The next presidential election is due in 1993.

President Gen. (retd) Suharto (since 1968)
Vice-president Lt.-Gen. (retd) Sudharmono (since 1988)

PRINCIPAL MINISTERS
Political affairs and security Adml. (retd) Sudomo
Economy, finance, industry and development supervision Radius Prawiro
Public welfare Gen. (retd) Supardjo Rustam
Internal affairs Gen. Rudini
Foreign affairs Ali Alatas
Defence and security Gen. Leonardus (Benny) Murdani

IRAN
Religious republic. Overall authority is exercised by the spiritual leader and executive power concentrated in the president. Elections to the majlis (parliament) were held in April-May 1992; the next are due in 1996. The last presidential election was in 1989; the next is due in 1993.

Spiritual leader Ayatollah Seyed Ali Khamenei (since 1989)
President Ali Akbar Rafsanjani (since 1989)

PRINCIPAL MEMBERS OF THE COUNCIL OF MINISTERS
Foreign affairs Ali Akbar Velayati
Interior; chairman of state security council Abdollah Nouri
Economic affairs and finance Mohsen Nourbaksh
Justice Hojatolislam Ismail Shostari
Defence and armed forces logistics Akbar Torkan
Intelligence and security Hojatolislam Ali Fallahiyan

IRAQ
Presidential republic. Governed by a Revolutionary Command Council (RCC) which elects the president. The Arab Ba'ath Socialist Party controls a majority in the 250-seat National Assembly. The last general election was in April 1989; the next is due in 1993.

President Saddam Hussein (since 1979)
Prime minister Mohammad Hamzah al Zubaydi

PRINCIPAL MINISTERS
Deputy prime minister Tariq Aziz
Interior Watban Ibrahim al Hasan
Foreign affairs Ahmad Husayn Khudayyir
Defence Ali Hasan al Majid
Finance Majid Abd Jafar
Oil Usamah Abd al Razzaq Hummadi al Hithi

IRELAND
Parliamentary republic. The president is directly elected for a seven-year term, most recently in November 1990. The lower house of parliament is the Dail Éireann with 166 members; the upper house is the Seanad Éireann with 60 members. Fianna Fail has governed in coalition with the Progressive Democrats since June 1989. The last general election was held in November 1992; the next is due by 1994.

President Mary Robinson (since 1990)
Prime minister Albert Reynolds

PRINCIPAL MINISTERS
Deputy prime minister John Patrick Wilson
Foreign affairs Gerard Collins
Finance Bertie Ahern
Defence Vincent Brady

ISRAEL
Parliamentary republic. Elections to the Knesset (the 120-member legislature) in June 1992 were a victory

for the Labour Party and ended 15 years of the right-wing Likud domination in Israeli politics. The next election is due in 1996.

President Chaim Herzog (since 1983)
Prime minister and minister of defence Yitzhak Rabin (replaced Yitzhak Shamir in Jun)

PRINCIPAL MINISTERS
Deputy prime minister; foreign affairs Shimon Peres (replaced David Levi in Jun)
Finance Avraham Shochat (replaced Yitzhak Moda'i in Jun)
Interior Arye Der'i
Housing and construction Binyamin Ben-Eliezer (replaced Ariel Sharon in Jun)

ITALY
Parliamentary republic. In a general election in April 1992 the Christian Democratic Party polled under 30% for the first time since 1946, but remained the largest party with 206 seats in the 630-member Chamber of Deputies.

President Oscar Luigi Scalfaro (replaced Francesco Cossiga in May)
Prime minister Giuliano Amato (DC) (replaced Giulio Andreotti in Jun)

PRINCIPAL MINISTERS
Deputy prime minister; justice Claudio Martelli
Foreign affairs Emilio Colombo (replaced Gianni De Michelis in Jun)
Interior Nicola Mancino (replaced Vincenzo Scotti in Jun)
Treasury Piero Barucci (replaced Guido Carli in Jun)
Budget Franco Reviglio (replaced Paolo Cirino Pomiciono in Jun)
Finance Giovanni Goria (replaced Salvatore (Rino) Formica in Jun)
Defence Salvo Ando (replaced Virginio Rognoni in Jun)
Education Rosa Russo Jervolino (replaced Riccardo Misasi in Jun)
Agriculture Gianni Fontana (replaced Giovanni Goria in Jun)
Environment Carlo Ripa di Meana (replaced Giorgio Ruffolo in Jun)

JAMAICA
Parliamentary monarchy. The head of state is the United Kingdom sovereign, represented by a governor-general. The People's National Party (PNP) has controlled the 81-member parliament since February 1989. The last general election was in 1989; the next is due by February 1994.

Governor-general Howard Cooke (since 1991)
Prime minister Michael Manley (since 1989)

JAPAN
Constitutional monarchy with power residing in a bicameral legislature (Diet), consisting of 512-member House of Representative (elected for up to four years) and 252-member House of Councillors (elected for six years, with half due for re-election every three years). The Liberal Democratic Party (LDP), which has been in government since its formation in 1955, lost its majority in the upper house in July 1989, but retained its overall majority in the lower house in the election of February 1990, winning 275 seats; the next election is due by February 1994.

Head of state Akihito, Emperor of Japan (succeeded in 1989)
Prime minister Kiichi Miyazawa (since 1991)

PRINCIPAL MINISTERS
Deputy premier; foreign affairs Michio Watanabe
Finance Yoshiro Hayashi (replaced Tsutomu Hata in Dec)
Agriculture, forestry and fisheries Masami Tanubu

International trade and industry Yoshiro Mori (replaced Kozo Watanabe in Dec)
Labour Masakuni Murakami (replaced Tetsuo Kondo in Dec)
Home affairs Keijiro Murata (replaced Masajuro Shiokawa in Dec)
Chief cabinet secretary Yohei Kono (replaced Koichi Kato in Dec, who replaced Misoji Sakamoto in Jul)
Director-general of management and co-ordination agency Michihiko Kano (replaced Junzo Iwasaki in Dec, who replaced Man Sasaki in Jul)
Director-general of Hokkaido and Okinawa development agencies Shuji Kita (replaced Tomoo Ie in Dec, who replaced Yoichi Tani in Jul)
Director-general of defence agency Toshio Nakayama (replaced Sohei Miyashita in Dec, who replaced Yukihiko Ikeda in Jul)
Director-general of economic planning agency Hajime Funada (replaced Takeshi Noda in Dec, who replaced Michio Ochi in Jul)
Director-general of science and technology agency Kanzo Tanigawa (replaced Akiko Santo in Jul)
Director-general of environment agency Taikan Hayashi (replaced Shozaburo Nakamura in Dec, who replaced Kazuo Aichi in Jul)
Director-general of national land agency Takashi Inoue (replaced Yoshiyuki Toya in Dec, who replaced Mamoru Nishida in Jul)

JORDAN
Constitutional monarchy. Political parties were legalised in mid-1991. Members of various groups are represented in the 80-member House of Representatives, including broadly pro-government forces, the Muslim Brotherhood and Palestinian and Arab nationalists. The last election to the house was in 1989; the next is due by November 1993.

Head of state Hussein, King of Jordan (succeeded in 1952)
Prime minister Sharif Zaid Ibn Shaker (since 1991)

KAZAKHSTAN
Former republic of the Soviet Union and a founder member of the Commonwealth of Independent States. In October 1990 a declaration of sovereignty was adopted by the Kazakhstan Supreme Soviet. A presidential election was held in December 1991.

President Nursultan Nazarbaev (since 1991)
Prime minister Sergei Tereshchenko (since 1991)

KENYA
Daniel T. arap Moi was officially declared the winner of Kenya's first multi-party elections in 26 years, held on December 29th 1992, with only 36% of the votes. He was sworn in immediately in a ceremony broadcast live on radio and TV. The three opposition parties say they were cheated by rampant ballot-rigging and tried to form an alliance to prevent President Moi taking power. The next presidential and legislative elections are due in 1997.

President Daniel T. arap Moi (since 1978)
Vice-president; minister of finance George Saitoti (vice-president since May 1989)

PRINCIPAL MINISTERS
Home affairs and natural heritage Davidson Kuguru
Foreign affairs and international co-operation Wilson Ndolo Ayah

KIRGIZSTAN
Former republic of the Soviet Union and a founder member of the Commonwealth of Independent States. In August 1991 the Kirgizstan Supreme Soviet voted to declare independence. In October 1991 the first direct presidential election was held.

President Askar Akaev (since 1991)
Prime minister Tursunbek Chyngyshev (since 1991)

KIRIBATI
Parliamentary democracy with a 41-member unicameral legislature, 39 members of which are popularly elected for up to four years. The president is elected for a four-year term from within the House of Assembly. The last general election was in May 1991, and a presidential election was held in July of the same year; the next general election is due by May 1995.

President Teatao Teannaki (since 1991)

NORTH KOREA
Single-party communist state. Nominal constitutional authority is held by the unicameral legislature, the 687-member Supreme People's Assembly (SPA), elected for a four-year term from a single list of candidates approved by the communist Korean Workers' Party, dominated since 1945 by Kim Il Sung. The last legislative elections were held in April 1990; the next elections are due by April 1994.

President Kim Il Sung (since 1972)
Prime minister Kang Song Sau (replaced Yon Hyong Muk in Dec)

SOUTH KOREA
Parliamentary democracy with legislative power exercised by 299-member National Assembly elected for four years. Executive power is exercised by an elected president who serves a five-year term. The Democratic Liberal Party was formed in 1990, since when it has controlled two-thirds of the Assembly seats. The last general election was held in March 1992; the next is due by March 1996. The president's term of office expires in February 1993, but a presidential election was held in December 1992. The ruling party candidate Kim Young Sam was elected as the next president to succeed Roh Tae Woo in February 1993. He will be the first civilian president in over 30 years.

President Roh Tae Woo (since 1988)
Prime minister Chung Won Shik

PRINCIPAL MEMBERS OF STATE COUNCIL
Deputy prime minister; head of economic planning board Choi Gak Kyu
Foreign affairs Lee Sang Ock
Home affairs Paik Kwang Hyun (replaced Lee Sang Yeon in Mar)
Finance Rhee Yong Man
Defence Choi Sae Chang
National unification Choi Young Choul (replaced Choi Ho Joong in Mar)
Environment Lee Jai Chang (replaced Kwon Hwi Hyuk in Mar)

KUWAIT
Monarchy ruled by the Emir who appoints a cabinet. The National Assembly was dissolved in 1986. Elections to an interim National Council were held in June 1990; a general election to the reconstituted 50-seat National Assembly was held in October 1992.

Head of state Jabir al Ahmad al Jabir al Sabah, Emir of Kuwait (succeeded in 1978)
Prime minister Crown Prince Sheikh Saad Al-Abdullah al Salim al Sabah (since 1978, reappointed in Oct)
Defence Ali Sabah Al-Salem
First deputy prime minister and foreign minister Sabah Al-Ahmad Al-Jaber

LAOS
People's republic. Political power rests in the hands of the Lao People's Revolutionary Party. National elections to a Supreme People's Assembly were held in 1989.

President Kaysone Phomvihane
Chairman of the council of ministers Gen. Khamtay Siphandon

LATVIA
Parliamentary republic, which became independent of the Soviet Union in September 1991. The 201-member Supreme Council, elected in March-April 1990, elects its own chairman, who is de facto president.

President Anatolijs Gorbunovs (since 1990)
Prime minister Ivars Godmanis

LEBANON
Presidential republic. No one political party has a majority in the National Assembly which, under the new electoral law of July 16th 1992, has equal representation of Muslims and Christians. The last general election was held in August-September 1992. In November 1989 the term of the National Assembly was extended until December 1994.

President Elias Hrawi (since 1989)
Prime minister; minister of finance Rafic El Hariri (replaced in Sep Rashid al-Solh, who had replaced Omar Karami in May)

PRINCIPAL MINISTERS
Deputy prime minister Michel al-Murr
Minister of national defence Mohsen Dalloul (replaced Michel al-Murr in Sep)
Finance Assad Diyab (replaced Ali al Khalil in May)
Foreign and expatriate affairs Fares Bouez
Interior Bichara Merhej (replaced Maj.-Gen. Sami al Khatib in Sep)

LESOTHO
Monarchy, ruled by military council. Political activity was banned in March 1986. The ruling military council took effective power from the king in February 1990, and in November he was replaced by his son. The present chairman of the military council took power in a bloodless coup in April 1991. The only contested election since independence in 1966 was in January 1977. The next election is scheduled for March 1993.

Head of state King Letsie III
Chairman of the military council Col. Elias Ramaema

LIBERIA
Presidential republic. A rebellion in 1990 brought about the collapse of the government and embroiled the country in a protracted civil war. Amos Sawyer was installed in November 1990 as interim president with the backing of a regional peace-keeping force, the Economic Community of West African States (ECOWAS) Monitoring Group (ECOMOG), and re-elected by a national conference in April 1991. The conference also decided that the transitional government should serve until January 1992, when it would hand over to an elected government, but political crisis and fighting postponed this process.

President Amos Sawyer (since 1990)
Vice-president Peter Naigow

LIBYA
People's republic since 1969, headed by Col. Muammar Qaddafi as "leader of the revolution". Local people's congresses form an electoral base for the General People's Congress.

Head of state Col. Muammar Qaddafi (since 1970)
Senior adviser Maj. Abdel-Salem Jalloud (since 1970)

LIECHTENSTEIN
Parliamentary principality. The Patriotic Union (VU) and Progressive Citizens' Party (FBP) have governed in coalition since 1938. The last general election was in

March 1989; the next is due by March 1993.

Head of state Hans Adam II, Prince of Liechtenstein (succeeded in 1989)
Head of government Hans Brunhart (vu) (since 1978)

LITHUANIA
Parliamentary republic, which became independent of the Soviet Union in September 1991. The 141-member Supreme Council was elected in February 1990, and its chairman, the de facto president, was elected in March. In October and November 1992 the first post-independence legislative elections were held. President Landsbergis's nationalist Sajudis coalition was defeated by their ex-communist rivals, the Democratic Labour Party. The next presidential election is scheduled for 1993.

President Algirdas Brazauskas (acting, replaced Vytautas Landsbergis in Dec)
Prime minister Bronislavas Lubys (replaced Aleksandras Abisala in Dec, who replaced Gediminas Vagnorius in May)

LUXEMBOURG
Parliamentary grand duchy. The Christian Social Party (PCS) has governed in coalition with the Socialists since July 1984. The last general election was in June 1989; the next is due by June 1994.

Head of state Jean, Grand Duke (succeeded in 1964)
Prime minister Jacques Santer (PCS) (since 1984)

MADAGASCAR
Presidential republic. The Vanguard of the Malagasy Revolution party holds the majority in the 137-seat National People's Assembly, the last elections for which were held in May 1989. The next are due in 1994. A presidential election, held in March 1989, secured a third seven-year term for the president. Under an agreement reached with the opposition in October 1991, an 18-month state of transition was established prior to the creation of a third republic, and the assembly was dissolved. The first round of presidential elections was held in November and failed to resolve the political crisis. The second round is due in January 1993.

President Adml. Didier Ratsiraka (since 1976)
Prime minister Willy-Guy Razanamasy (since 1991)

MALAWI
Presidential republic. The Malawi Congress Party is the sole legal political party and executive power is vested in its leader, Hastings Kamuzu Banda, who has ruled Malawi since independence in 1966. Legislative power is vested in a National Assembly to which 112 members are elected. The president has the power to appoint an unlimited number of deputies to the assembly. The last general election was held in June 1992; the next is due in 1997.

President Hastings Kamuzu Banda (since 1966)

MALAYSIA
Federal monarchy (rotating between nine hereditary sultans). Since the establishment of Malaysia in 1963, the United Malays National Organisation (UMNO) has been the dominant party in a series of National Front coalitions. The last election to the House of Representatives was in 1990; the next is due by October 1995.

Head of state Sultan Azlan Muhibbuddin Shah (since 1989)
Prime minister Mahathir Mohamad (since 1981)

PRINCIPAL MINISTERS
Deputy prime minister; national and rural development Ghafar Baba
Foreign affairs Abdullah Ahmad Badawi

Defence Najib Tun Razak
Finance Anwar Ibrahim
International trade and industry Rafidah Aziz

MALDIVES
Presidential republic. There are no political parties. Elections to the 48-member Citizen's Assembly (Majlis) were held in 1989. The next are due by November 1994.
President Maumoun Abdul Gayoom (since 1978)

MALI
Republic. In March 1991 the ruling Military Committee for National Liberation was overthrown in a military coup. A 25-member Transition Committee for the Salvation of the People (CTSP), was set up with 10 military and 15 civilian members. A national conference decided in November to extend the transition period to March 1992, until the presidential election. A presidential election was held in April 1992. The transitional government resigned and a new president appointed the prime minister.

President Alpha Oumar Konare (replaced Lt.-Col. Amadou Toumani Toure in Apr)
Prime minister Younoussi Toure (replaced Soumana Sacko in June)

MALTA
Parliamentary republic. In a general election in February 1992 the Nationalist Party secured its majority in the 69-member House of Representatives. The next general election is due in 1997.

President Vincent Tabone (since 1989)
Prime minister Edward Fenech Adami (since 1987)

MARSHALL ISLANDS
Parliamentary republic, with a compact of free association with the United States implemented in 1986, under which the US is responsible for defence and foreign policy. The 33-member legislature (the Nitijela) is elected for four years and chooses a president from among its members. The last presidential election was held in 1987.

President Amata Kabua (since 1987)

MAURITANIA
Presidential republic. The reintroduction of a National Assembly was decreed by the constitution of May 1992. In July 1991 legislation was introduced allowing political parties. Legislative elections were held in March 1992, which resulted in the Social Democratic Republican Party winning a majority of the 79-seats in the National Assembly.

President Col. Moaouia Ould Sidi Mohammed Taya (since 1984)
Prime minister Sidi Mohammad Ould Boubaker (since Apr)

MAURITIUS
Parliamentary democracy, with the United Kingdom sovereign as head of state, represented by a governor-general. Elections in September 1991 returned to power the ruling coalition of the Mouvement Socialiste Mauricien, the Mauritius Labour Party and the Organisation du Peuple Rodriguais. The alliance won 59 of the 62 directly elected seats in the 70-seat National Assembly. The next elections are due in 1996.

Governor-general Sir Veerasamy Ringadoo (since 1986)
Prime minister; defence; internal security Aneerood Jugnauth (MSM) (since 1982)
External affairs Paul Raymond Berenger

MEXICO
Federal republic. The Institutional Revolutionary Party has controlled the 564-member National

Congress since 1929. The last general election was in 1988; the next is due by July 1994.

President Carlos Salinas de Gortari (since 1988)
PRINCIPAL MINISTERS
Government Fernando Gutierrez Barrios
Foreign relations Fernando Solana Morales
Defence Gen. Antonio Riviello Bazan
Navy Adml. Luis Carlos Ruano
Finance and public credit Pedro Aspe Armella
Planning and federal budget Ernesto Cedillo Ponce de Leon

MICRONESIA
Federal republic, with a compact of free association with the United States implemented in 1986, under which the US is responsible for defence and foreign policy. The National Congress (which elects the president) has 14 members. The last election was in March 1991.

President Bailey Olter (since 1991)
Vice-president Jacob Nena (since 1991)

MOLDOVA
Former republic of the Soviet Union and a founder member of the Commonwealth of Independent States. In August 1991 the Moldovian Parliament proclaimed independence from the Soviet Union. In December 1991 a directly elected presidency was instituted.

President Mircea Snegur (since 1991)
Prime minister Andrei Sangeli (replaced Valeriu Muravsky in Mar)

MONACO
Parliamentary principality, with informal political groupings. The monarch nominates the minister of state from a list of three French diplomats submitted by the French government. The last election, in which the National and Democratic Union won all the 18-member National Council seats, was held in January 1988. The next is due in January 1993.

Head of state Rainier III, Prince (since 1949)
Minister of state Jacques Dupont (since 1991)

MONGOLIA
People's Republic, ruled by the standing parliament created in May 1990. The 430-seat Great People's Hural elects the president. The last general election was in June 1992; the next is due in 1996. A constitution is under discussion.

President Punsalmaagiyn Ochirbat (since 1990)
Prime minister Puntsagiin Jasari (replaced Dashiyn Byambasuren in Jul)
Defence Shagalyn Jadambaa

MOROCCO
Constitutional monarchy, with a government that is a coalition of political parties represented in the 306-member Chamber of Representatives. The last general election was held in September 1984; the next is scheduled for April 1993.

Head of state Hassan II, King (since 1961)
Prime minister Mohammed Karim Lamrani (replaced Azeddine Laraki in Aug)

PRINCIPAL MINISTERS
Finance Mohammed Berrada
Foreign affairs and co-operation Abdellatif Filali
Interior and information Driss Basri

MOZAMBIQUE
Presidential republic. A new constitution allowing for multi-party politics came into effect in November 1990. Previously the ruling Front for the Liberation of Mozambique (Frelimo) had been the sole legal political party since independence in 1975. Legislative elections were scheduled for 1991 following the

formal registration of political parties, but did not take place and now are expected in 1993.

President Joaquim Alberto Chissano (since 1986)
Prime minister Mario da Graca Machungo (since 1986)

MYANMAR (BURMA)
Republic ruled by military junta. All political power rests with the ruling junta, the State Law and Order Restoration Council (SLORC). The last general election in May 1990 resulted in a landslide victory for the opposition National League for Democracy (NLD). But at the end of 1992 the SLORC had still not transferred power.

Chairman (SLORC) Gen. Than Shwe (replaced Gen. Saw Maung in Apr)

NAMIBIA
Presidential republic. Became independent in March 1990. The Constituent Assembly, elected in November 1989, was converted into the lower house of a bicameral parliamentary structure by March 1991. The current president, with executive powers, was unanimously elected in February 1990 by the assembly. Legislative elections are due in 1994, a presidential election in 1995.

President Sam Nujoma (since 1990)
Prime minister Hage Geingob (since 1990)
Foreign affairs Hifikepunye Pohamba
Defence Peter Mueshihange

NAURU
Parliamentary democracy, with an 18-member unicameral parliament elected for up to three years. The new parliament elects the president (who serves as both head of government and head of state) from among its members. The last election was held in November 1992; the next is due by December 1995.

President Bernard Dowiyogo (since 1989)

NEPAL
Parliamentary monarchy. The Nepali Congress Party (NCP) won a majority in an election held in May 1991 to a newly created House of Representatives. The next election is due by May 1995. The number of NCP members in the 205-member house following the election was 110.

Head of state King Birendra Bir Bikram Shah Deva (crowned in 1975)
Prime minister Girija Prasad Koirala

NEW ZEALAND
Parliamentary democracy, with the United Kingdom sovereign as head of state, represented by a governor-general. The 97-member unicameral House of Representatives, elected for up to three years, is controlled by the conservative National Party which holds 68 seats. The last general election was in October 1990; the next is due in November 1993.

Governor-general Dame Catherine Tizard (since 1990)
Prime minister Jim Bolger (since 1990)

PRINCIPAL MINISTERS
Deputy prime minister; external relations and trade; foreign affairs Don McKinnon
Finance Ruth Richardson
Defence; local government Warren Cooper
Attorney-general, health, enterprises Paul East

NICARAGUA
Presidential republic. The ruling coalition party, the National Opposition Union (UNO) does not command an overall majority in the 90-member National Assembly. The last general election was held in 1990; the next will be held in November 1996.

President Violeta Chamorro (since 1990)

PRINCIPAL MINISTERS
Foreign affairs Ernesto Leal (replaced Enrique Dreyfus in Jan)
Interior Alfredo Mendieta (replaced Carlos Hurtado in May)
Finance Emilio Pereira
Presidency Antonio Lacayo

NIGER
Presidential republic. The current head of state has been in power since November 1987 and was last elected (unopposed) in December 1989. A national conference on the political future of the country, held with a view to the adoption of multi-party politics, began deliberating in July 1991. In August it suspended the constitution, stripping the president of his executive power, although he remains head of state. In November it handed executive power over to Amadou Cheiffou and made him prime minister during the period of transition to democracy which continues until 1993. Legislative power during the transition is vested in a 15-member Higher Council of the Republic.

President Brig.-Gen. Ali Saibou (since 1987)
Presidium president (national conference) André Salifou (since 1991)
Prime minister Amadou Cheiffou (since 1991)

NIGERIA
Federal republic, ruled by military council. The present regime took power in a coup in August 1985. The principal decision-making body is the Armed Forces Ruling Council (AFRC), composed of senior officers and members of the police force. The 21 state governors, along with the president, form the National Council of States. The last election at a national level was held in 1983. Local elections were held in 1990. In July 1992 elections to the 593-member House of Representatives took place. These were supposed to mark the penultimate step in the return of black Africa's most populous country to civilian rule in January 1993, but in October 1992 President Babangida cancelled presidential primaries and disbanded the leadership of the two army-created political parties. The timetable for the end of military rule and the general election was provisionally agreed for June–August 1993.

President Maj.-Gen. Ibrahim Babangida (since 1985)

PRINCIPAL MINISTERS
Vice-president Vice-Adml. (retd) Agustus Aikhomu
Budget and planning Chu Okongwu
External affairs Maj.-Gen. (retd) Ike Nwachukwu
Finance and economic planning Abubakar Alhaji
Internal affairs Maj.-Gen. (retd) A. B. Mamman
Petroleum resources Jibril Aminu

NORWAY
Parliamentary monarchy. A minority Labour government has been in power since November 1990. The last general election was in September 1989 for a fixed four-year-term parliament which cannot be dissolved prematurely.

Head of state Harald V, King of Norway (succeeded in 1991)
Prime minister Gro Harlem Brundtland (since 1990)

PRINCIPAL MINISTERS
Foreign affairs Thorvald Stoltenberg
Finance Sigbjørn Johnsen
Defence Johan Jorgen Holst

OMAN
Absolute monarchy. Ruled by the Sultan, who appoints a cabinet. There are no elections and no political parties.

Head of state Sultan Qaboos bin Said (succeeded in 1970)
Deputy prime minister Sayyid Fahr bin Taimour al Said (since 1989)

PAKISTAN
Parliamentary republic. The Islamic Democratic Alliance (IDA) controls an absolute majority in the National Assembly. A general election was held in October 1990; the next is due in 1995. A presidential election was held in December 1988; the next is due in 1993.

President Ghulam Ishaq Khan (since 1988)
Prime minister; defence; foreign affairs Nawaz Sharif (since 1990)

PRINCIPAL CABINET MINISTERS
Interior Choudhry Shujat Hussain
Finance and economic affairs Sartaj Aziz

PANAMA
Presidential republic. The coalition Democratic Civic Opposition Alliance (ADOC) has controlled the 67-member legislative assembly since December 1989. The last general election was in 1989; the next is expected in 1994.

President Guillermo Endara Galimany (since 1989)
First vice-president Ricardo Arias Calderon
Second vice-president Guillermo Ford

PRINCIPAL MINISTERS
Treasury and finance Mario Galindo
Foreign affairs Julio E. Linares

PAPUA NEW GUINEA
Parliamentary democracy, with the United Kingdom sovereign as head of state, represented by a governor-general. Traditionally, governments consist of loose and frequently shifting coalitions, based around individuals rather than ideologies. The last election was held in June 1992 and its results were the closest in the country's history. Both Paias Wingti and Rabbie Namaliu got 54% of the votes. The next election is due by June 1997.

Governor-general Wiwa Korowi (since 1991)
Prime minister Paias Wingti (replaced Rabbie Namaliu in Jul)

PARAGUAY
Presidential republic. The Colorado Party (ANR-PC) has controlled the 102-member National Congress since 1954. The last general election was in 1989 and the next is due by May 1993.

President Gen. Andres Rodriguez (since 1989)

PERU
Presidential republic. The ruling Change 90 (Cambio 90) movement does not command a majority in the 240-member Congress. The last general election was in 1990; the next is due in 1995. After an April 1992 coup President Fujimori promised direct elections within five months. With a little delay the legislative elections were held in November 1992. President's New Majority and Change '90 coalition won 44 of the 80 seats with 38% of the vote.

President Alberto Fujimori (since 1990)
Prime minister; foreign affairs Oscar de la Puente Raygada (replaced Alfonso de los Heros in Apr)

PRINCIPAL MINISTERS
Economy and finance Carlos Bolona Behr
Interior Gen. Juan Briones Davila
Defence Gen. E.P. Victor Malca

PHILIPPINES
Presidential democracy, with a powerful directly elected president whose supporters command a majority in the lower house of the bicameral

Congress but not in the Senate. The last presidential election was held in May 1992; the next is due in 1998. The last legislative elections were held in May 1992; the next are due in 1995.

President Fidel Ramos (replaced Corazon Aquino in May)

PRINCIPAL MEMBERS
Defence Gen. Renato de Villa
Finance Ramon del Rosario (replaced Jesus Estanislao in May)
Foreign affairs Roberto Romulo (replaced Raul Manglapus in May)

POLAND
Parliamentary republic with bicameral national assembly, consisting of the 460-seat Sejm (lower house) and the 100-seat Senate. The president is elected by universal suffrage. A general election in October 1991 resulted in a legislature with no clear party majority. The next general elections are due in 1995. The Polish parliament voted in July 1992 on the new cabinet.

President Lech Walesa (since 1990)
Prime minister Hanna Suchocka (replaced Jan Olszewski in Jul)

PRINCIPAL MINISTERS
Finance Jerzy Osiatynski (replaced Karol Lutkowski in Jul)
Justice Zbigniew Dyka
Minister-director of the central planning office Jerzy Kropiwnicki (replaced Jerzy Eysmontt in Jul)
National defence Janusz Onyszkiewicz (replaced Jan Parys in Jul)
Foreign trade Andrzej Arendarski
Internal affairs Andrzej Milczanowski (replaced Antoni Macierewicz in Jul)
Foreign affairs Krzysztof Skubiszewski
Agriculture and food economy Gabriel Janowski

PORTUGAL
Parliamentary republic. The president is elected for a five-year term. A general election to the 250-member Assembly of the Republic (elected for up to four years) was held in October 1991. The ruling Social Democratic Party (PSD) was returned with a majority of 135 seats. The next legislative and presidential elections are due in 1995.

President Mario Soares (since 1986)
Prime minister Anibal Cavaco Silva (since 1985)

PRINCIPAL MINISTERS
Defence Fernando Nogueira (replaced Carlos Brito in 1991)
Finance Jorge Braga de Macedo
Interior Manuel Dias Loureiro
Foreign affairs Joao de Deus Pinheiro

QATAR
Absolute monarchy ruled by the Emir who appoints a cabinet. There are no political parties, no elections and no legislature.

Head of state Sheikh Khalifa bin Hamad al Thani, Emir; prime minister (since 1972)
Heir apparent Sheikh Hamad bin Khalifa al Thani (since 1989)

ROMANIA
Presidential republic. The bicameral parliament comprises a 328-seat Chamber of Deputies and a 143-seat Senate. In the first multi-party general election in May 1990, the National Salvation Front, which took power after the overthrow of the Ceausescu regime in 1989 and was dominated by former Romanian Communist Party members, won an outright majority in the Chamber and in the Senate. The president was directly elected. A referendum in

December 1991 approved a new constitution. A general election was held in 1992 and took place in two stages: the parliamentary elections and the first round of the presidential election on September 27th and the second ballot in the presidential run-off on October 11th 1992.

President Ion Iliescu (since 1990)
Prime minister Nicolae Vacaroiu (replaced Theodor Stolojan in Nov)

PRINCIPAL MINISTERS
Foreign affairs Teodor Viorel Malescanu (replaced Adrian Nastase in Nov)
Defence Gen. Constantin Niculae Spiroiu
Finance Florin Georgescu (replaced George Danielescu in Nov)
Interior George Danescu (replaced Victor Babiuc in Nov)

RUSSIA
Former republic of the Soviet Union and a founder member of the Commonwealth of Independent States. Has taken over the international obligations of the Soviet Union. The 1,066-seat Congress of People's Deputies is the highest legislative body. The first presidential election was held in June 1991.

President Boris Yeltsin
Vice-president Alexandr Rutskoi
Prime minister Victor Chernomyrdin (replaced in Dec Yegor Gaidar, who had replaced Boris Yeltsin in April)

PRINCIPAL MINISTERS
Finance Vassily Barchuk
Defence Pavel Grachev
Foreign affairs Andrei Kozyrev
Economics Andrei Nechaev

RWANDA
Presidential republic. Executive power is vested in the president, who is elected for a five-year term. Legislative power is exercised jointly by the president and the 70-member National Development Council, whose members are also directly elected for five years from a list of candidates put forward by the sole legal party, the National Revolutionary Movement for Development. Presidential and legislative elections were held in December 1988. A new constitution providing for a multi-party system was drawn up in early 1991. A transitional government was formed in April and in August agreement was reached on political reforms.

President Maj.-Gen. Juvénal Habyarimana (since 1973)
Prime minister Dismas Nzengiyaremye (replaced Sylvestre Nsanzima in Apr)

ST CHRISTOPHER AND NEVIS
Parliamentary monarchy. The head of state is the United Kingdom sovereign, represented by a governor-general. The People's Action Movement has controlled the 23-member National Assembly since June 1984. The last general election was in 1989; the next is due by June 1994.

Governor-general Clement Athelston Arrindell (since 1983)
Prime minister Kennedy A. Simmonds (since 1983)

ST LUCIA
Parliamentary monarchy. The head of state is the United Kingdom sovereign, represented by a governor-general. The United Workers' Party (UWP) has controlled the 17-member House of Assembly since 1982. The last general election was held in April 1992; the next is due by May 1997.

Governor-general (acting) Stanislaus James (since 1988)

Prime minister John Compton (since 1982)

ST VINCENT AND THE GRENADINES
Parliamentary monarchy. The head of state is the United Kingdom sovereign, represented by a governor-general. The New Democratic Party (NDP) has controlled the 21-member House of Assembly since 1984. The last general election was in 1989 and the next is due by May 1994.

Governor-general David Jack (since 1989)
Prime minister James Mitchell (since 1984)

SAN MARINO
Parliamentary republic, with legislative power vested in a 60-member Grand and General Council. In the 1988 general election, a coalition government of the Communist Party and the Christian Democrat Party was returned to power. The next election is due by May 1993.

Heads of state Edda Ceccoli and Marino Riccardi, Captains-Regent

SAO TOME AND PRINCIPE
Presidential republic. In January 1991 the ruling Democratic Convergence Party won the first multi-party elections to the 55-member National Assembly.

President Miguel Trovoada (since 1991)
Prime minister Daniel Lima dos Santos Daio (since 1991)

SAUDI ARABIA
Absolute monarchy ruled by the king who also heads an appointed Council of Ministers. There are no political parties and no elections.

Head of state King Fahd ibn Abdul Aziz (succeeded in 1982)

SENEGAL
Presidential republic. The ruling Socialist Party obtained 103 of the 120 seats in the National Assembly in the general election in February 1988. Constitutional changes made in September 1991 limited the presidential mandate to two terms of seven years each and laid down that presidential and legislative elections would not be held simultaneously as before. The next legislative elections are due in 1993 and the presidential election in 1995.

President Abdou Diouf (since 1981)
Prime minister Habib Thiam (since 1991)

SEYCHELLES
Presidential republic. The present head of state seized power in a coup in 1977. Executive power is vested in the president, who is elected for a five-year term by direct suffrage and appoints the Council of Ministers. There is a unicameral National Assembly of 23 members elected for five years and two members appointed by the president. In July 1992 the country's first multi-party elections in 15 years gave President René and his ruling party, the Seychelles People's Progressive Front, a substantial victory, winning 58.4% of votes.

President Albert René (since 1977)

SIERRA LEONE
Presidential republic. The country was a one-party state under the All-Peoples Party from 1978 until in August 1991 a referendum overwhelmingly approved a new constitution providing for a multi-party system. In September 1991 the president formed an interim government to preside until a general election scheduled for 1992, but then postponed. In April 1992 after a military coup a National Provisional Defence Council was formed and the previous government denounced. The last

presidential election was held in 1985; the last legislative elections in 1986.

Head of state Capt. Valentine E. Melvin Strasser (replaced Maj.-Gen. Joseph Saidu Momoh in Apr)
Vice-president Lieut. Solomon A. James Musa (replaced Gen. Abdulai Conteh in Apr)

SINGAPORE
Parliamentary republic. The People's Action Party (PAP) has had a majority in parliament since 1959. The last general election was in 1991; the next is due by August 1996.

President Wee Kim Wee (since 1985)
Prime minister Goh Chok Tong (since 1990)
Senior Lee Kuan Yew

PRINCIPAL MINISTERS
Defence Yeo Ning Hong
Foreign affairs Wong Kan Seng

SLOVENIA
Former republic of Yugoslavia. In July 1990 the Slovenian Assembly declared sovereignty. In December 1990 a referendum endorsed independence proposals. Full independence was proclaimed on October 8th 1991. Slovenia is governed by a coalition of seven parties. The first post-independence presidential election was held in December 1992. Slovenia's ex-communist president was re-elected with 64% of the vote.

President Milan Kucan (since 1990)
Prime minister Janez Drnovsek (replaced Lozje Peterle in Apr)

SOLOMON ISLANDS
Parliamentary democracy, with the United Kingdom sovereign as head of state, represented by a governor-general. In 1989 the People's Alliance Party won control of the 38-member legislature, but in October 1990 the prime minister resigned from the party and formed a government of national unity. The last election was held in March 1989; the next is due in March 1993.

Governor-general Sir George Lepping (since 1988)
Prime minister Solomon Mamaloni (since 1989)

SOMALIA
Presidential republic. Was formed in 1960 from British Somaliland Protectorate and the UN Trust Territory of Somalia (former Italian colony). In October 1969 after a military coup led by Maj.-Gen. Mohammad Diyad Barre the constitution and the multi-party system were abolished. The Barre government was overthrown in January 1991 by the United Somali Congress (USC). Its leader was installed as interim president and a transitional government was created. In July 1991 the constitution of 1961 was re-adopted and elections were promised within two years. In May 1991 northern Somalia (former British Protectorate of Somaliland) declared its independence.

President Ali Mahdi Mohammed (since 1991)
Prime minister Umar Arteh Ghalib (since 1991)

SOUTH AFRICA
Federal republic. Under the constitution of 1984, there is a tricameral parliament, with a House of Assembly (178 members) representing whites, a House of Representatives (85 members) representing people of mixed race ("Coloureds"), and a House of Delegates (45 members) representing Indians, but no representation for the majority black population. Elections were held in September 1989 to all three houses, and F. W. de Klerk was then elected as the new executive state president by an electoral college composed of 50 members of the House of Assembly, 25 members of the House of Representatives and 13

from the House of Delegates. The National Party, the party of government since 1948, continues to command a majority in the House of Assembly. The next general election is due in 1993.
President F. W. de Klerk (since 1989)

PRINCIPAL MINISTERS
Foreign affairs Roelof F. Botha
Constitutional development Fanus Schoeman (replaced Gerrit van Viljoen in Dec)
Defence E. Louw (replaced Roelf Meyer in Apr)
Minerals and energy George Bartlett
Justice Kobie Coetsee
Finance Derek Keys (replaced Barend du Plessis in Apr)
Law and order Hernus Kriel
State expenditure A.A. Venter
Home affairs Louis Pienaar

SPAIN
Parliamentary monarchy. The Spanish Socialist Workers' Party (PSOE) has controlled a majority in the 350-member Congress of Deputies since 1986. The distribution of seats in Congress following a general election in October 1989 was finalised in April 1990, when the PSOE was allocated 175 seats, which was exactly half. The next general election is due by October 1993.

Head of state Juan Carlos, King of Spain (since 1975)
Prime minister Felipe Gonzalez (since 1982)

PRINCIPAL MINISTERS
Deputy prime minister Narcis Serra
Defence Julian Garcia Vargas
Interior Jose Luis Corcuera
Foreign affairs Francisco Fernandez Ordonez
Economy and finance Carlos Solchaga
Justice Tomas de la Quadra-Salcedo
Industry, commerce and tourism Claudio Aranzadi Martinez
Labour and social security Luis Martinez Noval
Education and science Javier Solana Madariaga
Agriculture Pedro Solbes Mira
Culture Jordi Sole Tura
Government spokeswoman Rosa Conde de Espina Gutierrez del Alamo

SRI LANKA
Presidential democracy. The United National Party has had control of the unicameral parliament since 1977. The last parliamentary election (using proportional representation for the first time) was in February 1989; the next is due by 1995. The president is elected directly; the last election was in December 1988; the next is due by 1994.

President Ranasinghe Premadasa (since 1989)
Prime minister Dingiri Banda Wijetunge (since 1989)

PRINCIPAL MINISTERS
Finance and defence Dingiri Banda Wijetunge
Foreign affairs Harold Herath

SUDAN
Republic, ruled by a 15-member Revolutionary Command Council, composed of military officers, since June 1989. The last general election was held in 1986. Voting for local electoral colleges began in May 1992. The election process was expected to take up to a year.

Chairman Lt.-Gen. Omar Hassan Ahmad al Bashir (since 1989)

PRINCIPAL MINISTERS
Deputy prime minister; interior Gen El Zubeir Mohammed Salih
Foreign affairs Ali Ahmed Sahloul
Finance and national economic planning Abdel Rahim Hamdi

SURINAM
Presidential republic. The New Front coalition has a majority in the 50-member National Assembly. The last general election was held in 1991; the next is due by 1996.

President Ronald Venetiaan (since 1991)
Vice-president; head of government Jules Ajodhia

SWAZILAND
Constitutional monarchy. Considerable executive power is vested in the king and is exercised by a cabinet appointed by him. The bicameral legislative body, the Libandla, composed of a Senate and House of Assembly, has limited powers. Elections to both houses are indirect; the last ones were in November 1987. All political parties are banned.

Head of state King Mswati III (succeeded in 1986)
Prime minister Obed Dlamini (since 1989)

SWEDEN
Parliamentary monarchy. The conservative Moderate Unity Party (M) has ruled in coalition with the liberal People's Party (FP), Centre Party (C) and the Christian Democratic Community Party (KDS) since October 1991. The last general election was held in September 1991; the next is due by September 1994.

Head of state Carl XVI Gustaf, King of Sweden (succeeded in 1973)
Prime minister Carl Bildt (M) (since 1991)

PRINCIPAL MINISTERS
Deputy prime minister Bengt Westerberg (FP)
Foreign affairs Margaretha af Ugglas (M)
Defence Anders Bjorck (M)
Finance Anne Wibble (Lib)
Industry and commerce Per Westerberg (M)
Labour Borje Hornlund (C)
Agriculture Karl Erik Olsson (C)
Environment Olof Johansson (C)
Immigration and cultural affairs Birgit Friggebo (Lib)
Justice Gun Hellsvik (M)
Transport Mats Odell (KDS)
Public administration Juger Davidsson (KDS)

SWITZERLAND
Federal republic. The Christian Democratic People's Party, the Social Democratic Party, the Radical Democratic Party and the Swiss People's Party have ruled in coalition since 1959. The last general election was in October 1991; the next is due in October 1995.

President René Felber
Vice-president Adolf Ogi

PRINCIPAL MEMBERS OF THE BUNDESRAT
Political (foreign) affairs René Felber (SPS)
Finance Otto Stich (SPS)
Interior Flavio Cotti (CVP)
Military (defence) Kaspar Villiger (FDP)

SYRIA
Presidential republic. The Ba'ath Party has been in power since 1963. Hafez Al-Assad was confirmed as president by referendum in December 1991. The last general election to the 250-member People's Assembly (the legislative organ) was held in April 1990; the next is due by April 1994. In 1992 the governing Ba'ath coalition promised more liberal economic policy, but ruled out the future launch of new political parties.

President Lt.-Gen. Hafez Al-Assad (since 1971)
Vice-presidents Abdel Halim Khaddam; Zuhqir Mashariqa
Prime minister Mahmoud Zubi

PRINCIPAL MINISTERS
Foreign affairs Farouq Al-Sharaa
Defence Lt.-Gen. Mustafa Tlaas

Interior Muhamed Harba

TAIWAN

Presidential republic. The government of Taiwan is derived from that which ruled the Chinese mainland before the 1949 communist revolution; it maintains its claim to mainland China and continues to designate itself the Republic of China. Under constitutional amendments passed in April 1991, parliamentary elections were held in December 1992. For the first time since 1948 all seats in the new 161-member parliament were up for election. Support for the ruling Kuomintang Party fell sharply and its candidates won 96 seats. The pro-independence Democratic Progressive Party won enough seats to initiate legislation and to be an important voting block.

President Lee Teng-hui (since 1988)
Vice-president Lee Yuan-zu
Prime minister Gen. Hau Pei-tsun

TAJIKISTAN

Former republic of the Soviet Union and a founder member of the Commonwealth of Independent States. In August 1990 the Tajik Supreme Soviet declared sovereignty. A directly elected president was instituted in November 1991, when a presidential election was held.

Speaker of Parliament (de facto President) Imoli Rakhmanov (replaced in Nov Akbarsho Iskandrov (acting president), who had replaced Rakhmon Nabiev (ousted Sep))
Acting prime minister Abdulmalik Abdullodzhanov (replaced in Nov Akbar Mirzoyev, who had replaced Maksud Ikramovln in Mar)

TANZANIA

Federal republic. Executive power is vested in the president, who is nominated by the sole legal political party, Chama Cha Mapinduzi (the Revolutionary Party of Tanzania), and is directly elected to a five-year term, renewable once only. The two vice-presidents, one of whom is the president of Zanzibar and the other the prime minister of the Union government, are appointed by the president. Legislative power is vested in the National Assembly, composed of 180 directly elected members and a number of ex-officio, nominated and indirectly elected members. The assembly's term is five years. The current president was elected for a second term in October 1990, when legislative elections were also held.

President Ali Hassan Mwinyi (since 1985)
First vice-president; prime minister John Malecela (since 1990)
Second vice-president; president of Zanzibar Salmin Amour (since 1990)

THAILAND

Monarchy. A new constitution took effect in December 1991. The victory by a pro-military coalition in March 1992 general election led to serious clashes in Bangkok in May. In June the House of Representatives was dissolved and an interim government was called and was held in September 1992.

Head of state Bhumibol Adulyadej (Rama IX), King of Thailand (succeeded in 1946)
Prime minister Chuan Leekpai (replaced Anand Panyarachun in Sep, who replaced Suchinda Kraprayoon in Jun, who replaced Anand Panyarachun in Mar)

PRINCIPAL MINISTERS
Defence Gen. Vichit Sukmark (replaced Gen. Banchop Bunnak in Sep, who replaced Adml. Praphat Krisanchan in Jun)

Finance Tarrin Nimmanahaeminda (replaced Phanat Simasathian in Sep, who had replaced Suthee Singgsaneh in Jun)
Foreign affairs Prasong Soonsiri (replaced Arsa Sarasin in Sep)
Interior Gen. Chavalit Yongchaiyudh (replaced Police Gen. Pow Sarasin in Sep, who had replaced Gen. Issarapong Noonpackdee in Jun)

TOGO

Presidential republic. A national conference to determine the political future of the country ended in August 1991 with legislative and presidential elections scheduled for the end of 1992, following a constitutional referendum. The Conference also elected a prime minister, with executive powers, to head a transitional government, and announced the dissolution of the Rally of the Togolese People (RPT), hitherto the ruling and sole legal party. A coup attempt in late 1991 ended with the formation of a national unity government.

President Gen. Gnassingbe Eyadema (since 1967)
Prime minister Koukou Koffigoh (since 1991)

TONGA

Constitutional monarchy, with a unicameral legislature, the majority of whose 29 members are either appointed or serve on a hereditary basis. The last elections were in February 1990; the next are due by February 1993.

Head of state King Taufa'ahau Tupou IV (succeeded in 1965)
Prime minister Baron Vaea (since 1991)

TRINIDAD AND TOBAGO

Parliamentary republic. The National Alliance for Reconstruction controlled the 36-member House of Representatives from December 1986 until the general election in December 1991, when the People's National Movement won a clear majority. The next national election is due by January 1997. President Noor Mohammed Hassanali (since 1987)

Prime minister Patrick Manning (since 1991)

TUNISIA

Presidential republic; the Constitutional Democratic Rally (RCD) controls the National Assembly, although other parties have been legalised since 1981. In the last general election in April 1989 the RCD won all 141 National Assembly seats despite competition from six opposition parties. The next general election is due in April 1994.

President Zine el Abidine Ben Ali (since 1987)
Prime minister Hamed Karoui (since 1989)

PRINCIPAL MINISTERS
Defence Abdelaziz Ben Dhia
Foreign affairs Habib Ben Yahya

TURKEY

Presidential republic, with a 500-seat Grand National Assembly elected by universal suffrage. Following the last general election in October 1991 a coalition government was formed by the True Path Party (DYP) and the Social Democratic Populist Party (SHP), which had won 178 and 88 seats respectively in the 500-seat legislature. The next general election is due by October 1996.

President Turgut Ozal (since 1989)
Prime minister Suleyman Demirel (since 1991)

PRINCIPAL MINISTERS
Deputy prime minister and minister of state Erdal Inonu
Minister of state Tansu Ciller
Foreign affairs Hikmet Cetin

National defence Nevzat Ayaz
Interior Ismet Sezgin
Finance and customs Sumer Oral

TURKMENISTAN

Former republic of the Soviet Union and a founder member of the Commonwealth of Independent States. Sovereignty was declared in August 1990. A referendum in October supported it, and from October 27th 1991 Turkmenistan became an independent state.

President Saparmurad Niazov (since 1990)
Prime minister Khan Akhmedov (since 1990)

TUVALU

Parliamentary democracy. The United Kingdom sovereign is head of state, represented by a governor-general. A 12-member unicameral legislature, elected for up to four years, chooses the prime minister. The last election was in 1989; the next is due by September 1993.

Governor-general Toaripi Lauti (since 1990)
Prime minister Bikenibeu Paeniu (since 1989)

UGANDA

Presidential republic, ruled by military council. The present ruler came to power in January 1986 at the head of the National Resistance Movement. The president is assisted by a prime minister and cabinet, composed of representatives of a number of political parties; although the parties continue to exist, political activity is banned, and elections held in February 1989 to the National Resistance Council (NRC) were conducted on a non-party basis. The first direct presidential election will be held in 1994. The NRC, consisting of 210 elected and 68 presidentially appointed members, is acting as a legislative body for the interim period until a new constitution has been framed.

President Yoweri Museveni, Minister of Defence (since 1986)
Prime minister George Cosma Adyebo (since 1991)

UKRAINE

Former republic of the Soviet Union and a founder member of the Commonwealth of Independent States. The Ukrainian Supreme Soviet declared sovereignty in August 1991. A directly elected president was instituted in December 1991.

President Leonid Kravchuk (since 1991)
Prime minister Leonid Kuchma (replaced Vitold Fokin in Oct)

PRINCIPAL MINISTERS
First deputy prime minister Igor Yukhnovsky (replaced Konstantin Masyk in Oct)
Foreign affairs Anatoly Zlenko

UNITED ARAB EMIRATES

Federation of seven emirates (Abu Dhabi, Dubai, Sharjah, Ras al Khaimah, Fujairah, Umm al Qaiwan and Ajman) represented by a Supreme Council of Rulers which elects the president and vice-president. There are no political parties and no elections.

President Sheikh Zaid bin Sultan al Nahayan (ruler of Abu Dhabi since 1966; president since 1971)
Vice-president; prime minister Sheikh Maktoum bin Rashid al Maktoum (ruler of Dubai since 1990, Vice-President of UAE since 1990)

UNITED KINGDOM

Parliamentary monarchy. The Conservative Party has had control of the 650-member House of Commons since May 1979. The last general election was held in April 1992; the next is due by April 1997.

Head of state Queen Elizabeth II (succeeded in 1952)
Prime minister John Major (since 1990)
CABINET MINISTERS
Lord President of the Council and leader of the House of Commons Tony Newton (replaced John McGregor in Apr)
Lord Chancellor Lord Mackay of Clashfern
Foreign affairs Douglas Hurd
Chancellor of the Exchequer Norman Lamont
Home secretary Kenneth Clarke (replaced Kenneth Baker in Apr)
Defence Malcolm Rifkind (replaced Tom King in Apr)
Education and science John Patten (replaced Kenneth Clarke in Apr)
Transport John McGregor (replaced Malcolm Rifkind in Apr)
Lord Privy Seal and leader of the House of Lords Lord Wakeham (replaced Lord Waddington in Apr)
Social security Peter Lilley (replaced Tony Newton in Apr)
Chancellor of the Duchy of Lancaster William Waldegrave (replaced Chris Patten in Apr)
Northern Ireland Patrick Mayhew (replaced Peter Brooke in Apr)
Agriculture, fisheries and food John Selwyn Gummer
Employment Gillian Shephard (replaced Michael Howard in Apr)
Wales David Hunt
Trade and industry Michael Heseltine (replaced Peter Lilley in Apr)
Health Virginia Bottomley (replaced William Waldegrave in Apr)
Environment Michael Howard (replaced Michael Heseltine in Apr)
Scotland Ian Lang
Chief Secretary to the Treasury Michael Portillo (replaced David Mellor in Apr)
National Heritage Peter Brooke (replaced David Mellor in Sep)

UNITED STATES
Federal democracy, embodying strict separation of powers between a president (popularly elected for four years), a bicameral legislature and an independent judiciary. The legislature consists of a 435-member House of Representatives (elected for two years) and a 100-member Senate (elected for six years, with one-third being renewed every two years). After legislative elections in November 1992 the Democrats had 258 seats in the House and 57 in the Senate. In the presidential election in November 1992 the Democratic candidate won the presidency. The next presidential election is due in November 1996.

President George Bush (to be replaced by Bill Clinton in Jan 1993)

CABINET MEMBERS
Vice-president Dan Quayle (to be replaced by Al Gore in Jan 1993)
State Lawrence Eagleburger (replaced James Baker in Dec; to be replaced by Warren Christopher in Jan 1993)
Treasury Nicholas Brady (to be replaced by Lloyd Bentsen in Jan 1993)
Defence Richard Cheney (to be replaced by Les Aspin in Jan 1993)
Interior Manuel Lujan (to be replaced by Bruce Babbitt in Jan 1993)
Agriculture Edward Madigan (to be replaced by Mike Espy in Jan 1993)
Commerce Barbara Franklin (to be replaced by Ron Brown in Jan 1993)
Housing and urban development Jack Kemp (to be replaced by Henry Cisneros in Jan 1993)
Transportation Andrew Card (replaced Samuel Skinner in Feb; to be replaced by Federico Pena in Jan 1993)
Health and human services Louis Sullivan (to be

replaced by Donna Shalala in Jan 1993)
Attorney-general William Barr (to be replaced by Zoë Baird in Jan 1993)
Labour Lynn Martin (to be replaced by Robert Reich in Jan 1993)
Energy James Watkins (to be replaced by Hazel O'Leary in Jan 1993)
Education Lamar Alexander (to be replaced by Richard Riley in Jan 1993)
Veterans' affairs Edward Derwinski (to be replaced by Jesse Brown in Jan 1993)

OTHER LEADING EXECUTIVE BRANCH OFFICIALS
White House chief of staff James Baker (replaced Samuel Skinner in Aug; to be replaced by Thomas McLarty in Jan 1993)
Director of office of management and budget (OMB) Richard Darman (to be replaced by Leon Panetta in Jan 1993)
Assistant to the president for national security affairs Gen. Brent Scowcroft (to be replaced by Anthony Lake in Jan 1993)
Representative for trade negotiations Carla Hills (to be replaced by Mickey Kantor in Jan 1993)
Director, central intelligence agency (CIA) Robert Gates (to be replaced by R. James Woolsey in 1993)
Chairman, president's council of economic advisers Michael Boskin (to be replaced in Jan 1993)
Director, office of national drug control policy Bob Martinez (to be replaced by Laura D'Andrea Tyson in Jan 1993)

LEGISLATIVE BRANCH
President of the Senate Dan Quayle (vice-president) (to be replaced by Al Gore in Jan 1993)
Senate majority leader George Mitchell
Senate majority whip Wendell Ford
Senate minority leader Robert Dole
Senate minority whip Alan Simpson
Speaker of the House Thomas Foley
House majority leader Richard Gephardt
House majority whip David Bonior
House minority leader Robert Michel
House minority whip Newt Gingrich
Chairman Senate Foreign Relations Committee Claiborne Pell
Chairman Senate Armed Services Committee Sam Nunn
Chairman Senate Budget Committee Jim Sasser
Chairman Senate Finance Committee Lloyd Bentsen (to be replaced by Daniel Moynihan in Jan 1993)
Chairman Senate Judiciary Committee Joseph Biden
Chairman House Foreign Affairs Committee Dante Fascell (to be replaced by Lee Hamilton in Jan 1993)
Chairman House Armed Services Committee Les Aspin (to be replaced in Jan 1993)
Chairman House Budget Committee Leon Panetta (to be replaced in Jan 1993)
Chairman House Ways and Means Committee Dan Rostenkowski
Chairman House Judiciary Committee Jack Brooks

THE SUPREME COURT
Chief justice William Rehnquist
Associate justices David Souter, Byron White, Harry Blackmun, John Paul Stevens, Sandra Day O'Connor, Antonin Scalia, Anthony Kennedy, Clarence Thomas

*Replacements subject to confirmation by Congress.

URUGUAY
Presidential republic. The ruling National Party (PN or Blancos) coalition government lacks a majority in the 129-member National Congress. The last general election was in 1989; the next is due by November 1995.

President Luis Alberto Lacalle Herrera (since 1990)
Vice-president Gonzalo Aguirre Ramirez (since 1990)

PRINCIPAL MINISTERS
Home affairs Juan Andres Ramirez
Foreign relations Hector Gros Espiell
Economy and finance Ignacio De Posadas (replaced Enrique Braga in Feb)
Defence Mariano Brito

UZBEKISTAN
Former republic of the Soviet Union and a founder member of the Commonwealth of Independent States. Sovereignty was declared in June 1990. The 500-member Supreme Soviet is the legislative body. The president is directly elected.

President Islam Karimov (since 1991)
Prime minister Abdulkhashim Mutalov (since Jan)

VANUATU
Parliamentary democracy, with a 46-member unicameral legislature controlled by the Vanuaaka Pati, which has held power since 1983. The last election was in December 1991; the next is due by 1995.

President Fred Timakata (since 1989)
Prime minister Maxime Carlot (since 1991)

VATICAN CITY
Religious state, with the Pope as head of state. The Pope is elected for life by the Sacred College of Cardinals. Since 1984 the routine administration of the Vatican has been delegated to the secretary of state and a Pontifical Commission, appointed by the Pope.

Head of state His Holiness Pope John Paul II (since 1978)
Secretary of state Cardinal Angelo Sodano

VENEZUELA
Federal republic. The ruling Democratic Action Party (AD) has no overall absolute majority in the 245-member National Congress. The last general election was held in 1988 and the next is due by December 1993. In February and April 1992 military coups were attempted.

President Carlos Andres Perez (since 1989)

PRINCIPAL MINISTERS
Interior Luis Pinerua Ordaz (replaced in Apr Virgilio Avila Vivas, who had replaced Alejandro Izaguirre in Feb)
Foreign affairs Gen. Fernando Ochoa Antich (replaced Armande Duran in Jun)
Finance Pedro Rosas Bravo (replaced Roberto Pocaterra in Feb)
Defence Gen. Ivan Jimenez (replaced Gen. Fernando Ochoa Antich in Jun)

VIETNAM
Socialist republic. The last general election to the 395-member National Assembly (Quoc-Hoi) was held in July 1992; the next is due by September 1996. A new constitution and a new election law were introduced in April 1992. A single president replaced the old Council of State which served as a collective presidency.

President Le Duc Anh (replaced Vo Chi Cong in Sep)
Prime minister Vo Van Kiet (since 1991)

PRINCIPAL MINISTERS
Foreign affairs Nguyen Manh Cam
National defence Gen. Doan Khue
Interior Lt.-Gen. Bui Thien Ngo
Finance Ho Te

WESTERN SAMOA

Parliamentary democracy, with an elected constitutional monarch and a 47-member unicameral legislature elected for up to three years. The Human Rights Protection Party won 26 seats in the election of April 1991; the next election is due by April 1994.

Head of state Susuga Malietoa Tanumafili II (since 1963)
Prime minister Tofilau Eti Alesana (since 1988)

YEMEN

Presidential republic resulting from the unification of North and South Yemen in May 1990, with a provisional parliament and a transitional cabinet. A general election was scheduled for November 1992, but was postponed until April 22nd 1993 due to tension within the government.

President Gen. Ali Abdullah Saleh (since 1990)
Prime minister Haider Abu Bakr al Attas (since 1990)

YUGOSLAVIA

The civil war since mid-1991 has torn apart the former federation, which consisted of the republics of Bosnia & Hercegovina, Croatia, Macedonia, Montenegro, Serbia (incorporating Vojvodina and Kosovo provinces) and Slovenia. The rump Yugoslavia now consists of Serbia and Montenegro. Despite total chaos in Yugoslavia a Serbian presidential election was held on December 20th 1992. President Slobodan Milosevic took a decisive lead over his election challenger, Federal Prime Minister Milan Panic.

Federal president Dobrica Cosic (replaced Stipe Mesic in Jul)
Montenegro president Momir Bulatovic
Serbia president Slobodan Milosevic

ZAIRE

Presidential republic. The unicameral National Legislative Council (CNL) is elected for a five-year term, all candidates being proposed by the Popular Movement for the Revolution (MPR). Political reforms were announced in April 1990, envisaging the introduction of a multi-party system after a one-year transitional period. Mobutu's term formally expired in December 1991 but a constitutional amendment allowed him to remain in office pending elections.

President Marshal Mobutu Sese Seko (since 1965)
Prime minister Etienne Tshisekedi (replaced Jean Nguza Karl-I-Bond in Aug)

ZAMBIA

Presidential republic. The sole legal political organisation was the United National Independence Party (UNIP) until September 1990 when the party agreed to allow multi-party elections in October 1991. The National Assembly is elected by direct popular vote for a five-year term. The multi-party elections resulted in a victory for Frederick Chiluba and the Movement for Multi-party Democracy.

President Frederick J. T. Chiluba (since 1991)
Vice-president Levy Patrick Mwanawasa (since 1991)

ZIMBABWE

Presidential republic. The Zimbabwe African National Union-Patriotic Front (ZANU-PF) led by Robert Mugabe holds 116 of the 120 elective seats in the 160-member House of Assembly. Presidential and legislative elections were last held in March 1990 and are due in 1996.

President Robert Gabriel Mugabe (since 1987)

PRINCIPAL MINISTERS
Vice-presidents Simon Muzenda; Joshua Nkomo
Senior minister, political affairs Didymus Mutasa
Senior minister, finance, economic Bernard Chidzero
Foreign affairs Nathan Shamuyarira
Defence Richard Hove

Verhältnis: Hauptanschlüsse zu BSP
Ratio of main lines to G.N.P.
Rapport: Lignes principales à P.N.B.
Relación entre líneas principales y PNB

		Kurzzeichen des Landes (ISO-Code) Abbreviation for country (ISO code) Désignation du pays (Code ISO) Abreviatura del país (Código ISO)	Versorgungsfaktor Service factor Taux d'équipement Factor de abastecimiento 1. 1. 1991	Hauptanschlüsse/100 Einwohner Main lines/100 inhabitants Lignes principales/100 habitants Líneas principales/100 habitantes 1. 1. 1991	Bruttosozialprodukt je Einwohner Gross national product per capita Produit national brut par habitant Producto nacional bruto por habitante US $ [1]) 1990
Ägypten		EGY	3,20	3,23	439
Argentinien		ARG	1,17	10,89	3 966
Australien [30. 6.]		AUS	1,10	47,08	17 928
Belgien		BEL	0,83	39,72	20 095
Brasilien		BRA	1,03	6,26	2 595
BR Deutschland		DEU	0,79	40,11	21 305
China, Rep. (Taiwan) [30. 6.]		TWN	1,75	32,54	7 853
Dänemark		DNK	0,94	56,64	25 310
Finnland		FIN	0,80	53,52	27 853
Frankreich		FRA	0,97	48,99	21 086
Griechenland		GRC	2,46	39,25	6 768
Großbritannien [31. 3.]		GBR	1,05	(45,46)	18 147
Hongkong [31. 3.]		HKG	1,34	42,67	13 372
Indonesien		IDN	0,38	(0,52)	594
Israel		ISR	1,31	34,90	11 265
Italien		ITA	0,82	38,76	19 736
Japan [31. 3.]		JPN	0,72	44,79	25 894
Kanada		CAN	1,07	57,68 *)	22 619
Luxemburg		LUX	0,78	49,65	26 619
Marokko		MAR	0,75	1,61	923
Mexiko		MEX	0,87	6,02	2 954
Neuseeland [31. 3.]		NZL	1,54	(48,66)	13 274
Niederlande		NLD	1,05	46,45	18 637
Norwegen		NOR	0,86	50,29	24 392
Österreich		AUT	0,84	41,80	20 871
Pakistan [30. 6.]		PAK	0,91	(0,78)	374
Paraguay		PRY	0,78	2,63	1 453
Peru		PER	0,93	2,53	1 175
Philippinen		PHL	0,69	1,09	683
Polen		POL	1,62	8,64	2 291
Portugal		PRT	1,50	22,60	6 370
Schweden		SWE	1,00	68,33	28 536
Schweiz		CHE	0,71	58,76	34 682
Spanien		ESP	1,03	32,35	13 273
Südafrika [31. 3.]		ZAF	1,33	9,40	3 030
Syrien		SYR	0,56	4,10	3 118
Türkei		TUR	2,49	12,23	2 107
Tschechoslowakei		CSK	2,47	14,91	2 581
UdSSR		SUN	2,29	(11,92)	2 234
Ungarn		HUN	1,12	9,44	3 607
Uruguay		URY	1,75	13,44	3 274
USA		USA	1,02	54,54 *)	22 477

[1]) zu Preisen 1991 und Jahresmittelkurs 1991
at constant prices 1991 and calculated with mid-point exchange rates 1991
fixé aux prix constants de 1991 et évalués au cours moyen annuel de 1991
a precios constantes de 1991 y calculado a la paridad media del año 1991

Internationale Fernmeldestatistik der Siemens AG / ▽ Auswertung mehrerer Quellen durch Siemens, hauptsächlich Geschäftsberichte der Fernmeldeverwaltungen
International Telecom Statistics from Siemens AG / ▽ Evaluation of several sources by Siemens mainly Annual Reports of Telecommunications Administrations

Der Versorgungsfaktor gibt an, um wieviel ein Land eine höhere (> 1) oder eine geringere Versorgung (< 1) mit Hauptanschlüssen besitzt als das mittlere Verhältnis bei zugehörigem BSP/Kopf des Landes.

Die Steilheit der Regressionsgeraden (> 45°) läßt erkennen, daß die Entwicklung der Hauptanschlüsse je 100 Einwohner gegenüber der Entwicklung des Bruttosozialprodukts überproportional zunimmt.

The service factor indicates whether the country's penetration of main lines is higher (> 1) or lower (< 1) than the mean value on the regression line in relation to the country's respective G.N.P. per capita.

The slope of the regression line (> 45°) reveals that the number of main lines per 100 inhabitants is increasing superlinearly relative to the development of the G.N.P.

Le taux d'équipement indique de combien supérieur (> 1) ou inférieur (< 1) est le nombre de lignes principales que possède un pays, par rapport à la moyenne du P.N.B./hab.

La pente de la droite de régression (> 45°) permet de constater que la progression du nombre de lignes principales pour 100 habitants est plus rapide que celle du P.N.B.

El factor de abastecimiento de un país indica si su abastecimiento de líneas principales, referido al respectivo PNB per cápita, es mejor (> 1) o peor (< 1) que la relación media.

La pendiente de la línea de regresión (> 45°) permite reconocer que el número de líneas principales por cada 100 habitantes crece más rápidamente que el producto nacional bruto.

Mittleres Verhältnis
Mean ratio
Rapport moyen
Relación media

Hauptanschlüsse je 100 Einwohner
Main lines per 100 inhabitants
Lignes principales par 100 habitants
Líneas principales por 100 habitantes

Bruttosozialprodukt (BSP) je Einwohner in US $[1]
Gross National Product (G.N.P.) per capita (U.S. $)[1]
Produit national brut (P.N.B.) par habitant en $ A[1]
Producto nacional bruto (PNB) por habitante en $ USA[1]

Stand: 1. Januar 1991
Status: January 1, 1991
Situation au 1er janvier 1991
Estado: 1° de enero de 1991

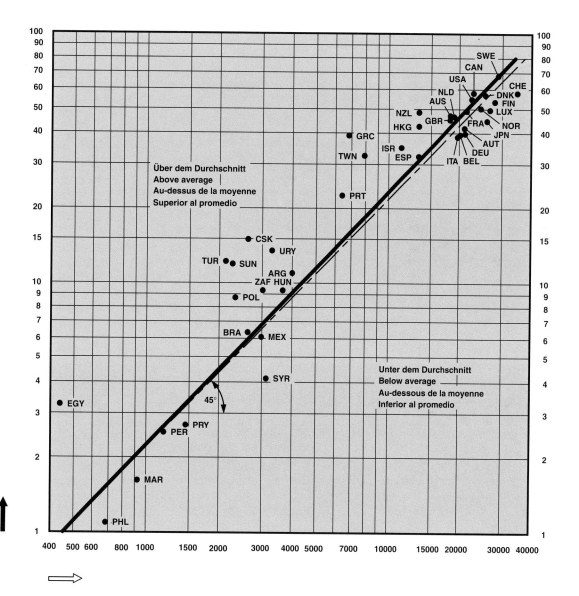

Über dem Durchschnitt
Above average
Au-dessus de la moyenne
Superior al promedio

Unter dem Durchschnitt
Below average
Au-dessous de la moyenne
Inferior al promedio

45°

Statistique internationale des télécommunications de Siemens AG /▽ Exploitation de plusieurs sources par Siemens surtout Rapports de Gestion par les Administrations des Télécommunications

Estadística internacional de telecomunicaciones de Siemens AG /▽ Evaluado por Siemens de varias fuentes, principalmente de las Memorias de las Administraciones de telecomunicación

Investitionen im Fernmeldewesen
Investments in telecommunications
Investissements dans les télécommunications
Inversiones en telecomunicaciones

Quelle:
Source: UIT
Origine: ▽
Fuente:

	US $[3]) 1990 ■	US $[3]) 1989 ■	US $[3]) 1988 ■
Algerien	...	163 948	185 932
Australien[1])	2 345 600	2 280 502	2 093 005
Belgien	836 800	652 900	494 067
Brasilien	2 100 000	2 600 000	2 000 000
BR Deutschland (ohne DDR)	11 936 800	9 470 305	9 617 117
Costa Rica	29 080	19 072	17 132
Dänemark	523 700	504 086	608 429
Ecuador	50 960	60 900	65 130
Finnland	808 600	685 554	611 977
Frankreich	6 073 100	4 827 260	4 881 800
Griechenland	376 350	303 545	239 244
Großbritannien[2])	5 063 700	5 056 818	4 855 957
Hongkong[2])	387 669	343 007	305 804
Indien[2])	1 800 000	1 552 663	1 404 291
Irland[2])	293 920	230 769	201 011
Island	14 370	11 570	12 610
Israel	372 752	338 747	314 012
Italien	8 124 200	7 526 921	5 602 183
Japan[2])	13 704 800	15 081 700	14 798 000
Jugoslawien	296 000	180 616	151 492
Kanada	3 663 400	3 521 800	3 145 500
Kolumbien	208 640	...	386 970
Korea, Rep.	2 964 300	3 010 966	1 793 199
Luxemburg	53 960	44 965	36 831
Malaysia	246 840	144 791	168 786
Mexiko	1 490 600	941 910	657 697
Neuseeland[2])	446 419	458 900	385 100
Niederlande	1 487 200	1 427 894	983 995
Norwegen	439 500	539 347	670 364
Österreich	1 158 300	877 406	897 351
Portugal	714 700	495 785	434 818
Schweden	1 288 700	1 204 104	1 139 657
Schweiz	2 151 200	1 557 855	1 636 516
Singapur[2])	257 520	114 448	97 220
Spanien	6 916 100	4 947 303	3 065 322
Südafrika[2])	...	512 220	559 502
Syrien	17 350	12 495	11 299
Thailand[4])	380 800	314 670	240 640
Tschechoslowakei	129 100	216 033	211 068
Türkei	801 100	400 808	631 493
Tunesien	58 670	...	23 896
Ungarn	222 850	223 395	232 799
USA	24 518 000	24 294 300	26 124 500
Vereinigte Arab. Emirate	140 630	165 221	103 561
Zimbabwe[1])	30 790	34 100	23 380

■ in Tausend
  in thousands   [1]) [1. 7. 1990 – 30. 6. 1991]   [3]) converted with mid-point exchange rates: 1 US-$ ≙ 1,61 DM (1990)
  en milliers   [2]) [1. 4. 1990 – 31. 3. 1991]   ≙ 1,87 DM (1989)
  en miles   [4]) [1. 10. 1989 – 30. 9. 1990]   ≙ 1,76 DM (1988)

Internationale Fernmeldestatistik der Siemens AG /▽ Auswertung mehrerer Quellen durch Siemens, hauptsächlich Geschäftsberichte der Fernmeldeverwaltungen
International Telecom Statistics from Siemens AG /▽ Evaluation of several sources by Siemens mainly Annual Reports of Telecommunications Administrations

Investitionen der Fernmeldeverwaltungen im Fernmeldewesen pro Jahr (einschließlich Gebäude und Grundstücke) als Anteil vom BIP (nominal in Landeswährung)
Total annual gross investments in telecommunications by Telecommunications Administrations (including land and buildings) as a share of GDP (at factor costs in national currency)
Total des investissements annuels brut par les Administrations des Télécommunications dans les télécommunications (terrains et bâtiments inclus) comme part du produit interieur brut (au coût des facteurs, en monnaie nationale)
Inversiones anuales brutas de las Administraciones de Telecomunicación en telecomunicaciones (incluidos terrenos y edificios) como parte del producto interior bruto (al coste de los factores, en moneda nacional)

	Durchschnitt / Average / Moyenne / Medio 1988 – 1990 ‰		Durchschnitt / Average / Moyenne / Medio 1988 – 1990 ‰
Algerien	3,5	Korea, Rep.	12,7
Australien [1]	8,1	Spanien	12,2
Belgien	3,9	Portugal	11,5
Brasilien	5,2	Neuseeland [2]	10,2
BR Deutschland (ohne DDR)	8,0	Schweiz	9,0
Costa Rica	4,3	Australien [1]	8,1
Dänemark	4,8	BR Deutschland (ohne DDR)	8,0
Ecuador	5,3	Israel	7,8
Finnland	5,9	Ungarn	7,8
Frankreich	5,6	Italien	7,6
Griechenland	5,3	Österreich	7,1
Großbritannien [2]	5,7	Türkei	7,1
Hongkong [2]	5,6	Kolumbien	6,9
Indien [2]	5,8	Irland [2]	6,7
Irland [2]	6,7	Kanada	6,4
Island	2,3	Südafrika [2]	6,3
Israel	7,8	Schweden	6,1
Italien	7,6	Finnland	5,9
Japan [2]	5,1	Malaysia	5,9
Jugoslawien	2,7	Indien [2]	5,8
Kanada	6,4	Norwegen	5,8
Kolumbien	6,9	Großbritannien [2]	5,7
Korea, Rep.	12,7	Frankreich	5,6
Luxemburg	5,5	Hongkong [2]	5,6
Malaysia	5,9	Luxemburg	5,5
Mexiko	5,3	Niederlande	5,4
Neuseeland [2]	10,2	Ecuador	5,3
Niederlande	5,4	Griechenland	5,3
Norwegen	5,8	Mexiko	5,3
Österreich	7,1	Zimbabwe [1]	5,3
Portugal	11,5	Brasilien	5,2
Schweden	6,1	Singapur [2]	5,2
Schweiz	9,0	Japan [2]	5,1
Singapur [2]	5,2	Dänemark	4,8
Spanien	12,2	USA	4,8
Südafrika [2]	6,3	Vereinigte Arab. Emirate	4,8
Syrien	0,8	Tunesien	4,6
Thailand [4]	4,5	Thailand [3]	4,5
Tschechoslowakei	3,8	Costa Rica	4,3
Türkei	7,1	Belgien	3,9
Tunesien	4,6	Tschechoslowakei	3,8
Ungarn	7,8	Algerien	3,5
USA	4,8	Jugoslawien	2,7
Vereinigte Arab. Emirate	4,8	Island	2,3
Zimbabwe [1]	5,3	Syrien	0,8

[1] [1. 7. 1988 – 30. 6. 1991]
[2] [1. 4. 1988 – 31. 3. 1991]
[4] [1. 10. 1987 – 30. 9. 1990]

Statistique internationale des télécommunications de Siemens AG / ▽ Exploitation de plusieurs sources par Siemens surtout Rapports de Gestion par les Administrations des Télécommunications
Estadística internacional de telecomunicaciones de Siemens AG / ▽ Evaluado por Siemens de varias fuentes, principalmente de las Memorias de las Administraciones de telecomunicación

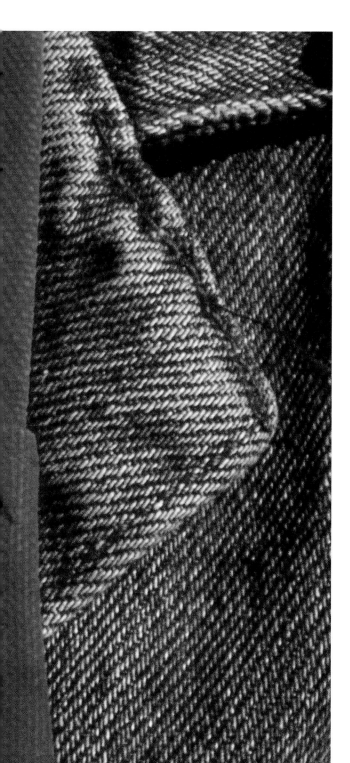

ECONOMIC AND FINANCIAL INDICATORS

Population and income

POPULATION GROWTH World population more than doubled between 1950 and 1990, up from 2.5 billion to 5.3 billion. The total will continue to rise but at a slower rate, reckons the United Nations, which forecasts a world population of 11.5 billion in 2150. Europeans have become relatively scarce: more than 15% of people were European in 1950, but only 9.4% of them were in 1990. If the UN's forecast is accurate, Europeans will be rarer still in 2150, accounting for just 3.7% of the total. The proportion of North Americans is forecast to fall, too, from 5.2% in 1990 to 2.7% in 2150. Africa's population is growing fastest, up from 8.8% of the total in 1950 to 12.1% in 1990. By 2150, says the UN, one person in four will be African.

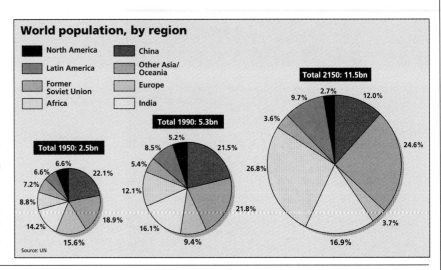

World population, by region

North America · China · Latin America · Other Asia/Oceania · Former Soviet Union · Europe · Africa · India

Total 1950: 2.5bn — 22.1%, 6.6%, 6.6%, 7.2%, 8.8%, 14.2%, 15.6%, 18.9%

Total 1990: 5.3bn — 5.2%, 21.5%, 8.5%, 5.4%, 12.1%, 21.8%, 16.1%, 9.4%

Total 2150: 11.5bn — 2.7%, 12.0%, 9.7%, 3.6%, 24.6%, 26.8%, 3.7%, 16.9%

Source: UN

Population and GDP

Looking at the full list of OECD members, the only country whose population declined between 1981 and 1991 was Belgium. Turkey had the fastest population growth; over the same period it rose by 26%. In 1991 Holland had the highest population density, with 367 more people per square kilometre than Australia or Iceland. United Nations' figures indicate a steadily ageing population: in 17 of the 24 OECD countries the average age will be more than 40 by 2015. By that date Germany is predicted to have the most mature population, averaging 46 years. This is 16 years more than Turkey, the only country with

	Australia	Austria	Belgium	Canada	Denmark	Finland	France	Germany*	Greece	Holland	Iceland	Ireland
Population, 000s												
1981	14,923	7,565	9,853	24,366	5,122	4,800	54,182	78,360	9,730	14,247	231	3,443
1991	17,336	7,823	9,840	27,023	5,154	5,008	57,050	79,819	10,269	15,065	260	3,520
Population density per sq km												
1991	2	93	323	3	119	15	104	224	78	369	2	49
Median age, years												
1995	33.4	37.2	38.0	35.4	38.2	37.8	36.0	38.9	37.3	36.1	31.4	28.6
2005	36.2	40.9	41.2	39.1	41.2	40.6	38.6	42.4	39.5	39.5	35.0	31.3
2015	38.4	44.3	43.7	41.2	44.6	42.4	40.9	45.9	41.9	42.7	38.0	34.2
Life expectancy, men/women, years												
1990-95	73.7/80.2	71.6/78.6	72.4/78.9	74.0/80.7	73.3/79.1	72.1/79.6	72.9/80.8	72.4/78.5	74.3/78.7	74.3/80.8	75.3/81.0	72.5/77.9
2000-05	75.2/81.2	73.5/80.1	74.1/80.3	75.5/81.7	75.0/80.5	73.8/80.7	74.5/81.8	74.0/80.0	75.6/80.2	75.7/81.8	76.4/81.9	74.1/79.5
2010-15	76.2/82.2	75.1/81.1	75.5/81.3	76.4/82.7	76.0/81.5	75.2/81.8	75.8/82.8	75.4/81.2	76.6/81.2	76.6/82.7	77.3/82.9	75.5/80.7
GDP, $bn												
1981	172.1	66.3	96.4	294.8	57.3	50.6	582.3	681.8	37.0	141.4	3.4	18.3
1991	291.8	163.9	197.1	587.2	130.1	126.1	1,198.7	1,562.2	69.6	286.6	6.3	43.5
GDP per head, at current prices, $												
1981	11,530	8,760	9,780	12,100	11,190	10,540	10,750	11,060	3,800	9,920	14,590	5,320
1991	16,830	20,950	20,030	21,730	25,240	25,180	21,010	24,360	6,780	19,020	24,230	12,360
GDP per head, at purchasing-power parities, United States = 100												
1981	77	76	75	91	76	71	82	85	37	77	81	44
1991	73	80	79	88	79	73	83	87	35	76	76	52

*Population–united Germany; GDP–western Germany

LONG-TERM GROWTH The chart, based on the figures calculated by Angus Maddison, an economic historian, tracks the relative ranking of countries' GDP per head over time. In 1870 Britain was the world's richest country, with purchasing power per head more than twice that of Germany. By early this century it had been overtaken by America, and more recently it has been passed by all the other big industrial economics. Another country to slip behind is Argentina. Indeed, at its peak in the late 1920s it was one of the richest countries in the world. Today it is somewhere around 70th. By contrast, Japan, which was little richer than India in 1870, has soared in the rankings in the past 40 years.

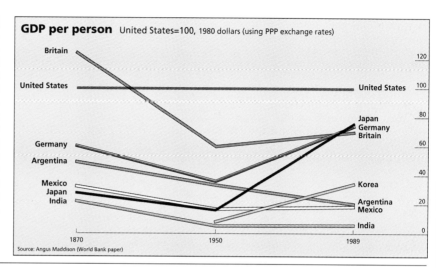

GDP per person United States=100, 1980 dollars (using PPP exchange rates)

Source: Angus Maddison (World Bank paper)

an average life expectancy below 70 in 1995.

The United States has the largest gross domestic product, two-thirds bigger than Japan's. The countries with the fastest growing dollar values in the ten years to 1991 were Japan, Spain, Italy and Portugal, (whose GDPs almost trebled). Switzerland had the highest income per head with $33,220. When comparing living standards between countries, however, it is better to use purchasing-power parities than current exchange rates; the most notable changes in the league table of GDP per head since 1981 were Japan (up from 16th to 5th), Luxembourg (up from 7th to 3rd) and Belgium (up from 13th to 9th). The poorest OECD countries in 1991, as in 1981, were Portugal, Greece and Turkey.

	Italy	Japan	Luxembourg	New Zealand	Norway	Portugal	Spain	Sweden	Switzerland	Turkey	United Kingdom	United States
Population, 000s												
1981	56,503	117,650	365	3,157	4,100	9,358	37,751	8,324	6,429	45,864	56,379	230,138
1991	57,783	123,920	375	3,396	4,262	10,580	39,025	8,617	6,860	57,700	57,370	252,688
Population density per sq km												
1991	193	328	145	13	13	114	78	19	166	74	235	27
Median age, years												
1995	37.8	38.8	38.3	32.4	36.6	34.0	34.7	39.4	38.9	23.6	36.1	34.8
2005	41.0	40.6	41.9	35.5	38.8	36.9	37.9	40.8	41.8	26.6	38.9	37.9
2015	44.8	43.3	44.8	38.4	41.8	39.8	41.1	42.8	44.8	29.8	41.2	39.6
Life expectancy, men/women, years												
1990-95	73.2/79.6	75.9/81.7	72.0/78.5	72.7/78.6	74.3/80.7	71.1/77.7	74.4/80.3	75.0/80.7	74.6/80.9	64.5/68.1	73.3/78.9	72.8/79.9
2000-05	74.8/80.8	76.8/82.6	73.8/80.1	74.3/80.2	75.6/81.8	73.0/79.4	75.6/81.3	76.0/81.7	75.7/81.8	68.0/71.9	74.8/80.4	74.5/80.9
2010-15	75.9/81.8	77.8/83.4	75.2/81.1	75.6/81.1	76.6/82.7	74.5/80.6	76.6/82.3	77.0/82.6	76.7/82.7	70.4/74.6	76.0/81.4	75.7/82.0
GDP, $bn												
1981	408.2	1,169.7	3.8	24.1	57.1	24.4	186.1	114.3	94.1	57.7	510.8	3,007.2
1991	1,146.1	3,363.3	8.9	42.2	105.6	68.4	527.7	237.2	227.9	107.3	1,012.8	5,549.3
GDP per head, at current prices, $												
1981	7,220	9,940	10,470	7,630	13,930	2,610	4,930	13,730	14,640	1,260	9,060	13,070
1991	19,830	27,140	23,730	12,430	24,780	6,470	13,520	27,530	33,220	1,890	17,650	21,960
GDP per head, at purchasing-power parities, United States = 100												
1981	74	71	80	69	73	38	51	80	102	14	68	100
1991	77	87	93	62	77	41	57	79	98	15	74	100

Economic and business forecasts

ECONOMIC FORECASTS Each month *The Economist* polls a group of forecasters, then calculates the average of their predictions for growth, inflation and the current-account balance in the 13 biggest industrial economies. The previous month's figure, where changed, is shown in brackets. The last two columns rank countries' overall performance for the current year and the next (1 is best, 13 is worst). This is derived from the sum of the individual rankings of the three measures. In January 1992 our seers trimmed their forecasts for GDP growth in ten of the 13 countries in the table. The biggest revision was in Britain: December 1991's forecast of 2.1% growth in 1992 was cut to 1.6%. Japan was expected to rank first in 1992, just as it had in 1991; Italy and Sweden were expected to be last.

The Economist poll of forecasters, January averages (previous month's, if changed)

	Real GDP % change		Consumer prices % increase		Current account as % of GDP		The Economist's ranking*	
	1991	1992	1991	1992	1991	1992	1991	1992
Australia	-1.3 (-1.0)	2.6 (2.8)	3.3 (3.4)	3.6 (3.8)	-3.7 (-3.6)	-3.8 (-3.7)	9= (9)	7 (7=)
Belgium	1.7	2.0	3.2 (3.3)	3.0 (3.1)	2.0 (2.1)	2.1 (2.2)	2	2
Canada	-1.0	2.5 (2.7)	5.7 (5.8)	2.8 (3.1)	-3.1 (-3.0)	-2.7 (-2.8)	11=	4 (4=)
France	1.3	1.8 (1.9)	3.1	2.9	-0.6	-0.5 (-0.6)	4	3
Germany†	3.1 (3.3)	1.6 (1.8)	3.5 (3.6)	3.8	-1.2 (-1.0)	-0.5 (-0.4)	5	8 (7=)
Holland	2.1	1.7	3.6 (3.7)	3.8	3.7 (3.6)	3.7 (3.6)	3	5= (6)
Italy	1.1	1.6 (1.9)	6.4	5.8 (5.7)	-1.4	-1.5 (-1.4)	9= (10)	12=(12)
Japan	4.3	2.6 (2.8)	3.3 (3.2)	2.3 (2.2)	2.0 (1.9)	1.8 (2.0)	1	1
Spain	2.5 (2.6)	2.9	6.0	6.0	-3.2	-3.1	8	10
Sweden	-1.2 (-1.1)	0.3 (0.5)	9.4 (9.3)	3.7 (3.9)	-1.9 (-1.8)	-1.8 (-1.6)	13	12=(13)
Switzerland	-0.3 (-0.1)	1.0 (1.3)	5.9	4.4	4.0 (4.2)	4.0 (4.1)	6	9 (10)
UK	-2.2 (-2.1)	1.6 (2.1)	5.9 (5.8)	4.1	-1.1 (-1.2)	-1.4 (-1.3)	11=	11 (9)
USA	-0.7 (-0.5)	1.8 (2.0)	4.2	3.3 (3.5)	-0.3 (-0.4)	-0.9 (-1.0)	7	5=(4=)

Source: BZW, EIU, Goldman Sachs, Hoare Govett, James Capel, Kreditbank, Lehman Brothers, Long-term Credit Bank, Merrill Lynch, JP Morgan, Morgan Stanley, Nomura, Nordbanken, Paribas, Royal Bank of Canada, Salomon Brothers, Scotiabank, UBS Philips & Drew, S.G. Wa
*Based on sum of rankings for the three measures.

ECONOMIC FORECASTS As 1992 wore on *The Economist*'s group of forecasters grew more pessimistic. By December they had trimmed their estimates for GDP growth in 1992 in all but two of the 13 countries in the table. In January they expected Japan's GDP to grow by 2.6%; by December that had been cut to 1.7%. Britain's GDP, for which they had forecast growth of 1.6% in January, was by December expected to decline by 0.8%. The exceptions to the gloom were America and France; by December 1992 growth for both countries was estimated at 1.9%, up a little from January's 1.8% forecast. In France, Germany, Holland, Italy and Spain our seers expect 1993 to be even more miserable than 1992. Overall, Spain is set to be 1993's worst performer.

The Economist poll of forecasters, December averages (previous month's, if changed)

	Real GDP % change		Consumer prices % increase		Current account as % of GDP		The Economist's ranking*	
	1992	1993	1992	1993	1992	1993	1992	1993
Australia	1.9 (2.1)	3.3 (3.4)	1.4 (1.3)	2.8	-3.4 (-3.5)	-3.7 (-3.9)	3 (2=)	6 (7=)
Belgium	1.4 (1.5)	1.5 (1.7)	2.5 (2.6)	2.5	2.4 (2.5)	2.4 (2.5)	6 (4)	2
Canada	1.3	2.6 (2.8)	1.6 (1.7)	2.1 (2.3)	-4.2 (-4.0)	-3.7 (-3.5)	7=	4=(3=)
France	1.9 (1.8)	1.2 (1.3)	2.9	2.4 (2.6)	0.1	nil (-0.1)	2 (2=)	3 (3=)
Germany†	1.1	0.3 (0.6)	4.0 (3.9)	3.5 (3.3)	-1.1	-0.9 (-0.8)	10	10=(11)
Holland	1.5 (1.4)	1.2 (1.3)	3.7 (3.6)	3.0 (3.1)	3.4	3.3 (3.4)	5 (5=)	4= (5)
Italy	1.2	0.4 (0.7)	5.4	5.6	-2.1	-2.0 (-2.1)	13	12
Japan	1.7 (1.8)	2.2 (2.4)	1.9	1.6 (1.7)	3.1 (3.0)	3.2 (3.1)	1	1
Spain	1.5	0.6	6.0 (6.3)	5.6 (5.8)	-3.7 (-3.5)	-3.7 (-3.6)	11	13
Sweden	-1.5 (-1.3)	-1.0	2.4	3.4 (2.7)	-0.9 (-0.8)	-0.4 (-0.3)	7=	10= (9)
Switzerland	-0.1 (0.2)	0.9 (1.2)	4.1 (4.0)	3.1 (3.2)	4.4 (4.3)	4.3 (4.2)	7=	7= (6)
UK	-0.8 (-0.9)	1.0 (1.2)	3.8 (3.7)	2.7 (2.9)	-1.9	-1.9 (-2.2)	12	9 (10)
USA	1.9 (1.7)	2.4 (2.3)	3.0	3.0	-0.9 (-0.8)	-1.1 (-0.9)	4 (5=)	7=

Source: BZW, EIU, Goldman Sachs, Hoare Govett, James Capel, Kreditbank, Lehman Brothers, Long-term Credit Bank, Merrill Lynch, JP Morgan, Morgan Stanley, Nomura, Nordbanken, Paribas, Royal Bank of Canada, Salomon Brothers, Scotiabank, UBS Phillips & Drew, S.G. Warburg, Williams de Broe.
* Based on sum of rankings for the three measures.   † Current-account figures now on all-German basis; others western Germany only.

BUSINESS CONFIDENCE Businessmen were feeling less confident than three months earlier in 11 of the 15 countries covered by Dun & Bradstreet's November 1992 survey of sales expectations. Comparing optimists and pessimists, a net 54% of American businessmen expected sales to rise in the fourth quarter of this year, down from 61% in the third quarter. In Japan pessimists outweighed optimists by 8%, but the Swiss were even gloomier, with a net 14% expecting lower sales. Britain has suffered the biggest slump in confidence: a net balance of only 2% of businessmen expected higher sales, down from 30% in the third quarter—the gloomiest response for 15 months. Only businessmen in Australia, Brazil, Canada and Mexico felt cheerier than in the previous quarter.

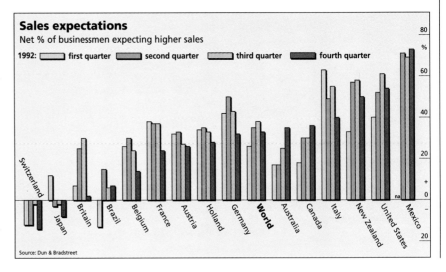

Sales expectations
Net % of businessmen expecting higher sales
1992: ☐ first quarter ☐ second quarter ☐ third quarter ■ fourth quarter

Switzerland, Japan, Britain, Brazil, Belgium, France, Austria, Holland, Germany, **World**, Australia, Canada, Italy, New Zealand, United States, Mexico

Source: Dun & Bradstreet

ASIAN ECONOMIES Despite the world recession, South-East Asian economies thrived in 1991. Nearly all enjoyed GDP growth of at least 4%; South Korea and Malaysia grew by more than 8%. The prospects for 1992 depended partly upon the impact of recovery in America on South-East Asia's exports, relative to the impact of slowdowns in Japan and Europe. The American market has become less important: its share of the region's exports slid from a third in 1985 to a fifth in 1991. Most of the countries export more to Japan and Europe combined than to America, and so were exposed to recessions there. American Express Bank forecast slower growth for most of the region in 1992, but still expected it to average 6%.

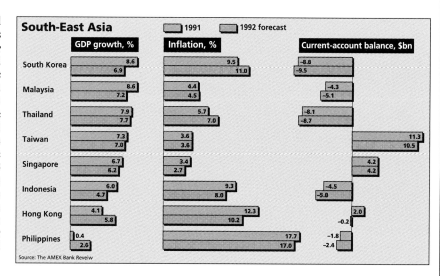

LATIN AMERICAN ECONOMIES The 1980s were a "lost decade" for Latin America but, thanks to economic reforms, the 1990s promise faster growth. The Economist Intelligence Unit (EIU), part of The Economist Group, forecast that Mexico's GDP would grow by an annual average of 4.2% in 1991-96, compared with 1.6% in the previous six years. Argentina's recovery could prove even more spectacular, with an average growth of 4.7% a year compared with an annual decline in output of 0.6% in 1985-90. The main exception is Brazil, where growth was expected to slow in the 1990s to 1.3% a year from 2.9% a year in 1985-90. Brazil's consumer prices have been rising at an annual rate of almost 1,000%, and even by 1996 the EIU expects inflation to be close to 300%.

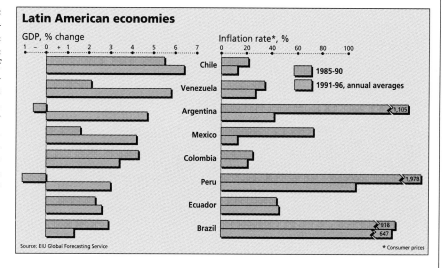

THIRD-WORLD DEBT Many poorer nations' finances look healthier than they have done for years, partly due to debt-reduction deals. Debt-service ratios—interest and debt repayments during the year as a proportion of exports—have plunged. The aggregate debt-service ratio has fallen from 22% in 1986 to 14% in 1991, and was expected to be 13% in 1993. The debt-service ratio for the 15 most indebted countries fell by even more, to 31% in 1991 from 45% in 1986. Against this trend, Sub-Saharan Africa's ratios were virtually unchanged in 1991. Total developing-country debt (excluding Eastern Europe and the former Soviet Union) rose by 4.9% in 1991; official debt's share of total debt fell in 1991, the first time since 1981, to 42%.

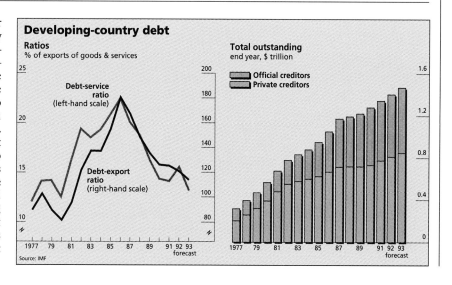

Economic growth

ECONOMIC GROWTH Industrial output will rise more slowly in 1993 than it did in 1992 in 14 of the 24 OECD countries, according to forecasts published in the *Economic Outlook* at the end of 1992. Growth is expected to slow in 1992's five-fastest growing economies. Turkey's growth rate—at 5.3%, the highest in 1992—is expected to fall to 4.5% in 1993. The two biggest industrial economies, America and Japan, buck the trend; both are expected to grow more quickly in 1993. Germany's output is expected to rise by 1.3% in 1993, compared with 1.4% in 1992. This hides sharp differences between the two old Germanies: west German output is expected to rise by a tiny 0.7%; eastern Germany's is expected to rise by 5%.

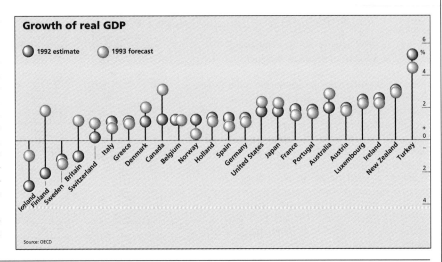

Growth of real GDP

1992 estimate   1993 forecast

Iceland, Finland, Sweden, Britain, Switzerland, Italy, Greece, Denmark, Canada, Belgium, Norway, Holland, Spain, Germany, United States, Japan, France, Portugal, Australia, Austria, Luxembourg, Ireland, New Zealand, Turkey

Source: OECD

Real GDP

Gross domestic product (GDP) is the total value of a country's output of goods and services. Gross national product (GNP), a measure used until recently by many larger economies, also includes net factor income from abroad such as profits and investment income. The United States switched to the GDP measure in 1991, and Japan and Germany started to focus more on GDP in 1992. The figures in the table for all three countries now show GDP. Growth rates are measured at constant prices to exclude the effects of inflation. The OECD's estimates and forecasts for Germany include the former East Germany.

% change on a year earlier

		Australia	Belgium*	Canada	France	Germany†	Holland	Italy	Japan	Spain	Sweden	Switzerland	United Kingdom	United States
1991	1st qtr	-1.2	na	-3.6	nil	4.7	1.9	1.2	5.4	2.7	-1.1	0.4	-2.4	-1.9
	2nd qtr	-1.9	na	-1.9	0.5	4.8	3.0	1.8	3.4	2.5	-2.5	-0.5	-3.5	-1.7
	3rd qtr	-1.3	na	-1.2	1.2	2.5	2.4	1.1	3.1	2.5	-1.7	-0.8	-2.2	-1.0
	4th qtr	-0.3	na	nil	1.7	1.5	1.7	1.7	2.6	2.7	-2.0	-0.9	-1.6	0.1
1992	1st qtr	0.4	na	1.7	2.8	2.2	3.2	1.8	2.7	2.3	-2.2	-0.6	-1.3	1.6
	2nd qtr	1.5	na	0.5	2.4	1.1	1.0	1.5	1.7	1.6	-0.7	-0.4	-0.7	1.6
	3rd qtr	2.4	na	0.7	1.6	0.9	1.3		0.9		0.1	-0.6	-0.7	2.1
	4th qtr	–	na	–	–	–	–	–	–	–	–	–	–	–

OECD estimates and forecasts, December 1992 % change on previous period at annual rate

		Australia	Belgium*	Canada	France	Germany†	Holland	Italy	Japan	Spain	Sweden	Switzerland	United Kingdom	United States
1992		2.0	1.3	1.3	1.9	1.4	1.4	1.2	1.8	1.4	-1.2	0.2	-1.0	1.8
	1st half			0.8	2.1	2.9		1.8	1.9				-1.9	2.0
	2nd half			2.1	0.6	-0.9		-0.4	1.5				-0.1	2.2
1993		2.9	1.3	3.2	1.6	1.2	1.2	0.8	2.3	0.9	-1.4	1.1	1.3	2.4
	1st half			3.3	1.6	1.6		1.0	2.5				1.5	2.3
	2nd half			4.0	2.4	2.5		1.5	2.9				2.1	2.7
1994		3.4	2.2	4.2	2.8	2.9	2.4	1.7	3.1	2.3	1.3	1.8	2.4	3.1
	1st half			4.2	2.9	2.9		1.5	2.9				2.3	3.1
	2nd half			4.3	3.1	3.2		2.2	3.7				2.7	3.5

Nominal GDP

		Australia	Belgium*	Canada	France	Germany†	Holland	Italy	Japan	Spain	Sweden	Switzerland	United Kingdom	United States
1992		3.5	4.0	2.3	5.2	6.9	4.5	5.7	3.7	8.4	-0.1	3.2	4.3	4.6
	1st half			1.3	5.6	8.1		4.5	4.1				3.6	4.9
	2nd half			4.1	3.9	4.4		5.1	3.2				3.8	4.5
1993		5.1	4.0	5.4	4.1	5.8	3.6	6.1	4.0	7.2	-0.6	4.3	6.3	4.7
	1st half			5.6	4.0	6.4		6.4	4.1				7.3	4.7
	2nd half			6.2	4.7	5.9		6.6	4.6				6.9	4.9
1994		5.7	4.9	6.3	5.0	6.3	4.6	7.0	4.8	7.5	2.8	4.5	6.6	5.0
	1st half			6.4	5.0	6.4		7.0	4.6				6.4	5.0
	2nd half			6.5	5.2	6.4		7.3	5.4				6.5	5.2

*Annual rates only. 1991 GNP 1.6% †Quarterly figures: Western Germany; OECD estimates and forecasts: pan–Germany.

Industrial output

INDUSTRIAL OUTPUT Americans are still obsessed with recession, yet the United States is the only country of the five in the chart where industrial production has risen substantially during 1992. Output in November was 1.5% higher than a year earlier. Japanese production has plummeted, falling by over 9% from its peak in the first quarter of 1991. Even so, since 1986 only western Germany's output—up by 20%—has grown by more than Japan's (up by 18.5%). British industrial production, which grew rapidly during the mid-1980s, has tumbled by 9% from its peak in the second quarter of 1990. In August it was a miserable 3.5% higher than in the first quarter of 1986, by far the worst performance of the five countries.

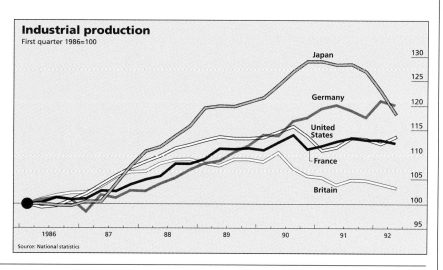

Industrial production
First quarter 1986=100

Source: National statistics

Industrial production

Industrial production indices measure movements in the output of the production industries. These generally include manufacturing, energy and utilities and, in some countries, construction. Output is measured in constant prices to give an indication of volume movements and so the effects of inflation are excluded. Industrial production accounts for as much as 30% of the United States's gross domestic product and 40% of Japan's. The 12-month percentage changes in our table are based on statistics from national sources, so definitions vary. Switzerland's indices are calculated quarterly.

% change on a year earlier

		Australia	Belgium	Canada	France	Germany*	Holland	Italy	Japan	Spain	Sweden	Switzerland	United Kingdom	United States
1991	Jan	-1.9	3.4	-5.6	1.5	5.6	4.8	-0.3	7.0	-1.6	-6.2		-3.1	-0.8
	Feb	-1.9	2.8	-7.0	2.3	3.7	18.9	-2.6	7.0	0.3	-6.7		-2.1	-2.6
	Mar	1.3	1.1	-7.1	-1.3	4.4	2.5	-3.3	4.3	-10.5	-5.3	-1.6	-3.3	-3.1
	Apr	-2.5	1.0	-6.1	nil	7.1	1.8	-3.6	4.6	6.8	-8.3		-6.9	-3.0
	May	-2.5	0.5	-5.4	0.6	3.8	8.4	-2.4	4.2	-2.7	-9.4		-5.9	-2.7
	Jun	-2.8	-0.3	-4.7	0.6	6.6	4.7	-0.4	1.0	-3.9	-8.6	0.9	-5.2	-2.5
	Jul	-6.0	-0.2	-4.5	-0.7	3.2	2.4	-2.3	2.1	0.4	0.9		-2.2	-2.1
	Aug	-0.8	-0.5	-3.4	-0.7	1.2	1.6	-6.6	0.2	-1.6	-9.5		-2.7	-2.3
	Sep	0.2	-1.4	-0.9	-0.1	0.8	-5.8	-2.2	1.3	1.3	-11.5	1.7	-2.0	-2.0
	Oct	-1.9	-1.9	-1.6	0.4	0.7	3.5	-1.5	-1.8	5.2	-12.7		-1.5	-1.4
	Nov	nil	-1.9	-0.2	1.4	1.6	4.6	1.1	-1.2	-1.7	-10.5		-0.3	-0.2
	Dec	-0.6	-2.0	-1.3	2.8	-1.6	-0.1	-1.7	-2.2	0.1	-12.1	3.4	-0.1	0.2
1992	Jan	1.6	-1.8	-0.5	0.1	0.2	3.6	-1.4	-3.6	-4.2	-7.3		-1.2	nil
	Feb	-0.6	-1.3	1.5	0.4	3.4	-5.0	0.3	-4.6	2.1	-6.5		-0.9	1.4
	Mar	-1.7	-0.8	1.4	2.7	0.2	6.4	0.3	-5.6	16.3	-9.2	-0.8	-1.8	2.0
	Apr	4.7	-0.6	1.2	1.2	-0.2	4.9	0.5	-6.0	-24.6	-3.7		1.3	2.5
	May	2.7	-0.3	-0.3	-0.5	0.3	-1.9	1.1	-8.9	-4.1	-1.6		0.3	2.3
	Jun	-0.2	-0.3	-0.6	-0.4	-3.9	-1.3	-2.6	-3.8	1.0	-7.3	-0.8	-2.5	1.1
	Jul	1.4	-0.3	-1.1	-1.1	-2.6	1.1	0.2	-6.1	-1.4	-7.1		-1.5	1.2
	Aug	1.9	0.3	1.0	-1.1	-0.8	-1.7	-0.3	-8.1	-5.8	-2.0		nil	1.0
	Sep	0.4	–	0.3	nil	-1.3	1.9	-3.5	-4.1	-0.6	-4.7	–	-0.1	0.4
	Oct	2.1	–	–	0.2	-3.6	–	–	-6.4	–	–		0.5	0.8
	Nov	–	–	–	–	–	–	–	–	–	–	–	–	1.5
	Dec	–	–	–	–	–	–	–	–	–	–	–	–	–

*Western Germany: consolidated figures for Germany not yet available.

Unemployment rates

Unemployment rates for most of the countries in our table rose in 1992 as the world economy continued to slow. The exception was Holland, the only country where unemployment consistently fell, until August's rise, and France, Italy and Japan, where rates stayed fairly constant throughout the year, albeit at very different levels. Japan's unemployment rate of 2.2% in October 1992 is the lowest in our table while Italy's rate of 10.6% in the same month is one of the highest. Spain started the year with the highest unemployment rate of the countries in the table. It slipped slightly mid-year but by October was back up to 15.0%. Sweden was an uncharacteristically poor performer in 1992 as its unemployment rate has leapt from 4.1% in January to 5.4% in November. The rates quoted in our table are those reported nationally, so definitions vary. Eurostat, the EC's statistical agency, and the OECD produce standardised series.

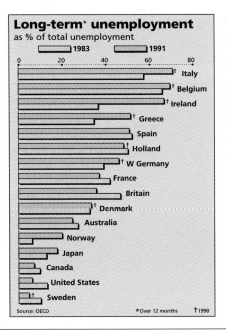

Long-term* unemployment
as % of total unemployment

Source: OECD   *Over 12 months   †1990

CHRONIC JOBLESSNESS Half of the 16 countries in the chart have seen a rise in the number of their long-term unemployed, expressed as a proportion of total unemployment, since 1983. Ireland saw the biggest increase, with 67% of its unemployed out of work for more than 12 months in 1991, up from 37% in 1983. That still leaves it behind Belgium (70%) and Italy (71%). Belgium's rate is little changed from 66% in 1983 while Italy's rate was 58% in 1983. In 1991, as in 1983, long-term unemployment in every European country except Sweden and Norway accounted for over one-third of total unemployment. In the United States, by contrast, the proportion was only 6.3%, down from 13.3% in 1983. Britain has seen the sharpest decline, from 47% of the total in 1983 to 36% in 1991. Although small in comparison with most countries, Japan's rate of 18% in 1991 is a marked increase on the 1983 total of 13%.

Unemployment

% of labour force

		Australia	Belgium	Canada	France	Germany*	Holland	Italy	Japan	Spain	Sweden	Switzerland	United Kingdom	United States
1991	Jan	8.7	7.4	9.9	9.1	6.3	4.8	10.1	2.0	15.3	2.3	0.9	6.7	6.2
	Feb	9.1	7.5	10.2	9.2	6.3	4.9	10.1	2.0	15.3	2.3	1.0	7.0	6.5
	Mar	9.7	7.4	10.5	9.2	6.3	4.9	10.0	2.1	15.3	2.2	1.0	7.4	6.8
	Apr	9.4	7.4	10.2	9.3	6.2	4.6	10.1	2.1	15.2	2.1	1.1	7.7	6.6
	May	9.4	7.4	10.2	9.5	6.3	4.6	9.9	2.1	15.2	2.1	1.1	7.9	6.8
	Jun	9.4	7.5	10.5	9.6	6.3	4.4	10.0	2.1	15.1	2.2	1.1	8.1	7.0
	Jul	9.8	7.5	10.4	9.7	6.3	4.2	10.3	2.2	15.0	2.8	1.2	8.4	6.8
	Aug	9.8	7.6	10.5	9.7	6.3	4.3	10.0	2.2	15.0	3.1	1.3	8.6	6.8
	Sep	10.2	7.6	10.2	9.8	6.3	4.3	10.3	2.1	14.9	3.1	1.3	8.7	6.8
	Oct	10.2	7.7	10.3	9.9	6.3	4.4	10.3	2.0	15.3	3.1	1.5	8.8	6.9
	Nov	10.5	7.7	10.3	10.0	6.3	4.4	10.2	2.1	15.4	3.2	1.7	8.9	6.9
	Dec	10.6	7.8	10.3	10.0	6.3	4.4	10.7	2.1	15.2	3.5	1.9	9.0	7.1
1992	Jan	10.4	7.8	10.4	10.1	6.2	4.5	10.6	2.1	15.0	4.1	2.2	9.2	7.1
	Feb	10.5	7.9	10.6	10.2	6.2	4.4	10.7	2.0	15.0	4.0	2.3	9.4	7.3
	Mar	10.5	8.0	11.1	10.1	6.3	4.4	10.9	2.1	15.1	4.2	2.5	9.4	7.3
	Apr	10.4	8.1	11.0	10.3	6.5	4.4	10.8	2.0	15.0	4.2	2.6	9.5	7.2
	May	10.6	8.1	11.2	10.3	6.5	4.2	11.0	2.1	14.7	4.4	2.7	9.6	7.5
	Jun	11.1	8.2	11.6	10.3	6.6	4.0	11.0	2.1	14.4	4.6	2.7	9.6	7.8
	Jul	11.0	8.2	11.6	10.3	6.7	3.8	11.1	2.2	14.1	5.3	2.9	9.8	7.7
	Aug	10.9	8.3	11.6	10.2	6.7	4.0	10.6	2.2	14.1	5.8	3.1	9.9	7.6
	Sep	10.8	8.3	11.4	10.3	6.8	4.0	10.6	2.2	14.5	5.2	3.3	10.1	7.5
	Oct	11.3	8.4	11.3	10.4	7.0	4.5	10.6	2.2	14.9	5.2	3.5	10.1	7.4
	Nov	11.4	–	11.8	–	7.1	–	–	–	15.3	5.4	3.9	10.3	7.2
	Dec	–	–	–	–	–	–	–	–	–	–	–	–	–

* Western Germany: consolidated figures for Germany not yet available.

Retailing

SHOP RENTS In Tokyo's busy Ginza it costs $7,632 to rent a square metre of shopping space for a year, the highest rate in the world, according to Healey & Baker's league table of shop rents. Hong Kong's Pedder Street has dropped from first to second place as rents fell to $5,758. In 13 of the 16 cities surveyed in both years, rents fell or remained flat. Leading the downward slide was Singapore, where rates on Orchard Road fell by a third on a year ago, to $3,130. Of the three streets in the survey where rents rose, the biggest jump came on Lisbon's Baixa (rents increased by half, to $1,303). The most expensive street in Europe is Munich's Kaufingerstrasse, where rents rose 4% on a year earlier to $2,890.

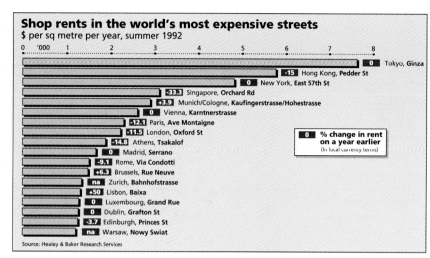

Shop rents in the world's most expensive streets
$ per sq metre per year, summer 1992

Source: Healey & Baker Research Services

Retail sales, volume

Retail sales provide an indicator of consumer demand, measuring the volume of sales in the shops. The 12-month percentage changes in our table are based on statistics from national sources and from the OECD. Definitions vary, covering different ranges of retailers. Where necessary the OECD has deflated the sales values by the appropriate consumer-price indices. In 1991 and 1992 consumers stayed away from the shops due to the world-wide recession and retail sales figures were either flat or falling. But American consumers started to spend again in 1992, with sales up by 3.8% in the 12 months to October 1992.

% change on a year earlier

		Australia	Belgium	Canada*	France	Germany†	Holland	Italy	Japan	Spain	Sweden	Switzerland	United Kingdom	United States
1991	Jan		10.4	-14.7	-0.3	14.9	4.4	-0.4	2.8	8.8	0.4	-1.0	-1.6	-5.6
	Feb		5.3	-11.6	-1.6	10.2	2.4	-10.9	1.8	7.5	-2.3	-1.9	-2.8	-3.0
	Mar	-1.3	8.5	-12.9	0.5	11.3	4.6	5.7	2.1	4.4	-5.2	-0.5	2.0	-2.0
	Apr		14.4	-11.9	0.4	9.8	-0.5	-12.4	1.8	13.5	-3.5	-7.9	-2.2	-2.1
	May		10.3	-9.1	-2.0	8.2	0.1	-9.6	2.9	3.3	-3.0	-1.7	-3.4	-1.0
	Jun	-2.2	13.2	-9.4	-2.5	12.4	4.0	-1.8	2.4	5.5	-5.2	-2.2	-0.5	-1.4
	Jul		21.4	-9.5	3.2	3.2	2.2	3.7	1.9	1.7	-0.3	-0.4	-0.6	-1.6
	Aug		14.2	-11.2	-0.8	-2.3	1.2	1.6	1.2	1.9	-1.6	-2.1	-0.2	-1.9
	Sep	-0.3	16.1	-9.4	-2.3	-0.1	-2.3	-2.6	0.8	-0.4	-3.0	-3.5	-0.7	-1.7
	Oct		16.4	-9.5	1.4	3.0	2.8	6.5	nil	1.1	1.7	2.5	-0.1	-1.0
	Nov		17.0	-7.3	0.7	-0.2	-0.7	7.5	-0.1	2.2	-2.5	-1.5	1.6	-1.9
	Dec	0.8	17.9	-7.7	-1.5	0.7	-1.7	5.0	-2.3	-3.1	-2.5	-3.3	-0.4	0.1
1992	Jan		5.5	2.6	0.2	-1.3	-0.4	–	0.1	2.2	-1.8	-2.3	0.8	4.4
	Feb		10.0	-0.6	3.3	-2.0	-0.8	–	1.1	4.4	1.1	-5.5	1.3	3.3
	Mar	1.7	-1.6	-0.2	-6.9	-5.0	-3.7	–	-4.4	-2.2	-3.5	-10.8	-3.2	0.7
	Apr		11.0	0.3	2.6	-2.4	1.1	–	-1.9	-1.6	-4.1	4.6	1.1	1.8
	May		2.3	-1.1	-0.9	-4.1	1.7	–	-3.5	4.4	-8.6	-2.9	1.9	1.2
	Jun	4.5	0.8	0.4	-1.3	-6.1	-2.8	–	-4.0	-3.0	-6.7	-3.9	0.5	0.9
	Jul		-4.4	0.5	-3.5	-4.2	0.9	–	-2.9	0.6	-5.3	-5.1	-0.3	1.9
	Aug		2.3	0.5	–	-1.5	1.3	–	–	-3.2	-8.1	-5.4	1.3	2.9
	Sep	1.7	–	–	2.4	-0.1	–	–	–	2.3	–	-2.2	1.5	3.1
	Oct		–	–	–	-2.2	–	–	–	-4.3	–	–	1.8	3.8
	Nov		–	–	–	–	–	–	–	–	–	–	0.7	–
	Dec		–	–	–	–	–	–	–	–	–	–	–	–

*From January 1991 indices exclude goods and services tax; previously included federal sales tax. † western Germany: consolidated figures for Germany not yet available.

Prices

INFLATION Since 1990 consumer-price inflation has fallen in all but five of the OECD economies. The exceptions are Austria, Germany, Holland and Turkey. Sweden and Iceland have seen the biggest drops in inflation in the past two years, in Sweden by eight and in Iceland by twelve percentage points. The inflation league seems to have turned upside-down. Germany and Switzerland used to be bastions of low inflation, but in September they were in the upper half of the league table. On the other hand, New Zealand and Australia, which have traditionally been high-inflation countries, had two of the lowest inflation rates. New Zealand's consumer prices have risen by a mere 1% over the past year.

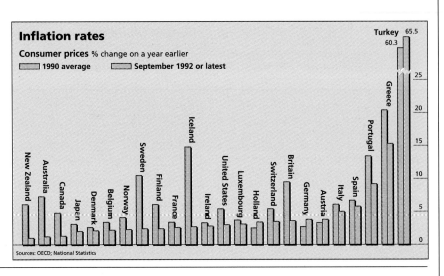

Inflation rates
Consumer prices % change on a year earlier
1990 average   September 1992 or latest

Sources: OECD; National Statistics

Consumer prices

The level of consumer-price inflation is one of the economic indicators which western governments are most sensitive about, as it is the benchmark against which most people measure the value of money in their pockets. The trends in the table below show a general decline in inflation from the beginning of 1991. The main exception was western Germany where the high costs of unification caused inflation to rise to 4.8% in March 1992, up from 2.8% in January 1991. Sweden saw the biggest reduction in inflation: from 12.6% in February 1991 to 1.3% in November 1992, the third lowest in our table.

% increase on a year earlier

		Australia	Belgium	Canada	France	Germany	Holland	Italy	Japan	Spain	Sweden	Switzerland	United Kingdom	United States
1991	Jan		3.9	6.8	3.5	2.8	3.2	6.5	4.0	6.8	10.0	5.5	9.0	5.7
	Feb		4.0	6.2	3.5	2.7	2.9	6.7	3.6	6.0	12.6	6.2	8.9	5.3
	Mar	4.9	3.3	6.3	3.2	2.5	3.1	6.6	3.6	5.9	9.9	5.8	8.2	4.9
	Apr		2.9	6.3	3.2	2.8	3.1	6.7	3.4	5.9	10.7	5.8	6.4	4.9
	May		3.3	6.2	3.2	3.0	3.3	6.7	3.4	6.2	10.1	6.3	5.8	5.0
	Jun	3.4	3.6	6.3	3.3	3.5	3.4	6.9	3.4	6.2	10.1	6.5	5.8	4.7
	Jul		3.8	5.8	3.4	4.4	4.5	6.7	3.5	6.0	9.1	6.5	5.5	4.4
	Aug		3.5	5.8	3.0	4.1	4.6	6.3	3.3	6.0	8.2	6.0	4.7	3.8
	Sep	3.2	2.5	5.4	2.6	3.9	4.4	6.2	2.7	5.8	8.1	5.7	4.1	3.4
	Oct		2.2	4.4	2.5	3.5	4.5	6.1	2.7	5.5	7.8	5.1	3.7	2.9
	Nov		2.7	4.2	3.0	4.2	4.8	6.2	3.1	5.8	7.9	5.5	4.3	3.0
	Dec	1.5	2.8	3.8	3.1	4.1	4.9	6.0	2.7	5.6	7.9	5.2	4.5	3.1
1992	Jan		2.3	1.6	2.9	4.0	4.1	6.1	1.8	6.0	5.2	4.9	4.1	2.6
	Feb		2.3	1.7	3.0	4.3	4.4	5.3	2.0	6.8	2.4	4.6	4.1	2.8
	Mar	1.7	2.7	1.6	3.2	4.8	4.3	5.5	2.0	6.8	2.4	4.9	4.0	3.2
	Apr		2.8	1.7	3.1	4.6	4.4	5.5	2.4	6.5	2.1	4.8	4.3	3.2
	May		2.8	1.3	3.1	4.6	4.2	5.7	2.0	6.5	2.1	4.2	4.3	3.0
	Jun	1.2	2.6	1.1	3.0	4.3	4.0	5.4	2.3	6.2	2.0	4.2	3.9	3.1
	Jul		2.6	1.3	2.9	3.3	3.1	5.4	1.7	5.2	1.8	3.8	3.7	3.2
	Aug		2.1	1.2	2.7	3.5	3.5	5.2	1.7	5.7	2.0	3.6	3.6	3.1
	Sep	0.8	2.3	1.3	2.6	3.6	3.4	5.1	2.0	5.8	2.4	3.5	3.6	3.0
	Oct		2.2	1.6	2.4	3.8	3.0	4.9	1.1	5.2	2.2	3.5	3.6	3.2
	Nov		2.2	1.7	2.1	3.7	2.9	4.8	–	5.1	1.3	3.3	3.0	3.0
	Dec	–	–	–	–	–	–	–	–	–	–	–	–	–

INFLATION The consumer-price index is the most popular measure of inflation. It measures the cost of a basket of goods and services bought by the average family. Producer prices (wholesale prices), in contrast, track the prices of domestically produced goods at the factory gate. In all six economies in the chart, consumer prices have grown faster than producer prices over the past five years. For example, Japan's consumer prices have increased 12% since the first quarter of 1988, compared with a 4% rise in producer prices. Britain's consumer prices have jumped by 34%, producer prices by 25%. Consumer-price indices include services, which tend to rise faster in price than goods because of slower growth in productivity.

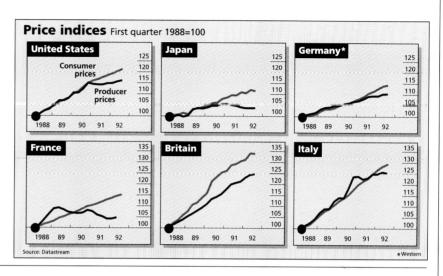

Price indices First quarter 1988=100

Source: Datastream

*Western

Producer prices

Movements in producer prices (which in most countries cover only manufacturing) provide a useful indicator of domestic cost pressures. Producer prices tend to fluctuate more than consumer prices (eg prices often fall over 12-month periods because they are more sensitive to changes to the price of raw materials). Eight of the countries in our table have experienced negative producer-price inflation in 1992. Britain had the highest rate of inflation: 3.3% in the 12 months to November. America's inflation over the same period stood at 1.2%, compared with a negative rate of 0.4% in January 1992.

		Australia	Belgium	Canada	France	Germany	Holland	Italy	Japan	Spain	Sweden	Switzerland	United Kingdom	United States
1991	Jan	5.1	-0.1	2.2		2.3	0.8	7.8	2.1	2.3	3.7	0.8	6.1	4.1
	Feb	4.0	-1.3	1.0		2.2	0.9	9.7	1.6	1.9	3.1	0.8	6.1	3.4
	Mar	2.3	-2.1	0.5	0.7	1.8	1.1	8.2	1.0	1.6	3.1	-0.1	6.1	3.3
	Apr	1.6	-1.2	nil		2.1	1.1	7.3	0.1	1.7	2.9	-0.1	6.2	3.5
	May	1.8	-0.5	-0.8		2.2	1.3	7.9	0.6	1.7	2.6	0.2	5.9	3.5
	Jun	2.6	0.2	-0.8	-0.7	2.3	1.8	7.2	0.6	1.9	2.4	0.5	5.7	3.2
	Jul	2.6	0.1	-0.8		3.3	2.7	6.9	0.4	2.2	2.2	0.6	5.7	2.7
	Aug	1.5	-1.6	-1.6		2.7	2.5	3.1	0.1	1.7	1.4	0.3	5.5	1.8
	Sep	0.0	-2.3	-2.5	-1.5	2.6	2.0	2.1	-0.4	1.1	0.4	-0.2	5.4	0.7
	Oct	-1.0	-2.0	-3.0		2.3	1.3	-0.3	-0.9	0.6	-0.1	0.6	5.0	-0.1
	Nov	-1.8	-1.0	-3.2		2.5	1.9	2.3	-1.3	1.0	-0.2	0.9	5.1	-0.2
	Dec	-1.0	-1.4	-3.4	-3.6	2.6	2.5	1.2	-1.6	0.7	-0.1	0.7	4.8	nil
1992	Jan	-0.3	-0.9	-3.5		1.6	2.2	0.8	-2.2	0.5	-1.6	0.3	4.5	-0.4
	Feb	0.3	0.6	-2.3		2.0	2.2	0.4	-1.6	0.9	-1.4	nil	4.4	0.5
	Mar	1.0	1.4	-1.5	-3.0	2.5	2.3	1.6	-1.4	1.3	-1.3	0.7	4.5	1.0
	Apr	1.2	1.1	-0.9		2.0	2.6	3.0	-1.2	1.5	-1.0	0.5	3.8	1.2
	May	1.4	1.3	nil		2.0	2.3	3.0	-1.4	1.5	-0.6	0.6	3.5	1.2
	Jun	1.4	1.2	0.4	-1.1	2.0	2.2	2.3	-1.5	1.8	-0.5	0.3	3.6	1.6
	Jul	1.6	0.9	0.8		1.1	1.1	2.3	-1.2	1.5	-0.7	nil	3.6	1.8
	Aug	2.1	-0.6	1.5		1.1	0.7	1.7	-1.1	1.4	-1.6	-0.5	3.4	1.6
	Sep	–	-0.7	2.1	-0.9	0.8	0.1	1.0	-1.1	1.2	-1.6	-0.2	3.4	1.7
	Oct	–	–	2.9		0.5	0.1	–	-1.3	–	-1.3	-0.3	3.3	1.6
	Nov	–	–	–		0.5	–	–	-1.3	–	–	-0.1	3.3	1.2
	Dec	–	–	–	–	–	–	–	–	–	–	–	–	–

Wages and earnings

PERSONAL INCOME TAX The chart, based on an OECD study, shows income taxes (central, state and local government) paid by a two-child family earning average manufacturing wages. In 1991 such a Danish family paid 36% of its earnings in income tax; at the other extreme, those in France, Iceland, Luxembourg and Portugal paid 1% or less. If non-standard tax reliefs, such as those on mortgage-interest payments are included, then in most countries the actual tax burden would be smaller. Adding in employees' social-security contributions and family allowances the average Danish worker is left with only 68% of his earnings; but Icelanders' net income amounts to 117% of their gross earnings, thanks to family allowances.

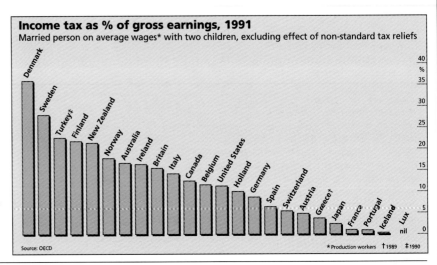

Income tax as % of gross earnings, 1991
Married person on average wages* with two children, excluding effect of non-standard tax reliefs

Source: OECD   *Production workers   †1989   ‡1990

Wages and earnings

The figures for more than half the countries in our table represent wage increases for all workers. Those for Belgium, Canada, Italy, Japan, Sweden and Switzerland refer to wages in industry or manufacturing only. Switzerland publishes wage figures only once a year. Out of all the countries in our table, Britain started 1992 with the second highest 12-month rate of increase in earnings (7.3%). But as unemployment rose and inflation fell, wage growth slowed to 5.5% in October. The biggest rate of decline was in Italy where the wage rate dropped from 10.9% in August 1991 to 3.5% in August 1992.

% increase on a year earlier*

		Australia	Belgium	Canada	France	Germany	Holland	Italy	Japan	Spain	Sweden	Switzerland	United Kingdom	United States
1991	Jan			5.2	5.2	5.9	2.4	7.9	1.8		8.0		9.5	3.7
	Feb	6.9		5.9		6.0	2.4	8.1	5.5		4.5		9.3	3.2
	Mar		5.3	5.4		6.7	2.4	8.1	4.2	8.2	4.8		9.0	3.2
	Apr			5.5	4.3	6.7	2.6	8.5	3.9		2.8		8.8	3.3
	May	3.0		4.8		7.2	3.7	10.4	4.0		4.8		8.5	3.4
	Jun		3.5	4.9		7.2	3.9	10.3	4.5	9.0	3.3		8.0	3.5
	Jul			4.6	4.7	7.2	3.1	10.4	1.9		4.1		7.8	2.9
	Aug	3.1		4.6		7.0	4.0	10.9	6.5		4.9		7.8	3.1
	Sep		4.4	5.0		7.1	4.1	10.8	2.8	8.4	4.4		7.8	2.9
	Oct			4.0	4.5	7.0	3.2	10.8	3.0		4.7	7.4	7.5	3.0
	Nov	2.2		3.6		6.8	3.2	10.7	2.7		5.0		7.5	2.9
	Dec		5.8	3.9		6.7	4.1	10.4	3.5	8.5	4.8		7.3	2.9
1992	Jan			4.0	4.1	7.1	3.7	9.4	4.7		4.6		7.3	2.8
	Feb	2.2		3.9		7.1	3.8	9.1	1.7		3.8		7.5	3.0
	Mar		4.2	3.8		6.3	3.9	9.1	2.2	8.5	2.7		7.5	3.0
	Apr			4.0	4.6	5.7	4.3	8.8	1.7		5.0		7.0	2.3
	May	4.2		3.8		5.6	4.0	4.6	1.2		4.4		6.3	2.3
	Jun		5.8	2.9		5.7	4.0	4.7	3.9	8.5	6.0		6.3	2.0
	Jul			3.2	3.8	5.5	4.2	4.0	2.5		3.7		6.0	2.3
	Aug	3.0		3.8		5.5	4.1	3.5	-1.6		4.7	–	5.8	2.7
	Sep		–	3.3		5.5	4.2	–	2.1	7.9	4.3		5.5	2.3
	Oct			–	–	5.3	4.2	–	1.9		4.7		5.5	2.4
	Nov	–		–		–	–	–	–		–		–	2.8
	Dec		–	–	–	–	–	–	–		–		–	–

*Hourly earnings for all employees except Australia, weekly earnings; Spain, quarterly earnings; UK, monthly earnings; Japan and Switzerland, manufacturing monthly earnings; Belgium, Sweden, industrial hourly earnings; Canada, Italy, manufacturing hourly earnings.

Focus on business

COMMERCIAL BANKS The world's six biggest commercial banks (measured by total assets) at the end of 1991 were all Japanese. Compare this with 1970, when there were no Japanese banks in a top ten dominated by America (six) and Britain (two). Barclays—fourth biggest in 1970—was 13th in 1991, with assets of $258 billion. Citicorp, America's biggest bank, languished in 20th place, while Bank of America, the world's biggest in 1970, was 47th in 1991. Does a similar fate await 1991's largest bank, Dai-Ichi Kangyo which had assets of $446 billion? Sumitomo was not far behind, with assets of $427 billion. Europe's biggest bank was Crédit Agricole, seventh in the world. Another French bank, Crédit Lyonnais, was Europe's number two.

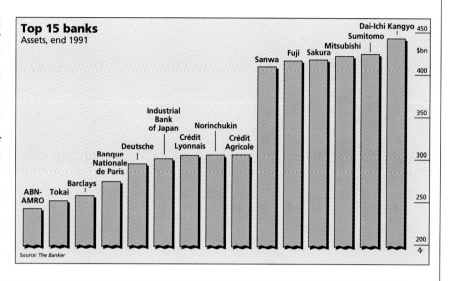

Top 15 banks
Assets, end 1991

Source: The Banker

BIG COMPANIES The fall in the Tokyo stockmarket has pushed Japanese firms down and out of the top 20 league table of the world's biggest companies as measured by market capitalisation. Just five years ago, nine of the world's 12 most valuable companies were Japanese. This fell to only two in June 1992. In the case of NTT, Japan's telecommunications giant, which held first place by a wide margin over the previous few years, fears of the effects of deregulation in Japan's telecoms industry has made its decline even more marked. Royal Dutch/Shell overtook its rival oil giant, Exxon, in 1992 to become the world's most valuable company, while hapless British Petroleum, in 15th place in 1991, fell out of the league altogether.

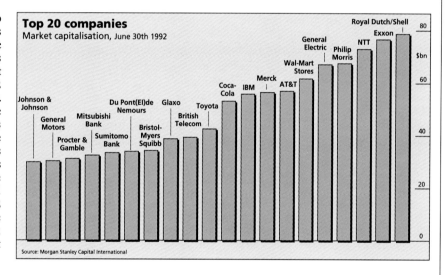

Top 20 companies
Market capitalisation, June 30th 1992

Source: Morgan Stanley Capital International

OFFICE RENTS Although city office rents were falling in the rest of the world, they continued to rise in continental Europe in 1991, according to Richard Ellis, an international property agency. Firms had been moving their offices in readiness for the completion of Europe's internal market, and to make the most of opportunities in Eastern Europe. At the end of 1991 London's office rents ($91 per square foot) were little higher than those of cities like Paris ($83). However, in total, London's offices were far more expensive than those in any city except Tokyo; tax and service charges added around 50% to the rent bill. In Berlin rents soared by 42% between June and December 1991. Office rents in Tokyo were nine times those in Amsterdam.

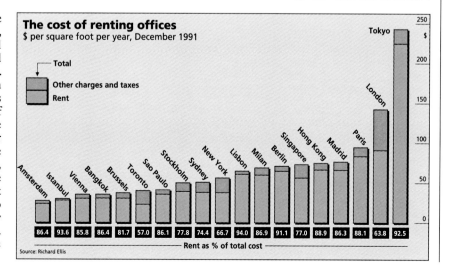

The cost of renting offices
$ per square foot per year, December 1991

Total
Other charges and taxes
Rent

Amsterdam	Istanbul	Vienna	Bangkok	Brussels	Toronto	Sao Paulo	Stockholm	Sydney	New York	Lisbon	Milan	Berlin	Singapore	Hong Kong	Madrid	Paris	London	Tokyo
86.4	93.6	85.8	86.4	81.7	57.0	86.1	77.8	74.4	66.7	94.0	86.9	91.1	77.0	88.9	86.3	88.1	63.8	92.5

Rent as % of total cost

Source: Richard Ellis

The Economist commodity-price index

Each week *The Economist* publishes a set of commodity-price indices. Our indices are based on 1985=100 and are weighted by the value of imports into OECD countries in 1984-86, net of intra-EC trade affected by the common agricultural policy. Over 1992 as a whole, *The Economist*'s all-items index measured in terms of SDRs, a basket of currencies, rose 6%, possibly marking the end of the slump in commodity prices which began in 1989. The dollar index edged up 2%, but the collapse in the pound pushed sterling prices higher in the last quarter and the index finished 26% up on the year. The SDR food index sank to a new low in September, of only 58% of its 1985 value. Grain prices eased as supplies recovered. America harvested a record maize crop–25% more than in 1991, and prices dipped to a four-year low of under $2 a bushel. Russia also had a good harvest; its difficulties in repaying grain loans forced wheat prices lower. There was a bumper soyabean crop in the United States. The United States and the EC reached agreement on oilseed production. Huge surpluses continued to depress cocoa and coffee prices. Fears of a low Brazilian coffee crop boosted prices in the final quarter. America's economic recovery began to boost demand for some industrial commodities. Timber prices ended the year at record highs. Natural rubber consumption rose 4% in 1992, and prices gained 8%. However, high metal stocks and the continuing flood of exports from former Soviet countries dampened prices again after a spate of investment buying had boosted the market until August. Stocks on the London Metal Exchange, already a record, soared by more than 60% to 2.6m tonnes. Metal producers planned cutbacks in 1993. Nickel fared worst; prices fell nearly 20%. Aluminium did best; prices rose 10%.

Weights in the index

Industrials, %		Foods, %	
Metals		Beef	6.7
Copper	28.4	Lamb	2.1
Lead	4.4	Wheat	4.9
Zinc	9.9	Maize	8.5
Tin	6.3	Coffee	33.3
Aluminium	41.8	Cocoa	10.7
Nickel*	9.2	Tea	3.0
NFAs*		Sugar	8.1
Wool 64s	10.5	Soyabean meal	7.6
Wool 48s	10.5	Soyabeans	10.3
Cotton	20.2	Soyabean oil	1.1
Jute	0.2	Groundnut oil	0.7
Sisal	0.3	Coconut oil	1.4
Hides	11.2	Palm oil	1.6
Rubber	14.2		
Timber	26.8	**Foods**	49.8
Soyabeans	4.4	**Industrials**	50.2
Soyabean oil	0.4	**Metals**	29.3
Coconut oil	0.6	**NFAs***	20.9
Palm oil	0.7	**All items**	100.0
*Non-food agriculturals			

Averages, 1985=100		Dollar index					Sterling index					SDR index				
		All items	Food	Industrial materials			All items	Food	Industrial materials			All items	Food	Industrial materials		
				All	NFAs	Metals			All	NFAs	Metals			All	NFAs	Metals
1987		111.5	93.1	129.9	131.7	128.6	87.1	72.8	101.3	102.9	100.0	87.4	73.0	101.7	103.3	100.6
1988		147.4	113.2	181.4	144.9	207.2	106.2	81.6	130.6	104.4	149.1	111.4	85.6	137.0	109.5	156.5
1989		139.5	108.0	170.7	137.3	194.4	109.0	84.4	133.3	107.5	151.6	110.4	85.6	135.2	108.8	153.8
1990		126.4	98.4	154.2	135.6	167.4	91.3	71.2	111.3	98.1	120.6	94.7	73.8	115.5	101.7	125.3
1991		110.5	89.2	131.6	122.7	137.8	80.3	64.9	95.6	89.4	100.1	82.0	66.2	97.7	91.2	102.3
1992		108.7	87.7	129.6	122.4	134.7	79.2	64.0	94.4	89.3	97.9	78.3	63.2	93.4	88.2	97.0
1991	Jan	115.1	89.6	140.5	124.5	151.8	76.4	59.4	93.3	82.6	100.8	82.1	63.9	100.3	88.8	108.3
	Feb	114.2	88.8	139.4	122.8	151.2	74.6	58.0	91.1	80.2	98.8	80.5	62.4	98.3	86.6	106.4
	Mar	114.6	90.9	138.1	120.7	150.3	80.6	64.0	97.2	85.0	105.8	83.9	66.6	101.1	88.4	110.1
	Apr	114.1	89.8	138.2	123.9	148.2	83.3	65.5	100.9	90.5	108.2	85.7	67.5	103.9	93.1	111.4
	May	110.8	86.3	135.2	132.4	137.0	81.8	63.7	99.8	97.8	101.2	83.7	65.2	102.1	100.0	103.5
	Jun	111.4	87.3	135.4	136.4	134.6	86.5	67.8	105.1	105.9	104.5	85.7	67.2	104.1	104.9	103.5
	Jul	111.1	89.1	132.9	128.8	135.7	86.5	69.3	103.5	100.3	105.7	85.3	68.4	102.1	99.0	104.2
	Aug	107.8	88.1	127.5	119.8	132.9	82.2	67.1	97.2	91.4	101.3	82.0	66.9	96.9	91.1	101.0
	Sep	108.0	90.3	125.5	116.7	131.8	80.2	67.0	93.2	86.6	97.8	80.9	67.7	94.1	87.5	98.8
	Oct	106.7	90.0	123.4	115.8	128.8	79.5	67.0	92.0	86.3	96.0	79.7	67.2	92.1	86.4	96.2
	Nov	107.4	89.8	124.9	118.3	129.5	77.2	64.5	89.7	85.0	93.0	78.6	65.7	91.4	86.6	94.7
	Dec	106.0	90.2	121.7	115.3	126.2	74.3	63.2	85.3	80.8	88.5	76.3	64.9	87.6	82.9	90.8
1992	Jan	107.1	89.9	124.2	119.2	127.8	75.6	63.4	87.7	84.1	90.2	77.0	64.6	89.3	85.7	91.9
	Feb	107.7	87.5	127.9	120.4	133.1	77.7	63.1	92.2	86.9	96.0	78.7	63.9	93.4	88.0	97.2
	Mar	109.4	88.5	130.2	124.1	134.5	81.1	65.6	96.6	92.0	99.7	81.2	65.7	96.6	92.1	99.8
	Apr	110.7	88.8	132.5	126.1	137.1	80.6	64.6	96.5	91.8	99.8	82.0	65.8	98.2	93.3	101.5
	May	110.7	88.6	132.7	125.8	137.6	78.2	62.6	93.7	88.8	97.2	80.9	64.7	96.9	91.8	100.5
	Jun	112.0	89.7	134.1	127.4	138.7	77.3	62.0	92.5	88.0	95.7	80.4	64.4	96.3	91.5	99.6
	Jul	111.8	87.7	135.8	122.5	145.1	74.7	58.6	90.7	81.8	96.9	78.6	61.7	95.4	86.1	102.0
	Aug	110.9	86.3	135.2	120.1	145.9	73.2	57.0	89.3	79.4	96.4	77.3	60.2	94.3	83.7	101.7
	Sep	108.7	85.5	131.7	119.7	140.1	74.7	58.8	90.5	82.4	96.3	75.3	59.2	91.2	82.9	97.0
	Oct	104.4	84.7	124.0	117.7	128.4	80.8	65.5	95.9	91.1	99.3	74.0	60.0	87.9	83.4	91.0
	Nov	103.7	86.5	120.9	119.5	121.8	87.2	72.7	101.6	100.4	102.4	76.0	63.4	88.6	87.6	89.3
	Dec	106.8	88.2	125.3	124.3	126.0	88.3	72.9	103.6	102.8	104.2	78.1	64.5	91.6	90.9	92.1

ECONOMIC AND FINANCIAL INDICATORS

1985=100		Dollar index					Sterling index					SDR index				
		All items	Food	Industrial materials			All items	Food	Industrial materials			All items	Food	Industrial materials		
				All	NFAs	Metals			All	NFAs	Metals			All	NFAs	Metals
1992 Jan 7		105.8	89.5	122.1	119.1	124.2	72.5	61.2	83.6	81.5	85.0	74.8	63.2	86.3	84.2	87.8
14		105.9	89.8	121.9	118.7	124.1	75.8	64.3	87.2	85.0	88.8	76.3	64.7	87.9	85.6	89.5
21		107.7	90.2	125.1	118.8	129.5	76.4	64.0	88.8	84.3	91.9	77.7	65.1	90.2	85.7	93.4
28		108.8	89.9	127.7	120.1	133.1	77.7	64.2	91.2	85.7	95.0	79.1	65.3	92.8	87.2	96.7
Feb 4		107.1	88.2	125.9	119.9	130.1	76.2	62.8	89.6	85.4	92.6	77.6	63.9	91.3	86.9	94.3
11		107.4	87.9	126.8	120.1	131.6	76.4	62.6	90.2	85.4	93.6	77.8	63.7	91.9	87.0	95.3
18		107.8	86.8	128.6	120.1	134.5	78.9	63.6	94.1	88.0	98.5	79.2	63.8	94.5	88.3	98.8
25		108.7	87.1	130.1	121.6	136.2	79.3	63.6	94.9	88.7	99.3	80.1	64.2	95.9	89.6	100.4
Mar 3		108.9	87.6	130.0	123.1	134.8	80.2	64.5	95.8	90.7	99.3	80.5	64.8	96.2	91.1	99.8
10		108.8	88.2	129.2	122.8	133.7	81.3	65.9	96.5	91.7	99.9	80.8	65.5	96.0	91.2	99.3
17		109.7	88.9	130.4	125.5	133.9	81.2	65.8	96.5	92.9	99.1	81.6	66.1	96.9	93.2	99.5
24		110.0	89.6	130.3	124.7	134.2	82.0	66.8	97.1	92.9	100.0	81.9	66.7	97.0	92.8	99.9
31		109.7	88.1	131.1	124.5	135.8	81.0	65.1	96.9	91.9	100.3	81.2	65.2	97.0	92.1	100.5
Apr 7		110.8	88.7	132.7	126.4	137.1	81.2	65.0	97.2	92.6	100.5	81.8	65.5	98.0	93.3	101.2
14		111.2	89.3	132.9	126.1	137.7	80.4	64.6	96.2	91.2	99.6	82.2	66.0	98.3	93.3	101.9
21		110.7	89.1	132.2	125.3	137.0	81.2	65.3	97.0	91.9	100.5	82.3	66.2	98.3	93.2	101.9
28		110.3	88.1	132.3	126.4	136.5	79.6	63.6	95.6	91.3	98.6	81.7	65.2	98.0	93.6	101.1
May 5		109.8	87.6	131.8	125.1	136.5	78.9	63.0	94.8	89.9	98.2	80.9	64.6	97.2	92.2	100.7
12		110.5	89.0	131.9	125.1	136.8	78.2	62.9	93.3	88.5	96.7	81.0	65.2	96.7	91.7	100.3
19		111.3	89.0	133.5	126.7	138.2	77.6	62.0	93.1	88.3	96.4	80.6	64.4	96.6	91.7	100.1
26		111.3	88.9	133.6	126.1	138.9	78.1	62.3	93.7	88.4	97.4	80.9	64.6	97.1	91.6	100.9
Jun 2		112.3	89.9	134.5	127.3	139.6	78.8	63.1	94.5	89.4	98.1	81.2	65.0	97.3	92.1	101.0
9		112.1	90.9	133.2	127.1	137.5	78.4	63.6	93.1	88.9	96.2	80.9	65.6	96.1	91.7	99.2
16		111.5	89.7	133.3	127.3	137.4	76.9	61.8	91.8	87.7	94.7	80.2	64.5	95.8	91.5	98.8
23		110.9	88.9	132.7	128.5	135.6	76.3	61.2	91.3	88.4	93.3	79.5	63.8	95.1	92.1	97.2
30		113.0	89.3	136.6	127.0	143.3	76.1	60.1	92.0	85.5	96.5	80.1	63.3	96.9	90.1	101.7
Jul 7		111.7	87.3	136.0	123.6	144.7	74.3	58.1	90.5	82.3	96.3	78.4	61.2	95.4	86.8	101.5
14		111.3	88.0	134.5	122.5	142.9	74.6	59.0	90.1	82.1	95.8	78.0	61.7	94.3	85.9	100.2
21		112.2	88.0	136.2	122.2	146.1	75.3	59.1	91.5	82.0	98.1	79.2	62.1	96.2	86.3	103.2
28		112.1	87.6	136.4	121.8	146.7	74.5	58.2	90.7	80.9	97.5	78.8	61.6	95.9	85.6	103.1
Aug 4		111.0	86.6	135.2	120.6	145.6	74.0	57.8	90.2	80.4	97.1	78.0	60.9	95.1	84.8	102.3
11		110.4	86.1	134.7	119.2	145.6	73.7	57.4	89.8	79.5	97.2	77.3	60.3	94.3	83.4	102.0
18		110.4	85.8	134.9	120.2	145.3	73.4	57.0	89.6	79.8	96.5	77.1	59.9	94.2	83.9	101.5
25		111.5	86.8	136.1	120.6	147.1	71.8	55.9	87.6	77.6	94.7	76.6	59.6	93.4	82.8	101.0
Sep 1		110.8	86.8	134.6	119.9	144.9	71.1	55.7	86.4	77.0	93.0	75.7	59.3	92.0	82.0	99.1
8		110.6	86.9	134.1	121.7	142.8	70.8	55.6	85.8	77.9	91.4	75.5	59.4	91.6	83.1	97.6
15		109.4	85.4	133.3	121.6	141.5	74.9	58.5	91.3	83.3	96.9	76.5	59.7	93.2	85.0	98.9
22		106.4	84.5	128.1	118.7	134.7	79.8	63.4	96.1	89.0	101.1	74.9	59.5	90.2	83.6	94.9
29		106.3	84.1	128.4	116.8	136.6	77.0	60.9	93.0	84.6	99.0	73.7	58.3	89.0	80.9	94.7
Oct 6		105.1	84.6	125.5	117.5	131.1	78.7	63.4	94.0	88.0	98.2	73.0	58.8	87.2	81.6	91.1
13		104.6	84.6	124.5	118.5	128.7	78.1	63.1	93.0	88.5	96.1	73.9	59.8	88.0	83.8	91.0
20		104.1	84.9	123.1	117.3	127.2	82.1	67.0	97.1	92.5	100.3	74.2	60.5	87.8	93.6	90.6
27		103.7	84.6	122.8	117.4	126.5	84.2	68.7	99.7	95.3	102.7	74.8	61.0	88.6	84.7	91.3
Nov 3		103.8	86.4	121.2	117.4	123.9	86.0	71.5	100.4	97.2	102.6	75.6	62.9	88.2	85.4	90.1
10		102.8	85.5	119.9	118.7	120.8	87.0	72.4	101.5	100.5	102.3	75.4	62.7	88.0	87.1	88.6
17		103.7	87.1	120.3	119.8	120.5	87.5	73.4	101.4	101.1	101.6	76.3	64.1	88.5	88.1	88.6
24		104.6	86.9	122.2	122.0	122.2	88.3	73.3	103.2	103.0	103.2	76.8	63.8	89.8	89.7	89.8
Dec 1		106.0	87.5	124.4	124.3	124.5	88.4	73.0	103.8	103.7	103.8	77.8	64.3	91.3	91.2	91.4
8		105.7	87.8	123.4	121.7	124.6	84.8	70.5	99.1	97.7	100.0	76.5	63.6	89.4	88.1	90.3
15		106.5	88.8	124.1	123.1	124.7	87.1	72.6	101.4	100.6	102.0	77.6	64.7	90.4	89.7	90.9
22		108.1	88.9	127.2	126.1	127.9	90.0	74.0	105.9	105.1	106.5	79.0	64.9	92.9	92.1	93.4
29		107.8	88.0	127.4	126.4	128.1	91.3	74.6	107.9	107.0	108.5	79.6	65.0	94.1	93.3	94.6

343

Focus on commodities

ALL ITEMS The slump in commodity prices could be coming to an end. After falling 40% from its peak at the beginning of 1989, to a low in October 1992, *The Economist's* all-items index, measured in SDRS (a basket of currencies) turned back up. It ended the year 6% higher than at the start. In sterling terms the index rose 26%. America's economic recovery began to boost demand for industrial materials such as rubber and timber. However, high stocks, and the flood of exports from former Soviet countries, continued to dampen metal prices. Food prices remained depressed. One exception was coffee, which gained 50% between August and end year. Bumper harvests and Russia's difficulties in repaying its grain loans were expected to hit wheat prices further in 1993.

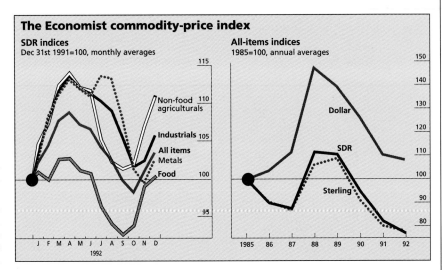

The Economist commodity-price index

SDR indices
Dec 31st 1991=100, monthly averages

Non-food agriculturals
Industrials
All items
Metals
Food

All-items indices
1985=100, annual averages

Dollar
SDR
Sterling

BEVERAGES Beverages were the big movers in *The Economist's* food index last year. Weighed down by huge surpluses, robusta coffee prices sank to 22–year lows in August. Fears that Brazil's 1992-93 coffee crop was below 20m bags (of 60 kg each) boosted prices in the last quarter. There was little progress towards negotiating a new Coffee Agreement. Although cocoa supplies were in deficit in 1991–92 for the first time in eight years, world stocks were still a massive 1.4m tonnes and prices dropped to new 17–year lows. Tea prices in London were the lowest for more than four years in January, but they had climbed 40% (in sterling terms) by end year. A production shortfall of 120m kilos owing to drought was partly off-set by a fall in Russian buying.

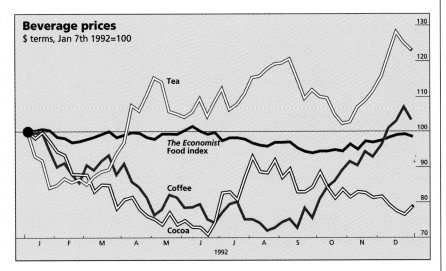

Beverage prices
$ terms, Jan 7th 1992=100

Tea
The Economist Food index
Coffee
Cocoa

OTHER AGRICULTURALS Global recession held down prices of non-food agricultural (NFA) commodities in 1992. Between January and June *The Economist's* NFA dollar index rose 11%, and ended the year 9% higher than at the start. Australian wool was hit by slack demand for textiles and prices fell to their lowest level in real terms this century. Floods hit Pakistan's cotton crop, but world stocks were forecast to end the 1992-93 season at 47% of consumption and prices slipped to six–year lows. The slump in car sales continued to depress the rubber market for much of the year. Bucking the trend, timber prices hit record levels in March after fears of a shortage. New Zealand wool, used for carpets, had climbed 27% by September, thanks to Chinese buying.

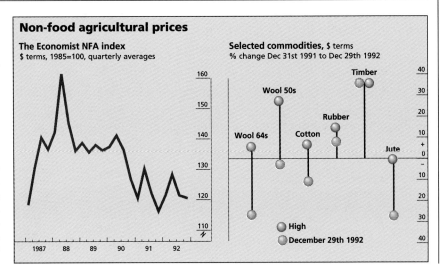

Non-food agricultural prices

The Economist NFA index
$ terms, 1985=100, quarterly averages

Selected commodities, $ terms
% change Dec 31st 1991 to Dec 29th 1992

Timber
Wool 50s
Rubber
Wool 64s
Cotton
Jute

High
December 29th 1992

METALS *The Economist* dollar-based metals index fell by 53% from its peak in June 1988 to a low at the beginning of 1992. It then climbed 19% by August before turning down again. Investment buying boosted prices during the summer, but fund managers then lost interest in metals. With no sign of an end to the economic gloom, there was little prospect of higher industrial demand, and prices plunged. Stocks on the London Metal Exchange reached a record 2.6m tonnes. Aluminium and nickel surpluses were swelled by heavy Russian exports. Chinese buying, which supported copper prices in the first half of the year, dried up; a rise in Chinese exports helped depress tin prices in the second half of the year.

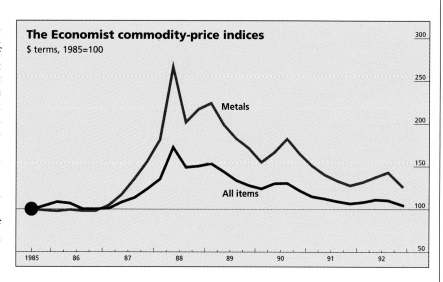

The Economist commodity-price indices
$ terms, 1985=100

GOLD The world gold boom has started to peter out. Production from western gold mines grew by only 2% in 1991, less than in any year since the boom began in 1980, according to *Gold 1992*, a survey by Gold Fields Mineral Services in London. Since then output in America and Australia has increased tenfold; but the boom has passed South Africa by: output has fallen by 11% and its share of production has halved to just 34%. Even though the country's average production costs were cut by 4.5% last year, to $325 an ounce, they remain above those of other big producers. With gold at less than $340 an ounce, 6% down on 1991's price, more South African mines look set to close—especially if buyers' disenchantment with gold as an investment persists.

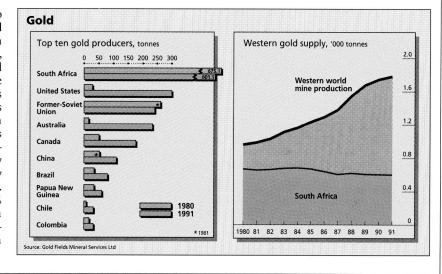

Gold

Top ten gold producers, tonnes

Western gold supply, '000 tonnes

Source: Gold Fields Mineral Services Ltd

OIL RESERVES Two-thirds of the world's proven oil reserves are in the Middle East. Saudi Arabia has by far the biggest reserves–258 billion barrels, or more than a quarter of the world's total. At present rates of production, that will last the kingdom 84 years. Kuwait's reserves will last 162 years and Iraq's will last 97 years at the rate they were pumping oil before the Gulf war; Abu Dhabi's will be good for 119 years. Iran, the fourth biggest producer in 1991, has enough oil to last 78 years. The United States produces more oil than Saudi Arabia, but its reserves could run out in just ten years; the reserves of the former Soviet Union, the biggest oil producer in 1991, could run dry in 15 years. However, this is unlikely thanks to new discoveries, and more efficient ways of extracting oil.

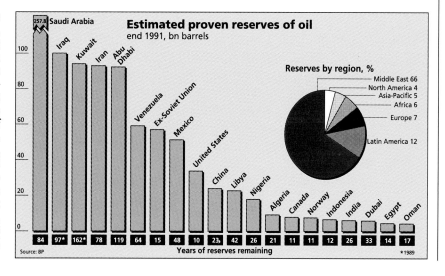

Estimated proven reserves of oil
end 1991, bn barrels

Reserves by region, %

Source: BP   Years of reserves remaining   *1989

345

World stockmarkets

The continuing recession throughout much of the industrial world made 1992 a jittery year for world stockmarkets. Tokyo was most bearish: despite the finance ministry's incentives to investors the Nikkei fell a massive 39.9% to a six-year low of 14,309 on August 18th, from its 1992 high on January 2nd. Wall Street had a turbulent 12 months, ending the year only 4.2% up. Renewed economic optimism sent the Dow Jones industrial average soaring in January and improved growth statistics in November prompted a 5.4% rally from October's year low. London fell to its 1992 low in August, though it bounced back at

Share-price indices

End month

		Australia	Belgium	Canada	France	Germany	Holland	Hong Kong	Italy
		All ordinaries index Jan 1st 1980=100	BEL 20 share index Jan 1st 1991=1,000	Toronto composite index Jan 1st 1975=1,000	CAC general index Dec 31st 1982=100	Deutscher Aktien index Dec 31st 1987=1,000	CBS All Share index Dec 31st 1983=100	Hang Seng Bank index July 31st 1964=100	Banca Commerciale index 1972=100
1991	Jan	1321.5	974.9	3272.9	419.2	1420.1	167.3	3243.3	496.2
	Feb	1405.6	1141.8	3462.4	465.6	1542.1	182.5	3552.1	572.5
	Mar	1444.2	1196.6	3495.7	479.8	1522.8	195.7	3746.0	581.2
	Apr	1534.2	1188.4	3468.8	479.6	1605.8	200.7	3588.4	575.8
	May	1510.0	1171.7	3546.1	488.5	1704.1	201.7	3707.0	609.6
	Jun	1506.2	1162.5	3465.8	470.8	1622.2	197.5	3668.6	586.2
	Jul	1572.4	1139.7	3539.6	464.5	1622.3	200.8	4009.6	573.4
	Aug	1540.4	1128.9	3517.9	486.7	1650.5	199.3	3998.3	555.4
	Sep	1562.1	1089.0	3387.9	496.4	1607.0	193.9	3956.7	539.1
	Oct	1683.0	1101.0	3515.8	494.7	1582.1	195.5	4038.7	515.7
	Nov	1605.7	1068.3	3448.5	477.4	1566.6	191.9	4149.8	518.5
	Dec	1651.4	1092.7	3512.4	476.7	1578.0	191.4	4297.3	507.8
1992	Jan	1619.5	1180.2	3596.1	504.7	1687.5	201.6	4601.8	541.4
	Feb	1614.2	1210.6	3581.9	526.5	1745.1	205.8	4929.1	536.0
	Mar	1582.6	1193.0	3412.1	529.5	1717.9	203.9	4938.3	502.5
	Apr	1655.9	1192.8	3355.6	547.3	1734.0	212.3	5269.6	504.8
	May	1678.3	1230.8	3387.9	547.9	1803.2	215.1	6080.2	496.6
	Jun	1644.7	1162.8	3387.7	517.9	1752.6	205.7	6103.9	454.2
	Jul	1617.7	1145.3	3443.4	488.1	1613.2	198.6	5881.1	401.7
	Aug	1547.2	1057.3	3403.0	468.0	1541.3	195.6	5628.6	390.9
	Sep	1485.0	1109.2	3297.9	463.1	1466.4	196.8	5505.4	363.6
	Oct	1425.8	1140.0	3336.1	460.9	1492.3	191.8	6290.7	439.0
	Nov	1448.1	1128.1	3282.8	463.5	1544.3	194.3	5810.6	438.3
	Dec	1549.9	1127.0	3350.4	484.5	1545.1	198.0	5512.4	446.3
1992 high		1684.5	1235.4	3666.0	555.9	1811.6	215.5	6447.1	551.6
1992 low		1357.2	1046.1	3195.4	441.7	1420.3	189.7	4301.8	354.9

Market capitalisation, $bn

	Australia	Belgium	Canada	France	Germany	Holland	Hong Kong	Italy
End 1991	141	67	246	319	342	121	119	145
End 1992	133	63	220	333	326	130	162	124

Top five companies by market capitalisation, November 30th 1992

	Australia	Belgium	Canada	France	Germany	Holland	Hong Kong	Italy
	BHP	Electrabel	BCE	Alcatel	Allianz	Royal Dutch	HSBC	Generali
	News Corporation	Petrofina	Northern Telecom	Elf Aquitaine	Siemens	Unilever	Hong Kong Telecom	Fiat
	National Australia Bank	Tractebel	Seagram	BSN	Deutsche Bank	ABN-AMRO	Hang Seng Bank	SIP
	CRA	Générale de Belgique	Thompson	LVMH	Daimler-Benz	International Nederlanden	Sun Hung Kai Properties	STET
	BTR Nylex	Générale Banque	Imperial Oil	L'Oréal	RWE	Elsevier	China Light & Power	Banca di Roma

Source: MSCI

the beginning of December as lower interest rates and a change in economic policy cheered investors and sent the FT-SE 100 to an all-time high. Cuts in German interest rates in September prompted the DAX to fall 8% to its low for the year in October. Paris ended 1992 1.6% up on the year. Encouraging noises in neighbouring China over economic and market reforms pushed share prices in Hong Kong 50% higher to an all-time high of 6,447 in mid-November. But rows over the colony's democratic future then sent the Hang Seng plummeting 23%. Zurich ended 1992 on a record high.

		Japan	Singapore	South Africa	Spain	Sweden	Switzerland	United Kingdom	United States	World
		Nikkei 225 share average	Straits Times Industrials Dec 30th 1966=100	JSE Industrials Sept 28th 1978=264.3	Madrid SE index Dec 30st 1985=100	Affarsvarlden General Feb 1st 1937=100	Swiss market index June 30th 1983=1500	FT-SE 100 Dec 30th 1983=1000	Dow Jones Industrials	Morgan Stanley Capital Int index* Jan 1st 1970=100
1991	Jan	23293.1	1267.3	2882.0	231.2	970.6	1434.3	2170.3	2736.4	477.4
	Feb	26409.2	1459.6	3218.0	264.1	1070.1	1578.7	2380.9	2882.2	520.6
	Mar	26206.9	1465.9	3389.0	284.3	1093.7	1649.4	2456.5	2913.9	504.3
	Apr	26111.3	1553.9	3542.0	274.1	1039.4	1659.5	2486.2	2887.9	507.2
	May	25789.6	1554.2	3608.0	284.2	1108.8	1740.8	2499.5	3027.5	517.8
	Jun	23291.0	1489.9	3817.0	277.0	1130.9	1664.3	2414.8	2906.8	484.8
	Jul	24120.8	1482.9	4085.0	269.5	1116.6	1727.2	2588.8	3024.8	506.8
	Aug	22335.9	1432.2	4114.0	273.2	1097.5	1736.6	2645.7	3043.6	504.2
	Sep	23916.4	1360.6	3974.0	274.4	1035.3	1664.7	2621.7	3016.8	516.4
	Oct	25222.3	1407.1	4263.0	263.8	1015.7	1683.9	2566.0	3069.1	524.1
	Nov	22687.4	1453.2	4220.0	246.4	954.8	1622.6	2420.2	2894.7	500.0
	Dec	22983.8	1490.7	4170.0	246.2	917.6	1670.1	2493.1	3168.8	533.4
1992	Jan	22023.1	1529.7	4402.0	255.0	970.1	1753.5	2571.2	3223.4	524.4
	Feb	21338.8	1477.4	4417.0	266.5	940.4	1840.6	2562.1	3267.7	514.4
	Mar	19346.0	1414.3	4485.0	255.5	999.9	1837.2	2440.1	3235.5	488.8
	Apr	17390.7	1437.0	4313.0	248.7	981.5	1880.1	2654.1	3359.1	495.0
	May	18347.8	1524.7	4665.0	261.1	991.5	1920.6	2707.6	3387.8	513.7
	Jun	15951.7	1481.1	4520.0	238.3	913.0	1854.8	2521.2	3318.5	495.4
	Jul	15910.3	1451.8	4242.0	216.3	861.7	1798.1	2399.6	3393.8	495.6
	Aug	18061.1	1378.5	4054.0	205.0	772.7	1751.6	2312.6	3257.4	506.6
	Sep	17399.1	1351.0	4211.0	193.0	696.6	1878.3	2553.0	3271.7	501.0
	Oct	16767.4	1383.9	4013.0	198.5	706.9	1911.1	2658.3	3240.3	486.4
	Nov	17683.7	1469.1	4192.0	213.9	901.4	1931.2	2778.8	3305.2	494.1
	Dec	16925.0	1524.4	4369.0	214.3	912.6	2107.0	2846.5	3301.1	497.1
1992 high		23801.2	1545.9	4689.0	266.5	1014.5	2107.0	2847.8	3413.2	542.1
1992 low		14309.4	1311.0	3936.0	179.5	639.0	1670.1	2281.0	3136.6	467.5

Market capitalisation, $bn

	Japan	Singapore	South Africa	Spain	Sweden	Switzerland	United Kingdom	United States	World
End 1991	2,945	79	160	113	95	187	908	3,168	9,832
End 1992	2,331	75	102	95	87	195	915	4,023	9,320

Top five companies by market capitalisation, November 30th 1992

Japan	Singapore	South Africa	Spain	Sweden	Switzerland	United Kingdom	United States	World
NTT	Singapore Airlines	De Beers	Telefonica	Astra	Nestlé	BT	Wal-Mart	Wal-Mart
Mitsubishi Bank	OCBC Bank	Anglo American	Endesa	Procordia	Roche	Glaxo	Exxon	Exxon
IBJ	Development Bank of Singapore	S.A. Breweries	Repsol	Ericsson	Sandoz	Shell T&T	Philip Morris	Philip Morris
Sumitomo Bank	Malayan Banking†	Gencor	Banco Bilbao Vizcaya	Asea	Union Bank of Switzerland	BAT	General Electric	General Electric
Dai-Ichi Kangyo Bank	Sime Darby†	Rembrandt	Iberdrola	Volvo	Ciba-Geigy	SmithKline Beecham	AT&T	NTT

Source: MSCI   * $ terms   †Malaysia.

Focus on stockmarkets

GERMANY The most widely quoted German stockmarket index is the Deutscher Aktienindex (DAX), an arithmetic index of the share prices of 30 blue-chip German firms, weighted by market capitalisation. It is updated every minute during the trading day. From the beginning of January 1992, it replaced the Commerzbank index in *The Economist's* weekly bourses table. The DAX represents 80% of total German market capitalisation, and covers all the country's exchanges. The Commerzbank index features 60 firms on the Düsseldorf exchange, but that market accounts for only 30% of German trading volume. Between the end of 1979 and November 1992 the DAX rose 224% in dollar terms, while the Morgan Stanley Capital International world index rose 270%.

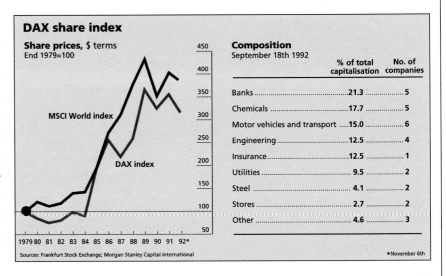

DAX share index

Share prices, $ terms
End 1979=100

MSCI World index

DAX index

Sources: Frankfurt Stock Exchange; Morgan Stanley Capital International

Composition
September 18th 1992

	% of total capitalisation	No. of companies
Banks	21.3	5
Chemicals	17.7	5
Motor vehicles and transport	15.0	6
Engineering	12.5	4
Insurance	12.5	1
Utilities	9.5	2
Steel	4.1	2
Stores	2.7	2
Other	4.6	3

*November 6th

CANADA Toronto has the world's sixth-biggest stockmarket by value, accounting for about three-quarters of total Canadian turnover. Its main share-price index is the Toronto Stock Exchange Composite index (TSE-300), which was introduced in January 1977, with its base year of 1975 set at 1,000. The TSE-300 is a capitalisation-weighted, arithmetic index of 300 companies, which accounts for 70% of the total value of shares listed in Toronto. In 1977 metals, minerals, gold and energy accounted for 35% of the index. In February 1992 their share was only 22%. Over the past decade Canadian shares have shown the smallest rise of the big stockmarkets. Since 1979 the TSE-300 has risen by only 71% in dollar terms, compared with a rise of 270% in the world share-price index.

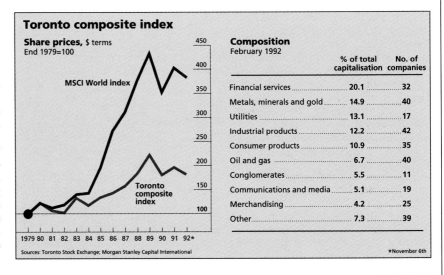

Toronto composite index

Share prices, $ terms
End 1979=100

MSCI World index

Toronto composite index

Sources: Toronto Stock Exchange; Morgan Stanley Capital International

Composition
February 1992

	% of total capitalisation	No. of companies
Financial services	20.1	32
Metals, minerals and gold	14.9	40
Utilities	13.1	17
Industrial products	12.2	42
Consumer products	10.9	35
Oil and gas	6.7	40
Conglomerates	5.5	11
Communications and media	5.1	19
Merchandising	4.2	25
Other	7.3	39

*November 6th

SWITZERLAND The most widely quoted stockmarket index in Switzerland is the Swiss market index (SMI). From April 1992 it replaced the Swiss Bank Corporation's industrial index in *The Economist's* table of world bourses. The SMI is a capitalisation-weighted, arithmetic index of 18 companies traded on the Basle, Geneva and Zurich stock exchanges. Zurich accounts for 70% of total turnover. The Swiss market's biggest sector, chemicals and drugs, includes three of the five biggest companies by capitalisation: Roche, Sandoz and Ciba-Geigy account for more than a third of the total index. Between December 1988 and November 1992 the SMI rose by 43% in dollar terms, compared with a 2% fall in the Morgan Stanley Capital International World index.

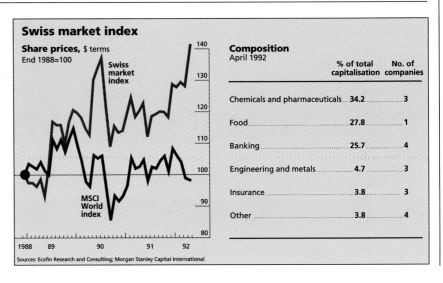

Swiss market index

Share prices, $ terms
End 1988=100

Swiss market index

MSCI World index

Sources: Ecofin Research and Consulting; Morgan Stanley Capital International

Composition
April 1992

	% of total capitalisation	No. of companies
Chemicals and pharmaceuticals	34.2	3
Food	27.8	1
Banking	25.7	4
Engineering and metals	4.7	3
Insurance	3.8	3
Other	3.8	4

ITALY Several Italian cities have small bourses, though much the biggest is Milan. By international standards, even that is tiny: its end-1991 market capitalisation of $154 billion represented only 14% of Italy's GDP. (New York's capitalisation was 66% of America's GDP; London's 95% of Britain's.) To make their market more attractive to investors and companies, the Italian authorities are overhauling the market's rules. Our table of world bourses shows the index compiled by the Banca Commerciale Italiana (BCI). This covers the 226 companies (all but two of them Italian) listed on the Milan exchange. Between the end of 1989 and November 1992 the index had fallen 41% in dollar terms, compared with a fall of 14% in Morgan Stanley's World index.

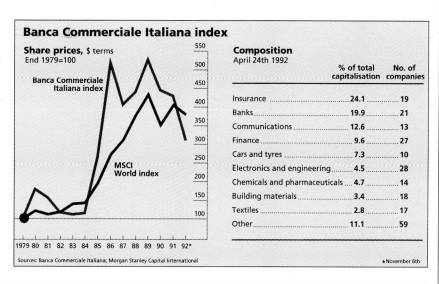

Banca Commerciale Italiana index

Share prices, $ terms
End 1979=100

Composition
April 24th 1992

	% of total capitalisation	No. of companies
Insurance	24.1	19
Banks	19.9	21
Communications	12.6	13
Finance	9.6	27
Cars and tyres	7.3	10
Electronics and engineering	4.5	28
Chemicals and pharmaceuticals	4.7	14
Building materials	3.4	18
Textiles	2.8	17
Other	11.1	59

Sources: Banca Commerciale Italiana; Morgan Stanley Capital International

*November 6th

AUSTRALIA The most widely quoted Australian index is the All-Ordinaries, which was introduced at the end of 1979 with about 260 companies. It now comprises 245 firms, which together account for 92% of shares listed in Australia and Papua New Guinea by market capitalisation, plus three actively traded New Zealand shares. The All-Ordinaries is a capitalisation-weighted arithmetic index, updated twice a minute during the trading day. The index encompasses two others, which are often quoted independently: the All-Mining index accounts for 17.6% of the All-Ordinaries; the All-Resources, 34.1%. In the 1980s the All-Ordinaries trailed the world average; but between December 1990 and November 1992 it rose 1.4% in dollar terms, against a world average of 5.4%.

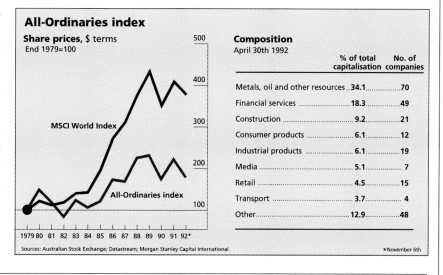

All-Ordinaries index

Share prices, $ terms
End 1979=100

Composition
April 30th 1992

	% of total capitalisation	No. of companies
Metals, oil and other resources	34.1	70
Financial services	18.3	49
Construction	9.2	21
Consumer products	6.1	12
Industrial products	6.1	19
Media	5.1	7
Retail	4.5	15
Transport	3.7	4
Other	12.9	48

Sources: Australian Stock Exchange; Datastream; Morgan Stanley Capital International

*November 6th

SPAIN The country's main stockmarket measure is the Madrid Stock-Exchange index, which was introduced in December 1940. In 1992 the index included the 92 biggest firms (according to market capitalisation) traded on the Madrid exchange, representing around 84% of the total value of the Madrid market. The index covered only 72 company stocks in 1985. To take account of changes in the relative size of the companies included, and to add new firms, the index is now re-weighted every year. Between 1985 and 1987 the Madrid index rose by more than three times as much as the Morgan Stanley Capital International index of world stockmarkets. Between the end of 1991 and November 1992, the index fell 31%, while the World index fell 8.1%.

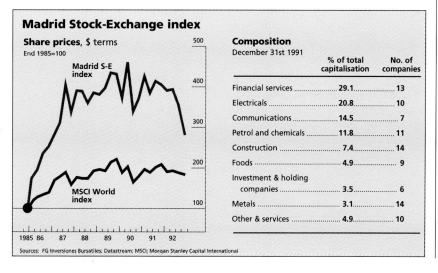

Madrid Stock-Exchange index

Share prices, $ terms
End 1985=100

Composition
December 31st 1991

	% of total capitalisation	No. of companies
Financial services	29.1	13
Electricals	20.8	10
Communications	14.5	7
Petrol and chemicals	11.8	11
Construction	7.4	14
Foods	4.9	9
Investment & holding companies	3.5	6
Metals	3.1	14
Other & services	4.9	10

Sources: FG Inversiones Bursatiles; Datastream; MSCI; Morgan Stanley Capital International

Money supply

Narrow*, % change on year earlier

		Australia	Belgium	Canada	France	Germany**	Holland	Italy	Japan	Spain	Sweden	Switzerland	United Kingdom	United States
1991	Jan	9.6	2.8	-1.3	-0.3	na	7.3	6.2	5.1	19.9	na	1.2	3.6	3.9
	Feb	7.7	0.8	-1.7	1.5	na	11.2	6.8	0.9	21.6	na	2.0	2.7	4.4
	Mar	8.0	1.8	3.1	0.6	na	10.8	7.9	1.1	20.9	na	-0.2	2.5	4.8
	Apr	5.7	0.8	9.1	2.3	na	7.3	6.3	0.3	17.0	na	2.5	1.5	4.4
	May	7.0	-0.4	4.6	1.2	na	9.9	7.2	3.1	16.9	na	3.0	1.6	5.5
	Jun	6.9	4.4	5.1	-0.3	na	4.7	7.8	6.6	16.8	na	0.6	2.0	5.9
	Jul	8.0	3.5	9.6	-0.5	na	5.0	7.2	6.1	15.9	na	2.7	2.1	6.2
	Aug	11.3	1.4	7.8	2.7	na	7.5	7.8	7.2	16.2	na	3.1	1.6	6.2
	Sep	8.2	4.7	7.1	2.1	na	nil	6.1	6.3	15.4	na	0.7	2.3	6.0
	Oct	10.1	2.9	2.5	-3.1	na	1.1	7.4	7.4	15.0	na	1.2	2.6	7.1
	Nov	10.4	3.5	6.0	0.8	na	5.3	9.0	9.2	14.6	na	0.4	3.0	8.2
	Dec	7.6	0.2	5.5	-4.6	na	4.5	10.5	8.7	13.5	na	-1.8	3.1	8.7
1992	Jan	12.2	1.1	6.0	-2.4	3.9	3.2	11.1	7.5	13.2	na	nil	2.1	10.2
	Feb	14.0	-2.9	7.2	-2.2	4.1	2.4	8.1	7.4	11.3	na	0.8	2.2	11.3
	Mar	13.4	2.5	5.3	-1.4	4.9	2.9	7.4	7.6	9.9	na	1.2	2.3	11.5
	Apr	15.4	1.8	4.7	-1.5	7.0	4.6	9.8	7.1	9.6	na	1.3	2.3	11.9
	May	14.6	3.4	3.6	1.7	5.8	8.3	9.4	6.9	7.6	na	-2.6	2.5	12.2
	Jun	14.8	2.4	4.8	-1.7	6.5	1.0	9.9	3.2	5.4	na	-1.3	1.3	11.0
	Jul	23.1	2.2	4.1	-0.7	5.5	-1.2	7.4	2.9	3.4	na	-3.0	2.5	11.7
	Aug	21.0	–	5.9	-1.6	6.0	1.9	5.3	3.7	3.8	na	-2.5	2.4	12.3
	Sep	24.4	–	6.2	nil	8.6	7.1	5.1	2.9	3.8	na	1.3	2.1	13.4
	Oct	21.7	–	9.9	1.6	8.4	12.8	5.4	2.4	1.7	na	–	2.4	14.3
	Nov	–	–	8.6	–	–	–	–	2.5	-0.1	na	–	3.0	14.3
	Dec	–	–	–	–	–	–	–	–	–	na	–	–	–

Broad†, % change on year earlier

		Australia	Belgium	Canada	France	Germany	Holland	Italy	Japan	Spain	Sweden	Switzerland	United Kingdom	United States
1991	Jan	9.9	5.0	8.5	7.4	2.4	7.1	7.6	6.0	11.6	6.7	2.7	11.2	1.5
	Feb	8.3	0.5	9.1	7.9	3.5	8.6	8.0	5.3	12.3	6.9	2.8	10.7	2.1
	Mar	8.0	2.5	9.7	7.9	4.2	7.5	9.0	6.8	12.8	10.1	3.1	9.9	2.2
	Apr	6.6	3.2	8.7	7.9	3.6	4.7	7.7	2.3	12.0	8.8	3.5	9.6	2.2
	May	7.1	3.2	8.6	7.3	3.8	9.1	8.2	4.2	11.6	11.2	3.8	9.2	2.2
	Jun	6.4	5.2	8.6	6.4	3.7	3.2	8.9	3.6	11.2	12.2	3.7	7.9	2.1
	Jul	6.2	6.0	8.9	6.4	4.0	4.4	8.1	2.9	11.1	13.0	4.1	7.6	1.6
	Aug	4.9	6.0	6.5	6.9	4.4	6.9	8.1	3.1	11.1	11.3	3.5	7.1	1.2
	Sep	3.9	6.3	6.5	5.4	4.6	0.8	7.0	1.2	11.7	12.4	2.3	6.7	0.9
	Oct	3.3	6.9	6.7	4.2	4.7	2.8	7.4	2.4	11.8	12.6	3.1	6.4	1.0
	Nov	2.1	6.1	6.5	4.9	5.1	5.1	8.3	2.2	11.8	11.0	2.7	5.7	1.2
	Dec	1.7	5.3	5.8	2.7	5.8	4.8	9.0	4.2	10.9	4.0	2.9	6.2	1.4
1992	Jan	3.2	4.4	5.8	3.8	6.3	5.3	9.4	3.4	9.7	5.7	2.5	6.2	1.2
	Feb	3.8	2.0	5.6	3.6	6.5	5.0	7.6	1.9	7.8	2.7	3.0	5.9	0.9
	Mar	2.7	6.2	5.7	4.1	7.0	5.3	7.4	0.2	6.9	3.2	2.6	5.8	0.6
	Apr	3.8	7.7	6.0	4.5	7.6	6.3	9.3	2.6	6.8	3.4	3.7	5.6	0.3
	May	3.3	7.8	5.0	5.8	7.8	7.6	9.0	0.8	6.6	2.7	3.5	5.1	0.2
	Jun	2.9	7.6	5.9	5.2	8.3	5.0	9.6	0.6	6.5	0.4	3.5	5.3	nil
	Jul	7.4	8.4	7.0	5.3	8.3	3.6	8.0	1.3	5.9	0.5	3.0	5.6	0.1
	Aug	8.1	–	8.1	5.1	8.7	5.0	6.5	0.3	5.7	1.1	3.0	5.5	0.4
	Sep	7.2	–	8.2	5.4	9.4	10.4	6.1	-0.4	5.1	-3.9	3.0	4.8	0.7
	Oct	6.6	–	8.3	7.2	10.4	10.2	7.2	-0.6	5.1	-3.8	–	5.4	0.6
	Nov	–	–	8.8	–	–	–	–	-0.6	0.1	0.7	–	4.7	0.6
	Dec	–	–	–	–	–	–	–	–	–	–	–	–	–

* M1 except UK M0   † M3 except Belgium, Holland, Italy M2, Japan M2 plus CDs, Spain M3 plus other liquid assets, UK M4   **From January 1991 % change from 4th quarter 1990 at annual rate. From January 1992 % change on a year earlier

Interest rates: money market

Overnight, %, last Tuesday of month

		Australia	Belgium	Canada	France	Germany	Holland	Italy	Japan	Spain	Sweden	Switzerland	United Kingdom	United States
1991	Jan	12.10	9.75	11.75	10.06	8.50	9.00	12.75	8.06	14.42	13.35	8.00	14.00	6.00
	Feb	12.00	9.10	10.25	9.19	8.70	8.84	13.13	8.19	14.57	12.25	7.44	14.00	5.50
	Mar	12.10	8.70	9.75	9.75	8.95	9.19	12.13	8.19	13.63	12.25	9.00	13.38	6.13
	Apr	11.50	8.30	9.44	9.25	8.85	9.16	11.75	8.16	13.21	12.10	8.38	8.63	5.94
	May	10.40	8.75	9.25	10.00	8.95	8.94	10.88	7.88	12.80	11.25	8.00	11.50	5.88
	Jun	10.50	8.75	8.75	10.13	8.85	8.72	10.88	7.94	12.81	10.15	7.75	10.31	5.81
	Jul	10.50	8.75	8.88	9.56	9.00	8.81	11.50	7.41	12.65	10.10	7.63	11.13	5.69
	Aug	10.55	8.90	8.50	9.06	9.15	9.06	11.13	7.44	12.59	10.10	8.00	10.63	5.50
	Sep	9.50	9.00	9.00	9.25	9.10	9.06	11.00	6.81	12.59	9.90	8.00	10.38	5.25
	Oct	9.20	9.10	9.00	8.93	9.10	9.19	10.75	6.69	12.39	10.60	8.13	9.00	5.11
	Nov	8.55	9.10	7.38	9.81	9.10	9.06	11.13	6.25	12.58	10.55	7.75	11.00	4.94
	Dec	8.50	9.30	7.75	10.50	9.50	9.88	12.63	5.72	12.73	14.25	8.50	10.00	4.09
1992	Jan	7.60	9.40	7.38	6.69	9.50	9.53	12.25	5.50	12.62	12.50	7.38	11.25	4.00
	Feb	7.50	9.30	7.25	9.75	9.50	9.25	12.25	5.56	12.48	11.90	7.75	11.00	3.97
	Mar	7.50	9.30	7.13	9.94	9.65	8.13	12.25	5.56	12.03	11.10	8.88	10.63	4.07
	Apr	7.50	9.30	6.88	9.94	9.65	9.44	12.50	4.69	11.99	11.60	8.75	8.63	3.50
	May	6.60	9.30	6.25	9.94	9.55	9.56	12.50	4.66	12.38	11.50	9.56	17.50	4.02
	Jun	6.50	9.30	5.63	10.00	9.70	9.47	13.50	4.69	12.37	11.40	9.13	10.00	3.88
	Jul	5.70	9.45	5.75	10.00	9.70	9.69	15.00	4.03	12.94	12.05	8.25	10.13	3.27
	Aug	5.75	9.60	4.88	10.06	9.75	9.75	15.38	4.03	12.96	12.90	7.88	7.00	3.29
	Sep	5.65	9.00	12.00	21.63	9.15	8.94	16.63	4.06	13.72	39.25	7.13	9.00	3.26
	Oct	5.70	8.75	8.00	9.88	8.85	8.81	15.81	3.97	13.09	12.55	6.00	9.00	2.95
	Nov	5.75	8.70	7.50	9.69	8.85	8.75	13.25	3.81	14.83	12.60	6.13	5.50	2.58
	Dec	5.80	8.60	6.75	10.75	8.90	8.66	13.63	3.88	14.64	11.10	6.88	6.00	2.74

Three-month, %, last Tuesday of month

		Australia	Belgium	Canada	France	Germany	Holland	Italy	Japan	Spain	Sweden	Switzerland	United Kingdom	United States
1991	Jan	11.85	9.86	10.70	10.06	9.13	9.18	13.63	7.64	15.04	12.85	8.13	13.88	6.92
	Feb	11.70	9.32	9.95	9.38	8.94	8.96	13.50	7.62	14.59	11.74	8.00	13.00	6.60
	Mar	11.60	9.41	9.78	9.38	9.13	9.12	12.50	7.65	13.28	12.25	8.56	12.50	6.29
	Apr	11.20	9.25	9.32	9.15	9.06	9.17	12.13	7.57	13.45	12.36	8.44	11.69	5.92
	May	10.00	8.92	8.90	9.25	8.88	9.03	11.63	7.46	12.46	11.18	8.13	11.44	5.91
	Jun	10.50	9.25	8.70	9.94	8.94	9.11	11.75	7.41	12.55	10.72	7.88	11.25	6.11
	Jul	9.90	9.31	8.90	9.58	9.25	9.22	12.00	7.08	12.91	10.71	7.88	11.13	6.00
	Aug	10.25	9.20	8.00	9.69	9.20	9.27	12.13	7.00	12.62	10.64	8.00	10.81	5.74
	Sep	9.50	9.26	8.42	9.44	9.20	9.26	11.88	6.47	12.35	10.42	8.06	10.31	5.52
	Oct	8.50	9.40	7.88	9.06	9.35	9.34	11.50	6.15	12.64	10.85	8.44	10.47	5.31
	Nov	8.10	9.50	7.44	9.68	9.40	9.41	10.15	6.19*	12.82	11.84	8.06	10.69	4.94
	Dec	7.35	9.75	7.25	10.25	9.55	9.68	13.19	5.75	13.02	13.34	8.31	10.94	4.45
1992	Jan	7.40	9.50	6.88	9.98	9.50	9.59	12.13	4.91	12.84	12.20	7.44	10.81	4.10
	Feb	7.40	9.50	7.25	10.00	9.50	9.52	12.25	5.16	12.90	12.05	7.63	10.31	4.20
	Mar	7.50	9.74	7.19	10.06	9.70	9.61	12.44	4.83	12.60	11.64	8.81	10.81	4.28
	Apr	6.95	9.63	6.67	9.97	9.75	9.49	12.50	4.69	12.49	11.98	8.75	10.50	3.96
	May	6.40	9.50	6.15	9.88	9.65	9.44	12.50	4.70	12.49	11.45	9.38	10.00	3.91
	Jun	6.30	9.56	5.36	10.06	9.70	9.49	14.13	4.50	12.65	11.58	9.25	10.13	3.81
	Jul	5.35	9.70	5.24	10.31	9.70	9.57	16.31	4.04	13.32	12.62	8.63	10.25	3.38
	Aug	5.65	9.75	4.83	10.50	9.87	9.82	16.19	3.76	13.46	14.52	8.00	10.81	3.48
	Sep	5.60	9.25	7.55	15.00	9.10	9.05	18.13	3.89	14.48	26.50	7.00	9.00	3.26
	Oct	5.60	8.50	6.05	9.81	8.70	8.60	14.81	3.82	13.68	12.87	6.50	8.75	3.47
	Nov	5.87	8.59	8.05	10.50	8.90	8.65	14.81	3.75	14.98	12.18	6.50	7.25	3.78
	Dec	5.73	8.50	7.03	11.25	8.80	8.66	13.44	3.75	14.94	10.20	6.25	7.13	3.55

*New series. Sources: Banco Bilbao Vizcaya, Chase Manhattan, Banque de Commerce (Belgium), Credit Lyonnais, Bank Nederland, Royal Bank of Canada, Svenska Handelsbanken, Westpac Banking Corp, The WEFA Group. These rates cannot be construed as offers by these banks.

Interest rates: prime

The prime rate is charged by banks for short-term loans to their best business customers. It is the key commercial borrowing rate in America, making headlines when altered, usually because of changes in the discount rate the Federal Reserve charges for lending to banks. In other countries it is more an indicative rate for business loans. In Belgium, Germany, Holland, Italy and Switzerland it is the rate charged to prime business customers for overdrafts. Britain's prime rate is banks' base rate plus 1%. In 1992 most countries' rates continued to decline as governments tried to give a boost to their slumping economies. America's prime rate fell from 9.5% at the start of 1991 to 6.0% in December 1992. Over the same period Britain's fell from 15.0% to 8.0%. Despite pleas and rumours of rate cuts, the German rate has remained at around 11.0% throughout 1991 and 1992. Japan's rate has dropped from 8.25% in January 1991 to 4.5% in December 1992.

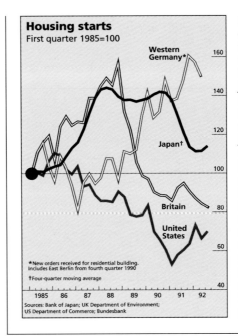

Housing starts
First quarter 1985=100

Western Germany*

Japan†

Britain

United States

*New orders received for residential building. Includes East Berlin from fourth quarter 1990

†Four-quarter moving average

1985 86 87 88 89 90 91 92

Sources: Bank of Japan; UK Department of Environment; US Department of Commerce; Bundesbank

HOUSING A good leading indicator of economic activity is residential construction. As interest rates rise, housing starts fall, indicating a downturn; a revival of house-building usually signals a recovery. Japan's slowdown was introduced by a fall in housing starts in the second half of 1991; starts in the third quarter of 1992 were down by a fifth from the peak of July-September 1990. In America starts rose steadily during 1991 and 1992, boosting hopes of economic recovery. However between the first quarter 1985 and the third quarter 1992 starts fell 30%. In Britain, the rise that began in summer 1991 was quickly interrupted and starts in the third quarter of 1992 were 45% lower than in the boom of summer 1988. House-building in western Germany was booming in the third quarter of 1991, starts were up 10% over the previous year, but fell in the first half of 1992, down 6.4% from the peak in 1991.

Commercial banks' prime-lending rates, %

Last Tuesday of month

		Australia	Belgium	Canada	France	Germany	Holland	Italy	Japan	Spain	Sweden	Switzerland	United Kingdom	United States
1991	Jan	15.50	13.25	12.25	10.15	10.50	10.50	13.00	8.25	16.50	14.00	10.25	15.00	9.50
	Feb	15.50	13.25	11.25	10.15	10.50	11.00	13.50	8.25	16.50	13.50	10.13	14.00	9.00
	Mar	15.50	12.75	11.25	10.15	10.50	11.00	13.50	8.25	16.50	13.00	10.88	13.50	9.00
	Apr	15.00	12.50	10.25	10.15	10.50	11.00	13.50	7.88	16.50	13.00	10.63	13.00	8.50
	May	14.25	12.75	9.75	10.15	10.50	11.00	12.88	7.88	16.50	13.00	10.13	12.50	8.50
	Jun	14.25	12.75	9.75	10.15	10.50	11.00	12.50	7.88	16.00	12.00	9.75	12.50	8.50
	Jul	14.25	12.75	9.75	10.15	10.50	11.00	12.50	7.63	16.00	12.00	9.38	12.00	8.50
	Aug	14.25	12.75	9.75	10.15	11.50	11.25	12.50	7.63	16.00	12.00	10.63	12.00	8.50
	Sep	13.50	12.75	9.50	10.15	11.50	11.25	12.50	7.38	16.00	12.00	10.13	11.50	8.00
	Oct	13.50	12.75	8.75	10.00	11.50	11.25	12.50	7.00	16.00	12.00	10.00	11.50	8.00
	Nov	12.50	12.75	8.50	10.00	11.00	11.25	12.50	6.63	16.00	12.00	9.88	11.50	7.50
	Dec	12.50	12.75	8.00	10.35	11.25	11.75	12.63	6.63	16.00	14.50	10.13	11.50	6.50
1992	Jan	11.75	13.25	7.50	10.35	11.00	11.75	13.00	5.88	16.00	14.50	9.38	11.50	6.50
	Feb	11.75	13.25	7.50	10.35	11.00	11.75	13.00	5.88	16.00	13.50	10.00	11.50	6.50
	Mar	11.75	13.25	8.25	10.35	11.00	11.75	13.00	5.88	13.00*	12.50	11.13	11.50	6.50
	Apr	11.75	13.25	7.75	10.35	11.00	11.75	13.13	5.25	13.00	12.50	11.13	11.50	6.50
	May	10.75	13.25	7.50	9.85	11.00	11.75	13.13	5.25	13.00	12.50	11.25	11.00	6.50
	Jun	10.75	13.25	7.00	9.85	11.00	11.75	13.50	5.25	13.00	12.50	10.88	11.00	6.50
	Jul	10.00	13.25	6.75	9.85	11.00	11.75	14.88	5.25	13.00	12.50	10.38	11.00	6.00
	Aug	10.00	13.25	6.50	9.85	11.50	11.75	15.38	4.75	13.50	13.00	9.88	11.00	6.00
	Sep	10.00	13.25	6.25	9.85	11.00	11.25	17.00	4.75	13.50	21.00	9.38	10.00	6.00
	Oct	10.00	12.75	7.75	9.85	11.00	11.00	17.00	4.25	13.50	16.00	7.88	9.00	6.00
	Nov	10.00	12.75	9.00	9.45	11.00	11.00	15.80	4.75	14.00	14.50	8.25	8.00	6.00
	Dec	10.00	12.75	7.25	10.00	11.00	10.75	14.75	4.50	14.00	13.00	7.63	8.00	6.00

*New series.

Interest rates: bank deposits

The table below lists indicative interest rates which commercial banks offer customers for deposits of large sums for three months' duration. Unlike regular deposits, the money is not available on demand; the customer must wait until maturity or pay a penalty for early withdrawal. In compensation the banks offer rates close to money-market interest rates. The Australian, Swedish, British and American rates are for certificates of deposit (CDs), an investment instrument which started in New York in the 1960s and is popular with commercial customers because it can be traded in secondary markets run by the banks themselves and discount houses. Because they are too large to be covered by deposit insurance, CDs are viewed as a slightly riskier investment than government guaranteed Treasury bills and consequently offer higher rates of interest. In December 1992 Japan had the lowest deposit rate and Sweden the highest.

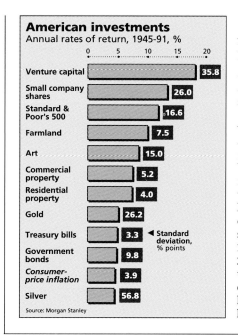

American investments
Annual rates of return, 1945-91, %

	Return	Standard deviation
Venture capital	35.8	
Small company shares	26.0	
Standard & Poor's 500	16.6	
Farmland	7.5	
Art	15.0	
Commercial property	5.2	
Residential property	4.0	
Gold	26.2	
Treasury bills	3.3	◄ Standard deviation, % points
Government bonds	9.8	
Consumer-price inflation	3.9	
Silver	56.8	

Source: Morgan Stanley

INVESTMENT RETURNS Since 1945 America's Standard & Poor's 500 index has yielded an average annual return of 11.8% in dollar terms, compared with only 4.8% on government bonds. But, according to Morgan Stanley, the standard deviation of the annual returns–a measure of how far returns vary from the mean–was almost twice as high for shares as for bonds. This means shares were much riskier, with big losses in one year offset by big gains in another. In general, investments with the highest average returns have the highest standard deviations. Venture capital has been the best performer since 1945, with an average return of 18%, but it had a standard deviation of 36 percentage points, compared with ten percentage points for bonds. The exceptions are gold and silver, which have had both low average returns and high standard deviations.

Three-month commercial-bank deposits, %

Last Tuesday of month

		Australia	Belgium	Canada	France	Germany	Holland	Italy	Japan	Spain	Sweden	Switzerland	United Kingdom	United States
1991	Jan	12.00	9.60	10.70	10.19	8.30	9.18	na	4.08	7.25	12.79	7.50	13.88	6.95
	Feb	11.70	9.05	9.95	9.56	8.14	8.96	na	4.08	9.50	11.74	7.25	12.97	6.67
	Mar	11.60	9.50	9.78	9.50	8.31	9.12	na	4.08	9.50	12.43	7.69	12.41	6.33
	Apr	11.20	9.15	9.30	9.28	8.30	9.17	na	4.08	9.50	12.40	7.69	11.69	5.90
	May	10.00	8.75	8.90	9.38	8.08	9.03	na	4.08	9.50	11.25	7.63	11.38	5.88
	Jun	10.50	9.25	8.70	9.81	8.13	9.11	na	4.08	9.00	10.65	7.13	11.25	6.04
	Jul	9.90	9.38	9.00	9.75	8.42	9.22	na	4.08	8.50	10.60	7.88	11.06	5.90
	Aug	10.25	9.05	8.56	9.44	8.37	9.27	na	3.75	8.50	10.70	7.50	10.81	5.66
	Sep	9.50	9.31	7.25	9.31	8.37	9.26	na	3.75	8.50	10.35	7.31	10.28	5.39
	Oct	8.50	9.20	7.00	9.16	8.51	9.34	na	3.75	8.50	11.10	7.69	10.44	5.28
	Nov	8.10	9.40	7.00	9.68	8.55	9.41	na	3.25	8.50	11.40	7.31	10.50	4.88
	Dec	7.35	9.50	7.37	10.07	8.69	9.68	na	2.75	8.50	13.55	7.56	10.88	4.30
1992	Jan	7.40	9.47	6.85	9.88	8.65	9.59	na	2.75	8.50	12.35	6.94	10.53	4.10
	Feb	7.40	9.50	7.00	10.00	8.65	9.52	na	2.75	8.50	12.30	7.13	10.19	4.19
	Mar	7.50	9.55	6.75	10.00	8.83	9.61	na	2.75	8.00	11.50	8.06	10.69	4.23
	Apr	6.95	9.63	6.25	10.00	8.87	9.49	na	2.15	8.00	11.75	8.25	10.38	3.91
	May	6.40	9.50	5.75	9.81	8.78	9.44	na	2.15	8.00	11.60	7.88	9.94	3.85
	Jun	6.30	9.56	5.50	10.00	8.83	9.49	na	2.15	8.00	11.70	8.75	10.00	3.89
	Jul	5.35	9.70	5.25	10.25	8.83	9.57	na	3.20	8.00	12.20	8.19	10.13	3.32
	Aug	5.65	9.75	4.75	10.94	8.98	9.82	na	2.80	8.00	14.20	7.50	10.69	3.35
	Sep	5.60	9.25	7.25	13.00	8.23	9.05	na	3.70	8.00	27.00	6.50	8.88	3.12
	Oct	5.60	8.50	5.75	9.75	7.92	8.60	na	3.57	8.00	13.40	6.00	7.81	3.40
	Nov	5.75	8.62	8.00	10.20	8.10	8.65	na	3.50	8.00	12.50	6.00	7.09	3.68
	Dec	5.73	8.38	6.63	11.00	8.01	8.35	na	3.73	8.00	10.95	5.88	7.00	3.37

Interest rates: government bonds

BOND YIELDS Long-term government-bond yields have fallen in most big economies since 1990. Japanese yields have tumbled from 8.7% in September 1990 to 4.7% in November 1992; real bond yields (deflated by the rise in prices over the previous 12 months) have fallen from 5.7% to 2.6%. In America, bond yields have fallen by less than inflation, so real yields have risen. Real yields in Britain appear to have jumped even more sharply, from 0.5% to 4.7%. But Britain's headline inflation rate has been distorted. Using an underlying rate, real yields in November 1992 were 4.5%. Nominal bond yields in Germany fell from 9.05% in September 1990 to 8.21% in November 1992, while its real yields fell from 5.9% to 3.4%.

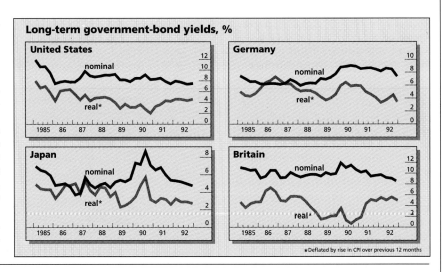

Long-term government-bond yields, %

United States · Germany · Japan · Britain

nominal / real*

*Deflated by rise in CPI over previous 12 months

Government-bond yields

Government bonds have a minimal risk of insolvency and provide a steady income not affected by stockmarket fluctuations. Yields shown in this table are for benchmark long-term bonds with maturities ranging from five years to 30 years. In Belgium, Canada, Japan and Spain yields are for a single bond; all others are the average of yields for bonds of similar maturity. Salomon Brothers, a New York investment bank, reckons the total of central government bonds outstanding for the countries listed below was $5.5 trillion at the end of 1991, 39.4% of all publicly-issued bonds outstanding.

%, last Tuesday of month

		Australia	Belgium	Canada	France	Germany	Holland	Italy	Japan	Spain	Sweden	Switzerland	United Kingdom	United States
1991	Jan	11.61	9.82	10.04	9.55	8.94	8.97	12.06	6.75	14.30	11.71	6.42	10.16	8.24
	Feb	11.47	9.21	9.67	9.04	8.40	8.57	11.90	6.34*	13.63	11.19	6.25	9.98	8.04
	Mar	11.38	9.40	9.75	9.13	8.55	8.74	11.64	6.55	12.68	11.69	6.14	10.18	8.31
	Apr	10.97	9.28	9.71	8.70	8.50	8.65	11.18	6.73	12.27	11.30	6.06	10.13	8.18
	May	10.45	9.16	9.89	8.87	8.40	8.55	11.15	6.66	11.54	10.49	5.89	10.22	8.28
	Jun	11.31	9.51	10.28	9.23	8.65	8.67	11.55	6.83	12.06	10.71	5.96	10.44	8.51
	Jul	11.00	9.61	10.13	9.25	8.90	8.89	11.93	6.59	12.44	10.71	6.01	10.06	8.40
	Aug	10.65	9.52	10.00	9.10	8.76	8.84	11.58	6.46	11.79	10.54	6.53	9.86	8.12
	Sep	10.41	9.38	9.63	8.89	8.68	8.80	11.20	5.99	11.32	10.03	6.12	9.44	7.88
	Oct	9.78	9.36	9.25	8.79	8.66	8.80	11.07	5.87	11.65	10.10	6.77	9.59	7.89
	Nov	9.81	9.40	9.29	8.94	8.58	8.76	11.03	6.40	11.97	9.88	6.67	9.83	7.95
	Dec	9.50	9.18	8.98	8.72	8.47	8.60	11.23	5.38	11.74	9.94	6.40	9.60	7.45
1992	Jan	10.12	8.76	8.97	8.41	8.04	8.38	10.91	5.26	11.32	9.38	6.17	9.30	7.67
	Feb	10.00	8.83	9.12	8.52	8.08	8.31	10.78	5.40	10.74*	9.54	6.15	9.20	7.95
	Mar	9.90	9.20	9.41	8.71	8.18	8.39	11.02	5.32	10.94	9.48	6.57	9.72	7.96
	Apr	9.75	9.09	9.47	8.73	8.26	8.32	10.93	5.67	10.89	9.65	6.60	9.09	8.05
	May	9.15	9.02	9.20	8.52	8.28	8.27	10.94	5.51	10.85	9.53	6.82	8.89	7.91
	Jun	8.95	9.09	8.97	8.79	8.41	8.31	11.60	5.28	11.45	9.74	6.98	9.07	7.78
	Jul	8.55	9.21	8.34	8.98	8.34	8.37	12.15	4.93	12.16	9.99	7.00	8.96	7.43
	Aug	8.82	9.20	8.28	8.96	8.49	8.31	12.13	4.64	12.34	11.35	6.95	9.27	7.47
	Sep	9.05	8.78	8.58	8.57	7.98	7.83	12.47	4.81	13.07	11.57	6.33	9.19	7.37
	Oct	8.84	7.92	8.38	8.28	7.48	7.52	12.06	4.77	12.38	10.91	5.98	8.70	7.61
	Nov	8.77	8.76	8.70	8.19	7.36	7.34	11.72	4.62	12.67	10.36	5.93	8.69	7.53
	Dec	8.70	7.65	8.55	8.16	7.25	7.24	11.77	4.53	12.44	9.75	5.48	8.61	7.36

*New series.

Interest rates: corporate bonds

Companies issue bonds to borrow money on terms which are often more favourable than those offered by banks. Unlike shareholders, investors buying the bonds do not have voting rights; however, corporate bonds do offer the guarantee of a steady stream of income, or should the company go bankrupt, a place in the queue of creditors. Corporations can issue bonds in both the domestic and overseas markets. Yields in this table are for domestic bonds, and for most countries represent the average for a sample of bonds of similar maturity; but in Belgium, Canada, Japan and Spain a single bond's yield is quoted. Maturities range from six years for Germany to 25 for Britain. Corporate-bond yields are usually higher in countries with high inflation rates. Investors also usually demand higher yields on corporate bonds than on government bonds because of the greater perceived risk of default.

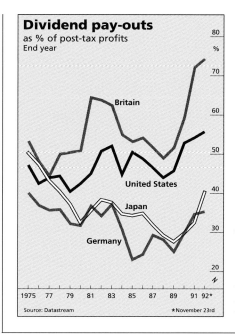

Dividend pay-outs
as % of post-tax profits
End year

Source: Datastream — ★November 23rd

COMPANY DIVIDENDS Where companies prefer to maintain their dividends to shareholders regardless of their own financial performance, you would expect pay-outs, calculated as a proportion of profits, to move counter to the business cycle. In Britain, especially, this has happened. As the chart shows, during the recessions of the early 1980s and 1990s dividends increased as a share of (dwindling) post-tax profits; during the mid-1980s, as the economy boomed, the ratio of dividend to profit fell. Equally striking is the growing divergence among the dividend ratios of the countries shown. In November 1992 Britain's dividend ratio was 74%. America's was 56%, Japan's 40% and Germany's 35%. In the mid-1970s, the ratios were closer, all lying between 40% in Germany and 53% in Britain. Financial deregulation in America (in the 1970s) and Britain (in the 1980s) may be part of the explanation.

Corporate-bond yields, %

Last Tuesday of month

		Australia	Belgium	Canada	France	Germany	Holland	Italy	Japan	Spain	Sweden	Switzerland	United Kingdom	United States
1991	Jan	12.25	9.85	11.02	10.34	8.96	9.98	12.33	7.29	14.46	12.75	7.14	11.89	9.36
	Feb	13.15	9.28	10.69	9.80	8.50	9.51	12.29	7.36	13.73	12.52	6.83	11.42	9.07
	Mar	13.15	9.42	10.62	9.80	8.60	9.48	12.23	7.51	13.36	13.00	6.80	11.44	9.22
	Apr	12.70	9.27	10.64	9.65	8.57	9.37	11.78	7.64	13.91	12.89	6.78	11.43	9.04
	May	12.10	9.13	10.64	9.66	8.42	9.43	11.23	7.60	13.76	11.73	6.62	11.45	9.16
	Jun	13.00	9.52	11.02	9.86	8.75	9.14	11.31	7.77	13.50	11.88	6.60	11.50	9.29
	Jul	12.70	9.63	10.83	9.87	9.05	9.47	11.42	7.44	14.19	11.83	6.66	11.44	9.17
	Aug	12.20	8.53	10.93	9.60	8.91	9.51	11.48	7.26	13.91	11.99	7.08	11.19	8.89
	Sep	11.83	9.45	10.69	9.55	8.79	9.49	11.55	6.56	13.91	11.57	6.77	10.76	8.69
	Oct	11.14	9.43	10.46	9.31	8.76	9.51	11.24	6.17	13.61	11.78	7.04	10.97	8.73
	Nov	11.01	9.49	10.19	9.51	8.71	9.49	11.27	7.86	13.41	11.73	7.08	11.21	8.70
	Dec	10.45	9.35	10.18	9.47	8.61	9.75	11.33	6.12	11.96	12.47	7.03	10.93	8.32
1992	Jan	11.42	8.98	9.98	9.10	8.08	9.55	11.21	5.73	11.46	11.72	6.84	10.62	8.45
	Feb	11.16	9.01	9.84	9.22	8.16	9.29	10.97	5.52	11.68	11.88	6.72	10.46	8.66
	Mar	10.95	9.20	10.12	9.40	8.29	9.42	11.16	5.29	11.46	11.72	6.90	10.87	8.62
	Apr	10.85	9.21	10.60	9.08	8.33	9.32	11.11	6.09	11.66	11.83	6.97	10.34	8.69
	May	10.11	9.21	10.18	9.21	8.35	9.55	11.27	5.96	11.56	11.88	7.16	10.04	8.52
	Jun	9.90	9.31	9.95	9.42	8.51	9.44	11.74	5.50	12.48	12.20	7.44	10.26	8.46
	Jul	9.21	9.41	9.56	9.61	8.43	9.29	12.37	5.82	12.87	12.47	7.41	10.17	8.17
	Aug	9.83	9.46	9.24	9.58	8.59	9.49	12.42	5.68	13.05	14.00	7.41	10.44	8.12
	Sep	9.90	8.93	9.64	9.34	8.00	8.92	13.84	5.69	13.92	13.90	6.91	10.53	8.08
	Oct	9.96	7.99	9.73	9.00	7.46	8.44	13.01	5.69	13.34	13.16	6.58	10.23	8.30
	Nov	8.77	8.76	8.70	8.19	7.36	7.34	11.72	4.62	12.67	10.36	5.93	8.69	7.53
	Dec	9.88	7.69	9.61	8.71	7.26	8.49	12.50	5.47	13.61	11.41	6.07	10.04	8.10

Interest rates: Eurocurrency deposits

A Eurocurrency is any currency deposited and lent outside its country of origin, for example, D-marks deposited in London are Euromarks. Eurodeposits are always lent for a fixed term, which can vary from overnight to five years. For each currency, the rate taken is the mid-point between the London bid and offer rates. Since January 1991 Eurocurrency deposit rates have fallen for many of the countries in our table. The Eurodollar rate has dropped to below half the level it was at the beginning of 1991, as America's Federal Reserve has eased its monetary policy to stimulate the economy. Eurosterling rates, which were falling gradually during 1991 and fluctuating around 10.5% in the first half of 1992, dropped sharply after sterling's withdrawal from the European exchange-rate mechanism in September 1992. Euromark rates, which were 9.13% at the beginning of 1991, have been substantially less volatile. They started 1992 at 9.88% and ended at 8.63%.

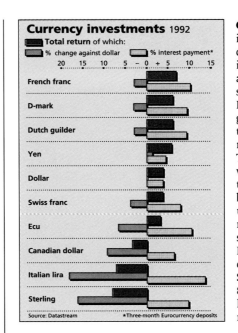

Currency investments 1992

■ Total return of which:
▨ % change against dollar ▢ % interest payment*

Source: Datastream   *Three-month Eurocurrency deposits

French franc
D-mark
Dutch guilder
Yen
Dollar
Swiss franc
Ecu
Canadian dollar
Italian lira
Sterling

CURRENCY YIELDS An international investor's total return on a currency deposits depends upon both the rate of interest paid on Eurocurrency deposits and movements in exchange rates. The shrewd investor put his money into the French franc, the D-mark, or the Dutch guilder in 1992. Despite slipping against the dollar, the franc yielded a high total return, thanks to a 10% interest payment. The D-mark yielded almost as much, but was a much less risky investment than the franc (which did so well largely because it was anchored to the mighty D-mark by the European exchange-rate mpechanism). At times in 1992, the franc seemed certain to follow sterling and the Italian lira, the year's worst-performing currencies in the chart, out of the ERM. Sterling yielded a total loss for the year of 8.89%, thanks to a 19% fall against the dollar. The dollar yielded a middling total return of 3.8% in 1992.

Three-month Eurocurrency deposit rate, %

Last Tuesday of month

		Australia	Belgium	Canada	France	Germany	Holland	Italy	Japan	Spain	Sweden	Switzerland	United Kingdom	United States
1991	Jan	11.56	9.81	10.44	10.13	9.13	9.06	12.25	8.19	14.25	13.00	8.25	13.91	7.06
	Feb	11.25	9.88	10.56	10.06	9.06	9.13	12.31	8.13	14.20	12.63	8.06	13.63	6.56
	Mar	11.53	9.38	9.44	9.38	9.13	9.13	11.63	8.16	12.95	12.30	8.50	12.44	6.38
	Apr	10.88	9.25	9.00	9.19	9.06	9.19	11.50	8.03	12.81	12.35	8.50	11.84	6.00
	May	10.00	8.88	8.63	9.31	8.94	9.00	11.00	7.72	12.00	11.25	8.13	11.34	6.00
	Jun	10.03	9.25	8.50	9.88	9.00	9.13	11.13	7.84	11.70	10.75	8.00	11.25	6.13
	Jul	10.13	9.25	8.69	9.63	9.31	9.19	11.38	7.41	12.56	10.62	7.88	11.10	6.00
	Aug	10.00	9.25	8.38	9.25	9.13	9.25	11.50	7.28	12.25	10.63	8.13	10.81	5.75
	Sep	9.44	9.19	8.13	9.38	9.19	9.19	11.25	6.50	12.06	10.30	8.13	10.31	5.50
	Oct	8.50	9.25	7.75	9.13	9.44	9.44	11.00	6.28	12.25	10.63	8.44	10.50	5.38
	Nov	7.75	9.44	7.38	9.81	9.38	9.44	11.75	6.19	12.22	11.38	8.13	10.69	4.94
	Dec	7.38	9.56	6.88	10.25	9.56	9.56	12.25	5.63	11.67	13.23	8.13	10.94	4.19
1992	Jan	7.38	9.44	6.81	9.94	9.88	9.44	11.50	5.16	12.48	12.13	7.44	10.59	4.19
	Feb	7.25	9.50	7.13	9.94	9.56	9.44	11.88	5.16	12.31	12.06	7.50	10.22	4.31
	Mar	7.31	9.75	7.56	10.06	9.69	9.63	12.00	5.06	12.37	11.53	8.63	10.81	4.31
	Apr	6.81	9.50	6.72	10.00	9.81	9.25	12.00	4.72	12.40	11.75	8.69	10.44	4.06
	May	6.19	9.50	6.09	9.88	9.63	9.38	12.00	4.72	12.25	11.29	9.19	9.93	3.94
	Jun	5.68	9.56	5.41	10.06	9.75	9.50	13.25	4.50	12.65	11.90	9.38	10.06	3.84
	Jul	5.44	9.69	5.13	10.50	9.75	9.56	15.25	4.03	13.25	12.35	8.56	10.19	3.38
	Aug	5.81	9.81	4.72	10.44	9.81	9.81	15.75	3.78	13.12	15.38	7.94	10.81	3.44
	Sep	4.56	9.25	6.97	14.25	9.06	8.88	17.75	4.06	15.00	16.00	6.94	8.94	3.25
	Oct	5.81	8.50	6.38	9.88	8.75	8.56	14.13	3.75	13.78	12.75	6.13	7.75	3.56
	Nov	5.69	8.63	8.63	10.75	8.75	8.63	14.50	3.78	14.87	11.75	6.44	7.19	3.63
	Dec	5.69	8.94	6.88	11.25	8.63	8.63	13.00	3.78	14.94	10.75	6.06	7.19	3.50

Interest rates: Eurobond yields

A Eurobond is issued by a company, or government, in a market outside that of its currency of denomination and is issued internationally, on the Euromarket, rather than in just one domestic market. Since Eurobonds are issued offshore, they escape any national financial regulations. The rates in the table, which are the averages of several issues in each currency, are collated by Credit Suisse First Boston, with the exception of Spain's, which are provided by the Ministry of Economics. There are no longer enough issues of Australian dollar Eurobonds to calculate an average. Over the past two years bond yields have fallen for most of the countries in the table as economies slipped into recession. Since January 1991 the yield on Eurodollar bonds has dropped by almost two percentage points, to 6.51%. Euromark rates have fallen by over one percentage point since June 1992 as Germany felt the effects of recession.

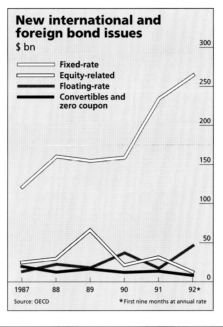

New international and foreign bond issues
$ bn

- Fixed-rate
- Equity-related
- Floating-rate
- Convertibles and zero coupon

Source: OECD   *First nine months at annual rate

1987 88 89 90 91 92*

BONDS New issues of international bonds have soared from $179 billion in 1987 to nearly $250 billion in the first three quarters of 1992, according to the OECD. Fixed-rate bond issues have increased the most. These pay a set amount of interest each year until redemption, when the issuer pays back the capital. Much of this growth reflects the need of European governments, especially those of Britain and Germany, to finance widening budget deficits. Recent political and currency uncertainty has increased the proportion of new bonds issued in dollars—the traditional safe haven in times of trouble. Issues of equity-related bonds, which pay interest but can be swapped for an agreed number of shares, have slowed. The bearish stockmarkets of recent years mean that these bonds have had little appeal to investors. In developing countries, bond issues continued to accelerate.

Eurocurrency-bond yields, %

Last Tuesday of month

		Australia	Belgium	Canada	France	Germany	Holland	Italy	Japan	Spain	Sweden	Switzerland	United Kingdom	United States
1991	Jan	11.97	9.87	10.59	9.95	8.88	9.38	11.31	6.80	13.73	12.07	6.96	11.20	8.32
	Feb	11.73	9.22	10.09	9.24	8.34	8.91	11.34	6.56	13.15	11.63	6.35	10.66	7.89
	Mar	12.17	9.42	10.21	9.21	8.26	8.88	11.29	6.87	12.55	11.82	6.67	10.67	8.09
	Apr	na	9.28	10.04	9.06	8.41	8.90	11.25	6.89	12.17	11.82	6.55	10.70	8.14
	May	na	9.21	9.99	8.97	8.31	8.85	10.38	6.86	11.70	10.89	6.36	10.80	8.13
	Jun	na	9.38	10.47	10.80	8.22	8.82	10.92	7.11	12.00	13.98	6.41	10.84	8.80
	Jul	na	9.48	10.28	9.10	8.68	8.91	10.26	6.85	12.06	10.92	6.54	10.59	8.13
	Aug	na	9.34	10.10	9.03	8.71	8.98	10.23	6.54	11.73	10.73	6.54	10.44	7.76
	Sep	na	9.22	9.64	8.83	8.40	8.90	10.25	6.07	11.61	10.61	6.72	10.01	7.40
	Oct	na	9.14	9.01	8.70	8.10	8.90	10.15	5.88	11.36	10.48	7.11	10.05	7.07
	Nov	na	9.22	9.16	8.85	8.08	8.87	10.25	5.92	11.77	10.28	6.86	10.43	6.81
	Dec	na	9.01	8.81	8.79	8.19	8.74	10.23	5.75	11.96	11.48	6.79	10.40	6.22
1992	Jan	na	8.71	9.03	8.47	7.67	8.35	10.10	5.36	11.24	10.80	6.58	10.00	6.57
	Feb	na	8.79	8.92	8.62	7.64	8.38	10.16	5.58	10.95	10.70	6.48	9.78	6.81
	Mar	na	8.90	9.31	9.02	8.19	8.56	10.98	5.58	11.06	10.00	6.77	10.25	7.58
	Apr	na	8.85	9.37	8.80	8.22	8.49	10.92	5.69	10.90	10.06	6.83	9.62	7.53
	May	na	8.77	8.40	8.40	8.14	8.44	10.91	5.57	10.87	9.96	6.98	9.35	7.21
	Jun	na	8.84	8.11	8.82	8.34	8.48	11.52	5.35	11.30	10.23	7.02	9.42	6.79
	Jul	na	8.94	7.35	9.27	8.36	8.54	12.38	4.95	12.59	10.43	6.88	9.39	6.17
	Aug	na	8.99	7.50	9.46	8.27	8.55	12.29	4.66	12.64	12.15	6.82	9.96	6.23
	Sep	na	8.63	8.08	8.57	7.77	7.78	12.38	4.83	14.25	12.24	6.46	8.89	5.91
	Oct	na	8.15	8.42	8.24	7.11	7.29	12.07	4.76	13.05	11.18	6.06	7.77	6.39
	Nov	na	8.03	9.13	8.20	7.07	7.28	11.64	4.77	13.14	10.03	5.59	7.82	6.64
	Dec	na	7.83	8.89	8.14	6.91	7.13	11.69	4.72	13.00	9.46	5.28	7.92	6.51

Focus on finance

CASH AND CREDIT More than 90% of Swiss, Dutch, German and French adults have bank accounts, but only 63% of Americans and 59% of Italians trust a bank to look after their money, according to a report in 1992 by Datamonitor. Americans love plastic: 60% of them carry credit cards, compared with only 33% in Britain. Japan, too, has caught the bug. More than 60% of Japanese wallets now contain a card, though it may be used infrequently. Plastic has yet to catch on in mainland Europe– only 1% of Dutch, Italian and German adults own a credit card. Nor is withdrawing money from cash machines easy in these countries–all have fewer than one-third as many cash machines per 10,000 people as Japan. Belgium has less than one cash machine per 10,000 people.

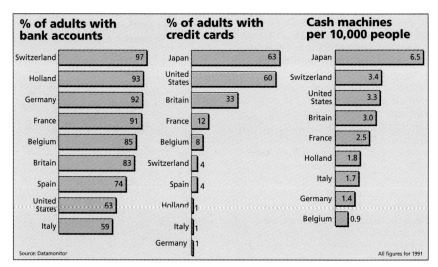

INSURANCE The Swiss are either the most accident-prone people in the OECD, or the most risk-averse. Financial statistics published in 1992 by the OECD showed that in 1990 insurance premiums equalled 13% of Switzerland's GDP. Switzerland also had the highest premiums per head in both life and non-life insurance–$1,792 and $2,515 per person, respectively. Britons were the next most cautious overall, with insurance premiums equal to 12.8% of GDP. But the Japanese had the second highest life-insurance premiums per head ($1,645) and Americans the second highest non-life premiums ($1,508). Among the countries in our chart, life-insurance premiums have been growing fastest in France, increasing by 22% a year between 1980 and 1990.

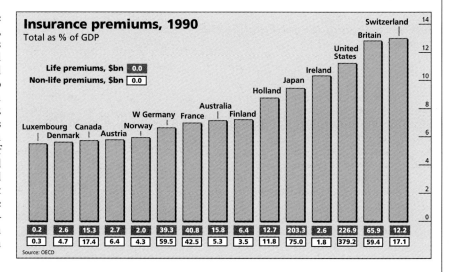

DERIVATIVES Swaps, futures and options have spread from America to Europe and Asia, multiplying on stock exchanges and on over-the-counter markets. Trading in these instruments is often cheaper than in the bonds or currencies that they "derive" from, so turnover often exceeds that of the underlying markets. Derivative contracts on interest rates and currencies were worth 25% of banks' international assets at the end of 1986, 75% four years later. But techniques for valuing derivatives have not kept up with their growing popularity. Banks and investment managers are only now establishing how to measure their value. They are not shown in balance sheets. A few American banks now have unreported assets worth several times those in their balance sheets.

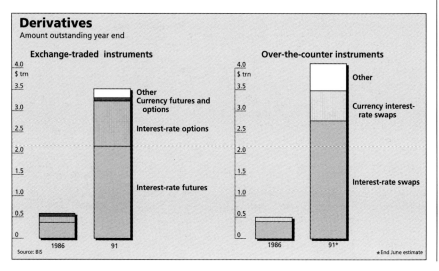

BUDGET DEFICITS Borrowing by OECD governments has risen sharply since 1989. Of the 18 countries in the chart, only Japan is estimated to have had a budget surplus in 1992. In 1989 seven countries boasted surpluses. The sharpest deteriorations have been in Finland, where a budget surplus of 2.9% of GDP in 1989 was transformed into an estimated deficit of 7.7% in 1992; and in Sweden where the budget swung from a surplus of 5.5% to a deficit of 4.1% of GDP. Greece has the biggest budget deficit of any industrial economy–a hefty 14.5% of its GDP–but it is one of the few economies that has trimmed its borrowing since 1989, from 17.7% of GDP. America is still the biggest borrower in absolute terms, but its deficit is only 3.8% of GDP.

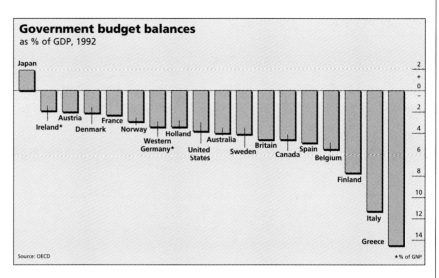

Government budget balances
as % of GDP, 1992

Source: OECD   *% of GNP

BIG COMPANY SHARES In nine of the countries in the chart, the ten biggest quoted companies accounted for over 30% of total stockmarket capitalisation at the end of April 1992. The smallest markets were the most concentrated. In Holland (with a total capitalisation of $132 billion) the ten biggest firms made up 74% of the market, with Royal Dutch Petroleum accounting for 33%. (Even that was down on April 1991, when it accounted for 39%.) At the other extreme, America's ten biggest companies accounted for only 15% of the total market ($3.7 trillion); the biggest stock was also an oil company, Exxon, which represented just 2% of the market's total value. Telecoms companies topped three countries' stockmarkets: Japan's NTT, Hong Kong Telecom and Telefonica de Espana.

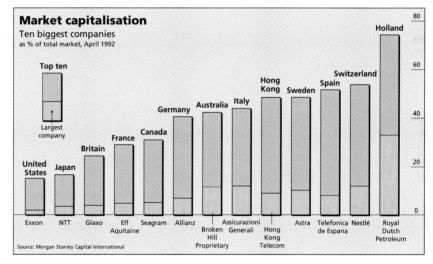

Market capitalisation
Ten biggest companies
as % of total market, April 1992

Source: Morgan Stanley Capital International

INTERNATIONAL MONETARY FUND Lending by the IMF fell to an annual rate of SDR4.2 billion ($6 billion) during the first eight months of 1992, a 43% fall from SDR7.4 billion in the whole of 1991. At the same time, countries' repayments to the Fund dipped only slightly, to an annualised SDR4.4 billion. As a result the IMF was a net recipient of money for the sixth time in seven years; 1991 was the exception. In 1992 three of the IMF's five biggest borrowers were in Latin America: Mexico (accounting for 17% of the Fund's outstanding loans, down from 18% in 1991), Venezuela (8%), and Argentina (6%). India's share increased to 10%, from 7% in 1991. Czechoslovakia (4%), which had benefited from recent increases in the IMF's lending to Eastern Europe, was fifth.

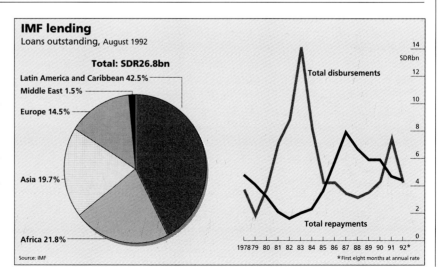

IMF lending
Loans outstanding, August 1992

Total: SDR26.8bn

Latin America and Caribbean 42.5%
Middle East 1.5%
Europe 14.5%
Asia 19.7%
Africa 21.8%

Total disbursements
Total repayments

1978 79 80 81 82 83 84 85 86 87 88 89 90 91 92*

Source: IMF   *First eight months at annual rate

Trade

Australia, France, Canada, Japan, Britain and America measure their visible-trade balance using exports free on board (fob) less imports fob, which means that goods are valued only up to the point of embarkation. Other countries in the table use cost-insurance-freight (cif) for imports. In these countries the valuation of goods imported includes all transport costs and insurance to their destination. Japan's 12-month visible-trade surplus has doubled since January 1991, to $131.5 billion in October 1992. Germany's annual visible-trade surplus fell by almost 80% in 1991 to $13.6 billion in December 1991, but has since widened to $25.6 billion in October 1992. France has witnessed the biggest turnaround, from a 12-month visible-trade deficit of $10.5 billion in January 1991 to a surplus of $4.4 billion in October 1992. America's 12-month visible trade-deficit increased in 1992 to $77.5 billion in October, from its low of $6.1 billion in February.

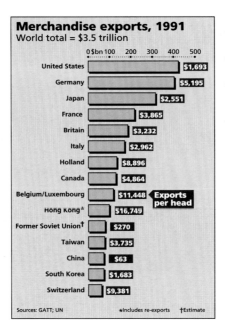

Merchandise exports, 1991
World total = $3.5 trillion

United States	$1,693
Germany	$5,195
Japan	$2,551
France	$3,865
Britain	$3,232
Italy	$2,962
Holland	$8,896
Canada	$4,864
Belgium/Luxembourg	$11,448 ◀ Exports per head
Hong Kong*	$16,749
Former Soviet Union†	$270
Taiwan	$3,735
China	$63
South Korea	$1,683
Switzerland	$9,381

Sources: GATT; UN   *Includes re-exports   †Estimate

EXPORTS The value of world trade grew by only 1.5% in 1991, the smallest gain since 1985; in 1990 its growth was 13.5%. The strongest growth was in Asia. Hong Kong which (including its re-exports) became the first developing country to make the world's top ten, saw a 20% jump in exports. At the other extreme the exports of the former Soviet Union fell by 25%, to $78 billion. America again overtook Germany as the world's biggest exporter; its exports rose by 7.5% in 1991, five times the world average. Ranking countries in terms of exports per head gives a different picture. Of the top 15 exporters in the chart, Hong Kong's exports amount to $16,749 per person, followed by Belgium at $11,448. Japan, however, exports only $2,551 per head, less than all the other industrial economies except the United States, which exported $1,693 per person in 1991. China exported only $63 per person in 1991.

Trade balances, $bn

12 months to date

		Australia	Belgium	Canada	France	Germany	Holland	Italy	Japan	Spain	Sweden	Switzerland	United Kingdom	United States
1991	Jan	0.99	-2.22	9.12	-10.45	57.71	5.83	-12.95	65.78	-32.97	2.72	-5.51	-31.82	-98.16
	Feb	0.94	-2.21	9.55	-10.90	53.25	5.79	-12.22	67.37	-33.06	3.11	-5.52	-30.65	-96.01
	Mar	1.44	-2.23	9.68	-11.41	47.19	6.50	-10.07	69.91	-32.56	3.35	-5.73	-28.42	-91.71
	Apr	1.60	-1.45	9.77	-11.22	42.07	6.19	-11.20	74.48	-33.03	3.77	-5.69	-26.42	-88.24
	May	1.96	-1.63	9.54	-10.70	34.43	7.26	-11.66	77.33	-32.96	3.66	-5.54	-25.48	-85.14
	Jun	2.24	-1.82	9.05	-10.66	29.82	7.21	-12.34	79.60	-32.81	4.03	-5.66	-23.20	-82.81
	Jul	2.48	-2.27	8.32	-10.57	23.92	6.85	-13.84	82.90	-33.28	4.29	-5.81	-20.82	-79.44
	Aug	3.18	-2.29	8.32	-10.38	20.95	7.37	-13.78	87.11	-32.86	4.41	-5.53	-19.61	-76.81
	Sep	3.24	-2.87	7.07	-9.07	16.82	7.59	-14.57	90.20	-33.04	4.53	-5.46	-19.73	-74.26
	Oct	3.29	-2.68	5.83	-6.73	12.67	7.34	-14.38	94.49	-32.89	4.94	-5.15	-18.96	-70.74
	Nov	3.21	-2.81	5.08	-6.27	12.67	7.87	-13.07	98.52	-32.61	4.98	-5.37	-18.67	-65.37
	Dec	3.57	-2.73	5.04	-5.46	13.59	7.64	-13.22	103.04	-32.89	5.30	-5.36	-18.21	-64.81
1992	Jan	3.76	-2.73	5.12	-3.53	12.67	7.82	-11.45	105.83	-32.66	5.67	-4.84	-17.68	-63.76
	Feb	3.87	-3.13	5.24	-2.61	12.18	8.05	-12.43	111.09	-32.83	5.75	-4.41	-17.95	-61.77
	Mar	3.64	-3.90	5.09	-1.21	13.35	6.89	-13.94	113.44	-34.00	5.69	-4.11	-17.87	-63.04
	Apr	3.73	-4.16	5.16	0.43	15.38	7.68	-13.62	114.95	-34.03	5.55	-3.65	-18.78	-65.85
	May	3.37	-3.84	5.57	1.79	16.47	7.93	-13.53	119.53	-34.67	5.90	-3.20	-18.71	-68.05
	Jun	3.03	-3.49	5.27	2.14	17.48	7.99	-14.50	121.61	-35.32	5.63	-2.76	-19.82	-70.17
	Jul	2.63	-3.16	5.29	3.99	18.20	8.40	-13.51	124.63	-36.08	6.43	-2.34	-20.93	-71.86
	Aug	2.17	–	5.62	4.09	20.35	7.96	-12.27	125.89	-36.80	6.66	-1.89	-21.73	-74.24
	Sep	2.03	–	5.97	4.77	23.22	–	-11.77	128.62	-36.88	6.37	–	-22.00	-76.35
	Oct	1.54	–	7.03	4.35	25.59	–	-10.52	131.54	-36.45	6.56	–	-22.35	-77.51
	Nov	–	–	–	–	–	–	–	–	–	6.72	–	–	–
	Dec	–	–	–	–	–	–	–	–	–	–	–	–	–

Current account

A country's current-account balance measures both visible and invisible (eg, services such as banking and insurance) trade. Germany's current-account balance has been calculated for the whole country since monetary union in July 1990. Germany had the biggest 12-month current-account surplus in the table in January 1991, but by October 1992 this had become a deficit of $21.9 billion. Japan's current-account surplus has tripled over the same period to $113.7 billion in the year to October 1992. America's annual current-account deficit narrowed to $3.7 billion in the fourth quarter of 1991, helped by contributions from foreign governments towards the cost of the Gulf war, then widened to $45.2 in the third quarter of 1992. Britain's current-account deficit fell through 1991 to $10.6 billion in the year to December, but has since increased to $19.7 billion in the 12 months to October 1992. Switzerland, Holland and Belgium remained in surplus.

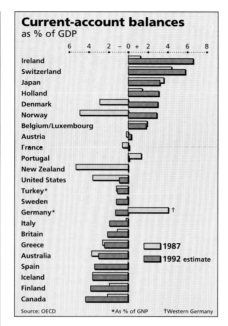

Current-account balances
as % of GDP

1987 / 1992 estimate

Source: OECD   *As % of GNP   †Western Germany

EXTERNAL BALANCES America may have the world's biggest current-account deficit in dollar terms (an estimated $56 billion in 1992), but this is a mere 0.9% of GDP, down from a high of 3.6% of GDP in 1987. Canada's current-account deficit, by contrast, amounts to a whopping 4.3% of GDP. Likewise, Japan's estimated current-account surplus of $119 billion in 1992 dwarfs those of all other countries, but at 3.2% of GDP it is less than half as big as Ireland's. Norway has seen the biggest turnaround over the five years, from an external deficit of 4.9% of its GDP in 1987 to an estimated surplus of 2.9% in 1992. Germany had a surplus of 4.1% of GDP in 1987, but in 1992 was expected to have a deficit of 1.3% of GDP. New Zealand's current account has been in broad balance in 1992, and the OECD has forecast a small surplus in 1993. If so, it will be New Zealand's first in the last 20 years.

Current-account balances, $bn

12 months to date

		Australia	Belgium	Canada	France	Germany	Holland	Italy	Japan	Spain	Sweden	Switzerland	United Kingdom	United States
1991	Jan	-14.0				38.7			36.4	-15.7	-6.8		-24.6	
	Feb	-13.9				33.6			37.6	-16.3	-6.6		-23.7	
	Mar	-13.1	4.1	-19.3	-13.7	22.2	10.6	-13.4	33.7	-16.9	-6.0	9.7	-21.5	-55.9
	Apr	-13.1				17.8			39.7	-16.8	-5.8		-18.6	
	May	-12.7				9.6			42.5	-17.0	-5.9		-16.8	
	Jun	-12.3	3.6	-20.6	-12.0	5.5	11.6	-15.9	44.5	-17.5	-5.7	9.8	-13.7	-32.1
	Jul	-12.1				-0.4			47.7	-17.0	-5.7		-11.7	
	Aug	-11.2				-4.7			52.4	-16.6	-5.4		-11.1	
	Sep	-11.2	3.8	-22.9	-9.5	-9.6	10.3	-20.2	56.7	-16.7	-4.9	9.9	-11.7	-19.2
	Oct	-10.9				-15.8			60.9	-16.3	-4.3		-11.3	
	Nov	-10.6				-15.7			66.3	-16.2	-3.8		-11.0	
	Dec	-9.9	4.3	-25.6	-6.3	-19.5	9.1	-21.5	72.9	-16.0	-3.3	10.4	-10.6	-3.7
1992	Jan	-9.4				-22.0			75.7	-15.8	-3.1		-10.2	
	Feb	-8.9				-23.2			80.6	-16.1	-3.0		-10.6	
	Mar	-9.2	4.9	-26.1	-3.1	-19.5	9.1	-22.5	90.2	-17.3	-3.6	11.2	-10.9	-21.8
	Apr	-8.9				-19.9			92.1	-19.1	-3.8		-12.7	
	May	-8.9				-19.5			97.4	-20.2	-4.0		-13.5	
	Jun	-9.3	4.1	-26.4	-0.6	-19.7	–	-23.9	100.4	-20.4	-4.3	12.4	-15.5	-42.0
	Jul	-9.7				-21.8			104.9	-23.3	-3.3		-17.1	
	Aug	-10.0				-21.1			106.5	-23.9	-3.5		-18.3	
	Sep	-10.1	–	-26.2	0.8	-22.9	–	–	109.5	-25.3	-3.8	14.4	-19.0	-45.2
	Oct	-10.5				-21.9			113.7	-25.2	-3.7		-19.7	
	Nov	–				–			–	–	–		–	
	Dec	–				–			–	–	–		–	

Focus on trade and aid

THIRD WORLD INVESTMENT While rich countries saw their inflows of foreign direct investment shrink by 20% in 1991, developing countries took up some of the slack, according to the Bank for International Settlements. After averaging $13 billion a year from 1985 to 1989, rising to $18 billion in 1990, net inflows of foreign direct investment into developing countries soared to $31 billion in 1991. The pattern changed too. In the late 1970s, when foreign investment in these countries averaged $7 billion a year, over half went to Latin America, with another quarter heading for Asia. In 1991, Asian countries accounted for 60% of gross inflows and Latin America for 28%. Other developing countries—mostly in Africa and Eastern Europe—accounted for only 12%.

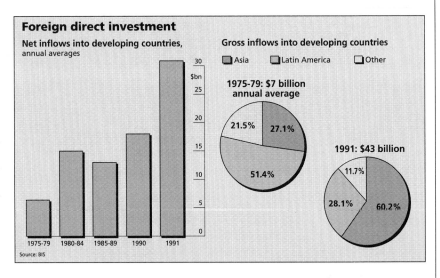

Foreign direct investment

Net inflows into developing countries, annual averages

Gross inflows into developing countries

■ Asia   ■ Latin America   □ Other

1975-79: $7 billion annual average

21.5%   27.1%   51.4%

1991: $43 billion

11.7%   28.1%   60.2%

Source: BIS

EASTERN EUROPE The pattern of trade between Eastern Europe and the rich OECD countries has changed dramatically. Between 1989 and 1991 exports to OECD countries increased by 31%, while imports from the OECD climbed by 32%. But trade among the former Comecon countries has collapsed—one of the main reasons for the continuing slump in the region. Morgan Stanley, an American investment bank, expects the picture to remain gloomy. In 1992 real GDP is estimated to have fallen by 16% in Eastern Europe. But Poland may be recovering: its industrial production is estimated to have risen by 2% in 1992. The longer-term prospects for East European exports also look good: the region's manufacturers enjoy a huge advantage in labour costs.

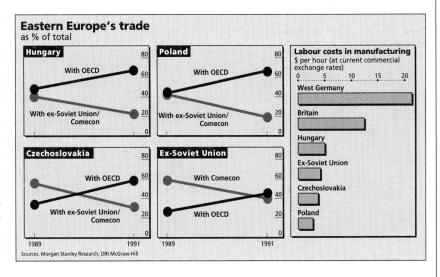

Eastern Europe's trade
as % of total

Hungary — With OECD / With ex-Soviet Union/Comecon

Poland — With OECD / With ex-Soviet Union/Comecon

Czechoslovakia — With OECD / With ex-Soviet Union/Comecon

Ex-Soviet Union — With Comecon / With OECD

Labour costs in manufacturing
$ per hour (at current commercial exchange rates)

West Germany, Britain, Hungary, Ex-Soviet Union, Czechoslovakia, Poland

Sources: Morgan Stanley Research; DRI McGraw-Hill

OVERSEAS AID Of the 20 rich countries in the chart, America is the biggest donor of official aid, giving $11.5 billion in 1991. But that was a tiny 0.2% of America's GDP—down from a still-mediocre average of 0.24% between 1978 and 1982. Contrast that with Norway's contribution. It donated only $1.2 billion in 1991, but that amounted to 1.14% of its GDP, up from 0.92% in 1978-82. Other Scandinavian countries are also generous. In 1991 Denmark donated $1.2 billion, 0.96% of its GDP; and Sweden gave $2.1 billion, 0.92% of GDP. Japan is almost as stingy as America; the $11 billion it sent overseas in 1991 was just 0.32% of GDP, up from 0.28% between 1978 and 1982. Ireland was meanest of all, giving only 0.19% of GDP in official foreign aid—a paltry $73m.

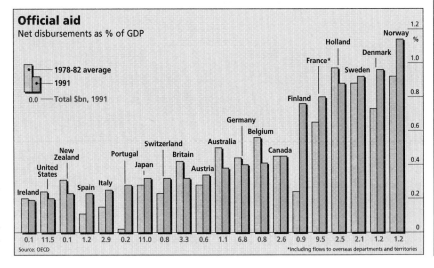

Official aid
Net disbursements as % of GDP

■ 1978-82 average
■ 1991
0.0 — Total $bn, 1991

Ireland, United States, New Zealand, Spain, Italy, Portugal, Japan, Switzerland, Britain, Austria, Australia, Germany, Belgium, Canada, Finland, France*, Sweden, Holland, Denmark, Norway

0.1 11.5 0.1 1.2 2.9 0.2 11.0 0.8 3.3 0.6 1.1 6.8 0.8 2.6 0.9 9.5 2.5 2.1 1.2 1.2

Source: OECD

*Including flows to overseas departments and territories

Exchange rates: trade-weighted

At the end of 1992 most currencies outside the European exchange-rate mechanism (ERM) were little changed from a year earlier. Pressure on the pound forced its withdrawal from the ERM in September and by October 1992 it had fallen to 78.4 from a high of 93.3 in June 1992. Similar pressures resulted in Italy's withdrawal from the ERM and Spain's devaluation. In consequence the lira's trade-weighted value dropped 17% and the peseta 8% from their mid-year highs. The yen index strengthened sharply after August, following a period of weakness, and it still remains the currency with the biggest increase from the base year of 1985. The D-mark continued its upward progress, but worries over the cost of German re-unification may account for its late decline. A run on the krona forced Sweden to devalue after 18 months pegged to the ecu. The indices used are those calculated by the Bank of England and the Reserve Bank of Australia.

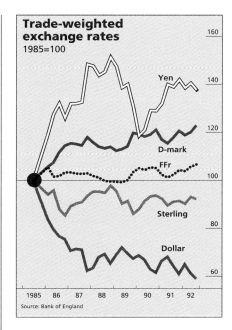

Trade-weighted exchange rates
1985=100

Yen
D-mark
FFr
Sterling
Dollar

1985 86 87 88 89 90 91 92
Source: Bank of England

CURRENCIES A good way to measure shifts in a country's exchange rate is to use its trade-weighted (or effective) exchange rate. This is an index of the average of all its bilateral rates, weighted by the pattern of trade with other countries. The yen has been the strongest currency over the past seven years; its trade-weighted value has gained 39% since 1985. At the other extreme, the dollar's rate reached a record low in 1992, 41% below its level in 1985. Since the currencies of the European exchange-rate mechanism are pegged to each other, and account for a big part of each other's baskets, their trade-weighted exchange rates tend to be much more stable. For example, other ERM currencies account for 72% of the French franc's trade-weighted basket and 60% of the D-mark's. Sterling's membership was suspended on Black Wednesday (September 16th) after loss of confidence resulted in widespread selling.

Trade-weighted exchange rate, 1985=100

End month

		Australia	Belgium	Canada	France	Germany	Holland	Italy	Japan	Spain	Sweden	Switzerland	United Kingdom	United States
1991	Jan	85.4	112.7	101.1	104.9	120.7	115.9	100.4	132.0	110.1	93.1	115.2	94.2	60.6
	Feb	86.0	112.4	102.8	104.3	120.0	115.3	100.6	132.7	110.3	93.2	112.3	93.8	61.5
	Mar	88.7	110.4	104.6	102.3	116.9	113.1	98.7	132.0	108.1	93.7	112.1	92.4	66.3
	Apr	89.5	110.0	105.1	102.1	116.0	112.7	98.9	137.0	107.8	94.1	112.5	91.4	65.9
	May	86.9	110.1	106.0	101.9	116.2	112.8	98.7	135.9	107.7	94.2	111.5	91.2	66.4
	Jun	88.7	109.5	107.2	101.2	115.3	112.1	97.8	139.9	105.2	92.6	109.7	89.5	68.0
	Jul	89.3	110.2	105.4	101.8	116.5	112.9	98.2	137.6	106.5	93.1	108.8	90.9	66.8
	Aug	89.9	110.2	106.4	101.8	116.3	112.9	98.2	138.4	107.0	93.0	108.6	90.5	66.7
	Sep	90.0	111.0	106.2	102.4	117.7	113.8	98.9	138.9	106.4	93.5	110.0	91.1	64.3
	Oct	88.1	111.0	107.0	101.9	117.5	113.7	98.5	141.7	106.8	93.5	109.0	90.8	64.2
	Nov	87.7	111.6	105.6	102.9	118.7	114.5	98.9	140.8	106.6	94.5	109.4	90.6	63.5
	Dec	83.1	112.8	102.0	104.3	120.5	115.9	99.5	141.9	107.9	95.9	109.3	91.4	60.8
1992	Jan	82.9	111.5	101.4	103.1	118.6	114.7	99.0	145.2	107.8	95.3	108.5	90.9	62.7
	Feb	84.4	111.6	101.3	103.3	118.4	114.5	98.9	142.3	107.3	95.2	106.2	90.7	64.0
	Mar	87.1	111.7	101.0	103.8	118.7	114.6	98.6	138.5	107.2	95.3	105.8	90.2	64.9
	Apr	84.6	111.2	100.5	103.9	118.1	114.2	98.5	138.2	107.5	95.4	104.5	92.4	64.9
	May	82.0	111.3	98.8	104.6	118.3	114.2	98.4	142.3	108.3	95.8	106.1	92.9	63.1
	Jun	81.3	112.3	98.4	105.7	119.9	115.3	99.0	140.5	108.3	96.6	107.8	93.1	61.2
	Jul	81.3	113.0	99.2	106.2	121.2	116.2	100.0	136.9	108.5	97.1	110.4	92.3	60.3
	Aug	76.7	114.2	97.2	106.6	123.0	117.7	100.1	138.2	107.9	97.6	111.5	92.0	58.6
	Sep	76.8	116.5	93.6	110.9	126.4	120.2	87.9	145.4	102.4	98.0	117.2	83.7	60.1
	Oct	77.1	115.9	96.2	109.0	124.5	119.2	89.4	148.7	99.4	96.4	113.3	78.4	63.7
	Nov	77.0	115.7	93.7	109.1	124.8	119.3	87.3	150.7	98.0	84.5	112.0	78.5	65.8
	Dec	77.4	116.2	95.1	108.8	125.0	119.5	83.6	151.6	99.9	83.0	111.5	79.6	66.3

Exchange rates: $ and £

Currency units per $ End month

		Australia	Belgium	Canada	France	Germany	Holland	Italy	Japan	Spain	Sweden	Switzerland	United Kingdom	United States
1991	Jan	1.28	30.5	1.16	5.03	1.48	1.67	1112	131	92.8	5.54	1.26	0.51	na
	Feb	1.27	31.4	1.15	5.20	1.53	1.72	1140	133	95.1	5.66	1.33	0.52	na
	Mar	1.29	35.2	1.16	5.78	1.71	1.92	1269	141	106.0	6.17	1.46	0.57	na
	Apr	1.28	35.3	1.15	5.80	1.72	1.93	1270	136	106.0	6.20	1.45	0.58	na
	May	1.32	35.7	1.15	5.90	1.74	1.96	1291	138	107.0	6.23	1.48	0.59	na
	Jun	1.30	37.3	1.14	6.15	1.81	2.04	1348	138	114.0	6.55	1.56	0.61	na
	Jul	1.28	36.0	1.15	5.94	1.75	1.97	1302	137	109.0	6.34	1.53	0.59	na
	Aug	1.27	36.0	1.14	5.94	1.75	1.97	1304	137	109.0	6.34	1.53	0.59	na
	Sep	1.25	34.3	1.13	5.66	1.66	1.87	1244	133	105.0	6.07	1.45	0.57	na
	Oct	1.29	34.4	1.12	5.70	1.69	1.88	1250	131	105.0	6.10	1.47	0.57	na
	Nov	1.28	33.6	1.14	5.55	1.63	1.83	1225	130	103.0	5.96	1.44	0.56	na
	Dec	1.32	31.3	1.17	5.18	1.52	1.71	1151	125	96.7	5.53	1.36	0.53	na
1992	Jan	1.33	33.2	1.17	5.50	1.61	1.82	1213	126	101.5	5.86	1.43	0.56	na
	Feb	1.33	33.7	1.18	5.57	1.64	1.84	1229	129	102.9	5.95	1.49	0.57	na
	Mar	1.30	33.8	1.19	5.57	1.64	1.85	1239	133	103.8	5.98	1.50	0.57	na
	Apr	1.32	34.1	1.20	5.60	1.66	1.86	1247	134	104.1	5.99	1.52	0.60	na
	May	1.32	33.6	1.20	5.41	1.61	1.81	1214	128	100.4	5.80	1.46	0.55	na
	Jun	1.34	31.4	1.20	5.13	1.53	1.72	1155	126	96.4	5.51	1.38	0.53	na
	Jul	1.34	30.5	1.18	5.00	1.48	1.69	1119	127	94.3	5.37	1.32	0.52	na
	Aug	1.40	29.1	1.20	4.81	1.41	1.59	1078	123	91.5	5.15	1.26	0.50	na
	Sep	1.40	29.1	1.25	4.76	1.41	1.59	1233	119	99.0	5.29	1.23	0.56	na
	Oct	1.44	31.6	1.24	5.21	1.54	1.73	1314	123	109.2	5.78	1.37	0.64	na
	Nov	1.47	33.0	1.29	5.43	1.60	1.80	1399	125	115.4	6.86	1.45	0.66	na
	Dec	1.45	33.3	1.27	5.53	1.62	1.82	1474	125	114.6	7.07	1.47	0.66	na

Currency units per £ End month

		Australia	Belgium	Canada	France	Germany	Holland	Italy	Japan	Spain	Sweden	Switzerland	United Kingdom	United States
1991	Jan	2.51	60.0	2.29	9.88	2.90	3.27	2185	258	182	10.9	2.47	na	1.96
	Feb	2.44	59.9	2.20	9.92	2.92	3.28	2177	254	181	10.8	2.53	na	1.91
	Mar	2.24	61.2	2.01	10.00	2.96	3.34	2207	246	183	10.7	2.53	na	1.74
	Apr	2.20	60.9	1.99	10.00	2.96	3.33	2190	235	183	10.7	2.50	na	1.72
	May	2.25	60.6	1.95	10.00	2.95	3.33	2193	235	182	10.6	2.52	na	1.70
	Jun	2.11	60.4	1.85	9.95	2.94	3.31	2183	223	184	10.6	2.52	na	1.62
	Jul	2.17	60.6	1.94	10.00	2.94	3.31	2194	232	184	10.7	2.57	na	1.68
	Aug	2.14	60.5	1.92	9.98	2.94	3.31	2192	230	183	10.7	2.57	na	1.68
	Sep	2.19	60.0	1.98	9.92	2.91	3.28	2180	233	184	10.6	2.54	na	1.75
	Oct	2.24	60.0	1.96	9.94	2.90	3.27	2178	228	183	10.6	2.55	na	1.74
	Nov	2.25	59.3	2.00	9.80	2.87	3.23	2162	230	183	10.5	2.53	na	1.76
	Dec	2.46	58.5	2.16	9.70	2.84	3.20	2149	234	181	10.4	2.54	na	1.87
1992	Jan	2.39	59.3	2.11	9.80	2.88	3.24	2161	225	181	10.4	2.56	na	1.79
	Feb	2.34	59.1	2.08	9.78	2.88	3.24	2160	227	181	10.4	2.61	na	1.76
	Mar	2.26	58.9	2.07	9.68	2.85	3.21	2154	231	180	10.4	2.60	na	1.74
	Apr	2.34	60.4	2.12	9.90	2.93	3.30	2204	237	184	10.6	2.69	na	1.77
	May	2.42	60.5	2.20	9.87	2.94	3.31	2213	234	183	10.6	2.66	na	1.83
	Jun	2.55	59.7	2.28	9.76	2.90	3.27	2193	240	183	10.5	2.62	na	1.90
	Jul	2.59	58.5	2.28	9.60	2.84	3.20	2149	245	181	10.3	2.53	na	1.92
	Aug	2.76	57.5	2.37	9.50	2.79	3.14	2135	244	181	10.2	2.49	na	1.98
	Sep	2.49	52.0	2.22	8.52	2.52	2.84	2207	214	177	9.5	2.20	na	1.78
	Oct	2.25	49.6	1.94	8.17	2.41	2.71	2060	193	171	9.1	2.15	na	1.56
	Nov	2.21	49.7	1.95	8.19	2.41	2.71	2109	188	174	10.3	2.17	na	1.51
	Dec	2.20	50.3	1.93	8.36	2.45	2.75	2231	189	174	10.7	2.22	na	1.51

Exchange rates: SDR and ecu

Currency units per SDR End month

		Australia	Belgium	Canada	France	Germany	Holland	Italy	Japan	Spain	Sweden	Switzerland	United Kingdom	United States
1991	Jan	1.83	43.8	1.67	7.24	2.14	2.40	1604	188	134	7.97	1.82	0.73	1.43
	Feb	1.81	44.4	1.63	7.35	2.16	2.43	1615	188	135	8.01	1.87	0.74	1.42
	Mar	1.74	47.5	1.56	7.83	2.31	2.60	1706	190	143	8.20	1.97	0.78	1.35
	Apr	1.72	47.8	1.54	7.85	2.32	2.68	1717	184	143	8.31	1.96	0.79	1.34
	May	1.76	47.6	1.54	7.84	2.31	2.61	1718	185	143	8.29	1.97	0.78	1.34
	Jun	1.71	49.1	1.50	8.08	2.38	2.68	1772	181	149	8.60	2.05	0.81	1.31
	Jul	1.72	48.0	1.54	7.92	2.33	2.63	1740	184	146	8.45	2.03	0.79	1.33
	Aug	1.70	46.9	1.53	7.91	2.33	2.62	1738	183	145	8.45	2.04	0.79	1.34
	Sep	1.71	46.9	1.55	7.75	2.28	2.56	1704	182	144	8.30	1.98	0.78	1.37
	Oct	1.74	47.2	1.54	7.82	2.29	2.58	1713	179	144	8.34	2.01	0.78	1.37
	Nov	1.77	46.0	1.58	7.64	2.23	2.52	1686	180	142	8.18	1.98	0.78	1.39
	Dec	1.88	44.7	1.65	7.41	2.17	2.45	1647	179	138	7.91	1.94	0.76	1.43
1992	Jan	1.86	46.4	1.64	7.69	2.25	2.54	1695	176	142	8.19	2.00	0.78	1.40
	Feb	1.83	46.6	1.63	7.70	2.26	2.55	1698	179	142	8.21	2.05	0.78	1.38
	Mar	1.79	46.4	1.63	7.64	2.25	2.54	1700	183	142	8.20	2.06	0.79	1.37
	Apr	1.80	46.7	1.64	7.67	2.27	2.55	1708	183	143	8.20	2.09	0.78	1.37
	May	1.84	46.9	1.68	7.56	2.25	2.53	1695	179	140	8.09	2.04	0.77	1.40
	Jun	1.91	44.9	1.71	7.35	2.19	2.46	1653	180	138	7.89	1.97	0.75	1.43
	Jul	1.94	44.0	1.71	7.22	2.14	2.44	1616	184	136	7.76	1.90	0.75	1.44
	Aug	2.08	43.1	1.77	7.13	2.09	2.36	1599	182	136	7.64	1.87	0.75	1.48
	Sep	2.06	42.8	1.84	7.02	2.08	2.34	1815	176	146	7.79	1.81	0.83	1.47
	Oct	2.02	44.4	1.74	7.33	2.16	2.43	1847	173	154	8.12	1.93	0.90	1.41
	Nov	2.02	45.5	1.77	7.49	2.21	2.48	1929	172	159	9.46	1.99	0.92	1.38
	Dec	2.00	45.7	1.76	7.69	2.25	2.50	2026	172	158	9.73	2.02	0.91	1.38

Currency units per ecu End month

		Australia	Belgium	Canada	France	Germany	Holland	Italy	Japan	Spain	Sweden	Switzerland	United Kingdom	United States
1991	Jan	1.77	42.2	1.61	6.96	2.05	2.32	1539	182	128	7.66	1.74	0.70	1.38
	Feb	1.72	42.2	1.55	6.98	2.05	2.32	1538	180	128	7.64	1.79	0.70	1.35
	Mar	1.55	42.4	1.39	6.98	2.06	2.32	1532	181	127	7.40	1.75	0.69	1.20
	Apr	1.53	42.4	1.37	6.96	2.06	2.32	1524	162	126	7.37	1.72	0.70	1.19
	May	1.57	42.3	1.37	6.98	2.06	2.32	1527	165	128	7.42	1.77	0.70	1.19
	Jun	1.48	42.3	1.30	6.96	2.05	2.32	1529	156	129	7.43	1.77	0.70	1.13
	Jul	1.51	42.3	1.36	6.98	2.05	2.32	1532	162	129	7.46	1.80	0.70	1.18
	Aug	1.50	42.3	1.34	6.98	2.05	2.31	1533	161	128	7.45	1.80	0.70	1.18
	Sep	1.54	42.2	1.39	6.98	2.05	2.31	1531	164	130	7.48	1.78	0.70	1.23
	Oct	1.57	42.1	1.37	6.99	2.05	2.31	1533	159	129	7.45	1.79	0.70	1.22
	Nov	1.60	42.0	1.42	6.99	2.03	2.29	1530	162	130	7.44	1.79	0.71	1.25
	Dec	1.76	41.9	1.55	6.95	2.04	2.29	1542	169	130	7.45	1.82	0.72	1.34
1992	Jan	1.69	42.1	1.49	6.96	2.04	2.30	1536	160	129	7.42	1.82	0.71	1.27
	Feb	1.66	42.1	1.48	6.95	2.05	2.30	1536	161	129	7.42	1.86	0.71	1.25
	Mar	1.61	42.0	1.48	6.92	2.04	2.30	1541	165	129	7.41	1.86	0.71	1.24
	Apr	1.64	42.2	1.49	6.93	2.05	2.31	1543	166	129	7.41	1.88	0.70	1.24
	May	1.69	42.3	1.54	6.90	2.06	2.32	1549	164	129	7.40	1.87	0.70	1.28
	Jun	1.80	42.2	1.61	6.89	2.05	2.31	1550	169	129	7.40	1.85	0.71	1.34
	Jul	1.85	42.0	1.63	6.89	2.04	2.30	1544	176	130	7.41	1.82	0.72	1.38
	Aug	2.02	41.8	1.71	6.91	2.03	2.28	1549	179	132	7.41	1.82	0.73	1.43
	Sep	1.96	40.6	1.72	6.66	1.97	2.20	1731	167	138	7.40	1.72	0.79	1.40
	Oct	1.84	40.5	1.59	6.67	1.97	2.21	1680	157	140	7.40	1.76	0.82	1.28
	Nov	1.80	40.3	1.58	6.68	1.96	2.20	1714	153	141	8.41	1.77	0.81	1.23
	Dec	1.75	40.3	1.54	6.69	1.96	2.20	1783	151	139	8.55	1.76	0.80	1.21

Focus on other economies

AUSTRIA The Austrian economy has been one of the OECD's stars in recent years. Although most economies had slowed sharply in 1991, Austria's hardly faltered; its GDP grew by 3%. The OECD, in its 1992 report on the economy, forecast that growth should continue at just less than 3% in 1992 and 1993. Austria also had one of the lowest inflation rates in the OECD, at slightly over 3% in 1991. Its unemployment rate was forecast to rise to 3.8% in 1992, only half the average unemployment rate in other rich countries. In the 1992 report the OECD advised the Austrian government to do more to control public spending and to cut its budget deficit, which was roughly 2% of GDP. But even that was only half the size of the average European budget deficit.

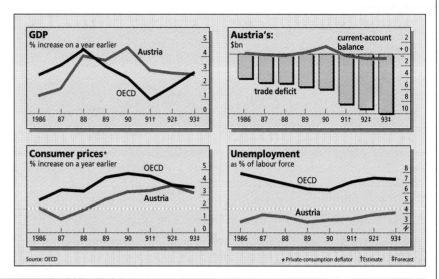

Source: OECD *Private-consumption deflator †Estimate ‡Forecast

ICELAND With its fish catch falling in 1991 for the fourth year in a row, Iceland's economy slipped into recession. According to the OECD, the GDP of its smallest member was expected to fall by 2.6% in 1992, and barely grow in 1993. With the price of aluminium (after fish, Iceland's biggest export) dropping too, exports have suffered: they did no more than match imports in 1991 and were forecast to do the same in 1992. Iceland's current-account deficit, swollen in 1991 by pre-election fiscal laxity, was forecast to stick at around $300m (5% of GDP) in both 1992 and 1993. A government-trade union accord in 1990 helped bring inflation down to 6.8% in 1991 from 21% in 1989. In 1992 prices were forecast to rise by just 4.5%, the smallest increase since 1967.

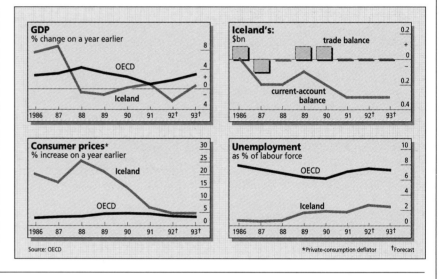

Source: OECD *Private-consumption deflator †Forecast

NORWAY The collapse in oil prices in 1986 dealt the Norwegian economy a blow from which it has not yet fully recovered. The OECD forecast that, thanks to growing private consumption and economic recovery, Norway's real GDP would grow by 2% in 1992 and by 2.9% in 1993—close to the OECD average. Consumer-price inflation was forecast to fall to 2.8% in 1993, while the unemployment rate was expected to edge down to 4.8%. Oil is still the mainstay of the Norwegian economy. Growth in oil output should help increase the current-account surplus to $7.1 billion in 1993—almost 6% of GDP. The OECD reckoned Norway could use its oil wealth more efficiently—by which it meant using fewer petro-kroner to subsidise inefficient non-oil industries.

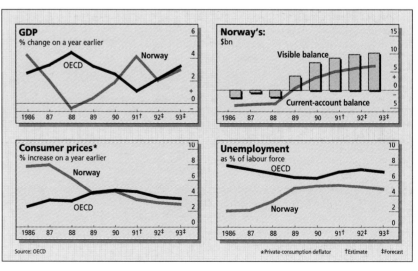

Source: OECD *Private-consumption deflator †Estimate ‡Forecast

TURKEY The Gulf war and political uncertainty slowed Turkey's economic expansion in 1991, as public-sector borrowing soared and inflation worsened. Real GDP growth slumped to 1.5% in 1991, close to the OECD average; it grew by 9.2% in 1990. Generous state wage increases and agricultural subsidies agreed on the eve of October's 1991 election led to a sharp rise in Turkey's public-sector deficit to 12.6% of GDP in 1991, up from 10.5% in 1990. The annual inflation rate grew to 66% in 1991, up from 60.3% the previous year. Sluggish domestic demand led to a current-account surplus of $272m in 1991, reversing a deficit of $2.6 billion in 1990. Turkey's urban unemployment rate rose sharply to 11.5% in 1991, up from 10% in 1990. Growth in 1993 was expected to slow to 3.7%.

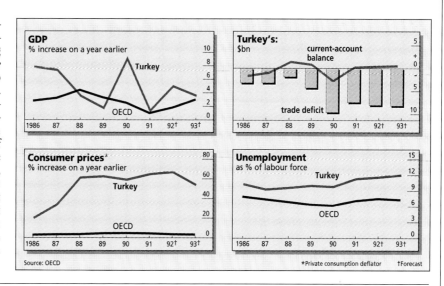

EMERGING ASIAN STOCKMARKETS
India's share prices soared between December 1991 and April 1992, doubling in dollar terms. This was a vote of confidence in the government's massive deregulation programme. But prices plunged following the discovery of scandal on the Bombay stockmarket. Of other Asian markets in our chart only Malaysia and Thailand stood as high at the end of 1992 as they were in January 1990. Taiwan's share prices fell by three-quarters between January and September 1990, reflecting a collapse in liquidity, and remained well below half their January 1990 level in 1991 and 1992. South Korean share prices also fell sharply during the past three years, down by more than 50% at their trough, then recovered slightly in the last quarter.

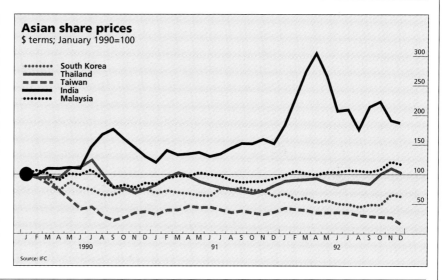

LATIN AMERICAN STOCKMARKETS
Tighter fiscal and monetary policies, coupled with supply-side reforms, sent share prices soaring during 1991 and 1992 in all the countries in the chart except Brazil. These gains, however, reflected the markets' low starting points as much as the success of reforms. Venezuela's stockmarket—the star performer, with a rise of more than 900% in 1990 and 1991—fell heavily in 1992 because of attempted coups in February and November. Brazil's stockmarket fell by two-thirds in dollar terms in 1990, and then recouped it all in 1991, but prices slipped back in 1992, unsettled by continuing political uncertainties. Share prices in Argentina rose by more than 500% in the 18 months to June 1992, on the back of radical reforms, but then fell by over 50%.

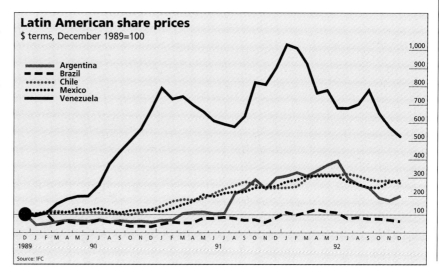

Other economies

JOBLESS RATES By the end of 1992 almost 8% of the labour force in industrial economies was unemployed. The chart shows how jobless rates vary among the 24 OECD members, using a standardised definition (in a few countries this differs substantially from the national measure). In late 1992 Spain and Ireland had the highest jobless rates, both at 17.5%; at the other extreme, Luxembourg's was only 1.4%. Some of the biggest increases in unemployment in recent years have been in countries which once boasted the lowest rates. Sweden's has risen from 1.4% in 1989 to 5.3% in 1992. Most spectacular of all is New Zealand: its unemployment rate averaged 0.5% in the 1970s, but in late 1992 stood at 10.1%.

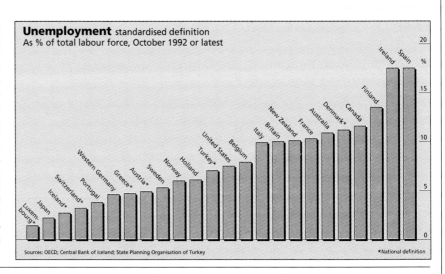

Unemployment standardised definition
As % of total labour force, October 1992 or latest

Sources: OECD; Central Bank of Iceland; State Planning Organisation of Turkey

*National definition

	Austria	Denmark	Finland	Greece	Iceland	Ireland	Luxembourg	New Zealand	Norway	Portugal	Turkey
GDP, % change on year earlier											
1991	3.1	1.2	-6.5	1.8	1.5	2.5	3.1	-1.8	1.9	2.1	0.3
1992	2.0	1.2	-2.0	1.2	-2.8	2.6	2.5	3.1	1.3	1.9	5.3
Industrial production, % change on year earlier											
1991 Q1	3.0	nil	-5.8	-3.2	na	4.8	1.3	-5.8	3.8	5.0	-4.3
1991 Q2	1.9	3.1	-9.8	-2.7	na	1.9	0.3	-8.9	4.1	-0.5	1.9
1991 Q3	2.5	6.8	-11.8	5.3	na	1.6	-1.1	-3.0	0.6	-1.3	6.4
1991 Q4	0.3	1.6	-6.7	-5.2	na	5.3	1.5	-0.1	-0.2	-3.1	2.8
1992 Q1	nil	nil	-2.9	-1.6	na	8.6	2.4	4.1	3.8	-1.5	10.0
1992 Q2	1.2	3.1	5.9	-1.9	na	10.1	-1.9	–	4.2	–	4.4
1992 Q3	-2.2	–	5.8	–	na	–	–	–	9.9	–	2.8
1992 Q4	–	–	–	–	na	–	–	–	–	–	–
Unemployment, % of labour force											
1991 Q1	7.1	11.0	5.9	4.0	1.9	14.1	1.2	9.5	5.3	4.1	7.4
1991 Q2	5.3	10.2	6.8	4.7	1.1	14.8	1.3	10.1	5.3	3.8	–
1991 Q3	4.7	10.2	7.9	5.0	1.0	15.2	1.4	10.7	5.6	4.2	8.3
1991 Q4	6.2	10.7	9.9	4.7	1.7	15.2	1.4	10.6	5.8	4.1	–
1992 Q1	7.1	12.0	12.0	4.6	3.0	15.4	1.4	11.1	5.8	3.8	8.3
1992 Q2	5.2	10.9	12.3	5.0	2.7	15.9	1.5	10.1	6.0	4.2	–
1992 Q3	4.8	10.8	13.2	–	–	16.5	1.5	10.3	6.0	4.1	–
1992 Q4	–	–	–	–	–	–	–	–	–	–	–
Consumer prices, % increase on year earlier											
1991 Q1	3.4	2.5	4.9	21.7	6.3	2.7	3.3	4.5	3.9	13.0	62.7
1991 Q2	3.5	2.7	4.5	20.3	6.2	3.1	3.1	2.8	3.7	12.0	63.2
1991 Q3	3.5	2.3	3.7	18.4	7.0	3.6	3.6	2.2	3.5	11.1	68.8
1991 Q4	3.0	2.2	3.5	17.9	7.8	3.6	2.5	1.0	2.7	9.5	68.2
1992 Q1	4.1	2.4	2.8	18.2	7.0	3.6	2.9	0.8	2.4	8.3	78.3
1992 Q2	4.1	2.5	2.6	15.6	4.9	3.7	3.6	0.9	2.5	9.6	69.8
1992 Q3	3.9	2.1	2.5	14.7	2.8	2.9	3.1	1.0	2.3	9.3	66.4
1992 Q4	–	–	–	–	–	–	–	–	–	–	–

	Austria	Denmark	Finland	Greece	Iceland	Ireland	New Zealand	Norway	Portugal	Turkey
Stockmarkets										
Index	Credit Aktien	Copenhagen stock exchange	HEX index	ASE Composite index	VIB Icelandic stock index	ISEQ Overall	NZSE 40 Capital index	Oslo stock exchange industrials	BTA index	ISF Composite index
Base date	Dec 30th 1984=100	Jan 3rd 1983=100	Dec 28th 1990=1,000	1980=100	Jan 1st 1987=100	Jan 4th 1988=100	Jan 31st 1957=100	Jan 2nd 1983=100	April 1st 1977=100	Jan 3rd 1986=100
End of period										
1991 Q1	502.3	346.4	1,156.7	1,242.9	747.2	1,483.0	1,329.0	716.5	2,419.4	4,520.0
1991 Q2	480.8	367.4	974.9	954.4	797.4	1,365.0	1,435.0	756.8	2,246.8	3,587.4
1991 Q3	455.7	364.2	851.3	841.8	794.0	1,443.5	1,474.0	753.1	2,188.1	2,887.3
1991 Q4	374.6	352.6	781.8	809.7	760.3	1,380.2	1,562.9	671.0	1,977.7	4,369.2
1992 Q1	428.5	330.2	826.7	868.3	740.0	1,372.1	1,480.6	712.6	2,057.3	4,076.6
1992 Q2	390.8	321.4	763.1	842.8	663.1	1,310.8	1,604.4	693.9	2,077.9	4,407.7
1992 Q3	326.6	262.8	611.6	648.3	659.9	1,144.1	1,532.5	589.0	1,865.7	3,976.4
1992 Q4	313.0	261.6	829.0	672.3	681.0	1,227.4	1,566.8	666.8	1,637.9	4,004.2
1992 low	291.4	250.4	541.0	558.9	760.3	1,094.9	1,365.4	532.4	1,637.9	3,142.0
1992 high	458.6	365.3	935.9	1,009.5	628.6	1,469.6	1,597.5	772.7	2,156.4	5,128.9
Market capitalisation, $bn										
End 1991	22.4	47.6	13.8	13.4	0.7	4.6	16.1	22.9	9.3	15.5
End 1992	17.5	35.3	14.6	9.5	0.4	4.2	15.5	22.8	8.7	9.9
Discount rate, %										
End 1991	8.00	9.50	8.50	19.00	21.00	10.75	8.30	10.00	14.50	45.00
End 1992*	8.25	9.50	9.50	19.00	16.00	13.75	7.10	11.00	14.50	45.00
Exports, $bn										
1991	42.51	35.89	23.02	8.69	1.55	24.27	8.99	33.47	16.25	13.60
1992 First half	22.15	17.95	11.57	–	0.74	19.78	5.17	11.53	8.62	6.94
Imports, $bn										
1991	49.25	32.32	21.69	21.52	1.72	20.76	7.86	24.91	26.07	21.08
1992 First half	26.50	16.73	10.57	–	0.80	11.53	4.28	8.34	14.07	10.36
Current-account balance, $bn										
1991	-0.1	2.2	-6.6	-1.5	-0.3	1.9	nil	5.0	-0.7	0.3
1992 OECD f'cast	0.6	4.3	-4.3	-1.9	-0.2	3.2	nil	3.3	0.1	-1.3
Exchange rates, end of period, per $										
1991 Q1	12.06	6.46	4.05	184.16	59.66	0.64	1.71	6.55	148.96	3,704
1991 Q2	12.76	7.02	4.28	198.60	62.97	0.68	1.73	7.07	157.67	4,335
1991 Q3	11.70	6.41	4.05	184.98	59.20	0.62	1.76	6.61	143.90	4,723
1991 Q4	10.69	5.91	4.13	175.28	55.62	0.57	1.85	5.97	134.18	5,080
1992 Q1	11.57	6.37	4.48	190.70	59.19	0.62	1.83	6.45	141.61	6,248
1992 Q2	10.75	5.86	4.15	185.62	55.53	0.57	1.83	5.97	127.48	6,875
1992 Q3	9.91	5.47	4.52	180.90	53.82	0.54	1.86	5.72	125.28	7,325
1992 Q4	11.34	6.28	5.23	214.65	63.94	0.62	1.95	6.92	146.45	8,591
Reserves, end of period, $bn										
1991 Q1	9.03	8.82	8.24	2.94	0.31	5.30	3.88	14.13	13.02	3.76
1991 Q2	8.57	8.12	7.41	3.12	0.31	5.53	3.41	13.89	14.56	5.08
1991 Q3	9.81	7.92	6.11	4.97	0.30	5.91	3.42	13.57	18.57	5.04
1991 Q4	10.33	7.40	7.61	5.19	0.45	5.74	2.95	13.23	20.63	5.14
1992 Q1	10.37	6.29	6.91	4.17	0.51	5.83	3.17	13.10	21.90	3.79
1992 Q2	11.36	7.08	6.97	4.53	0.55	5.70	2.98	16.07	25.33	4.39
1992 Q3	13.85	7.98	5.96	4.27	0.54	3.89	3.15	14.95	22.92	5.72
1992 Q4	–	–	–	–	–	–	–	–	–	–

* Or latest available

Other economies

Former Soviet Republics

	Bulgaria	Czechoslovakia	Hungary	Poland	Romania	Former-Yugoslavia	Former-Soviet Union
Population, m							
1985	9.0	15.5	10.7	37.2	22.7	23.1	277.5
1995 f'cast	9.0	15.9	10.5	39.4	23.8	24.4	298.6
Population density per sq km							
1990	81	123	113	123	98	93	13
Population under 15 years, %							
1985	21.3	24.4	21.4	25.5	24.7	23.9	25.2
1995 f'cast	18.7	21.0	17.8	23.5	21.8	21.1	24.8
Population 65 years and over, %							
1985	11.3	11.0	12.4	9.4	9.5	8.5	9.6
1995 f'cast	14.5	12.0	14.3	10.9	11.4	11.1	10.9
GDP/GNP, $bn							
1981	na	35.0	22.9	54.0	42.0	62.9	na
1991	6.2	33.2	32.8	75.5	23.2	na	60.0
GDP/GNP per head, $							
1981	na	2,313	2,124	1,504	1,860	2,790	na
1991	725	2,129	3,177	1,975	1,000	na	216
GDP/GNP, % change on a year earlier							
1990	-12	-4	-4	-12	-10	-6	-4
1991	-23	-15	-10	-9	-15	-18	-17
1992 f'cast	-10	-4	-3	-2	-8	na	na
Consumer prices, % increase on a year earlier							
1990	19	10	28	586	4	583	8
1991	334	58	35	70	175	117	86
1992 f'cast	100	14	20	46	175	na	2,000
Exports, $bn							
1990	2.4	5.9	9.6	13.6	5.9	14.3	50.3
1991	2.2	8.3	9.7	14.9	4.1	14.0	46.6
1992 f'cast	3.5	7.3	10.2	15.3	4.6	na	67.7
Imports, $bn							
1990	3.8	6.5	8.7	8.2	9.1	18.9	65.2
1991	2.9	8.8	9.3	15.5	5.3	14.7	54.2
1992 f'cast	3.7	7.5	9.1	14.3	5.6	na	70.2
Current-account balance, $bn							
1990	-1.1	-1.0	0.3	0.8	-1.7	-2.4	-5.0
1991	-0.8	0.3	0.4	-2.4	-1.2	-1.4	-5.8
1992 f'cast	-1.2	0.4	1.0	-0.6	-1.0	na	-9.8

Exchange rate, end year, per $

	Lev	Koruny	Forint	Zloty	Lei	New Dinar	Rouble
1990	2.15	28.00	61.45	9,500	34.71	10.66	5.61
1991	19.00	27.84	75.62	10,957	189	19.74	123
1992	24.20	29.42	84.16	15,792	433	775	445

	Population, m 1990	Population density per sq km, 1990	GDP/GNP as a % of former-Soviet Union, 1990	GDP/GNP at PPP* rate, $m, 1990
Armenia	3.3	110.5	0.96	17,184
Azerbaijan	7.1	82.3	1.45	26,057
Belorussia	10.3	49.4	3.96	71,100
Estonia	1.6	45.1	0.79	13,351
Georgia	5.5	78.3	1.47	26,446
Kazakhstan	16.7	6.1	4.47	80,400
Kirgizstan	4.4	22.0	0.82	14,752
Latvia	2.7	41.7	1.20	21,633
Lithuania	3.7	57.1	1.31	23,559
Moldova	4.4	129.4	1.26	22,606
Russia	148.0	8.7	61.41	1,102,800
Tajikistan	5.2	36.7	0.70	12,610
Turkmenistan	3.6	7.4	0.73	13,021
Ukraine	51.8	5.9	16.27	292,100
Uzbekistan	20.3	45.4	3.20	57,500

Notes

In Eastern Europe and the former-Soviet Union, estimates of economic statistics can vary, those used above are: United Nations (population), Economist Intelligence Unit (GDP/GNP and forecasts), International Monetary fund (trade, current account and exchange rates), Moscow National Bank (rouble rate) and PlanEcon (all former Soviet Republics statistics)

*Purchasing–power parities

Other economies

	China	Hong Kong	India	Indonesia	S Korea	Singapore	Taiwan	Thailand	S Africa	Argentina	Brazil	Mexico
Population, m												
1985	1,060.0	5.5	769.1	167.3	40.8	2.6	19.1	51.6	31.6	30.3	135.6	79.4
1995 forecast	1,223.0	6.1	946.7	201.8	44.7	2.9	21.2	59.6	39.3	34.2	165.0	98.0
Population density per sq km												
1990	119	5,599	259	97	432	4,407	574	109	29	12	18	45
Population under 15 years, %												
1985	29.7	23.1	37.6	38.7	30.0	24.4	30.4	36.5	37.7	30.5	36.4	40.9
1995 forecast	26.3	18.8	36.0	33.4	23.0	23.2	21.6	29.3	36.5	28.3	33.7	35.0
Population 65 years and over, %												
1985	5.3	7.6	4.3	3.6	4.3	5.2	4.9	3.6	4.1	8.6	4.3	3.6
1995 forecast	6.3	10.1	4.8	4.4	5.4	6.4	9.0	4.4	4.3	9.6	5.1	4.2
GDP/GNP, $bn												
1981	318.0	31.1	189.8	85.1	70.9	13.3	63.1	35.8	78.9	55.3	253.0	216.1
1991	367.8	81.2	256.5	114.8	283.0	40.0	175.7	91.9	107.6	184.9	435.4	282.5
GDP/GNP per head, $												
1981	320	6,080	270	560	1,830	5,450	3,297	750	2,730	1,930	2,040	3,000
1991	318	13,900	305	628	6,540	14,487	8,600	1,605	3,049	5,653	2,840	3,216
GDP/GNP, % change on a year earlier												
1990	5.2	3.0	5.0	7.4	9.2	8.3	4.9	10.0	-0.5	0.4	-4.0	4.4
1991	7.0	3.9	2.0	6.6	8.4	6.7	7.3	7.5	-0.6	5.0	1.2	3.7
1992 forecast	11.0	6.0	4.3	7.0	7.1	5.6	7.3	7.2	-0.5	5.5	0.5	3.0
Consumer prices, % increase on a year earlier												
1990	2.1	9.8	9.0	7.4	8.6	3.5	4.1	6.0	14.4	2,314.4	2,928.0	26.7
1991	3.4	12.0	14.0	9.2	9.7	3.4	3.6	5.7	15.3	171.6	441.0	22.7
1992 forecast	7.0	10.0	11.5	8.3	7.8	2.4	4.0	6.5	13.5	25.3	877.0	16.4
Exports, $bn												
1990	51.5	82.2	18.9	26.8	63.1	50.7	66.7	22.8	23.4	12.4	31.7	26.8
1991	58.9	98.2	18.5	29.1	69.5	56.8	75.5	25.4	23.8	12.1	31.6	27.1
1992 forecast	67.8	123.8	21.1	32.4	76.2	59.8	85.6	29.4	26.1	13.5	33.6	28.7
Imports, $bn												
1990	48.8	82.8	26.0	20.7	65.1	55.8	52.1	29.5	17.0	3.7	20.7	31.3
1991	42.4	100.3	22.2	24.5	76.6	61.0	59.8	32.5	17.5	7.4	21.0	38.2
1992 forecast	50.2	126.7	24.2	27.4	81.7	64.9	68.9	35.4	20.6	11.9	21.9	44.2
Current-account balance, $bn												
1990	12.0	na	-8.9	-2.4	-2.2	2.4	11.2	-7.1	2.3	1.9	-2.2	-7.1
1991	13.8	na	-5.2	-4.5	-8.8	4.0	12.0	-7.5	2.7	-2.5	0.0	-13.3
1992 forecast	9.9	na	-4.3	-4.8	-6.9	3.1	11.5	-7.9	1.1	-5.4	0.4	-17.3
External debt, end year, $bn												
1991	47.8	5.4	76.7	58.3	38.7	3.7	0.8	29.9	18.4	62.8	114.0	101.9
Exchange rate, end year, per $												
	Yuan	Dollar	Rupee	Rupiah	Won	Dollar	New Taiwan $	Baht	Rand	Peso	Cruzeiro	Peso
1990	5.22	7.80	18.07	1,901	716.4	1.74	26.90	25.29	2.56	0.56	177	2,812
1991	5.43	7.80	25.83	1,992	760.8	1.63	26.80	25.28	2.74	1.00	1,068	3,018
1992	5.80	7.74	28.94	2,059	788.4	1.64	25.40	25.33	3.05	0.99	12,242	3,120

Foreign reserves

Official foreign reserves are roughly equivalent to a nation's bank balance. They consist of foreign currencies, special drawing rights (SDRS) and the country's reserve position in the International Monetary Fund. The figures in the table do not include gold: holdings often remain unchanged for years though the market value will vary with the price of gold. Changes in reserves can reflect a country's underlying trading problems or the amount of official intervention in the currency markets. The unprecedented leap in German reserves in September 1992 followed intervention in the currency markets in support of sterling and other ERM currencies. This was mirrored by a fall in the reserves of weaker ERM currencies before the enforced withdrawal of sterling and the lira and the devaluation of the peseta. Sweden abandoned efforts to peg the krona to the ecu after reserves were threatened by an outflow of capital.

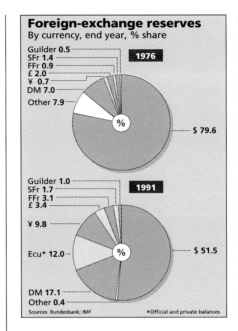

Foreign-exchange reserves
By currency, end year, % share

1976
Guilder 0.5
SFr 1.4
FFr 0.9
£ 2.0
¥ 0.7
DM 7.0
Other 7.9
%
$ 79.6

1991
Guilder 1.0
SFr 1.7
FFr 3.1
£ 3.4
¥ 9.8
Ecu* 12.0
%
$ 51.5
DM 17.1
Other 0.4

Sources: Bundesbank; IMF   *Official and private balances

OFFICIAL RESERVES Government reserves of foreign currencies, gold and special drawing rights can be used to pay for imports, lessen the impact of economic shocks, service a country's debt and defend its exchange rate. The chart shows the composition of world foreign-exchange reserves at the end of 1991, compared with 1976. Though the dollar was still much the preferred currency going into 1992, its share of total assets had fallen to 51.5%—down from 79.6% in 1976. The second most popular currency, the D-mark, increased its share from 7% to 17.1%. Sterling's popularity grew, from 2% to 3.4%. The ecu, non-existent in 1976, is also proving attractive to EC governments: official and private ecu assets account for 12% of the global total. In 1976 the yen accounted for only 0.7% of global reserves; 15 years later its share was 9.8%. Holdings of other currencies have fallen from 7.9% to 0.4%.

Official foreign reserves, $bn

End month

		Australia	Belgium	Canada	France	Germany	Holland	Italy	Japan	Spain	Sweden	Switzerland	United Kingdom	United States
1991	Jan	16.1	12.0	18.1	35.8	68.2	17.9	62.4	79.1	53.0	20.8	26.0	36.1	74.0
	Feb	16.2	12.0	16.8	36.3	66.4	17.6	62.8	79.5	53.0	20.3	26.0	39.1	71.1
	Mar	15.5	10.5	17.0	36.1	59.1	17.0	61.1	72.8	51.6	18.2	26.6	37.3	66.9
	Apr	15.6	10.5	15.8	35.2	59.7	16.0	59.5	70.8	54.5	17.6	25.3	38.5	67.2
	May	16.3	10.6	17.2	34.2	60.5	16.3	57.3	71.1	58.3	20.9	25.4	38.5	67.2
	Jun	15.5	10.1	16.5	32.0	57.7	15.8	54.4	70.7	57.4	21.0	25.1	38.2	63.9
	Jul	15.7	10.6	16.7	33.3	59.5	16.5	55.4	70.4	59.8	20.2	24.3	39.3	63.8
	Aug	15.7	10.7	16.1	33.5	60.2	16.3	54.7	69.8	60.6	18.3	24.9	39.3	62.5
	Sep	16.2	11.2	18.1	34.5	61.2	16.8	57.0	69.9	61.9	18.1	25.5	40.4	63.7
	Oct	16.2	11.1	16.9	33.9	60.4	16.6	53.9	70.1	61.3	17.2	25.6	39.9	63.5
	Nov	16.5	11.4	17.3	30.5	61.5	17.0	52.1	70.9	63.2	14.4	26.3	40.5	63.6
	Dec	16.5	12.2	16.3	31.3	63.0	17.8	48.7	72.1	65.8	18.3	29.0	41.9	66.7
1992	Jan	14.7	11.2	16.1	30.5	60.8	16.8	45.0	71.7	64.0	20.5	26.9	41.1	64.8
	Feb	13.6	11.3	16.0	32.7	61.5	16.7	44.1	71.2	64.4	22.4	27.0	40.9	64.0
	Mar	13.7	11.1	14.7	32.9	61.6	16.6	42.7	71.1	65.8	22.2	27.1	40.1	63.6
	Apr	13.6	11.4	14.9	33.8	63.2	16.8	39.5	71.1	66.7	18.9	26.6	40.9	63.7
	May	13.6	11.6	14.8	33.9	62.6	17.1	36.6	71.0	68.4	23.4	26.8	41.7	63.5
	Jun	13.9	14.6	14.7	33.5	64.1	17.7	34.8	70.5	72.1	23.7	27.8	42.6	66.0
	Jul	14.3	14.2	15.1	32.5	63.3	17.7	26.8	71.1	70.5	22.9	27.2	43.3	66.3
	Aug	12.9	14.9	15.1	31.7	67.1	18.2	23.6	72.2	70.4	17.5	28.2	43.4	67.4
	Sep	12.6	12.8	12.2	29.1	120.3	22.2	28.1	72.3	56.4	20.7	28.8	40.2	67.5
	Oct	11.2	11.5	12.7	–	88.4	20.8	22.6	71.3	52.3	–	27.8	39.5	63.1
	Nov	11.0	9.9	9.8	–	85.5	20.2	26.0	71.4	42.6	–	29.5	38.5	61.1
	Dec	–	–	–	–	–	–	–	–	–	–	–	–	–

376

377

380

381

THE ECONOMIST'S EDITORIAL STAFF

Susannah Amoore, *managing editor*
John Andrews, *Asia editor*
Amanda Attersley, *editorial assistant*
Robert Banbury, *reprographics manager*
Carol Banks, *editorial assistant*
Graham Bayfield, *editorial systems supervisor*
Jenny Bielenberg, *assistant to the editor*
Matthew Bishop, *finance journalist*
Andrew Bristow, *pre-press technician*
Ian Cable, *pre-press technician*
Frances Cairncross, *environment editor*
Duncan Campbell-Smith, *New York bureau chief*
Edward Carr, *resources/trade correspondent*
Geoffrey Carr, *science journalist*
Nicholas Colchester, *deputy editor*
Liz Conway, *cartographer*
Fiona Cooper, *researcher*
Una Corrigan, *senior designer*
Chris Coulman, *statistician*
Andrew Cowley, *Moscow correspondent*
Clive Crook, *economics editor*
Roland Dallas, *foreign affairs journalist*
Peter David, *international editor*
Rebecca Deacon, *editorial assistant*
Graham Douglas, *cartographer*
Marsh Dunbar, *editorial assistant*
Emma Duncan, *Britain journalist*
Celina Dunlop, *picture editor*
Michael Elliott, *Washington bureau chief*
Miranda Ellis, *editorial assistant*
Bill Emmott, *business affairs editor*
Caron Fan, *Hong Kong office manager*
Peter Farren, *head of publishing systems*
Edmund Fawcett, *Germany correspondent*
Daniel Franklin, *Britain editor*
Andrew Freeman, *banking correspondent*
Penny Garrett, *head of design department*
Martin Giles, *European business correspondent*
Anthony Gottlieb, *surveys editor*
Charles Grant, *Brussels correspondent*
Jean Greaves, *telex room supervisor*
John Grimond, *foreign editor*
Peter Haynes, *information technology correspondent*
John Heilemann, *media/entertainment correspondent*
Peter Holden, *deputy head of research*
Carol Howard, *head of research*
Stephen Hugh-Jones, *special features editor*
Ian Jones, *communication systems manager*
Stella Jones, *statistician*
Anita Lawrence, *pagination co-ordinator*
David Lipsey, *Britain journalist*

Daniel Litvin, *Britain journalist*
Judith Liverman, *editorial assistant*
Suzy Lyttle, *graphic designer*
Sebastian Mallaby, *Tokyo correspondent*
David Manasian, *business editor*
Liz Mann, *statistician*
Paul Markillie, *transport correspondent*
Carol Mawer, *letters editor*
Sharon McGowan, *deputy editorial systems manager*
David McKelvey, *research assistant*
John Micklethwait, *Los Angeles correspondent*
Andrew Mitchell, *pre-press technician*
Pauline Molyneux, *editorial systems manager*
Edwina Moreton, *diplomatic editor*
Oliver Morton, *science editor*
Virginia O'Riordan, *deputy editorial systems manager*
Hiroko Ofuchi, *Tokyo office manager*
John Parker, *Moscow correspondent*
Sophie Pedder, *Britain journalist*
John Peet, *finance journalist*
Rupert Pennant-Rea, *editor*
Keith Potter, *researcher*
Gideon Rachman, *South-East Asia correspondent*
Krysia Rejt, *senior designer*
Carrie Robinson, *New York librarian*
Caroline Robinson, *editorial assistant*
Jim Rohwer, *Asia correspondent*
Chris Rowles, *pre-press technician*
Cornelia Rudat, *Berlin office manager*
Yvonne Ryan, *picture researcher*
Craig Santus, *cartographer*
Roy Saunders, *publishing systems manager*
Tom Scott, *pre-press production manager*
Xan Smiley, *political editor*
Barbara Smith, *foreign affairs journalist*
Peter Sonderskov, *cartographer*
Merril Stevenson, *finance editor*
Ruth Taylor, *cartographer*
Tony Thomas, *Arts, Books and Sport editor*
Ian Troy, *pre-press supervisor*
Brooke Unger, *Germany business correspondent*
Vijay Vaitheeswaran, *Latin America correspondent*
Nick Valery, *Tokyo bureau chief*
Avril Walker, *Washington office manager*
Nick Wiseman, *statistician*
Anna Wolek, *researcher*
Chris Wood, *Tokyo finance correspondent*
Pam Woodall, *economics journalist*
Adrian Wooldridge, *Britain journalist*
Kenneth Wright, *researcher*
Ann Wroe, *America editor*